AMERICA AND THE FIGHT FOR IRISH FREEDOM

1866–1922

OTHER BOOKS BY CHARLES CALLAN TANSILL

The Canadian Reciprocity Treaty of 1854, 1921

Robert Smith (in the *American Secretaries of State and Their Diplomacy*), 1927

Documents Illustrative of the Formation of the Union of the American States, 1927

Proposed Amendments to the Constitution, 1889–1927, 1927

The Purchase of the Danish West Indies, 1931

The United States and Santo Domingo, 1798–1873, 1938

America Goes to War, 1938

The Diplomatic Relations Between the United States and Hawaii, 1885–1889, 1940

The Foreign Policy of Thomas F. Bayard, 1885–1889, 1940

Canadian-American Relations, 1875–1911, 1944

The Congressional Career of Thomas F. Bayard, 1869–1885, 1946

Back Door to War, 1952

Daniel F. Cohalan

America and the Fight for Irish Freedom 1866-1922

AN OLD STORY BASED UPON NEW DATA

Charles Callan Tansill

PROFESSOR OF AMERICAN DIPLOMATIC HISTORY

GEORGETOWN UNIVERSITY

ILLUSTRATED

New York, The Devin-Adair Co., 1957

Copyright 1957 by Charles Callan Tansill. All rights reserved.
No portion of this book may be reproduced
in any form without written permission
of the publisher, The Devin-Adair
Co., 23 E. 26th St., New York 10,
except by a reviewer, who may
quote brief passages in connection
with a review.
Canadian agent: Thomas Nelson
& Sons, Ltd., Toronto
Library of Congress Catalog card
number: 57–8866
Manufactured in the United States of America
by H. Wolff, New York

to

DANIEL F. COHALAN

JOHN DEVOY

Valiant Fighters for Irish Freedom

CONTENTS

ILLUSTRATIONS *between pages* 244 *and* 245

PREFACE *ix*

1 IRELAND: THE FIRST HALF-CENTURY UNDER THE UNION, 1801-1851 *3*
2 THE EMERGENCE OF PARNELL AS A STATESMAN *28*
3 THE DEATH OF PARNELL DELAYS FOR DECADES HOME-RULE LEGISLATION FOR IRELAND *59*
4 THE CLAN-NA-GAEL HELPS TO GIVE SUBSTANCE TO THE DREAM OF IRISH INDEPENDENCE *102*
5 JOHN REDMOND RELUCTANTLY DISCOVERS THAT BETRAYAL IS AN OLD ENGLISH POLITICAL PRACTICE *136*
6 ROGER CASEMENT AND THE EASTER REBELLION *169*
7 PRESIDENT WILSON FAVORS THE PRINCIPLE OF SELF-DETERMINATION FOR EVERY PEOPLE BUT THE IRISH *215*
8 CARDINAL O'CONNELL MAKES A FERVID PLEA FOR IRISH SELF-DETERMINATION *251*
9 JUDGE COHALAN IS SHARPLY REBUFFED BY PRESIDENT WILSON *284*
10 THE SENATE REJECTS A TREATY WHICH MAKES NO PROVISION FOR IRISH SELF-DETERMINATION *312*
11 PRESIDENT DE VALERA COURTS A QUARREL WITH JUDGE COHALAN *340*
12 IRISH-AMERICAN UNITY IS SPLIT THROUGH THE EFFORTS OF DE VALERA AND HIS LIEUTENANTS *369*
13 THE BLACK AND TANS BEGIN A LONG CHAPTER OF ARSON AND MURDER *397*
14 IRELAND ACCEPTS DOMINION STATUS AS A STEPPING STONE TO EVENTUAL INDEPENDENCE *418*

APPENDIX *443*

BIBLIOGRAPHY *451*

INDEX *461*

PREFACE

In writing this study of Irish-American relations I have played the role of pioneer. The wealth of data in the National Archives and in the Library of Congress has hitherto been largely untouched. I have been particularly fortunate in having had access to the papers of the late Judge Daniel F. Cohalan, which shed a great deal of significant light upon every phase of Irish-American relations from the turn of the twentieth century until the end of the Wilson Administration.

There have been many difficulties in the way of writing an objective study of Irish-American relations during the period from 1914 to 1922. The activities of De Valera during eighteen tempestuous months in America have been the subject of widely different accounts. Patrick McCartan, in his monograph *With De Valera in America,* has written the official defense of the De Valera mission to the United States. The mistakes in that volume are so numerous that one wonders if they are not an integral part of a long tirade of misrepresentation. Other books written by members of the De Valera clique draw their inspiration from the McCartan volume and repeat obvious errors.

In these books written by the De Valera court historians, the villain of the piece is always Judge Daniel F. Cohalan. There are many examples of this hysterical scholarship. It has been obvious that some historian should endeavor to redress this lack of balance and write a new volume based upon data recently made available. I have assumed this task with a clear realization that many critics, both here and in Ireland, will sharply disagree with my interpretation of these new data. It will not be the first time I have stirred up controversy and I hope it will not be the last. A great deal of historical truth often emerges from a spirited historical discussion even though the accents at times become somewhat strident.

As one looks through the large volume of data dealing with Irish-American relations, it soon becomes obvious that Judge Cohalan had many enemies who were far more articulate than his friends.

But these detractors of the Judge have been greatly embarrassed by the fact that one of his most ardent friends was John Devoy, the greatest of all the old Fenians. Their glib explanation is the alleged fact that Devoy fell under the spell of the masterful Cohalan and became his unthinking mouthpiece. No one who knew Devoy or who has read his copious correspondence could accept such a specious explanation of his devotion to the Judge. Devoy followed the lead of no man. He was a bold, independent spirit who charted his own path through the mazes of the Irish question. He often molded opinion; he seldom accepted the viewpoints of others without radical amendment.

The real reason for the quarrel between Judge Cohalan and De Valera has been conveniently overlooked. Cohalan was, above all, an ardent American whose loyalties to his native country were basic and compelling. This accent of Americanism is clear in everything he wrote or did. The cause of Ireland was dear to his heart but his affection for Erin was secondary to his devotion to the United States. De Valera could never understand the make-up of the Judge, and he expected an immediate and unquestioning response to his calls for action even when these calls would compromise the policy of the United States.

I wish to record my deep obligation to the members of the staff of the Library of Congress. Mr. Verner W. Clapp, Chief Assistant Librarian, is a friend to all scholars. Mr. David C. Mearns, Chief of the Division of Manuscripts, has gone far out of his way to be of assistance, and this helpful spirit has also been shown by Dr. Charles P. Powell, Dr. Elizabeth McPherson, Mr. John de Porry and Miss Katherine Brand.

In the National Archives one can always count upon the courteous help of Dr. Philip Hamer. In the Division of State Department Archives I have had the advantage of the counsel of Dr. Carl Lokke, and the active and very efficient assistance of Mrs. Kieran Carroll and Mrs. William A. Dowling.

In Georgetown University I have enjoyed the inspiration of the Rev. John M. Daley, S.J., Dean of the Graduate School. The staff of the Georgetown University library, headed by Rev. James B.

Preface

Horigan, S.J., and Philipps Temple, has been of the greatest service to me. My old friend, Dr. Tibor Kerekes, Chairman of the Department of History, has graciously extended to me many favors.

I am happy to record the help of two old and intimate friends, Dr. Harry Elmer Barnes and George Sylvester Viereck.

There are many other personal friends whose assistance I should like to record: Rev. Henry F. Wolfe, Captain Miles DuVal, Rear Admiral John Heffernan, Dr. Louis M. Sears, Dr. Reinhard H. Luthin, Dr. Rocco Paone, Mr. Anthony Kubek, Professor John Carroll, Dr. Carmelo Bernardo, Miss Mary Ann Sharkey, Mr. William R. Tansill, Miss Susan Sharkey, Mr. Louis Carroll, Mr. Charles B. Tansill, Mr. Raymond T. Parker, Mrs. Grace Lee Morton, Mrs. Mary Ann Sharkey, Mrs. C. Bernard Purcell, Dr. Samuel F. Bemis, Dr. Charles Seymour, Mr. Fred G. Tansill, Mrs. Grace M. Carpenter, Miss Amy Holland, Dr. Harry Sievers, S.J., Mrs. Natalia Summers, and the Reverend Joseph Costanzo, S.J.

I cannot forget the inspiration of my intimate friend the late Dr. Gerald G. Walsh, S.J., whose wise counsel often restrained my slightly impetuous nature. One friend who has been of great help and inspiration to me in the preparation of this book is Dr. Herbert J. Clancy, S.J. It would be impossible for me to indicate more than a fraction of my debt to him.

For the editing of the manuscript and proofs for publication, I am grateful to Mr. T. O'Conor Sloane III, editor of the Devin-Adair Co.

It is difficult adequately to record the assistance constantly given to me by a long-suffering wife who repeatedly read the manuscript, offered many corrections, and with characteristic diplomacy indicated improvements in organization. I have paid her by slightly increasing the ardor of my already warm affections.

Charles Callan Tansill

Georgetown University

AMERICA AND THE FIGHT FOR IRISH FREEDOM

1866–1922

1 IRELAND: THE FIRST HALF-CENTURY UNDER THE UNION, 1801-1851

A. THE IRISH NATION

Philip Guedalla once remarked that imperialism is much like an open window—if you open it you welcome *fresh air;* if the other fellow opens it you complain of a *draft.* For the Irish nation, British imperialism meant a strong draft that blew freedom and prosperity to the four winds. Under home rule and independence, freedom has been recovered. Prosperity is still around the corner of a distant tomorrow.

The story of Ireland is the epic of a subject people who never lost the memory of an ancient greatness and who kept alive the vision of a future nation endowed with bright promise and dedicated to large achievement. Under English domination the Irish people were for a brief period ruled by a so-called Irish Parliament that was completely subordinate to English desires. As a conquered people, they were denied admission to this legislative assembly. Under severe penal laws they were deprived of all opportunities for education and were forbidden to hold property. Even the consolations of their religion were denied them, and a price was put upon the heads of their priests.

The English ruling class ardently hoped that these far-reaching restrictions would kill the Irish spirit and produce a nation of helots who would obey without question the dictates of their masters. They could never realize that Irish nationality was a spiritual entity born of a meeting of minds and a union of hearts and therefore was something that was unconquerable and indestructible. Through dreary centuries it defied all the brutalities of English rule. The cruelties of Cromwell and the pillage and murder visited upon Ireland by the Black and Tan arson squads of Lloyd George failed to break the spirit of a nation that had gained immortality through the death of its political form. When resurrection came in 1921, the whole world paid tribute to a modern miracle.

B. THE BURDEN OF ENGLISH IMPERIALISM

In America, English imperialism was a burden borne by a people far removed from the center of empire and who had, moreover, a large amount of political and economic freedom. Ireland was a conquered country and its people were fitted into an economic vise that seldom permitted them more than a marginal existence. Absentee landlords were chiefly interested in rack rents and not in peasant rights. Their agents in Ireland were equally mercenary. The agricultural system worked like a screw press; the increase in "the rent of any farm at the close of any half-year might be small, but the screw still went on revolving, the pressure increasing until, at last, human nature could no longer endure it." [1]

As early as 1724 Swift complained that the rents in Ireland had recently been "enormously raised and screwed up" to some two million sterling a year, and a third of this large sum was transmitted to landlords who were "perpetual absentees in England." [2] The plight of the masses was so tragic that he felt compelled to write his grim *Modest Proposal for Preventing the Children of Poor People from Being a Burden to their Parents of the Country*. He would spare the rod and eat the child.

Sir William Petty was more realistic in his approach. He was certain that sheep breeding and cattle raising were more suited to the economic picture in Ireland than subsistence farming. It would be expedient, therefore, to remove a million persons from Ireland and leave behind a mere three hundred thousand who would take

---

1. Daniel Corkery, *The Hidden Ireland* (Dublin, 1925), p. 23.
2. Jonathan Swift, "Drapier's Letters," *Works* (London, 1907), VI, 188.

care of millions of sheep and cattle. From the cattle industry alone there would be some £500,000 available for payment to the British Crown and to needy landlords.[3] For the poor peasants in Ireland, political economy was indeed the "dismal science."

The British Government made no attempt to move a million persons from Ireland, but it did encourage a clearance movement in favor of large-scale grazing operations, and in 1735 it shifted the burden of maintaining the Established Church upon the shoulders of the Catholic peasantry.[4] To English statesmen, Ireland was merely one factor in a long equation of mercantilism. Their sole concern was how Ireland could best serve the interests of empire. No serious competition between Irish and English exports to world markets must be allowed, so Irish wool shipments were restricted to the English market. When this market was barricaded by high tariff barriers, the inevitable result was the disappearance of the Irish woolen industry.[5]

The linen industry in Northern Ireland received more favorable treatment from English mercantilists, who grudgingly granted some preferential duties upon Belfast exports to English markets. In subsequent decades this economic tie drew Ulster close to London.

In contrast with this modest prosperity enjoyed by the linen trade, the provisions industry had a precarious existence. Some profits were made from the sale of foodstuffs to ships entering the harbors of Cork, Waterford, and Wexford and from exports to Europe and to the overseas empire, but the economic situation in Ireland continued to be so unfavorable that it was only through broad smuggling operations that a large number of people were able to live.

3. Sir William Petty, "A treatise of Ireland, 1687," in the *Economic Writings of Sir William Petty* (Cambridge, 1899), pp. 545-621.
4. Eric Strauss, *Irish Nationalism and British Democracy* (London, 1951), p. 15.
5. George A. T. O'Brien, *Economic History of Ireland in the Eighteenth Century* (Dublin, 1919), p. 179.

C. ENGLAND'S DIFFICULTY IS IRELAND'S OPPORTUNITY

Ireland's opportunity to break some of the chains of English mercantilism came when England was faced with revolution in its overseas empire in America. English distress was very evident when France intervened in the struggle, and in 1782-3 Irish leaders like Henry Grattan were able to extract from a reluctant English Government the concession of an independent parliament. The moment had also arrived to push the question of Catholic emancipation. A start had been made in 1778, and this movement was given additional impetus under the terms of legislation enacted in 1793. Most of the provisions of the penal code were repealed, but Catholics were still denied the right to serve in the Irish Parliament. These concessions did not proceed from a belated recognition of basic rights. The wars of the French Revolution had started fires all over Europe. Concessions to Ireland might prevent sparks of revolt from igniting social tinder that was ready for the flame.[6]

The sharp social cleavage that existed in Ireland was clearly illustrated in the attitude of Grattan towards the repeal of the penal laws. Pitt wished to have the suffrage franchise placed upon a broad social basis that would admit some 30,000 Irish forty-shilling freeholders to the polls. The opposition of the upper-class Irish to this liberal extension of the franchise was immediate and vehement. In the recollections of Lord Donoughmore the situation is clearly described:

> We found that Pitt and Dundas, after two or three interviews . . . said they would advise the prayer of their [the Irish delegation] petition being granted, and that the qualification should be forty shillings. Upon this, Grattan and I [Lord Donoughmore] asked to see Dundas, and we had different interviews with him in which we stated that the Catholics [in Ireland], in asking for a qualified franchise, had never thought of less than £20 a year and that they would be content even with £50. We urged again and again the impolicy of so low a fran-

6. Patrick S. O'Hegarty, *A History of Ireland Under the Union, 1801-1922* (London, 1952), pp. 19-20.

chise; and all we could get from Dundas was that it must be the same as it was in England.[7]

Catholic emancipation was merely one item on the Irish agenda. The moment had arrived for striking off the shackles of English mercantilism. Foster's Corn Law of 1784 placed a premium upon Irish grain exports. This was a direct challenge to English opposition to any expansion of Irish agriculture. Further defiance of England found expression in protective-tariff duties upon English cotton goods. An Irish cotton-goods industry seemed in the making.

But the alliance between the progressive wing of the Irish country gentlemen and the urban middle class did not long survive these triumphs. Grattan was basically pro-British, and his followers realized that British armed support was necessary for the maintenance of the privileged position of the landlords. Political connection with England remained a social imperative. To the urban bourgeoisie of Northern Ireland, this tie was not so essential. They had felt a deep interest in the American Revolution, in which their kinsmen had played an important part, and the French Revolution of 1789 seemed to indicate the path to a better way of life. The society of the United Irishmen which Wolfe Tone had helped to found in 1791 became more radical after extorting some English concessions. Tone himself was a disciple of Danton and Tom Paine and wished to establish an Irish republic by armed force. Realizing that this objective could be realized only through French assistance, Tone went to Paris in 1796 and inspired the French Directory to send several expeditions—which never reached Ireland. Captured on one of these fruitless attempts to break the English hold upon Ireland, Tone cheated the hangman by cutting his own throat on November 12, 1798, and died a few days later.[8]

When it became apparent that the spirit of the society of United Irishmen was definitely revolutionary, the Catholic freeholders who had just been given the elective franchise took alarm and withdrew from further association with the followers of Wolfe Tone. Needless

7. *The Creevy Papers*, ed. by Sir Herbert Maxwell (New York, 1904), p. 521.
8. Frank MacDermot, *Theobald Wolfe Tone* (London, 1939); Leo McCabe, *Wolfe Tone and the United Irishmen* (London, 1937).

to say, Flood and Grattan had little sympathy with the fiery gospel of a Dublin coachmaker's son who would put a torch to the existing social structure. But Tone had sounded a note that swelled into a great chorus when the Sinn Fein revolution of April 1916 ushered in a new era. Tone was the herald of Irish nationality; a nationality that united every race, every class, every creed. The present Irish Free State is the lengthened political shadow of a man who dared to dream a dream that would never die.

D. THE CRAFT OF CASTLEREAGH PUTS AN END TO GRATTAN'S PARLIAMENT

The rising tide of nationalism in Ireland during the period of Grattan's Parliament menaced the favored position of England according to mercantilist principles. The best way to stem this dangerous tide was to bring Ireland back within the legislative control of England. The stage was set for parliamentary union.

The rebellion of 1798 hastened this event. The savage measures of repression adopted to crush the revolt were enough to convince many faint-hearted persons that conformity with English desires was the safest course to pursue. Coercion was the order of the day, and the loyalty of "the wealthy Catholics and of the prelacy was brushed aside and the Government exploited the patent disaffection of the Catholic masses and a good many members of the lower clergy as justification for a strictly Orange terror regime." [9] But terror was not the only weapon used against Catholics. The sweet bait of possible Catholic admission to a united parliament was dangled before the dazzled eyes of wealthy Catholics, and Castlereagh's well-filled purse made many compromises acceptable.

Presbyterian dissenters in Northern Ireland were bought over by another means of bribery. If the Presbyterian clergy were in receipt of an annual bounty that would ease their economic distress, their fealty to the Crown would be securely established. Under Castlereagh's arrangements the Government agreed to pay to each minister an annual sum that in many cases reached the respectable

9. Strauss, *op. cit.*, p. 55.

figure of £100. There was no longer any doubt about the "zealous loyalty" of these clerics, who now looked to London for a large part of their subsistence:[10] "The Northern Presbyterians ceased to be an independent, liberal and positive community, and became a narrow, bigotry-ridden negative community. . . . The Presbyterian community became merely a part of England's Garrison."[11]

E. THE ECONOMIC CONSEQUENCES OF THE UNION

Terror, bribery, and false promises were the more important solvents that crumbled the main supports of Grattan's Parliament. When the Act of Union was finally pushed through in 1800, it was not long before Ireland felt the weight of a crushing economic burden. Castlereagh had estimated that the number of workers in Irish cotton mills was between thirty and forty thousand.[12] In 1822 they were placed at the low figure of from three to five thousand.[13] As early as September 1810, Daniel O'Connell complained in a speech in Dublin that since 1800 Ireland had seen "her artificers starved, her tradesmen begging, her merchants become bankrupts, her gentry banished, her nobility degraded."[14]

In Ulster the economic outlook was much brighter. Although the cotton-spinning industry was soon in sore straits, the linen trade moved slowly forward. Handloom weavers were still able to make a bare living working for English textile manufacturers, and new industries like shipbuilding in Belfast and shirtmaking in Derry helped to place Northern Ireland in a favored position.[15] These factors helped to integrate Ulster into the economic pattern of England and thus widened the gulf between the northern and southern

---

10. Viscount Castlereagh, *Correspondence, Despatches and Other Papers* (London, 1849), IV, 287.
11. O'Hegarty, *op. cit.*, p. 15.
12. Castlereagh, *op. cit.*, III, 252.
13. *Edinburgh Review*, June 1822, p. 98.
14. Daniel O'Connell, *Select Speeches* (edited by John O'Connell, Dublin, 1860), I, 17 *et seq.*
15. Select Committee on the State of Ireland (Lords), *British Parliamentary Papers*, 1825, ix, 34-37; Report on the Linen and Cotton Manufacture in Ireland, *ibid.*, 1840, xxiii, 772-800.

counties of Ireland. In the southern counties there was no longer any opportunity for the growth of an urban middle class, and in many towns the closing of cotton mills imposed serious economic distress upon a large number of families. The disappearance of industry placed most of Ireland in an economic strait jacket that squeezed all classes into the narrow confines of a semifeudal land system.

But even this outmoded system worked very profitably during the wars of the French Revolution, which shut off from England most of the grain imports from Continental Europe. Thanks to this monopoly, the shipments of grain and flour from Ireland to English ports increased in value from £598,370 in 1792 to £1,641,583 in 1812.[16] After the defeat of Napoleon in 1815, the war boom collapsed. Continental grain once more poured into the English market and the Irish grain trade nearly collapsed. The mass of the Irish people were too poor to buy this surplus grain, and they continued to manage a bleak existence upon the scanty harvests gleaned from the few acres allotted to potato production. The landlords, alarmed by the fall in grain prices, turned once more to cattle grazing. As one Irish Tory remarked in 1825: "The landlords of Ireland are at length deeply convinced that, though a stock of cattle or sheep will afford profits, a stock of mere human creatures, unemployed, will afford none." [17] It is evident that the position of the Irish laborer was becoming increasingly hopeless, and the period from 1815 to 1845 was a real Thirty Years' War which ended in the great famine. Starvation by the million was the unescapable result of this economic dislocation, and English statesmen seemed unable or unwilling to take any effective action that would prevent this tragic situation.

16. Select Committee on the Corn Trade of the United Kingdom, *British Parliamentary Papers,* 1812-1813, iii, 27; *Edinburgh Review,* April 1809, p. 168.
17. Select Committee on the State of Ireland, *British Parliamentary Papers,* 1825, ix, 59.

F. CATHOLIC EMANCIPATION

The deep and unending distress of the farm population of Ireland led to the formation of numerous secret societies designed to exert pressure upon harsh landlords. They were given many colorful titles—Thrashers, Caravats, Carders, Whitefeet, Blackfeet, Rockites, Michael Coffeys, and Molly Maguires. They were generally described as Ribbonmen and were the forerunners of the Irish Republican Brotherhood. They lacked effective leadership, a common program and a close-knit organization, but they gave great concern to the landlords and were looked upon with open disfavor by the Catholic middle class, composed of lawyers, doctors, merchants, minor officials, and well-to-do farmers. This Catholic middle class was outspoken in its loyalty to England and Dublin Castle saw no reason to question its sincerity. The political creed of these Catholics was clearly expressed by Bishop Doyle in 1825: "If we were freed from the disabilities under which we labour, we have no mind, and no thought, and no will but that which would lead us to incorporate ourselves most fully and essentially with this great kingdom." [18]

The leaders of the Catholic middle class saw the evident importance of harnessing the explosive force of the Irish masses in order to blow aside the barriers that kept Catholics out of Parliament. Needless to say, none of the members of the Irish masses would be able to qualify for entrance into Parliament under any scheme devised by the middle-class leaders. Emancipation would free only Catholics who had some property, but this fact was not made clear to the people.

Pressure-group tactics required the temporary fusing of the middle class with the masses, and this was managed by founding the Catholic Association. Members of the middle class subscribed a guinea a year to the funds of the association; members of the masses contributed a penny per month. Thanks to the steady contributions of the Irish people, the income of the Association reached

18. *Ibid.*, viii, 210.

the large total of £1,000 per week. It was widely believed that these funds would secure concessions for all Catholics. The average Irishman did not realize that a deal was in the making whereby wealthy Catholics would be able to go to Parliament but thousands of Catholic forty-shilling freeholders would lose their elective franchise.

When the Catholic Emancipation Bill finally became law on April 13, 1829, not only were wealthy Catholics now eligible to stand for Parliament but a large number of offices were open to them. In the passage of this emancipation bill, Daniel O'Connell had played an important and effective role.[19]

G. ANTI-CLIMAX AT CLONTARF

After securing the passage of the emancipation bill, O'Connell pushed vigorously for the repeal of the Act of Union. As an orator he was unexcelled. Indeed, no man in Irish history spoke with such authentic accents the language of the Irish people. When he addressed the "monster meetings" all over Ireland, his eloquence was sufficient to "carry away the most callous, and to influence the most prejudiced; the critic . . . almost forgot his art, and men of very calm and disciplined intellects experienced emotions the most stately eloquence of the Senate had failed to produce." [20]

It was not long before O'Connell realized that a program that contained the single item of repeal was not broad enough to enlist the ardent support of the Irish masses, so he soon included other items like fixity of land tenure, abolition of tithes, and the democratization of politics along the lines stressed by the Chartists. He firmly believed that these objectives could be eventually achieved by pursuing a policy of Parliamentarianism—pressure in the House of Commons by Irish representatives. But this pressure had little effect upon a phalanx of 558 political foes from different parts of the United Kingdom.

19. Rev. Patrick Rogers, "Catholic Emancipation," in *Daniel O'Connell* (Dublin, 1949), pp. 115-150; Denis Gwynn, *Daniel O'Connell* (Cork, 1947), pp. 145-180.
20. O'Hegarty, *op. cit.*, pp. 147-164.

This O'Connell pressure took the form of loud talk and bitter epithets against English statesmen. The Irish masses were regaled with a spicy repast of bold phrases that were a sharp challenge to English officials in Ireland.

In his Address to the People of Ireland, February 18, 1839, he closed with the following ominous words: "We are Nine Millions! —and the period is gone by when a Nation of Nine Millions can be insulted and degraded with impunity and without redress." At Mallow, on the evening of June 11, 1843, his words carried the same menace:

> Are we to be called slaves? Are we to be trampled underfoot? Oh, they shall never trample me at least [tremendous cheering for several minutes]. I was wrong—they may trample me underfoot—I say they may trample me, but it will be my dead body they will trample on, not the living man. . . . I hope my dream of conflict will never be realized—that it is an empty vision.[21]

At Tara Hill, on August 15, 1843, O'Connell spoke to a vast throng of 700,000 people in these familiar accents of belligerency, which reached a crescendo at Roscommon on August 20. He was especially critical of the attitudes of the Duke of Wellington and of Sir Robert Peel. They had met his arguments for repeal with "beastly bellowings" that had not weakened his firm resolution. He was now ready openly to defy them:

> They thought to frighten us. They spoke at once of putting us down by military force. . . . I knew they would not attack anybody, and then I defied them in your name. I told them that we would not fight them by attacking them, but I defied them to come and attack you, and I want to know if there is any man here who would not fight if he were attacked [tremendous cheers]. There is music in that shout and a mighty pretty tune it is. Now that shout is exactly what I told them, as I merely translated it into English for them.[22]

These were real fighting words in favor of repeal, but O'Connell had no stomach for actual armed conflict. He had moved all over

21. O'Hegarty, *op. cit.*, pp. 141-142.
22. *Ibid.*, pp. 146-147.

Ireland with earthquake feet that shook the masses out of their lethargy, but when the tremors of revolution began to shake the political structure he lost heart and began to eat his words. He had played upon the strings of Irish hearts with a bold touch that had made them vibrate with martial ardor, and he had demanded repeal with an urgency that left no real alternative but revolution. There is no doubt that his words were an incitement to revolt if his program were rejected by English statesmen, but when he looked at that stern contingency he quailed and disavowed the plain purport of his addresses.

His bluff was finally called at Clontarf, where another monster meeting was to be held on October 8, 1843. The English Government grew weary of O'Connell's repeated challenges and determined upon action that would show the Irish people that their champion was a man of bold words and faint heart. On October 6 the Dublin *Evening Mail* published a statement indicating that the meeting at Clontarf would be forbidden by the English Government. On the next day the expected proclamation was issued and the decision as to the meeting was placed squarely before O'Connell. He hurriedly announced that the meeting was canceled and thus showed all Ireland that their leader was a man with little vision and less courage. His campaign for repeal had moved the Irish nation to its depths. Catholic emancipation had been a cheat that had deprived a vast number of forty-shilling freeholders of their votes, but repeal had been sold to them as a general panacea that would solve all their difficulties. The masses were willing to fight for it—to die for it if necessary. That was the evident meaning of that great shout that thundered from the throats of more than five hundred thousand enthusiasts at the Roscommon meeting. The word surrender was not in their minds that day, but O'Connell kept it constantly in view, and when England challenged him to a fight he immediately raised a white flag and submitted to terms. He would save the Irish masses for the great starvation of 1845-1847.[23]

23. *Ibid.*, p. 164.

H. O'CONNELL MISSES THE MEANING OF IRISH NATIONALISM AND PROVOKES A QUARREL WITH THE LEADERS OF YOUNG IRELAND

It is apparent that O'Connell had little conception of Irish nationalism and therefore could give it no adequate expression. He constantly stressed the importance of material considerations like loss of trade, rack rents, landholdings, and similar problems. The spiritual fact of the Irish nation and its dynamic expression in terms of a fervid, all-embracing gospel of nationalism was something which he never clearly grasped. But there were others in Ireland who had this national vision and the courage and ability to voice it. The *Nation*, founded by Charles Gavan Duffy, Thomas Davis, and John Blake Dillon, began publication on October 15, 1842. Duffy was the editor and proprietor but Davis did most of the writing. His task was to give intellectual leadership to the movement for Repeal and thereby erect a significant milestone along the road to Irish nationalism.

Duffy knew that to love one's country it is necessary for the rank and file to know its history and to exult in the achievements of its great men. Ireland did not have to be large in geographical extent to be a great nation. Sweden and Prussia had proved the falsity of such a conception. In the past, Ireland had played an important role in world history. This fact had been recognized by Dr. Johnson, who made the sage observation that "Ireland had civilized and Christianized a great part of Europe." The intellectual ability of Irishmen had been illustrated by the fact that they had won conspicuous places in every country where a career was open to them. Ireland should aim to be completely Irish, not Anglo-Irish, because vigor and health belonged to men and nations that followed their own natures and not those of a foreign mold. There was an individual quality to Irish genius which should be recognized and fostered.[24]

In the columns of the *Nation*, Duffy and Davis preached a gospel

24. Charles Gavan Duffy, *Young Ireland, 1840-45* (London, 1896), I, chaps. iii-iv.

of nationalism that had first been given expression by Wolfe Tone. They gave it new depth and fuller meaning and the *Nation* became the reading habit of Irish intellectuals, who became known as the Young Irelanders. But this gospel of nationalism had implications of independence which gave concern to London. O'Connell, Duffy, and other Irish leaders of the repeal movement were arrested and charged with conspiracy and sedition. In the arguments against them it was emphasized that O'Connell had endeavored to put a benign appearance upon the repeal movement by constantly appealing to his followers to avoid all types of violence. Under this innocent mask, sedition and treason had lurked. The jury was convinced by this charge and found the prisoners guilty. The application for a new trial was rejected, and on May 29, 1844, O'Connell was sentenced to twelve months of imprisonment and the other prisoners, with one exception, to nine months of confinement. But life in Richmond Prison was not harsh. Sir John Gray, of *The Freeman*, and Gavan Duffy continued to write for their periodicals, and there was no attempt to prevent the prisoners from seeing their friends. In the meantime an appeal had been carried to the House of Lords, and to the amazement of most Englishmen the five Law Lords sustained the appeal. On September 6, O'Connell and his companions were released.

But this short period of confinement nearly broke the spirit of O'Connell. His voice had lost its accustomed fire and his gait was slow and faltering. The old stormy petrel would no longer defy the winds of English opposition. But he could still engage in conflict with his old acquaintances in Ireland, and in 1845 he broke with Gavan Duffy on the question of federalism.[25] Duffy and other members of the Young Ireland group had preached the gospel of separatism; repeal was to them merely a halfway house along the road to independence. To O'Connell this ultimate objective was distinctly repellent. He wanted no repetition of Clontarf with its accompanying jail sentence.

A break between O'Connell and the members of Young Ireland

25. Charles Gavan Duffy, *My Life in Two Hemispheres* (New York, 1898), I, chap. vi.

became inevitable after the death of Thomas Davis in September 1845. He had been the chief writer for the *Nation,* and his ardent nationalism had inspired large numbers of the Irish middle class with a passionate devotion to their native land. After his death there was no remaining member of Young Ireland who could speak with the same accents of authority or who would be listened to with the respect that utterances of Davis always commanded. In the autumn a whispering campaign against the Young Irelanders spread over many parts of the island. They were accused of being anti-Catholic, disloyal to O'Connell, and dangerously separatist in sentiment. On November 22, 1845, the *Nation* published an editorial provoked by an article in an English newspaper concerning the ease with which Ireland, because of its railway system, could be overrun by English military forces. The editorial in the *Nation* challenged these statements and indicated how sabotage could seriously affect the operation of Irish railways. To O'Connell this editorial was needlessly provocative and he promptly informed Duffy of his displeasure at this type of inflammatory writing. To conciliate English opinion, O'Connell prepared a long report which he submitted to a meeting of the Repeal Association. It was a condemnation of any belief in physical force as a means of achieving measures favorable to Ireland: "We emphatically announce our conviction that all political amelioration . . . ought to be sought for . . . only by peaceable, legal and constitutional means." When John Mitchel, a prominent member of the Young Ireland group, refused to accept the implication that "no national or political rights ought, at any time, or under any circumstances, or by any people, be sought for with an armed hand," O'Connell immediately attacked him as an advocate of open warfare to attain Irish objectives.[26]

Gavan Duffy took up the gage thrown down by O'Connell and on July 18 he attacked the idea that Ireland should never contemplate the use of force to attain her independence. The memorable slogan of O'Connell, "England's weakness is Ireland's opportunity," seemed to have lost its meaning. John O'Connell, the verbose and ineffective son of an aged and ailing father, belligerently suggested

26. O'Hegarty, *op. cit.,* pp. 243-245.

that the Young Irelanders withdraw from the Repeal Association. After a stormy meeting in which personalities were freely exchanged, the Young Ireland group followed this suggestion, leaving only the members who obeyed without question the dictates of the elder O'Connell. It was not long before the revenues of the association declined to the point where all its properties, including the Conciliation Hall, were sold to pay its debts. The repeal movement had collapsed and the person most responsible for this debacle was Daniel O'Connell. It was the age-old question of rule or ruin.[27]

I. THE IRISH MASSES ARE EXHORTED BY THE GREAT IRISH LEADER TO STARVE IN QUIET DIGNITY

The collapse of the Repeal Association left the Irish masses without any important organization that could look after their interests. Unity in Ireland was desperately needed in the fall of 1845 when the specter of starvation began to stalk along Irish highways. O'Connell was entirely aware of this fact, and if he had been a real statesman he would not have pushed his quarrel with the Young Irelanders. He knew all the implications of crop failures, and he must have seen that the so-called famine would soon turn into the great starvation. As George Bernard Shaw so clearly points out in his *Man and Superman*, in 1845 and through 1847 Ireland was faced with starvation, not famine. In his play, when Violet referred to the famine in the black year 1847, she was immediately corrected by Malone who bitterly remarked: "No, the Starvation. When a country is full o' food, and exporting it, there can be no famine. Me father was starved dead; and I was starved out to America in me mother's arms. English rule drove me and mine out of Ireland." [28]

The situation in Ireland in 1847 was never painted in truer colors than Shaw used in this picture of English imperialism in action. It was all the more tragic because of the large population in Ireland, which had rapidly increased by more than two million people during

27. Gavan Duffy, *My Life in Two Hemispheres,* I, 92-194.
28. George Bernard Shaw, *Man and Superman* (New York, 1930), pp. 147-148.

the period 1827-1846.[29] A simultaneous reduction in the acreage devoted to crop cultivation seemed to many observers an indication that the gloomy doctrine of Malthus would soon be proved beyond doubt.

The first signs of the potato blight appeared early in 1845 and rapidly gave evidence of national disaster, because the Irish masses lived largely upon the potatoes they raised on the small lots devoted to their cultivation. The Irish countryside grew numerous other crops—wheat, oats, barley, turnips, and carrots, but these were exported to England to pay the rack rents exacted by absentee landlords. The Duke of Wellington described the role of these landlords when a minor famine descended upon Ireland in 1830:

> It is starvation because it is the fact that, although there is abundance of provisions in the country of a superior kind . . . those who want in the midst of plenty cannot get [food] because they do not possess even the small sum of money necessary to buy a supply of food. . . . The proprietors of the country, those who ought to think for the people . . . are amusing themselves in the Clubs in London . . . and the Government . . . must find the remedy for it where they can, anywhere excepting in the pockets of Irish Gentlemen.[30]

These Irish gentlemen had to enjoy their clubs even though the Irish people starved and the English Government, whether Tory or Whig, was not disposed seriously to interfere with their enjoyment. The cure for the situation was evident to the Very Reverend Dr. McEvoy, of Kells:

> With starvation at our doors, grimly staring us, vessels laden with our sole hopes of existence, our provisions, are hourly wafted from our every port. . . . Self-preservation is the first law of nature. The exports of food from Ireland should be immediately halted. The right of the starving to try and sustain existence is a right far and away paramount to every right that property confers.[31]

29. Michael J. Mulhall, *Dictionary of Statistics* (New York, 1903), p. 13.
30. Wellington to Northumberland, July 7, 1830, *Despatches, Correspondence and Memoranda of Field Marshal Arthur, Duke of Wellington* (London, 1878), VII, 111-112.
31. John Mitchel, *The Last Conquest of Ireland (Perhaps)* (New York, 1873), pp. 207-208.

These stirring words of Dr. McEvoy, written and published in October 1845, were a real call to arms. While O'Connell was bent upon disciplining Gavan Duffy, John Mitchel, and other Young Irelanders for their separatist dreams and their incendiary words, McEvoy was issuing this clarion call to the Irish masses to stop the exportation of food from Irish ports. There was really only one way to stop these exportations and that was through force. But O'Connell hated to contemplate such a desperate contingency. Pressure in the House of Commons was the only method he believed would save the situation, and when the Whig Government of Lord John Russell came into power in 1846 his hopes rose rapidly. Soon there was a strong rumor that a pact had been established between the Whig Government and O'Connell. If this was so, there was no proof of it in the matter of Irish policy. Lord John Russell was seemingly indifferent to starvation in Ireland and he was resolutely opposed to any serious interference with what he regarded as the basic laws of economics: "He proposed to leave the trade as much liberty as possible. He believed that the markets would be best supplied without interference of Government. He did not propose to interfere with the wholesale or retail trade." [32]

The niggardly relief measures adopted by the government of Lord John Russell made a favorable impression upon O'Connell, who in September 1846 went so far as to say that it was "consoling to see the exertions which are being made by Government to relieve distress." [33] These faint-hearted exertions were not preventing starvation throughout Ireland, and O'Connell should have been completely familiar with this fact. But he still believed in his favorite formula of pressure in the House of Commons, and this pressure was still along the lines of repeal of the Act of Union. He finally perceived that this objective could not be realized in the near future, so he shifted his pressure in favor of public works, the taxation of absentee landlords, and the purchase and importation of food. He did not ask for the only remedy that would save the situation—the retention in Ireland of the food produced by Irish

32. O'Hegarty, op. cit., p. 306.
33. Ibid., p. 310.

farmers. In this supreme crisis he still counseled "endurance and petition, and no violence, no attempt to prevent the removal from the countryside of the food which alone could save the people." [34]

To O'Connell it seemed preferable for the Irish people to die on their knees in a last petition to Parliament (that was indifferent to their suffering) rather than rise in desperate revolt and die on their feet in a countrywide attempt to retain the ample crops they had raised. There was no real fighting blood in O'Connell, but there was plenty of it in other Irishmen in Clare, Limerick, Tipperary, and King's County in the autumn of 1847. So many tenants withheld "both rent and produce" from the landlords that the Government flooded Ireland with troops to such an extent that Lord Clarendon, the Viceroy, remarked that he felt at "the head of a provisional Government in an half-conquered country." [35]

In some parts of Ireland the people did not have enough strength to rise in revolt. When John Mitchel visited Galway he saw

> cowering wretches, almost naked in the savage weather, prowling in turnip-fields, and endeavoring to grub up roots which had been left but running to hide as the mail-coach rolled by. . . . Around those farmhouses which were still inhabited were to be seen hardly any stack of grain; the poor-rate collector, the rent agent, the county-cess collector had carried it off; and sometimes I could see in front of the cottages little children leaning against a fence when the sun shone out, for they could not stand, their limbs fleshless, their bodies half-naked, their faces bloated yet wrinkled, and of a pale greenish hue—children who would never . . . grow up to be men and women.[36]

When half-famished Irishmen refused to follow the prescription of O'Connell which insisted that they refrain from violence and be content to starve with dignity upon their tiny, blighted farms, they were promptly fed the usual English diet of beatings and bullets. The real tragedy was that they did not die fighting. They had little to lose but their economic chains, and if O'Connell had

34. O'Hegarty, op. cit., p. 302.
35. Spencer Walpole, *Life of Lord John Russell* (London, 1891), I, 460; Nassau Senior, *Journals, Conversations and Essays Relating to Ireland* (London, 1868), I, 227.
36. Mitchel, *Last Conquest of Ireland*, pp. 207-208.

called out in stentorian tones for a countrywide rising in 1845 he might have changed the history of Ireland in a most significant way. Many thousands would have died in a rain of bullets, but the English Government would have been compelled to alter its policy of starvation. World opinion would not have permitted the slaughter of the million that died for want of food.

But the great starvation did produce some secret societies that kept alive a spirit of resistance to English coercion. It was not long before the Irish Republican Brotherhood was founded upon a basis of independence gained through open revolt. These brave men had the courage to face the situation boldly and squarely. The time would come when England's weakness would really be Ireland's opportunity. An opportunity not to be thrown away according to the O'Connell prescription of Parliamentary palaver, but one to be grasped boldly with the iron fist of revolution.

J. THE RESULTS OF THE GREAT STARVATION

One of the ablest students of Irish economic history has expressed the opinion that English statesmen deliberately refrained from adopting measures that would have prevented the great starvation. In other words, both Whigs and Tories pursued a policy of "depopulation" in order to weaken Ireland. In this regard they were grimly successful. Canon O'Rourke estimates that during the black years from 1845 through 1847 there were "one million two hundred and forty thousand deaths resulting from the Irish Famine and the pestilence which followed in its track." [37] This is one of the most damning facts in all British history, and Joseph Stalin in 1931 in looking for a precedent to justify the starvation of millions of kulaks could have placed with satisfaction his broad finger upon this one. Sir Robert Peel and Lord John Russell had far less excuse than Stalin, who had a long background in terrorism and violence. They did, however, represent a school of English statesmen who placed British interests far ahead of humane considerations. The Opium

37. Canon John O'Rourke, *History of the Great Irish Famine of 1847* (Dublin, 1902), pp. 498-499.

War in China is a classic example of English policy in the Far East. Geography did not alter this British policy. There was no reason to expect that the Irish people would receive better treatment than the Chinese. The Irish were starved because English statesmen believed that the rapidly growing population on the island constituted a menace to English safety. As an able Irish historian expresses the matter: "There is justification for the view that the Government policy under which over a million died, and over a million emigrated in five years, was a deliberate policy of extermination, in pursuance of English political advantage." [38]

There were many members of the Irish middle class who saw through this policy of starvation, depopulation, pauperization, and emigration, and they had a leader in John Mitchel who refused to adhere to the O'Connell policy of constant submission. Mitchel himself tells how so many of his friends endured the ordeal of the starvation period and how finally "a kind of sacred wrath" took possession of them and they were ready for revolt.[39] They clearly saw the futility of petitioning an English Parliament for the redress of ancient wrongs when that same Parliament was content to have the Irish people starve in order to insure English political advantage.

Mitchel was a member of the Irish Confederation that had been organized by the Young Irelanders when they broke with O'Connell, and the radical tone of his writings alarmed many of his associates. The O'Connell tradition of submission was still strong even among men like Gavan Duffy and Smith O'Brien, who had once challenged O'Connell himself for his policy of weakness. Mitchel had grown weary of inaction. There were "far worse things going on around us than bloodshed." To give pungent expression to his viewpoint, Mitchel began, February 12, 1848, the publication of his own journal, the *United Irishman*. For sixteen weeks he poured out his fiery gospel: "The Irish people have a first and indefeasible right to this island and to all moral and material wealth and resources thereof, to possess and govern the same for their own use, maintenance, comfort and honour as a distinct Sovereign State." To English eyes this dec-

38. O'Hegarty, *op. cit.*, p. 328.
39. Mitchel, *op. cit.*, p. 201.

laration of independence was treason in its most heinous form, but many of the Young Irelanders took new heart at these bold words and the Irish Confederation adopted a more resolute stand. It was not long before the *Nation* became as forthright in its utterances as the *United Irishman*. The English Government did not allow these incendiary remarks to pass unnoticed. In May, 1848, Smith O'Brien, Mitchel, and Thomas Francis Meagher were charged with sedition. O'Brien and Meagher were put on trial but the jury disagreed and they were released. To be certain that Mitchel would not escape the Government net, Parliament rushed through a Treason-Felony Act, and it was under the terms of this broad legislation that Mitchel was tried and convicted May 27, 1848. He was sentenced to fourteen years' transportation to Van Diemen's Land (Tasmania), from which it was expected that no echoes of liberty could reach Ireland.[40]

The brutal treatment accorded Mitchel moved other members of the Irish Confederation to prepare for open revolt. But the Government was prepared to act with vigor. In July 1848 Gavan Duffy and several of his associates were arrested. Duffy was held for trial, but his associates were released because it was felt that they did not have the spirit for a real revolt. But disaffection continued to grow despite the passage by Parliament of a special bill to suspend the writ of habeas corpus in Ireland. The insurrection when it came was a dismal affair with no chance for success. The only solace for the former Young Irelanders was the fact that Duffy, after five trials, was released. He was able once more to publish the *Nation* but the soul had gone out of it, and Ireland, after being tortured with starvation and coercion, was a broken land.[41] There remained some bold spirits who still dreamed of Irish independence gained through revolution, but they had to nurse these dreams in deep secrecy because the middle class and the Church were fearful of any more conflicts with the English Government. These fighting Irish had to face social ostracism and Church displeasure, but they kept alive the spark of revolt that burst into flame in the rising of 1916, and

40. O'Hegarty, *op. cit.*, pp. 349-352.
41. Denis Gwynn, *Young Ireland and 1848* (Dublin, 1949).

it is to them that Ireland owes her present independence. Many of these bold spirits rallied under the banner of the Irish Republican Brotherhood or its counterpart in America, the Fenians. Their program will be discussed in the following section.

K. THE FOUNDING OF THE IRISH REPUBLICAN BROTHERHOOD AND THE FENIANS

The great starvation during the years 1845-1847 affected landlords as well as the Irish masses, and the Government hurried through the Encumbered Estates Act, which would give them financial relief. Under the terms of this legislation, Commissioners were empowered to sell any estate on petition of the owner or creditor. In the eight years following its enactment there were 7,489 estates sold for twenty million pounds. The new landlords were speculators who bought for investment and profit, and they continued the system of rack rents which had kept the Irish peasants down to a mere marginal existence. But the number of these laborers was fast diminishing. The old system of tillage was being replaced by large enclosures devoted to grazing. Between 1826 and 1870 the prices of agricultural products rose very slowly while the prices of beef, mutton, and pork more than doubled. This transition from tillage to grazing brought about a fundamental change in the social structure in Ireland. There was no longer a crowded countryside. In 1869, Friedrich Engels found the country districts in Ireland almost deserted, while Wilfrid Scawen Blunt noticed in 1886 that there were still "traces of old evictions everywhere in the little potato plots, with their marked ridges and furrows, now under grass, and here and there the site of a house long swept away." [42]

Dire poverty still existed in Ireland under a system that emphasized grazing and a money economy. The low wages paid to laborers kept the mass of the population in straitened circumstances and acted as a spur to emigration. Large numbers of the middle class also were adversely affected by the economic stagnation after 1848, and like Gavan Duffy they sought new opportunities in far-

42. Eric Strauss, *Irish Nationalism and British Democracy*, pp. 135ff.

flung British colonies or in America. The Irish middle class generally accepted with resignation the fact of English domination, and Dublin Castle loomed ever larger in their eyes. These "Castle Catholics" were delighted to receive the faintest nod of social recognition, and they were rewarded for their loyalty with minor Government posts and an occasional title. The Church also followed this line of least resistance and Cardinal Cullen initiated a policy of the "discouragement of aggressive Irish nationalism, acceptance of English domination . . . and a general acceptance of the theory that by remaining a subject race we were spreading the true religion and that we should get our reward in Heaven." [43] The Cardinal's action in keeping priests out of politics aroused the indignation of Gavan Duffy, who exclaimed: "Exclude the priests from politics! It was for this object that English intrigue laboured for the last half-century." If this policy prevailed, he was of the opinion that the Irish masses, "hopeless of agitation, would fly to secret societies and violence." [44] This prediction was completely vindicated.

The activities of secret societies were revealed in the legislation enacted by Parliament to suppress them—the Crime and Outrage Acts of 1851, 1856, 1858, and 1860, and the Unlawful Oaths Acts of 1853, 1854, and 1855. The driving force behind the organization of these secret societies came from Irish leaders who had fled to America, where they nursed in safety their hatred of England. Michael Doheny, Thomas D'Arcy McGee, Richard O'Gorman, John O'Mahony, and James Stephens were implicated in the revolution of 1848 and escaped to America.[45] Later they were joined by Thomas Francis Meagher and Terence Bellew McManus. In the autumn of 1853 John Mitchel escaped from Australia and hurried to New York City, where he began the publication of a paper which he called *The Citizen*. He was soon in hot water. In an open letter to Archbishop Hughes he voiced a hostility he had long felt towards the Catholic Church: "I mean to say, Bishop, that your Grace, and

---

43. O'Hegarty, *op. cit.*, p. 408.
44. Charles Gavan Duffy, *The League of North and South* (London, 1886), p. 339.
45. John O'Leary, *Recollections of Fenians and Fenianism* (London, 1896), I, 78.

the whole hierarchy of your Church, and the priesthood of it, too, so far as the hierarchy can control it, is an enemy of Irishmen, to the rights, the manhood, and the very lives of Irishmen."[46] Such utterances helped to confirm the hostility felt by the Archbishop towards radical Irishmen and their secret societies.

On April 13, 1854, Mitchel helped to found the first pre-Fenian society in New York City, the "Irishmen's Civil and Military Republican Union," which had for its objective the liberation of Ireland from the oppressive yoke of England. But his hostility towards Archbishop Hughes adversely affected the circulation of his paper, so he sold out to John McClenahan and moved to Tennessee. His old associates in New York City continued their agitation against England, and in the autumn of 1857 they sent a letter to James Stephens, in Dublin, asking him to found a society in Ireland which would work for independence. Stephens agreed to undertake this task but he was dependent upon Irish agitators in America for funds. When these were raised he founded in Dublin, on March 17, 1858, the Irish Revolutionary Brotherhood.[47] The American branch of this organization was founded in April 1859 and was called the Fenian Brotherhood.[48]

Although John Mitchel, Thomas Francis Meagher, and D'Arcy McGee refused to join the Fenians, the brotherhood grew rapidly and was soon an important factor in the American political equation. When it dissolved under the impact of Papal pressure, another brotherhood, the Clan-na-Gael, was founded by patriotic Irish-Americans who refused to let their dreams of Irish independence be extinguished by any authority either clerical or civil.

46. *The Citizen,* September 9, 1854.
47. Joseph Denieffe, A *Personal Narrative of the Irish Revolutionary Brotherhood* (New York, 1906), chap. iii.
48. William D'Arcy, *The Fenian Movement in the United States, 1858-1886* (Washington, 1947), pp. 12-15. John O'Mahony was responsible for the name "Fenian" as applied to this brotherhood. He was engaged in translating Geoffrey Keating's *History of Ireland* and was struck by the name of the Irish militia in pre-Christian times—Feonin Erin. The Fenian Brotherhood was to be a modern replica of this ancient institution.

2 THE EMERGENCE OF PARNELL AS A STATESMAN

A. THE FENIAN PROGRAM, "NOW OR NEVER," FAILS TO FREE IRELAND IN THE REVOLT OF 1867

The fiasco of '48 had been a serious blow to the leaders of the Young Ireland movement and they soon faded out of the political picture. Doheny was the only one of the Young Irelanders who stayed in the foreground and who continued his activity against England by becoming an ardent Fenian. The main body of the Fenians, as a matter of fact, came from different social and economic strata than the intellectuals who had eagerly read the stirring columns of the *Nation* in the days of Charles Gavan Duffy, Thomas Davis, and John Blake Dillon. The great starvation of 1845-1847 and the Encumbered Estates Act (1849) had wrought an economic revolution in Ireland. Emigration on a large scale had greatly reduced the number of agricultural laborers, while the shift from tillage to grazing, together with the replacement of a domestic economy by a money economy, had fundamentally changed the countryside of Ireland. Many members of the middle class had moved up to the position of landlords. They showed little sympathy for the economic distress of the laborers, and they pushed the collection of rack rents with the same cold tenacity that had marked the operation of estates by the former landlords. They were making money out of the existing situation and were strongly opposed to any forces of discontent that had revolutionary implications.

The agricultural laborers, shopworkers, and artisans still had a hard time maintaining a mere marginal existence. They were the rank and file of the Fenian societies. As John O'Leary remarked: "If I were to judge from my own experience . . . I should say that we had a great proportion of shopmen. . . . I should say that the men in the shops, as compared with the men in the workshops, were relatively more important in '65 than in '48. But of course these last were also most numerous in our movement."[1] Servant boys and farm laborers "formed from the start a large part of the active strength of the Fenian body, and counties like Kilkenny, where the condition of the laborers was described as particularly bad, were amongst the best organized districts in the country."[2]

The ritualism of the Fenians was short and simple: an oath of allegiance to an "Irish Republic now virtually established"; an emphasis upon the use of force to gain this political objective; and an expression of belief that armed action against English domination should soon be taken. After 1867 this note of urgency was definitely muted. It is significant that the Fenian program contained no items that expressed a demand for social and economic rights. All classes could march under the banner of nationalism, and Fenians seemed unaware of the fact that political inclinations often follow economic and social lines. The well-to-do Irish middle class had grown accustomed to looking to London for political directives and it scorned Fenian propaganda that aimed at independence. John O'Leary was one of the few Fenians who completely understood this fact:

> Your average bourgeois may make a very good sort of agitator, for here he can be shown, or at least convinced, that his mere material interests are concerned, and that he may serve them with little or no material risk. A rebel, however, you can rarely make of him, for here the risk is certain and immediate, and the advantage, if material advantage there should be, doubtful and distant.[3]

In the *Irish People*, a periodical founded by James Stephens in November 1863, O'Leary was bitterly critical of the indifference shown by the upper classes to the ideal of Irish nationalism:

1. John O'Leary, *Recollections of Fenians and Fenianism*, II, 238.
2. Eric Strauss, *Irish Nationalism and British Democracy*, p. 146.
3. O'Leary, *op. cit.*, I, 31.

Twenty years ago Thomas Davis appealed to the aristocracy to save the people with their own hands. We make no appeal to the aristocracy. For we know that, though we spoke with the tongues of men and angels, our appeal would be in vain. The hearts of these cruel aristocrats are hard as the nether millstone. . . . It is a waste of time, and labour, or worse, to endeavour to arouse the upper and middle classes to a sense of the duty they owe their country.[4]

The editorials in the *Irish People* were chiefly written by John O'Leary, Charles J. Kickham, and Thomas Clarke Luby.[5] They did not have the literary polish of the editorials that had appeared in the *Nation*, but they were direct and hard hitting. They were particularly severe upon the antics of Alexander M. Sullivan, the new editor of the *Nation*. On October 30, 1858, Sullivan wrote a long article in which he trenchantly declared that any person who entered a secret society was "an enemy to his country and a deadly foe to the cause of her Freedom."[6] In some of his articles he came close to being an informer against members of secret societies, and for this reason he aroused a virulent hatred in the breasts of most Fenians. In the *Irish People* John O'Leary poured bitter scorn upon men like Sullivan. He had nothing but contempt for

> dilletanti patriots, who perhaps meant well to their country, but certainly always with the saving clause that they suffered little ill themselves. Those drawing-room rebels could sing the loves of Ireland in more or less melodious verses, and perhaps accompany themselves on the piano, but they no more meant "to strike one blow for thee, dear land," than to scale the heights of Olympus. Elegant verses and eloquent speeches they can give in abundance, but that is all.[7]

But the Fenians had to contend with a much more formidable foe than the leaders of the Irish middle class. The Catholic Church early entered the lists against them and carried on the contest with

---

4. P. S. O'Hegarty, *History of Ireland Under the Union, 1801-1922*, pp. 435-436.
5. For interesting pen portraits of O'Leary, Luby, and Kickham, see John Devoy, *Recollections of an Irish Rebel* (New York, 1929), pp. 280-318.
6. *Ibid.*, chap. v.
7. O'Hegarty, *op. cit.*, p. 430.

increasing bitterness. As early as October 3, 1858, the parish priest of Kenmare sent to Dublin Castle certain particulars concerning secret societies in his neighborhood. In this regard he was in close accord with Cardinal Cullen. Cullen had been rector of the Irish college in Rome during the revolt against Papal authority in 1848, and he regarded the Fenians as an Irish version of the Italian secret society, the Carbonari. To the Fenians the Cardinal was afflicted with a distressing malady which they called "Carbonari on the brain." [8] His open hostility towards all Fenians was strikingly illustrated in the matter of the burial of Terence Bellew McManus.

McManus had not been a Fenian but he had participated in the rising of 1848. He had fled to America and finally settled in San Francisco. When he died in January 1861, many Fenians were struck by the thought that their secret society would be widely advertised and enormously strengthened if the body of McManus were taken back to Ireland and buried under impressive Fenian auspices. In New York, Archbishop Hughes not only made arrangements for a Mass in St. Patrick's Cathedral but he also preached a sermon upholding the right of an oppressed people to strike for freedom.[9] Cardinal Cullen, however, was not so broad-minded. He refused to allow Mass to be said in the Cathedral for McManus. The Fenians, therefore, took the body to the Mechanics Institute and the funeral was conducted from there. It was one of the most significant in Irish annals. The cortège which marched to Glasnevin Cemetery was seven miles long and was watched by a vast throng of spectators, including many priests like Father Kenyon, of Templederry, and Father Meehan, of Dublin.[10]

In Ireland the Fenians continued to flourish despite the unceasing enmity of the Church. In America this hostility was by no means universal. In October 1864 Archbishop Martin Spalding, of Baltimore, sent a circular letter to the American Catholic hierarchy asking their opinion of Fenianism. It had already been denounced by

8. William D'Arcy, *The Fenian Movement in the United States, 1858-1886*, p. 19.
9. Michael Cavanagh, *Memoirs of Thomas Francis Meagher* (Worcester, 1902), pp. 419-422.
10. John Devoy, *Recollections of an Irish Rebel*, pp. 22-23.

the bishops of Chicago and Philadelphia and the archbishop of Cincinnati. In their replies to Archbishop Spalding a majority of the hierarchy advised a delay before taking action against Fenianism because it was not clear that the Fenians were a secret society in the sense of the Pontifical decrees. The Fenians soon secured a copy of this letter of Archbishop Spalding and made good use of one of the phrases he had used when he was Bishop of Louisville: "The Fenians are not to be disturbed." [11]

But the Fenians in America were profoundly disturbed by the outbreak of the Civil War. Thousands of members of the society enlisted in the armies of the North and the South and thus postponed the day when they could be of service to Ireland. Thomas Francis Meagher commanded a brigade that fought with distinguished gallantry for the North, and an Irish brigade under Patrick Cleburne helped to write a bright page in the military history of the South. Leading Fenians like Thomas Clarke Luby refused to come out in favor of the North and in the *Irish People* he sharply attacked the activities of recruiting agents sent to induce the Irish youth to enlist in the federal military service: "We consider the Irishman who leaves Ireland at present expressly to join the Northern ranks, not a true soldier of freedom, but a miserable hireling, guilty of conduct almost as unprincipled . . . as that of the Irishman . . . who becomes the mercenary tool of English tyranny." [12]

There was one aspect of the American Civil War that gave some consolation to many Fenians—through their service in the armies of the North and South there were thousands of Fenians who would receive an excellent apprenticeship in arms. This fact led James Stephens to announce secretly that towards the end of 1865 there would be a revolt in Ireland against English domination. After the Civil War had ended he had high hopes of securing from America a large supply of military equipment that was no longer needed. He knew that he would have many officers who had been

11. William D'Arcy, *op. cit.*, p. 49.
12. O'Hegarty, *op. cit.*, p. 436. For some interesting comments upon the enlistment of Irish recruits in the armies of the North, see Frank L. Owsley, *King Cotton Diplomacy* (Chicago, 1931), pp. 517-526.

trained in the hard school of experience. As for recruits, he could count upon some 100,000 Fenians who were sworn members of the society. A considerable number of these Fenians were in the armed forces of England. Of the 26,000 regular troops that England had stationed in Ireland, sixty percent were Irish and it is estimated that 8,000 of these were Fenians. Of the militia force of 12,000, one half were Fenians, while in the army in England the Fenians numbered 7,000. If Stephens could have started a revolt in 1865 it would have been a formidable affair.[13]

But there were many factors that wrecked his bold plans. There was a woeful lack of efficient organization with reference to actual military planning and there was a great dearth of military equipment. The split in the Fenian Brotherhood in America had seriously retarded the shipment of arms to Ireland. Moreover, the Fenians in America were planning an invasion of Canada and they required most of the equipment they had been able to store away. While Stephens was considering some means of overcoming the difficulties that grew more serious each day, the English Government suddenly decided to arrest the more important Fenians who were known to be plotting a revolt. On September 15, 1865, a strong force of police entered the office of the Fenian periodical, the *Irish People*, and arrested everyone they found upon the premises. Others were arrested in their residences. Thomas Clarke Luby, John O'Leary, and O'Donovan Rossa were quickly apprehended and in November, James Stephens, Charles J. Kickham, Hugh Brophy, and Edward Duffy were taken into custody. By the time the English Government had suspended the writ of habeas corpus, February 17, 1866, hundreds of prisoners were awaiting trial.[14]

But James Stephens, who had been rescued from jail, continued his efforts to prepare a revolt against the English armed forces. He did not seem to realize how great were the odds against him, and when the rising finally came on March 5-6, 1867, it was easily crushed. The English jails were now overflowing with Irish prisoners whose trials would be speedily pushed through.

13. Devoy, *op. cit.*, chaps. x-xi.
14. *Ibid.*, chaps. xii-xxxiv.

B. FENIAN ACTIVITIES THREATEN TO CAUSE A CRISIS IN ANGLO-AMERICAN RELATIONS

Plans for a rising in Ireland against English armed forces were widely discussed in America, and a diversionary attack upon Canada seemed to many Fenians as an important means of contributing to the success of the Irish venture. Many bold spirits were not content to remain in America and play a secondary role. Hundreds of Irish-Americans who had served in the armies of the North and South during the struggle for Southern independence sailed for Ireland and were soon taking part in the preparations for a revolt. On February 17, 1866, the English Government suspended the writ of habeas corpus; one of the main reasons for this action was the decision to take prompt action against these former residents of Ireland. According to the English doctrine of indefeasible allegiance, all Irish-Americans, despite their American citizenship, were still British subjects and could be treated as such. It was the belief of William West, the American consul in Dublin, that the Government action relative to suspension of the writ was taken so that all Americans in Ireland could be placed in jail "without having to assign any cause for their committal, the existing laws of the country being found inadequate to the occasion." [15]

To lend assistance to these imprisoned Americans, a meeting was called in New York City on March 4. Archbishop McCloskey opposed this rally and issued a circular letter to be read in all the Catholic churches in the city. He asked all Catholics to refrain from attending the rally, which he condemned as a profanation of the Lord's day. His appeal fell on deaf ears, since 100,000 Fenians and their sympathizers turned out and listened to a vigorous address by Captain John McCafferty, fresh from a jail in Ireland.[16]

The Fenians were particularly concerned about the fate of American prisoners in Ireland awaiting trial. In response to Ameri-

15. West to Secretary Seward, February 17, 1866, Dublin, *Consular Despatches,* IV, *MS.*, National Archives.
16. New York *Herald,* March 5, 1866.

can protests voiced by the American Minister in London, Lord Clarendon declared that "no British-born subject could ever or under any circumstances, renounce, or be absolved from, his allegiance to his sovereign." [17] The reply of Secretary Seward was equally uncompromising:

> The United States will find themselves entirely unable to acquiesce in the course which is indicated . . . in the case of John H. and Joseph Gleason and other British born, but naturalized citizens of the United States. . . . There has been no reservation on the part of the United States in regard to the principle that the process of naturalization in this country completely absolves the person complying with it, from foreign allegiance.[18]

Lord Clarendon readily saw the dangers of this impasse, so he issued instructions that the Fenian prisoners in Ireland, both naturalized and native-born citizens of the United States, should be gradually released if they would promise to return to the United States.[19]

While this diplomatic duel was taking place between Seward and Lord Clarendon, the Fenians were preparing for an invasion of New Brunswick from the Maine border that skirted the St. Croix River. This attempt was easily thwarted by General Meade on April 19, and thus ended another Fenian fiasco. But failure at Campo Bello did not prevent the Fenians from attempting another invasion. This was to be a two-pronged affair. Brigadier General Samuel S. Spear was to command the army that would cross the frontier at St. Albans, Vermont, while Brigadier General W. F. Lynch would be in charge of the detachment that would move into Canada at a point near Buffalo. On May 31 Colonel John O'Neill crossed the Niagara River and occupied the village of Fort Erie. On June 2 he marched to Black Creek and then moved on to Ridgeway to inter-

17. Lord Clarendon to Sir Frederick Bruce, British Minister at Washington, March 10, 1866, F. O. 115, 449, Transcripts from Public Record Office, London, Library of Congress.
18. Secretary Seward to Adams, March 22, 1866, Great Britain, *Instructions*, XX, *MS.*, National Archives.
19. Clarendon to Bruce, April 14, 1866, F. O. 115: 450.

cept a Canadian force under Colonel Booker. This volunteer force was easily dispersed, but when an enemy column of 1,400 troops began to move to the rear of the Fenian expeditionary force, it was decided to beat a rapid retreat. On June 3 Colonel O'Neill and his small force hurriedly retreated to American territory. Fenian raids had merely a nuisance value.[20]

On the political scene these Fenian raids were of more importance. In Congress there was a spirited competition for the "Irish vote," and Robert C. Schenck, of Ohio, introduced a resolution in the House of Representatives urging the Department of State to recognize the Irish nation as a belligerent.[21] Although Secretary Seward paid little attention to this resolution, the mere fact that it had been introduced gave great concern to British Minister Bruce in Washington, who regarded it as an indication of the "strength of the Irish vote" in the United States.[22] Bruce was also worried about the naturalized Fenians who were in Canadian and British prisons, and he expressed to Clarendon the hope that they would be treated with leniency. Stiff prison terms might cause serious difficulties between the United States and Britain.[23]

On June 18 a resolution was introduced in the House of Representatives calling upon the President for information concerning the Fenian prisoners in Canada and Ireland.[24] The fact that it passed unanimously indicated the political implications in the Fenian question, and Seward pressed Bruce for the release of these prisoners on condition that they would immediately return to the United States. Bruce was able to satisfy this request, and during July and August 1866 the Fenians who had been confined in Irish prisons were released and conducted by the constabulary to ships bound for America.[25] The British Government was well aware of the fact that Seward had done his best to handle the Fenian

20. Frank H. Severance, "The Fenian Raid of '66," *Buffalo Historical Society Publications*, XXV (1921), 263-285.
21. *Journal* of the House of Representatives, 39 Cong., 1 sess., 816-819.
22. Bruce to Lord Clarendon, June 12, 1866, F. O. 115: 453.
23. Bruce to Clarendon, June 18, 1866, F. O. 115: 453.
24. *Journal* of the House of Representatives, 39 Cong., 1 sess., 860.
25. Secretary Seward to Adams, June 9, 1866, Great Britain, *Instructions*, XX, MS., National Archives.

question so that a minimum amount of friction would be aroused. From London, Adams reported that he had received "the most marked and pointed" expressions of appreciation in all circles in London with reference to Seward's conduct of foreign relations.[26] But the British Minister in Washington had apprehensions as to the course Congress would follow during its next session, and he feared that political factors might influence the decisions of President Johnson:

> I feel much uncertainty as to the course the President may adopt, if he is placed in the dilemma of sacrificing the Irish vote, or of allowing the Fenians to take their chance. I think he is honest, & Mr. Seward pacifist—but his honesty may be put to too severe a trial, & Mr. Seward's continuance in office becomes every day more problematical.[27]

The fate of the Fenians in Canadian prisons was a source of special concern to Mr. Bruce. The Montreal *Gazette* had expressed the viewpoint of multitudes of Canadians with reference to these Fenians. It regarded them as "mere land-pirates coming among us . . . to rob and subjugate us, or, if we refused to do their behests, to murder us. The laws of civilized warfare do not and cannot apply to them." [28]

During the trials in Toronto in October and November, twenty-six Fenians had been acquitted, but the death sentence had been imposed upon several of them, including John McMahon, a Catholic priest from Anderson, Indiana. The indignation in Fenian circles aroused by this news caused Seward to exert pressure upon Bruce. He soon reported that the executions would not be carried out, and on March 4, 1867, the sentences were commuted to long prison terms.[29] Two years later, after considerable further correspondence, McMahon was finally released.

In May 1870 Colonel John O'Neill staged his long-threatened

26. Adams to Secretary Seward, June 21, 1866, Great Britain, *Despatches,* XCII, MS., National Archives.
27. Bruce to Lord Stanley, *Confidential,* August 2, 1866, F. O. 115: 454.
28. November 5, 1866.
29. Bruce to Secretary Seward, November 27 and December 8, 1866, Great Britain, *Notes,* LXXXIII, MS., National Archives.

foray across the Canadian frontier near Franklin, Vermont. It was easily repelled and O'Neill and other Fenian leaders were arrested and, after conviction of violation of American neutrality laws, were given prison terms. The Fenian menace to Canada was now at an end and Anglo-American relations could run a smoother course.[30]

C. THE MANCHESTER MARTYRS

The treatment of Fenian prisoners in Britain became more rigorous after the Manchester incident of September 18, 1867. In August of that year Colonel Thomas J. Kelly, a prominent Fenian who had escaped arrest after the rising in Ireland in March, called a convention of the Irish Republican Brotherhood to meet in Manchester. After making plans to infuse a new spirit of confidence into dejected Fenian hearts, it was decided to heal the split in the Fenian Brotherhood in America by forming a compromise organization named the Clan-na-Gael. The Clan, during its existence, had an important role in furthering the cause of Irish freedom. But the activities of Colonel Kelly attracted the attention of the Manchester police, who arrested him and Captain William Deasy on September 11, 1867. A week later they were rescued by a group of Fenian volunteers who stopped the police van carrying the prisoners from the police court back to jail. During the rescue one of the policemen was accidentally killed and the population of Manchester was set ablaze with indignation.[31]

The Fenians in America hailed the release of Kelly and Deasy as an act of heroism. Their attitude is revealed in the following excerpt from a Fenian newspaper published in New York City: "The Fenians have at last fought their first real fight and won their first real victory. They have met, attacked and vanquished an armed band of English hirelings in the center of England herself." [32]

In Manchester twenty-eight Irishmen were quickly arrested and held for examination. Five were finally put on trial—W. P. Allen,

30. Lester B. Shippee, *Canadian-American Relations, 1849-1874* (New Haven, 1939), pp. 238-239.
31. Devoy, *op. cit.*, pp. 237-250.
32. The *Irish World*, October 5, 1867.

O'Meagher Condon, Michael Larkin, Edward Maguire, and Michael O'Brien. The evidence against Maguire was so dubious that he was released, but public opinion in Manchester demanded some victims and they had to be supplied. Condon and O'Brien were American citizens and appealed to the American Minister in London for assistance. On November 19 he received a telegram from Secretary Seward instructing him to intercede for O'Brien and Condon.[33] Adams took no action with regard to O'Brien, but he did push the case of Condon, who was granted a reprieve.[34] After a farcical trial, Allen, Larkin, and O'Brien were convicted of murder and executed on November 23, 1867.

In America the execution of the three Fenians aroused widespread indignation. *The New York Times,* long known to be hostile to Fenianism, expressed the opinion that the manner in which the trial in Manchester had been conducted was a blot upon the English legal record: "Thousands on both sides of the Atlantic believe that the dead had not a fair trial, and this conviction prevails widely even among those who have always condemned the Fenian movement."[35] The movement itself was greatly stimulated by these executions, and the Fenians girded themselves for another assault upon the British empire. But they ran into a major obstacle when, on January 12, 1870, the Fenian Brotherhood was condemned by the Catholic Church.[36]

This condemnation was not based upon the charge that it was a secret society whose aims were unknown. The brotherhood was condemned because it "worked for the overthrow of British rule in Ireland. According to the teaching of the Catholic Church a rebellion is justified only if a tyrannical government is oppressing a country; if force is the only means of remedying the condition; if there is a reasonable chance of success; if conditions in the country will be improved by the overthrow of the tyrannical government.

33. Secretary Seward to Adams, November 19, 1867, Great Britain, *Instructions,* XXI, *MS.,* National Archives.
34. Adams to Secretary Seward, November 22, 1867, Great Britain, *Despatches,* LXXXXIV, *MS.,* National Archives.
35. November 25, 1867.
36. *Acta Sanctae Sedis* (5th ed., Rome, 1872-1911), I (1872), 290.

According to the decree, none of these conditions applied to Ireland. In the course of seven hundred years the British Government had become legitimate in Ireland." [37]

D. THE EMERGENCE OF CHARLES STEWART PARNELL AS A STATESMAN

The Papal decree condemning Fenianism did not convince a large number of American Fenians that English government in Ireland was legitimate and therefore should not be overthrown by force. The brotherhood still had strength enough to launch another futile invasion of Canada (May 1870) and to exert pressure upon the Department of State to press for the release of Fenian prisoners in the United Kingdom. In December 1870 the British Government responded to this pressure and announced the release of certain prisoners, who would be required to take passage for the United States. The first contingent of these refugees arrived in New York in January 1871 and included such well-known persons as John Devoy, John McClure, Henry S. Mulleda, Charles Underwood O'Connell, and Jeremiah O'Donovan Rossa. The "Cuba Five," as they were called after the name of the vessel that transported them to America, were destined to have an important role in keeping alive an anti-English spirit in the United States, and John Devoy lost no time in announcing a program:

> Our aim will be to create an Irish party in this country, whose actions in American politics will have for its sole object the interests of Ireland. But Devoy immediately made it clear that the Fenians would have no part in this program: We will also hold aloof from all the different sections of Fenians. I may tell you that most of us are sick of the very issue of Fenianism, though as resolved as ever to work for the attainment of Irish independence.[38]

This hostility of John Devoy towards the American brand of Fenianism was typical of the attitude of large numbers of once-

---

37. William D'Arcy, *The Fenian Movement in the United States, 1858-1886* (Washington, 1947), pp. 330-331.
38. The Boston *Pilot*, February 4, 1871.

Parnell as a Statesman

ardent members of the brotherhood. Bitter divisions within their ranks; the failure of repeated invasions of Canada, and the continued hostility of the Catholic Church finally destroyed an organization which had started with such high hopes. In November 1885 the Fenians held their last convention in the United States, and during the following year the brotherhood disbanded.[39] Its tradition of securing Irish independence through armed force was carried by the "physical force" men of the Clan-na-Gael.

In Ireland the situation was quite different. The thunders of the Church did not frighten Irishmen who continued to cherish the objective of independence through the use of armed force. They would never regard English rule in Ireland as legitimate and they continued their activities in spite of every obstacle. It was noted that Cardinal Cullen was in Rome attending the Vatican Council when the decree condemning Fenianism was issued. It was also remembered that in 1867 Cardinal Manning had once devoted a whole pastoral to an attack upon the brotherhood. The Vatican decree had been anticipated by some Fenians and when it came they were not deeply disturbed by it. When their activities continued there were some politicians who hoped to use the brotherhood to advance their political fortunes.

In the forefront of this group was Isaac Butt, who had served as the legal counsel for some of the more important Fenians during the state trials. He believed this service might attract many Fenians who would welcome his advice on political matters. In 1870 he founded the Irish Home Rule League, whose real purpose was to perpetuate leadership in the hands of the landlords and the upper middle class. He was distinctly fearful of the leveling effects in England of the Parliamentary reform bill of 1867, and he thought that the best way to keep this liberal contagion from reaching Ireland was to have some form of home rule. It was his opinion that there were "no people on earth less disposed to democracy than the Irish. The real danger of revolutionary violence is far more with the English people. The time may not be far distant when a separate Irish Parliament might be, in the best sense of the word, a Conserva-

39. William D'Arcy, *op. cit.,* pp. 406-408.

tive element in the British Constitution." [40] If he could harness the energies of the Fenians to some scheme of Home Rule, there was little doubt that the movement would be greatly strengthened. In this way, moreover, he could keep them from advocating any dangerous revolutionary reforms.

Two outstanding Fenians who co-operated with the Home Rule party were Joseph Biggar and John Barry, both of whom were wealthy businessmen. Biggar became a troublesome thorn in the side of English statesmen by pushing in Parliament a policy of legislative obstructionism. The nuisance value of this policy soon became apparent, and compromises were often wrung from reluctant English leaders. But progress was slow and Cardinal Manning in 1873 remarked with satisfaction that Home Rule had divided "the Irishmen and reclaimed many Fenians. Without in any way committing myself to it I have been very tolerant about it, believing it to be 'like vaccination to small-pox.'" [41]

As long as Isaac Butt was the outstanding leader in Ireland, the conservative movement so dear to his heart was the main factor in the political equation. But his position as leader was soon challenged by a young man of wealth and assured social position—Charles Stewart Parnell. In his biography of Parnell, St. John Ervine takes great pains to prove that the Parnells had no Celtic blood in their veins. To him it seemed incredible that a member of the Anglo-Irish aristocracy could have any real devotion to the idea of Irish nationalism—nationalism that would embrace every creed, every race, every class. Parnell was a puzzle to him and he could not comprehend how a man with such superior talents could misuse them for such a dubious cause as Irish independence.

It is this note of independence that clearly distinguishes Parnell from other Irish leaders like O'Connell. O'Connell was never a separatist who wished to dissolve the ties that bound Britain to Ireland. He never dreamed of an Ireland outside the political confines of the Empire, but Parnell constantly stressed the ideal of independence. As Mr. O'Hegarty reminds us:

40. Isaac Butt, *Irish Federalism* (London, 1874), p. 39.
41. Shane Leslie, *Henry Edward Manning* (London, 1921), p. 207.

Parnell as a Statesman

> To Parnell the issue of national independence or self-government was the primary and dominating issue. . . . The effect of Parnell was a Separatist effect. His appeal was to Separatist sentiment and his support came from Separatist sentiment. . . . He saw that an Irish revolutionary movement must have two sides, an open one and a secret one, co-operating but not uniting . . . and he did do his best to secure that co-operation.[42]

Parnell was not a man of wide reading and highly developed intellectual tastes, and according to his wife his knowledge of Shakespeare was pathetically meager.[43] But he was a political realist who had the courage of his convictions. One of these convictions was a fervent belief in the cause of Irish independence, no matter how secured, and this fact made him willing to work with the Fenians. His interest in this brotherhood was first awakened when the "Manchester Martyrs" were hurriedly hanged by the English in November 1867. The brutal manner in which these executions had been handled made an unfavorable impression, which grew stronger as he watched from his seat in the House of Commons the British Government in action. After he had taken his seat in Parliament, April 22, 1875, he was content for many months to see much and say little, but on June 30, 1876, he was shocked into vehement utterance. Sir Michael Hicks-Beach, the Chief Secretary for Ireland, speaking on the matter of Home Rule, referred to the "Manchester Martyrs" as the "Manchester Murderers." He was at once interrupted by Parnell, who shouted out in sharp protest, "No! No!" Black Michael regarded the young member from Meath with astonishment and then remarked in icy tones: "I regret to hear that there is an honourable member in this House who will apologize for murder." Parnell believed that the best way to settle this situation was to raise his eyebrows and not the roof. After listening to angry shouts of "Withdraw! Withdraw!," he arose with quiet dignity and calmly addressed Sir Michael: "The right honourable gentleman looked at me so directly when he said that he regretted that any member of the house should apologize for murder that I

---

42. O'Hegarty, *op. cit.*, pp. 597-598.
43. Katharine O'Shea, *Charles Stewart Parnell* (2 vols., London, 1914), I, 174.

wish to say as publicly as I can that I do not believe, and never shall believe, that any murder was committed at Manchester." [44]

This declaration was not intended by Parnell for just the ears of the members of the House of Commons—he was really addressing himself to Irishmen all over the world, and the echoes of his bold words gave particular delight to the Fenians who had lost hope in the program of Isaac Butt. As leader of the Irish party in Parliament, Butt had tried conciliation without success and had imposed upon his followers a policy of moderation. To depose Butt as leader was a task that would require new Parliamentary tactics, and Parnell was ready to follow the path indicated by Joseph Ronayne. Ronayne had seen the scanty political harvests that Butt had gleaned from plowing furrows of acquiescence in English legislative fields; a nuisance policy of obstruction might bring far greater returns. He explained his formula to Joseph Biggar as follows: "The English stop our bills. Why don't we stop their bills? That's the thing to do. . . . Butt's a fool—too gentlemanly." [45]

Joseph Biggar was impressed with the wisdom of this counsel, which he promptly put into action. But he was not of the mold of a party leader. A successful pork procurer from Belfast with some of the crudity that went along with his business, he was not the diplomat that was needed to bring unity to the Irish delegation in the House of Commons. He was a fighter, not a leader. Parnell saw the situation at a glance. He would work with Biggar in a policy of legislative obstruction, but he would so direct the proceedings that the public eye would be chiefly fastened upon him. John Morley has criticized Parnell for lack of a "constructive faculty," but he had to admit that the Irish leader "knew what he wanted." [46]

There is little doubt that Parnell knew exactly what he wanted, and in 1877 he adopted a policy of legislative obstructionism as the best path to that goal. At first his tactics aroused English bewilderment and then loudly expressed wrath. Mr. Henry Lucy com-

---

44. R. Barry O'Brien, *The Life of Charles Stewart Parnell*, pp. 95-96.
45. *Ibid.*, pp. 93-94.
46. *Life of Gladstone* (New York, 1903), p. 304.

plained that Parnell had "no redeeming qualities unless we regard it as an advantage to have in the House a man who unites in his own person all the childish unreasonableness, all the ill-regulated suspicion, and all the childish credulity of the Irish peasant, without any of the humour, the courtliness, or dash of the Irish gentleman." [47]

Parnell was tired of the constant courtesy that Isaac Butt had shown in the House of Commons towards his English associates, and he had no desire to make a reputation for Parliamentary courtliness. On the evening of April 12, 1877, the situation came to a climax. Parnell and Biggar had been goading Mr. Gathorne-Hardy with sharp verbal pricks that caused him to tremble with rage. Some Irish members who felt a little ashamed at Parnell's performance rushed to Isaac Butt, quietly reposing in the smoking room, and requested his assistance in quieting the obstreperous member from Meath. Butt lost no time in reaching the Chamber and reproving Parnell: "I must express my disapproval of the course taken by the honourable member for Meath. It is a course of obstruction, and one against which I must enter my protest. . . . I disapprove entirely of the conduct of the honourable member for Meath." [48]

Parnell remained perfectly calm under this rebuke and finally rose to remark: "The honourable and learned gentleman was not in the House when I attempted to explain why I had not put down notice of my amendments." [49] This defiant answer marked the decline of Butt's leadership in the House of Commons. He had chided a bold Irishman for an obstructionist policy which had been adopted as the only means for securing justice for Ireland. Moreover, he had not been present in the Chamber during the debate but had acted merely upon glib hearsay. This incident received further elaboration when the *Freeman's Journal,* Dublin, published some correspondence between Parnell and Butt. It was apparent to many observers that Butt had written his last political will and testament. A new and bolder hand would soon guide the Irish

47. *The Irish World,* March 29, 1876.
48. O'Brien, *op. cit.,* pp. 110-112.
49. *Ibid.,* pp. 112-113.

Party in Parliament, and Fenians throughout the world began to take an increased interest in a leader who was not afraid to beard British lions in their legislative den.

E. PARNELL VISITS AMERICA AND RECEIVES A MILD REBUFF FROM PRESIDENT GRANT

Parnell's deep-seated dislike of England came to him very naturally. His mother was a daughter of the distinguished American Commodore Charles Stewart who had fought some spirited battles with English frigates during the War of 1812. As a young boy Parnell heard from his mother long recitals of his grandfather's successful encounters with perfidious Englishmen who well deserved to be beaten. When Barry O'Brien talked to Parnell's mother in 1896 he asked why "Charles had such an antipathy to the English." She responded with explosive vigor: "Why should he not? Have not his ancestors been always opposed to England? My grandfather Tudor fought against the English in the War of Independence. My father fought against the English in the War of 1812, and I suppose the Parnells had no great love for them." [50]

Parnell had a romance with an American girl which, unlike his father's, did not have a story-book ending. He paid a visit to the United States in 1871 in order to persuade her to become his wife, but she calmly rejected his suit because "he was only an Irish gentleman without any particular name in public." [51]

His next visit to America was more auspicious. In the summer of 1876 a meeting of "advanced Nationalists" was held in Dublin at which an address was "voted to General Grant congratulating the American people on the centenary of American independence." Parnell and Mr. O'Connor Power were deputed to present this address to General Grant. When they reached Washington in October 1876, they ran into diplomatic difficulties. The Secretary of State,

---

50. *Ibid.*, pp. 28-29.
51. John Howard Parnell, *Charles Stewart Parnell* (New York, 1914), pp. 74-78.

Hamilton Fish, was out of the city and he had left his vigilant assistant, J. C. Bancroft Davis, in charge of diplomatic protocol. The *Diary* of Davis tells how Parnell and Mr. Power were prevented from presenting to Grant an address from the "Irish nation" to the "American people":

> October 17: the President spoke about the Irish address. I explained the custom and what they ought to do and said I had cursorily looked at the address as it was in a side room at the White House . . . and I was satisfied that I could not assist in presenting it without the knowledge of the British Minister. He agreed with me and in the afternoon Sniffin brought me a note he had written to Messrs. Power and Parnell saying it must be sent for approval to the State Department and the Minister's [British] assent. I altered it a little and it was to be sent. I had seen Sir Edward [Thornton] a moment in the morning and he was anxious to avoid a question, and to do what he could.

On the following day Parnell and Mr. Power called upon Mr. Davis at the Department of State. They were "very quiet and gentlemanly and said they could not well submit their address to Sir Edward Thornton, but thought it proper I should. I explained the practice and agreed to send it and did with a note to Sir Edward Thornton." [52]

Parnell did not appreciate this lesson in diplomatic procedure and he later blurted out to his brother John that he thought President Grant was a "vulgar old dog." [53] But Congress was more considerate than the President. On December 20, 1876, Mr. Holman introduced in the House of Representatives a resolution calling attention to the address of the "Irish nation" congratulating the American people on the centenary of their independence.[54] Although this resolution was buried in the files of the Committee on Foreign Affairs, Mr. Caulfield, on March 3, 1877, secured the unanimous approval of a similar resolution which expressed the "grateful recognition" of the "people of the United States" for this

52. J. C. Bancroft Davis, *Diary*, October 16-18, 1876, *Hamilton Fish Papers*, Library of Congress.
53. Parnell, *op. cit.*, p. 146.
54. *Congressional Record*, December 20, 1876, 44 Cong., 2 sess., 321-322.

Irish address.[55] Mr. Power could take back to Ireland an expression of warm friendship from the House of Representatives.

F. FAMINE YEARS IN IRELAND LEAD TO THE ESTABLISHMENT OF A LAND LEAGUE

In 1877 it was apparent to Parnell that he was moving more and more into the public eye. The very fact that he had been chosen to present to President Grant the address of the advanced Nationalists was an indication that he was being regarded as a leader by an ever-widening circle of devoted followers. It was also evident that leadership of a high quality was imperatively needed. A prolonged season of hard times had descended upon Ireland and some solution had to be found. This economic recession had begun in England. After the repeal of the Corn Laws in 1846 England had opened her ports to a flood of foodstuffs that poured in from all over the world. Cheap food was an important essential to the English factory workers as exports soon reached unprecedented heights. But English prosperity came to an abrupt end in the last months of 1873 and "there began the greatest depression trend of modern times which was to reach its limit in 1896 with a price index of 61." England was at the end of an era. From 1815 to 1875 English investors had exported a capital surplus of half a billion pounds, a great part of this sum coming between the years 1850 and 1873, when prices were surging upward during years of mounting prosperity. This golden tide suddenly ebbed in 1873. England found it difficult to balance her requirements of food and raw materials with the manufactured goods she was able to export and the freights her merchant marine could earn.[56]

Economic recession in England meant hard times in Ireland. Competition with overseas exports of food to England had driven down the prices of Irish products in the seventies. After 1875 the

---

55. *Ibid.*, March 3, 1877, p. 2237.
56. Leland H. Jenks, *The Migration of British Capital to 1873* (New York, 1927), pp. 330-333; Sir Robert Giffen, *Economic Inquiries and Studies* (London, 1904); Stephen Bourne, *Trade, Population and Food* (London, 1880).

bottom fell out of the English market. Butter, which had sold for 110s. per cwt. in 1870 fell to 61s. in 1879; while during the same period the minimum price of beef had dropped from 70s. to 50s.[57]

In this era of falling prices it was inevitable that friction between landlords and tenants in Ireland should increase. Any factor that would adversely affect the disposition of crops would also affect the rent equation, and this equation was the most important part of the land problem. In Ireland, in preconquest days, the land arrangement had been tribal and every member had a right to an allotment of land. This tradition of communal ownership continued to survive in Irish minds, and it was responsible for the widespread belief that each tenant had a "possessory right" to the land on which he lived.[58] In 1881 the Bessborough Commission commented on this very fact: "There has in general survived to him [the Irish tenant] through all vicissitudes . . . a living tradition of possessory right such as belonged in the more primitive ages of society to the status of the men who tilled the soil." [59] This tradition of ownership was regarded with definite sympathy by England's leading economist: "The land of Ireland, the land of every country, belongs to the people of that country." [60] To thousands of Irish tenants this statement of John Stuart Mill had the authority of Scripture.

Although the Land Act of 1870 had recognized that the claims of the tenants to an interest in their holdings had a valid basis, it had not gone far enough to provide any real settlement of the land question. One of its main purposes had been to make the eviction of tenants by landlords a costly process; it had also made provision for the payment by landlords for improvements of a permanent nature made by tenants. But in Ireland the Act of 1870 was regarded largely as a "fair weather law," [61] and it was apparent that

57. Bessborough Commission, *British Parliamentary Papers*, 1881, XVIII, question 1627.
58. D. P. Conyngham, *Ireland, Past and Present* (New York, 1889), pp. 206-221; W. E. Montgomery, *The History of Land Tenure in Ireland* (Cambridge, 1889), pp. 27-30.
59. Bessborough Commission, *op. cit.*, 4.
60. *Principles of Political Economy*, I, 411.
61. A. G. Richey, *The Irish Land Laws* (London, 1881), pp. 58-67; M. F. Sullivan, *Ireland of Today* (Philadelphia, 1881), p. 421.

the landlords, when they wished to violate its provisions, could usually drive "a coach and four" through them.[62] It became increasingly obvious that additional legislation was needed to protect the Irish tenants.

In the 1870s these tenants numbered more than 600,000. Fully five-sixths of them lived precariously as tenants-at-will; the others occupied their holdings under leases that varied greatly as to years of tenure. Nearly 300,000 tenants lived on holdings of fifteen acres or less, and as James H. Tuke grimly remarked: "Farms under ten, fifteen or twenty acres of land . . . are too small to support a family." [63] According to J. J. Clancy's survey of the situation in Ireland, there were "thousands of Irish families that have nothing between themselves and starvation but a paltry patch of watery potatoes." In 1880 these paltry patches produced few potatoes, and starvation began to stalk the Irish countryside.[64]

Famine did not descend suddenly upon Ireland. Trouble began in 1877 when inclement weather reduced the size of the potato crop. The following year was no better, and 1879 was the worst since the great famine of 1848. The potato crop of 1876 had been valued at £12,500,000; in 1879 the value of the crop dipped to the perilously low figure of £3,350,000.[65] To the registrar-general it seemed obvious that a food crisis had arrived, and he issued a warning about the imminence of famine.[66] At least one half of the peasant population in the West of Ireland had no money, no credit, and no work. Their desperate plight was given graphic description in a letter from Mitchell Henry to the Lord Lieutenant: "The condition of the West is daily becoming worse. The people have neither food nor clothes, no credit to buy them, nor work to earn them. Pale, thin and bloodless, silent and without a smile, their condition is absolutely without hope." [67] When great landlords

---

62. T. A. Gibbons, *The Irish Land and Irish Landlords* (New York, 1880), p. 14.
63. *Irish Distress and Its Remedies: A Visit to Donegal and Connaught in the Spring of 1880* (London, 1881), p. 91.
64. *Land League Manual* (New York, 1881), p. 12.
65. David B. King, *The Irish Question* (New York, 1882), p. 101.
66. T. P. O'Connor, *The Parnell Movement* (New York, 1891), pp. 166-167.
67. Dublin *Evening Mail*, December 30, 1879.

like Lord Lifford and Lord Kenmare denied that their tenants were in distress and did nothing to help them,[68] it was inevitable that popular indignation would soon reach dangerous heights: when this distress was accompanied by an increasing number of evictions, the situation became ominous.[69] Isaac Butt once remarked that "to evict a tenant in Ireland from his bit of land is to reduce him to beggary,"[70] and Gladstone during a debate on the Irish Land Act of 1881 expressed the opinion that a sentence of eviction in Ireland "is equivalent to a sentence of death."[71] This fact was painfully apparent to large numbers of Irishmen who were determined that some solution of the land problem would have to be found at once. Perhaps the establishment of a land league would be the answer they were anxiously seeking!

G. PARNELL AND THE ESTABLISHMENT OF THE LAND LEAGUE

The idea of a land league came from the fertile brains of two Fenians who had served prison terms for their activities, Michael Davitt and John Devoy. According to Desmond Ryan, "Michael Davitt came from prison with the Land League in his brain."[72] This was undoubtedly true, but John Devoy played an important role in the movement, and Frank H. O'Donnell looked upon him as the "Father of the Land League" with Davitt merely as "his leading lieutenant at the outset of the institution."[73] Devoy was an ardent separatist who realized that the political factor was not enough to balance the uneasy Irish equation. In 1848, in the fight for Repeal, James Fintan Lalor came to the opinion that it would be wise to broaden the basis of the struggle for Irish rights: it

68. Letter of Lord Lifford in the London *Times*, March 17, 1880.
69. The number of annual evictions rose from 2470 in 1878 to 10,457 in 1880. See Sir James O'Connor, *History of Ireland, 1798-1924* (London, 1925), II, 55.
70. Quoted in J. J. Clancy, *Land League Manual*, pp. 39-40.
71. Norman D. Palmer, *The Irish Land League Crisis* (New Haven, 1940), p. 18.
72. *The Phoenix Flame* (London, 1937), p. 247.
73. *History of the Irish Parliamentary Party*, I, 375-378.

would be expedient to "link Repeal to some other question, like a railway carriage to an engine; some question possessing the intrinsic strength which Repeal wants." The main question that had motive power to spare was the one dealing with the distribution of land in Ireland, and Lalor pushed this point with great force.[74] In 1848 the question of mere survival had top priority in Ireland and the land problem was temporarily shelved, but in the late 1870s Davitt and Devoy gave it new emphasis and linked it to the issue of Home Rule and eventual independence. Both the Home Rulers and the Fenians were looking for leadership, and it was not long before their eyes fell upon Parnell.

With reference to Parnell's early ties with the Fenians, Barry O'Brien makes the following comment: "It would not be accurate to say that the Fenians made Parnell. Parnell made himself. But it would be accurate to say that in Fenianism he found the lever on which his power turned."[75] The devotion of the Fenian leaders to the cause of Irish independence made a strong appeal to Parnell, and he was happy to have their support in his fight to fashion a creed of Irish nationalism that would move men's hearts and not just their lips. His availability as a leader of the advanced Nationalists led Dr. William Carroll, of Philadelphia, Chairman of the Executive of the Clan-na-Gael, to pay a visit to London in 1877, where he had a conference with Parnell. James O'Kelly was with Parnell as an adviser and he continued in this role for many years. At this London conference O'Kelly had a sharp argument with John O'Leary which "prevented a formal agreement with Parnell who was quite willing to come to an understanding with Dr. Carroll."[76]

Parnell did not permit this argument in London to keep him from perfecting close connections with the Fenians. In January 1878 he met Davitt and three other well-known Fenians, Corporal Thomas Chambers, Sergeant Charles McCarthy, and John P. O'Brien, as they

74. Nathaniel Marlowe, ed., *James Fintan Lalor: Collected Writings*, pp. 3, 57-61, 87-97.
75. R. Barry O'Brien, *Life of Charles Stewart Parnell*, p. 121.
76. Devoy, *op. cit.*, p. 283.

reached Dublin after serving long terms in English prisons. When he took them to breakfast at Morrison's Hotel, McCarthy was taken so violently ill that he died within a few moments. His troubled demise made a lasting impression upon Parnell.[77] McCarthy had suffered and died for Ireland: no man could do more for the national cause. If these stalwart Fenians could be effectively fused with the Home Rulers there was real hope for Irish independence. This was the basis of the famous "new departure" which John Devoy and Michael Davitt hoped would lead to the destruction of landlordism and finally to the establishment of Irish independence. Close cooperation with Parnell was essential to the success of their plans.

John Devoy was fully aware of this fact and in 1878 he sent a cable to Parnell offering the support of the Clan-na-Gael "on certain conditions." This cable was first sent to Charles Kickham and requested him to give it to Parnell. Kickham merely forwarded it without comment. Devoy then went to Paris in December 1878 to attend a meeting of the Irish Republican Brotherhood, and his proposal to Parnell was supported by the "Executive of the Clanna-Gael, as well as John Boyle O'Reilly, Patrick A. Collins . . . Robert Dwyer Joyce and other prominent men." [78] Devoy then had a conference with Parnell at Boulogne early in 1879 and later paid a visit to Ireland for further conferences.

In the meantime Parnell had made an address at Tralee that deeply stirred a large crowd of supporters. He frankly stated that "nothing short of a revolution would bring about a change in the land laws." When he stressed the need for the establishment of a tribunal for fixing rents and then urged the creation of a peasant

77. O'Brien, *op. cit.*, pp. 151-152. According to a statement of Dr. William A. Carroll in 1906, he was in Dublin on the morning of this breakfast and later had a conversation with Parnell. He asked Parnell if he was "in favour of the absolute independence of Ireland." Parnell replied "that he was and that so soon as the people so declared he would go with them." I then told him that we would be his friends and would ask our friends there to support him in all he did towards that end. *Devoy's Post Bag, 1871-1928* (ed. by William O'Brien and Desmond Ryan, Dublin, 1948), p. 298.
78. Devoy, *op. cit.*, p. 284.

proprietary, someone shouted that it would take an earthquake to settle the land question. Parnell's reply was straight to the point: "Then we must have an earthquake." [79]

Parnell knew that a social earthquake was even then threatening to destroy the social and economic structure of Ireland. One day he asked Charles Kickham if the people thought "very keenly on the land question." "Yes," said Kickham, "they would go to Hell for it." [80] Davitt and Devoy would save them from Hell by doing away with the institution of landlordism and by bestowing upon the peasants the land they thought was theirs. Davitt summed up his program in a speech he delivered in Cooper Union in New York City: "It is our intention to shoot Irish landlordism, and not the landlords." [81] James Redpath outlined the program of Davitt and Devoy in the same pithy manner: "This crusade is not a Donnybrook Fair fight, to break the heads of the landlords, more or fewer, but a democratic uprising for the immediate and total abolition of landlordism in Ireland. It is not a mad riot against men, but a holy war against a system." [82]

It should be remembered, however, that both Davitt and Devoy were using this drive against landlordism as a steppingstone to the goal of national independence. As for Parnell the record is not so clear, but his "last link" speech at Cincinnati on February 23, 1880, has the ring of separatism in every line:

> When we have given Ireland to the people of Ireland, we shall have laid the foundation upon which to build up our Irish nation. The feudal tenure and the rule of the minority have been the cornerstone of English rule. Pull out that cornerstone, break it up, destroy it, and you undermine English misgovernment. . . . And let us not forget that that is the ultimate goal at which all we Irishmen aim. None of us . . . will be satisfied until we have destroyed the last link which keeps Ireland bound to England.[83]

79. O'Brien, *op. cit.*, p. 174.
80. *Ibid.*, p. 183.
81. This speech was delivered on November 8, 1880, and was printed in the *Irish World*, November 20, 1880.
82. The *Irish World*, December 18, 1880.
83. *As it Was Said* (Dublin, 1886), pp. 14-16.

In the spring of 1879 Parnell may not have understood all the implications of the "new departure" of Devoy and Davitt, but he must have been well acquainted with the general outlines of their program. In June of that year he had a conference with Devoy at Morrison's Hotel, in Dublin, and a so-called "full working agreement" was concluded.[84] In the meantime Davitt had arranged for a meeting of tenant farmers at Westport on June 8, 1879.[85] The Archbishop of Tuam denounced the idea of such a meeting because it was sponsored by Fenians,[86] and Parnell was advised to stay away from Westport. He scorned this advice and made a memorable address in which he coined a slogan for the Land League: "You must show them [the landlords] that you intend to hold a firm grip on your homesteads and lands."[87]

Parnell's speech at Westport was followed by a series of engagements at Tipperary, Tullow, and Cork, and on October 12 he addressed some 20,000 enthusiastic followers at Navan, in County Meath, where he was hailed as "the New O'Connell." It was evident that he was the leader of the movement for a radical reform of the system of landholding in Ireland. To give this movement the advantage of an effective organization, the Irish National Land League was founded in Dublin on October 21, 1879, with Parnell as its President. The objectives of the League were briefly stated in the following resolution: "To bring about a reduction of rack rents; second, to facilitate the obtaining of ownership of the soil by the occupiers of the soil."[88]

Seeing that the membership of the Land League was growing with amazing rapidity, the Government took belated steps to curb its development. On November 19, 1879, Michael Davitt, James Daly, and J. B. Killeen were arrested on the charge of using seditious language at a meeting held in Gurteen, County Sligo. It was

84. Devoy, *op. cit.*, p. 284; Desmond Ryan, *The Phoenix Flame*, p. 263.
85. The date of the Westport meeting is somewhat in doubt. It may have been on June 7.
86. The role of the Archbishop in this matter is described in Michael Davitt, *The Fall of Feudalism in Ireland* (London, 1904), p. 153.
87. *Ibid.*, p. 154.
88. M. F. Sullivan, *Ireland of Today* (Philadelphia, 1881), pp. 362-365.

significant that no charge was leveled at Parnell, who addressed a large protest meeting on November 21 in Dublin. The trial of the prisoners showed how deep-seated was the sentiment in favor of the Land League. No jury, unless it were Government-packed, would bring in a verdict of guilty against Davitt and his confederates, and they were soon released.[89] The Land League, with Parnell as its uncompromising leader, had won its first victory.

But the League needed funds to carry on its activities, so Parnell decided to visit America for the dual purpose of raising money to be used for League expenses and for much-needed assistance to the thousands of Irish farmers who were near the point of starvation. There is little doubt that he was now devoted to the ideal of eventual Irish independence, and he knew that he would receive ardent support from the Clan-na-Gael on that point. He was anxious to talk over this matter with the leaders of the Clan, and this was one of the main reasons for his trip to America. He and the members of the Clan had something fundamental in common—"they both hated England. Between him and the British Minister there was nothing in common. He would accordingly use the Clan, as he would use every Irish organization, to fight the Britisher." [90] In Brooklyn, on January 24, 1880, he struck the keynote that he sounded so often in America on subsequent speeches:

> The high heart of our country remains unquelled, the will and courage of our race unquenched, and they are strengthened by the great power of our people in this free land. . . . The day is very near at hand when we shall have struck the . . . first vital blow at the land system as it now exists in Ireland, and then we shall have taken the first step to obtain for Ireland that right to nationhood for which she has struggled so long and so well.[91]

Parnell's visit to America was a tour of triumph. Governors of States were glad to welcome him, important politicians were anxious to be seen in his company, and the streets were lined with large

---

89. Michael Davitt, *The Fall of Feudalism in Ireland*, pp. 178-186.
90. O'Brien, *op. cit.*, p. 200.
91. *Ibid.*, p. 202.

crowds who cheered him lustily. In two months he visited sixty-two cities and traveled nearly 11,000 miles. The climax of the tour was a trip to Washington to plead the case of Ireland before the American Congress. Shortly after Parnell had arrived in America, the Clan-na-Gael sent a letter to the Speaker of the House of Representatives inviting him and the other members of the House to be present on the evening of February 2 to hear the great Irish leader speak on "the present suffering in Ireland." In the House of Representatives Thomas Lowry Young, of Ohio, offered a resolution accepting this invitation. When it was adopted, Samuel Sullivan Cox, of New York, moved that Parnell be invited to deliver his address in the hall of the House of Representatives. When this motion was agreed to, preparations were made to receive Parnell.[92]

On the evening of February 2, with Speaker Randall in the chair, Parnell addressed a crowded chamber filled with all the important politicians of both parties. After discussing the situation in Ireland, with desperate poverty threatening the lives of thousands of farmers, he emphasized the importance of giving to every "occupying farmer in Ireland" the opportunity "to become the owner of his own farm." He was certain that "American public opinion would be of the greatest importance in enabling the Irish people to obtain a settlement of the Irish question." [93]

After a cordial reception at the White House on February 4, Parnell made a flying trip to Canada where, in Montreal, he was hailed as the "uncrowned king of Ireland." He returned to New York and there helped to organize an American Land League. His mission to America was now completed, and he carried back to Ireland the glad news that he had raised a large sum of money to assist the starving people of his native land.[94] It is the opinion of Michael J. McCarthy that Parnell's American tour was "one of the most important landmarks in the modern history of Ireland," because it focused the attention of the world upon the "condition of Ireland and raised the dispute between Irish landlords and

92. *Congressional Record*, January 13, 1880, 46 Cong., 2 sess., 393.
93. Washington *Star*, February 3, 1880.
94. It is estimated that he raised in America the considerable sum of $200,000. See O'Brien, *Charles Stewart Parnell*, p. 204.

tenants from the level of a sordid quarrel to a political issue of ... world-wide interest." [95]

Ireland had at last found a leader who was not afraid to lead. He was not an orator like O'Connell but he could forge phrases that stirred the popular imagination and served as slogans for great national movements. And above all he had courage—courage to lift his eyes to the distant horizon of an Ireland that was free from all the ties of oppression that had long bound her to Britain. He knew that the price of leadership was high and the burden of responsibility would be more than his uncertain health could stand, but he never counted the cost of personal sacrifice in his fight for the freedom of a people he knew so well and loved so deeply. For a half century after his death there was in Glasnevin Cemetery in Dublin no monument honoring the memory of Parnell; there was no memorial that could do him justice.

95. The *Irish Revolution* (Edinburgh, 1912), I, 94; Joan Haslip, *Parnell* (New York, 1937), pp. 103-114.

3 THE DEATH OF PARNELL DELAYS FOR DECADES HOME-RULE LEGISLATION FOR IRELAND

A. GLADSTONE CRUSHES THE IRISH LAND LEAGUE AND PURSUES A POLICY OF COERCION AND CONCILIATION

When Parnell returned to Ireland in March 1880 he found agitation on the land question at high tide. The old refrain, "We want the land that bore us, we'll make that cry our chorus," was gaining rapidly in popularity. In order to make this chorus a reality, the starving peasants in Galway were engaging in violent demonstrations against process servers with eviction notices. In January 1880, at the tiny village of Carrarol, process servers were attacked by a crowd of several hundred men, women, and children. Sixty police who had been sent to handle the situation were able to throw a mantle of protection around the two men who carried the hated eviction notices, but it was soon learned that 116 out of 120 warrants had not been served. Intimidation had proved to be a most successful weapon against the landlords.[1]

While violence against process servers continued during the spring of 1880, emphasis was placed upon the importance of the approaching elections. In its manifesto of March 12 the Land League made a strong appeal for the support of its program: "If you give your vote to a landlord candidate, you are voting for

---
1. A. M. Sullivan, *New Ireland*, p. 578; Brian O'Neill, *The War for Land in Ireland* (New York, 1933), p. 73.

famines, rack rents, evictions, workhouses and extermination."[2] This manifesto had a tremendous effect upon the voters, who placed themselves in overwhelming numbers under the banners of the League. In County Mayo, a stronghold of Catholicism, an Ulsterman and a Protestant, the Reverend Isaac Nelson, was elected purely because he was in favor of the League program.[3]

Flushed with success achieved in the elections, the Land League supporters continued their agitation during the summer of 1880. When a note of violence was occasionally struck, the landlords became increasingly fearful and the Dublin *Evening Mail* was certain that beyond the river Shannon "society is being resolved into its elements."[4]

But Gladstone, the new Prime Minister, was unaware of the crisis in Ireland, which he later confessed rushed upon him "like a flood."[5] In order to extricate himself from this dangerous tide he sponsored the Compensation for Disturbance Bill which provided a measure of relief for Irish tenants in a period of unusual distress. In the House of Lords, Lord Lansdowne, owner of a huge estate in County Kerry, made a vehement attack upon this proposed legislation, and other landlords followed suit. The bill was finally defeated by the imposing majority of 282 to 51. At the conclusion of the vote, T. P. O'Connor arose in the House of Commons and moved the abolition of the upper chamber.[6] The *Freeman's Journal* strongly echoed this sentiment. It was confident that the action of the House of Lords would "deepen the intense feeling that from the Parliament of England no relief is to be expected. It will embitter the relations between landlord and tenant in Ireland."[7] In Ireland it was soon evident that the prediction in the *Freeman's Journal* was a classic understatement.

Joseph Chamberlain had been apprehensive that the rejection by the House of Lords of the Compensation for Disturbance Bill

2. Quoted in the Dublin *Evening Mail*, March 13, 1880.
3. London *Times*, April 12, 1880.
4. July 1, 1880.
5. John Morley, *Life of Gladstone*, III, 48.
6. *Evening Mail*, September 1, 1880.
7. London *Times*, August 5, 1880.

would usher in civil war in Ireland.[8] These apprehensions were soon realized. In Parliament the members representing Ireland had delivered speeches "of a nature sufficient to drive a nation of saints to revolution."[9] The members of the Land League were not primarily interested in sainthood but they were distinctly ready for a social revolution in Ireland. On September 19 an important meeting was held at Ennis, the chief town in County Clare. When Parnell arrived at 4:00 A.M. he was met by a large delegation carrying torches. In his speech that afternoon he sounded a note that soon swelled into a mighty chorus:

> When a man takes a farm from which another has been evicted, you must show him on the roadside when you meet him, you must show him in the streets of the town, you must show him at the shop-counter, you must show him in the fair and in the market-place, and even in the house of worship, by leaving him severely alone, by putting him into a moral Coventry, by isolating him from his kind as if he was a leper of old—you must show him your detestation of the crime he has committed, and you may depend upon it that there will be no man so full of avarice . . . as to dare the public opinion of all right-thinking men and to transgress your unwritten code of laws.[10]

Parnell had produced a formula that would soon lead to violence in many parts of Ireland. The popular imagination had been kindled with the fire of bitter opposition to landlordism, and Parnell fanned the flames with speeches that moved thousands to action. On October 3, 1880, the Land League sponsored fourteen large meetings in Ireland, and at Cork, Parnell was hailed by a crowd that numbered close to 100,000 persons. To Michael McCarthy, Parnell was "so instinct with power" that he reminded him of a "Greek god come to take part in a festival organized by his votaries."[11]

The rallying cry for the members of the Land League was "Ireland for the Irish and the land for the people." Fanny Parnell

8. Herbert Paul, *A History of Modern England* (New York, 1904-1906), IV, 165, no. 2.
9. Clifford Lloyd, *Ireland Under the Land League* (London, 1892), p. 1.
10. R. Barry O'Brien, *Life of Charles Stewart Parnell*, p. 237.
11. Michael J. F. McCarthy, *The Irish Revolution* (Edinburgh, 1912), I, 126.

pitched this cry on a high and ominous note in her poem, "Hold the Harvest," with its stirring lines:

> Rise up! and plant your feet as men
> Where now you crawl as slaves,
> And make your harvest fields your camps,
> Or make of them your graves.

The popular response to this call to arms was immediate and effective. Its most famous expression took place in County Mayo, where Captain Charles S. Boycott was the agent on the estate of the Earl of Erne. He was a harsh man whose years of military training led him to believe that the Irish peasantry could be most effectively controlled by force rather than by conciliation. When some of his tenants refused to pay their rents he summoned a process server armed with writs of eviction.[12] In retaliation for this summary action, the peasants ordered all the employees of Captain Boycott to leave his service. When they complied with these demands the crops on Lord Erne's estate were threatened with ruin. He at once wrote to the London *Times* to complain of the pressure that was being applied to him, and soon a large number of armed laborers from Ulster, under the command of Mr. Manning and Mr. Goddard, were sent to County Mayo to meet this emergency. Hundreds of soldiers and police accompanied them as an escort. According to the *Freeman's Journal*, "fully seven thousand men, military and police, more than a sixth of the whole available force of British military power in Ireland," were finally enlisted in this expedition to succor the hard-pressed Captain Boycott.[13] The crops were saved but the power of the Land League was so clearly demonstrated that many Englishmen believed that anarchy would soon be rampant throughout Ireland. According to the London *Times*, the only cure for lawlessness in Ireland was to "sink the island fifty feet below the level of the ocean for forty-eight hours and then to lift it up and commence anew." [14]

12. Michael Davitt, *The Fall of Feudalism in Ireland*, pp. 275ff.
13. Norman D. Palmer, *The Irish Land League Crisis*, p. 304.
14. December 31, 1881.

In November 1880 the Attorney General instituted proceedings against important Land League leaders like Parnell, Biggar, Thomas Brennan, Patrick Egan, and T. D. Sullivan, but on January 26, 1881, the jury brought in a split verdict of ten to two for acquittal.[15] It was apparent that some gesture of conciliation towards the Irish peasantry would have to be made before the tumult over the land question could be quieted. In July 1880 the Queen had appointed a commission to examine into the workings of the Land Act of 1870. This so-called Bessborough Commission reported in January 1871 and strongly advocated reforms on the basis of the famous "Three F's"—fixity of tenure, fair rent, and free sale.[16] But Gladstone believed that coercion should precede conciliation, so on March 2, 1881, the bill for the Protection of Life and Property in Ireland became law. Under its terms the Habeas Corpus Act was suspended and the authorities were empowered to imprison any "reasonably suspected" person. Parnell and his Irish "rapscallions" carried on a determined legislative fight against the bill but their efforts were in vain. The Government had resolved to crush the rebellious spirit in Ireland and was given the support of the average Englishman in this regard. The Queen had expressed the opinion of the upper classes in a letter to the Marquis of Hartington: "The Queen trusts that means will be found to prevent the dreadful Irish people from succeeding in their attempts to delay the passing of the important measure of coercion." [17]

After pushing through coercive legislation, Gladstone was ready for the conciliatory Irish Land Act of August 22, 1881. It was primarily his Act, and Lord Hartington shrewdly summarized the situation when he remarked that "the Parliamentary history of the year was the history of a single measure carried out by a single man." [18] Gladstone had assured the House of Commons that he had been guided by a "divine light" in the preparation of his pro-

15. Davitt, *op. cit.*, pp. 286-295.
16. "Report of Her Majesty's Commissioners of Enquiry into the Workings of the Landlord and Tenant Act of 1870 and the Acts Amending the same," *Parliamentary Papers*, 1881, XVIII-XIX.
17. Margaret Barton and Osbert Sitwell, *Victoriana: A Symposium of Victorian Wisdom* (London, 1931), p. 132.
18. London *Times*, August 27, 1881.

gram,[19] but there were few Irishmen who accepted that assurance. Although the Land Act and its companion Land Bill attempted to carry out the "Three F's," the complexities of the new legislation baffled even its most ardent supporters. As the Bishop of Limerick wrote to the Archbishop of Dublin: "Since the Apocalypse was written, nothing so abstruse has appeared." [20]

Despite these complexities the landlords in Ireland clearly realized the menace of this new legislation, and one of their ablest spokesmen, Standish O'Grady, published a long lament in which he outlined the drift of events in Ireland: "The stone which Michael Davitt set rolling, now rolls irrecoverable to the abyss." The institution of landlordism was doomed. A few large landowners might survive the flood of democracy but they would be few and far between "like the scattered peaks of a submerged world." [21]

The Irish Nationalists refused to believe that the Land Act would work the destruction of the landlord class, and the *Irish World* referred to it as Gladstone's "quack remedy for Irish grievances." [22] In the face of an increasing number of evictions it was hard to believe in the sincerity of the program pushed by the Prime Minister. In the second quarter of 1881 the number of evictions reached 5,262, and for the quarter ending on September 30 it moved upwards to the alarming total of 6,496.[23] In response to these evictions, violence spread to many parts of Ireland, and the London *Times* reported that anarchy "reigns in many districts." [24]

Gladstone's answer to this wave of increasing violence was the application of more coercion. On October 7, at Leeds, he delivered an address in which he unsparingly denounced the Land League and its leaders. He was playing an astute game. If he could provoke Parnell into a fiery reply he could then take drastic action against him.

There is little doubt that Parnell was eager to enter this verbal

---

19. 3 *Hansard*, CCLX, 926.
20. Patrick J. Walsh, *William J. Walsh* (London, 1928), pp. 108-109.
21. *The Crisis in Ireland* (Dublin, 1882), pp. 3-5, 18.
22. Quoted in the *Evening Mail*, August 12, 1881.
23. T. P. O'Connor, *The Parnell Movement*, pp. 231, 244.
24. June 7, 1881.

battle. He knew he was treading upon thin political ice that might break at any moment, but he could not afford to remain quiet in the face of Gladstone's attack. At Wexford, on October 9, he made a speech that played directly into the hands of the Prime Minister. He assured his audience that their activities so far had "gained but a fraction of that to which you are entitled, and the Irishman who thinks that he can now throw away his arms just as Grattan disbanded the volunteers in 1783, will find to his sorrow and destruction when too late, that he has placed himself in the power of the perfidious and cruel and relentless English enemy." He then openly defied Gladstone by referring to him as that "masquerading knight errant, that pretending champion of the rights of every other nation except the Irish." As a final challenge to the Prime Minister he boldly declared that it was not in Gladstone's power to "trample on the aspirations and rights of the Irish nation." [25]

Gladstone was quick to strike back. On the morning of October 13 Parnell was arrested at Morrison's Hotel and taken to Kilmainham Jail. The arrest of the other leaders of the Land League provoked a riot in Dublin and led to the issuance (October 18) of the famous "No Rent Manifesto," which called upon the tenant farmers to "pay no rent under any circumstances to their landlords until the Government relinquishes the existing system of terrorism, and restores the constitutional rights of the people." Parnell signed the manifesto with many misgivings. He realized, as well as did its author, William O'Brien, that it was "unquestionably, in spirit and in language, the product of a country in full revolution." [26]

Parnell's forebodings were soon realized—the Church came out in sharp opposition to the manifesto. Even Dr. Croke, Archbishop of Cashel, who had long been an unswerving champion of the Land League, wrote a letter to *Freeman's Journal* in which he condemned the manifesto and prophesied that it would lead to "nothing but disintegration and defeat." [27] The Archbishop followed this attack with a pastoral in which he declared that the manifesto "assailed

25. Joan Haslip, *Parnell* (New York, 1937), pp. 203-204.
26. *Recollections* (London, 1905), p. 367.
27. Michael MacDonagh, *Life of William O'Brien* (London, 1928), p. 57.

the eternal law of God and struck at the foundations on which society rests."[28]

Taking advantage of the hostility of the clergy to the manifesto, W. E. Forster, Chief Secretary for Ireland, on October 20 issued a proclamation suppressing the Land League.[29] This action was the signal for widespread violence throughout Ireland. As Parnell had predicted, "Captain Moonlight" took over when the League leaders were thrown into Kilmainham Jail. Landlords were shot down "like partridges in September,"[30] and on November 21 the *Evening Mail* presented the stark fact that Ireland was in just "as bad, if not a worse condition than it was twelve months ago." A week later the *Mail* expressed the opinion that the Land League had left "nothing . . . save the havoc it has made."[31] But Michael Davitt thought otherwise. To him the League had "found the Irish peasant a virtual slave on the land of Ireland. It has 'rooted' him in the soil on which he was but a rent-earning machine, and has given him a right of property, where he was previously but a trespasser, equal to that of his former master."[32]

B. PARNELL'S RELATION WITH THE CLAN-NA-GAEL

It should be remembered that Davitt's chief interest in the creation of a land league was to use that organization as the spearhead of a drive towards the achievement of the eventual independence of Ireland.[33] The so-called "New Departure" was based upon that separatist ideal. In the Devoy-Parnell-Davitt pact of April–June 1879, there had been complete agreement that nothing should be done to "impair the vitality of the Fenian movement or to discredit its ideal of complete National Independence, to be secured by the eventual use of physical force."[34] In June 1881, in the midst of the

28. David B. King, *The Irish Question* (New York, 1882), pp. 333-336.
29. *Parliamentary Papers*, 1882, C.-3125.
30. Clifford Lloyd, *Ireland Under the Land League* (London, 1892), p. 224.
31. November 29, 1881.
32. "Report of the Parnell Commission," *Nineteenth Century*, XXVII, March 1890, 382.
33. *Ante*, pp. 52, 54-55.
34. *Devoy's Post Bag, 1871-1928*, II, 2.

struggle of the Land League against the landlords, Thomas Willis Beach (better known under his pen name, Major Henri Le Caron) had an interview with Parnell. According to Beach, Parnell was ready to use the turmoil in Ireland as an opportunity to stage an insurrection if he had the necessary military equipment:

> He [Parnell] said: 'You furnish the sinews of war. . . . The whole matter rests in your hands. . . . There need be no misunderstanding. We are working for a common purpose—for the independence of Ireland, just as you are doing; for I have long ceased to believe that anything but force of arms will ever bring about the redemption of Ireland.' . . . He told me that he did not see any reason . . . why a successful insurrectionary movement should not be inaugurated in Ireland.[35]

This testimony of Beach before the Parliamentary Parnell Commission in 1888 is partially corroborated by two letters Beach wrote to John Devoy on June 18, 1881. One deals with an interview with Parnell and is quite explicit upon the Irish leader's attitude towards an insurrection against English authority:

> The night before leaving I had a long interview with Mr. P [arnell] and thinking I should see you soon, desired me to say to you from him that his purpose, as you should know, has been other than the mere present agitation. Such is his desire still. His first proposition was to send 'E' over here at once, the next was to get you over to Paris, at once, so that you could return before the August convention, not for the purposes of laying before that body details of any understanding or alliance that might be formed, but to enable the governing body to shape the future policy of the org [anization] on this as well as the other side and to eradicate the antagonistic policy that has been pursued by the home org [anization] or at least individuals—the org [anization] here and parties representing the same there. His programme in detail for the future, though more in detail, was almost identical with that of Mr. E. [Patrick Egan]. He desired that I should convey to you his ideas, intentions and desires, and I think they are upon a basis that you and every liberty-loving revolutionist can agree upon, hence as I have written you his desire to see you.[36]

35. *Report of the Special Commission to Inquire into Charges and Allegations against Certain Members of Parliament and Others, 1888,* C.-5891, XII, 49-50.
36. *Devoy's Post Bag, 1871-1928,* II, 89-90.

The second letter conveys Parnell's earnest desire to have Devoy visit Paris at once for consultations.[37]

There is little doubt that Parnell was in close contact with members of the Clan-na-Gael in the spring of 1881. On February 18 William Mackey Lomasney wrote to Devoy about a meeting he had arranged with Parnell. This meeting made such a favorable impression upon Lomasney that he assured Devoy that Parnell was "eminently deserving of our support, . . . and he means to go as far as we do in pushing the business."[38] On April 22, 1881, John O'Leary wrote in the same vein to Devoy: "It seems to me as if Emerson [Parnell] and Co. must go, sooner or later, into something like our line of business. This will, I suppose, seem good news to you, and *may* be good, but as to whether it is or not, will I think depend fully as much upon how we act as upon how they do."[39]

Devoy goes into this matter of the relations between Beach (Le Caron) and Parnell in two articles in the *Gaelic American*, September 8 and 15, 1923. It is apparent that he had forgotten about the two letters Beach had written to him on June 18, 1881, or he wished to shield the memory of Parnell. In his article of September 8 he remarks:

> Parnell, with his invariable caution, did not confide anything to him, and the statements to that effect in Le Caron's book are all inventions. Parnell gave him no message for me. When I met him on his return, Le Caron told me verbally that Parnell wanted me to go over to Ireland, but he had not a line in writing to show that the message was genuine.

Parnell was just as evasive as John Devoy. In his testimony before the Parliamentary Special Commission his denials were very sweeping. He stated that the Le Caron version of an interview with him was "entirely untrue." He had never intimated that the redemption of Ireland could be secured only through "force of

---

37. Thomas Willis Beach to John Devoy, June 18, 1881, *ibid.*, p. 88.
38. *Ibid.*, 39-40.
39. *Ibid.*, 71.

arms." He was certain that he had never "even thought it." Moreover, he had "no recollection" of any meetings with Devoy and Davitt in June 1879 relative to the proposed Land League, and he denied having had any contacts with any members of the Clan-na-Gael in 1881.[40] It is apparent that his testimony in this regard was an exercise in mendacity.

C. THE KILMAINHAM TREATY TRANSFORMS PARNELL FROM A REVOLUTIONARY AGITATOR INTO AN OPPORTUNIST STATESMAN

The comments of Beach upon Parnell after 1882 are interesting: "I will tell you briefly what I think of Mr. Parnell. There can be no question that up to the time of his imprisonment in 1881 he was exceedingly revolutionary in his ideas, believing in the most extreme measures against the English Government, but iron bars had a singularly happy effect in moderating his views."[41] Parnell's chief reason for hating his imprisonment in Kilmainham Jail was the fact that it kept him from being with Mrs. O'Shea, who had recently given birth to a child that he had fathered. His relations with Mrs. O'Shea had become so well known to members of the English Cabinet that Chamberlain sent Captain O'Shea, who had long acquiesced in the dubious relations between Parnell and his amorous wife, to Kilmainham Jail to work out the terms of an agreement whereby the Irish leaders would be released upon the promise that they would help to restore some measure of peace in Ireland. Parnell was eager to come to terms. In a very short time the articles of the so-called Kilmainham Treaty were put into acceptable form: "The Government were to introduce a satisfactory Arrears Bill, and Parnell was to 'slow down' the agitation."[42] In a letter to Captain O'Shea, Parnell even went so far as to promise that in the future he hoped to "co-operate cordially" with the "Liberal Party in forwarding Liberal principles."[43] As Michael

40. *Report of the Special Commission*, XX, 123-126.
41. *Devoy's Post Bag*, II, 50-51.
42. O'Brien, *op. cit.*, I, 350.
43. Haslip, *Parnell*, pp. 222-223.

Davitt remarked, the Kilmainham Treaty had transformed Parnell from a "revolutionary reformer" into an "opportunist statesman." [44]

But tragedy in Dublin upset all of Parnell's plans. One of the reasons why he had been released from jail was the belief that he could put an end to much of the violence that was stalking the countryside. He had alluded to the probable exploits of "Captain Moonlight" in the event of the imprisonment of the leaders of the Land League, and there is no doubt that at times he had been in close relations with some Irish extremists. Kilmainham Jail had interrupted these relations and had turned his mind to thoughts of peace. From his viewpoint the Liberal Party had abandoned its policy of coercion and was ready to press for the enactment of legislation that would materially benefit tenant farmers. There was a bare possibility that the stage was being set for "something like Home Rule." [45]

In Irish Nationalist circles the Kilmainham Treaty was received with exultation. M. M. O'Hara thought it would not be "easily possible to admire too highly the statesmanship of Parnell throughout the affair," [46] and T. P. O'Connor thought that the great Irish leader had "beaten all the mighty resources, from soldiers to gaols, of the Government, and he stood supreme, more unchallenged than ever, in his control of the Irish people." [47]

On May 6 Parnell went down to Portland to greet Michael Davitt upon his release from prison. On the way back to Dublin, Parnell expressed his pleasure at the turn of events and he criticized his sister for her activities in connection with the Ladies' Land League. When Davitt praised her for keeping "the ball rolling," Parnell replied with acerbity: "I don't want her to keep the ball rolling any more." While Parnell was talking to Davitt the ball of violence began to roll down the streets of Dublin and it completely smashed all his plans for conciliation and progress. Mr. T. H. Burke, an under-secretary at the Castle, and Lord Frederick Cavendish, the

---

44. *Devoy's Post Bag, 1871-1928*, II, 116.
45. Davitt, *op. cit.*, p. 356.
46. *Chief and Tribune* (London, 1919), p. 208.
47. *Memoirs of an old Parliamentarian* (London, 1929), I, 240.

new Chief Secretary for Ireland, were assassinated by a group of "Invincibles" in full sight of the windows of Viceregal Lodge.

D. GLADSTONE PURSUES A POLICY OF COERCION AND CONCILIATION

Parnell was so crushed by this turn of circumstance that he sent word to Gladstone that he would resign his seat in the House of Commons if such action would help the Prime Minister to handle the ominous situation that had arisen. Gladstone replied that Parnell's departure from public life would not assist him in any way in formulating a program for Ireland, and for a brief period it seemed as though the Prime Minister would hold firm against the pressure in Parliament in favor of strong measures that would place the Irish nation in a legal strait-jacket. As John L. Hammond aptly remarks: "It was clear that if England could act with magnanimous common sense, the Irish people might be won and coercion might be avoided." [48]

But Balfour and Salisbury attacked the Liberal leader with such a torrent of abuse that he was persuaded to sponsor the Crimes Act of 1882. This was the legislation that Dublin Castle had long demanded. The Viceroy was authorized to forbid public meetings and suppress newspapers; the Attorney General could change venue whenever he desired and magistrates were empowered to compel the attendance of witnesses and question them in secret. In other words, the ordinary processes of law were suspended; trial by jury was set aside in favor of trial by judges who could decide questions of fact as well as questions of law.

Parnell tried in every way to soften the rigors of the proposed Crimes Act, but Gladstone unwisely followed the counsel of his chief lieutenants, Harcourt and Spencer, who advised the rejection of some suggested amendments by Parnell. The Prime Minister's failure to adopt these amendments was probably his "chief tactical blunder in this disastrous summer." [49]

48. *Gladstone and the Irish Nation* (London, 1938), p. 284.
49. *Ibid.*, p. 299.

Gladstone did, however, adhere to his promise concerning an Arrears Bill, which extended to tenant farmers much needed help with reference to arrears and which also prevented eviction on a wide scale. But the Prime Minister had great difficulty in trying to maintain a balance between conciliation and coercion. He was constantly fearful of evoking further venomous attacks from Conservative leaders, and for this reason he refused to give favorable consideration to several constructive proposals from Parnell. The Irish leader was too much of a statesman to let these rebuffs lead him to adopt a policy of opposition to every item in the Gladstone program. He continued to discourage outrage in Ireland and he founded the Irish National League for the purpose of furthering political objectives like the restitution of the Irish Parliament and the establishment of local government upon a popular basis. He was also deeply interested in important agrarian reforms that could be achieved by amending the Land Act.[50]

Through Mrs. O'Shea, Gladstone kept one ear open to these proposals from Parnell, but he kept his other ear attuned to vindictive counsels from men like Hartington and Harcourt, who were determined that the Irish question should not find a rational answer. In Irish eyes Gladstone was suspect as a man who had talked glibly of a program that was aimed at a settlement of ancient wrongs and bitter quarrels, but the olive branch he extended to Dublin was so old and withered that it looked more like a rod to chastise than a staff to lean upon.

This feeling was given confirmation by W. E. Forster's savage attack upon Parnell in February 1883. In the previous month new evidence had been unearthed against the secret society whose members had plotted the murders in Phoenix Park, and twenty of them were arrested and brought to trial. It soon developed that some officials of Parnell's Land League were incriminated in these murders, and Forster pointed the finger of suspicion straight at Parnell. On the following day (February 23, 1883) Parnell made a characteristic reply. He was not interested in making any attempt

50. Lord Eversley, *Gladstone and Ireland*, p. 246.

to impress the British public with his innocence in the matter of the murders. The only public opinion with which he was concerned was that of his native country. Mr. Forster's speech had made it clear that the former Chief Secretary was the person best fitted for the "congenial work of the gallows in Ireland." The Gladstone Government should send him back to Dublin to carry on the task of "misgoverning and oppressing" a long-suffering people. But the time would come when even the English voters would "reject their present leaders, who are conducting them into terrible courses into which the Government appear determined to lead Ireland." [51]

Some of the attempts to strike at Parnell were indirect and subtle. Perhaps the Irish people would respond to Papal pressure! Towards the end of 1882 an Irish Catholic Whig, Mr. George Errington, decided to visit Rome. Before starting on this journey he called on Lord Granville, at the Foreign Office, and casually remarked that he might have an opportunity to discuss Irish affairs with the Pope. Granville immediately saw the drift of this hint and gave to Errington a letter of recommendation which he could show to the Papal Secretary of State. This document might serve as an indication that England might be ready to establish diplomatic relations with the Vatican. It was a very plain intimation that Granville "wished to use the Pope to put down Parnell, and to control Irish affairs generally in the English interest." [52]

In the autumn it became widely known that Parnell's estate at Avondale was burdened by a large mortgage of some £14,000. In order to prevent a foreclosure, Archbishop Croke came forward with a proposal to raise a National tribute to Parnell for his "splendid public services." The Vatican countered with a Papal rescript condemning this national subscription. Papal thunders, which duly resounded in all Catholic churches, were muted to an unheard whisper across the Irish countryside which gave a full ear to the pleas for Parnell. In December 1883, when the collections were closed, the Parnell tribute reached the surprising sum of

51. O'Brien, *op. cit.*, II, 10-11.
52. *Ibid.*, 24.

£40,000.⁵³ Irish nationalism was a high tide that Papal dykes could not confine in 1883 or in subsequent years.

But the Gladstone Government was not greatly disturbed by the failure of the Errington mission to Rome. It was apparent that Parnell was far more potent in Irish affairs than most English observers had believed possible. As a friendly gesture in the direction of Ireland, the Liberals decided to force through the House of Commons a Franchise Bill that would greatly enlarge the electorate in Ireland. This legislation of 1884 increased the number of voters from 200,000 to 700,000,⁵⁴ and there was little doubt that most of these new voters would rally to the standard of Parnell.

E. PARNELL PREPARES FOR A POLITICAL EXCURSION WITH THE CONSERVATIVES

In the summer of 1885 Parnell had grown thoroughly tired of the roller coaster tactics of the Liberal Government towards Ireland. At one period they would follow a policy of coercion which was a direct denial of liberal principles. Under pressure from an adverse public opinion they would swing to the other extreme and enact legislation which was of great and permanent benefit to the Irish nation. But this lack of consistency annoyed Parnell and his colleagues and they were ready for a new political orientation. The Maamtrasna incident hastened change along the political front.

In August 1882 a crime was committed at Maamtrasna, in the wild mountain country of Connemara, which had momentous political implications. A father, mother, and three children were killed. Parnell expressed the opinion that the murder was the outcome of a quarrel between members of a Ribbon Society over the alleged misuse of certain funds. The evidence on which three men were hanged and five were condemned to penal servitude for life was sharply challenged, and the Archbishop of Tuam appealed to the Viceroy, Lord Spencer, for an inquiry into the manner in which

53. Haslip, *op. cit.*, p. 255.
54. Paul Dubois, *Contemporary Ireland*, p. 8.

the trial in Dublin had been handled. Spencer decided that the verdict and sentence of the court had been just, and by taking this stand he opened a Pandora's box of difficulties for the Liberal Party. In October 1884 the conduct of Spencer was debated with great vehemence in the House of Commons, and in Ireland it was widely believed that the Maamtrasna incident tended to confirm the impression that English justice was a farce. In England the incident convinced a large number of people that the situation in Ireland had gone from bad to worse.[55]

To Parnell it appeared obvious that the time had come for a new political alliance. On June 8-9 he joined forces with the Conservatives to defeat the budget. In the new Salisbury Ministry Lord Carnarvon was appointed to the office of Viceroy of Ireland, and his earnest desire to find a real settlement of the Irish question offered an opportunity that Salisbury did not have the courage, or disposition, to grasp. He had a deep-seated distrust of the Irish leaders and he had no inclination towards Home Rule. Birth, breeding, and assured social position made him the ideal representative of British conservatism; his ample girth afforded cartoonists an excellent model for the John Bull of the latter nineteenth century. In the field of foreign affairs he is generally supposed to have shown unusual ability, yet in the field of Anglo-American relations, especially in the Venezuelan boundary controversy, he was distinctly inept.[56] In dealing with Ireland he and his breed showed little heart and less sense. And in this regard he kept step with Queen Victoria, who seldom tried to hide her cordial dislike of the Irish people because of their refusal to suffer in silence under a regime of British brutality.[57] Any move in the direction of Home Rule was to her nothing less than treason. It was soon apparent to Parnell and his followers that they could not remain long in Conservative circles, where hatred of Irish aspirations was the most important article in their creed.

55. J. L. Hammond, *Gladstone and the Irish Nation*, p. 322.
56. Charles C. Tansill, *The Foreign Policy of Thomas F. Bayard* (New York, 1940), pp. 621-777.
57. George Buckle, *Letters of Queen Victoria, Second Series*, III, 222, 301, 711, 714.

F. THE IRISH QUESTION TAKES ON AN AMERICAN ASPECT

Parnell had no illusions about the real attitude of the Conservatives towards the Irish people. He knew that British misrule stemmed from a strong feeling of dislike for the Irish way of life whenever it failed to fit into an approved English pattern. This pattern emphasized constant service to British masters, whose authority was not to be questioned. If the heavy hand of oppression moved some bold spirits to active opposition, Dublin Castle had an ancient prescription that quickly quieted Irish dissent—swift execution or long terms of penal servitude. For English officials, Ireland was outside the pale of civilized nations, and the ordinary rules that governed relations between nations could be suspended when dealing with the Irish people. Because of this age-old mistreatment of Ireland, it seemed to Parnell to be a waste of time to appeal to the "moral sense of England." Much the English care, he remarked, "for the shooting of a few landlords in Ireland. They murder and plunder all over the world, and then they howl when somebody is killed in Ireland because the killing is of no use to them." [58]

Parnell was primarily a Nationalist and he knew that Irish independence was the only real solution for the Irish question. Only halfway measures could be pushed through a hostile House of Commons. This fact he strongly stressed: "I do not wish to attach too much importance to what can be gained by the action of your members [Irish delegation] in the House of Commons." After these brief words of introduction he went to the heart of the matter in words that lingered long in the memories of ardent Fenians: "Much good will result from an independent parliamentary representation, but I have never claimed for parliamentary action anything more than its just share of weight." [59] He was heart and soul a separatist and the driving force of his personality aimed always at that goal. Although after 1882 he was often at odds with the extremists, he clearly realized that, if parliamentary action could never bring

---

58. O'Brien, *op. cit.*, I, 374.
59. *Ibid.*, 378.

independence, the program of these extremists was the only prescription that pointed to national salvation.

Many of these extremists lived in America, where the Clan-na-Gael flourished. Parnell never lost touch with some of the leaders of the Clan, and he depended upon them for funds which were badly needed for the national cause. On April 25, 1883, a large Irish convention was held in Philadelphia. Parnell had been invited to attend, and many hoped he would deliver a keynote address that would serve as a summons to Irish all over the world to enlist under the banner of independence no matter what the cost. But he refused to be stampeded in this matter. The letter he sent to the Philadelphia convention was mild and carefully phrased. He advised the leaders to adopt a platform that would make it possible for the Irish at home to "continue to accept help from America, and at the same time to avoid offering a pretext to the British Government for entirely suppressing the national movement in Ireland. . . . I have perfect confidence that by prudence, moderation, and firmness the cause of Ireland will continue to advance; and . . . before many years have passed we shall have achieved those great objects for which through many centuries our race has struggled." [60] To many Fenians the note of independence sounded by Parnell in this letter was so faint it could scarcely be heard.

During the sessions of the convention it was decided to organize a National League of America to co-operate with the National League of Ireland. This new organization would take the place of the American Land League. It was obvious that the Clan-na-Gael would largely control the policy of the National League. Towards the end of 1883 the Clan-na-Gael itself was divided into two branches. One was known as the United Brotherhood; the other was called The Triangle because of the fact that its governing body consisted of a committee of three. Bitter feeling existed between these two branches of the Clan, and John Devoy poured out all the vials of his wrath against Alexander Sullivan, who was the leader of the Triangle. In a speech made in Chicago in 1889, Devoy described Sullivan in the following picturesque language:

60. *Ibid.,* II, 18.

"The Chairman of the Triangle is the cross-born offspring of an English cad, born in a British camp, nursed in a British barrack, with the Union Jack flying over it, fed on British rations, and educated in British schools. There is nothing Irish about him except his name, which does not properly belong to him." [61] Devoy charged that the Triangle had spent $128,000 without the permission of the home organization, the Irish Republican Brotherhood. The majority report of the Trial Committee appointed by both branches of the Clan acquitted Sullivan of the more serious charges made against him, and Parnell and Davitt were in his favor. But the minority committee was hostile to Sullivan and Devoy hated him with increasing bitterness after the murder of Dr. P. H. Cronin, who had pushed charges against Sullivan.[62]

This obvious rancor between the two branches of the Clan-na-Gael did not prevent the execution of a program of terrorism in England. From 1883 to 1885, attempts were made to blow up London Bridge and the offices of the Local Government Board. In order to prevent other plots from being carried out, "special guards of police and soldiers were placed in charge of public buildings, and the streets of London presented the appearance of a town under the sway of some despotic ruler who feared the vengeance of his people." [63]

Although Parnell felt some repugnance for the drastic program of Irish-American extremists, he continued his relations with the Clan. In 1883 he sent a cautious cablegram to the Clan convention in Philadelphia and in the following year he sent William Redmond to attend another convention in Boston. As for the morality of the dynamite plots, Parnell, according to his best biographer, did not think "about them at all."

> He regarded the moral sermons preached by English statesmen and publicists as the merest cant, and looked upon the 'Times' denunciations of the 'Irish World' as a case of the pot calling the kettle black. Morality was the last thing the English thought of in their dealings

61. *Devoy's Post Bag*, II, 234; *Gaelic American*, January 17, 1925.
62. *Devoy's Post Bag*, II, 236; J. T. McEnnis, *The Clan-na-Gael and the Murder of Dr. Cronin* (Chicago, 1889).
63. O'Brien, *op. cit.*, II, 29.

with Ireland. ... He was content to call the dynamitards fools, and to laugh at the moral pretensions of the House of Commons.[64]

In America many politicians and the public in general did not take this program of terrorism in Ireland so calmly. The British Legation in Washington was profoundly disturbed by the actions of the Irish extremists, and the Minister sought assistance from the Pinkerton detective agency in trying to learn of plots that were being hatched by members of the Clan-na-Gael. But he confessed to Lord Granville that he had been "quite unable to ascertain what the Fenians are doing in this country." He was certain, however, that the feeling in America against bomb outrages was rising rapidly. There were a few members of Congress who posed as ardent champions of Ireland, but "if they would tell the truth, as they sometimes do to me, they hate the Irish no less than the majority of their countrymen." [65]

One of these so-called champions of Ireland was James G. Blaine, who apparently had a "general dislike for all foreigners, and especially the English." [66] The British Minister could only hope that if he were the Secretary of State in the new Garfield Cabinet he would "prove more amenable to reason than he has hitherto appeared to be." As far as the American public was concerned, Mr. Thornton was pleasantly surprised. There was little real sympathy for the Irish cause and there was distinct irritation at the obstructive course followed by Parnell in Parliament:

> The tone of most of the respectable Newspapers with regard to the Irish question is entirely favourable to the measures which are being

64. *Ibid.*, 32.
65. Edward Thornton to Lord Granville, Washington, February 8, 1881, "Private Letters from the British Embassy, 1880-1885," printed in the *Annual Report of the American Historical Association*, Washington, 1942, I, 116.
66. In her able monograph, *The Foreign Policy of James G. Blaine* (Minneapolis, 1927), Dr. Alice F. Tyler makes the following comments upon Blaine: "The attitude of Blaine toward England and toward Canada was always suspicious, sometimes hostile, never entirely friendly. ... Of Revolutionary stock he had grown up during the days of 54° 40″ or fight, and of the Aroostook wars. For more than twenty years he had been a citizen of Maine. It is perhaps not surprising that he was not always entirely unbiased in his attitude toward England and her daughter Canada."

taken by Her Majesty's Government, except that many think that it would have been completely justified in acting with greater rigour towards Mr. Parnell and his adherents. . . . Indeed, there are many thoughtful Americans who fear that serious questions will some day arise in this country with the mass of Irishmen living here, who have from time to time shown symptoms of being troublesome.[67]

Even Mr. Blaine proved surprisingly cordial to the British Minister. During Mr. Thornton's first interview with the new Secretary of State he was assured that he would discover no note of hostility towards England during the conduct of diplomatic relations. After repeated visits to the Department of State he found this assurance was based upon fact, but he still regarded Blaine as "an impulsive and dangerous man, and that in case of any serious questions between us, he will require very careful management." [68]

Thornton's successor in Washington, Victor Drummond, found Blaine very co-operative with reference to alleged Fenian plots against England. The British Government was deeply worried about the construction of a torpedo boat by Delamater and Company, of New York, which, it was rumored, was being built to attack British warships. On August 31 Drummond had a conversation with Secretary Blaine with regard to this torpedo boat and to the general question of Fenian plots to place infernal machines on board British merchant ships. Blaine called Drummond's attention to the "strong feeling on the part of the American people & that shown by the respectable portion of the Press & their indignation with Irish schemes. . . . He said that if infernal machines were used and any passenger ship with Americans on board was destroyed, the Irish would be exterminated here—that no Irishman's life would be safe." [69]

When Parnell was arrested and placed in jail on October 13, 1881, Drummond reported that the "respectable people" in America felt that such action was "well deserved." [70] Some ten days later

---

67. Thornton to Granville, February 22, 1881, *Annual Rept. of Amer. Hist. Assoc.*, 1942, I, 117-118.
68. Thornton to Granville, May 17, 1881, *ibid.*, 133.
69. Victor Drummond to Lord Granville, New York, September 7, 1881, *ibid.*, 147.
70. Drummond to Granville, October 18, 1881, *ibid.*, 148.

he assured Lord Granville that the American Government was well disposed towards England. If the Fenians attempted "any nonsense" in America they would be promptly "crushed." [71]

When Lionel Sackville-West assumed the duties of British Minister at Washington in November 1881, these friendly relations continued. The wives of Cabinet members conveniently overlooked their usual scruples and made no serious fuss about attending functions at the British Legation even though their hostess was the illegitimate daughter of the British Minister. Washington bachelors refused to become disturbed by the dubious background of this handsome hostess, and it was rumored that even President Arthur pressed upon her in vain a proposal of marriage.[72]

The British Minister himself was a second-rate diplomat who had walked through life along the easy levels of instinct. From his photographs he appears as a man crushed by the heavy burdens of life, but his amatory adventures prove that he was possessed of unusual energy and virility. It is a pity that these qualities were not in evidence in his practice of diplomacy in Washington. His main worry was with the Fenians, who seemed forever fomenting plots against England. For his peace of mind they often transferred their activities to the British Isles and thereby provoked much correspondence concerning naturalization.

It was undoubtedly true that certain naturalized American citizens who had been born in Ireland were occasionally homesick for their native land. They soon discovered that the British Government was suspicious of all homesick Irishmen and was often disposed to let them view the Irish countryside through the bars of a safe Irish prison. This harsh treatment led to many warm protests to the American Minister in London, and finally, on January 31, 1882, a resolution was adopted by the House of Representatives calling for information with reference to these arrests and imprisonment.

As early as December 23, 1881, the American Minister in London had addressed an inquiry to Lord Granville with reference to the arrest of Dennis H. O'Connor. There had been no question about

71. Drummond to Granville, October 24, 1881, *ibid.*, 150.
72. V. Sackville-West, *Pepita* (New York, 1937), p. 171.

the naturalization of Mr. O'Connor. Other cases of imprisonment were brought to the attention of the American Secretary of State, and inquiries began to pour into the British Foreign Office.[73] The case of Michael Hart aroused considerable attention. When the American vice-consul at Queenstown pressed the inspector of police for particulars, he was bluntly informed that Hart was a "dangerous, good-for-nothing, troublesome character, who was perhaps involved in more serious matters than those which led to his arrest." [74]

Secretary Frelinghuysen could not accept this vague indictment of Mr. Hart's character, so he asked Mr. Lowell, the United States Minister in London, for further information. In his detailed reply, March 14, 1882, Lowell discussed the general situation in Ireland. He stated his belief that the Coercion Act was "arbitrary and severe and contrary to the spirit and fundamental principles of the British constitution." But the British Government insisted that "the condition of Ireland was such that nothing short of an extreme measure like this could meet the difficulty." Lowell had little sympathy with naturalized Americans who disturbed the serenity of the American Legation in London, but he was conscious of the fact that the Administration in Washington was fearful of the political implications of these arbitrary arrests.[75]

On March 29 Bancroft Davis, Under-Secretary of State, paid a visit to the British Legation to explain that President Arthur had reason to believe that Mr. Lowell had not made it clear to the British Government that wholesale arrests of American citizens in Ireland could not continue. The Foreign Office must not get the impression that the repeated protests from the Secretary of State were mere "bluster." [76] In his reply to this American pressure, Lord Granville went into a long explanation of the troubled state of affairs in Ireland and the necessity for a Coercion Act. He wished

---

73. Mr. Lowell to Lord Granville, December 23, 1881; Granville to Lowell, January 26, 1882, *Foreign Relations, 1882,* pp. 192-193.
74. Mr. Lowell to Secretary Frelinghuysen, March 4, 1882, *ibid.,* pp. 200-201.
75. Lowell to Frelinghuysen, March 14, 1882, *ibid.,* pp. 201-206.
76. Lionel Sackville-West to Lord Granville, April 4, 1882, *Rept. of Amer. Hist. Assoc.,* 1942, I, 166.

to emphasize the interesting fact that the imprisonment of naturalized Americans in Ireland was not "a measure of punishment, but of prevention." Her Majesty's Government was not "desirous of detaining unnecessarily in prison any persons from whom no danger to the public peace is to be apprehended." [77]

On April 3 a mass meeting was arranged in Cooper Union in New York City at which resolutions were adopted denouncing Mr. Lowell, the American Minister in London, and calling for the prompt release of American citizens in Irish jails.[78] The British Minister in Washington did not take too seriously these protests from pressure groups, and he assured Lord Granville that there was "really no sympathy" in the United States "with Irish agitation." [79]

After the murder of Lord Frederick Cavendish and T. H. Burke in Phoenix Park (May 6, 1882), the British Minister expressed the opinion that the crime had been plotted in America "by the irreconcilable or Fenian section of the Irish Land League party here." [80] Although the American press strongly condemned terrorism in Ireland, there remained a persistent feeling that American citizens should not be dealt with in an arbitrary manner when they visited their native land. When Henry George was repeatedly arrested by police in the summer of 1882, Secretary Frelinghuysen sent a long instruction to Lowell protesting against this course of action.[81]

Along with these difficulties concerning the arrest and imprisonment of American naturalized citizens in Ireland, there were points of friction in Anglo-American relations caused by inflammatory articles in the *Irish World*. The British Government objected to these articles as incitements to outrage in the British Isles. Blaine, out of office, was sharply critical of the Irish-American press and

77. Granville to West, April 6, 1882, *Foreign Relations, 1882*, 317-319.
78. New York *Tribune*, April 4, 1882.
79. West to Granville, April 18, 1882, *Rept. of Amer. Hist. Assoc.*, 1942, I, 167.
80. West to Granville, May 16, 1882, *ibid.*, 169.
81. Secretary Frelinghuysen to Mr. Lowell, October 3, 1882, *For. Rel.*, 1882, 296-298.

of Secretary Frelinghuysen for not taking a more positive stand against the publication of articles that might lead to crimes in foreign countries:

> He [Blaine] . . . remarked on the articles which had appeared in the newspapers respecting the note which I had addressed to Mr. Frelinghuysen on the subject of the incentives to murder and outrage which had lately been published in certain New York papers, and said that he thought it was time something should be done. He went on to say that putting aside relations with other Countries it was a disgrace to permit the United States to be made the refuge for the scum of Europe, and he did not hesitate to affirm that Congress ought summarily to deal with the matter. . . . There had been of late too much "demagogy" on the part of the Government in dealing with the Irish element in New York. It must not be forgotten that although it dominated the State and City of New York it was a foreign element and in no sense an American one, and that as such it might become a very dangerous one to American institutions.[82]

Despite these bold words, Blaine made no attempt to press for legislation to curb the freedom of the American press. In private he was very free in his criticism of the Arthur Administration for a course of action which he would have adopted had he been in office. The correspondence of Sackville-West with Lord Granville affords an inside view of Blaine that confirms the general impression of his chameleon character.

G. GLADSTONE MAKES A TRY AT HOME RULE

Parnell's courtship of the Conservatives was short-lived and fruitless. Salisbury had set his mind against any form of Home Rule, and in this regard the Queen was one of his most ardent supporters. It had been Gladstone's hope that some plan for Home Rule could be worked out upon a bipartisan basis, and he was ready to cooperate with Salisbury in the formulation of a feasible program. He soon discovered that bipartisanship was really anathema to Salisbury. The November-December elections resulted in an interesting

---

82. Memorandum of a conversation between Sackville-West and Mr. Blaine, April 1, 1883, *Rept. of Amer. Hist. Assoc.*, 1942, I, 175.

Decades Home-Rule Legislation for Ireland

balance of power—335 Liberals, 249 Conservatives, and 96 Home Rulers. It seemed clear to Gladstone that an effort should be made to meet Irish desires for the establishment of an Irish legislative body "to handle domestic affairs." [83] But the Conservatives had no intention of acting with a clear vision of the realities of the situation. Instead, there was new talk of a policy of coercion that would crush all the hopes of Home Rulers.

Parnell knew that such ill-advised action would usher in a period of serious disorder in Ireland. Hoping to avert such a grave contingency, he made several overtures to Gladstone for co-operation. But Gladstone wished to give the Conservatives an opportunity to carry out the plain mandate of the recent elections with reference to Home Rule. When he realized that Salisbury could think only in terms of coercion, he was ready for the co-operation for which Parnell had been pleading. On January 26 the Conservatives announced a new Coercion Bill, and that evening the Liberals and Irish Nationalists finally united and administered to the Conservatives the defeat that was long overdue. As the new Prime Minister, Gladstone was determined to open the Home Rule door on which opportunity was loudly knocking. He did not realize that many of his Liberal followers would refuse to hear that knock.

On April 8, 1886, Gladstone moved in the House of Commons the first reading of a Home Rule Bill for Ireland. It provided for the establishment of an Irish Parliament and an Irish Executive for the direction of Irish affairs, reserving certain matters for the control of the Imperial Parliament. There was no longer any doubt that Gladstone was ready to provide a real answer to a problem that had long clamored for settlement. If the members of his party had possessed the same vision and courage, Ireland would have been spared all the "blood, sweat and tears" of the decade from 1916 to 1927. Perhaps it took that eventful decade to prove to the world that Irishmen would gladly die for a political ideal that was immortal.

But in England in 1886 there were many important members of the Liberal Party who cordially disliked any step towards Irish

83. Hammond, *op. cit.*, p. 458.

independence, and they were determined to defeat the Home Rule Bill. The tactics of Chamberlain, as leader of the Radicals, and Lord Hartington, as the leader of the Whig autocracy, are a familiar story.[84] The Bill was defeated by 343 to 313, with 93 Liberals led by Chamberlain, Hartington, and John Bright voting against the measure.

Gladstone had not clearly realized the persistence of a fundamental disinclination to do justice to Ireland, and to many persons it seemed extraordinary that he could persuade himself that a simple appeal to England's conscience could in some magic manner dissolve most of the opposition to Irish Home Rule. The "adverse forces included not only the wealth and social power, but the intellect of England. . . . Herbert Paul gives a list of the men eminent in science and literature who now declared against him [Gladstone], most of whom had been his supporters: Huxley, Tyndall, Tennyson, Browning, Lecky, Seeley, Froude, Goldwin Smith, Martineau, Jowett, Herbert Spencer."[85] The case against Home Rule had been summed up as follows by the London *Times*: "We cannot make Ireland like Canada, first because Canadians are our friends, whilst the majority of Irishmen are our enemies, and second because Canada is 3,000 miles away, and Ireland is at our door."[86]

To Lord Salisbury, leader of the Conservatives, the "majority of Irishmen" were "enemies" who had to be governed with a stern hand. In a speech at St. James's Hall, May 15, 1886, he frankly stated his viewpoint:

> My alternative policy is that Parliament should enable the Government of England to govern Ireland. Apply that receipt honestly, continuously, and resolutely for twenty years, and at the end of that time you will find that Ireland will be fit to accept any gifts in the way of local government or repeal of coercion laws that you may wish to give her.

84. J. L. Garvin, *Life of Joseph Chamberlain*, II, 159-262; Stephen Gwynn, *Life of the Rt. Hon. Sir Charles W. Dilke* (London, 1917), II, 222ff.; George M. Trevelyan, *Life of John Bright* (London, 1913), pp. 454-455.
85. Hammond, *op. cit.*, p. 524.
86. December 19, 1885.

What she wants is government . . . that she cannot hope to beat down by agitation at Westminster.[87]

This appeal to the deep-seated hatred and distrust that so many Englishmen had for centuries cherished against Ireland had its effect, and at the end of the July elections the results were all that Salisbury had desired—316 Conservatives, 191 Liberals, 85 Nationalists and 78 Liberal-Unionists. When Parnell introduced in Parliament a bill to relieve hard-pressed Irish tenants, the Salisbury Government promptly rejected it. Arthur Balfour, Salisbury's nephew, was now made Chief Secretary for Ireland and he applied the prescription that Salisbury had advocated in his speech at St. James's Hall, May 15, 1886—coercion until the spirit of Ireland was broken. He tempered this drastic policy with concessions like the Land Act of 1887 and the establishment of the Congested Districts Board in 1891, but force and brutality were never absent from the Irish picture. To make sure that the Coercion Bill would be carried out with relentless rigor, Balfour made Edward Carson, a briefless barrister in Dublin, the Crown Prosecutor. His choice of lieutenants and his ruthless attitude towards the Irish earned for him in a short time the well-merited title *Bloody Balfour.*

Randolph Churchill soon discovered that the repressive legislation affecting Ireland was not regarded by the Government as a "hateful necessity" but as "something good in itself, producing a salutary effect upon the Irish people and raising the temper of the Ministerial party." He was offended by the calm assumption of social and racial superiority displayed, as a matter of course, by the Ministers towards "their Irish opponents, and the studied disregard of Nationalist sentiments."[88] But Balfour had no qualms or scruples as to his course of action. He believed that he must "restore respect for authority by making authority dreaded. Intimidation was thus his object, and pursuing it he did not flinch from any action however arbitrary, or any method however careless of

87. Lady Gwendoline Cecil, *Life of Lord Salisbury* (London, 1881), III, 303.
88. Winston S. Churchill, *Lord Randolph Churchill* (London, 1952), p. 655.

justice." [89] In such an atmosphere it was inevitable that false charges would be leveled against Parnell. As an advocate of Home Rule, indeed as a real advocate of separatism, he should be destroyed. The means selected was a clumsy one, and Parnell was vindicated before a Special Parliamentary Commission, but the shadow of defeat was already moving across his path. A similar shadow had recently destroyed the career of Sir Charles Dilke. It would work with the same devastating effect upon Parnell.

H. THE PARNELL PARLIAMENTARY COMMISSION

To the Salisbury Government, the destruction of Parnell's political career was a political imperative. The strong and at times violent Irish dissatisfaction with English rule had found impressive personal expression in Parnell. If he were eliminated from the political scene there was no other Irish leader who could carry the torch of legislative independence with the same assurance and the same popular support. In a way, he had made rebellion against English domination seem respectable even in high clerical circles. In 1887 Gerard Manley Hopkins wrote to Cardinal Newman in sharp complaint against the outrages in Ireland. He must have been greatly surprised at the tenor of the reply: "If I were an Irishman, I should be (in heart) a rebel." [90] The spirit of understanding was not to the liking of Conservatives. It must be destroyed. This could best be accomplished by showing Parnell in the dubious light of a conspirator who was behind the murders in Phoenix Park in May 1882. If this were possible, the "respectable elements" in society would surely be aligned against him. It was necessary, therefore, to secure or manufacture evidence that would purport to show that Parnell had secret dealings with the Irish extremists who used murder as a means of furthering political ends.

This dubious evidence was finally supplied to the London *Times* by Richard Pigott, a forger and a scribbler whose pen wrote freely

---

89. Hammond, *op. cit.*, p. 575.
90. Wilfrid P. Ward, *Life of John Henry, Cardinal Newman* (New York, 1912, 2 vols.), II, 527.

when necessity nudged his elbow. After securing letters purporting to be Parnell's, the *Times* in April 1887 began the publication of a series of articles entitled *Parnellism and Crime*. Salisbury assured large audiences that this evidence against Parnell was authentic, and in an address to the Primrose League (April 20) he scored Gladstone for having dealings with the Irish leader: "You may go back to the beginning of British Government, you may go back from decade to decade, and from leader to leader, but you will never find a man who has accepted a position, in reference to an ally tainted with the strong presumption of conniving at assassination, which has been accepted by Mr. Gladstone at the present time."[91]

When a former follower of Parnell, F. H. O'Donnell, brought action for libel against the *Times* on the basis that he had been mentioned in the articles on *Parnellism and Crime*, the Salisbury Government permitted the Attorney General to represent the *Times*. The grave impropriety of this action did not disturb the head of the Conservative Party. Indeed, Salisbury and his followers lost all sense of decency in their attempts to ruin Parnell. They refused to heed his suggestion that a Select Committee be appointed to look into the charges against him. Instead, they introduced a bill into Parliament to provide for an inquiry, by a Commission, into certain allegations that had been made against members of Parliament and "others." This legislation would authorize an extended investigation into every aspect of the situation in Ireland. Having pushed through this measure by use of the closure, the Conservatives then nominated three judges, who were well-known opponents of Home Rule, to serve on the Commission.[92]

To blacken Parnell and his followers, the Commission permitted the Attorney General, as counsel for the *Times*, to summon a long procession of witnesses who testified as to the dark days of terrorism that had long existed in Ireland. During this testimony a special effort was made to fix the blame for many outrages upon the influence of the Land League. At last, in February 1889, the matter

91. London *Times*, April 21, 1887.
92. Hammond, *op. cit.*, pp. 586-587.

of the letters supposedly written by Parnell came before the Commission. As a star witness for the *Times,* the Commission heard the testimony of Captain O'Shea. It was soon evident that the husband of Parnell's mistress was very anxious to ruin the man who had pushed him from a marriage bed which he had found attractive only when the sheets were covered with bank notes furnished by a generous wife. O'Shea was an accountant rather than a lover.

The lengthy proceedings before this special commission fill eleven large folio volumes and they constitute a damning indictment of the British legal procedure. Finally, on February 13, 1890, the Commission dismissed the charges against Parnell. Richard Pigott, the author of the forged Parnell correspondence, fled to Spain after he had been unmasked, and committed suicide in a gloomy Madrid bedroom. But Salisbury was unmoved by the turn of events, and in Parliament the grievous wrongs inflicted upon Irish members were passed over in silence. Why should anyone worry about injured Irish feelings! The Opposition in the House of Commons, however, staged a sharp attack upon the Conservatives, and Gladstone made one of his greatest oratorical efforts in exposing the dangerous rancor of the Salisbury Government towards all things Irish.[93] This rancor would soon find full expression in a new drive against Parnell. As Winston Churchill remarked with his usual wit: "The downfall of Parnell was at hand. Her Majesty's Government regained in the Divorce Court the credit they had lost before the Special Commission." [94]

I. THE WAY OF A MAID WITH A MAN

In the "downfall of Parnell," Joseph Chamberlain played a prominent part. His warm dislike of Home Rule inevitably made him distrust and despise Parnell. It was only natural for him to encourage Captain O'Shea to press a divorce suit that would seriously compromise Parnell in his relations with Gladstone and thereby put an end to all Irish dreams of a large share of self-government.

93. John Morley, *Life of Gladstone,* III, 408-412.
94. *Lord Randolph Churchill,* p. 720.

When O'Shea wrote to Chamberlain on October 13, 1889, and asked whether "some strong action" should be taken with reference to Parnell's relations with Mrs. O'Shea, Chamberlain promptly replied in a letter that was a plain incitement to divorce proceedings: "I am not sure that the boldest course is not always the wisest." [95] On Christmas Eve, 1889, Captain O'Shea's lawyers instituted legal action against Parnell and thus began a suit that destroyed for decades Irish hopes for Home Rule.

Just before divorce proceedings had been instituted, Parnell paid a visit to Hawarden to talk with Gladstone about the Irish question. The discussions proceeded along friendly lines and Gladstone reported to his colleagues that nothing could have been "more satisfactory" than Parnell's frank statements.[96] It was most unfortunate for Parnell that he was not equally frank in connection with the divorce suit. He was fearful that if he strongly contested the statements of O'Shea the divorce would not be granted and Mrs. O'Shea would still be married to a man she had learned to despise. O'Shea was quick to take advantage of Parnell's refusal to offer any defense against the charges that were hurled against him. Evidence designed completely to blacken Parnell's character was brought forward and was not called into question by cross-examination.[97]

The case itself did not come into court until November 15, 1890, and two days later Captain O'Shea got his divorce. In commenting upon the case, the London *Times* expressed the opinion of the average Englishman:

> Domestic treachery, systematic and long-continued deception, the whole squalid apparatus of letters written with the intention of misleading, houses taken under false names, disguises and aliases, secret visits and sudden flights make up a story of dull, ignoble infidelity, untouched, so far as can be seen, by a single ray of sentiment, a single flash of passion, and comparable only to the dreary monotony of French middle-class vice, over which M. Zola's scalpel so lovingly lingers." [98]

95. J. L. Garvin, *Life of Joseph Chamberlain*, II, 400.
96. Hammond, *op. cit.*, p. 603.
97. *Annual Register, 1890*, p. 231.
98. November 18, 1890.

It was obvious that the *Times* regarded the divorce suit as a glorious opportunity to strike back at the great Irish leader who had so recently been vindicated before the Special Commission. The forged letters of Richard Pigott had exploded in the face of Mr. MacDonald, the manager of the *Times*, but where forgery had failed, the love of a man for an unworthy woman had given the *Times* a new weapon of such atomic fury that Parnell was soon blasted from the Irish scene. A few months earlier he had appeared as an Irish Ajax who calmly defied all the bolts of verbal lightning that British opponents hurled at him with increasing hatred. Now he had been blackened by filth that made him take on the appearance of a man of low character who had seduced a beautiful woman and then lived in terror of the castigation of an outraged husband.

The *Times* insisted upon depicting Parnell as a cold-blooded villain who had conducted his campaign for the affections of Mrs. O'Shea without a "single flash of passion." Quite the opposite is true. If Parnell's passion had not been so ardent and so self-sacrificing he would have insisted, when the romance was young, upon taking Mrs. O'Shea to Avondale and thus would have forced the hysterical husband to resort to the divorce court. But Katherine O'Shea did not love Parnell enough to follow such a course. In her personal equation the factor of money was the dominant one. For many years she had lived on the bounty of a rich aunt, Mrs. Benjamin Wood, and she was apprehensive lest the stench of scandal should offend the delicate nostrils of this benefactress. She could not bear the thought of disinheritance, and Parnell's warm affection could never balance the scales that were tipped against him by a weighty pile of British guineas. In 1889 this wealthy aunt died and left her entire fortune to Mrs. O'Shea, but her brothers and sisters immediately contested the will and she was thus denied the funds with which she might have bought off Captain O'Shea.[99]

Parnell was more in need of loyal friends than ample funds. As early as November 4, 1890, Gladstone wrote to Arnold Morley and

99. Henry Harrison, *Parnell Vindicated* (New York, 1931), pp. 131-217.

remarked that he feared a thundercloud would soon "burst over Parnell's head, and I suppose will end the career of a man in many respects invaluable." [100] John Morley was more optimistic. On November 13 he dined with Parnell and gave some credence to assurances that the divorce proceedings would not lead to political disaster.[101] These same assurances Parnell gave to Davitt and William O'Brien. When O'Brien had been married in London, Parnell was the guest of honor and made a brief talk that was "dignified and graceful and delivered in the best parliamentary manner." Wilfrid Blunt attended the wedding and Parnell's talk made a most favorable impression upon him: "It [the talk] raised my opinion of him immensely, for hitherto I have rather underrated his intellectual qualities." [102]

Gladstone did not underrate the intellectual qualities of Parnell, but he confided to Lord Acton his fear that the Irish leader had lost all his "moral force" [103] and therefore would have to retire from an active role in politics. In many ways it was Gladstone who forced this retirement. If he had given any support to Parnell, the Irish leader would never have lost his hold upon his followers. As a close student of English history, Gladstone knew there was an excellent precedent for such support. In June 1836 Lord Melbourne was accused by George Norton of adultery with his wife. His future lay in the hands of Wellington, who stoutly refused to take political advantage of an alleged lapse in Melbourne's morals.[104]

Gladstone did not have the courage and iron will of Wellington, and he was much more sensitive to political considerations. The central item in his political program was Home Rule, and he began to fear that unless Parnell retired from the leadership of the Irish Party all Home Rule legislation was doomed to failure. Cardinal Manning encouraged him in this belief. He expressed to Gladstone the opinion that Parnell could not be "upheld as a leader. No politi-

---

100. Morley, *op. cit.*, III, 429.
101. Hammond, *op. cit.*, pp. 614-615.
102. *The Land War in Ireland*, p. 70.
103. Hammond, *op. cit.*, p. 632.
104. William T. Torrens, *Memoirs of William, Second Viscount Melbourne* (London, 1878, 2 vols.), II, 191.

cal expediency can outweigh the moral sense." [105] Gladstone, however, was very cautious in dealing in moral overtones, and when Harcourt pressed him to take action against Parnell on the ground that "immorality itself had made him unfit and impossible," Gladstone countered with the remark that his position as leader of the Liberals did not make him a judge of "faith and morals." [106]

Under pressure from members of his Cabinet circle, Gladstone finally decided to convey to Parnell, through Justin McCarthy and John Morley, the word that he could not continue to advocate Home Rule legislation if Parnell insisted upon remaining the leader of the Irish Party. In the meantime, on November 18 the Executive of the Irish National League had resolved unanimously to support Parnell. On the following day, T. P. O'Connor, William O'Brien, and John Dillon, who were on a visit to America to raise funds for the national cause, came out in the American press in strong support of Parnell. O'Connor called Parnell the "greatest parliamentary leader that the Irish ever had." O'Brien could see no reason why he should not stand "firmly" for Parnell, while Dillon believed that nothing of great consequence had occurred that would make it necessary to "alter the leadership of the Irish Party in the House of Commons." [107]

On November 20 a large meeting was held in Leinster Hall, Dublin. Timothy Healy arose from a sick bed to attend this meeting and lead the cheers for Parnell. He was very insistent in his assurances to the audience that Parnell was "less a man than an institution. . . . I say we would be foolish and criminal if we . . . upon an occasion of this kind . . . surrendered the great Chief who has led us so far forward." Justin McCarthy was in strong support of the position taken by Healy:

> I ask you, suppose a man has gone morally wrong in some case . . . is that the least reason to excuse him from doing his duty to the people he is leading to victory? . . . Can we say to that man: 'We can do without you?' No! We know we cannot say it—we cannot possibly say

105. Manning to Gladstone, November 21, 1890, Shane Leslie, *Henry Edward Manning* (New York, 1921), p. 436.
106. Hammond, *op. cit.*, p. 640; A. G. Gardiner, *Life of Harcourt*, II, 84-85.
107. O'Brien, *op. cit.*, II, 240-241.

it [applause]. We say to him: 'We want you to lead us, as you have done; and we recognize no reason why you should be exempted from the great public duty of leading the Irish Party and the Irish people to a public victory.[108]

On that very day (November 20) T. P. O'Connor and Mr. Dillon were again interviewed and once more they were in strong support of Parnell. O'Connor expressed the opinion that Ireland was "socially, enthusiastically and fiercely on the side of the Irish leader," while Dillon declared that he had the "utmost confidence in Parnell." [109] But Gladstone had lost his faith in Parnell as the leader of the Irish Party, and he was determined to compel his abdication. He immediately wrote two notes, one to Justin McCarthy and one to John Morley. They clearly indicated Gladstone's fixed opinion that Parnell should retire as a leader of the Irish Party. McCarthy saw Parnell just before the meeting of the party and apparently did not express to him in forceful terms Gladstone's viewpoint. At the party caucus on November 25 the reception given to Parnell was "enthusiastic in the extreme." Thomas Sexton promptly proposed the re-election of Parnell as leader of the party. This motion was seconded by Colonel Nolan and agreed to with loud applause. Parnell must have felt quite secure after listening to this vociferous support.

It was not long, however, before sharp notes of discord were heard outside Committee Room No. 15. When leading Liberals heard that Parnell had been re-elected as leader of the Irish Party they fell into transports of rage. According to Lewis Harcourt, "Our men were mad, frantic, cursing, crying, the whole place in an uproar. A terrible scene which I could not stand." [110] At this moment John Morley sought out Parnell and told him of Gladstone's position in the matter. Parnell then remarked that the feeling against him was merely a "storm in a teacup." If he retired from the leadership of his party in the House of Commons he "should never return to it; that if he once let go, it was all over." He had decided to

108. *Ibid.*, 242-244.
109. *Ibid.*, 245.
110. Haslip, *Parnell*, p. 380.

stick "to his present position in his party until he was convinced . . . that it was impossible to obtain Home Rule from a British parliament."[111]

After Morley had discussed the situation with Gladstone it was decided to give to the *Pall Mall Gazette* the letter that Gladstone had written to Morley with reference to Parnell's retirement as the leader of the Irish Party. Morley then talked once more with Parnell and told him that the letter had been given to the press. Parnell was not disturbed by this bit of news. "Yes," he remarked, "I think Mr. Gladstone will be quite right to do that; it will put him right with his party."[112]

The letter put Gladstone right with his party but it fell like a bomb in the ranks of the Irish Party. The morning after the Gladstone letter to Morley was published, Barry O'Brien went to the Irish Press Agency and talked with a member of the Irish Party who believed that many of his colleagues would now be inclined to demand the retirement of Parnell. This expression of opinion made O'Brien's blood boil and he hotly exclaimed:

> You have all condoned Parnell's moral offense; you have had your Leinster Hall meeting . . . the meeting of the parliamentary party, the enthusiastic re-election of Parnell as leader. And now, in an instant, at the bidding of an Englishman, you eat your own words and you abandon your own leader. . . . Parnell is of more importance to Ireland than Mr. Gladstone and the Liberal Party, and for that matter than the Irish Party too, all put together. Let him go, and Home Rule will go with him for this generation.[113]

On November 26 the Irish Party had another meeting in Committee Room No. 15. With Parnell in the chair, John Barry arose and suggested that Parnell should retire "for a brief period" from the leadership of the party. On the previous afternoon Thomas Sexton had proposed the re-election of Parnell as party leader. Now he believed that the matter of leadership should be reconsidered. On November 20, at the great meeting in Leinster Hall,

---

111. Morley, *op. cit.*, III, 440.
112. *Ibid.*, 440-441.
113. O'Brien, *op. cit.*, II, 254-255.

Dublin, Justin McCarthy had been vehement in his belief that even though Parnell had been "morally wrong" in the O'Shea divorce case he should be retained as leader of the party. He was the only member who could lead the "Irish party and the Irish people to a public victory." On November 26 he was ready to abandon this outstanding leader because Gladstone demanded the sacrifice.

Two nights later there was a dramatic scene in the apartment of Dr. Fitzgerald, who was a member of the Irish Party. Parnell summoned a number of his colleagues to meet him at this apartment for the purpose of reading a manifesto he had written on the policy pursued by Gladstone. It was an acrid critique of Gladstone and threw suspicion upon his program for Home Rule. When Parnell finished reading the draft of the manifesto, Justin McCarthy burst out excitedly: "I disapprove of every word in that manifesto." When Parnell inquired as to his specific objections, McCarthy once more exclaimed: "I object to everything in it." His final comment was to the effect that the wording in places was "offensive to our English allies." He particularly objected to Parnell's reference to "English wolves" who were howling for his destruction.[114]

On the morning of November 29 Parnell's manifesto appeared in the press and the Liberals joined with the Conservatives in a concerted attack upon the Irish leader. They soon attracted recruits from the ranks of former Parnell supporters. On November 19 T. P. O'Connor, William O'Brien, and John Dillon had come out in the American press in strong support of Parnell, and on the following day they had repeated their protestations of loyalty. On November 30 they suddenly reversed their stand and began a drumfire of criticism on the position of Parnell.[115]

This reversal of stand was not approved by many influential members of the Clan-na-Gael. John Devoy cabled to James O'Kelly to support Parnell: "If Parnell yields to English, clamour will destroy American movement. No other man or men can keep it together. Retirement means chaos, leaving Ireland at mercy of English whims and Irish cranks. . . . Assure him [Parnell] may count on unswerv-

114. *Ibid.*, 258-267.
115. *Devoy's Post Bag*, II, 326.

ing support and increased financial aid of American Irish, with or without liberals." [116]

The rank and file of Irish in America had deep affection for Parnell, and they were not favorably impressed with the sudden shift in the attitudes of T. P. O'Connor, William O'Brien, and John Dillon concerning the leader of the Irish Party. When this Irish delegation prepared to leave New York, the Irish servants in the hotel made a tight ring around Tim Harrington and cried out in voices choked with emotion: "Mr. Harrington, don't desert Parnell —don't give him up." [117]

But there were many members of the Irish Party who were entirely ready to abandon the man they had so lately sworn to uphold. Parnell soon discovered that bonds of loyalty and ties of personal friendship melt easily in the hot fires of political expediency. On December 6 the struggle for leadership came to a bitter close. When Tim Healy rose to speak in favor of Parnell's retirement as leader, there were many persons who remembered his fervid words on the evening of November 20 when he loudly declared that it would be foolish and criminal if the Irish Party surrendered "the great Chief who has led us so far forward." Parnell had kept in mind those ardent words of praise and he now looked with contempt upon the little Bantry clerk he had raised from the gutter: "Mr. Healy has been trained in this warfare. Who trained him? Who saw his genius first: Who telegraphed to him from America? Who gave him his first opportunity and chance? Who got him his seat in Parliament? That Mr. Healy should be here today to destroy me is due to myself." [118]

Healy had made the statement that Parnell owed his position to the Irish Party. Parnell hotly denied this statement:

> My position has been granted to me not because I am a mere leader of a parliamentary party, but because I am the leader of the Irish nation. It has been granted to me on account of the services which I have rendered in building up this party, in conciliating prejudices, in sooth-

---

116. *Ibid.*, 316.
117. O'Brien, *op. cit.*, II, 273.
118. *Ibid.*, 282.

ing differences of opinion, and in keeping together the discordant elements of our race within the bounds of moderation.[119]

With his back to the wall, Parnell showed a native eloquence that surprised even his more ardent supporters, but it was a fight he was bound to lose. Finally, at the meeting on December 6, Justin McCarthy arose abruptly and declared that it was "idle to continue the proceedings." Without any more ado he hurriedly left Committee Room No. 15, followed by forty-four adherents. Parnell remained with a mere twenty-six faithful followers.[120] The old English chain of command was still working. An English statesman had spoken with authority, and alleged Irish Nationalists immediately threw down their arms and helped to break a great leader upon a wheel of poor politics and sham morals. The man who was the most active in turning that wheel to the tune of gross obscenities was Tim Healy. The language of the gutter seemed to be his mother tongue.

The attempts of Parnell and his devoted followers to find some compromise that would save the situation are too well known to require repetition. The meetings at Boulogne and Calais (December 1890-February 1891) were futile, and Parnell found that his enemies scorned his suggestion that he be succeeded in the leadership of the party by either William O'Brien or John Dillon. He had no recourse but to fight a rear-guard action, which the bye-elections proved to be a rout. In July 1891 the Catholic hierarchy adopted a resolution which denounced Parnell as "wholly unworthy of the confidence of Catholics," [121] and during this same month the *Freeman's Journal* suddenly turned its editorial guns upon him.[122]

In his fight against overwhelming odds Parnell overtaxed his strength, and on September 27, 1891, at Creggs, in County Roscommon, he was suddenly taken with a chill that forecast the end. When the news of his death at Brighton, October 6, 1891, reached Ireland, Tim Healy, in the columns of the *National Press*, exulted

---

119. *Ibid.*, 286.
120. T. P. O'Connor, *Memoirs of an Old Parliamentarian*, II, 210-235; T. M. Healy, *Letters and Leaders of My Day* (London, 1928, 2v.), I, 326-356.
121. *Freeman's Journal*, July 3, 1891.
122. July 31, 1891.

in the belief that the influence of Parnell was at an end: "No
Parnellite, however honestly mistaken in the past, can now honestly
persevere in his delusion." [123] But there were thousands in Ireland
who had loved Parnell and who had winced at every defeat he
had suffered in the by-elections. They knew he had been hated
in England because he had dared to dream of eventual independence for Ireland and had lifted weary Irish eyes to distant political
horizons they would never forget. They realized that the widespread English rancor against him was the measure of his strength
as a statesman. Katharine Tynan speaks of the hysterical devotion
lavished upon him by multitudes in Dublin when he visited that city
after his deposition as leader of the Irish Party:

> All Dublin was mad for Parnell. . . . I don't think anyone outside
> Ireland can understand what a charm Mr. Parnell has for the Irish
> heart; that wonderful personality of his, his proud bearing, his hand-
> some, strong face, the distinction of look which marks him more than
> anyone I have ever seen.[124]

It was a tragedy for Ireland when Parnell, broken in body and
spirit, finally gave up the struggle for Irish self-government and
eventual independence and came home to rest in the land he loved
so well. Betrayed by some of his most trusted followers, purposely
misunderstood by some who had helped to prepare his program of
action, and ruined by a woman who thought far more of pursuing
an elusive inheritance than of contributing to the happiness and
well-being of her lover, Parnell is the most arresting figure in the
history of modern Ireland. Intellectually he was far below the high
level of many brilliant Irishmen of his day, and morally he was
never a bright light upon a commanding hill. He was not a great
orator or a great writer. But he was a great leader of men devoted
to the cause of Ireland. He had helped to acquaint his followers
with the ideal of Irish nationality; an ideal that gained immortality
when the English destroyed its political form. He was the embodi-
ment of an Irish spirit that refused to quail before English threats

---

123. October 8, 1891.
124. *Twenty-five Years: Reminiscences* (London, 1913), pp. 325-327.

and that pointed out to the Irish people the path to a bright political future. As he said in the last meeting of the Irish Party on December 6: "I am [not] a mere leader of a parliamentary party . . . I am the leader of the Irish nation." This was a statement of fact that the rank and file of the Irish people never doubted. It took his political martyrdom and death to make this fact apparent to a legion of his faithless followers.

4 THE CLAN-NA-GAEL HELPS TO GIVE SUBSTANCE TO THE DREAM OF IRISH INDEPENDENCE

A. JOHN REDMOND SUCCEEDS PARNELL AS THE LEADER OF THE IRISH PARLIAMENTARY PARTY

After Parnell's death the anti-Parnellites sounded a strong note of conciliation that was designed to appeal to the sensitive ears of John Redmond, who was carrying the banner of his lately deceased chief. In this regard the *Freeman's Journal* played an important role: "What has divided the Irish party is not a question of principle, but a question of personality."[1] But Redmond remained unresponsive to these overtures, and on October 21, 1891, he issued a statement which was a counterblast to the soft, friendly tones affected by the *Freeman's Journal:*

> The plain issue before the electors of Cork is—are they prepared to put the destinies of Ireland into the hands of a party whose independence was sold to an English statesman for the price of his continued countenance and support, or are they prepared to vindicate Parnell's memory and rescue Ireland from the shame that is sought to be cast upon her by those whose action undoubtedly had the effect of sending him to an early grave.[2]

1. October 19, 1891.
2. Francis S. L. Lyons, *The Irish Parliamentary Party, 1890-1910* (London, 1951), pp. 30-31.

Although the election at Cork went against Redmond by a decisive majority, he indicated that he had just begun to fight. In December 1891 he entered into a bitter contest with Michael Davitt for a vacant seat in Waterford. Redmond won the electoral fight and Davitt was given a black eye by one of the voters, who cast more than his ballot. Davitt did not appreciate this token of dislike and complained that Redmond's triumph at Waterford was the result of "Toryism and terrorism." [3] It was apparent to the anti-Parnellites that Justin McCarthy's notes of conciliation in the direction of Redmond had turned very sour, so in the early summer of 1892 John Dillon and T. P. O'Connor made overtures to him for some sort of understanding. Discussions in Dublin, in the presence of an Irish-American arbitrator, were held for a while but no progress was made.[4] In the general election of 1892 the full force of the Church was thrown against the Parnellites, who were reduced to the insignificant number of nine. Their opponents had captured seventy-one seats, and this overwhelming victory killed any further efforts at conciliation.

The anti-Parnellites were harassed by a bitter struggle between Dillon and Healy for leadership. The mantle of Parnell was not an easily-won prize. Healy had certain advantages in the contest for party control and he used them to the limits of his ample abilities. His conduct towards Parnell had shown him to be ruthless and not above betraying a friend if it served to speed his progress. He was a master of destructive criticism, but the bilge of billingsgate he had poured upon Parnell was of little help in his fight with Dillon, who was skilled in the arts of political manipulation. Moreover, Dillon was a political realist who had carefully analyzed the reasons for Parnell's mastery over men. Party unity had been the watchword for the political successes of the great Irish leader who had forced his followers to accept a stern discipline that required obedience without any embarrassing questions. Dillon decided to enforce a similar discipline, and he rallied his cohorts with a party whip that fell upon many resentful shoulders. In following the path blazed

3. *Irish Times,* December 26, 1891.
4. T. M. Healy, *Why Ireland is Not Free* (Dublin, 1898), p. 72.

by Parnell, he occasionally failed to see the faint signs that his chief had placed along all the political highways of Ireland, and he lacked the instinct that all great leaders possess in meeting emergencies with decisions that are supremely successful. It was easy to step into Parnell's shoes, but they no longer had the wings that had propelled the master of Avondale with swift speed along roads that now seemed uncertain and endless.

Dissensions within the Irish Party did not help the cause of Home Rule in 1893, when Gladstone's bill was successfully pushed through a hesitant House of Commons and then buried under a huge adverse vote in the House of Lords (419 to 41). When Lord Rosebery followed Gladstone as the new leader of the Liberal Party (March 1894), he dampened Irish hopes of new legislation by frankly announcing that before any measure of home rule could be granted to Ireland, "England as the predominant partner of the Three Kingdoms will have to be convinced of its justice and equity." [5]

Tim Healy was dissatisfied with this Delphic utterance and refused to lend his support to Liberal measures. Dillon, on the other hand, placed all his political eggs in the basket of Home Rule and he followed Liberal leadership because he ardently believed that Lord Rosebery could safely hatch them under a warm blanket of expediency. Healy's strong doubts in this regard widened the breach between him and Dillon and finally led to his expulsion from the party in the early months of 1897. Dillon was now firmly in the saddle, but in the general election of 1895 the Conservatives returned to power with all the old implications of coercion and conciliation. Many members of the Irish Party began to believe that neither Dillon nor Healy possessed the genius necessary for successful leadership, so in 1900 all the factions of the party were united under the banner of John Redmond. It was ironic that Redmond, supposedly dedicated to the political ideals of Parnell, soon abandoned the chief item in the Parnell program—the independence of Ireland.

5. Lord Crewe, *Lord Rosebery* (London, 1921, 2 vols.), II, 444-445.

B. PRESIDENT CLEVELAND USES THE FISHERIES CONTROVERSY WITH CANADA TO MAKE A BID FOR THE IRISH VOTE

In America the Clan-na-Gael never lost the vision of an independent Ireland, and its members ardently hoped that English involvement in a major war would some day afford an opportunity for a successful rebellion against English rule. When this major war failed to develop, the Clan used every minor Anglo-American diplomatic difficulty to harass the British Government.

One of these minor difficulties that was welcomed by Irish-Americans grew out of the use by American fishermen of Canadian inshore fisheries. In 1885, at the beginning of the first Cleveland Administration, the articles in the Treaty of Washington that had conferred upon American fishermen the liberty to fish within the three-mile limit along Canadian coasts had been terminated by action of Congress. In June 1885, by a *modus vivendi,* Secretary Bayard had been able to extend for several months (until January 1886) the liberty to use the Canadian inshore fisheries.[6] He ardently hoped that some compromise could be made with Canadian officials that would obviate the friction that had existed before the Treaty of Washington.

A fundamental change in American fishing practices seemed to indicate a path of accommodation. The purse seine made it possible for American fishermen to catch mackerel outside the three-mile limit and thus eliminated the necessity of resorting to Canadian ports to purchase bait for this type of inshore fishing. Any bait bought in these ports would be used only in open-sea fishing, and therefore the old limitations of the Treaty of 1818 were no longer pertinent.[7] But Canadian authorities clung to the old restrictions, and in 1886 the American fishing vessel *David J. Adams* was seized for purchasing bait in a Canadian port. As the seizures of American

6. Secretary Bayard to Sir Lionel West, June 19, 20, 22, 1885, *British Legation, Notes to,* XX, MS., National Archives.
7. Charles Callan Tansill, *Canadian-American Relations, 1875-1911* (New Haven, 1943), chaps. i-ii.

vessels continued, the usually pacific Secretary Bayard grew increasingly indignant and complained to the American Minister in London that the actions of Canadian officials in this matter had become "almost intolerable." If the British Government did not soon take steps to adjust these difficulties, the United States would deal with the Canadians in a very "practical way." [8] Henry Cabot Lodge, a young Congressman from Massachusetts, attracted wide attention by a fervid declaration designed to compel prompt action: "Whenever the American flag on an American fishing smack is touched by a foreigner, the great American heart is touched." [9]

Outraged public opinion forced Congress to act, and in March 1887 legislation was enacted that looked towards commercial nonintercourse with Canada. This situation had such dangerous implications that an Anglo-American Joint High Commission was appointed to recommend a solution of the fisheries problem. On February 15, 1888, the Bayard-Chamberlain Treaty was signed and placed before the Senate for its consideration. To gain political capital during the Presidential election of 1888, the Republicans in the Senate decided to debate the treaty in open session. In hopes of attracting the Irish-American vote in certain industrial centers in the East, the claim was made that the treaty made too many concessions to England.

Senator Riddleberger, of Virginia, took the lead in a bitter attack upon Britain. He could see no use in having a treaty with such a faithless nation, and he was certain that America could never "have a national government until we have whipped England for her deeds. . . . England has never kept a treaty; she has never made one that she did not violate." [10] Senator Teller, of Colorado, was equally Anglophobe in his sentiments, and he made a particular gesture in the direction of the Irish vote. He thought it should be evident to most Americans that England had always been the "most aggressive, the most bloodthirsty, the most destructive of the human race until it has become a proverb . . . that the Anglo-Saxon

---

8. Secretary Bayard to E. J. Phelps, November 6, 1886, *Bayard Letter Book*, III, *Bayard Papers*, Library of Congress.
9. New York *Nation*, May 19, 1887, XLIV, 417.
10. *Congressional Record*, 50 Cong., 1 sess., XIX, 7155-7157.

is the cruelest of all men. . . . By her course of procedure at one time . . . she [England] put a million and a quarter of Irish people in the grave, starved to death, or dying with sickness from starvation." [11]

These attacks upon the Bayard-Chamberlain Treaty were so popular that Democratic senators refused to support the foreign policy of the Cleveland Administration. The vote in the Senate on the treaty was significant (August 21, 1888): Yeas—27, Nays—30, Absent—19.[12] It was obvious that both Republicans and Democrats were anxious to attract the Irish vote in the fall elections. This fact was made crystal clear when President Cleveland (August 23) sent a special message to Congress calling for retaliatory legislation against Canada that would "subserve the interests of our people and maintain the high standard and the becoming pride of American citizenship." [13] Irish-American reaction to this bold Presidential message was immediate and favorable, and Cleveland was deluged "with a snowstorm of telegrams from a host of Rileys, Murphys and Ryans who applauded this slap at Britain. 'God bless you for your devotion to old Erin,' telegraphed one." [14]

C. SIR LIONEL WEST FURNISHES IRISH-AMERICANS WITH AMMUNITION TO FIRE A BLAST AT BRITAIN

Republican politicians had been quick to perceive the importance of making political capital out of the fisheries controversy with Canada. They were equally quick to take advantage of a grievous error of judgment on the part of the British Minister in Washington in 1888 and raise a cry that President Cleveland had British support in his bid for re-election. The opportunity to raise this cry came during the late summer of 1888, when a California fruit grower named George Osgoodby wrote a letter to the British Minister, Sir Lionel Sackville-West, and asked his advice with reference to the

---

11. *Ibid.*, 7220.
12. *Ibid.*, 7768.
13. James D. Richardson, *Messages and Papers of the Presidents*, VIII, 620-621.
14. Thomas A. Bailey, *A Diplomatic History of the American People* (New York, 1946), p. 440.

approaching Presidential election. He represented himself as a naturalized citizen of English birth and signed the letter as Charles F. Murchison. He said he was especially anxious to hear from Sir Lionel because if the advice from the Minister was favorable to the Democratic Administration he would be able to "assure many of our countrymen that they would do England a service by voting for Cleveland." [15]

The guileless British Minister fell at once into this obvious political trap and expressed an opinion favorable to Cleveland. Osgoodby turned this correspondence over to some members of the Republican Executive Committee of California, and on October 21, 1888, the letters were published in the Los Angeles *Times*.[16] The Republicans were delighted with this opportunity to denounce Cleveland as a tool of England, and there was no doubt that many Irish-Americans were deeply disturbed by this turn of events. On October 25 John Boyle O'Reilly, editor of the Boston *Pilot*, sent a terse telegram to the President: "British Minister's letter regarded as deep offense. His withdrawal ought to be the consequence." [17] On the following day J. D. Plunkett sent to Cleveland a letter along the same line: "I must raise my voice against the continuance in power here of Lord Sackville. For more reasons than time would warrant here to mention, I am of the opinion that a demand for his recall is the proper thing to do. In this opinion I am supported by the intelligent Irish Citizens of America." [18]

Colonel Lamont, the President's private secretary, talked over the situation with E. A. Moseley, who believed that drastic action should be taken at once. He was certain that no one was "nearer the Irish-American pulse than Mr. O'Reilly, and his words are very significant." He felt it in his "bones that if he [Sir Lionel Sackville-West] at least is not figuratively 'kicked' out of Washington it will be bad business for us." He had shown O'Reilly's telegram to

---

15. *House Ex. Doc.* 1, pt. 1, 50 Cong., 2 sess., 1667-1668.
16. Charles C. Tansill, *The Foreign Policy of Thomas F. Bayard* (New York, 1940), chap. 11.
17. John Boyle O'Reilly to President Cleveland, October 25, 1888, *Cleveland Papers*, Library of Congress.
18. J. D. Plunkett to President Cleveland, October 26, 1888, *ibid.*

Commissioner Bragg, who expressed the opinion that Sir Lionel should be recalled at once, and Commissioner Schoonmaker was explosive in his comments upon the British Minister: "If his [Sir Lionel's] backsides are kicked out at once without any delay it will counteract the trouble. If not, things will grow worse." [19]

Under the impact of this vehement correspondence, President Cleveland drafted a brief note to Secretary Bayard. He was "very much concerned about this matter and almost feel that if this stupid thing does not greatly endanger or wreck our prospects, it will only be because this wretched marplot is recalled. John Boyle O'Reilly of the Boston *Pilot* who is doing good work will falter or worse if this is not done and I am afraid it is too much just what the enemy wants to have him remain here." [20]

John Boyle O'Reilly and Congressman Patrick Collins rushed to Washington and had a long conference with President Cleveland, who apparently gave assurances that the British Minister would be given his passports if he were not recalled by the British Government within three days.[21] Colonel A. K. McClure advised the President to "knock out Lord Sackville with your biggest boot and best kick, and you've got 'em. *Hesitation is death.*" [22] A similar message was sent to the President by Leverett Saltonstall, who said that the Irish element in Massachusetts regarded the Murchison letter as a "very serious matter." [23]

It was apparent to Cleveland that the British Minister would have to be abruptly dismissed. There was no time to discuss the matter with the British Foreign Office. On October 30, at a Cabinet meeting, it was decided to hand Sir Lionel Sackville-West his passport and inform him that he was *persona non grata*. When this decision was carried out, Joseph F. Tobias sent the following telegram to Secretary Bayard: "A thousand cheers for our American President. The old flag still floats triumphantly." [24]

19. E. A. Moseley to Colonel Lamont, October 26, 1888, *ibid*.
20. President Cleveland to Secretary Bayard, October 26, 1888, *Bayard MS*.
21. New York *World*, October 28, 1888.
22. Colonel A. K. McClure to President Cleveland, October 27, 1888, *Cleveland MS*.
23. Leverett Saltonstall to William C. Endicott, October 27, 1888, *ibid*.
24. *Bayard MS*., Library of Congress.

The British press believed that the Star Spangled Banner should droop quite low after such an incident. The London *Times* expressed the opinion that a "more ridiculous spectacle has rarely been witnessed in any civilized country than the flurried and unmannerly haste with which the Government of President Cleveland has endeavoured to put a slight on this country . . . before Her Majesty's ministers could deal, one way or the other, with the alleged indiscretion of the British representative at Washington." [25] The London *Standard* was equally caustic. It was certain that the Salisbury government could not "without loss of reputation, permit our ambassador at Washington to be expelled from the United States as though he had been guilty of some heinous crime." [26]

Just what form of reprisal Lord Salisbury should take in this matter was not indicated by the *Standard*. Salisbury himself decided that the easiest way out of the embarrassing situation was to refrain from appointing, during the remainder of the Cleveland Administration, any new British Minister to the United States. He was determined, however, to make known to the American Government his irritation over the way the incident had been handled. In an official note to Mr. Phelps, in London, he expressed the opinion that there was "nothing in Lord Sackville's conduct to justify so striking a departure from the circumspect and deliberate procedure by which in such cases it is the usage of friendly states to mark their consideration for each other. I will abstain from comment upon the considerations, not of an international character, to which you refer as having dictated the action of the President." [27]

Secretary Bayard had little sympathy with Lord Sackville. To him it seemed obvious that the British Minister knew that the struggle of the Irish people for

> home rule or a separate government is the controlling question today in the heart of every man of Irish birth or blood in the United States. He knew that no man could be advocated by England without losing the vote of every sympathizer with Ireland in the United States. . . .

25. November 1, 1888.
26. November 2, 1888.
27. Lord Salisbury to E. J. Phelps, December 24, 1888, *Great Britain, Despatches*, CLX, MS., N.A.

He knew thoroughly the arguments and efforts made in this canvass to obtain the Irish vote by alleging British sympathies of the President and his administration. And so informed, he receives the letter of 'Murchison' and promptly answers in complete sympathy.[28]

The Lord Sackville incident finally took on a ludicrous aspect when the Minister himself published a pamphlet in which he stated that "the keeper of a dime museum on Broadway" had written to him and offered a salary "to exhibit himself daily to the public." [29] It is a pity that the American public was denied this opportunity to see a titled ass bray for money.

D. LORD SALISBURY EXPERIENCES AT AMERICAN HANDS ANOTHER DIPLOMATIC DISAPPOINTMENT

In 1897 Lord Salisbury experienced at American hands another diplomatic disappointment. In 1895-1896 Anglo-American relations were seriously disturbed over the possibility of conflict concerning the boundary between British Guiana and Venezuela.[30] Kaiser Wilhelm II helped to quiet this difficulty by sending (January 3, 1896) to President Kruger, of the South African Republic, a famous telegram congratulating him upon the capture of Dr. Jameson, who led an English raiding expedition into Boer territory. This telegram transformed the Kaiser into a lightning rod which drew off from America much of the indignation that was boiling in British breasts against American intervention in the Venezuelan boundary controversy. On February 2, 1897, Lord Salisbury was persuaded to sign a treaty with Venezuela which provided for arbitration of the dispute relative to the boundary of British Guiana.

This pacific ending of a serious controversy that came perilously near to war seemed to turn British and American minds towards the topic of arbitration. On January 11, 1897, Secretary Olney and Sir Julian Pauncefote, the British Ambassador at Washington,

28. Secretary Bayard to E. J. Phelps, November 19, 1888, *Bayard MS.*
29. Secretary Bayard to President Cleveland, October 24, 1895, *Bayard Letter Book,* III, *Bayard MS.*
30. Carl Schurz to Ambassador Bayard, January 12, 1897, *Schurz MS.*, Library of Congress.

signed a treaty which provided for the arbitration of all "questions in difference" which the two powers had been unable to adjust by "diplomatic negotiation." The Senate was soon flooded with telegrams and letters of approval. Carl Schurz was quick to express the opinion that the "Arbitration Treaty which has just been signed crowns the beneficent efforts that have been made in that direction. All mankind must be congratulated upon this great achievement." [30] To Ambassador Bayard, in London, the treaty appeared as an "upward step in the march of civilization and will check the wild and wicked selfishness of brute force." [31]

To the Senate of the United States the arbitration treaty with England did not wear a beneficent expression, and many members of that body viewed it with deep misgivings. After the treaty had been before the Senate a month, Secretary Olney began to fear that it would be "talked to death, the Senatorial idea being that the interest in the question is subsiding and that the time will come when the Treaty can be rejected without any particular objection . . . on the part of the public." [32]

To stem this deadly tide of words, President McKinley (March 4, 1897) urged favorable action upon the treaty, "not merely as a matter of policy, but as a duty to mankind." [33] But the Senate seemed more concerned with its amending powers than with any broad humanitarian purposes, and on May 5, 1897, the treaty failed to receive the necessary two-thirds majority vote.

Richard Olney, who as Secretary of State under Cleveland had signed the arbitration treaty, sent letters of explanation to England. He believed that one of the more important reasons for the defeat of the treaty in the Senate was the hostile attitude of the Senators from the silver-producing states in the American Union against Great Britain as the "most conspicuous and efficient supporter" of the gold standard. [34]

31. Bayard to George Gray, January 29, 1897, *Bayard MS.*
32. Secretary Olney to J. L. Nelson, February 11, 1897, *Olney MS.*, Library of Congress.
33. J. D. Richardson, *Messages and Papers of the Presidents,* XIII, 6242.
34. Richard Olney to Henry White, May 8, 14, 1897, *Olney Papers,* Library of Congress.

But Mr. Olney did not tell the whole story. One of the most potent forces against the ratification of the arbitration treaty was the hostility of Irish-Americans. This fact was made clear in an editorial in the Boston *Pilot:* "Had Irish-Americanism anything to do with the failure of the English arbitration treaty? We trust so, and believe so. We should be very much ashamed of our fellow citizens of Irish blood if they had not done their utmost to baffle the attempt to place this republic before the world as a mere colony of Great Britain." [35]

E. MANY IRISH-AMERICANS WELCOME THE BOER WAR AS AN OPPORTUNITY TO EMBARRASS HARD-PRESSED ENGLAND

It was significant that during the Boer War (1899-1902) a majority of Americans favored the Boers despite the fact that during the recent Spanish-American War the British Government had adopted a friendly attitude towards the United States. Americans who held the seats of the mighty, however, were strongly Anglophile. Secretary Hay, who was given a free hand by President McKinley in the field of foreign policy, was strongly in support of Great Britain. As Tyler Dennett aptly remarks:

> Hay was not what might be called an 'under-dog' man. . . . In England his friends were perhaps not exclusively Tories, but at least always among the ruling classes. He believed in the British Empire. . . . He could see no redeeming virtue in the Boers' defiance of England, and as for their American sympathizers, he regarded their motives as usually partisan, unworthy, and insincere. . . . The most active and troublesome advocates in America of the Boer cause were German and Irish immigrants for whom, as a class, Hay had often expressed his distrust. It probably appealed to his sense of humor that the Irish were even willing to support in South Africa a government so aggressively Protestant that Catholics were by law excluded from holding office.[36]

After the Boer War broke out in October 1899, Theodore Roosevelt, serving as Governor of New York, was at first strongly Anglo-

35. *Literary Digest,* May 29, 1897, XV, 140.
36. *John Hay* (New York, 1933), pp. 240-241, 246.

phile. He believed that the Boers were "battling on the wrong side in the fight of civilization and will have to go under. . . . The interests of the English-speaking races and of civilization demand the success of British arms."[37] When a group of "belated Fenians" called upon him and inquired about his attitude in the event they launched an invasion of Canada, he promptly warned them that if they went ahead with such a scheme he would call out the militia "and clap them all in jail."[38] When the New York Assembly was inclined to adopt a resolution expressing sympathy for the Boers he used his influence to defeat such a move.[39] He regarded as "scoundrels" Congressmen who favored a similar resolution.[40] He was distinctly contemptuous of the activities of the Irish-American pressure groups, and lost patience with people who kept "howling" against England after knowing about the friendly attitude the British Government had displayed towards the United States during the Spanish-American War.[41]

The Irish-Americans, however, were not unduly disturbed by Roosevelt's hostility towards them. In February 1900 a "very prominent and thoroughly trustworthy Irishman" pressed upon the agent of the Transvaal Government in the United States a scheme to send five thousand men to help the Boers in their war with England. He had arranged with a French company to transport these recruits to Delagoa Bay. The Irish societies in the United States would pay a portion of the transportation expenses. The Boer agent in the United States placed this proposal before W. J. Leyds, the official representative of the Transvaal in Europe, but he had no authority to carry out such an arrangement, so it was finally abandoned.

But the Irish-American societies were persistent in their schemes to send help to the Boers. Their most fruitful scheme was the decision to send a Red Cross corps to the South African Republic

37. John H. Ferguson, *American Diplomacy and the Boer War* (Philadelphia, 1939), p. 208.
38. Roosevelt to Cecil Spring Rice, January 27, 1900, *Roosevelt Papers*, Library of Congress.
39. Roosevelt to Arthur Lee, January 30, 1900, *ibid*.
40. Roosevelt to Henry Cabot Lodge, *Selections from the Correspondence of Theodore Roosevelt and Henry Cabot Lodge* (New York, 1925), I, 444.
41. Roosevelt to Sewall, April 24, 1900, *Roosevelt MS*.

under the auspices of the Geneva Red Cross Society. The Ancient Order of Hibernians raised funds for this purpose, and on February 15, 1900, a group of fifty persons, with Dr. John R. MacNamara in charge, left New York for Delagoa Bay.[42] Before their departure the members of the corps executed affidavits to the effect that their expedition wished merely to serve as an ambulance corps in the Boer War, and this action made it possible for them to obtain official recognition from the American National Red Cross.[43]

The British Ambassador submitted evidence purporting to show that these messengers of mercy were expert sharpshooters who could lend effective assistance to the Boer military forces. United States secret service agents expressed grave doubts about the real motives of the members of this Red Cross corps, but these had covered their trail so carefully that no legal action could be taken against them. After they reached the Transvaal in April 1900, Consul Adelbert Hay, at Pretoria, sent a terse telegram that the "Irish-American ambulance almost all preparing to fight."[44] It was not long before the corps proved that Consul Hay's telegram was one hundred per cent correct.

Consul Hay was Secretary Hay's eldest son, and his appointment to the office at Pretoria evoked widespread criticism from many Irish-Americans. This was bitterly resented by Secretary Hay, who wrote a typical complaint to Whitelaw Reid, the American Ambassador in London: "Thank you for your kind mention of Del. Nothing ever said of me annoyed me so much as the attack upon him by Croker and Bourke Cockran. But I don't know that anything matters much."[45]

Another major annoyance for Hay was the drive for American

42. There is an extended account of the organization and purpose of the Irish-American Ambulance Corps in the Chicago *Times-Herald,* February 10, 1900. According to Colonel John F. Finerty, the corps was going to South Africa "to assist wounded Boers and not to take up arms against the English."
43. Clara Barton to Secretary Hay, April 25, 1900, *Miscellaneous Letters,* State Dept. Archives, 1900, III, National Archives.
44. Adelbert Hay to Secretary Hay, April 18, 1900, *Pretoria, Consular Letters,* I, MS., National Archives, hereafter cited as N.A.
45. Secretary Hay to Whitelaw Reid, September 20, 1900, *Hay Papers,* Library of Congress.

mediation between the Boers and Britain. Hay was strongly opposed to such a move. In a letter to Henry White on the eve of the outbreak of the Boer War he insisted that the "one indispensable feature of our foreign policy" should be a "friendly understanding with England." If war actually came he ardently hoped that England would "make quick work of Uncle Paul [Kruger]." [46] Uncle Paul and his brave Boers proved doughty warriors, and Britain suffered a series of defeats. When the American public became enthusiastic over the exploits of the surprising Boers, Hay sneered at this ardor: "I have the greatest admiration for the Boers' smartness, but it is their bravery that our idiotic public is snivelling over." [47]

After the war had lasted several months with no end in sight, the movement for American mediation was launched by the pro-Boer element in America. The first step in this drive was the proposed appointment of General James R. O'Beirne as Commissioner Extraordinary from the government of the Transvaal.[48] But both the South African Republic and the Orange Free State were advised that it was contrary to American practice to receive one of its own citizens as the diplomatic agent for a foreign power. This action prompted the United States Senate to adopt a resolution requesting the President to make known any protests that had been made against such an appointment.[49] It was evident that some senators suspected that a protest from the British Foreign Office had made up the mind of Secretary Hay. He was glad of an opportunity to deal a slap at the Senate and formally report that no protests had been filed against the appointment of General O'Beirne as the representative of the South African Republic. He was not honest enough to report that in 1867-1868 Anson Burlingame had been received by Secretary Seward as the diplomatic agent of the Chinese Empire and signed with Seward the famous treaty with China that permitted unrestricted Chinese immigration into the United States.

46. Secretary Hay to Henry White, September 24, 1899, *White Papers*, Library of Congress.
47. Secretary Hay to Henry Adams, June 15, 1900, *Hay MS.*
48. Secretary of State for the South African Republic to the U.S. Secretary of State, October 5, 1899, *South African Republic and Orange Free State, Notes to*, I, MS., N.A.
49. *Congressional Record*, 56 Cong., 1 sess., January 19, 1900, 976-982.

Even before the O'Beirne episode a famous Irish-American orator had taken the initiative in trying to find a pattern of peace which would solve the situation in South Africa. On August 24, 1899, Bourke Cockran wrote a long letter to President McKinley in which he made a strong plea for American mediation:

> It can hardly be questioned that a proffer of friendly mediation by you would suffice to delay, if not prevent, the threatened invasion of the Transvaal. . . . An Anglo-American alliance can hardly be a force for the maintenance of justice and the spread of civilization as its advocates contend, if England's foreign policy be marked by respect for justice while the two countries are estranged, and by wanton acts of aggression while the relations are cordial. . . . A friendly but urgent tender of your good offices would undoubtedly evoke a full and complete statement of the grounds on which the peace and integrity of the Transvaal are threatened. Such a statement would be a powerful obstacle to hostilities, for it would enable the civilized world to form a judgment on the merits of the controversy.[50]

When this letter was turned over to Secretary Hay he made the following typical comment: "Mr. Cockran's logic is especially Irish. He assumes that we have an alliance with England, and, therefore, demands that we oppose England in the Transvaal. His facts are as shaky as his inferences." [51]

The President's response to this pressure from Bourke Cockran and other pro-Boer enthusiasts was made public on October 12 in a statement to the press: "As to taking sides with either party to the dispute, it is not to be thought of. As regards mediation, the President has received no intimation from the countries, and in the absence of such intimation from both parties there is nothing in international rules or usages to justify an offer of mediation in the present circumstances." [52]

General O'Beirne immediately challenged this statement and reminded Secretary Hay that he had furnished copies of cablegrams from the Transvaal requesting American mediation. The New York

50. Bourke Cockran to President McKinley, August 24, 1899, *McKinley Papers*, Library of Congress.
51. Secretary Hay to President McKinley, September 6, 1899, *ibid*.
52. Washington *Star*, October 12, 1899.

World remarked that the President was using "diplomatic language that was invented to conceal the truth," and it recalled that just a few days previous to the Presidential statement, President Kruger had expressed, in a cablegram to the *World*, his readiness to accept mediation.[53]

It was true that no strictly *official* request for mediation had arrived in the Department of State asking for American mediation, and Secretary Hay had refused to pay any attention to appeals in the press or to any documents furnished by General O'Beirne, inasmuch as he had not been recognized as a representative of the South African Republic. He took the position that requests for mediation would have to come from both disputants before mediation could be offered by the United States. His stand in this regard was quite dubious. Under international law it is possible to offer mediation even though neither party to the dispute has requested it. As a matter of fact the McKinley Administration itself in March 1900 offered mediation after having received merely a request from the Boer Government, and in the face of a probable British rejection of this American offer.[54]

The request from the Boer republics for mediation was formally made on March 5, 1900. Secretary Hay was very loath to present this to Britain but was compelled to do so by an aroused American public opinion favorable to the Boers. As he explained to Henry White, the Irish-Americans and German-Americans had "joined their common lunacies" and were too powerful as pressure groups to be ignored.[55] When the Boer appeal for mediation was presented to the British Foreign Office, Lord Salisbury postponed a reply for three days. On March 13 he had an interview with Henry White and made the following curt reply: "Her Majesty's Government cannot accept the intervention of any other power."[56]

There was a storm of indignation in many American quarters at

53. October 13, 1899.
54. John W. Foster, *The Practice of Diplomacy* (Boston, 1906), pp. 349-350; L. Oppenheim, *International Law, a Treatise* (London, 1920), II, 11-13.
55. Allan Nevins, Henry White, *Thirty Years of American Diplomacy* (New York, 1930), pp. 151-152.
56. Henry White to Secretary Hay, March 13, 1900, *Great Britain, Despatches*, CXCIX, MS., N.A.

this abrupt refusal of the British Government to entertain a proposal for mediation, and on March 26, 1900, in Faneuil Hall, in Boston, Bourke Cockran delivered one of his finest orations. It was an acrid attack upon British imperialism:

> This war on the Boers is a renewal of the old attempt by the governing class of England to undermine the institutions to which the English people have always been attached. . . . This is a war of the London smart set, the Stock Exchange gamblers and the street mobs. It has never been approved by the sober judgment of the English people; it is abhorrent to the conscience of the American people. It is a fashionable war on both sides of the Atlantic; it is a popular war on neither side.[57]

When the three envoys from the Boer republics visited the United States in May 1900, Cockran made a famous speech of welcome in Washington. But his eloquence was in vain. Secretary Hay was determined that no action should be taken by the Department of State that would in any way contribute to the success of the Boer mission. He received it with scant courtesy and purposely misunderstood the attempts of the envoys to secure a favorable hearing.

Some months later, a young Irish-American attorney in New York City who was rapidly attracting favorable notice as an orator, Daniel F. Cohalan, denounced American imperialism in the Philippines and expressed the deep regret of Irish-Americans generally that the Department of State had become so Anglophile that it "feared to express the hope entertained by nine-tenths of the people of America that the two struggling republics of South Africa should be victorious in their magnificent fight for existence lest the feelings of England should be ruffled."[58]

Thanks to the influence of Secretary Hay and other prominent Republicans, the Republican national convention at Philadelphia adopted a platform with a plank that gave little comfort to Boer

---

57. James McGurrin, *Bourke Cockran, a Free Lance in American Politics* (New York, 1948), pp. 199-200.
58. Address delivered by Daniel F. Cohalan at the Hoffman House, August 1900, *Cohalan Papers*.

sympathizers. The Democratic national convention which met at Kansas City in June 1900 gave ample evidence that the members of the platform committee had been impressed with the importance of making some friendly gesture towards the friends of the Boers. In the platform as finally agreed upon there was a plank that clearly revealed the fact that someone had read or heard the speeches of Bourke Cockran and Daniel Cohalan. The Democratic Party "viewed with indignation the purpose of England to overwhelm with force the South African republics." [59]

But this political honey attracted few voters. In the election of 1900 Bryan received a smaller electoral and popular vote than he had received in 1896. Popular action against the pro-Boer senators was devastating. Fourteen of them stood for re-election and nine were defeated. The Irish vote in Boston probably saved the seat of George F. Hoar, but it is clear that in the field of national politics the Irish-American pressure group had much to learn about propaganda and procedure. It was fortunate for them that two sagacious leaders like Daniel F. Cohalan and John Devoy were available to direct their future activities. In the fight for Irish freedom, as far as America was concerned, Cohalan and Devoy furnished the brains and the courage to prepare a program that met with wide acclaim in Irish-American circles. It was a program that advocated physical force in the struggle against England.

F. THE CLAN-NA-GAEL ADVOCATES A PROGRAM OF PHYSICAL FORCE IN THE FIGHT FOR IRISH FREEDOM

In Ireland many important leaders, like John Redmond, were ready to abandon the program of Parnell for Irish independence. In America that dream was kept alive by the Clan-na-Gael, and Daniel F. Cohalan and John Devoy were the most important leaders of the Clan in the New York area. Through their constant efforts towards conciliation the two divisions of the Clan were united in 1900 and new life was infused into the work of the organization.

59. Edward Stanwood, *A History of the Presidency from 1788 to 1916* (Boston, 1916), II, 63.

Cohalan was born in Middletown, New York, December 21, 1865, and moved to New York City in September 1889. He was graduated from Manhattan College in 1885 and was admitted to the Bar in 1888. His mother and father had been born in County Cork, Ireland, and he cherished a deep affection for their native land. As an ardent believer in Jeffersonian democracy he hoped that the Irish question could be solved by the incorporation of these democratic principles into the political structure of Ireland. Like John Devoy, he believed that democracy in Ireland could flourish only if independence were secured. Home Rule within the bonds of the British Empire would be merely a palliative and not a cure for the political ills of Ireland.

After his admission to the Bar in 1888 it was apparent to young Cohalan that Middletown was too small a field in which to make an important name in legal practice. In the following year he moved to New York City and soon made a favorable impression. He was an unusually gifted person who put his genius into his living and his talents into the cause of Irish independence. He believed this cause could best be promoted by the work of the Clan-na-Gael, and he devoted a good deal of his time to preparing a program of action. At the convention held by the Clan in July 1900, a declaration of principles was adopted, and it was made very clear that Irish independence was the main item in a long list of objectives. Independence could be secured only through "physical force," and the Clan did not shrink from all the implications that went along with this program:

> The object of the Clan is the complete independence of the Irish people and the establishment of an Irish Republic, and to unite all men of our race in all lands who believe in the principles of Wolfe Tone and Emmet. We pledge ourselves to the principle that physical force is the only engine a revolutionary organization can consistently and successfully use to realize the hopes of lovers of freedom in lands subject to the bonds of oppression. . . . Our duty is to nerve and strengthen ourselves to wrest by the sword our political rights from England.[60]

60. Circular issued to members of the Clan-na-Gael, October 10, 1900, *Cohalan MS.*

All members of the Clan were pledged not to aid in any way the parliamentary movement which aimed at securing some form of Home Rule for Ireland. On October 26, 1901, Cohalan issued a circular to all members of District One of the Clan in the New York City area to attend a meeting held in Brevoort Hall on the evening of November 3. The attendance at this meeting would indicate that the members had no sympathy with the activities of the Irish Parliamentary Party. The members of the Clan should realize that Irish independence could be secured only "by means of physical force." [61]

G. DOUGLAS HYDE AND THE ESTABLISHMENT OF THE GAELIC LEAGUE

It is very apparent that there was no thought of compromise in the plans of Cohalan and Devoy with reference to the establishment of Irish independence. As realists they saw clearly that England would never voluntarily agree to any arrangement that would result in eventual independence for Ireland. That would come through force alone. But they knew very well that in Ireland the majority of landowners, a very large section of the professional classes, many small industrialists and shop owners and the more prominent members of the Catholic clergy looked with deep suspicion upon any movement towards securing independence through the employment of force. Nationalism in Ireland was a sentiment that had few strong overtones of independence. These overtones would have to be supplied by organizations that would create a deeper and more pervasive feeling throughout Ireland of an essential Celtic unity that demanded political independence as the only real basis for the complete expression of the Celtic spirit. One of the outstanding creative spirits in producing this feeling of Celtic unity was Douglas Hyde, who wished to restore to its proper place in Irish life the old Irish language.[62]

In 1892 he delivered to the National Literary Society of Dublin a

61. *Cohalan MS.*
62. Ernest A. Boyd, *Ireland's Literary Renaissance* (New York, 1916), chap. iii.

Substance to the Dream of Irish Independence 123

stimulating address on the "Necessity for de-Anglicizing Ireland." Throughout his address he emphasized the importance of language as a factor in the development of nationalism:

> In Anglicizing ourselves wholesale we have thrown away with a light heart the best claim which we have upon the world's recognition of us as a separate nationality. . . . In order to de-Anglicize ourselves we must at once arrest the decay of the language. . . . We must strive to cultivate everything that is most racial, most smacking of the soil, most Gaelic, most Irish because in spite of the little admixture of Saxon blood in the north-east corner, this island *is*, and will *ever* remain Celtic at the core.[63]

In 1893 Douglas Hyde, Father Eugene O'Growney, and John MacNeill founded the Gaelic League. Hyde was a young Protestant graduate of Trinity College. He was of Ascendancy pedigree but rapidly proved that he was really a passionate Gael who was determined that the Gaelic literature he had learned to love should not remain merely a source of study for linguists and antiquarians. Father O'Growney was Professor of Irish at Maynooth College and had written a popular Irish grammar that became an essential textbook for members of the League. He emphasized the fact, however, that he had no desire to banish the English language from Ireland. Irishmen in the past had expressed in imperishable prose and poetry, in the English language, many of the thoughts that lay closest to Irish hearts. He advocated a system of bilingual education that would afford the Irish youth an opportunity to learn and appreciate both Gaelic and English classics. MacNeill was a civil servant from the Glens of Antrim whose ardent interest in Gaelic literature made him anxious to have it more widely known and more deeply appreciated.

As President of the Gaelic League, Hyde pushed a vigorous program that resulted in the establishment, within a decade, of some 500 branches. It was soon publishing Irish primers, Irish grammars, texts of old Irish prose and poetry, and a weekly paper in Irish. It

---

63. *The Revival of Irish Literature: Addresses by Gavan Duffy, Dr. Sigerson, and Douglas Hyde* (Dublin, 1894), pp. 117 *et seq.*

had an important share in the revival of Irish dancing and Irish music and thus was an important agency in giving expression to the ever-present but partly concealed spirit of Irish nationalism.[64]

H. THE IRISH LITERARY AWAKENING AND ITS IMPLICATIONS OF NATIONALISM

It was inevitable that the Gaelic League would help to produce a literary awakening in Ireland. The names of William Butler Yeats, Lady Gregory, Edward Martyn, Katharine Tynan, Ethna Carbery, George W. Russell, George Bernard Shaw, J. M. Synge, and James Stephens are outstanding stars in a firmament that included many lesser lights. Yeats had long been interested in Irish nationalism and for a while was closely associated with the I.R.B. In his stories of Red Hanrahan he wished to attract the interest of the Irish peasants, but he was also anxious to make a potent appeal to the upper strata of Irish society. In a letter to Alice Milligan he outlines this objective: "I feel that the work of Irishmen of letters must not be so much to awaken or quicken or preserve the national idea among the mass of the people, but to convert the educated classes to it on the one hand . . . and . . . to fight for moderation, dignity and the rights of the intellect among their fellow Nationalists." [65]

In 1899 Yeats, Lady Gregory, and Edward Martyn organized the Irish Literary Theatre and in October 1900 they presented a one-act comedy by Douglas Hyde, *The Twisting of the Rope*. It was the first time an Irish play, in Irish, had been presented in an Irish theatre. But the high point of the literary awakening came on the evenings of April 2, 3, and 4, 1902, when the inspired and patriotic one-act play by Yeats, *Cathleen ni Houlihan*, was presented in St. Teresa's Hall in Dublin. With Maude Gonne in the title role, the play was so deeply moving that it created a sensation in Ireland. As Yeats remarked, concerning the acting of Maude Gonne: "She made Cathleen seem like a divine being fallen into our mortal infirmity." [66]

64. Patrick S. O'Hegarty, *A History of Ireland Under the Union, 1801-1922*, pp. 615-19.
65. Joseph M. Hone, *William Butler Yeats, 1865-1939* (London, 1942), p. 143.
66. *Ibid.*, p. 175.

John J. Horgan, who saw the original performance in Dublin, remarks as follows with reference to the profound impression the play made upon him:

> Simple in plot, yet deeply moving and poetic, this play depicted the scene in a peasant's house at Killala during the French invasion of 1798. We see the eldest son leave his prospective bride to join the French invaders at the bidding of a poor old vagrant woman who is no other than Cathleen ni Houlihan—the spirit of Ireland. Few who saw the original performance, as I did, will forget the great climax of the play when Michael goes out to follow the strange old woman, and his father asks the younger son if he saw an old woman going down the path. "I did not," replies the boy, "but I saw a young girl and she had the walk of a queen." No more potent lines were ever spoken on an Irish stage.[67]

Although Yeats was proving to be of tremendous service in strengthening the spirit of nationalism in Ireland, there were some American critics who thought that he overemphasized the contributions of the Gaelic League and the Irish Literary Theatre. He appeared to overlook the important services of the Clan-na-Gael. This viewpoint was acidly expressed in a letter from John Devoy to Daniel F. Cohalan:

> Many things are occurring which have chilled my enthusiasm for the Gaelic League. The worst is that Yeats has managed to fill every American editor with the idea that his theatre company is a product of the Gaelic League, has Hyde's endorsement and by inference that he approves the "Playboy" [of J. M. Synge]. It is repeated almost every day, as in a *Times* editorial today, and we are lectured as being "out of touch" with Ireland by people who never knew Ireland. Hyde lets this go. Until he comes out with a denial I will personally do no more for the Gaelic League. . . .
> The time of our men is constantly taken up with raising money for the League, to the neglect of our own work. Hardly anybody else does anything, and yet everything is done to please those who are hostile or indifferent and every recommendation by us or our friends is ignored. Hyde is making nonsensical speeches about the Irish having "got their land and going to get their Nationality." This is politics and the Gaelic League is supposed to be non-political. Hyde is constantly cater-

[67]. John J. Horgan, *Parnell to Pearse* (Dublin, 1949), pp. 93-94.

ing to Redmond, who does nothing for him and whose friends here are hostile to the League. It is time we insisted upon being treated seriously. . . .

Shane Leslie is a young man of much promise and he may or may not develop. He has much to learn and one of the things he must learn quickly is that he must not talk such rot as he talked in Dublin before leaving for America—"Don't mind your customs or excise—the only important thing is education." That was a pointed reference to what ought to be in the Home Rule Bill and was political heresy. Some of the Ulster Unionists who are coming round, with their hard heads, balk straight at that question.[68]

Devoy greatly disliked Synge's "Playboy of the Western World" and sharply criticized it in the columns of the *Gaelic American*. He believed it was uncouth and did not give a true picture of the Irish people. John Quinn, an eminent Irish-American lawyer whose ample funds helped to support the literary activities of William Butler Yeats, resented these criticisms of Devoy and wrote to Cohalan a letter of bitter protest:

> When the "Playboy" was first published I had an early copy of it and took it with me one evening to New Rochelle where I was to dine with Judge and Mrs. Keogh. Devoy was also there for dinner. After dinner I read out certain passages from the book and they all enjoyed the richness and imagery of the style. I came back on the train with Devoy and said to him that the book had two or three rather strong phrases. But he replied that he *did not object to the language; that the Irish were the plainest-spoken people in the world;* and he told me on the train, and at the Belmont cafe where he had some supper with me, several stories to illustrate their freedom and frankness of speech. . . . He did say that he objected to the play on one ground, that it would give an opening to the English to claim that the Irish were a lawless or brutal people. . . .
>
> In the eyes of the world of letters Synge is today one of the few modern Irish writers of genius and thousands of readers have a better understanding and are moved with sympathy for the lives of the Irish people because of his "Riders to the Sea," his wonderful book on the Aran Islands, his "Deirdre of the Sorrows," his poems, and even his "Playboy" itself. But my point is that in his paper for weeks and weeks Devoy railed at the *language* of the "Playboy" as foul, un-Irish, in-

68. John Devoy to Daniel F. Cohalan, November 29, 1911, *Cohalan MS.*

decent, blasphemous, and so on. . . . I don't recognize his credentials as a dramatic or literary critic. . . . I used to respect and admire him. Now I can't help feeling that his usefulness is ended.[69]

Cohalan, of course, did not agree with this snap judgment of John Quinn, and he continued to maintain cordial relations with Devoy. He knew that Synge was not popular in Dublin, and that fact was equally known to Quinn, despite his heated remarks concerning Devoy's criticisms. On February 15, 1905, Yeats had written to Quinn to deplore the fact that very small audiences had attended the presentation of Synge's "Well of the Saints":

> We had rather thin audiences for Synge's play but they were always sufficient to play to and make expenses and a little more. . . . The audiences always seemed friendly, but the general atmosphere has for all that been one of intense hostility.[70]

I. DAVID P. MORAN SEEKS TO STRENGTHEN IRISH NATIONALISM BY PROMOTING IRISH INDUSTRIES

There were many important Irishmen who were glad to support the activities of Douglas Hyde and the Gaelic League, and some of these enthusiasts had other strings to their bow of nationalism. David P. Moran, who was a warm advocate of all the items in the Hyde program, also believed that Irish nationalism could be strengthened and confirmed by the establishment of a system of Irish industries. During the years from 1898 to 1900 he published in the *New Ireland Review* a series of articles in which he expressed his deep anxiety that Irish nationalism was about to expire. This led him to examine into the essentials of nationalism:

> A characteristic way of expressing thought, a distinct language, is usually the most prominent part of a nation. Then there will be found a native colour in arts, industries, literature, social habits, points of view, music, amusements, and so on, throughout all the phases of human activity. It is scarcely necessary to point out that of the things which go into the making of a nation, some, such as art, practically do not exist in

---

69. John Quinn to Daniel F. Cohalan, undated, *Cohalan MS.*
70. Hone, *op. cit.*, p. 206.

Ireland; others, such as the language we speak and the literature we read, are borrowed from another country. There are certainly some traits to be found in Ireland which stamp the people as a distinct race even yet; but they characterize her torpor and decay rather than her development. . . . In other words, all the national life is to be left to bleed out of us, until we come by our right to make laws for the corpse.[71]

Moran was certain that the Protestant Parliament and the non-Gael generally were not Irish at all but simply "English who happened to be born in Ireland." Literature written in English by Irishmen was not really Irish literature no matter how patriotic its theme. The time had come when Irishmen should cease to believe that political agitation was the "begin-all and end-all of Irish nationhood." They should realize the importance of two other movements that clamored for serious consideration. One was the "movement which aims at making the best of Ireland's economic opportunities, and the other, that for reviving a universal interest in all that appertains to the Gael and his language." [72]

In 1900 Moran established a weekly paper, *The Leader*, in which he endeavored to emphasize the importance of promoting Irish industries by applying the principle of voluntary protection. Loyal Irishmen should insist upon purchasing *Irish* manufactured goods and should not be content with English substitutes. His constant propaganda in this regard was partly responsible for the establishment of the Industrial Development Societies and the Irish Trade Mark Association. No one helped more to clothe Irish nationalism in a garb of its own manufacture.

J. SIR HORACE PLUNKETT AND THE CO-OPERATIVE MOVEMENT IN IRELAND

While David P. Moran was preparing plans for an industrial revival in Ireland, the lot of the farmer was rapidly improving. The Salisbury policy of coercion and concessions had led to the passage of the Land Acts of 1887, 1891, 1896, and 1903. Their purpose was to

71. David P. Moran, *The Philosophy of Irish-Ireland* (Dublin, 1905), pp. 1-3.
72. *Ibid.*, pp. 30-31.

assist Irish tenants to become the owners of the farms they tilled. The Act of 1903 had provided £112,000,000 to broaden the base of tenant ownership.

In 1898 the Local Government Act vested local government in Ireland in popularly elected Urban Councils, Rural Councils, and County Councils. The old Grand Jury system under which local affairs had been managed by a small and sometimes corrupt landlord class was now swept away. The Conservatives had purposed to kill Home Rule with kindness; instead they had helped prepare the way for eventual Home Rule. In commenting upon the social and political changes that had been introduced by the Local Government Act and the land acts, P. S. O'Hegarty sagely remarks: "The new Lord of the soil was the tenant. The new Lord of the political world was the common Irishman." [73]

Under this new regime, in the picturesque phrase of Standish O'Grady, some of the old landowners just "rotted off the land." But outstanding men like Sir Horace Plunkett continued to take a deep interest in all agrarian questions. He was primarily concerned with the idea of co-operation and founded in 1879 a Consumers' Co-operative Society in his native village of Dunsany. After some years of serious illness which compelled an exile in western America, he returned to Ireland and in 1894 became the leading spirit in the establishment of the Irish Agricultural Organization Society. The co-operative movement was now successfully launched and Plunkett rendered invaluable service in improving the lot of the average Irish farmer. His politics changed as the co-operative movement developed. At first a firm Unionist, he gradually broadened his political outlook and finally worked for an Irish Dominion. Economics is often a close companion of political progress.

K. ARTHUR GRIFFITH MAKES SINN FEIN TAKE ON SEPARATIST OVERTONES

The political progress that was closest to some Irish hearts was one that aimed at eventual independence. This had been the dream of

73. *Op. cit.,* p. 620.

the Fenians and of Parnell, but it died in the hearts of lesser men like Redmond, who worked for some type of Home Rule within the bonds of the British Empire. The I.R.B., however, still dared to dream of Irish independence, and their dream was shared by the Clan-na-Gael in America. When Lord Salisbury, in the House of Commons, threw into the faces of the Irish members the taunt that England, during the Boer War, had been able to withdraw from Ireland all able-bodied soldiers and hold the island with a small force of cripples, he rendered a distinct service to the cause of Irish independence. The I.R.B. gave careful consideration to that taunt and began to gather recruits against the day when a real fight for freedom should be launched.

On March 4, 1899, Denis Devereux began the publication of the *United Irishman*, with Arthur Griffith as editor. Its chief slogan came straight from Wolfe Tone: "We must have Ireland, not for certain peers, or nominees of peers, in College Green, but Ireland for the Irish." In his first leading article Griffith threw out a bold challenge to everyone who thought in terms of political compromise:

> We believe that when Swift wrote to the whole people of Ireland 170 years ago, that by the law of God, of nature, and of nations they had a right to be as free a people as the people of England, he wrote commonsense. . . . We trust we have made ourselves perfectly plain, we have not endeavoured to do aught else. Lest there might be a doubt in any mind, we will say that we accept the Nationalism of '98, '48, and '67 as the true Nationalism and Grattan's cry 'Live Ireland—perish the Empire' as the watchword of patriotism.[74]

The *United Irishman* had a restricted circulation among politically conscious persons who had separatist leanings. Through John Devoy it received financial assistance from the Clan-na-Gael, and its editorial columns reflected at times the viewpoint of the Clan.[75] The selection of Griffith as the editor was especially fortunate. He had read widely and wisely in the field of Irish political literature, and

74. *Ibid.*, p. 635.
75. Major John MacBride to John Devoy, June 10, 1902, *Devoy's Post Bag*, II, 350.

his nationalism was ardent and separatist. He had no faith in the Home Rule program of the Irish Parliamentary Party. Thoroughly familiar with all the checks and balances in English political practices, he knew that with reference to Ireland most Englishmen had read history with their prejudices rather than with their eyes.

On March 15, 1900, he published an important article entitled "A National Organization—a Suggestion." He referred to the "few associations" in Ireland that were "working for the old cause and the old ideals." If these associations were under some central authority their efforts would be much more effective and far-reaching. A common program could be immediately adopted which would be aimed at the general diffusion "of knowledge on all matters Irish, to undertake the education of the people in the history, literature and language of their country, to teach them to appreciate Irish art, and to induce them to study the resources of Ireland . . . and to revive throughout the land the spirit of brotherhood." [76] In conclusion he made it clear that a more ardent Irish nationalism should be developed. This new nationalism should have no affection for Home Rule:

> For years past the word Nationalist has been sadly abused, and the man who shouted for cheap land and the man who yelled for Home Rule told the people they were Nationalists and the simple people believed them. Let it be clearly understood that Home Ruler and Nationalist mean wholly opposite and irreconcilable things. The Home Ruler acknowledges the right of England to govern this country. . . . The Nationalist . . . totally rejects the claim of England or any other country to rule over or interfere with the destinies of Ireland.

After considerable correspondence between leading Irishmen in different parts of the island, on September 30, 1900, a national organization of Irish societies was founded. It took the name of Cumann na nGaedheal and announced an ambitious program for training along nationalist lines. This provisional organization was approved at a convention held on November 25, 1900, and thus a National Council was formally launched with John O'Leary as President. At the turn of the century it represented merely an ar-

76. O'Hegarty, *op. cit.*, pp. 637-638.

dent aspiration in the direction of eventual independence. Thanks to Arthur Griffith, this movement towards independence was given an accelerated pace.

In October 1902, at a convention of the Cumann na nGaedheal, a carefully phrased proposal of Griffith was adopted:

> Whereas, the practice of sending Irishmen to represent the Irish people in the Imperial Parliament of Great Britain is an acquiescence in a "usurpation and fraud" on the Irish nation, and further, that the practice and policy of Parliamentarianism . . . has proven barren and useless . . . be it resolved that we call upon our countrymen abroad to withdraw all assistance from the promoters of a useless, degrading and demoralizing policy until such time as the members of the Irish Parliamentary Party substitute for it the policy of the Hungarian Deputies of 1861, and refusing to attend the British Parliament or to recognize its right to legislate for Ireland, remain at home to help in promoting Ireland's interests and to aid in guarding its national rights.[77]

This "Hungarian Analogy" to which Griffith adverted in his long proposal, which the convention adopted, was further developed in a pamphlet which he published in 1904. This pamphlet received wide circulation and its influence went very deep and spread very far. It purported to show that Hungary became a nation only after she ceased to follow the political lead of Austria. Ireland had sacrificed nationality on the altar of expediency and compromise. In his penetrating study of the fight for Hungarian freedom, Griffith found many of the factors that were present in the Irish political equation: religious discord, absentee landlordism, and the decline of the Hungarian language and culture. The saviors of Hungary were two brilliant young men, Francis Deak and Louis Kossuth. Kossuth favored the formula of revolution against Austrian misrule, but Deak believed that Hungary's lot could best be improved by insisting that the Pragmatic Sanction had given Hungary legislative independence and therefore the Austrian claims to rule in Budapest were unconstitutional. The policy of Deak finally prevailed and Hungary, by insisting upon her constitutional rights, gained legislative independence. Following this analogy, Griffith contended that

77. *Ibid.*, p. 642.

Substance to the Dream of Irish Independence 133

the Renunciation Act passed by England in 1783 had made it clear that, in the future, Ireland was to be controlled only by laws enacted by the King and the Parliament of Ireland. The Act of Union with Great Britain in 1801 was never valid because the Irish Parliament had no legal right to terminate its own existence. If Irishmen would follow the example of Deak and stand upon the Renunciation Act of 1783, they could win their legislative independence. As a first step along this line he recommended the withdrawal of the Irish members from Westminster and the establishment of a Council of Three Hundred which would determine national policy. The decrees of this council would be carried out by the Country Councils and other local bodies.[78]

It was soon evident that the writings of Griffith had awakened unusual interest in a separatist policy. New branches of the Cumann na nGaedheal and the National Council in Dublin were organized along with the creation of a number of Dungannon Clubs. As this tide of separatist sentiment rose higher it was decided that Griffith himself, during the meetings of the National Council in November 1905, should announce what he called the Sinn Fein policy. The Irish words Sinn Fein meant merely "ourselves," and the program to be adopted was explained by Griffith as follows: "National self-development through the recognition of the duties and rights of citizenship on the part of the individual, and by the aid and support of all movements originating from within Ireland, instinct with national tradition, and not looking outside Ireland for the accomplishment of their aims." [79]

Shortly after the announcement of this Sinn Fein policy, some of the separatists became convinced that it was essential to bring about a unification of the organizations advocating this new departure. In April 1907 the Cumann na nGaedheal amalgamated with the Dungannon Clubs under the title The Sinn Fein League. The following year (September 1908) the League and the National Council merged into Sinn Fein. The constitution boldly proclaimed

---

78. Arthur Griffith, *The Resurrection of Hungary: A Parallel for Ireland* (Dublin, 1904).
79. O'Hegarty, *op. cit.*, p. 650.

that the object of Sinn Fein was the "re-establishment of the Independence of Ireland."

Griffith, however, realized that his program was a long-range one. His remarks to Mr. O'Hegarty were revealing: "I am a separatist. The Irish people are not separatists. I do not think that they can be united behind a separatist policy."[80] But he did not give up hope that eventually the many factors of nationalism would balance the uneasy Irish equation.

But there were many disappointments that Griffith and his Sinn Feiners had to face. In 1907 one of the younger Irish members of Parliament, Mr. C. J. Dolan, North Leitrim, resigned his seat and offered himself for re-election as a Sinn Feiner. His defeat by a large majority of votes was a setback that deeply disturbed many young voters who had fondly believed that Sinn Fein had caught the popular fancy. They were given additional concern by the fact that Griffith had to suspend the publication of a Sinn Fein daily paper for want of adequate support. The most serious blow to Sinn Fein hopes came when the Liberals in England returned to power in 1906 and soon made strong gestures of conciliation in the direction of the Irish Parliamentary Party. The center of political gravity quickly shifted from Dublin to London, and Redmond and the majority of Irish voters expected that some measure of Home Rule would be pushed through Parliament. The Sinn Fein organization, after being a serious threat to the Irish Parliamentary Party in 1907, declined until, "at the time of the insurrection, it was practically confined to one central branch in Dublin."[81]

The age-old hope of securing Irish independence through physical force had been abandoned by most Irishmen and was cherished chiefly by some stout-hearted men of the I.R.B. who would stage the rising of 1916. The uncertain solution in the Irish national test tube could be precipitated only by the blood of heroes who were not afraid to die in order that a nation might live. It is apparent that the Gaelic League, Sinn Fein, patriotic societies of all sorts, and devoted friends of Ireland in every country had merely helped to

80. *Ibid.*, p. 652.
81. P. S. O'Hegarty, *The Victory of Sinn Fein* (Dublin, 1924), pp. 6-7.

create a national sentiment that waited for decades for some great moment of expression. That moment came on April 24, 1916, when the I.R.B. suddenly staged a revolution and the cry that had long choked in Irish throats burst forth in a roar of defiance that echoed all over the world. In America, Daniel Cohalan and John Devoy had long anticipated this cry, and through their constant and untiring efforts help had been sent to Ireland that made it possible to keep alive a spirit of rebellion. The anthem of Ireland had many American notes.

5 JOHN REDMOND RELUCTANTLY DISCOVERS THAT BETRAYAL IS AN OLD ENGLISH POLITICAL PRACTICE

A. MAURICE HEALY SUCCESSFULLY CHALLENGES THE LEADERSHIP OF JOHN REDMOND

In Ireland, during the Redmond era, political affiliations were distinctly fluid. The unity of the Parnell period was sadly lacking even after Redmond had become the accepted leader of the Irish Party. William O'Brien was one of the dissidents who continued to give trouble despite many overtures from Redmond. In January 1908 O'Brien and Tim Healy, with four of their associates, rejoined the party, but in 1909, when the Liberal Government introduced a land bill to amend the financial provisions of the Land Act of 1903, O'Brien immediately indicated his opposition to the proposed legislation. When his views were given scant consideration, he announced another retirement from public life and went to Italy to gather strength for further conflicts.

His departure left a vacancy in the city of Cork, and in April 1909 George Crosbie was selected by a group of local Nationalists to succeed O'Brien. His candidacy was welcomed by Redmond, who made a visit to Cork to advocate Crosbie's election. But the opposition showed surprising strength and Maurice Healy was the victor by a narrow margin. The Irish Party refused to accept him as a member, and a new political feud began which was further complicated by a serious general strike in Cork that led to the creation of the Citizen's Army, a workers' volunteer force. This force played a prominent part in the rising of 1916. Moreover, the irrepressible William O'Brien returned to Ireland to help Sinn Fein become a formidable spearhead of revolt against English rule.[1]

B. THE LIBERAL PARTY CLIPS THE POLITICAL WINGS OF THE HOUSE OF LORDS

The revolt in Cork in 1909 against the leadership of John Redmond was a portent of things to come rather than a signal of immediate political change in Ireland. The program of the Liberal Party called for Home Rule legislation of a far-reaching character, and not only the younger generation but seasoned politicians like Joe Devlin, Tom Kettle, and Dick Hazleton were glad to endorse Redmond's support of the Asquith Government.

As a preliminary to Home Rule it was necessary to abolish the legislative veto that the House of Lords could use as a barrier along the road to the enactment of any measure granting some form of political independence to Ireland. When the House of Lords rejected the Lloyd George budget of 1909 it was decided to take prompt action in favor of a fundamental constitutional change. Asquith was not a fearless fighter who enjoyed strenuous political battles, but the strong radical leaven in Liberal ranks compelled him to act boldly. In the January (1910) elections the issue was placed squarely before the voters.

In Ireland the Parliamentary Party lost some ground but still retained some seventy pledge-bound members. In the new House of Commons the balance was precarious—275 Liberals, 273 Conservatives, and 40 Labor members. The Irish Party held the balance of power, and for a while it seemed prepared to make the most of its favored position. Asquith was disturbed over the situation and complained that Redmond was "cold and critical if not avowedly hostile."[2] Concession was in the air and Asquith hurriedly threw out bait which he knew would attract the support of the Irish Party. The

1. John J. Horgan, *Parnell to Pearse* (Dublin, 1949), pp. 172-176.
2. J. A. Spender and Cyril Asquith, *Life of Lord Oxford and Asquith,* p. 273.

first item in his program was the destruction of the veto power of the House of Lords. On May 10, 1910, three resolutions passed the House of Commons. It was now provided that in the future the House of Lords would not have the power to veto any money bill. Also, any other measure which passed the House of Commons in three successive sessions, in spite of a negative by the Lords, would automatically be submitted to the King for his approval.

This proposed legislation was of such far-reaching importance that it was thought advisable to hold a constitutional conference between the leaders of the two parties. During the sittings of this conference, which lasted from August until November, the Irish Party was not accorded any representation. After it broke up without accomplishing anything of importance, Parliament was dissolved on November 28 and another general election was held. The Liberal coalition made a net gain of only two seats, and once more it was apparent that the Irish Party controlled the balance of power. In the face of this situation the House of Lords finally (August 10) approved the Parliament bill without amendment, and eight days later it received the royal assent. The way was now clear for the long-awaited Home Rule legislation that Redmond had promised the Irish people.[3]

C. ULSTER BIDS DEFIANCE TO THE HOME RULE PROGRAM OF THE LIBERAL PARTY

The Royal Assent to the Parliament Bill aroused the deepest concern in Ulster, and the Orangemen were apprehensive that Home Rule legislation would soon be pushed through the House of Commons. Their fears were somewhat allayed in November 1911, when Balfour retired as the leader of the Conservative Party and his place was taken by Bonar Law. Canadian born but raised in Glasgow, Scotland, in an atmosphere of deep devotion to the Crown, Law never forgot that his family had for generations lived in Ulster, and he was surprisingly emotional when anything arose which af-

---

3. Lord Oxford, *Fifty Years of British Parliament* (Boston, 1926), II, 88-169; John Morley, *Recollections* (New York, 1917), II, 291-325.

fected Northern Ireland. One of his chief weapons, which he used with deadly effect in the House of Commons, was a faculty for vituperative language that flayed his opponents with such severity that few members wished to arouse his enmity. The Prime Minister was the main target for his frequent verbal barrages and he asked and gave no quarter. At the opening of the first session of 1912 the Prime Minister and Law were walking side by side from the House of Lords, where they had been listening to the King's Speech, when Law remarked to Asquith: "I am afraid I shall have to show myself very vicious this session. I hope you will understand." [4]

It used to be said that one of the reasons why Balfour retired in 1911 lay in the fact that he was too subtle to be highly effective in the rough and tumble verbal encounters in the House of Commons. Unionists grew restive under the sharp attacks of Lloyd George and they needed some champion who could "rain cudgel blows upon the Liberals, or spray them with the liquid fire of sarcasm." [5] But Bonar Law was not just a common scold who beat down the opposition by strident accents they could not match. He had the gift of effective leadership and he moved from one success to another until he reached the high post of Prime Minister. His background was very different from that of previous Prime Ministers. He was of obscure Colonial origin. He was not the product of any famous English school and he was not a graduate of Oxford or Cambridge. When other prospective Conservative leaders were making reluctant progress in Eton or Harrow, he was a mere clerk in the office of a Glasgow merchant. He was neither of the land nor of the aristocracy, but there was a hard core of character that carried him forward, and he was said to be "honest to the verge of simplicity." There is no doubt that he was a man of hard blows and reckless speech, and his intemperate utterances concerning Home Rule were so incendiary that they seemed designed to incite revolution throughout Northern Ireland. If John Redmond had dared to employ the same verbal pyrotechnics in support of Home Rule, he

4. Henry A. Taylor, *The Strange Case of Andrew Bonar Law* (London, 1932), pp. 170-171.
5. *Ibid.*, p. 170.

would have been banished to America and the members of the Irish Party would have been thrust into cold jails to dampen their excessive ardor.

Such political ardor was permissible only if it had an Ulster flavor. This fact was clearly perceived by Bonar Law's closest associate in the fight against Home Rule, Sir Edward Carson. Carson was born in Dublin and was educated in Trinity College. Like De Valera, he inherited a Latin strain from his father. From his mother's side he was descended from a general in Cromwell's army and he possessed to a marked degree the cold tenacity of a Roundhead soldier. He was not an orator in the popular sense, but his sharp, incisive manner of speech made an indelible impression upon his audiences. As a lawyer he was known for his unusual ability as a cross-examiner who could either break a witness or elicit from him the most damaging testimony. His soubriquet of "Coercion Carson" was well earned. His evident ability led Conservative leaders to name him Solicitor General for Ireland in 1892, and his rise in the party was steady if not spectacular. In 1911 he was a member of the Privy Council and a Conservative Member of Parliament for Dublin University. When the Liberal Party introduced its program providing for Home Rule, he immediately signified his bitter opposition. It was a fight to the finish and Carson emerged the victor.

Under the inspiration of Carson, in January 1911 the Ulster Women's Unionist Council opened the fight on Home Rule by adopting a resolution which declared that "we will stand by our husbands, our brothers, and our sons in whatever steps they may be forced to take in defending our liberties against the tyranny of Home Rule." Another slogan, written in 1886 by Lord Randolph Churchill, was enthusiastically adopted by belligerent Orangemen: "Ulster will fight and Ulster will be right." [6]

On April 9, 1912, at Balmoral, Bonar Law attended a large demonstration at which Carson was the principal speaker. After Law had denounced with unbridled violence any thought of Home Rule for Ulster, Carson arose, and after saluting Law, he shouted to the audience: "He will have no shrinking and no compromise.

6. Denis Gwynn, *The Life of John Redmond* (London, 1932), pp. 190-200.

We thank him for coming here to see face to face the manhood of the nation once more determined to express before him what I called at Craigavon the political tenets of our faith—that under no circumstances will we submit to Home Rule. Raise your hands! Repeat after me—'Never under any circumstances will we submit to Home Rule.' "[7]

Two days after this bitter outburst from Carson, the third and last Home Rule Bill was introduced in the House of Commons (April 11, 1912). It made provision for an Irish Parliament that would have authority to enact legislation covering everything except strictly imperial matters, and it gave Ireland forty-two members in Westminster.[8] In Parliament the opposition to Home Rule grew increasingly hysterical, and the strength and vehemence of the Unionists made such an impression upon some of the Liberals that on June 11 Mr. Agar-Robartes proposed an amendment that would exclude from the operation of the Home Rule Bill the four counties of Antrim, Armagh, Derry, and Down. In Derry the Catholics had a minority of 41.1%, and in Armagh the figure rose to almost half (45.3%). But Carson was not satisfied with this proposal. He would never agree "to leave out Tyrone and Fermanagh" even though both counties had Catholic majorities. Such a stand meant that he was strongly opposed to any Home Rule legislation that would affect Ulster.

The Home Rule Bill had been based upon the assumption that Ireland would be dealt with as a unit, and Birrell had stated that without Ulster, Home Rule would be "truncated." Lloyd George

7. *Ibid.*, p. 201; Ian Colvin, *The Life of Lord Carson* (London, 1934), II, 109-112.
8. The Irish Parliament would consist of a Senate of 40 members and a House of Commons of 164 members. Ulster would have 59 members of Parliament and would be safeguarded by the provision that the Irish Parliament would not be empowered to make any law, "either directly or indirectly to establish or endow any religion or prohibit the free exercise thereof, or give any preference, privilege or advantage or impose any disability or disadvantage on account of religious belief or religious or ecclesiastical status." It could not legislate on matters of peace and war, the Navy, the Army, foreign relations, trade outside Ireland, the coinage or legal tender. The executive was to remain vested in the sovereign or his representative, and 42 members from Ireland were to be elected to the British House of Commons.

informed the House of Commons that the Cabinet had carefully considered the claims of Ulster but had decided that "no geographical dividing line could be drawn." Carson's reply was a bold defiance of the Liberal Government: "We will accept the declaration of war. We are not altogether unprepared. I think it is time that we should take a step forward in our campaign, and I will recommend that to be done." On June 18 Bonar Law repeated the belligerent accents of Carson: "They know that if Ulster is in earnest, that if Ulster does resist by force, there are stronger influences than Parliamentary majorities. They know that in that case no Government would dare to use their troops to drive them out." [9]

It is not necessary to repeat all the inflammatory challenges thrown out by Ulster leaders to the Liberal Party. Mr. John J. Horgan's interesting compilation, *The Complete Grammar of Anarchy*, contains the more important of these incitements to violence. All through the summer of 1912 a series of demonstrations was held in Ulster denouncing any form of Home Rule, and prominent English Conservatives like Lord Salisbury and Lord Hugh Cecil, together with leading Irish Unionists like Lord Londonderry, the Duke of Abercorn, and Lord Charles Beresford, took part in a campaign to influence the Liberals in favor of compromise measures. This movement of opposition to Home Rule reached its peak in Belfast on Ulster Day, September 28, 1912. Carson was in attendance and took great pains to place his signature at the head of a long list of Covenanters. The purpose of this meeting was to place on record a formal announcement: "We Will Not Have Home Rule." [10]

To implement this spirit of defiance, the leaders in Ulster began to organize the Ulster Volunteers. This body of volunteers soon reached the large total of 100,000 men, and Lord Roberts was re-

9. The province of Ulster contained nine counties—or eleven, including Belfast and Derry City. It returned seventeen Home Rulers and sixteen anti-Home Rulers, and if the large city of Belfast were excluded, the Catholics would have been in the majority. They had a large minority in the four Protestant counties: 41.1% in Derry; 45.3% in Armagh; 31.6% in Down, and 20.3% in Antrim. Although the Catholic minority in Belfast was only 24.1%, the Catholics in Derry City reached a majority of 56.2%.
10. Ronald J. McNeill, *Ulster's Stand for Union* (London, 1922), pp. 116-117.

quested to train them. He refused, but recommended the appointment of Lieutenant General Sir George Richardson, who had learned warfare the hard way in bitterly fought campaigns against the Afghans.[11] It was not long before Richardson was bending all his energies to making the Volunteers an effective fighting force.

It was evident to Richardson that the efficiency of the Ulster Volunteers would be greatly increased if they could be equipped with rifles and ammunition. In Ulster it was not difficult to raise funds for the purchase of guns and ammunition in Europe. Some £70,000 was quickly collected for this purpose. The real task was to select some capable person who could smuggle these arms into Northern Ireland. It was finally decided to select Fred Crawford for this adventure in gun running. He had long been interested in this very job and had the complete confidence of the Ulster leaders. When he asked Sir Edward Carson if he was willing to "back him to the end," Carson "rose to his full height, looking me in the eye; he advanced to where I was sitting and stared down at me, shook his clenched fist in my face and said in a steady determined voice which thrilled me . . . 'Crawford, I'll see you through this business if I should have to go to prison for it.'"[12]

Crawford bought the arms and ammunition in Hamburg—thirty thousand rifles and three million rounds of ammunition. He finally stored them in a little boat, *The Fanny*, which ran for safety into a little bay on the Welsh coast, where the cargo was transferred to the *Mountjoy*. At 10:30 on the night of April 24, 1914, the *Mountjoy* came alongside the landing stage at Larne, where she was met by Ulster Volunteers who made short work of unloading the cargo. Fifty thousand Volunteers had been secretly mobilized for this venture, and control of Larne was securely in their hands. As Ian Colvin remarks: "The whole community was in it heart and soul. . . . At every crossroads sentinels were ready to direct the motorcars and vans, which carried Crawford's well-calculated bundles throughout the length and breadth of Ulster."[13]

11. Ian Colvin, *The Life of Lord Carson* (London, 1934), II, 86-187.
12. *Ibid.*, II, 363.
13. *Ibid.*, 374.

Although Asquith announced that "in view of this grave and unprecedented outrage . . . His Majesty's Government will take, without delay, appropriate steps to vindicate the authority of the law," nothing was done and the men of Ulster knew that the Liberals did not have the courage of their convictions. This fact was equally apparent in Southern Ireland, where the Nationalists came to the conclusion that Home Rule had best be defended by the organization of the Irish Volunteers.

D. BELLIGERENCE IN BELFAST LEADS TO THE CREATION OF THE IRISH VOLUNTEERS

The mad antics of Sir Edward Carson and Bonar Law were watched with particular interest in Southern Ireland by the members of the I.R.B. who hoped to be able to fish with profit in the troubled waters of Anglo-Irish relations. Men like Sean MacDiarmuda, Bulmer Hobson, Sean McGarry, and Tom Clarke had kept alive their separatist dreams and were only awaiting an opportunity to invoke a physical-force program that might lead to Irish independence. As they bided their time, Professor Eoin MacNeill, Vice President of the Gaelic League and Professor of Early Irish History in University College, Dublin, asked in the official organ of the Gaelic League a very pertinent question: "If Ulstermen can arm and organize to defeat Home Rule, can we not arm to defend it?" [14]

The fact that Dr. MacNeill was at the time a supporter of John Redmond and was not suspected of Sinn Fein sympathies made him an ideal leader of a movement to create a force of Irish Volunteers. A Provisional Committee met at Wynn's Hotel, Dublin, near the end of October 1913 to discuss the situation. Eight of the thirteen members of the committee belonged to the I.R.B.[15] On November 25, 1913, at a public meeting in the Rotunda Rink in Dublin, the Irish Volunteers were formally launched. A new Provisional Com-

---

14. Piaras Beaslai, *Michael Collins and the Making of a New Ireland* (London, 1926), pp. 31-33.
15. *Ibid.,* pp. 33-34.

mittee of twenty-eight was named, nine of whom were members of the I.R.B. and six were members of Sinn Fein.

At this Rotunda meeting a *Manifesto to the Irish People,* drafted by Eoin MacNeill, was approved with a few verbal alterations. It opened with a sharp criticism of the actions of the leaders of the Conservative Party and the Ulster extremists. It seemed apparent that "a plan has been deliberately adopted by one of the great English political parties . . . to make the display of military force and the menace of armed violence the determining factor in the future relations between this country and Great Britain." The object of the Irish Volunteers was "to secure and maintain the rights and liberties common to all the people of Ireland. Their duties will be defensive and protective, and they will not contemplate either aggression or domination." [16]

The slogan adopted by the Provisional Committee of the Irish Volunteers was "Defence, not Defiance," and by the end of 1913 the members reached 10,000. The Supreme Council of the I.R.B. had feared that the Liberal Government would take some adverse action against the organization of the Irish Volunteers, and their apprehensions were relieved when, on December 6, 1913, the London *Gazette* contained a proclamation merely prohibiting the importation of arms and ammunition into Ireland. For the time being, at least, the recruiting of the Irish Volunteers could continue, and the defiant actions of the Ulster leaders with special reference to the landing of guns and ammunition at Larne, April 24, 1914, swelled the ranks of Irish Volunteers to the impressive total of 160,000.

To John Redmond the rapid development of the Irish Volunteers was a challenge to his leadership. His political future was in the hands of the leaders of the Liberal Party, and Home Rule, even in an attenuated form, was to his mind an important political victory. The separatist dreams of Parnell were no longer cherished by the Irish Party, which was entirely content with something resembling dominion status within the empire. To secure this concession from the Liberal Party, Redmond was willing to meet Asquith more than

16. Patrick S. O'Hegarty, *A History of Ireland Under the Union, 1801-1922,* pp. 690-671.

half way with regard to satisfying the demands of Ulster. On February 2, 1914, he had an interview with the Prime Minister, who first gave assurances that "he and his colleagues were all firmly opposed to the exclusion of Ulster, or any part of Ulster, even temporarily," from the operation of Home Rule. After this bid for Redmond's good will, Asquith then spoke with evident apprehension of the tactics of the Opposition in connection with the passage of essential legislation. A "very serious crisis had arisen with regard to the Navy Estimates," and he anticipated "the very gravest trouble and danger not merely from a possibility of hostile votes, but from a general feeling of dissatisfaction and disappointment, which from the Whigs' point of view constituted a very grave menace that was likely to lead at any moment to accidents in the Division lobby." It was obvious that some concessions would have to be made to Ulster.[17]

Lloyd George was quick to press for some compromise on the issue of Home Rule. In a memorandum he presented to the Cabinet he advocated the immediate passage of the Home Rule Bill. If in Ulster certain counties wished to have the operation of Home Rule postponed until after a general election, this privilege should be extended to them. The wedge of separation was thus offered to Asquith. He promptly presented it to Redmond, who found himself in a difficult position. His program of co-operation with the Liberals compelled him to go along with Asquith, but he had to face the possibility of rising opposition in Ireland to any thought of even a temporary separation of the Ulster counties. On March 2, 1914, he had a long conference with Asquith and Lloyd George and finally agreed to the right of certain Ulster counties to "opt for remaining outside the jurisdiction of the Irish Parliament . . . for three years, covering the period when a General Election must take place." On March 9, Asquith moved the second reading of the Home Rule Bill, and the proposal was adopted that "any Ulster county might, by a majority of its Parliamentary electors, vote itself out of the operation of the Bill for six years."[18]

17. Denis Gwynn, *John Redmond*, pp. 250-252.
18. *Ibid.*, pp. 267-273.

But these concessions were not enough to allay the spirit of resistance in Ulster. It had been coddled by important military officers whose Ulster sympathies were stronger than their oaths of allegiance to the Crown. In this regard the *Diaries* of Sir Henry Wilson are illuminating. On November 9, 1913, he paid a visit to Bonar Law and frankly "told him there was much talk in the Army, and that if we were ordered to coerce Ulster there would be wholesale defections. . . . I then told him of Cecil's idea that Carson should pledge the Ulster troops to fight for England if she was at war. I pointed out that a move like this would render the employment of troops against Ulster more impossible than ever." [19] In March 1914 the determination of many British officers to refuse any service against Ulster reached a focus in the "affair of the Curragh." The Curragh was a vast common of springy turf which constituted the finest ground of exercise for men and guns and horses in all Ireland. The pride of the Curragh was the Third Cavalry Brigade. To the officers of this brigade the question of possible service against the men of Ulster was put very frankly. The first telegram of reply that Brigadier General Gough sent to the War Office contained the alarming news that "the officers of two regiments of Lancers were resigning their commissions." The second telegram was even more alarming: "Regret to report Brigadier and 57 officers, 3rd Cavalry Brigade, prefer to accept dismissal if ordered North." "Thus by Friday night the British Army at the Curragh had crumbled in the hands of its Commander-in-Chief. The full effects of the disintegration were not realised till next day, when it became plain to the quick brains of Mr. Churchill and Mr. Lloyd George . . . that . . . combined operations 'to anticipate and crush the resistance of Ulster' could not be carried through." [20]

In answer to all these threats of mutiny the ranks of Irish Volunteers swelled to such unexpected numbers that Redmond decided to attempt to take over the control of the movement. Without his

19. Sir Charles E. Callwell, *Field Marshal Sir Henry Wilson* (London, 1927, 2 vols.), I, 131.
20. Colvin, *op. cit.*, II, 319-336. For a recent and colorful account of the "affair of the Curragh," see A. P. Ryan, *Mutiny at the Curragh* (London, 1956).

direction it could amount to a serious challenge to the program of the Irish Parliamentary Party. With the expectation of securing quick control over the Irish Volunteers, he wrote a letter (June 9, 1914) to the press in which he suggested "that the Provisional Committee [of the Irish Volunteers] should be immediately strengthened by the addition of twenty-five representative men from different parts of the country, nominated at the instance of the Irish Party, and in sympathy with its policy and aims." [21] When the Provisional Committee suggested an alternative plan that would not give Redmond control over the Volunteers, he threatened to organize a rival volunteer force under his complete control and to attract from the existing force every member he could influence.[22]

The Provisional Committee finally gave way under the impact of this threat, and Redmond was able to have twenty-five members who could always be counted upon to respond to his wishes. He next proceeded to issue an appeal for funds to be collected, both in Ireland and in America, which would be expended only under his direction. He knew that if he succeeded in dominating the Irish Volunteers the Liberal Party would have no apprehensions concerning it. But events moved faster than Redmond anticipated. In May 1914 Erskine Childers joined a small committee formed in England to supply the Irish Volunteers with arms. He and a friend purchased in Hamburg 1,500 rifles, which were transferred to Childers' yacht off the Dutch coast on June 27, 1914. Finally, after some exciting episodes, most of the guns were landed at Howth on July 26, where the Volunteers were waiting for them, some so overwrought with emotion that they were in tears. But they did not have the situation as well in hand as the Ulster Volunteers had had at Larne. As the Irish Volunteers marched towards Dublin they were stopped by police who demanded the rifles. In the confusion that followed, most of the Volunteers who carried rifles were able to elude the police, who then gained dubious satisfaction by firing

---

21. Bulmer Hobson, *History of the Irish Volunteers* (Dublin, 1918), pp. 109-110.
22. *Ibid.*, p. 120.

Is an Old English Political Practice 149

upon an unarmed crowd of civilians in Bachelor's Walk, killing three and wounding thirty-eight. The contrast between the tragedy in Bachelor's Walk and the unmolested march of the Ulster Volunteers from Larne to different parts of Ulster was too striking to be overlooked. Redmond at once arose in the House of Commons and demanded a full judicial and military inquiry. Although this was promptly accorded, it did not mean the disarming of the Ulster Volunteers, nor did it bring back to Irish households the men, and the woman, who had been killed in Bachelor's Walk. It was merely another instance of "much ado about nothing" and it did not quiet the tension in Ireland.[23]

E. BRITAIN BOLDLY BETRAYS HER PROMISES OF HOME RULE FOR IRELAND

While the excitement in Ireland with reference to the tragedy in Bachelor's Walk was mounting to a danger point, events in Europe pointed to the outbreak of a World War. England's necessity would be Ireland's opportunity if there were an Irish statesman who had any political vision and a desire for Irish independence. Liberal statesmen would have to accede to any demands Redmond might make. He had abandoned Parnell's dream of independence but he had long supported a program which emphasized Home Rule. The realization of this program was now possible if he merely continued his pressure.

In Europe the shadows of war grew longer and darker. The assassination of the Archduke Franz Ferdinand on June 28 meant an inevitable showdown between Serbia and Austria-Hungary. Vienna knew that the only way to stop the dangerous intrigues of the Serbian Black Hand Society was to insist upon Austro-Hungarian representation upon commissions of inquiry that would deal with the activities of certain Serbian national societies. Vienna also knew that the Government at Belgrade would never

---

23. John J. Horgan, *op. cit.*, pp. 310-312; Dorothy Macardle, *The Irish Republic* (Dublin, 1951), pp. 116-122.

grant such representation, and a localized war against Serbia was planned by the War Office. Vienna did not know that the British Foreign Secretary, Sir Edward Grey, had made far-reaching promises of support to France in the event of a European war. As a matter of fact most of the British Cabinet were ignorant of the role played by Grey, and they did not know that since 1906 he had made so many commitments to France that England was in honor bound to support any French Government that became involved in war.[24]

As the Liberal Government moved down the road to war the necessity to conciliate Ireland seemed fundamental. A loyal and friendly Ireland was a national imperative. But the Liberal leaders knew they had Redmond in leading strings and they also believed that Redmond dominated the Irish situation. If they knew about the I.R.B. and its program of Irish independence, they must have burst into Homeric laughter. A handful of fanatics aroused no concern in Asquith's mind unless they marched under Ulster banners.

It was this Ulster threat that led Asquith to consent to compromise, even though this policy meant a betrayal of Irish hopes for Home Rule. On June 23 the House of Lords introduced a bill to amend the proposed Home Rule legislation. It largely embodied the proposals made by the Asquith Government in March. Lord Crewe invited further changes in the Home Rule Bill, and this action led to some important conferences between Redmond and Lord Murray of Elibank. Murray, in his most soothing manner, informed Redmond that both Carson and Bonar Law had expressed the opinion that "Home Rule was inevitable, and that the inclusion of Ulster in a comparatively short time was, in their judgment, inevitable also." Bonar Law was most "anxious" to find some path to compromise and was showing a "most conciliatory" disposition. But this so-called "conciliatory disposition" was merely a mask to cover a desire to increase the plebiscite area in Ulster to include Antrim, Derry City, Derry, Down, North and Mid-Armagh, and North Fermanagh.

24. For recent informing and critical evaluations of the foreign policy of Sir Edward Grey see Francis Neilson, *The Churchill Legend* (Appleton, 1954), pp. 214-232; Russell Grenfell, *Unconditional Hatred* (New York, 1953), pp. 3-23.

Redmond told Murray that the proposals of Carson and Bonar Law were "quite impossible," and negotiations bogged down.[25]

At the War Office, Sir Henry Wilson contributed to this adamant attitude of the Ulster leaders. Even though he felt that a European war was inevitable and that English intervention would be a matter of course, he still supported a line of conduct in Ulster that might lead to civil war in Ireland. During the first week of July, 1914, he had a talk with Lord Milner and immediately disclosed his sympathies with the attitude of the Ulster extremists. Milner said there was a strong possibility that Carson would soon "set up a Provisional Government" in Ulster and would take over such Government offices as he could without bloodshed. This action would bring "matters to a head." He then inquired what the Army would do if Carson took the course he had indicated. Wilson promptly replied that "much depended on the way the picture was put to us [the War Office]. I thought that if Carson and his Government were sitting in the City Hall, and we were ordered down to close the hall, we would not go." [26]

On July 8 the Amending Bill in the House of Lords was newly phrased so as to include the permanent exclusion of the whole province of Ulster from Home Rule. Five days later Redmond had an interview with Asquith and Birrell on this latest amendment to the Home Rule Bill. Asquith said he did not believe this proposal was meant to be seriously considered, and he then proceeded to discuss "the question of the area of possible exclusion." Redmond made the terse comment that it would be impossible "to make any further concession on the question of area." On July 21 an important conference was held at Buckingham Palace between Asquith, Lloyd George, Bonar Law, Lord Lansdowne, Redmond, Dillon, Carson, and Captain Craig. When the exclusion of the entire province of Ulster from Home Rule was proposed, Redmond and Dillon "vehemently repudiated it." On the following day Carson proposed the exclusion of the whole province of Ulster or six counties as a minimum. This suggestion was not acceptable to Redmond, who

25. Denis Gwynn, *John Redmond*, pp. 328-330.
26. Callwell, *op. cit.*, I, 148.

then asked whether any settlement not based upon exclusion would be given any consideration if the Nationalists would offer "very large concessions" along other lines. When this question failed to elicit any favorable replies, it was evident that the conference would close upon a note of complete failure.[27] In speaking of the sessions of the conference, Asquith made the following pithy comment: "Nothing could have been more amicable in tone or more desperately fruitless in result." [28]

While the sessions of the conference were moving towards a deadlock, the tides of a European war were rapidly rising and members of the Cabinet began to take alarm at the situation. On July 23 an Austrian ultimatum was presented to the Serbian government, and the Serbian reply, two days later, was regarded by Vienna as so unsatisfactory that war was declared. Russia had long viewed the war as the only means of securing control over Constantinople and, fortified with Poincaré's promise of support, on July 25 the Russian militarists ordered some preparatory mobilization measures. When this was followed by an order of general mobilization (July 30), a general European war was just around the corner of a weekend. In this regard Professor Sidney B. Fay cogently remarks: "It was the hasty Russian general mobilization, assented to on July 29 and ordered on July 30, while Germany was still trying to bring Austria to accept mediation proposals, which finally rendered the European war inevitable." [29]

On July 30, while the Russian War Office was issuing the fateful order of general mobilization, the House of Commons assembled to consider the Amending Bill. The course to be followed by the Liberal Government was clear and simple. The Amending Bill should have been rejected at once, and Home Rule legislation, without any reference to the exclusion of any counties in Ulster, should have been passed and sent to the King for the Royal Assent. Asquith chose the coward's course of postponing the issue for some weeks. Redmond could have brought the matter to an immediate

27. Denis Gwynn, *John Redmond*, pp. 341-343.
28. *Memories and Reflections* (Boston, 1928), II, 7.
29. Sidney B. Fay, *The Origins of the World War* (New York, 1929), II, 554.

and favorable decision by a stern demand for action, but he listened instead to the blandishments of Mrs. Asquith, who wrote him a brief note expressing the view that he should go "to the House of Commons on the Monday and in a great speech offer all his soldiers to the Government." This would be a very "dramatic thing to do at such a moment, and it might strengthen the claim of Ireland upon the gratitude of the British people." [30] Redmond closed his eyes to the fact that he was being asked to pay in Irish blood, sweat, and tears for the dubious privilege of being betrayed. In the spirit of an Irish lackey he replied that he was "very grateful" for the suggestion and hoped he might be able to carry it out.[31]

On Monday, August 3, Redmond was in the House of Commons and heard Sir Edward Grey make public for the first time the intimate connections he had forged with France from 1906 to 1914. He also heard Grey, after this recital of secret commitments that were morally binding, make the astounding claim that his hands were still free and that Parliament could act as it pleased with reference to intervention in the war that was about to break over Europe. Upon the eve of a World War the members of Parliament were more emotional than rational, and Redmond seemed particularly touched by Grey's brief reference to the Irish question: "The one bright spot in the very dreadful situation is Ireland. The position in Ireland—and this I should like to be clearly understood abroad—is not a consideration among the things we have to take into account now." [32]

This obvious British bait was eagerly seized by Redmond, who was now in a highly overwrought condition. During the course of Grey's speech he asked his colleague, John Hayden, if he should make some remarks. Hayden answered: "That depends on what you are going to say." Redmond excitedly remarked: "I'm going to tell them they can take all their troops out of Ireland and we will defend the country ourselves." Hayden advised him to speak out at once, but T. P. O'Connor, thinking of the excitement in Ireland

---

30. Margot Asquith, *An Autobiography* (New York, 1922), II, 23-24.
31. Denis Gwynn, *John Redmond*, p. 354.
32. Sir Edward Grey, *Twenty-Five Years* (New York, 1925), II, 308-326.

caused by the recent incident in Bachelor's Walk, thought the moment was not opportune for a pledge of support. But Redmond could not be silenced. In an atmosphere tense with the knowledge that war was at hand and that the attitude of Ireland was of supreme importance, Redmond arose in the Commons and walked right into the trap that Margot Asquith had baited for him. His delicate sensibilities would not permit him to touch upon any "controversial topic" at this hour of Empire crisis. The question of Home Rule for Ireland could be passed over in silence. But he was quite certain that the "democracy of Ireland" would turn with the "utmost anxiety and sympathy" to England in every "trial and every danger that may overtake it." This sympathy was supported by Redmond's pledge of help: "I say to the Government that they may tomorrow withdraw every one of their troops from Ireland. I say that the coast of Ireland will be defended from foreign invasion by her armed sons. . . . Is it too much to hope that out of this situation there may spring a result which will be good, not merely for the Empire, but good for the future welfare and integrity of the Irish nation." [33]

Stephen Gwynn has described how the Tory members of the Commons broke out with ejaculations of "bewilderment and delight" during Redmond's speech, and the Unionists "stood up to cheer him." [34] Redmond was naïve enough to believe that these cheers meant that the Unionists would now meet him halfway and that Home Rule was now assured. He was shocked when he had a meeting with Carson on August 5 and found the Ulster leader "absolutely irreconcilable." In a letter to Asquith on the same evening he expressed the opinion that the Liberal Party had the "greatest opportunity that has ever occurred in the history of Ireland to win the Irish people to loyalty to the Empire. . . . I beg of you not to allow threats . . . to prevent you from taking the course which will enable me to preach the doctrines of peace, goodwill and loyalty in Ireland." [35]

33. Denis Gwynn, *John Redmond*, p. 356.
34. *John Redmond's Last Years* (London, 1919), pp. 132-133.
35. Denis Gwynn, *John Redmond*, p. 363.

While Asquith was pondering this course as outlined by Redmond, the sentiment in Ireland was surprisingly cordial towards England. The recent excitement caused by the gun running at Howth quickly died down, and when the King's Own Scottish Borderers emerged from their barracks in Dublin, the incident in Bachelor's Walk was forgotten and they were received with cheers and every sign of good will. But some flies began to appear in this ointment of cordiality. When Asquith persuaded Lord Kitchener to replace him as Secretary of State for War, the old suspicion of Ireland became manifest. On August 7 Redmond had a long conversation with Kitchener and found him so frigid that he felt compelled to write a letter of protest to Asquith. The new Secretary of War wished to have nothing to do with the Irish Volunteers; he was distinctly disinclined to rely upon them for the defense of Ireland. To Redmond, this attitude was very discouraging, and he feared that unless prompt action was taken the "rising enthusiasm" in Ireland would soon decline.

This decline actually started with the appointment of Kitchener as Secretary of State for War. Asquith soon discovered that Kitchener posed as an authority "on Irish politics," and it was not long before he gathered around him in the War Office some of the Ulstermen who had been connected with the gun running at Larne. His influence in favor of Ulster was quickly noticed and deeply deprecated. It was obvious that he was strongly opposed to arming the Irish Volunteers.

To Irish Nationalists, this attitude on the part of Kitchener was shortsighted and dangerous. In a letter to Asquith (August 22), Redmond expressed the fear that any postponement of Home Rule legislation would be interpreted as a "betrayal of our hopes, as a sham." It was difficult to exaggerate the intensity of the "sympathy which is now felt for England and of enthusiastic approval of her cause in entering into the war with Germany. . . . But all this splendid temper may be destroyed if there be any postponement of the Home Rule Bill." [36]

But this ardent desire to be of service to England did not awaken

36. *Ibid.,* pp. 375-376.

any real response on the part of the Prime Minister, who recorded in his *Diary* (August 31) that he wished he could "submerge the whole lot of them [the Irish] and their island for, say, ten years under the waves of the Atlantic." [37] He then went ahead and submerged the hopes of many Irishmen by putting the Home Rule Bill on the Statute Book, but he attached to it a Suspensory Bill that would prevent its operation until the end of the war.[38] Further to dampen Irish hopes, Asquith issued a warning that the Home Rule Bill could not go into effect "until Parliament has had the fullest opportunity, by an Amending Bill, of altering, modifying, or qualifying its provisions in such a way as to secure the general consent both of Ireland and of the United Kingdom."

It was now very evident that the Amending Bill would embody exclusion of at least four of the counties of Ulster, and it might contain other changes that would be equally distasteful to Irish Nationalists. But Redmond did not seem unduly disturbed by these ominous possibilities. Although he frankly admitted that the action of the Liberal Government had inflicted "a severe disadvantage upon us," he still favored a policy of co-operation. Indeed, his remarks in the Commons showed how completely he had fallen under the spell of Asquith even when the Prime Minister's conduct was most dubious. He was constantly emphasizing the enthusiasm in Ireland for the cause of England:

> In this war I say, for the first time, certainly for over a hundred years, Ireland feels that her interests are precisely the same as yours. She feels and will feel that the British democracy has kept faith with her. She knows that this is a just war. . . . I say for myself that I would feel myself personally dishonoured if I did not say to my fellow-countrymen . . . that it is their duty, and should be their honour, to take their place in the firing-line of this contest.

Redmond's enthusiasm for the course taken by the Asquith Government reached the heights of hysteria when he justified the passage of the Suspensory Bill: "When everybody is preoccupied by

37. *Memories and Reflections*, II, 36.
38. *Hansard's Debates*, September 15, 1914, *Irish Affairs*, cols. 2763-2770.

the War, and when every one is endeavouring . . . to bring about the creation of an Army, the idea is absurd that under these circumstances a new Government and a new Parliament could be erected in Ireland." [39]

Redmond's complete surrender to the English viewpoint on Home Rule brought him tremendous popularity in the Commons, where his role in betraying Ireland was immediately recognized and appreciated. And there seemed to be no limits to the lengths he would go in his servility to the cause of England. On September 18, 1914, the House of Commons listened to the Royal Assent to the Home Rule Bill, and when this farce was finished, Will Crooks, the Labor leader, led the members in the singing of *God Save the King*. Later he called out in a loud voice: "God Save Ireland." Redmond, now thoroughly drunk with English emotion, called back in stentorian tones: "And God Save England too." To thousands of Irishmen who were sick and tired of broken English promises, these words of Redmond were nothing short of blasphemy.

F. THE CLAN-NA-GAEL AND THE IRISH VOLUNTEERS

To the members of the Clan-na-Gael, the speeches and actions of Redmond were extremely distasteful. The clan had kept alive Parnell's dream of Irish independence and it sharply repudiated Redmond's viewpoint that a limited amount of Home Rule was sufficient. The Clan constantly looked forward to the day when, through physical force, independence would be gained for Ireland, and it kept a steady stream of funds moving into the treasury of the I.R.B. It was also ready to support any organization that promoted the growth of Irish nationalism. When P. H. Pearse founded St. Enda's College he was in desperate need for funds. He could raise them only in America, and one of his friends who gave warm support to his project was Daniel F. Cohalan.[40]

It was with reference to the Irish Volunteer movement that the

---

39. *Ibid.*, cols. 2782-2784.
40. Bulmer Hobson to John Devoy, October 11, 1913, *Devoy's Post Bag*, II, 415-416, 430.

Clan-na-Gael made its most important contribution. On April 6, 1914, The O'Rahilly wrote to John Devoy and made an appeal to "the sincere Irish in America" for funds for the purchase of arms and ammunition with which to equip the Volunteers: "It is our finances and not our organization that are weak." He believed that "never was such an opportunity in our time, and if we don't grasp it, the next political development may destroy the chance." [41]

After receiving this appeal from The O'Rahilly, Devoy circulated a printed circular setting forth the objectives and needs of the Irish Volunteers. According to Tom Clarke, Redmond, during the Easter recess, offered to provide adequate finances for the Volunteers "on condition of being given control" over them. Devlin had made similar offers to Sir Roger Casement.[42]

These offers were refused, and Redmond redoubled his efforts to capture control over the Irish Volunteers. On June 16 a majority of the existing Provisional Committee agreed to accept Redmond's nominees to the committee. They did this reluctantly and merely "to preserve the unity of the Volunteers and, at the same time to maintain the non-party and non-sectional principle of organisation . . . pending the election of a . . . governing body by a duly constituted Volunteer convention." [43]

Bulmer Hobson, General Secretary and Quartermaster of the Irish Volunteers, was one of the members of the Provisional Committee who voted in favor of accepting Redmond's nominees. His action in this regard stirred the enmity of Tom Clarke and Sean MacDermott and led Devoy to terminate Hobson's services as correspondent of the *Gaelic American*. When Devoy learned the whole story concerning the attitude of Hobson, he reappointed him as correspondent of the *Gaelic American*, but between "postal difficulties" and the British ban on the papers, no further articles by Hobson appeared in the *Gaelic American*.[44]

41. *Ibid.*, 425-427.
42. Louis N. Le Roux, *Tom Clarke and the Irish Freedom Movement*, pp. 131-132.
43. The O'Rahilly to John Devoy, June 25, 1914, *Devoy's Post Bag*, II, 450-451; Dorothy Macardle, *The Irish Republic*, pp. 106-115.
44. *Devoy's Post Bag*, II, 456.

One of the strongest supporters of Hobson in the matter of accepting the Redmond nominees on the Provisional Committee was Sir Roger Casement. Casement arrived in New York City on July 20, 1914, and immediately got in touch with Devoy. When Devoy expressed his indignation at the way Hobson had acted, Casement warmly defended him and on the following day wrote a long letter to Devoy giving the details of the situation. He believed that if Hobson had fought the matter of concessions to Redmond, there would have been a "hideous scuffle" and the Volunteers would have been disbanded. The only thought "influencing Hobson was that that swayed me—to save the Volunteers from disruption and Ireland from a disgraceful faction fight in which all original issues would have gone by the board." [45]

G. REDMOND IS DETERMINED TO CONTROL THE IRISH VOLUNTEERS OR WRECK THE ORGANIZATION

The role of Redmond in the matter of the Irish Volunteers was one of rule or ruin. His constant support of the program of the Liberal Party led to an inevitable split in the ranks of Irish Nationalists, and his determination to control the Irish Volunteers sprang from his fear that the new organization was a menace to his dominant position in Irish circles. He had a deep-seated dislike for the I.R.B. and he was apprehensive that any funds they might secure from America would be used for striking a blow for Irish independence.[46] Such an objective was no longer attractive to him. In 1914 he played the very dubious role of trying to induce the youth of Ireland to die for an empire that had betrayed them. In his numerous

---

45. *Ibid.*, 461-463.
46. The funds raised for the Volunteers came from two sources. Redmond's Volunteer Fund, raised through the Irish World, amounted merely to some $5,000, but the campaign for its collection "obstructed the Clan-na-Gael's work and lowered the amount that otherwise would have been sent in." The Irish Volunteer Fund raised by John Devoy reached the impressive amount of $50,000. When this was supplemented by the Clan-na-Gael's remittances to the I.R.B., the total sum raised was close to $100,000. These were the funds that "supplied the men of Easter week with the means of striking their historic blow." John Devoy, *Recollections of an Irish Rebel*, p. 393.

speeches he never tired of repeating the British line of propaganda that the Allies were fighting a crusade against a wicked enemy that threatened to destroy the bases of civilization.

In this regard his speech at Woodenbridge, September 20, 1914, is typical:

> The duty of the manhood of Ireland is twofold. Its duty is at all costs to defend the shores of Ireland from foreign invasion. It has a duty more than that, of taking care that Irish valour proves itself on the field of war as it has always proved itself in the past. The interests of Ireland, of the whole of Ireland, are at stake in this war. This War is undertaken in defence of the highest principles of religion and morality and right, and it would be a disgrace for ever to our country, a reproach to her manhood, and a denial of the lessons of her history, if young Ireland confined their efforts to remaining at home to defend the shores of Ireland. . . . I say to you, therefore, your duty is twofold. . . . Go on drilling and make yourselves efficient for the work, and then account for yourselves as men, not only in Ireland itself, but wherever the fighting line extends, in defence of right and freedom and religion in this war.[47]

Redmond's burning loyalty to England was evident in every line of this speech, and it deeply angered thousands of Irishmen who had no desire to die for the ruling class of a country that for centuries had made Irish oppression a main article in its creed. The original Provisional Committee of the Irish Volunteers took immediate action and expelled Redmond's nominees from the committee. Redmond retaliated by organizing a separate body of his own under the title of The National Volunteers. From the viewpoint of numbers he won a significant victory. The enrollment of the Irish Volunteers had reached a total of more than 160,000 men. After the split the Provisional Committee merely controlled some 10,000, but they were picked members who, according to P. S. O'Hegarty, comprised "all the separatists and I.R.B. men and practically all the intelligent patriotism of the body." [48]

As the directing force behind the National Volunteers, Redmond became merely a recruiting sergeant for the British Army. He was

---

47. Stephen Gwynn, *John Redmond's Last Years* (London, 1919), pp. 154-155.
48. *Ireland Under the Union*, p. 688.

able to induce Asquith to visit Dublin on September 26 and make a speech of conciliation. The Prime Minister apparently supported the idea of "an Irish brigade—better still an Irish Army Corps." Irish recruits would not lose their identity "and become absorbed in some invertebrate mass, or . . . artificially distributed into units which have no national cohesion or character." The same conditions that had enabled Carson to raise the Ulster Division would govern the formation of the new Irish Divisions. As Denis Gwynn wryly remarks: "No pledges could have been more clearly given, but they were ignobly disregarded." [49]

Redmond never seemed to understand that Asquith was a master of double-talk, and he took the pledges of the Prime Minister at face value. In his speeches he repeated the assurance that "after the War was over the Volunteers would remain as a recognized permanent force for the defence of the country," and he made public a letter from Asquith stating that Kitchener would soon issue the announcement that "the War Office has sanctioned the formation of an Irish Army Corps." Needless to say, Kitchener never issued such an announcement. With reference to Home Rule, Redmond still clung desperately to his faith in Asquith even when signs began to multiply that he was being trifled with. In Ulster, Carson (September 28) had boastfully informed his audiences that the Home Rule Bill "is nothing but a scrap of paper. . . . We are never going to allow Home Rule in Ulster. . . . Our Volunteers are going to kick out anybody who tries to put it into force in Ulster." At the same time Bonar Law spoke in a similar vein, and his belligerent words awakened many fears in other parts of Ireland.[50]

While Redmond was touring Ireland, misinforming recruits by repeating the faithless pledges of Asquith, Lord Kitchener, at the War Office, was revealing his fixed determination to prevent the formation of an Irish Army Corps. On October 16 Lieutenant General Sir Lawrence Parsons wrote a conciliatory note to Redmond indicating that "three essentially Irish Brigades" formed the 16th Division, which had every claim, therefore, to be called an "Irish

---

49. *Life of John Redmond*, p. 394.
50. *Ibid.*, p. 395.

Division." But Redmond's pleasure at this news was soon clouded over by another note from General Parsons (October 26) which frankly stated that Lord Kitchener was issuing an order to "disperse the Irish recruits." Parsons also plagued Redmond by rejecting practically every candidate he recommended for a commission. Redmond was well aware of the fact that the Ulster Division had taken over the cadre of the Ulster Volunteers and their officers were automatically given commissions to command the men from their own districts. The situation was very different with regard to the National Volunteers. Parsons was able, as a special concession, to give commissions to two National Volunteer leaders, but he insisted that they bring recruits with them. He rejected suggestions that some of the thousands of Irishmen living in England be permitted to enlist in the new Irish Division. He feared they would be nothing more than "slum-birds." With reference to officer material he was highly selective. In the 16th Division he had particularly favored Irish Protestants, not one colonel in the whole Division being a Catholic.[51]

Although the refusal of General Parsons to grant a commission to Redmond's son deeply angered the leader of the Irish Party, he continued to recruit young Irishmen to fight the battles of Britain. Other members of the Irish Party were not so steadfast in their support of the Liberal Government's program. John Dillon soon became convinced that Redmond had gone too far in his efforts to please Asquith, and he began to lose faith in Liberal leadership.

This loss of faith in the program of the Liberal Party became more widespread in the early summer of 1915, when Asquith decided that a Coalition Government should be formed. He repeatedly asked Redmond to become a member of his new Cabinet. He knew that the leader of the Irish Party would lose face in Ireland if he did so, and he must have had his tongue in his cheek when he pressed for Irish representation. Carson had no qualms about entering the Cabinet and neither did Bonar Law, whose inflammatory addresses had helped to kindle a flame of opposition to Home

51. *Ibid.*, pp. 396-400.

Rule. The appointment of J. H. Campbell as Attorney General for Ireland was especially distasteful to Irish Nationalists who remembered his Ulster activities. Redmond wrote a plaintive letter to Asquith opposing the Campbell appointment: "There is a limit to our patience.... The feeling in Ireland is of the most intense character." [52] This feeling would grow even more intense when the Coalition Cabinet took final shape, with half of its members Unionist politicians who had been warmly sympathetic with Ulster's stand against Home Rule.

The strange actions of Asquith reduced in a radical manner Redmond's popularity in Ireland. There was particular bitterness concerning the broken pledges of the Prime Minister concerning the treatment of Irish troops. In the retreat from Mons, the 2d Battalion of the Royal Munster Fusiliers had fought a gallant rear-guard action and had nearly been wiped out while waiting for orders that never arrived. Disaster attended the landing of the 29th Division on the end of the Gallipoli peninsula, and the Munster and Dublin Fusiliers were badly cut up. Their gallantry in action had received little publicity, and it was soon evident that Irish regiments could expect no favorable notice. At Suvla Bay, in the Dardanelles campaign, the fighting was so sanguinary that the 10th Irish Division virtually ceased to exist as an effective unit, but it received no recognition whatever for its heroic efforts. For Irish troops there were no paths of glory leading to famous graves. They died without any purple paragraphs of praise, and it was widely known that they had been needlessly slaughtered. As Denis Gwynn aptly pictured the situation: "It was tragically clear that the first of the three Irish divisions of the New Army had been all but exterminated within a few days—and in an attack so hopelessly mismanaged that even the generals in command did not know what they were attempting." [53]

It was impossible for Redmond to maintain Irish interest in a catalogue of military disasters the most bloody items of which in-

52. *Ibid.*, p. 431; O'Hegarty, *Ireland Under the Union*, p. 696.
53. Denis Gwynn, *John Redmond*, p. 440.

volved Irish troops. Warm praise of Irish heroism might have assuaged some of the bitterness that grew in Irish hearts as hundreds of households received from the War Office tidings of the deaths of sons along far-flung frontiers. Kitchener, however, was a man whose granite features matched a granite heart, and the War Office did little in Ireland to soften the rigors of war. Regiments from Ulster, Australia, or Canada received ardent encomiums in the British press; men from southern Ireland died unwept, unhonored, and unsung. And in spite of this official neglect, recruits kept rushing to the colors. By October 1915 over 75,000 men had enlisted, and it was necessary to provide 1,100 a week to replace casualties at the Front. On January 18, 1916, Redmond proudly announced that between "recruits for the Army and Navy, reservists, and men in the old Army," there were 150,000 Irishmen with the colors. It was an impressive showing as far as military service was concerned, but there was fast developing in Ireland a feeling that this sacrifice had been in vain. Redmond's role in pushing Irish men and boys into the fiery furnace of a war for the British Empire looked more dubious each day. Recruits began to lose interest in the National Volunteers and began to move into the ranks of Sinn Fein and the I.R.B. Revolution was just around the corner of a few months.

H. ARTHUR GRIFFITH CHALLENGES THE LEADERSHIP OF JOHN REDMOND

It was easy for Arthur Griffith to see how Redmond was being deceived by Liberal leaders who made pledges they never expected to carry out. Home Rule was merely a device to secure slavish obedience from the members of the Irish Party so that Liberal legislative programs could be safely pushed through the House of Commons. In March 1914 Griffith pointed out that Ireland had paid

> for the Home Rule in eight years of slavish support of the Liberal Party in meek acquiescence in increased taxation and prohibited trade. . . . Who on this side of sanity believes that England six years hence would use force to compel Ulster to do what it will not compel it to do now? . . . This Bill [Home Rule] if passed into law on the basis of

the exclusion of part of the island will accentuate those fatal divisions which have kept Ireland poor and impotent.[54]

With reference to the war in Europe, Griffith was under no illusion that England was fighting a crusade. He made it clear that Ireland was

> not at war with Germany. She has no quarrel with any Continental power. England is at war with Germany, and Mr. Redmond has offered England the services of the Irish Volunteers to 'defend Ireland.' What has Ireland to defend and whom has she to defend it against? . . . Our duty is not in doubt. We are Irish Nationalists, and the only duty we can have is to stand for Ireland's interests, irrespective of the interests of England or Germany or any other foreign country.[55]

To Redmond this talk smacked of treason, and Griffith and the Sinn Feiners were roundly denounced as "pro-German" and life was made increasingly difficult for them. In its last number, December 1914, *Irish Freedom* gave a trenchant account of the situation in Ireland:

> Today in Ireland there are men dismissed from their employment and banished from their homes, there are men in jail because they have dared to stand in the trench that the Irish Parliamentary Party tried to hand over to the enemy. And those things, starvation, imprisonment, death maybe, lie at the door of Mr. Redmond and Mr. Dillon and Mr. Devlin, and their Party and their Press. . . . The "two weekly and one monthly papers" which disquiet the soul of the "Times," and which Mr. John Redmond terms "execrable little rags," may be assassinated. But their voices will be remembered in Ireland long after Mr. Dillon and his like have been relegated to the Seventh Hell.[56]

This spirit of defiance could not be snuffed out by Mr. Redmond and his followers, and members of Sinn Fein and the I.R.B. continued to cherish their dreams of Irish independence. They merely awaited the moment when England's necessity was Ireland's opportunity.

54. O'Hegarty, *Ireland Under the Union,* p. 689.
55. *Ibid.,* p. 690.
56. *Ibid.,* pp. 692-693.

I. REDMOND'S POPULARITY IN AMERICA RAPIDLY FADES AWAY

Redmond's popularity in America declined far more rapidly than it did in Ireland. The organization that had sponsored his program was the United Irish League of America, and its President was Michael J. Ryan, an able and frank Irish-American who did not mince words. Redmond's speech in the House of Commons on August 3, with its pledge of support to England, was profoundly disturbing to many members of the League. In explaining his stand to Ryan, Redmond assured him that he and his followers still dominated the Irish scene:

> The Home Rule Bill will receive the Royal Assent tomorrow and the one pretext on which Sinn Feiners and others of that kidney have been able to rely in their campaign against us will absolutely disappear. They really have no following whatever in the country. . . . The general sentiment of our people is unquestionably on the side of England in this war.

Ryan's reply (October 2, 1914) candidly informed Redmond that the decision to support England had "left him cold." It should be clearly understood "that no money worth speaking of can be raised in this country from the Irish people to even indirectly aid England. . . . All my sympathies are with Germany, and I believe that nine-tenths of the Americans of Irish blood think as I do." [57]

Mr. Fitzpatrick, the National Treasurer of the United Irish League, was just as pessimistic as Mr. Ryan with reference to the future of the League. In a letter to Redmond he enclosed a note from General Moloney, who asked the question that was in thousands of Irish-American minds—"Why should Irish-Americans be requested to provide funds for arming Irish Volunteers when the British Government had apparently agreed to train and equip them?" It seemed to Mr. Fitzpatrick and Mr. Ryan that it was high

57. Denis Gwynn, *John Redmond*, pp. 417-418.

time that the affairs of the United Irish League be wound up and the organization cease to function.[58]

Redmond soon discovered that practically every Irish newspaper in America was sharply critical of his policy of stanch support of England in the war that had just started. His intimate friend, Edward J. Gallagher, editor of the Lowell *Sun*, explained the situation clearly and frankly: "The old guard of Boston, as you know, is dead, and as for New York, you can hardly rely upon a single man of them." Redmond tried to stem this tide of defeat by assuring members of the League that in Ireland things were going along very favorably. He believed that the Irish Party had not lost "a single man who was a genuine supporter of ours for the last few years." But the United Irish League was rapidly disintegrating, and all the efforts of Redmond could not stop this dissolution.[59]

While Redmond was trying to persuade Irishmen to die for the British Empire, members of the I.R.B. were preparing for a rising that might speed the progress of Irish independence. They carefully counted the cost of this proposed rising and were not disheartened by all the ominous entries on the debit side of the ledgers of revolution. Those figures in red were a faint indication of the blood that Irish patriots would shed in a desperate fight for freedom. The men who planned to challenge English control over Ireland were ready not only for death but for the scorching hatred of the followers of Redmond, who were Englishmen first and Irish a bad second. They knew they would have to face the bitter hostility of prelates who would countenance revolution only if it could be justified by pertinent paragraphs from some textbook on moral theology. The great majority of the Irish people, muddled and confused by Redmond, would condemn a revolution that seemed to threaten the future operation of Home Rule. The only solace that members of the I.R.B. could hold close to their hearts was the thought that they would kindle a spark of independence that all the King's horses and all the King's men could never stamp out. The

58. *Ibid.*, pp. 417-419.
59. *Ibid.*, pp. 420-422.

flame that would eventually burn down the Imperial edifice in Ireland was, at first, fanned by the breath of just a handful of men, whose chief regret was that each had only one life to lose for the cause of independence.

It was inevitable that such burning zeal would lead some patriots to hasty decisions that were of dubious benefit to the cause of Irish freedom. The history of every revolution contains at least one chapter of tragic, misspent effort. In this regard the story of Roger Casement is typical. It now needs retelling with data supplied from American archives. Sympathies in the United States were deeply aroused on behalf of a gallant gentleman whose bravery outran his judgment and whose mind had been darkened by the shadows of human suffering. The execution of Casement clearly showed that hysteria was holding the reins of the British Cabinet carriage. As far as Ireland was concerned this was an ordinary occurrence.

6 ROGER CASEMENT AND THE EASTER REBELLION

A. CASEMENT ENLISTS IN THE MOVEMENT FOR IRISH INDEPENDENCE

The story of Roger Casement is proof of the oft-repeated statement that truth is stranger than fiction. Although born in Dublin, September 1, 1864, he was of an Ulster family and was raised in County Antrim. His father, Roger Casement, had been a captain in the 3rd Dragoon Guards and later was an officer in the Antrim Militia. His mother, Annie Jephson, had once been a Catholic but her four children were brought up as Protestants. During a visit in Wales, however, she arranged to have her children baptized by a Catholic priest.

Roger Casement was educated in the diocesan school kept by Dr. King in Ballymena until his seventeenth year, when he began to study for the Civil Service. He soon lost interest in preparing for such a career and finally decided to accept a position with the Elder Dempster Shipping Company of Liverpool. In his twenty-first year he made a voyage to West Africa as a purser on one of the company's steamers, and the lure of African exploration led him to become a member of one of the numerous expeditions of General Henry Sanford into the Congo. In 1876 an International Conference meeting in Brussels had organized the Association for the Exploration and Civilisation of Central Africa, with King Leopold of Belgium as its President. Less than a decade later an Independent Congo State was erected for the ostensible purpose of "promoting the civilization and commerce of Africa, and other humane and benevolent purposes." King Leopold was made its first President and therefore exercised tremendous power over a territory in Central Africa comprising more than a million square miles of territory and some twenty million natives.[1]

The British Government was deeply interested in the fate of this Congo Free State and kept a close watch upon its progress. Its boundaries must never be permitted to encroach upon the upper waters of the Nile. Diversion of these waters would have a catastrophic effect upon Egypt. British colonies in West Africa would eventually have intimate economic ties with this Belgian experiment, so young British civil servants were carefully trained for colonial careers. It was not long before Casement was appointed by the Colonial Office to serve as Traveling Commissioner in the Nigerian Protectorate, and in 1895 he was elevated to the post of Her Majesty's Consul at Lourenço Marques, the seaport of Portuguese East Africa on Delagoa Bay. His service in this new post was so meritorious that he soon received the Queen's South Africa Medal. In 1900 he was made Consul at Kinchassa in the Independent State of the Congo, and in the following year he held a similar position in the French Congo Colony. In 1903 he was instructed by the British Foreign Minister, Lord Lansdowne, to make a personal survey of conditions existing in the Congo basin and to report in detail at the earliest possible moment.

During the summer of 1903 Casement made a trip lasting two and a half months through a large part of the Congo basin. His long report was a mass of carefully tested data upon every phase of the effects of imperialism upon the natives of the Congo, and its sharp criticism of Belgian brutality evoked a strong demand all over Europe for basic reforms in the Congo Free State. In Belgium, Casement was denounced as a tool of British Protestantism working to discredit the important humanitarian endeavors of a great Catholic State. Cardinals and bishops entered into the lists against him, and Catholic missionaries were quick to testify that Casement's dark pictures were merely figments of his overheated imagination.

---

1. The best general account of the Congo Free State is contained in Arthur B. Keith, *The Belgian Congo and the Berlin Act* (Oxford, 1919).

In America bitter attacks were made upon him "by the Irish-American organs which were afterwards to make the utmost use of his reputation as the champion of the oppressed natives in Africa. 'English Want Congo Trade' . . . was the large headline that figured over four columns of denunciation of him by the Irish World." [2]

The British Foreign Office was taken aback at some of the statements in Casement's Congo Report and was exceedingly cautious about taking any action. Casement was furious at such inaction, and in his letters to friends he vented his indignation. He was certain that the Foreign Office was "sincerely sorry I was born." In a letter to E. D. Morel he fairly exploded: "It is the dirty, cowardly, knock-kneed game the Foreign Office have played that puts me out of action. They *know* the truth, and yet deliberately . . . prepare to throw over an honest and fearless official they deliberately thrust forward last year when it suited their book. They are not worth serving." As he pondered the situation his indignation grew: "The F.O. have certainly not played the game—for they have lifted no finger to indicate that they trusted me. . . . That is what I resent. It is so cowardly and mean. They shove me into the forefront . . . and then they slink off and leave me exposed to vulgar abuse and openly expressed contempt. . . . I have an overmastering contempt for them." He had bitter scorn for Balfour: "That cur is incapable of any honest or straightforward act of human sympathy. . . . What a swinish lot of pigs are these." He had little use for Sir Edward Grey, the Foreign Secretary: "I don't think there is very much real, sincere, humane feeling in him [Grey] at all . . . who strikes me as cold. . . . I feel pretty sure that Grey has been a traitor all along. . . . They make me sick these paltry English statesmen with their opportunist souls and grocers' minds." [3]

2. Denis Gwynn, *The Life and Death of Roger Casement* (London, 1930), pp. 106-107. Giovanni Costigan, in his able article, "The Treason of Sir Roger Casement," *American Historical Review*, LX (January, 1955), 285, remarks: "It is well known how Casement's Congo Report, with its calm and detailed exposure of the iniquities of Belgian rule, became the basis for Morel's heroic and almost single-handed attack on King Leopold's regime."
3. Mr. Costigan is the first historian to exploit the correspondence of Casement in the archives of the London School of Economics. See his article already referred to in the *American Historical Review*, LX, 285-289.

Casement never got over this deep suspicion of British statesmen, and it was not difficult for him to grow increasingly indignant over the wrongs inflicted upon Ireland. His labors in the Congo had seriously impaired his health, so he decided to spend an extended vacation in Ireland. He soon shared the vision of the Ulster nationalists who rejected the "traditions of Protestant Ulster." The program of these nationalists made a profound appeal to Casement. He ardently wished to promote the economic development of Ireland so that it could be self-supporting and self-reliant. He was anxious to encourage a devotion to native traditions and to foster the study of the ancient Irish tongue. When he discovered that Mrs. J. R. Green and Bulmer Hobson were writing a pamphlet to discourage young Irishmen from enlisting in the British Army, he asked permission to assist them in their task. As he later remarked in his *Diary:*

> I was . . . so well occupied in Ireland trying to keep Irishmen out of the British Army and in dreaming of an Ireland that might yet be free that I gave no second thought to that after-dinner suggestion [made to him by a friend of Lord MacDonnell's at Mrs. Green's house], any more than a later one of Sir Eric Barrington, that Stockholm was vacant and might be offered to me.[4]

But daydreaming in Ireland proved expensive, and soon Casement had to accept other posts in the foreign service of Britain. From 1906 to 1910 he held consular posts in Brazil, finally retiring as Consul General at Rio de Janeiro. In July 1910 he left England, with a commission to investigate conditions in the rubber reserves of the upper Amazon basin. The Peruvian Amazon Company, controlled by J. C. Arana, was the corporation whose practices were to be studied with particular care. Casement's actual stay in the Putumayo region lasted from September 22 to November 16, 1910. He was back in London on January 1, 1911.

His report upon the abuses inflicted upon the natives in the Putumayo region was as sharply critical as his classic indictment of conditions in the Congo. The crimes that were "charged against

4. Denis Gwynn, *Casement,* p. 111.

many men now in the employ of the Peruvian Amazon Company are of the most atrocious kind, including murder, violation, and constant flogging. The condition of things revealed is entirely disgraceful, and fully warrants the worst charges brought against the agents of the Peruvian Amazon Company and its methods of administration in the Putumayo."[5]

The British Foreign Minister was deeply impressed with Casement's report. In June 1911 he wrote Casement a cordial letter informing him that his name would be included "for a knighthood in the Birthday Honours list at the end of June." After another trip to the Putumayo region, Casement returned to County Antrim, and in August 1913 he retired from the British foreign service on a small pension. He soon found plenty to do in Ireland.

Since 1907 he had been deeply interested in Irish nationalism, and his correspondence with Bulmer Hobson revealed his eagerness to keep abreast of every phase of the nationalist movement. Before he went to Santos, Brazil, to serve as consul, he gave Hobson a small subsidy for his paper, *The Republic,* and when it stopped circulation he wrote to express his regrets concerning its demise: "When I read the last number I guessed it was the swan song. I knew that such defiance meant neck or nothing." In August 1907 he was in Donegal on a visit to the Cloghaneely Gaelic School that he was subsidizing. In an enthusiastic letter to Hobson he expressed his delight at being in a place where only Gaelic was spoken and "English is scarcely heard." Some months later he was in Dublin with Arthur Griffith, and his letters to his friends are filled with praise for the Gaelic League and Sinn Fein.[6]

In 1908 and 1909 he continued his generous subsidies to Irish Nationalist publications, but he was fearful that the proper spirit of sacrifice did not exist in Ireland. In a typical letter to Bulmer Hobson he poured forth his apprehensions and doubts: "I've been only a poor help. We've got no money. John Bull takes too good care of our purse. And what John Bull leaves is far above the reach

---

5. *Ibid.,* p. 164.
6. William J. Maloney, *The Forged Casement Diaries* (Dublin, 1936), pp. 134-135.

of an Irish revolutionary. Revolutions have been made without money, but then it was by men and women prepared to die."[7]

As his sympathies with the cause of Ireland became more ardent he began to look around for some nation that might break the British chains of servitude. Perhaps Germany would serve this useful purpose! In 1909 he wrote to a friend and expressed his high regard for the German race: "I like the Germans and believe in them." He was bitterly opposed to the Moroccan policy of the British Foreign Office: "I would have invited Germany into Morocco or anywhere else she wanted to go—to Brazil, for one—where her expansion would not hurt the British Empire. Now the miserable effort at bottling up Germany has gone so far that it is hard to get back to sober statesmanship."[8] He was in New York when he received the news of the German defeat at the Marne, and with tears in his voice he murmured to his friend John Butler Yeats: "Poor Kaiser, poor Kaiser."[9]

This ardor for Germany was matched by his dislike for Americans. He was particularly disgusted with Theodore Roosevelt: "It is impudent in the extreme for this man to go around Europe haranguing people on their duties to civilization when his own country permits one of the most lawless aspects of modern life the whole world affords. . . . The more I see of Americans, the less I believe in them." By 1911 he had lost all hope "in the U.S.A. The New World is not so healthy as the Old. The pulling down of slavery will not come from Uncle Sam. . . . The Monroe Doctrine is fast becoming a crime against the human race."[10]

Because of his intimate knowledge of the personnel of the British Foreign Office and of the main trends in world politics, he became convinced that a World War would break out in 1915. With this conviction in mind he took a strong stand against the enlistment of Irishmen in the British Army. These activities helped to sever his last ties with England.

7. *Ibid.*, p. 135.
8. Giovanni Costigan, "The Treason of Sir Roger Casement," *op. cit.*, 296-97.
9. John Butler Yeats, *Letters to His Son, W. B. Yeats and Others* (London, 1944, ed. Joseph Hone), p. 195.
10. Costigan, *op. cit.*, 297.

In July 1913 he wrote a challenging article in the *Irish Review* under the pen name *Shan Van Vocht*. His theme was familiar in Sinn Fein circles: "I propose to show that Ireland, far from sharing the calamities that must necessarily fall upon Britain from defeat by a Great Power, might conceivably thereby emerge into a position of much greater prosperity."[11]

He was now frankly and ardently an Irish Nationalist[12] and he was deeply disturbed in 1913 when the Cunard Steamship Company announced that its steamers would no longer make Queenstown a port of call. He realized that this new policy was a declaration of economic warfare against Cork. To counter this move he made repeated efforts to persuade the Hamburg-Amerika Line to make Queenstown a port of call for their steamers bound for Boston. The liners *en route* to New York could also call at Queenstown. Casement hoped that these economic ties with Germany might develop political implications that would be of distinct service to Ireland. His efforts seemed to promise success when the Hamburg-Amerika Line, in January 1914, announced that the steamer *Rhaetia* would leave Hamburg on January 17 and call at Queenstown three days later. But British Foreign Office pressure soon dispelled Irish hopes in this regard. The Hamburg-Amerika Line published a new announcement to the effect that their steamers would not call at Queenstown, and Casement saw clearly that Ireland could secure assistance from Germany only in time of war. When the World War broke out in August 1914, he began to give serious consideration to a mission to Germany.[13]

On the eve of the World War, Casement played an important role in the gun running at Howth on July 26, 1914. According to his biographer, Casement was able to persuade his friends to subscribe at least one half the funds needed for the purchase of guns and ammunition in the Hamburg market. It was his intimate friend

11. Maloney, *op. cit.*, 138.
12. Lord Birkenhead, who sentenced Casement to hanging, expressed the false idea that Casement's "interest in his native country was of recent origin." Lord Birkenhead, *Famous Trials of History* (London, 1917), p. 258. He was unfamiliar with Casement's deep devotion to the cause of Ireland after 1906.
13. Denis Gwynn, *Casement*, pp. 213-217.

Erskine Childers who supplied the yacht that carried the guns to Ireland.[14]

Before the guns had landed at Howth, Casement decided to visit the United States to raise funds for the Volunteers. He arrived in New York City on July 20 and immediately telephoned to John Devoy, the famous old Fenian. He established a close accord with Devoy by informing him that his father, "although the Colonel of an English cavalry regiment, was a Fenian in principle." They apparently had much in common and both believed that it would be possible to secure important assistance from Germany during the continuance of the World War. Shortly after the war had commenced, a special committee of the Clan-na-Gael paid a visit to the German Club in New York City for an important talk with Count Bernstorff, the German Ambassador, and Captain Franz von Papen, the Military Attaché at the Embassy. The spokesman for the Clan informed the German Ambassador that it was the intention of some Irish Nationalists "to use the opportunity presented by the war to make an effort to overthrow English rule in Ireland and set up an Independent Government; that they had not an adequate supply of arms, had no trained officers, and wanted Germany to supply the arms and a sufficient number of capable officers to make a good start, but that we wanted no money." [15]

Count Bernstorff listened to the spokesman of the Clan with "evident sympathy" and promised to send a despatch to Berlin dealing with this important matter. Further statements containing the program of the Clan-na-Gael were also sent to Berlin through the agency of John Kenny. After Kenny succeeded in reaching the German capital and handed to von Buelow in person the message with which he had been entrusted, he then went to Ireland and told Tom Clarke and some other members of the I.R.B. the details of what had been done by the Clan. Meanwhile, on August 2, Devoy and Casement had attended in Philadelphia a "demonstration" of protest against the shooting of Irish civilians on July 26 in the Bachelor's Walk in Dublin. Snapshots of Devoy and Case-

---

14. *Ibid.*, p. 235.
15. John Devoy, *Recollections of an Irish Rebel*, p. 403.

ment caused Casement to fear "that it would lessen his chances of escaping detection by the English in case he wanted to go on any mission unknown to them. He was evidently even then thinking of going to Germany, although he had not mentioned it up to that time." [16]

As a background for this mission, Casement drew up an address to the Kaiser which was signed by all the members of the Clan-na-Gael Executive and sent to Berlin in the diplomatic pouch. It gave assurance to the Kaiser that millions of Americans either of Irish birth or descent had a feeling of

> sympathy and admiration for the heroic people of Germany, assailed at all points by an unnatural league of enmity. . . . We feel that the German people are in truth fighting for European civilization at its best and certainly in its less selfish form. We recognize that Germany did not seek this war, but that it was forced upon her. . . . We wholeheartedly hope for the success of the German people in this unequal struggle forced upon them.
> We draw Your Majesty's attention to the part that Ireland necessarily, if not openly, must play in this conflict. . . . The British claim to control the seas of the world rests chiefly on an unnamed factor. That factor is Ireland. . . . We are profoundly convinced that so long as Great Britain is allowed to control, exploit and misappropriate Ireland and all Irish resources . . . she will dominate the seas. . . . Ireland must be freed from British control.[17]

After waiting some weeks, Casement decided to issue a statement to the press with reference to the situation in Ireland. He consulted with John Quinn and Bourke Cockran about the expediency of issuing this statement, and they both tried to dissuade him from doing it. At this time Cockran was cautious about taking any decided stand regarding the policy to be pursued in Ireland, but according to John Devoy, after the Easter rising his sympathies were quite openly revealed. John Quinn was quite a different personality. A very successful lawyer in New York City, he had long been friendly with Devoy, Judge Cohalan, and other members of the Clan-na-Gael, but after the outbreak of the World War he be-

16. *Ibid.*, p. 417.
17. *Ibid.*, pp. 404-406.

came ardently pro-Ally and strongly hostile to the policy of the Clan.[18] According to Arthur Willert, he was the "staunchest supporter that the Allies . . . had among the Irish-American leaders." [19]

Casement rejected the advice of Cockran and Quinn and published in the American press and in the *Irish Independent,* in Dublin, a long letter giving his views on the Irish question. It was dated September 17, 1914:

> Ireland has no blood to give to any land, to any cause but that of Ireland. Our duty as a Christian people is to abstain from bloodshed: and our duty as Irishmen is to give our lives for Ireland. Ireland needs all her sons. . . . Ireland has suffered at the hands of British administrators a more prolonged series of evils, deliberately inflicted than any other community of civilized men. . . . It was not Germany who destroyed the national liberties of the Irish people. . . . There is no gain, moral or material, Irishmen can draw from assailing Germany. . . . Speaking as one of those who helped to found the Irish Volunteers, I say in their name that no Irishman fit to bear arms in the cause of his country's freedom can join the Allied millions now attacking Germany, in a war that at the best concerns Ireland not at all, and that can only add fresh burdens and establish a new drain in the interest of another community.[20]

In the third week in October 1914, Casement was ready to undertake a hazardous trip to Germany for the purpose of organizing an Irish Brigade out of the Irish prisoners in German camps. He might also be able to persuade the German Government to send much-needed arms and ammunition to Ireland and thus prepare the Irish Volunteers for an eventual blow for freedom. He took passage on the Norwegian steamer *Oskar II* and took along as his companion Adler Christensen, whom he had met in New York.[21]

---

18. *Ibid.,* p. 406.
19. *The Road to Safety* (London, 1952), p. 75.
20. Denis Gwynn, *Casement,* pp. 251-252.
21. Charles E. Curry, *Sir Roger Casement's Diaries* (Munich, 1922), chap. ii.

B. CASEMENT DISCOVERS THAT GETTING RID OF ANTAGONISTS IS MERELY A ROUTINE AFFAIR WITH BRITISH DIPLOMATS

Shortly after Casement landed in Christiania he made his way to the German Legation, where he was told to return on the following morning to secure papers that would ensure a safe passage to Berlin. For safety's sake he sent his companion, Adler Christensen, out to do some necessary shopping, and it was soon evident that the British secret service was hot on his trail. Christensen was accosted by a man who induced him to pay a visit to No. 79 Drammensveien, where he was sharply interrogated with reference to Casement's whereabouts. When he professed ignorance of the identity of Casement, he was permitted to leave and promptly returned to tell Casement about his adventure. A short search through the city directory indicated that the place he had visited was the British Legation. On the following day Christensen paid another visit to the British Legation and the Minister, Mr. de C. Findlay, blandly informed him that if someone "knocked Casement on the head" he would get "well paid for it." But Christensen's Roman virtue remained unsullied despite this large reward he would get if he murdered Casement, who safely arrived in Berlin on October 31, 1914.[22]

On November 2 Casement went to the German Foreign Office to see Zimmermann, the under-secretary. While waiting for this audience he made some interesting entries in his diary. He had "no regrets and no fears." If he suffered

> victory or defeat, it is all for Ireland. And she cannot suffer from what I do. . . . My country can only gain from my treason. . . . If I win all it is national resurrection—a free Ireland, a world nation after centuries of slavery. . . . If I fail—if Germany is defeated—still the blow struck today for Ireland must change the course of British policy towards that country. Things will never be again quite the same. The "Irish Question" will have been lifted from the mire

22. *Ibid.*, pp. 41-64.

and mud and petty, false strife of British domestic politics into an international atmosphere." [23]

He found Herr Zimmermann a cordial person who seemed glad to see him and who was intensely interested in the antics of Mr. Findlay, the British Minister at Christiania. When Casement described the plot against him, Zimmermann expressed the view that such conduct was "dastardly" but was only what the British had "always done when their interests are at stake. They stick at nothing." [24]

On November 6 Casement sent, through the German Foreign Office, the following message to Judge Cohalan in New York City:

> Lody's identity discovered by enemy who are greatly alarmed and taking steps to defend Ireland and possibly arrest friends. They are ignorant here purpose of my coming Germany, but seek evidence at all cost. Here everything favorable: authority helping warmly. Send messenger immediately to Ireland fully informed verbally. No letter [upon] him. He should be native-born American citizen, otherwise arrest likely. Let him despatch priest here via Christiania quickly. German Legation there will arrange passage: also let him tell Bigger, solicitor, Belfast, conceal everything belonging to me.[25]

As the relations between Casement and the German Foreign Office became more intimate, he persuaded Zimmermann, on November 20, 1914, to issue a statement concerning the official German attitude towards Ireland:

> The Imperial Government formally declares that under no circumstances would Germany invade Ireland with a view to its conquest or the overthrow of any native institutions in that country. Should the fortune of this great war . . . ever bring in its course German troops to the shores of Ireland, they would land there, not as an army of invaders to pillage and destroy, but as the forces of a Government that is inspired by goodwill towards a country and a people for whom

23. *Ibid.*, pp. 70-71.
24. *Ibid.*, pp. 71-72.
25. *Documents Relative to the Sinn Fein Movement* (London, 1921), Cmd. 1108, pp. 3-4. Lody was a German spy who was arrested at Killarney on October 2, 1914, and executed in the Tower on November 6, 1914.

Germany desires only NATIONAL PROSPERITY and NATIONAL FREEDOM.[26]

So far Casement's mission had been an unqualified success. His next task was the raising of an Irish Brigade out of Irish prisoners in German camps. Such a brigade would be of small military value, but its moral effect, according to the German viewpoint, was worth some "ten army corps." In a letter to Eoin MacNeill, November 28, 1914, Casement reported on the progress of his mission. He was certain that if Ireland would do

> her duty, rest assured Germany will do hers towards us, our cause, and our whole future. . . . I am entirely assured of the goodwill of this Government towards our country, and beg you to proclaim it far and wide. They will do all in their power to help us win national freedom. . . . Tell me all your needs at home, viz., rifles, officers, men. Send priest or priests at all costs—one not afraid to *fight* and die for Ireland. . . . We may win everything by this war if we are true to Germany.[27]

On December 5 the German Embassy in Washington sent a message to Berlin which had some important news for Casement. He was informed that a "confidential agent" had arrived in Ireland at the end of November. "The declaration of the German Foreign Office has made an excellent impression. The priest starts as soon as the leave of absence which he requires has been granted. This is expected soon. Judge Cohalan recommends not publishing statement about attempt on Casement's life until actual proofs are secured." [28]

Casement took Judge Cohalan's advice and set out to secure these "actual proofs" of Findlay's plot to capture or kill him. When Findlay increased the reward for Casement's capture to £10,000, Casement wryly remarks in his Diary: "I am mounting up in value." He now talked the matter over with the German Chancellor, Bethmann-Hollweg, who was amazed at the recital of Findlay's activ-

---

26. *Ibid.*, p. 4.
27. *Ibid.*, p. 5.
28. *Ibid.*, p. 6.

ities. "It is incredible, a man in Findlay's position so to act with an unknown, with your servant." "Yes," said Casement, "but that is the English character. You see I know them better than you. To get me, to crush an Irish national movement, they would commit any crime today, as in the past. They have no conscience when it comes to collective dealing. . . . Collectively they are a most dangerous compound and form a national type that has no parallel in humanity." [29]

On November 28 Casement received a letter from his friend Kuno Meyer, in New York City, telling of his having met "Cohalan, McGarrity, Devoy and John Quinn. They all disapprove the publication of the Christiania incident." [30] It was imperative for him, therefore, to secure proofs of Findlay's disposition to waylay or to kill him. Finally, on January 23, 1915, the evidence he sought was available in Berlin. Christensen had extracted from Findlay a most compromising document written on the official stationery of the British Legation at Christiania. It was a brief note from Findlay to Christensen:

> On behalf of the British Government I promise that if, through information given by Adler Christensen, Sir Roger Casement be captured either with or without his companions, the said Adler Christensen is to receive from the British Government the sum of £5,000 to be paid as he may desire. Adler Christensen is also to enjoy personal immunity and to be given a passage to the United States should he desire it.

This note carried the signature of Mr. Findlay, the British Minister at Christiania.[31]

Casement spent the next week composing an open letter to Sir Edward Grey, the British Foreign Minister, telling in detail the dubious conduct of Mr. Findlay. He stressed his devotion to the cause of Ireland and remarked that "to save Ireland from some of the calamities of war was worth the loss to myself of pension and

29. Curry, *op. cit.*, p. 132.
30. *Ibid.*, p. 140.
31. *Ibid.*, p. 170.

honours, and was even worth the commission of an act of technical 'treason.' " He had been prepared "to take all the risks and to accept all the penalties the Law might attach" to his action, but he had not bargained "for the risks and penalties that lay outside the law as far as my own action lay outside the field of moral turpitude. In other words, while I reckoned with British law and legal penalties and accepted the sacrifice of income, position and reputation as prices I must pay, I did not reckon with the British Government."

He had been entirely ready to face charges in a court of law. He had not been prepared to meet "waylaying, kidnapping, suborning of dependents or 'knocking on the head'—in fine, all the expedients your representative in a neutral country invoked when he became aware of my presence there." Mr. Findlay had been brutally frank in his offers of bribes to Christensen to murder or kidnap Mr. Casement. He made assassination seem very profitable. When emphasizing this fact, Mr. Findlay had asked Christensen a very pertinent question: "I suppose you would not mind having an easy time of it for the rest of your days?" In view of this scandalous conduct on the part of an important member of the British diplomatic service, Mr. Casement thought he was impelled to sever every connection he ever had with the British Government. For this reason he decided to return his decorations—the "insignia of the Most Distinguished Order of St. Michael and St. George, the Coronation Medal of His Majesty King George V, and any other medal, honor or distinction conferred upon me by His Majesty's Government." [32]

The story of the Findlay incident was soon broadcast in the press of the world, and Casement believed that it would strike a major blow at the prestige of the British Government. He was too naïve to realize that in Europe the practice of diplomacy had long been called the craft sinister. Diplomats were surprised that Casement, who had held important posts in the British consular service, should believe that Sir Edward Grey would be shocked to learn that Findlay was ready to resort to the ancient method of assassination in

32. *Ibid.*, pp. 184-191.

order to remove a troublesome adversary. In the British Foreign Office conscience was a watchdog that barked only at strangers.

C. IRISH SOLDIERS IN GERMAN PRISON CAMPS REFUSE TO JOIN AN IRISH BRIGADE RECRUITED BY CASEMENT

Casement regarded the outcome of the Findlay affair as a signal triumph that would greatly help his mission. He had proved to the world that the British Government would stoop very low to conquer its enemies, and he had high hopes that other successes would attend his efforts in Germany. But he soon discovered that it would be impossible to raise an Irish Brigade from the prisoners in German prison camps. In the last week in December 1914 he signed a so-called treaty with the German Foreign Office which outlined the terms on which the Irish Brigade was to be organized. It would fight under "the Irish Flag alone"; the soldiers would wear a "special distinctively Irish uniform"; and they would have only Irish officers. The brigade was to be "clothed, fed and efficiently equipped with arms and munitions by the Imperial German Government." Under certain circumstances the German Government would send the Irish Brigade "to Ireland with efficient military support, and with an ample supply of arms and ammunition to equip the Irish National Volunteers in Ireland who may be willing to join them in the attempt to recover Irish national freedom by force of arms." In the event of the Irish Brigade landing in Ireland and carrying on military operations "resulting in the overthrow of British authority and the creation of a native Irish Government, the Imperial German Government will give the Irish Government . . . its full moral support and . . . will contribute with all sincerity to the establishment of an independent government in Ireland." [33]

But the difficulties in the way of raising this brigade were enormous, and Casement quickly found out that this project would have to be abandoned. The story is simply and briefly told by Denis Gwynn:

33. Devoy, *op. cit.*, pp. 434-435.

The method which he employed to obtain recruits for his Irish Brigade was characteristic of his inability to appreciate any view but his own. To ask the regular soldiers who had taken part in the retreat from Mons to desert their regiments showed a strange blindness to realities. It was chiefly noncommissioned officers, who had almost all been with their regiments for ten years at least, that he addressed his first appeal, believing they would respond immediately and that the rest would follow their example. . . . Before Christmas of 1914 he had already seen the utter futility of his plan; and his later half-hearted attempts to do propaganda among them were little more than a demonstration of his own earnestness to impress the German Government, which suspected throughout that he was in Germany as a British spy.[34]

Under the strain of his failure to organize an Irish Brigade, Casement's health began to fail. In his diary he complained that he was "sick at heart and soul with mind and nerves threatening a complete collapse." His condition grew so alarming that St. John Gaffney, former United States Consul General at Munich, was anxious to arrange some means of transporting Casement back to the United States. The details were left in the hands of a friend of Gaffney, a Norwegian of German descent named Shirmer. Shirmer was to go at once (February, 1916) to New York and get in touch with some of Casement's friends.[35] Shirmer would take with him the documents in the Findlay case, which were to be turned over to Judge Daniel F. Cohalan for safekeeping.[36]

While Casement was awaiting news from America, word came from Robert Monteith, who had been helping him to organize the Irish Brigade, that big events in Ireland would soon take place. The German General Staff had summoned Monteith to Berlin and had informed him that a message had been received from John Devoy requesting the landing in Ireland of guns and ammunition in order

34. Denis Gwynn, *Casement*, pp. 14-15.
35. In a financial statement sent to Devoy, September 25, 1915, Casement acknowledged that he had received from the Clan-na-Gael, through Devoy, the sum of $7,740. Devoy, *Recollections of an Irish Rebel*, pp. 421-422; *Devoy's Post Bag*, II, 477-480.
36. Denis Gwynn, *Casement*, pp. 364-365. For a description of the overwrought condition of Casement's nerves see Evelyn, Princess Blücher, *An English Wife in Berlin* (New York, 1920), pp. 131, 138.

to prepare for a "rising." The German War Office was ready to meet this request.

Casement was deeply depressed that the German General Staff had preferred to deal with Monteith rather than with himself, and he was certain that they were not sincere in this matter of sending guns and ammunition to Ireland: "They lie always." His main desire now was to send word to Ireland that the German Government would not send adequate assistance with which to start a rebellion. He decided that John M'Goey was the person best qualified to be the bearer of these evil tidings to Ireland, and when the German General Staff realized what was behind the M'Goey mission they sharply chided Casement for his action.[37]

The German General Staff also had difficulties with Casement regarding what functions the proposed Irish Brigade would perform. Only a handful of men (53) had responded to Casement's entreaties, and they proved very hard to handle. German military authorities wished to send them to Ireland with Casement, but he refused this suggestion. He was convinced that they would not be of real assistance in any rebellion in Ireland, and he feared they would be quickly captured and shot. When the General Staff learned of Casement's objections to any rebellion in Ireland in the near future they bluntly told him—"no revolution, no rifles." It was finally decided that the Brigade would not be transported to Ireland. Only Casement and two companions would be landed on the Irish coast.

Before he embarked upon this last part of his mission, Casement had heard from America that the Findlay documents had been turned over to Judge Cohalan.[38] He had placed in American hands incontrovertible evidence that would clearly demonstrate the lengths the British Government would go in its practice of diplomacy. Judge Cohalan was very glad to get these documents, and he fully sympathized with Casement with reference to all the difficulties he had encountered in carrying out his mission. But neither he

37. See excerpts from Casement's *Diary* published in the *Irish Independent*, April 12-24, 1922.
38. Curry, *op. cit.*, pp. 168-169. These Casement documents are in the possession of the Cohalan family in New York City.

nor John Devoy was as pessimistic as Casement with regard to the projected Easter rising in Ireland. It was Devoy's belief that Casement's actions after he landed in Ireland were one of the real reasons for the failure of the rising.

The main reason why Casement wished to visit Ireland was to stop the projected Easter rebellion. Indeed, before he set out upon his trip to Ireland he had prevailed "upon two Irish-Americans whom he knew in Berlin to go straight to London with a message from himself to Asquith and Sir Edward Grey. They had agreed, after infinite persuasion, to do as he asked. He had told them that it was the only means of saving Ireland from a tragedy that would involve untold bloodshed and the defeat of all their hopes for generations to come. Germany had betrayed him, and was about to betray the Irish people in a miserable effort to evade its commitments to the Irish-Americans by sending a wretched cargo of rifles which would be utterly useless for military purposes." [39] After promising to carry Casement's letter to Sir Edward Grey, the two Irish-Americans suddenly decided that such an adventure was not only dangerous but might be very harmful to Irish interests. There was still a possibility that adequate German assistance would be sent to Ireland, and this possibility should be nursed and not destroyed.

There was nothing left for Casement to do but go in person to Ireland as soon as a submarine could be placed at his disposal. There was still hope that he could arrive in Ireland in time to stop the projected rising. In the early morning hours of April 21 he and two companions, Lieutenant Robert Monteith and Serjeant Julian Beverley (or Bailey), were landed on the bleak Kerry coast. Later that morning, John McCarthy, a farmer of Curraghane, noticed a boat that the tide had washed in. After he had summoned his neighbor, Pat Driscoll, they found three Mauser pistols and a bag of ammunition. Three sets of footsteps could be seen leading along the seashore.

When this news was taken to the Ardfert police barracks, a search was made of the countryside and Casement was found in a ruin called McKenna's Fort. He was quickly taken to Dublin by

39. Denis Gwynn, *Casement*, p. 376.

train and then imprisoned in the Tower of London. One of his companions, Julian Beverley, was soon arrested and turned King's evidence against Casement. Monteith escaped to America and recently published an absorbing narrative of the Casement incident. It was an incident that revealed how the British Government was not content with taking Casement's life. It sank so low as to forge a diary that made Casement appear as a moral leper who was so unclean as to deserve no sympathy for the misfortunes that dogged his last days. A British diplomat at Christiania had plotted his death and had kept his intrigue alive for a considerable period. Scotland Yard plotted the assassination of his character and its plans worked so well that in America some of Casement's close friends believed the unspeakably filthy smears that began to cloud his reputation. In America, for more than a century, British propaganda had been extremely effective. In 1916 there were few Americans who doubted any story that had a London postmark.

D. THE FIRST IRISH RACE CONVENTION

The first suggestion for the calling of an Irish Race Convention came from Richard McGinn of Paterson, New Jersey, in a personal letter to John Devoy, October 12, 1915. He thought it was important for Irish-Americans to prove that they were not in support of the program of John Redmond. This could best be done by calling a convention that would go on record as to its position with reference to the war then raging in Europe. He thought that Irishmen all over America looked to Mr. Devoy as the leader of the Nationalist cause: "You can urge a National Convention of the Irish race and the *Irish World* will back up your appeal. You need have no doubts or fear of the Convention being stampeded by an enemy of the race or by the friends of Ireland's traitors." [40]

Devoy talked this matter over with Judge Daniel F. Cohalan, T. St. John Gaffney, Richard F. Dalton, Jeremiah A. O'Leary, and Laurence J. Rice, who advised that a call for an Irish Race Con-

---

40. *Devoy's Post Bag,* II, 480-481.

vention be issued in the early months of 1916. Finally, on February 9, 1916, a printed call, signed by more than three hundred and fifty prominent Irish-Americans, was issued. The convention was scheduled to meet in New York City on March 4-5.

It opened in the Hotel Astor in an atmosphere of fervid enthusiasm, and the chief speakers were Judge Daniel F. Cohalan, Judge John W. Goff, Victor Herbert, Colonel Conley of the Sixty-ninth Regiment, the Honorable Patrick H. O'Donnell, of Chicago, and Judge O'Neill Ryan of St. Louis. The convention leaders lost no time in launching an important Irish-American organization—the Friends of Irish Freedom, with Victor Herbert as its national president. "The real leader and spokesman of this new organization was Daniel F. Cohalan, Justice of the New York Supreme Court, a distinguished authority on international politics and one of the leading jurists of the country." [41] One item in the constitution of the Friends of Irish Freedom was significant. It clearly stated that the prime object of the organization was "to encourage and assist any movement that will tend to bring about the National Independence of Ireland."

This frank statement represented the spirit of the Clan-na-Gael, and it was soon obvious that the Clan dominated the committees of the Friends of Irish Freedom. Of the seventeen members of the executive committee, fifteen were members of the Clan. T. St. John Gaffney was appointed as the European representative of the Friends. A bureau was established in Stockholm, with Gaffney in charge, and from there, and in Berlin, he maintained relations with the German Government. He was with Casement during his last days in Germany and did everything possible to make his mission a success.[42]

Before closing the sessions of the Irish Race Convention, the Executive Committee presented a Declaration of Principles and Policy, which was quickly adopted. It was a sharp challenge to England:

41. James McGurrin, *Bourke Cockran*, pp. 236-237.
42. T. St. John Gaffney, *Breaking the Silence* (New York, 1930), chap. xii.

For a generation past we have been flooded with literature, overrun with lecturers, thundered at from pulpits, and hectored from controlled editorial sanctums to convince us that we could not, or should not, stand alone, and that we had a divine mission, in common with England, to spread the gospel of Anglo-Saxon civilization, and the cult of British world supremacy. . . . But England never for one moment during this time has swerved from her changeless course of hostility and antagonism to America and to the old teachings of Americanism. . . . In her conduct of the present war she has flung caution to the winds and openly and brazenly has ridden roughshod over our neutral rights and our self-respect as a nation. . . . Such a state of affairs is intolerable to a freeborn and high-spirited people. Therefore we demand, in the name of American citizenship . . . that such acts must be stopped. . . . But it is to Ireland we must turn in order to see the most finished result of English misgovernment and selfishness. . . .

Today the alert and masterful enemies of England realize that for the peace of the world England must be deprived of mastery and dominion over Ireland. . . . We appeal to the Concert of the Powers, and particularly to America, if she be represented in such Council, to recognize that Ireland is a European and not a British Island; to appreciate that its complete Independence and its detachment from the British Empire are vital to the freedom of the seas . . . and we . . . demand in the name of liberty and of the small nationalities . . . that Ireland may be cut off from England and restored to her rightful place among the nations of the earth.[43]

E. THE BACKGROUND OF THE EASTER RISING

While the Irish Race Convention was holding its sessions in New York City, the I.R.B. were already pushing a plan for a rising to take place in Ireland on Easter Sunday, April 23. They had planned a rebellion for many months, and one of the reasons for the Casement mission to Germany was the possibility that he might be able to secure from the German War Office arms and ammunition that would make this rebellion successful. Casement's requests for the transport to Ireland of war matériel received support from the German Embassy in Washington. On October 6, 1915, George von Skal, one of the assistants of Captain Franz von Papen, sent word to the Foreign Office that it was important to send a "number

43. Devoy, *op. cit.*, pp. 451-457.

of rifles together with ammunition" to Fenit, located "seven miles from Tralee." These rifles would be put to very good use by a "group organized in Ireland to resist recruiting." [44] The German Admiralty Staff passed this communication on to the High Sea Command, November 10, and received the reply that owing to an insufficient depth of water in Tralee Bay it would be impossible for submarines to carry on any operations there. If arms were to be transported to that area it would be necessary to use trawlers of English design. They should be manned by Irish crews that would not have to make the hazardous trip back to Germany.[45]

Some weeks later (February 5, 1916), John Devoy was surprised by a visit from Tommy O'Connor, who brought a message in code from the Supreme Council of the I.R.B. As the main member of the Revolutionary Directory of the Clan-na-Gael, Devoy immediately decoded the cipher message and discovered that the I.R.B. had decided to "strike on Easter Sunday, April 23." It was imperative for the Clan to arrange for a shipment of arms to Limerick Quay between April 20 and April 23. As Devoy remarks in his *Recollections,* the Supreme Council of the I.R.B. had not asked "our advice; they simply announced a decision already taken; so, as we had already recognized the right of the Home Organization to make the supreme decision, our plain duty was to accept it and give them all the help we could." [46]

The members of the I.R.B. knew that the Clan had sent to Ireland every cent that could be scraped together. There were no further funds available for the purchase of arms and ammunition, and even if war matériel could have been purchased, it would have been impossible to ship it from an American port. There was nothing to do but make an appeal to Germany. On February 10, through the agency of the German Embassy in Washington, a message was sent to the German Foreign Office. It expressed the opinion that action in Ireland could not be postponed "much longer." Any delay would be "disadvantageous." The message then

---
44. Karl Spindler, *The Mystery of the Casement Ship* (Berlin, 1931), pp. 237-238.
45. *Ibid.,* pp. 238-239.
46. Devoy, *op. cit.,* p. 459.

quoted information from the I.R.B. in Ireland: "We can now put up an effective fight. . . . Initiative on our part is necessary. . . . We have therefore decided to begin action on Easter Saturday. Unless entirely new circumstances arise we must have your arms and munitions in Limerick between Good Friday and Easter Saturday." [47]

Six days later (February 16), the Revolutionary Directory of the Clan-na-Gael sent a long memorandum to the German Government. In this communication the date of the rising is put on Easter Sunday, *not Saturday*. It gave a detailed description of the strength of the British military establishment in Ireland, and indicated the importance of sending to Limerick 25,000 or, better, 50,000 rifles "with a proportionate number of machine guns and field artillery and a few superior officers." If 100,000 rifles could be sent it would be possible in Ireland to make good use of them. A successful rising in Ireland would divert some 500,000 British soldiers from employment on the Continent.[48]

On February 18, Count Bernstorff informed the Foreign Office that he had learned from John Devoy that the rising was to begin in Ireland "on Easter Saturday. Please send arms to [arrive] Limerick, west coast of Ireland, between Good Friday and Easter Saturday. To put it off longer is impossible." [49] After consulting with the Admiralty Staff the German Foreign Office sent word to Bernstorff, March 4, 1916, that "between 20th and 23rd April, in the evening, two or three steam-trawlers could land 20,000 rifles and 10 machine guns, with ammunition and explosives at Fenit Pier in Tralee Bay. Irish pilot boat to await trawlers at dusk, north of Island of Inishtooskert . . . and show two green lights close to each other at short intervals. Please wire whether the necessary arrangement in Ireland can be made secretly through Devoy." [50] A week later (March 12) a message came back to the German Foreign Office from Washington: "Irish agree to proposition. Necessary steps have

---

47. *Documents Relative to the Sinn Fein Movement,* London, 1921, Cmd. 1108, p. 9.
48. *Ibid.,* pp. 246-247; *Devoy's Post Bag,* II, 485-487.
49. *Documents Relative to the Sinn Fein Movement,* p. 10.
50. *Ibid.,* p. 10.

been taken." [51] Other details concerning signals to be used by trawlers and submarines were discussed in later communications between Washington and Berlin.

As the date of the projected rising approached, telegrams from Washington to Berlin became more urgent. On April 18 Berlin was told that the "delivery of arms must take place punctually on Sunday, April 23rd, in the evening. This is of the highest importance," and on the following day further word arrived from Washington: "The Irish desire to know if submarines are coming to Dublin Harbour; if not, do they intend to blockade the harbour and, if possible, Limerick Harbour? The landing of a body of troops, however small, is urgently desired, and they further suggest a simultaneous strong demonstration by airships and at sea." On April 18 the German Embassy sent a short message which carried the notation:

> Cohalan requests me to send on the following: The Irish revolt can only succeed if assisted by Germany, otherwise England will be able to crush it, although after a severe struggle. Assistance required. There would be an air raid on England and a naval attack timed to coincide with the rising, followed by a landing of troops and munitions and also of some officers, perhaps from an airship. It might then be possible to close the Irish harbours against England, set up bases for submarines and cut off food export to England. A successful rising may decide the war.[52]

On the very day that this message was sent to Berlin (April 18), United States Secret Service agents raided the office of the German Consul General in New York City and confiscated the files of correspondence found there. It was apparent from the communications of John Devoy to Berlin that a rising in Ireland was planned for Easter Sunday, April 23. Devoy's letters were turned over immediately to the British Embassy by the Department of State. The

51. *Ibid.*
52. *Ibid.*, pp. 12-13. On September 21, 1917, Judge Cohalan, in a statement to the press, denied that he had sent this message to Germany: "I never sent or requested the sending of the remarks attributed to me." Patrick McCartan, *With De Valera in America* (New York, 1932), pp. 18-19. In this regard see the remarks of John Devoy on p. 463 of his *Recollections of an Irish Rebel*.

plans of the I.R.B. were thus fully disclosed to the British Government, which took measures to intercept any ships from Germany bringing arms and ammunition to Tralee Bay. The message from Judge Cohalan to Berlin was treasured by the Wilson Administration, which saw in this communication a means of seriously embarrassing an Irish-American who had earned the bitter dislike of the President. The very fact that Cohalan was anti-English was enough to damn him in Wilson's eyes.

This Anglophilism on the part of the President was clearly revealed shortly after the outbreak of the war. During a conversation with Spring Rice, the British Ambassador in Washington, the topic of Prussian militarism was the subject of some caustic comments. The President turned to the Ambassador and in the most solemn manner remarked that if Prussian military prowess overcame the Allies it would be necessary for the United States "to give up its present ideals and devote all its energies to defense, which would mean the end of its present system of Government." Spring Rice then deftly turned the course of the conversation to certain aspects of English literature and alluded to the memorable sonnets of William Wordsworth written at the time of the Napoleonic Wars. When the President murmured that he knew those sonnets by heart and "had them in his mind all the time," Spring Rice approvingly replied: "You and Grey are fed on the same food and I think you understand." As the British Ambassador laid this accolade of appreciation upon the President's sensitive shoulders, the latter's eyes were wet with tears, and Spring Rice was sure that as far as England's interests were concerned, the American Chief Executive had an "understanding heart." [53]

This Presidential leaning toward the Allies was strongly accentuated by the sinking of the *Lusitania* on May 7, 1915. Some weeks later the Chief Executive took certain steps that secretly revealed he had lost all interest in maintaining a neutral attitude toward the belligerents. Calling for William J. Flynn, the Chief of the

---

53. Spring Rice to Sir Edward Grey, September 8, 1914, *The Letters and Friendships of Sir Cecil Spring Rice* (Boston, 1929, 2 vols. ed. by Stephen Gwynn), II, 223.

United States Secret Service, he instructed him to make "a discreet but thorough investigation of the activities of Count von Bernstorff and his staff, as it had been reported they were violating all the rules of neutrality, and the President wanted facts." To make this check on the activities of Bernstorff and his attachés, it was thought necessary to tap the telephone wires of the German and Austro-Hungarian embassies in Washington. This procedure was "approved by the State Department and carried out by the best telephone men in America." [54] It also required a staff of competent linguists, who made a record of conversations which took place in several languages. Each night a stenographic report of these conversations was placed in the hands of Mr. Flynn, who turned them over to the Department of State. In some reports there were "uncomplimentary references to high personages in the White House and in the State Department." Of what avail then were Bernstorff's eloquence and expressions of good faith "if reports of this type poisoned the minds of the President and of the Secretary of State." [55]

Needless to say, the very fact of this tapping of the wires of the German and the Austro-Hungarian embassies indicates how the Wilson Administration made a sorry joke of pretensions of neutrality. But not content with this telephone tapping, the Secret Service went so far as to steal the briefcase of Dr. Heinrich Albert, an able lawyer attached to the German Embassy. During the last days of July 1915 George Sylvester Viereck and Dr. Albert boarded the Sixth Avenue "L" at Rector Street. They were closely shadowed by Mr. W. H. Houghton and Mr. Frank Burke. After a brief conversation with Mr. Viereck, Dr. Albert lapsed into a comfortable doze from which he was suddenly awakened when the "L" glided into the 50th Street station. Still half asleep, Dr. Albert hurried from the train, leaving his bag of documents upon the seat. Mr. Burke at once seized the bag and rushed it to the Secret Service headquarters in New York City. After a cursory examination the documents were taken to Washington for a further examination by

54. William J. Flynn, "Tapped Wires," *Liberty*, June 2, 1928, pp. 19ff.
55. *Anonymous*, "War Propaganda," *Saturday Evening Post*, August 17, 1929, p. 43.

Secretaries Lansing and McAdoo. The more incriminating ones were handed over to the New York *World* for publication. Although most of them were "duds" which the *World* could not explode, the impression was created in the American public mind that Germany was plotting against American interests. It was merely a part of the plan to produce a climate of opinion very hostile to Germany.

The raid of the Secret Service agents upon the office of the German Consul General in New York City on April 18, 1916, was merely a routine affair for these Government detectives, who were throwing aside all the barriers that usually protected the diplomatic representatives of foreign countries. When they sorted out the files of correspondence they discovered the message that apparently Judge Cohalan had sent on that very day to Berlin. John Devoy, in his *Recollections*, expresses the opinion that this message was

> surreptitiously added to the von Igel papers to furnish a pretext for attacks upon Judge Cohalan. It was used for that purpose and the attacks were intensified a year later when the United States entered the World War. A crusade was started against Cohalan through which it was sought to have him removed from the Bench, arrested and impeached; the Administration at Washington made every effort to secure evidence that would incriminate or place him in a false light. But these tactics failed because no such evidence existed.[56]

F. THE EASTER REBELLION MEANS POLITICAL RESURRECTION FOR IRELAND

The decision to start a rebellion in Ireland was arrived at by the Supreme Council of the I.R.B., in August 1914. The opportunity to strike during a major war in which England was engaged was not to be overlooked. The purpose of such a rising was twofold. In the first place it would revive a drooping national spirit and in the second place it would call the attention of the world to the Irish question and pave the way for favorable action at the eventual peace conference. The Supreme Council set up a small military committee to fix the details of this rebellion. It would be necessary for

---

56. Devoy, *op. cit.*, p. 463.

members of the I.R.B. to infiltrate into the Irish Volunteer organization for the purpose of controlling it when the hour to strike finally arrived. The leaders of the movement were Tom Clarke and Sean MacDermott. They boldly pushed aside Bulmer Hobson, who had been a member of the Supreme Council, and put their faith in Padraic Pearse, who became "Director of Organization" in the Volunteers. In that office he could assume powers which really belonged to Eoin MacNeill, who was Chief of Staff but whose indolence made it easy for more enterprising spirits to adopt a program with which he was in decided disagreement. Along with Pearse, Clarke, and MacDermott were Thomas MacDonagh, Joseph Plunkett, and Eamon Ceannt. They were men of direct action who feared little and hoped much.[57]

The Military Committee set up by the I.R.B. Supreme Council was supposedly subordinate to it, but it was difficult to put any halters upon men like Clarke, MacDermott, and Pearse, who did much as they pleased. They had feared that James Connolly, who controlled the Irish Citizen Army, might give them a little trouble, so they kidnaped him and then employed such powers of persuasion that he finally accepted their program. There is little doubt that the main items in this program were prepared by Clarke, MacDermott, Pearse, and Connolly, with only nominal consultation with the members of the Volunteers, the Citizen Army, or the I.R.B. At the meeting of the I.R.B. Supreme Council in January 1916 it had been decided that there would be no rebellion unless and until affirmative action was taken at a subsequent meeting. This second meeting never took place.

For the purpose of creating the false impression that the Government was planning to adopt far-reaching coercive measures, Joseph Plunkett fabricated a document which he claimed came from the "files in Dublin Castle." It provided for the suppression of Sinn Fein, the Irish Volunteers, the Irish National Volunteers, and the Gaelic League, and the arrest of their executives and the occupation of their premises. Although the authenticity of this alleged document was at once challenged, it had the effect of in-

57. O'Hegarty, *Ireland Under the Union*, pp. 697-698.

creasing the apprehensions of many persons with reference to coercive Governmental measures.

It was evident, however, that a large majority of the people had no wish for a rebellion. For this reason the members of the I.R.B. Military Committee at first thought in terms of merely a Dublin rising which would be a bloody sacrifice for principle without any real hope of success. Sean MacDermott was of the opinion that the rebellion would soon be stifled: "We'll hold Dublin for a week, and save Ireland." [58]

Perhaps the arrival of arms and ammunition from Germany would alter the situation, and that consideration was the reason for the appeal to John Devoy and his pressure upon the German Government. In response to this pressure the German General Staff decided to send to Ireland some 20,000 rifles, 10 machine guns, and five million cartridges. On April 4 Lieutenant Karl Spindler received orders to take command of the small steamer *Libau*, which was rechristened the *Aud* and furnished with Norwegian papers. On the night of April 20 the *Aud* reached Fenit Bay and remained there twenty hours without making contact with anyone to whom the arms and ammunition could be given. On the same night the U-19, with Casement and his two companions on board, cruised in this same bay without seeing the *Aud*. Finally the *Aud* put out to sea and was intercepted by a British patrol boat. Spindler then scuttled the *Aud* and was taken prisoner. Thus the arms and ammunition from Germany were not landed on the Irish coast and the Irish rebels were deprived of this armament.[59] It is significant to remember that the United States Secret Service agents, in their raid upon the office of the German Consul General in New York City, had discovered communications from John Devoy which alluded to the projected visit of this German steamer laden with arms and ammunition. The British Government was immediately given copies of these documents, and patrol boats were stationed along the Kerry Coast to intercept any trawlers or small steamers from Germany.

58. *Ibid.*, p. 700.
59. Karl Spindler, *op. cit.*, pp. 255-282.

the Easter Rebellion 199

In the meantime Casement and his two companions had landed on the Irish coast. Although he was soon captured he did manage to send news to Eoin MacNeill that helped to destroy any chance for a successful rising. This story is best told by John Devoy in a letter to Lawrence de Lacy, July 20, 1916:

> Casement landed on Friday and sent a message to MacNeill to stop it [the rising]; that it was hopeless etc. MacNeill got it on Saturday and issued his countermand. He [Casement] got one message up by Monteith, who, of course, was obeying his orders, and sent another by a priest, for whom he sent after his arrest. MacNeill had only been told of the decision on Good Friday, which was a great mistake. He was at first shocked, but on hearing of the shipload of arms consented. The Limerick and Kerry men got word to him of the sinking of the ship, and that, with the request from Roger, decided him and he issued the fatal order and took care that it reached everybody.[60]

Clarke, MacDermott, and Connolly refused to heed the countermand of MacNeill and they issued orders for "maneuvers" on Easter Monday, April 24. At noon on that day the rebellion broke out in Dublin, and detachments of the Irish Citizen Army and of the Irish Volunteers soon occupied the General Post Office and various other buildings. Pearse then read to some amazed passersby a proclamation announcing the birth of the Irish Republic. It was signed by Thomas J. Clarke, Eamon Ceannt, James Connolly, Sean MacDiarmuda, Thomas MacDonagh, Patrick Pearse, and Joseph Plunkett. For several days there was heavy fighting in Dublin and the rebels showed gallant courage in holding back greatly superior forces. But on Saturday, April 29, Pearse surrendered unconditionally, and this order was conveyed to the various units in Dublin and the country. Although most of the fighting had been confined to Dublin, there had been some action in County Dublin and County Meath. In Wexford the Volunteers occupied Enniscorthy for a few days, and in Galway some rebels went out to the hills under the leadership of Mellowes but did not come into contact with any British forces.[61]

60. *Documents Relative to the Sinn Fein Movement*, Cmd. 1108, pp. 19-20.
61. Piaras Beaslai, *Michael Collins and the Making of a New Ireland* (London, 1926), I, 72-107.

G. REACTION IN IRELAND TO THE EASTER REBELLION

In Ireland the reaction to the Easter rebellion was generally hostile. According to P. S. O'Hegarty, the insurrection came upon the people like a thunderbolt:

> They had not been expecting it, and they did not want it. . . . The great mass of the people still hazily believed in the Allies and did not want England embarrassed. The insurrection was therefore universally and explosively unpopular. The population fraternized with the British soldiers during the fighting, gave them food and supplies. . . . If Ireland as a whole could have got hold of Tom Clarke and his comrades during that week it would have torn them to pieces.[62]

The press in Ireland was quick to denounce the rebellion. The Irish *Times* was profoundly shocked at the rising:

> The crime has been committed; the explosion has occurred; and we have gained at least one advantage. We know now beyond yea or nay, the extent, the power, and motives of the seditious movement in Ireland. . . . The State has struck, but the work is not yet finished. The surgeon's knife has been put to the corruption in the body of Ireland, and its course must not be stayed until the whole malignant growth has been removed. . . . The rapine and bloodshed of the past week must be finished with a severity which will make any repetition of them impossible for generations to come.[63]

The *Freeman's Journal* did not call so loudly for revenge but it had no sympathy for the rebels. The insurrection had been

> brought about by men without authority, representative character, or practical sanity. Beyond all doubt the leaders of this insane revolt would have been utterly powerless to marshal even a corporal's guard for their dread work but for the factionists, critics, and cranks of all stripes and vestures, who have been labouring these years past to undermine the power and authority of the popular constitutional leaders and the popular constitutional movement.[64]

62. *The Victory of Sinn Fein* (Dublin, 1924), pp. 3-4.
63. April 28, 29, May 1, 1916.
64. May 5, 1916.

The *Irish Independent* was equally caustic. It believed that "no terms of denunciation that pen could indite would be too strong to apply to those responsible for the insane and criminal rising of last week." [65]

Carson, speaking in the House of Commons, indicated his readiness to "put down these rebels now and for evermore," [66] and Redmond immediately went on record in a sharp denunciation of the "insane movement" which led to the rising. His first feeling on hearing of the rebellion had been one of "horror, discouragement, almost despair. . . . Was the insanity of a small section of her people once again to turn all her marvellous victories of the last few years into irreparable defeat?" [67]

The Protestant Archbishop of Dublin shared with Redmond this feeling of "detestation and horror" at the very thought of rebellion against English rule, and he called for stern measures of repression: "This is not the time for amnesties and pardons; it is the time for punishment, swift and stern." [68]

Prominent Catholics did not hesitate to denounce the rebellion. According to the teachings of the Church, a revolution must not be started unless it is against a government that practices intolerable oppression. Moreover, all legitimate means of redress should have been tried before any resort to violence. The revolutionary movement should have widespread popular support, and it should have a reasonable prospect of success.[69] After applying these criteria to the Easter Rebellion, John J. Horgan is sharply critical of the leaders of the rising: "This small body of conspirators by putting nationalism before religion . . . placed themselves outside the pale of the Church." [70]

Sir John Maxwell, in command of the British troops in Ireland, apparently believed that the conspirators had placed themselves outside the pale of civilization. He decided to follow the injunction of

65. May 4, 1916.
66. London *Times,* April 28, 1916.
67. Denis Gwynn, *John Redmond,* pp. 480-481.
68. Letter to the *Times,* May 4, 1916, signed "John Dublin."
69. Rev. H. Davis, S.J., *Moral and Pastoral Theology* (Dublin, 1938), II, 89.
70. *Parnell to Pearse,* p. 289.

the Protestant Archbishop of Dublin. The so-called justice he meted out to the men who participated in the Easter Rebellion was "swift and stern." A succession of courts-martial began in Dublin, and soon fifteen of the important rebels were executed. The seven leaders who had signed the proclamation announcing the birth of an Irish Republic were quickly shot, and eight others who were judged to be their chief supporters were hurried before firing squads. De Valera was reprieved only because there was a possibility that he was an American citizen.

According to statistics given in the *Documents Relative to the Sinn Fein Movement*, 450 persons were killed in the Easter Rebellion and 2,164 were wounded. Some 3,430 men and 79 women were arrested. Out of this total, 1,424 men and 73 women were released after enquiry. Of the 170 men and one woman who were tried by courts-martial, 159 men and one woman were convicted. The remaining prisoners, 1,847 men and five women, were sent to England for internment. Long terms of penal servitude were decreed for many of the persons convicted by the courts-martial: 10 were given penal servitude for life, 33 for ten years, and 18 for five years.[71]

H. AMERICAN REACTION TO THE EASTER REBELLION

In America, in official circles, there was little sympathy for Casement and the leaders of the Easter Rebellion. In the press there was a sharp division of sentiment. The New York *Herald*, a strong Administration paper, was distinctly hostile to the leaders of the rebellion: "The stronger Germany becomes the weaker becomes the rest of the world. And the fact that Sir Edward Carson was a sort of Roger Casement before the war does not make the treason any the less, nor does it make Home Rule or independence for Ireland any nearer." [72] The Washington *Star* expressed the viewpoint that "every friend of Ireland and the Irish people must deeply deplore

71. Cmd. 1108, London, 1921, p. 14.
72. April 28, 1916.

the lamentable blunder of revolution, with its inevitable train of disastrous consequences." [73] The Chicago *Tribune* believed that the rebel leaders were "not helping the cause of Ireland. They are not advancing their land toward freedom." [74] Hysteria marked the comments of *The New York Times*. The conduct of Casement was criticized as "treacherous and perfidious." [75] The Washington *Post* had no intention of defending Casement's conduct, but it was of the opinion that his execution would serve no useful purpose: "Casement, as a prisoner, kept out of mischief until the end of the war, would be practically forgotten; Casement, executed in the Tower, would become a martyr, enshrined in Irish hearts." [76] The Dallas *News* shared this view that clemency for Casement would be a wise policy: "Bring their heads [of the leaders] to the pump, not to the block." [77] The Philadelphia *Inquirer* favored a policy of magnanimity. It would be wise merely to sentence Casement to life-long incarceration. "That will meet the claims of justice and Irish susceptibilities will at the same time be spared." [78]

Some of the American newspapers were openly sympathetic with Casement after his arrest. The Birmingham *Age-Herald* thought that Sir Roger was both "picturesque and pathetic." While it might not be "possible to excuse him in the eyes of the law, there can be little doubt that he was actuated by lofty motives and had the welfare of Ireland at heart when he ventured upon his seditious venture." [79] The St. Louis *Globe-Democrat* could not wholly condemn Casement: "His fate will likely be determined more by policy than by justice. His personal statement was a confession of technical guilt, yet it will win him sympathy. He is either a marvelous actor and the British Government is partly a piece of inconceivable machinery, or he belongs to the long roll of lovers of Ireland who have let their devotion to the cause of independence

73. May 1, 1916.
74. May 2, 1916.
75. April 26, 1916.
76. April 26, 1916.
77. May 3, 1916.
78. April 26, 1916.
79. June 30, 1916.

overcome all considerations of self and all counsels of prudence." [80] The Cleveland *Plain Dealer* did not try to hide its sympathy for Casement: "There is something inherently abhorrent in the hanging of an able and efficient public man under the provisions of a statute of the fourteenth century." [81]

I. WHITE HOUSE DELAYS MAKE THE EXECUTION OF CASEMENT A CERTAINTY

The leaders of the Easter Rebellion[82] were quickly tried by a court-martial and sentenced to be shot. Sir Roger Casement was not treated in this summary manner. After all, he had been an important member of the British foreign service. First, all the honors he had received from the King were formally stripped from him. Then, on June 26 he was put on trial for treason in the King's Bench Division of the High Court. The judges composing the Court were the Lord Chief Justice Viscount Reading, Mr. Justice Avory, and Mr. Justice Horridge, and they sat with a jury. The prosecution consisted of Attorney General Sir Frederick Smith, Solicitor General Sir George Cave, Mr. A. H. Bodkin, Mr. Travers Humphreys, and Mr. G.A.H. Branson. For the defense there was A. M. Sullivan, K. C., Second Sergeant of the Irish Bar, Mr. Artemus Jones, and Mr. J. H. Morgan. Mr. Michael Francis Doyle, of the American Bar, was also in court for the defense, but he was not admitted to any of the consultations and the line of defense was not disclosed to him. He had been added to the defense counsel upon the insistent plea of Casement's sister, Mrs. Agnes Newman. Inasmuch as she was

80. June 30, 1916.
81. July 1, 1916.
82. In the United States the attitude of the Church and the Catholic press towards the Easter rising was anything but cordial. There were some Catholic clerics who could detect the accents of God in the pronouncements of officials in the Wilson Administration and who quickly reflected the opinions of the President. Reverend John A. Ryan was typical of this group. He sharply denounced the Easter Rising and expressed the view that everyone who aided the Sinn Feiners should feel the heavy hand of the British Government. It is interesting to note that during World War II Dr. Ryan went to an extreme in his support of the Roosevelt Administration.

hard-pressed financially, she was not able to pay any fee to Doyle for his services.

Because of her fervid importunities, Doyle wrote to Joseph Tumulty, a friend of long standing and private secretary to President Wilson, and inquired if it would be possible for the President to intervene in any way on behalf of Casement. Tumulty turned this letter over to the President and wrote upon it a brief question: "What reply shall I make to this?" The President's answer was terse and negative: "We have no choice in a matter of this sort. It is absolutely necessary to say that I could take no action of any kind regarding it." [83]

As the trial of Casement proceeded, it was significantly ironic that the Attorney General who would press the case against Casement was Sir Frederick Smith who, two years before in Ulster, had made many reckless statements against Home Rule which were so violent in tone that they could be regarded only as incitements to rebellion. No one knew the anatomy of violence any better than he. The closing words of his presentation of Casement's record were forceful and dramatic and made a deep impression upon the court and jury: "This prisoner, blinded by a hatred to this country, as malignant in quality as it was sudden in origin, has played a desperate hazard. He has played it and he has lost it. Today, the forfeit is claimed."

Despite a brilliant defense by Sergeant Sullivan there was no doubt about the verdict of the jury. Before the Lord Chief Justice passed sentence upon him, Casement was permitted to make a statement in his own defense. He denied that he ever "asked an Irishman to fight for Germany." He also denied that the rations of Irish soldiers had been reduced because they refused to join the Irish Brigade. With reference to the story that he had accepted large sums of German gold in order to further his intrigues, he stated that he had "never asked for nor accepted a single penny of

---

83. Michael F. Doyle to Tumulty, April 29, 1916; Tumulty to President Wilson, May 1, 1916; President Wilson to Tumulty, May 1, 1916, Casement file, *Wilson Papers*, Library of Congress.

foreign money. . . . Money was offered to me in Germany more than once . . . but I rejected every suggestion of the kind, and I left Germany a poorer man than I entered it." [84]

On June 29 the jury returned a verdict of guilty of high treason and then Casement was permitted a final presentation of his case. To many persons he was cogent and convincing:

> With all respect I assert this Court is to me, an Irishman, not a jury of my peers to try me in this vital issue, for it is patent to every man of conscience that I have a right . . . if tried at all, under this statute of high treason, to be tried in Ireland before an Irish Court and by an Irish jury. . . . Place me before a jury of my own countrymen, be it Protestant or Catholic, Unionist or Nationalist, Sinn Feineach or Orangemen, and I shall accept the verdict and bow to the statute and all its penalties. . . .
>
> I would add that the generous expressions of sympathy extended me from many quarters, particularly from America, have touched me very much. In that country, as in my own, I am sure my motives are understood and not misjudged—for the achievement of their liberties has been an abiding inspiration to Irishmen and to all men elsewhere rightly struggling to be free in like cause. . . .
>
> In Ireland alone in this twentieth century is loyalty held to be a crime. . . . If we are to be indicted as criminals, to be shot as murderers, to be imprisoned as convicts because our offence is that we love Ireland more than we value our lives, then I know not what virtue resides in any offer of self-government held out to brave men on such terms. Self-government is our right. . . . A thing no more to be doled out to us or withheld from us by another people than the right to life itself. . . . Ireland is treated today among the nations of the world as if she was a convicted criminal. If it be treason to fight against such an unnatural fate as this, then I am proud to be a rebel.[85]

After this statement by Casement the Lord Chief Justice passed sentence of death. Upon hearing it, Casement turned and left the dock with a smile tugging at the corners of his mouth. Erect and quite self-possessed, he disappeared behind the green curtain.[86] He had already taken the first step along the path to the gallows.

84. Geoffrey de C. Parmiter, *Roger Casement* (London, 1936), p. 298.
85. *Ibid.*, pp. 302-313.
86. It was Casement's fixed belief that Ireland could be redeemed only through the death of men devoted to her cause. Padraic Colum, *The Road Round Ireland* (New York, 1926), pp. 129-132.

Some of his friends still hoped that a plea for clemency might save his life. Ambassador Page, at London, hoped that no such plea would be made by the Department of State. In a letter to Secretary Lansing he remarked: "I fear that request to the British Government in this matter will produce a very disagreeable impression. Not only does Casement, a British subject, stand convicted of treason but I am privately informed that much information about him of an unspeakably filthy character was withheld from publicity. . . . If all the facts about Casement ever became public it will be well that our Government had nothing to do with him or his case even indirectly." [87]

As this letter from Page indicates, the British Government was spreading a filthy smear upon Casement's character in order to kill any plea of clemency from the American Government. Michael F. Doyle recorded the fact that when he arrived in London on June 13 the smear was already circulating. He soon discovered that it was "common gossip among the newspapermen and others." [88] On June 30 the London *Daily Express* referred to a Casement diary that was unusually filthy, and it characterized Casement as an "extremely degenerate traitor." This comment was promptly reproduced in *The New York Times* and went the rounds of the American press. As Mr. Maloney convincingly argues, the smear upon Casement's character was concocted in Scotland Yard out of a diary that Casement had preserved among his papers. It had been written in Spanish by one of the officials of the Peruvian Amazon Company and the translation was in Casement's handwriting. Eamon Duggan was shown the diary in 1921, and after a careful examination of it came to the conclusion that it was "a diary copied by Sir Roger during the Putumayo investigation." [89]

---

87. Ambassador Page to Secretary Lansing, London, July 3, 1916, Casement file, *Wilson MSS.*
88. W. J. Maloney, *The Forged Casement Diaries*, pp. 13-14.
89. *Ibid.*, p. 175. For comments right or wrong about this alleged Casement Diary, see Denis Gwynn, *Traitor or Patriot* (New York, 1931), p. 19; Henry W. Nevinson, *Last Changes, Last Chances* (London, 1928), p. 115; Blanche Patch, *Thirty Years with G.B.S.*[haw] (London, 1951), pp. 100-103; E. S. P. Haynes, *A Lawyer's Notebook* (London, 1932), p. 32. It was significant that Sir Basil Thompson, head of Scotland Yard in 1915, was

In a letter to Gavan Duffy, September 9, 1916, John Quinn told how English officials were "circulating reports of Casement's degeneracy. They came to me from all quarters. I was finally shown what purported to be photographic copies of his diary, and the handwriting looked like his. But I wrote to the ambassador . . . stating that I thought it was a dirty piece of business to circulate such reports . . . and that if this stuff . . . were continued I would open up again. . . . I think that my word of warning worked." [90] As a matter of fact Quinn's words of warning were completely disregarded by the British Government, which continued to circulate the unfounded smear upon Casement's character. There is no doubt that it created in many American minds a feeling that Casement was not worth saving.

But Michael Francis Doyle did not have this viewpoint and he once more turned to Tumulty in an effort to save Casement's life. He was confident that the President could persuade the British Government to commute Casement's sentence to life imprisonment:

> I am about to cable you asking if the President will not be good enough to write a letter to Sir Edward Grey or Mr. Asquith asking the British Government to spare the life of Sir Roger Casement. Of course I know he can do nothing officially, but a personal request from the President *will save his life.* An appeal has been lodged and will be heard July 17. It will be decided immediately; but if dismissed, execution of the sentence takes place within a few days. . . . There is absolutely no doubt that Casement never intended to assist Germany. His sole object was to defend Ireland. . . .
>
> John Redmond and Lord Northcliffe both told me the President's word would save him. His great services to the world in exposing the Congo outrages and in South America surely would justify the President, to say nothing of the Irish question. Attempts have been made lately to discredit his character by spreading vile stories concerning him. It is done by his enemies, and his counsel at this time

---

later apprehended by the police in Hyde Park on a morals charge. In his book, *Queer People* (London, 1922), p. 92, he claimed that the alleged *Diary* of Casement indicated that "some mental disintegration" must have occurred to Casement.

90. *Ibid.*, p. 27.

have not been able to verify them. They may have reached your ears by this time, but they should not affect the President. The charge against him is treason and that only.[91]

Doyle realized that in the United States there was a rising tide of sympathy for Casement and he wished to make use of it. In the latter part of June, eight Congressmen had petitioned the President to use his good offices to save Casement's life.[92] When nothing came of this move there were new attempts to exert pressure upon the British Government on Casement's behalf. Tumulty himself was very much worried about the implications of the Casement affair during an election year. The Irish vote in the industrial East was an important factor that could not be disregarded. In order to influence the President's mind he arranged for an interview between Franz H. Krebs, an important newspaperman, and the Chief Executive. On July 7, 1916, Krebs talked with the President about the Casement matter and then wrote a brief memorandum of their conversation:

> I told the President that the first time I saw Sir Roger this year was on February 12th and that he was merely a shadow of what he was when I . . . saw him in April, 1915. I also told the President that he was . . . suffering from a severe nervous breakdown. . . . President Wilson gave me a most sympathetic hearing when I spoke to him about the great work Sir Roger had done in collecting the evidence on which the British Parliament had acted and did away with King Leopold's rule in the Congo; further when I mentioned Sir Roger's

91. Michael F. Doyle to Tumulty, London, July 6, 1916, Casement file, *Wilson MSS*.
92. John M. Blum, *Joe Tumulty and the Wilson Era* (Boston, 1951), p. 107. With reference to the smear upon Casement's good name, William Butler Yeats wrote a poem of protest, some verses of which I quote as follows:
> I say that Roger Casement
> Did what he had to do.
> He died upon the gallows,
> But that is nothing new.
> Afraid they might be beaten
> Before the bench of Time,
> They turned a trick by forgery
> And blackened his good name.

work in connection with stopping the Putumayo outrages, President Wilson signified that he was fully informed regarding Sir Roger's activities in the past. . . . The general feeling in Washington is that the death penalty will be commuted.[93]

Tumulty felt hopeful after he talked with Krebs, and finally on July 20 he wrote a short memorandum to the President and inquired what he intended to do with reference to Casement. The reply from the Chief Executive gave him quite a jolt: "It would be inexcusable for me to touch this. It would involve serious international embarrassment." [94]

The Senate of the United States now moved into the picture and on July 29 adopted a resolution amended by Senator Pittman, of Nevada, requesting the President to transmit to the British Government their plea for clemency for Casement.[95] The resolution was mailed to the White House on July 29 and mysteriously stayed there for several days without any action being taken with regard to it. It did not reach the Department of State until after 11:00 A.M. "on August 2d, and was enciphered and sent in a cablegram to the Embassy in London at 1:00 P.M. on the same day." [96]

The American Embassy in London hurriedly decoded the message from the Department of State enclosing the Senate resolution asking for clemency for Casement. On August 3, Irwin Laughlin, First Secretary of the Embassy, took it to the Foreign Office. He was fearful of offending the sensibilities of Sir Edward Grey, so he made no reference to the Casement affair. During the course of his conversation on many topics of Anglo-American relations the Casement incident was alluded to by Grey, who commented upon the Senate resolution asking for clemency. Laughlin then remarked that he happened to have a copy of the resolution with him and inquired if the Foreign Secretary would like to have it. Grey replied that he would like to have a copy of the document. After

93. Memorandum of Franz H. Krebs with reference to a conversation with President Wilson, July 7, 1916, Casement file, *Wilson MSS*.
94. President Wilson to Joseph Tumulty, July 20, 1916, *Wilson MSS*.
95. *Congressional Record*, July 29, 1916, LIII, 11782-83.
96. Secretary Lansing to Joseph Tumulty, September 2, 1916, Casement file, *Wilson MSS*.

he read it over with deliberation he turned to Laughlin: "This is a very interesting document," he said when he had finished. "Would you have any objection if I showed it to the Prime Minister?" Of course this "was precisely what Mr. Laughlin did wish, and he replied that this was the desire of his government. The purpose of his visit had been accomplished, and he was able to cable Washington that its instructions had been carried out. . . . Simultaneously with his communication, however, he reported also that the execution of Roger Casement had taken place. In fact, it was being carried out at the time of the interview." [97]

Casement's execution in Pentonville prison on August 3 created a great stir in America, and Senator Phelan and many of his colleagues wanted to know why the Senate resolution had been so long delayed in the White House. The situation became so embarrassing to Mr. Tumulty that he wrote a long letter to Secretary Lansing requesting him to prepare a letter which would explain the situation, so as to relieve the increasing pressure from Irish-Americans who were furious over the Casement execution. He sketched the type of letter he thought Lansing should write and added a final note of warning: "As I told you this morning, this is of the most vital importance." [98]

But Secretary Lansing was in no mood to save Tumulty's face with a ready-made fabrication. In his letter of reply he did not mince matters:

> Of course you know . . . that the resolution [the Senate resolution asking for clemency for Casement] was transmitted to this Department from your office with the request that it be forwarded to London on the morning of the day preceding the Casement execution. It was received at 11:00 A.M., and was on the wires at 1:00 P.M. of that day. The embarrassment is that it reached the Department so late, as 1:00 P.M. would correspond to 6:00 P.M. London time. It probably could not, with all diligence, have reached our Embassy before midnight, where it had to be then deciphered. Now I am sure that you would not expect us to make an incorrect statement about the matter,

---

97. Burton J. Hendrick, *The Life and Letters of Walter H. Page* (Garden City, 1923), II, 167-168.
98. Joseph Tumulty to Secretary Lansing, September 7, 1916, *Wilson MSS.*

and I would not be willing to do so whatever the consequences might be." [99]

It was apparent that Secretary Lansing would not lie to save the President's face, so Tumulty turned to the Assistant Secretary of State, Frank K. Polk, who wrote a letter that fitted the Tumulty prescription.[100] But prominent Irish-Americans were not diverted by this evident red herring drawn across the Casement trail, and they continued to attack the Administration. Father Edward Flannery thought that he had a remedy that would save the situation. In a letter to Mr. Tumulty he placed a great deal of blame upon the Clan-na-Gael:

> It is the only organization you have to fear much. . . . The members of that society vote as they are told. . . . Let me outline the situation for you: If you see the *Gaelic American,* edited by John Devoy, you know what that has been saying, in a most scurrilous fashion, against the President. Now most of the Clan take the utterances of that sheet as if they were inspired. . . . The mystery comes when it is remembered that the *Gaelic American* is largely owned by Daniel Cohalan, the New York Surrogate and intimate adviser of Mr. Murphy, of Tammany. I told Mr. McCormick that the man to silence Devoy and his paper was the Judge.[101]

There was not much chance of getting Judge Cohalan to exert pressure upon John Devoy so that he would cease his criticism of President Wilson. The Presidential election would mean a great deal to Irish-American voters, and Devoy was anxious that they should vote against the Wilson Administration. In the last week in

99. Secretary Lansing to Joseph Tumulty, October 2, 1916, *Wilson MSS.*
100. Franklin K. Polk to Secretary Lansing, August 3, 1916, *Lansing Papers,* Library of Congress; Franklin K. Polk to Mr. Tumulty, October 5, 1916, *Wilson MSS.* It is interesting to note that Sir Edward Grey was distinctly annoyed at the temerity of the Senate in adopting a resolution requesting clemency for Casement. In a letter from Sir Edward Grey to Colonel House the following complaint is made: "We are not favourably impressed by the action of the Senate in having passed a resolution about the Irish prisoners." *The Intimate Papers of Colonel House* (Boston, 1926, edited by Charles Seymour, 2 vols.), II, 318.
101. Rev. Edward Flannery to Mr. Tumulty, August 10, 1916, *Wilson MSS.*

(above) Daniel O'Connell

(right) John E. Redmond

Theobald Wolfe Tone

Michael Davitt

Charles Stewart Parnell

John Mitchel

Douglas Hyde

(left to right, seated) W. Bourke Cockran, Daniel F. Cohalan, Congressman William E. Mason. *(standing)* U.S. Senator Thomas J. Walsh of Montana, Frank P. Walsh. Taken in Washington, D.C., December 12, 1919.

Judge Cohalan, Eamon de Valera, and Judge John W. Goff

Senator William E. Borah of Idaho
(International News photo)

James Cardinal Gibbons, Archbishop of New York, and Judge Cohalan at the Irish Race Convention in Philadelphia, February 22, 1919.

Sir Roger Casement

(top) William Cardinal O'Connell, Archbishop of Boston

(above) John Devoy

September he paid his respects to the President in one of his most vitriolic editorials in the *Gaelic American*:

> That President Wilson hates the Irish with the implacable hatred of the Ulster Orangeman—the stock he comes of—has been shown so many times since he became President that there can be no successful denial. . . . Mr. Wilson's mean and despicable attack on the Irish at the unveiling of the Barry monument in Washington on May 16, 1914, was deliberate and premeditated. And it was as cowardly as it was mean and untruthful, for he was protected by the character of the occasion from the possibility of reply or rebuke. . . . Since then Mr. Wilson has never missed an opportunity of repeating his false accusations of disloyalty against a race that proved its loyalty on the bloody battlefields of the Civil War fighting for the Union, while his relatives were fighting to destroy it and his father was desecrating a Christian pulpit by ranting in favor of human slavery.

The President had a long memory and he never forgave or forgot. He remembered how Judge Cohalan and the braves of Tammany had fought against his nomination at the Baltimore Convention of 1912. He was certain that Cohalan had plotted with the Germans to start a rebellion in Ireland whenever England was so hard pressed she could take no effective action to suppress it. To him, the rising in Dublin on Easter morning had a distinct Cohalan flavor. His deep devotion to England made him despise Irish-Americans who dreamed of an independent Ireland and who believed that the World War was Ireland's great opportunity to strike for freedom. As John Devoy pithily expressed it, Woodrow Wilson "imbibed with his mother's milk" an "implacable hatred of the Irish." This same hatred made it impossible for the Irish to get a real hearing at the Peace Conference at Versailles in 1919, and it encouraged Winston Churchill and Lloyd George to scourge Ireland with the Black and Tan murder squads in 1920. It was fortunate for Ireland that a new Presidential Administration came into office in the United States in 1921. In the election of 1920 the Irish-Americans were an important pressure group that helped to bury the Treaty of Versailles and thereby destroy Wilson's handiwork at Paris. The leader of this pressure group was Judge Daniel F. Cohalan. Succeeding chapters will emphasize his role in postwar American politics.[102]

102. In the early months of 1956 a new biography of Casement appeared in London. It is entitled *Roger Casement: A New Judgment*. Its author is René MacColl, a British journalist. Mr. MacColl has a long discussion of "Casement's Black Diaries—those discovered in his trunks at Ebury Street by the police after his arrest and which contained a voluminous and detailed record of homosexual behaviour." Mr. MacColl has a lengthy account of these diaries, pp. 278-291.

In 1936 William J. Maloney published his able volume on the *Forged Casement Diaries*, in which he made out a good case against the authenticity of the diaries as a record of any actions by Casement. In 1954 Herbert Mackey, F.R.C.S., brought out a notable book entitled *The Life and Times of Roger Casement*.

Mr. MacColl differs from Maloney and Mackey and supports the official British version that Casement was a confessed homosexual. His evidence is distinctly weak. He bases his opinions first upon remarks alleged to have been made by Serjeant Alexander Martin Sullivan during a conversation with MacColl on November 16, 1954. Sullivan, as the chief counsel for Casement, is an important witness with reference to the character of the Irish hero. According to MacColl, Sullivan was quite frank in his comments upon the homosexuality of Casement.

Any student looking over the account by MacColl is struck by two facts. First of all, there is no written evidence that Sullivan actually made the remarks attributed to him by MacColl. It is significant that MacColl does not publish any letter to him from Serjeant Sullivan relative to Casement's alleged homosexuality. He merely cites comments alleged to have been made by Sullivan during a conversation in November 1954. His evidence is far from convincing. One should also remember that in 1954 Sullivan was over ninety years of age. It would have been difficult for him to remember with exactitude remarks made to him by Casement in 1916.

MacColl also refers to some hearsay evidence which the late Senator Biggar confided to a nameless resident of Cork. Senator Biggar related that his uncle, F. J. Biggar, had some Casement papers that proved the degeneracy of Casement. He burned the papers and then became a gossip. His gossip is not impressive evidence on the matter of the charges against Casement.

7 PRESIDENT WILSON FAVORS THE PRINCIPLE OF SELF-DETERMINATION FOR EVERY PEOPLE BUT THE IRISH

A. PRESIDENT WILSON TRIES TO COMPEL CONGRESS TO DECLARE WAR UPON GERMANY

It is evident that President Wilson had scant sympathy for the Irish patriots who were summarily executed by British firing squads for participation in the Easter Rebellion. It has already been demonstrated how the President delayed sending to the British Foreign Office a Senate resolution asking clemency for Roger Casement. This White House tactic of delay ended any hope that Senate pressure might soften the hearts of British statesmen whose traditional formula for settling Irish unrest had been a sinister combination of the gallows and the firing squad.

As the spot light is shifted from Dublin to Washington for a closeup of the situation, it is evident that President Wilson felt deeply dedicated to the complete support of British foreign policy no matter what the cost might be in terms of American lives and treasure. Any thought of a rebellion in Ireland against British rule would naturally be most repugnant to him. In furtherance of his policy of Anglophilism he sent Colonel House to Europe in January 1916 to talk with the British Foreign Secretary regarding the course America should pursue. Colonel House had already assured Sir Edward Grey that he believed that the American people would be willing to "go to limits unthinkable to bring about a just solution" of the questions involved in the war then being waged in Europe. This just solution, of course, would be a peace based upon Allied military success.[1]

With Colonel House in this ardent Anglophile mood, it was inevitable that he should favor the signature of a document that would place America's manpower and treasure at the call of England. On January 11, 1916, the voluble Colonel assured Lloyd George that the "United States would like Great Britain to do those things which would enable the United States to help Great Britain to win the war."[2] A few weeks later House tried to banish French fears of defeat. If any crisis should arise that would threaten the fate of France, her statesmen should issue a call for assistance and he was certain that the President would not only arrange for American intervention in the war but would also guarantee "a settlement based upon justice."[3]

After giving these glib assurances of American assistance, the Colonel then proceeded to sign on February 22, 1916, the well-known House-Grey Agreement. This agreement was an invitation to war. In accordance with its terms President Wilson, after hearing from Britain and France, would issue a call to the belligerent powers to attend a peace conference. If Germany should refuse to heed this summons, the United States would enter the war against her. If Germany should attend the conference and then display an "unreasonable" attitude relative to peace terms, America "would leave the Conference as a belligerent on the side of the Allies."[4]

To implement this House-Grey Agreement, the President, on February 21, 1916, called to the White House important Congressional leaders like Senators Stone and Kern and Congressman Flood. He then boldly informed them that "the United States by entering the war now might be able to bring it to a conclusion by midsummer, and thus render a great service to civilization."[5] Sen-

1. Sir Edward Grey to Colonel House, September 22, 1915, *House MSS.*, Yale University Library.
2. *The Intimate Papers of Colonel House*, II, 124.
3. *Ibid.*, 163.
4. *Ibid.*, 201-202.
5. *Congressional Record*, LIII, Appendix, 833.

ator Stone, Chairman of the Senate Committee on Foreign Relations, had been a firm supporter of the domestic policies of the President, but he grew very excited when he realized the real meaning of this White House conference and loudly exclaimed: "By God! Mr. President! I shall not follow you into war with Germany." [6]

Senator Kern and Representative Flood were equally unenthusiastic about going to war with Germany, and they frankly told the President of the pacific disposition that prevailed in Congress. On the following morning the famous "Sunrise Conference" was held at the White House. Several important members of Congress, headed by Speaker Champ Clark, heard the President repeat his arguments for intervention into the war. When they frankly voiced their opposition to intervention he quickly shifted his position. It would not be smart politics to press for war when Congress was wedded to peace. Calling Senator Stone to the White House, he suddenly cooed like a dove and insisted that he was a passionate pacifist. He was so successful in this maneuver that Senator Stone gave a statement to the press in which he remarked that he believed the President did not wish to plunge America into war. After seeing the success of this deception, the President then had Colonel House send a cablegram to Sir Edward Grey announcing White House approval of the House-Grey Agreement with only a minor amendment.[7] But the American people were not lied into war at this time. Sir Edward Grey decided to await the outcome of the next great battle in France before invoking the House-Grey Agreement. The Battle of the Somme consumed most of the summer of 1916, and before it was over the President was in the midst of a close battle for re-election. The strongest argument used by the Democrats was a slogan that coined a lie—"He kept us out of war."

6. Charles C. Tansill, *America Goes to War* (New York, 1938), p. 466.
7. *Intimate Papers of Colonel House*, II, 203.

B. IRISH-AMERICANS STRONGLY PROTEST AGAINST
BRITISH BRUTALITY IN IRELAND

While President Wilson was trying to push Congress down the road to war, Irish-Americans were endeavoring to induce the Department of State to intervene on behalf of Irish prisoners who had been brutally treated after the last embers of the Easter Rebellion had been stamped out. The severity of British military rule in Ireland had deeply shocked American public opinion, and Irish-Americans began to ask Senators and Representatives to make every effort to put a stop to this bloody regime. On May 4, 1916, Senator Borah read on the floor of the Senate an editorial in the New York *Sun* expressing the hope that Britain would now be lenient in her treatment of Irish political prisoners.[8] Senator Martine followed this lead on May 19 with some sharply critical remarks upon British policy in Ireland:

> I feel that England in her effort to quell a local disturbance in the city of Dublin, Ireland, has gone rank mad and is both blind and deaf to all thoughts of humanity and civilization. . . . It seems to me humanity will rebel the world over at this recent act upon the part of this brutal and tyrannous Power.[9]

On May 16, 1916, the County Clare Association of California passed resolutions calling upon Senator James D. Phelan to take some action with reference to these atrocities. He immediately sent a vigorous letter to Joseph P. Tumulty, secretary to President Wilson, in sharp protest against the "secret trials and secret executions" that had become commonplace in Ireland:

> American citizens of Irish birth have been arrested and held without trial, and there are reports that one such citizen has been condemned by court martial to capital punishment. . . . You have in the name of humanity protested to other foreign Governments against the recklessness of power. The divine right of revolution is inherent in every

8. *Congressional Record*, LIII, 7439.
9. *Ibid.*, 8316.

people. . . . This is a right for which the unconquerable spirit of the Irish people has contended for centuries. . . .

We cannot as Americans look with indifference upon these events, because if our emotions do not respond under such circumstances our own liberties and independence are in danger. . . . Therefore, I repeat, in the name of humanity and liberty you should protest against these practices which all history, modern enlightenment, as well as political sagacity, condemn.[10]

Tumulty referred this letter to Frank L. Polk, the Counselor of the Department of State, for serious consideration. Polk replied that "in so far as the rights of Americans are concerned every effort will be made by the Department to see that they are fully protected. . . . As to the treatment of Irishmen, as they are not citizens of the United States, this Government has no right to speak. . . . Under the circumstances, this Government would not be in a position to make any protest." [11]

Tumulty would not accept this glib denial of his request for some official action by the Department of State. On June 9 he wrote again to Polk a word of warning: "I would like to discuss this matter with you before a reply is made to the Senator. There is so much dynamite in it that we ought to proceed with care." [12]

While Polk was making up his mind as to what action he should take, Robert P. Troy, President of the Knights of St. Patrick, San Francisco, California, telegraphed to Senator Phelan and inquired why his telegram to President Wilson had not been acknowledged: "Our members have been rather puzzled to understand this." [13] Phelan at once sent this telegram to Tumulty, who placed it before the President. On July 7 a reply from the Chief Executive was finally sent to Mr. Troy:

> Where the fate of an American citizen was involved, I have secured favorable action, and the Secretary of State, in answer to a resolution of the Senate of the United States on June 2, 1916, requesting cer-

10. Senator James D. Phelan to Joseph P. Tumulty, May 22, 1916, *Woodrow Wilson Papers*, Library of Congress.
11. Frank L. Polk to Joseph P. Tumulty, June 3, 1916, Wilson MSS.
12. Tumulty to Frank L. Polk, June 9, 1916, *ibid*.
13. Robert P. Troy to Senator James D. Phelan, June 23, 1916, *ibid*.

tain action and having in view the protest of your Society, the letter of Senator Phelan and many others, put forth a strong plea which I sincerely trust will be heeded. My natural sympathies are with men struggling for freedom, and concerning whose sincerity as patriots, seeking solely the welfare of their country, cannot be questioned. . . . In view of the conditions in other lands, Americans should be doubly thankful for the form of Government which has been transmitted to them by their ancestors, won by valor and sacrifice, under which they enjoy self-government. Please convey my thanks to your Society for having called my attention to the events and reciting precedents for such action as might be necessary on behalf of this government.[14]

C. IRISH-AMERICAN OPPOSITION TO AMERICAN INTERVENTION IN THE WORLD WAR

The ardent sympathies of President Wilson with the Allied cause were well known to many Irish-Americans who feared that he would push America into the war in order to preserve the British Empire. This might mean that American troops would be stationed in Ireland to prevent any further rebellions. It might also mean that American intervention in the war would lead to the enactment of stringent legislation dealing with espionage. Irish-American activities aimed at England could be interpreted as treason to the United States. In view of these facts the Friends of Irish Freedom, on February 10, 1917, prepared an address to President Wilson which set forth cogent reasons why America should stay out of foreign wars. It also protested against proposed legislation which provided for the suppression of "so-called revolutionary conspiracies against friendly foreign Governments." [15] Although this pressure may have had some influence in preventing drastic espionage legislation, it was significant that the legislation that was hurriedly pushed through Congress was phrased in such a manner as to awaken the mounting fears of many Irish-Americans. They knew that war hysteria might insist upon an unfriendly interpretation of this new espionage act as far as their activities were concerned.

In an effort to acquaint the Administration with the strength of

14. President Wilson to Robert P. Troy, July 7, 1916, *ibid.*
15. *The New York Times*, February 11, 1917.

Irish-American feeling towards the "Irish Question," a large meeting was held on April 8, 1917, in Carnegie Hall in New York City. Judge John W. Goff and Judge Daniel F. Cohalan were the principal speakers, and they were largely responsible for the preparation of a telegram to President Wilson and a letter to Speaker Clark. The telegram to the President pledged the support of Irish-Americans for any measures he might advocate for the "maintenance and protection of America's honor and interests," and it expressed the hope that he would raise his voice in a "demand for justice to Ireland which can only be secured by establishing her independence." In the letter addressed to Speaker Clark an appeal was made to Congress to "take such action as will secure the Independence of Ireland, not at the end of the war when 'scraps of paper' may be safely torn up, but now when America's intervention will count for more than at any time in the future." [16]

As a result of this meeting in Carnegie Hall, Representatives McCormick (April 9), Gallagher (April 13), and Mason (May 14) introduced resolutions calling for American support of the fight for Irish freedom. Needless to say, these resolutions were placed in convenient pigeonholes in the ample filing cabinets in the rooms of the House Committee on Foreign Affairs.

In order to present to the American mind the real meaning of the Irish Question, a debate was carried on in the columns of the Jesuit weekly *America*, which welcomed articles on current questions. The first contributor to this debate was Shane Leslie, who was closely connected with the British Embassy in Washington. Leslie was also one of the editors of a weekly periodical entitled *Ireland*, which was published in New York City. This periodical ardently supported the policies of John Redmond and had scant sympathy for any thought of Irish independence. In 1916 it had attacked the decision to hold an Irish Race Convention in America and had published a garbled version of a speech that John Devoy had made at that convention. Devoy answered Leslie in several bitter editorials in the *Gaelic American*. The following quotations are typical. In dealing with the falsifications printed in *Ireland*, Devoy

16. *Ibid.*, April 9, 1917.

remarked: "The man who made that falsification for the benefit of the British Government would do anything, no matter how mean, criminal or dishonest, to serve it." [17] Some weeks later, with reference to Leslie's comments upon the Easter Rebellion, Devoy returned to the attack: "Shane Leslie has selected the *Tribune* . . . as the medium through which to defame the dead who died for Ireland under the pretence of defending them as visionaries and lunatics. . . . What he does represent is the British Government, for which he is carrying on a propaganda in America through a paper with a fraudulent name, started with English money." [18]

In April 1917, shortly after America had entered the World War, Leslie continued his English propaganda, and this time he chose the columns of *America*. The title of his article was challenging: "What Does Ireland Want?" Apparently there was no doubt in his mind that he spoke for the Irish people. He was confident that the average Irishman was not clamoring for revenge or for a republic. What he really desired was Home Rule within the framework of the British Empire:

> All sects and classes, all the social strata left behind by Irish history, should find interest, representation and pride in a Dublin parliament. . . . The ideal as it exists in many minds outside Ireland is disturbed by emotion and distance and demands more than Ireland herself wants. Ireland wants less than any other small nationality in Europe today. She asks to possess and enjoy that full colonial independence enjoyed by Canada.[19]

The Reverend Sigourney W. Fay, S.T.D., devoted all his vast learning to prove a point which most people had long known—that Daniel O'Connell had never advocated independence for Ireland.

17. *Gaelic American,* March 25, 1916.
18. *Ibid.,* May 13, 1916. Arthur Willert, in his *The Road to Safety* (London, 1952), makes the following comments upon the activities of Shane Leslie in 1916-1917: "Tough, independent and unpaid, Shane Leslie was the nearest approach to a secret propagandist that we had in the United States. But he never got into trouble, and to me he was, in my newspaper and other work, a pleasant and useful ally with his quick brain, his sardonic humour, his quiet and tireless energy and his wide and exact knowledge of the personalities and problems within his sphere of action." Pp. 90-93.
19. *America,* April 28, 1917, pp. 56-57.

If O'Connell had never dreamed of anything more than Home Rule for Ireland, why should some loud-mouthed Irish agitators in 1917 ask for anything more? [20]

Father Fay was a convert to Catholicism who did not permit his conversion to dampen in any way his ardent support of England during World War I. He was a close friend of Shane Leslie, who spent much of his time in the British Embassy in Washington. Judge Cohalan had little patience with the viewpoints of Leslie and Fay. He was confident that "if a plebiscite were taken tomorrow, a large majority of the men and women of Ireland would declare themselves in favor of independence and of an Irish republic." Thanks to skillful British propaganda, the world had been sold on the idea that "the Irish are an unruly, turbulent people, who, being unable to rule themselves, have been raised to a half-civilized state by the unselfish and devoted efforts of England." This British propaganda had been successful even among certain Irish who had been "indoctrinated with the belief" that the notion of an Independent Irish republic was only the "dream of an enthusiast." The articles of Shane Leslie and Dr. Fay were strong proof of that fact. But these Anglo-Irish had overlooked the lessons of the Easter Rebellion, which had "stimulated and vitalized the determination of the men and women of Ireland to break the last link that binds them to England." When this last English tie had been finally broken, the old differences that had long bedeviled Ireland "will be forgotten and the people will unite without regard to old lines of cleavage and division upon the solution of the pressing problems of national progress." [21]

Mrs. Hanna Sheehy-Skeffington hastened to confirm the views of Judge Cohalan: "Ireland recognizes that complete independence is the only policy that will give her self-respect and abiding peace; that any system that unites her even by the slightest thread to the 'predominant partner' will never be administered for her own good." [22]

20. *Ibid.*, June 9, 1917, pp. 209-210.
21. *America*, May 19, 1917, pp. 133-135.
22. *Ibid.*, June 2, 1917, pp. 184-186.

John Devoy was entirely in accord with the sentiments of Judge Cohalan and Mrs. Skeffington. As a convinced separatist he ardently believed that real freedom for Ireland could be found only "in national independence and total separation from England." The separatists constituted the only group "in Ireland who have a consistent and continuous policy, kept alive and rigorously adhered to in spite of the vicissitudes of constant conflict with the British Government. . . . No matter what England does, or what may be the attitude of the Parliamentary party, the Separatists will hold out for national independence, fully confident that, if they do not win immediately, Ireland will fare better for their steadfastness and resolute adherence to principle." [23]

There was little doubt in the minds of most Irish-Americans that the articles of Judge Cohalan, Mrs. Skeffington, and John Devoy struck a political keynote that would continue to vibrate until Irish independence was finally secured. Some months later, Shane Leslie ruefully admitted that he had been "pulverized" by their cogency and power of statement.[24]

D. JOHN REDMOND DISCOVERS THAT THE "IRISH QUESTION" DEFIES A GLIB SOLUTION

As the minds of Irish-Americans leaned more and more towards independence as a solution of the Irish Question, John Redmond still sought some formula of settlement within the framework of the British Empire. This persistence in following British political paths helped to destroy his popularity in America. It was also true that his silence concerning the bloody excesses of British military government in Ireland had been widely regarded as a manifestation of weakness. He had adhered to his pledge to Asquith even though it meant political suicide. On May 15 Michael J. Ryan, President of the United Irish League of America, cabled to him that the Irish executions after the Easter Rebellion had "alienated every

23. *Ibid.*, June 30, 1917, pp. 293-294.
24. *The Irish Issue in its American Aspect* (New York, 1917), p. 203.

American friend and caused a resurgence of ancient enmities. Your life-work destroyed by English brutality." [25] Four days later the British Ambassador in Washington cabled to Sir Edward Grey the same story: "I fear that recent events have alienated from us almost the entire Irish Party [in America]." [26]

In Ireland, the division in Nationalist ranks began to widen rapidly and Redmond's leadership was under serious fire. This fact made him very cautious of new proposals from Lloyd George with reference to a plan to bring the "Home Rule Act into immediate operation." The Carsonites demanded the permanent exclusion of the six northern counties of Ireland from any application of Home Rule, and Redmond knew that he dared not make such a concession. He could not go further than to agree to immediate Home Rule for twenty-six counties with a provision for the final settlement of the Ulster question after the war. After some weeks of negotiations during the early summer of 1916 the matter reached an impasse. Carson then scored a cheap triumph in the House of Commons by suggesting that Redmond shake hands with him as "a fellow-Irishman." When Redmond made no effort to meet this proffer of false friendship, Carson posed before the world as a statesman who had offered in vain an olive branch to an old opponent who had closed his mind to any compromise.[27]

Redmond had not worried too much about the antics of Carson as long as Asquith remained Prime Minister. He believed that Asquith had a hard core of character upon which he could safely depend, but on December 6 the Asquith Government fell and Lloyd George became the new Prime Minister. This change in political control was a serious challenge to the plans of Redmond. He was familiar with every aspect of Lloyd George's political career and he knew that the wily Welshman was a politician first and a statesman second. The negotiations concerning Home Rule which had broken down in July had revealed very clearly that Lloyd

25. Denis Gwynn, *Life of John Redmond*, p. 500.
26. *Letters and Friendships of Sir Cecil Spring Rice*, II, 331.
27. Denis Gwynn, *John Redmond*, pp. 491-523.

George had given way before the relentless pressure of Carson. As Prime Minister, would he be more resolute against the demands of the iron man of Ulster?

The answer to this question might be furnished by American intervention in World War I on April 6, 1917. There was no doubt that the Irish-Americans would be a factor to be considered in the new equation. According to the British Ambassador in Washington, the Irish-Americans were

> of very great political importance at the present moment. The question is one which is at the root of most of our troubles with the United States. . . . The President is by descent an Orangeman and by education a Presbyterian. But he is the leader of the Democratic Party in which the Irish play a prominent part, and he is bound in every way to give consideration to their demands.[28]

Cablegrams from Shane Leslie and other friends in America told Redmond much the same story. Perhaps something could be accomplished if Balfour, during his visit to America, could be approached and the pressing matter of immediate Home Rule could be placed cogently before him. It was finally arranged that Colonel Robert T. Emmet, Justice Morgan J. O'Brien, John Quinn, Father Wynne, S.J., Father Sigourney Fay, Lawrence Godkin, and Mayor John F. Fitzgerald, of Boston, should go to Washington and have a conference with Balfour on May 3. John Quinn described the purpose of this meeting as follows: "There will be no oratory, no attempt to embarrass Mr. Balfour, but an earnest talk with him to try to impress upon him the fact that the way to take the wind out of the sails of the irreconcilables, the way to put them out of business, is to have home rule be given to an undivided Ireland. That will settle the Irish question, and it is the only thing that can settle it." [29]

On May 3 this committee of Irish-Americans had their audience with Balfour, who remarked that although he had no authority to

---

28. Spring Rice to Lord Robert Cecil, April 13, 1917, *Letters and Friendships of Sir Cecil Spring Rice*, II, 392-393.
29. John Quinn to Otto Carmichael, April 30, 1917, *Wilson MSS.*

speak for the British Cabinet he had been "profoundly impressed by the representative character of the delegation and the moderation of the views expressed. . . . He added that he would cable to the Cabinet the opinion of the delegation that a prompt settlement of the home rule question, without excluding any part of Ireland, would be hailed with satisfaction not merely by representative Irishmen but by Americans generally." [30]

In the New York *World*, letters from representative Americans dealing with the question of Home Rule were published. Ex-Presidents Theodore Roosevelt and William H. Taft were among the contributors to this symposium. Roosevelt believed that "both permanently and as regards this particular war it would be an immense advantage to the empire to give Ireland home rule." Taft expressed the opinion that such action would "help solidify and hearten American public sentiment in the great cause." Cardinal Gibbons thought that the Irish Question arose "from the fear of the minority in Ulster that they will be coerced into a union with the rest of Ireland which will be their ruin. . . . The only way I see out of the difficulty is the way of guarantees. The present position is impossible. Ireland cannot be sacrificed to a few counties in Ulster. These few counties cannot be sacrificed to the rest of Ireland." [31]

To Sir Horace Plunkett it seemed very evident that the many letters that had appeared in the American press concerning Home Rule indicated that there was "a pretty deep feeling on the subject in Irish circles." [32] Tumulty, as the President's private secretary, was well aware of this "deep feeling" in Irish circles in America. Among the numerous communications that poured into the White House was one from John D. Crimmins, of New York City. In an-

---

30. Shane Leslie, *The Irish Issue in its American Aspect* (New York, 1917), pp. 199-201.
31. New York *World*, April 26, 1917. On April 24, 1917, Archbishop Christie, of Portland, Oregon, wrote to President Wilson and suggested that he make a public statement favoring Home Rule. When this letter was turned over to Secretray Lansing he suggested that Tumulty should write merely a "brief acknowledgment" of the letter from the Archbishop. Tumulty followed this advice and thus refused to have the President dragged into this matter of Home Rule. *Wilson MSS.*
32. Sir Horace Plunkett to Colonel House, April 28, 1917, *House MSS.*

swer to his letter of April 28, Tumulty wrote to assure him that the President had a "keen interest" in the Irish Question and "in every way he properly can, is showing his sympathy with the claims of Ireland for Home Rule." [33] On May 12 this letter of Tumulty was printed in the New York *World*. This led John D. Moore, President of the Friends of Irish Freedom, to address a letter to Tumulty on the matter of Home Rule:

> If you mean by "Home Rule" the pitiful travesty upon self-government which went on the statute books, September 18, 1914, then you may be assured that Ireland is not making any "claim" for that sort of thing. What Ireland wants . . . is complete independence, and nothing short of it. The Irish people want to be free to exercise "the privilege of men everywhere to choose their way of life and of obedience" for which the President asked us to enter the war.[34]

A Home Rule arrangement, dictated by British necessities, meant little to earnest Irishmen, who realized that a great opportunity had arisen for Ireland to secure independence. This fact was particularly clear to the Irish prisoners who had been dragged from one English prison to another since the Easter Rebellion. As a gesture of good will to American public opinion, these prisoners were released on June 18. Patrick McCartan met them on the boat to Ireland and suggested that he take to America a statement of their views on the future of Ireland. Professor Eoin MacNeill wrote the suggested statement and it was signed by twenty-six of these recently released prisoners, including Eamon de Valera, Diarmuid Lynch, Tom Ashe, Desmond Fitzgerald, James J. Walsh, and John McGarry.

While writing this statement, Professor MacNeill had before him the message of President Wilson to the Provisional Government of Russia, May 26, 1917. The ringing words of the President concerning national self-determination awakened many echoes in the hearts of these Irish, and they referred to them in their appeal for Irish freedom:

33. Tumulty to John D. Crimmins, May 8, 1917, *Wilson MSS*.
34. John D. Moore to Joseph P. Tumulty, May 12, 1917, *ibid*.

We, the undersigned, who have been held in English prisons, and have been dragged from dungeon to dungeon, in heavy chains, cut off since Easter Week, 1916, from all intercourse with the outside world, have just had an opportunity of seeing the printed text of the message of the United States of America to the Provisional Government of Russia. We see that the President accepts as the aim of both countries the "carrying of the present struggle for the freedom of all peoples to a successful consummation." . . . "We are fighting," writes the President to the Government of Russia, "for the liberty, self-government and undictated development of all peoples. . . . Wrongs must first be righted and then adequate safeguards must be created to prevent their being committed again. Remedies must be found as well as statements of principle that will have a pleasing and sonorous sound." . . .

We trust that such remedies . . . will be held to include the right of each people . . . to defend itself against external aggression, external interference and external control. It is this particular right that we claim for the Irish people, and not content with statements of principle . . . we are engaged and mean to engage ourselves in the practical means for establishing this right.[35]

Dr. McCartan took this signed memorial to the United States, where he discussed with Joseph McGarrity and John Devoy the best procedure to follow relative to presenting it to the President. He also wished to have prepared a memorandum addressed to the President and to the Congress of the United States expressing the aspirations of the Irish people. After Devoy and McGarrity had assisted him in the writing of this memorandum, he journeyed to Westport, New York, to visit Judge Cohalan. After the Judge had made some further emendations in the phraseology of the memorandum, McCartan went back to New York City to have further conferences with John Devoy. As a result of this joint authorship the memorandum was uncompromising in its demand for Irish independence.[36]

On July 23, McCartan, flanked by James K. McGuire and John D. Moore, went to the White House and presented to Tumulty the memorial signed by the twenty-six members of Sinn Fein re-

35. *Wilson MSS.* This memorial was dated June 18, 1917.
36. Patrick McCartan, *With De Valera in America* (New York, 1932), pp. 8-14, 245-249.

cently released from prison and the memorandum which set forth in strong terms the aspirations of the Irish people. Tumulty referred these documents to Frank L. Polk, Counselor of the Department of State, who thought the "best thing to do would be to file the papers and not reply." [37] Tumulty followed this advice and for the time being the matter was closed.

But President Wilson realized that this Irish Question had many dangerous political implications. He felt that something should be done about extending Home Rule to Ireland. If this could be done in a manner that would not seriously affect British interests, it would remove an irritant that had long disturbed Anglo-American relations. On April 10, 1917, he sent the following instructions to Ambassador Page:

> Please convey to the Prime Minister in the most confidential manner the information that the only circumstance which seems now to stand in the way of an absolutely cordial co-operation with Great Britain by practically all Americans who are not influenced by ties of blood directly associating them with Germany is the failure so far to find a satisfactory method of self-government for Ireland. This appeared very strikingly in the recent debates in Congress upon the war resolution and appeared in the speeches of opponents of that resolution who were not themselves Irishmen or representatives of constituencies in which Irish voters were influential, notably several members from the South. If the people of the United States could feel that there was an early prospect of the establishment for Ireland of substantial self-government, a very great element of satisfaction and enthusiasm would be added to the co-operation now about to be organized between this country and Great Britain. Convey this information unofficially, of course, but as having no little significance. Successful action now would absolutely divorce our citizens of Irish birth and sympathy from the German sympathizers here with whom many of them have been inclined to make common cause.[38]

A week later Ambassador Page reported that he had invited the Prime Minister to his residence in order to have a confidential conversation concerning the President's instruction:

37. Frank L. Polk to Joseph P. Tumulty, August 8, 1917, *Wilson MSS.*
38. President Wilson to Secretary Lansing, April 10, 1917, 841D.00/103½ *MS.*, National Archives.

He instantly understood and showed that he already knew the facts that I presented and was glad that the President had instructed me to bring the subject up. He had had the American situation in mind during the whole discussion of Home Rule and he was doing his best. Then he asked me to request the President to give his views to Mr. Balfour as soon as possible after his arrival. Our country has no better English friend than Mr. Balfour and he belongs to the party that before the war opposed Home Rule. The enlistment of his influence would be a great help and the Prime Minister feels sure of a good result of a frank explanation to him by the President. I am, on my own account, without mentioning the President's instruction, expressing my private opinion to the same effect to other influential members of the Government.[39]

As a result of this Presidential pressure, Lloyd George wrote to John Redmond and outlined a plan to "introduce a Bill for the immediate application of the Home Rule Act to Ireland, but excluding therefrom the six counties of North-east Ulster, such exclusion to be subject to reconsideration by Parliament at the end of five years." If no agreement could be reached along these lines, he proposed the calling of a convention of Irishmen "of all parties for the purpose of producing a scheme of Irish self-government." Redmond replied on May 17 in a letter which rejected the proposed new scheme for Home Rule but which accepted the idea of a Convention "to devise a constitution for all Ireland." [40]

For the purpose of testing Irish-American opinion on this proposed convention in Dublin, Dr. J. M. A. Maloney, on May 24, 1917, initiated in the New York *Evening Post* a symposium of letters. On the following day Judge Cohalan expressed his opinion as follows:

There would be little difficulty in giving the answers evidently desired in the adroit questions of Dr. Maloney if the gathering to be called in Ireland were a convention actually representative of the people of Ireland, and if there were any honest intention on the part of England to meet the viewpoint of the people when expressed by such a

39. Ambassador Page to Secretary Lansing, April 18, 1917, London, 841D.00/106, *MSS.*, N.A.
40. Denis Gwynn, *John Redmond*, pp. 547-551.

gathering. The majority of the people of Ireland want independence.[41]

Judge John W. Goff had no faith in this proposed Lloyd George convention. It was merely a "proposal for a convention of government appointees . . . to meet in secret session under the presidency of a government-appointed chairman who would direct and control its procedure. That is not a convention either in the American sense or the true sense of the word."[42] Richard F. Dalton saw clearly through this scheme of Lloyd George: "I see a palpable effort of the present British Ministry to placate American public opinion and to square with our declaration of purpose in entering the war by ostensibly presenting to the Irish people an opportunity to settle their own affairs. . . . The aspirations and the purpose of the Irish in Ireland continues to be absolute independence."[43] Dr. Thomas Addis Emmet, Victor Herbert, and James K. McGuire signed a joint statement declaring that they regarded the proposal of a convention as an "insidious pretence, impracticable in its operation, and because of its lack of democratic honesty, foredoomed to failure."[44]

Redmond soon learned that these opinions of Cohalan, Goff, Dalton, and Victor Herbert were representative of the sentiments of most Irish-Americans concerning the proposed Dublin convention. In America there was a deep and widespread suspicion that the British Government was not inclined to be straightforward in its dealings with Ireland. The cruel and repressive policy which had been in force since the Easter Rebellion gave the lie to any pretensions of honesty. T. P. O'Connor, who had been sent to America by Redmond to collect funds for the Nationalist cause, was received coldly by Irish-Americans, and he complained that he had found his task quite difficult: "Feeling here about the executions and England was far more violent even than in Ireland. . . . I have no reason to doubt that the majority of clerical opinion

41. New York *Evening Post,* May 25, 1917.
42. *Ibid.,* May 25, 1917.
43. *Ibid.,* June 2, 1917.
44. *Ibid.,* May 25, 1917.

is either hostile to the War or not very enthusiastic. None of them has come to see me yet." [45]

In Ireland, Redmond faced further disappointments. Two by-elections became necessary through the deaths of Paddy O'Brien and Willie Redmond. Mr. de Valera was nominated by Sinn Fein to fill Willie Redmond's seat, and his election by an impressive majority was a heavy blow to the Nationalists. The leadership of Redmond received another sharp challenge in the election of Mr. Cosgrave in East Kilkenny. Cosgrave and De Valera had been heroes of the Easter Rebellion, and their elections meant that the tide of Sinn Fein was rapidly rising. It was also significant that the Lloyd George's proposed convention had been quickly repudiated by Sinn Fein. When the convention finally assembled on July 25, it was soon evident that the task of finding some path to conciliation and agreement was almost insuperable.[46] As the sessions of the convention dragged through long, weary weeks it took an invincible optimist to predict any worth-while results. Only a few Irishmen belonged in this class.

E. IRISH-AMERICANS DISCOVER THAT THE WILSON ADMINISTRATION COULD BE VERY VINDICTIVE

It came as a distinct shock to many of the leaders of the Friends of Irish Freedom to discover that the Wilson Administration sharply resented any agitation in America for Irish independence. Such agitation was regarded as evidence of a German plot to promote disunity between the Allies and thus sabotage the war effort. During the summer of 1917 the Executive Committee of the Friends prepared a petition calling for Irish independence. It was circulated throughout the United States and soon secured several hundred thousand signatures. It merely urged the President and the Congress to insist that the British Government grant to Ireland "complete national independence." The President responded by direct-

---

45. T. P. O'Connor to John Redmond, July 9, 1917, Denis Gwynn, *op. cit.*, pp. 563-564.
46. *Ibid.*, pp. 555-589.

ing agents of the Secret Service to call upon John D. Moore and other leaders of the Friends of Irish Freedom and submit them to a rigorous examination concerning the finances of the organization. Did German gold supply the funds that made it possible for the Friends to print and circulate the petition? Mrs. Hanna Sheehy-Skeffington, who was under contract with Mr. Moore to speak in many parts of the United States in support of the petition, found herself in great difficulties. She was bitterly denounced by important newspapers as a dangerous person who was endeavoring to stir up trouble for our British Ally. The British themselves resorted to the tactics they had used against Casement in Norway, and one attempt was made to kidnap her and spirit her across the Canadian border. Once on British soil, she could be given condign punishment.

But the Wilson Administration was after bigger game than Mrs. Sheehy-Skeffington. The outstanding leader of the Irish-Americans was Judge Daniel F. Cohalan, and every effort was made to discredit and ruin him. Secretary Lansing looked forward to this task with apparent pleasure. In his campaign against the German Government, while America was still a neutral, he had not hesitated to twist international law into strange forms that answered the demands of British propaganda. Professor Borchard has clearly demonstrated the fact that the first sharp note sent by the Department of State to Germany on February 10, 1915, was "founded on the false premise that the United States was privileged to speak not only for American vessels and their personnel, but also on behalf of American citizens on Allied and other vessels. No other neutral country appears to have fallen into this error." [47]

It is remarkable that Mr. Lansing could have made this mistake that led America straight down the road to war. He was well known as an authority in the field of international law and it is distinctly surprising that he proved to be so ignorant of principles that were familiar to the merest novice. There is a strong possibility,

47. Edwin M. Borchard and William P. Lage, *Neutrality for the United States* (New Haven, 1937), p. 183.

of course, that his anxiety to get America into the war caused him to write a note which he knew was based upon a "false premise."

Perhaps it was this same anxiety that pushed him down the road to mendacity. On January 18, 1916, in a well-known note on the status of armed merchant ships, he leaned towards the German viewpoint that such ships were really ships of war that could be sunk without any warning. Under pressure from Colonel House, he completely abandoned this logical position and finally condemned the viewpoint he once held. Then, in order to convince dubious senators and representatives of the soundness of his reversal of viewpoint, he prepared a memorandum which presented a false interpretation of the historic attitude of the Supreme Court towards armed merchant ships. Chief Justice Marshall had delivered an important opinion in the *Nereide* case, in which he stated that it was impossible for a prize court to distinguish between different degrees of armament. An armed merchant ship was a "ship of force" and should be so regarded. In Lansing's memorandum this important opinion of Justice Marshall was purposely garbled, and the version that he sent to members of Congress was "so false as to constitute practically a forgery." [48]

If Secretary Lansing would descend to forgery in order to confuse and mislead important senators and representatives, it is apparent that he would have few qualms about trying to crush Judge Cohalan by altering certain documents. The actions of the Judge were deeply disturbing to Britain, and therefore he should be silenced and discredited. Lansing thought he had some explosive revelations that would accomplish this purpose.

On April 18, 1916, United States Secret Service agents raided the offices of the German Consul General in New York City and confiscated the files of correspondence found there. Through some remarks made in letters from John Devoy to German authorities in Berlin, it was evident that a revolution was being planned in Ireland for Easter Sunday. These letters were at once turned over

---

48. *Hearings* on S. 3474, Committee on Foreign Relations, U. S. Senate, 74th Cong., 2 sess., January 10-February 5, 1936, p. 185.

to the British Embassy in Washington. No time was then lost in sending cables to London with the news of Casement's expected arrival in Ireland and of the shipment of German arms and ammunition to aid Irish revolutionaries. One of the documents alleged to have been seized in this raid upon the German Consulate was a message from Judge Cohalan to Berlin, April 18, 1916, concerning the extent of German assistance needed to make the revolution a success.

In September 1917 Secretary Lansing decided to have some of these documents published in the press. On September 23 the New York *World* and other newspapers broke the story of Cohalan's alleged collusion with German officials in Berlin. Several days before this story was published, the Judge had received an intimation as to what would happen. He talked the matter over with some intimate friends, and his version of the affair appeared on the same day that the story broke into print:

> In May, 1916, very shortly after the revolution in Ireland, I was warned by one who had the entree to the British Embassy, that the British authorities were determined, if possible, to destroy me as they would like to destroy every well-wisher of Ireland. I was later informed that about May 6, 1917, it was stated in the British Embassy in the presence of Shane Leslie, Lord Eustace Percy, Captain William J. Maloney and one or two others, that what they had in mind to do against me would prove to be a boomerang and injure their interests in this country.[49]

In a statement given to the press on July 9, 1921, Captain Maloney wrote in detail about the meeting in the British Embassy on May 3, 1917. He had gone to the Embassy to see an old friend, Lord Eustace Percy, and during the ensuing conference Shane Leslie, who was present, made some interesting remarks about evidence that could "silence Cohalan." It is very likely that Leslie's remark had reference to the data that had been seized in the office of the German Consulate in New York City. The lengthy letter that Captain Maloney gave to the press on July 9, 1921,

49. New York *World,* September 23, 1917.

is of a decidedly dubious nature. Depositions of Judge Cohalan and John Devoy, July 14, 1921,[50] and a personal letter to the author from Monsignor Patrick A. O'Leary, October 29, 1954, clearly demonstrate the falsity of many of Maloney's statements. It is probably true, however, that the British Embassy in May 1916 believed that the documents turned over to it by the Department of State would ruin Judge Cohalan. It should be remembered that the Judge did not sign any document that was sent to Berlin. The alleged document that connected his name with the proposed shipment of German arms to Ireland was in the third person, ostensibly quoting Cohalan. In a letter to the New York *World*, September 23, 1917, the Judge definitely denied that he had in any way inspired this message from New York to Berlin. It would have been very easy for Secretary Lansing to garble a document taken from the office of the German Consul General in the same way that he had garbled a famous decision of John Marshall in the *Nereide* case. If he had committed a "forgery" in one case it would have been very easy for him to repeat this dubious exercise.[51]

It had been Lansing's expectation that this exposure in the press on September 23 would ruin Judge Cohalan and lead to his removal from the New York Bench. This expectation was not only doomed to disappointment but the opponents of Cohalan were soon placed upon the defensive. Martin Coyne, President of Division I of the Ancient Order of Hibernians, W. P. Kilcawley, President of the Friends of Irish Freedom, and John J. Ryan, Chairman of the Irish National Committee, sent an open letter to the press, October 1, 1917, reciting the facts in Judge Cohalan's communication to the New York *World* on September 23. It made particular reference to the threats made against the Judge in the British Embassy in the presence of Captain Maloney, Lord Eustace Percy, and Shane Leslie:

50. *Cohalan MSS.*
51. The documents seized in the raid upon the office of the German Consul General in New York City were given official publication in the *Official Bulletin*, September 27, 1917, pp. 6-8.

You know and your readers know that the very first action taken by the representatives of the Associated Press as well as by the leading journals of New York, Washington and other cities throughout the country, all of which have correspondents in Washington, was to interview Lord Eustace Percy, Shane Leslie and Captain William J. Maloney for the purpose of ascertaining whether the scheme so specifically charged against the British Embassy actually was discussed in the Embassy in their presence on the date mentioned. Is there a leak in the British Embassy? Do the leaders of the Irish movement know what is going on within the British Ambassador's official residence? The charge made by Judge Cohalan is in detail. It leaves nothing to the imagination. . . . Why have not replies made to the press by the witnesses named been published? Each and every one of them would instantly have denied the charge were it not true.[52]

When newspaper reporters went to the British Embassy, they were given a cold brushoff. This action led John Devoy to make another attack upon the British Government. In the *Gaelic American* he published a facsimile of the original letter written by the British Minister at Christiania, Norway, in 1914 to Adler Christensen offering him £5,000 for the betrayal of Sir Roger Casement into British hands. He also published a copy of Casement's letter in which he told of the Minister's suggestion to Christensen to knock Casement "on the head" and thus put him out of the way. In his editorial comment upon these documents he savagely criticized the impudence of Anglophiles in America who were constantly repeating the refrain that "working for the independence of Ireland is Treason or disloyalty to the United States. . . . Every act they charge against Irishmen was committed, if at all, before America entered the war." [53]

The Wilson Administration responded to Devoy's remarks by publishing on October 10 some documents, dated January 1916, which were alleged to be copies of cables from Count Bernstorff to Berlin indicating, as men who would do sabotage work in the United States, Joseph McGarrity, John T. Keating, and Jeremiah O'Leary. Keating had died on June 24, 1915, some six months

---

52. *Cohalan MSS.*
53. *Gaelic American,* October 6, 1917.

before the date of these alleged cablegrams. Both McGarrity and O'Leary challenged Lansing to produce a scrap of evidence connecting them with any act of sabotage. But O'Leary was already in serious trouble with indictments against him for conspiring to obstruct recruiting and to commit treason. He was captured in his hiding place on the Pacific Coast and brought to New York for trial. When taken before Federal Judge Hand he pleaded not guilty but was remanded to the Tombs for trial. On October 8, 1917, his satirical periodical, *Bull*, was suppressed. Two weeks later, October 24, his trial began, but he was so ill with influenza that it had to be postponed. His account of the brutalities imposed upon him in the Tombs is revolting reading. When his trial was formally opened on January 27, 1919, it was evident that there was really no case against him. On March 23 the jury gave a verdict of not guilty on four of the five counts in the indictment, and disagreed by a vote of nine to three in favor of an acquittal on the fifth count. On March 29 O'Leary was released from the Tombs, and on May 25, at the Lexington Theatre in New York City, he was welcomed by thousands of Americans who were indignant over the rank injustice that had been inflicted upon him. The attempt of the Wilson Administration to blacken his reputation and to send him to jail for a long term had ended in a dramatic vindication that made him a hero. President Wilson and Secretary Lansing were doubtless quite happy that they were in distant Paris and therefore well insulated against the clamor of thousands of persons who felt that the Administration had outraged every article in the American creed of decency.[54]

While these attempts to ruin McGarrity and O'Leary were being pushed with ruthless vigor, a drive against John Devoy was also initiated. But Devoy could not be intimidated. In the *Gaelic American* he showed his contempt for the entire Wilson Administration. The following excerpt from one of his editorials is typical:

54. For a full discussion of every aspect of the trial of Jeremiah A. O'Leary, see his book, *My Political Trial and Experiences* (New York, 1919), pp. 159-468.

> We are not asking for immunity or special favors, but standing on our rights and demanding only justice. We make no promises and will continue to insist on Ireland's right to Independence as we have been doing all along. If the paper is to go down, it will be with its colors nailed to the mast., confident the Irish cause will eventually triumph whether the paper lives or dies.[55]

Although the drive against McGarrity, Devoy, and O'Leary failed, others were directed against any persons devoted to Irish independence. Patrick McCartan and Liam Mellows were the victims of a long and sustained attack. McCartan had arrived in New York City on July 1, 1917, as the "envoy of the Provisional Government of Ireland." Early in October 1917 he endeavored to arrange a passage to Russia, where he intended to press upon the Kerensky Government the cause of Ireland. He was to be accompanied by Liam Mellows. McCartan got as far as Halifax, where he was arrested and brought back to New York. Mellows never got started.

While in jail in New York City, McCartan was told that there was a possibility that the Wilson Administration would permit the British Government to conscript, for military service, Irish citizens who were resident in the United States. On February 17, 1918, he hurriedly addressed a letter to Secretary Lansing in which he strongly argued against conscription.[56] This letter was then given to the press which made a sensational story out of it. It was soon apparent that the administration had no intention of permitting Britain to carry on any conscription activities in the United States.

E. THE "IRISH QUESTION" GIVES PRESIDENT WILSON INCREASING CONCERN

It is obvious that British officials were very conscious of the explosive nature of the Irish Question as far as Anglo-American relations were concerned, and they watched with deep interest the reaction of President Wilson to pressure from Irish-Americans. On January 11, 1918, he granted an audience to Mrs. Sheehy-Skeffing-

---

55. November 17, 1917.
56. Patrick McCartan, *op. cit.*, pp. 252-258.

ton and listened carefully to her plea for the "recognition of an Irish Republic virtually in existence since April 1916." To her friends she disclosed the fact that when she reminded the President of his "Irish ancestry" he snapped back: "Scotch-Irish, Madam!"

On the same day he received a delegation of Irish-Americans headed by Senator Phelan, who made a strong plea for Irish independence. The President answered him in a very adroit manner. He would not snap at the bait of Irish independence, and Shane Leslie wrote to Joseph Tumulty to express his pleasure that the President had called Senator Phelan's attention to the fact that an Irish convention was at that time in session in Dublin considering the question of the best form of government for Ireland.[57] Leslie was confident that the President would be "the best representative Ireland can have at the Peace Conference."[58]

While President Wilson was trying to discuss the Irish Question upon a high level of diplomatic double-talk, Eamon de Valera made a speech on January 18, 1918, at the Mansion House, Dublin, which was distinctly provocative:

> We want Ireland to be set up as an Independent State with no closer bonds between us and England than there will be between it and America, or between it and Germany or between it and France. That ought to be clear enough for anybody. We say that if those who go about mouthing about self-determination do not take that interpretation of it, they are hypocrites, and we tell President Wilson, in view of the statements he has made, if he does not take that view of it, he is as big a hypocrite as Lloyd George.[59]

The President's name was being drawn more and more into this Irish Question. In the third week in January, Ambassador Page reported that telegrams to London newspapers from their Washing-

---

57. On February 7, 1918, Eamon de Valera wrote to McCartan in sharp criticism of the Dublin Convention: "The Lloyd George Convention was handpicked by the English Government, was by no means representative of Irish opinion, and was bound hand and foot by the terms of reference (excluding the only genuine solution—Separation), by the guarantee to Ulster and by the fact that any agreement . . . had to pass as an Act through . . . the English Parliament." *Devoy's Post Bag*, II, 522-523.
58. Shane Leslie to Joseph P. Tumulty, January 16, 1918, *Wilson MSS.*
59. *Freeman's Journal*, January 19, 1918.

ton correspondents had given the impression that President Wilson favored a plan whereby Congress would "vote a large sum of money to Ireland to help Home Rule cause." Although subsequent telegrams had disavowed this misinformation, Mr. Page was fearful that the "incident may not be so clearly understood in Ireland." The Lloyd George convention in Dublin was not making any substantial progress towards finding a solution of the problem of Irish government. Sir Horace Plunkett had confidentially informed Page that the biggest threat to the success of the convention lay in a possible "Sinn Fein effort to force a declaration in favor of secession from Great Britain and setting up an independent Republic. . . . There is a general feeling in political circles that if the Convention fails, a quick solution of the problem must be made in some other way." [60]

While the situation in Ireland grew more critical each day, Sir Frederick Smith (later Lord Birkenhead) paid a visit to the United States and made some very unfortunate remarks. In discussing the work of the Dublin convention, he made the following characteristic comment:

> It would be very inconvenient if anything should happen just now to overturn the attempt to bring about a settlement. In a few months, whatever happens, it won't amount to a damn. . . . Nothing ever gave me greater delight than the execution of Casement.[61]

These undiplomatic remarks were resented at the British Embassy, and Sir Frederick was induced to return to England at the end of January 1918. He had given great umbrage to Irish-Americans and had indicated that many Ulsterites had a definite contempt for the Dublin convention but wished it to continue its deliberations until England was ready for a showdown with Ireland. This showdown was precipitated by British insistence upon adopting a policy of conscription in Ireland.

60. Ambassador Page to Secretary Lansing, January 26, 1918, *MS.*, American Embassy Archives, 1918, 800/Ireland, N.A.
61. Boston *Post*, January 14, 1918.

On April 5, 1918, the Dublin convention finally adjourned after some fifty-one meetings. Fewer than half the members of the convention signed the main report, which proposed Home Rule with an Irish Parliament that would have no power over matters affecting the Crown, peace and war, Army and Navy, the customs and excise. It was a makeshift proposal that evoked little support, and it was widely realized that the convention had been a tragic failure. This fact aroused deep concern in many circles in Ireland and in America. John Quinn, a prominent Irish-American and an ardent supporter of the Allied cause, had gone on record in the late summer of 1917 in favor of the convention. He had expressed the view that it would find some compromise that would be agreeable to all factions in Ireland: "My prediction is that the convention will agree and that the country will ratify the verdict." [62] In May 1917, George W. Russell (A.E.), in a series of articles in the *Irish Times*, had warmly pleaded for a spirit of understanding among all the factions in the convention. The people in Ireland, "like the rest of the world must rise above ourselves and our differences if we are to manifest the genius which is in us and play a noble part in world history." [63] On June 25 Sir Horace Plunkett had delivered at Dundalk a strong defense of the convention and had tried to present a convincing argument in favor of an "all Ireland" support of its alleged objectives.[64]

But, despite all these pleadings and arguments, the convention had really been a flat failure, and on April 9 Lloyd George decided to press for immediate legislation authorizing military conscription in Ireland. His excuse for this pressure was the great German offensive along the Western Front in the spring of 1918. It is very likely that he would have been more hesitant about pushing this program if John Redmond, the Nationalist leader, had not died on March 6. He had always been embarrassed when Redmond had vehemently pointed out how England had repeatedly failed to

62. *The Irish Home-Rule Convention* (New York, 1917), p. 94.
63. *Ibid.*, p. 155.
64. *Ibid.*, pp. 172ff.

keep her promises to Ireland. There was no other Nationalist leader whose criticisms would cause the slightest pause in the Lloyd George drive for conscription.

In America, T. P. O'Connor, who was visiting San Francisco, grew greatly excited over the news of proposed conscription in Ireland. In a sharp telegram to President Wilson he tried to point out the baleful effects of such legislation: "Conscription will paralyze friends and encourage bitterest enemies in this country. This insane blunder would again render futile best efforts Irish leaders everywhere. . . . Your knowledge American opinion will suggest to you effect in this country." [65]

Maurice Francis Egan, former United States Minister to Denmark and an outstanding Irish-American, sent the President a brief note of protest. He had attended a meeting at the Catholic University of America at which were present three American cardinals and a "very representative group of bishops." The consensus was that conscription, if applied in Ireland, would awaken the most "terrible resistance." Moreover, "the effect on the Irish in this country will be bad." [66] The President at once replied that he realized the "critical significance" of the conscription issue and he wished "there were some proper way" in which he could help "to guide matters, but, so far, unfortunately, none has opened before me." [67]

T. P. O'Connor returned to the attack upon conscription in a letter to Senator Phelan. He feared that conscription could not be

> carried out without bloodshed and I feel certain that in the conflict between the Irish population and the English military forces that women and quite likely children will be killed as well as men. You will know better than I the effects such unfortunate results will have upon American opinion and morale. I am strongly of the opinion that it will dreadfully inflame the Irish race in America and Australia and have a profound effect upon the feelings of the English-speaking world. . . . I suggest having you consider appropriateness of laying these aspects of the case before the President in the hope that it will bring about in London a reversal of the plan for conscription.[68]

65. T. P. O'Connor to President Wilson, April 9, 1918, *Wilson MSS.*
66. Maurice Francis Egan to President Wilson, April 10, 1918, *ibid.*
67. President Wilson to Maurice Francis Egan, April 12, 1918, *ibid.*
68. T. P. O'Connor to Senator James D. Phelan, April 13, 1918, *ibid.*

Shane Leslie had much the same viewpoint, and he expressed to Mr. Tumulty the opinion that President Wilson was the only person who could effect any real solution of the Irish Question: "It is his due to command the Irish sentiment in the world." [69] On the following day he wrote another note to Tumulty to inform him that he had talked with the British Ambassador, Lord Reading, who had assured him that "Home Rule was certain and immediate, and that he had done his share from this side. 'The Prime Minister has given me his word,' he said. 'May I tell Mr. Tumulty that the Prime Minister will keep his word?' He nodded, a just and hard-pressed man, but fully realizing that the President alone can hold and wield the Irish sentiment in the world." [70]

T. P. O'Connor paid a special visit to Washington to discuss the situation with Lord Reading. He was firmly of the opinion that Ireland should "contribute her due proportion of the fighting forces of the Allies," but he thought that the actual raising of military forces in Ireland should be the task of an Irish, and not an English, Parliament. He was confident that the conscription legislation that was being pushed by Lloyd George could not be carried out even though Ireland were subjected to severe military pressures: "The most moderate and prudent leaders of public opinion in Ireland have always been the Bishops of the Catholic Church and the members of the legal profession. They have combined with the masses in pledging themselves to resist conscription." [71]

The most influential Irishman to write to President Wilson against conscription was Sir Horace Plunkett. He had spent a good deal of time in America and had, since 1913, been a regular correspondent with the President. As the presiding officer during the sessions of the recent Dublin convention, he knew the situation in Ireland far more intimately than the average leader, and both the President and Colonel House gave careful attention to his viewpoint. On April 29, in a letter to Colonel House, he endeavored to describe the Irish situation in realistic terms:

69. Shane Leslie to Joseph P. Tumulty, April 22, 1918, *ibid*.
70. Leslie to Tumulty, April 26, 1918, *ibid*.
71. T. P. O'Connor to Joseph P. Tumulty, April 26, 1918, *ibid*.

Ireland is quite justified in holding that immunity from conscription during the last two years was a recognition of her political grievances and that she had the strongest moral right to furnish her quota of manpower in her own way and through the instrumentality of her Government. . . . No one will appreciate more fully or clearly than you will the difficulty in which the Government are now placed. They have committed themselves to a policy which they ought to have known would have the most formidable opposition. Yet to withdraw from it would be a confession of weakness. . . .

The Irish people, more united than ever before, and incited by their Church to resist the British authority, are about to submit their grievance to the President. . . . Therefore he might think well of averting possible diplomatic and domestic embarrassment by expressing his opinion upon the issues raised in some appropriate manner. He might thus have an opportunity to relieve, if not save, an Irish situation far more dangerous than the British Government realize.[72]

In New York City, on May 4, a large meeting of Irish-Americans was held in Madison Square Garden which was addressed by Bourke Cockran, Congressman John J. Fitzgerald and Rev. A. A. Berle. Resolutions were adopted calling upon President Wilson and Congress "to use their influence to have this action [conscription] by the British Parliament reversed." [73]

While prominent Irish and Irish-Americans were exerting pressure upon President Wilson in favor of repeal of conscription, in Ireland the tide of sentiment against such a measure rose to dangerous heights. On April 18, in Dublin, a conference of representative men, convened by Lord Mayor O'Neill, assembled at the Mansion House. John Dillon, Joseph Devlin, Eamon de Valera, William O'Brien, T. M. Healy, and many other outstanding Irish leaders were present. An anticonscription pledge was presented to the meeting and at once adopted. It was uncompromising in its terms:

Denying the right of the British Government to enforce compulsory service in this country, we pledge ourselves solemnly to one another to

72. Sir Horace Plunkett to Colonel House, April 29, 1918, *House MSS.*, Yale University Library.
73. *New York Times*, May 5, 1918.

resist Conscription by the most effective means at our disposal. . . . The passing of the Conscription Bill by the British House of Commons must be regarded as a declaration of war on the Irish nation.[74]

On that same evening, the Catholic bishops, meeting at Maynooth, issued a manifesto that was just as sharp a challenge as the anti-conscription pledge adopted at the Mansion House:

> We consider that Conscription forced in this way upon Ireland is an oppressive and inhuman law which the Irish people have a right to resist by every means that are consonant with the law of God.[75]

It was apparent that events in Ireland would soon reach a critical stage. Some prominent officials in England were glad of this increasing tension. It would give the British Government an excuse for placing Ireland under a military administration so rigorous that armed resistance was almost inevitable. This resistance would be welcomed as an opportunity to shoot Irishmen. This fact was quite clear to a competent American observer, W. H. Buckler, who wrote to Colonel House the following revealing note:

> I have just had a talk with G. H. Fitzmaurice, of the Foreign Office, whose opinion is interesting as that of a man in close touch with official and Admiralty circles, yet personally, by race and religion in closest sympathy with Ireland. His extreme pessimism is based on his conviction that the authorities controlling the military and police in Ireland . . . have made up their minds to push matters to the limit. Their view . . . is that the bluff of the Irish must be called, and that if it be necessary to shoot a few hundred people the result will be worth it.[76]

If conscription had actually been attempted in Ireland, there would have been far more than a "few hundred people" killed. Public opinion had become so aroused over this senseless policy that serious civil war would have attended any determined government efforts to enforce it. Mr. Buckler was entirely correct in his

---

74. Dorothy Macardle, *The Irish Republic*, p. 250.
75. *Ibid.*, p. 251.
76. W. H. Buckler to Colonel House, May 10, 1918, *House MSS.*

estimate of the situation. His viewpoint was confirmed by a letter from Philip Harold-Berry, High Sheriff of the County of Cork, to the Prime Minister:

> I feel it my duty as High Sheriff of the County of Cork, to submit to you my convictions on the Conscription Crisis in this country. It is possible that you may think lightly of engineered agitation. The view of politicians and public men may not always be the real view of the people. . . . I have lived my life among the people, away from politics, my ancestors have been landlords and Unionists, my intimate friends are largely of the same class, but I do know the people in their homes, on their farms. . . . I assure you with all of the earnestness and solemnity that I can command, that whatever there may have been of bluff or demonstration in past agitations, there is now in the mind, not of the young men only, but of every man and woman of the land, outside a small class of Unionists, not any trace of bluff . . . but a fearfully quiet, earnest determination to die rather than accept Conscription from an English Parliament. Such unity as there now is, has never been known in Ireland. . . . But I would impress on you that never before have the Irish Bishops given countenance to such opposition as is now pledged.[77]

Ray Stannard Baker, who was very close to President Wilson, wrote a significant letter to Frank L. Polk, Counselor of the Department of State:

> I have just spent ten days in Ireland and have held long conversations with Dillon, Plunkett, Gwynn and Devlin in the South, with Sir George Clark and other leaders in Ulster and among many others, with the principal leaders of Labour and the Sinn Fein movement. . . . The leaders agree that the situation could hardly be more serious. . . . The Government has received a pressing appeal from British Labour "to avert the appalling disaster which now threatens our country and our national good name." The *Daily News* and other Liberal newspapers have expressed strong opposition to the Government, and the Manchester *Guardian* warns against the "murder of a nation." Never the less, the Government is supported by a large party of determined

---

[77]. Philip Harold-Berry to the Prime Minister, April 24, 1918, 800 I/113, *MSS.*, N.A. The opposition of the Catholic Bishops to conscription was strengthened by a statement of Cardinal Logue in which he urged the people of Ireland to try "by every legitimate means to save this country from the law of conscription." 800 I/55, N.A.

but unimaginative British public opinion convinced that Ireland must be compelled to do its duty in all justice.[78]

With Ireland on the verge of civil war, it suddenly occurred to some British statesmen to try the old smear tactics that had been so successful on previous occasions. These tactics could best be employed by charging that Irish leaders were engaged in a conspiracy with German agents to bring about Allied defeat. Evidence of a definitive nature would not have to be adduced to prove this charge, and the very fact that the charges were leveled against Irish leaders would afford sufficient grounds for their imprisonment without bail. Now that America had entered the war, it was obvious that the average American was most anxious to have the Allies gain a speedy and decisive victory. He would sharply resent any effort to sabotage the war effort. Smearing Irish leaders with the charge of treason would help to destroy the old bonds of friendship that had tied America so closely to Ireland, and it would afford President Wilson an excuse to refrain from pushing the claims of Ireland at the peace conference that would be held at the conclusion of hostilities. There is little doubt that he was anxious that some excuse should arise.

Some short-sighted Irish, with strong English inclinations, had a fixed idea that the President would welcome an opportunity to speak on behalf of Ireland with reference to Home Rule. By Home Rule they meant a certain political pattern approved by British politicians. Shane Leslie, attached to the British Embassy in Washington, was constantly calling upon the President to "command the Irish sentiment in the world." On June 12, 1918, he went so far as to say that Irishmen should place themselves "unconditionally at the service of the President. . . . He has the first right to the service of the Irish race all over the world." [79] Leslie had closed his eyes to the fact that President Wilson had no desire to be the spokesman for the Irish race "all over the world." He was determined not to embarrass the British Government by suggesting a

78. Ray Stannard Baker to Frank L. Polk, May 16, 1918, London Archives, 800 I/109, MSS., N.A.
79. Shane Leslie to Joseph P. Tumulty, June 12, 1918, Wilson MSS.

settlement of the Irish Question, and he did not appreciate Mr. Leslie's admonition to all Irishmen to place themselves "unconditionally at the service of the President." Some of his bold statements concerning the proper principles of international conduct had won wide approval among subject peoples, but he wished to sidestep any talk of their application to the condition of affairs in Ireland. He wished particularly not to be reminded of his address to Congress, February 11, 1918, with its sharply challenging sentences on national self-determination: "National aspirations must be respected; peoples may now be dominated and governed only by their own consent. 'Self-determination' is not a mere phrase. It is an imperative principle of action which statesmen will henceforth ignore at their peril."

These fiery phrases were verbal chickens that had come home to roost, and the President did not wish to have Shane Leslie serve as a chanticleer whose loud crowing would keep the world aware of their presence in the White House barnyard. He was glad, therefore, when charges were suddenly made that many Irish leaders were conspiring with German agents to bring about an Allied defeat. These charges were designed to act as a red herring that would shift American sentiment from sympathy with the plight of Ireland to sharp condemnation of Irish leaders. It was significant that United States Secret Service agents helped to create this red herring, whose noisome odor clung to the clothes of these agents and made them a stench in the nostrils of thousands of Americans.

8 CARDINAL O'CONNELL MAKES A FERVID PLEA FOR IRISH SELF-DETERMINATION

A. THE UNITED STATES SECRET SERVICE TRIES TO PIN A PLOT UPON SOME IRISH LEADERS

In dealing with the actions of the Wilson Administration, it should be kept clearly in mind that the President was usually quite willing to use his vast powers to prevent any possibility of the erection of an Irish Republic. Home Rule, upon conditions prescribed by the British Government, was as far as he was inclined to go. With regard to outstanding Irish-Americans, we have seen that he permitted Secretary Lansing to forge very dubious evidence in an attempt to encompass their ruin. Forgery soon became an accepted practice in certain branches of the government service.

In this regard, the agents of the United States Secret Service earned a questionable reputation. They were unceasing in their attempts to furnish evidence that would seriously compromise Irish-Americans and certain Irish patriots who kept alive their dream of an Irish Republic. In the autumn of 1917 Liam Mellows and Patrick McCartan, equipped with faked identification papers, had endeavored to leave the United States on a mission that they hoped would advance the cause of Irish independence. Mellows was arrested before he left New York City. McCartan was taken into custody in Halifax and shipped back to New York, where he and Mellows had to undergo a long inquisition by Secret Service agents. The methods and procedures of these agents were sharply criticized by John Devoy:

They [the Secret Service agents] manufactured a "confession" of Mellows which Mellows never made, put words in his mouth he never used and made him implicate certain men in the "plot" which does not exist. They began by describing Mellows as having been "deserted" by the men whom they described as being associated with him in the "plot"; said they had abandoned him to his fate, failed to procure bail for him, left him without counsel to defend him and acted as poltroons and cowards. They knew when they published this statement [*New York Times*, October 27, 1917] that a lawyer of ability was in daily conference with Mellows preparing his defence, seeing him sometimes several times a day, and doing everything for him that a lawyer could do. They wanted him released on bail so as to use him as a bait to entrap others, in the desperate hope that they could frame up a conspiracy case. . . .

His lawyer got the whole story from Mellows and he [Mellows] has given the lie direct to the infamous falsehood that he made a confession implicating Judge Cohalan, John Devoy and Jeremiah O'Leary in a 'plot' which he emphatically declares does not exist.[1]

When Diarmuid Lynch, a leader in the Easter Week rising, arrived in America in May 1918, he issued an explicit denial of any "plot" to begin another insurrection in Ireland.[2] He had been a member of the Supreme Council of the I.R.B. prior to the Easter Rebellion of 1916, and subsequently he became a member of the Executive of that Council and a member of the Executive Committee of Sinn Fein. If there had been any plot in America or in Ireland with reference to an insurrection, he would have known the whole story.

B. ENGLAND REGARDS THE GROWING STRENGTH OF SINN FEIN WITH INCREASING APPREHENSION

The British Government was delighted that agents of the United States Secret Service should take an important role in the dubious procedure of trying to pin upon Irish-Americans and Sinn Fein leaders a so-called "plot" to start an insurrection in Ireland. De

1. November 1, 1917, *Gaelic American*.
2. Diarmuid Lynch made his statement, concerning the alleged "plot" to start an insurrection in Ireland, during the course of an address at the Second Irish Race Convention, May 18-19, 1918.

Valera in Ireland was as much a thorn in the flesh as Judge Cohalan was in America. In July 1917 he had stood for election in Clare and surprised his opponents by an easy victory. A month later an election was held in Kilkenny city, and William Cosgrave, one of the heroes of the Easter Rebellion, was elected by an overwhelming vote. As a reprisal for this show of independence, police and military carried out a series of raids for arms which took them into even the homes of priests. It was not long before some eighty-four Republicans were placed in prison. Prisons under British administration had always been distinctly unhealthful for Irishmen of spirit, and it was not surprising that Thomas Ashe soon died from the far-from-tender ministrations of his jailers.[3] The reaction in Ireland to this exercise in brutality was so violent that it was apparent to the Lloyd George ministry that the situation was fast mounting to a crisis.

Resentment in Ireland had gone so deep and spread so far that membership in the Sinn Fein clubs grew rapidly and the I.R.B. was becoming every day a more important factor in the Irish equation.[4] Cathal Brugha and De Valera were not favorably impressed with the secret operations of the Brotherhood, and they endeavored to persuade Harry Boland and Austin Stack to withdraw from active membership. They refused to respond to this pressure and continued to hold positions of influence in the I.R.B. They were glad, however, to co-operate in calling together a large assembly of Sinn Fein to agree upon a new constitution and to elect a president.

The preamble to the new constitution was submitted to the convention (or Ard-fheis) on October 25, 1917, and the objectives outlined met with prompt approval:

> Sinn Fein aims at securing the international recognition of Ireland as an independent Irish Republic. Having achieved that status the Irish people may by Referendum freely choose their own form of Government.

3. Dorothy Macardle, *The Irish Republic*, pp. 227-229.
4. Piaras Beaslai, *Michael Collins and the Making of a New Ireland*, I, chap. viii.

The important question of leadership was settled by selecting De Valera as President of Sinn Fein. In his speech of acceptance he clearly indicated that the time had not arrived for choosing the final form of government for Ireland:

> This is not the time for this, for this reason, that the only banner under which our freedom can be won at the present time is the Republican banner. It is as an Irish Republic that we have a chance of getting international recognition. Some of us would wish, having got that recognition, to have a Republican form of government. Some might have fault to find with that and prefer other forms of government. . . . This is not the time for that; this is the time to get freedom. Then we can settle by the most democratic means what particular form of government we may have.[5]

The growing influence of De Valera was given additional confirmation on November 19, 1917, when the reorganized Irish Volunteers, at their third convention, elected him president. It was significant, however, that the influence of the I.R.B. in the Volunteers was strong enough to insure the choice of Michael Collins as Director of Organization, Diarmuid Lynch as Director of Communications, and Sean McGarry as General Secretary. Their role in the new organization would not be an inactive one.

As for De Valera himself, it was apparent that he felt it was his duty to speak out in stentorian tones about the progress of the republican movement in Ireland. To Lloyd George these statements had treasonable implications that could not be overlooked. On October 23, in the House of Commons, he alluded to the speeches of "the honourable Member for East Clare":

> They are not excited and so far as language is concerned they are not violent. They are plain, deliberate, and I might also say cold-blooded incitements to rebellion. . . . It is the case of a man of great ability, . . . deliberately going down to the district . . . to stir people up to rebellion against the authorities. . . . There is a great deal of talk among the Sinn Feiners which does not mean Home Rule. It does not mean self-government. It means complete separation . . . it means

---

5. Dorothy Macardle, *op. cit.*, p. 918.

secession. The words which are used are "sovereign independence." This country could not possibly accept that under any conditions.[6]

The ancient English prescription for handling any manifestation of Irish independence was coercion. The Lloyd George program made no deviation from this practice. In December 1917 the House of Commons enacted legislation that would pave the way for a redistribution of Parliamentary representation in Ireland. The new plan would assign Ulster Unionists seven or eight additional seats. Dillon denounced the measure as one that would throw the whole body of "Nationalists in Ireland into the Sinn Fein camp," and Redmond declared that the position of the Nationalists had been rendered completely "futile: We are never listened to."[7]

The progress of coercion soon began to gather momentum. On February 23, 1918, Sir Bryan Mahon, Commander-in-Chief of the British military forces in Ireland, issued an order prohibiting throughout Ireland the carrying of arms by unauthorized persons, and four days later Clare was proclaimed a military area. The climax was reached when conscription in Ireland was enacted by the House of Commons on April 16. The Irish responded by a nationwide pledge against conscription that was signed by Irishmen of all descriptions. On April 23 a general strike in Ireland paralyzed many activities, and it was obvious that dissatisfaction was reaching high tide. But Lloyd George went ahead despite these warning signals, and Field-Marshal Lord French, who had been appointed "His Majesty's Lord Lieutenant General and General Governor of Ireland," pointedly remarked to Lord Riddell that he would name a day "before which recruits must offer themselves in the various districts. If they do not come, we will fetch them."[8]

These preparations to enforce conscription were confirmed and extended by the appointment of the Right Honorable Edward Shortt as Chief Secretary and General Sir Frederick Shaw as the Commander-in-Chief of the British military forces in Ireland. It was

6. *Ibid.*, p. 236.
7. *Freeman's Journal,* December 5, 1917.
8. Lord G. A. R. Riddell, *Intimate Diary of the Peace Conference and After, 1918-1923* (London, 1933), p. 330.

evident that the Government was prepared to move ahead with scant regard for Irish opinion. In order, however, to assure British sympathies for this program of compulsion, it was suddenly announced that a "German plot" had been discovered. If Sinn Fein could be stigmatized by charges of treason, it might be possible to alienate from it a large part of American good will that had been so manifest since the outbreak of the Easter Rebellion. Such charges could also weaken any chance that an Irish delegation would have to present the case of Ireland at the peace conference that would follow the close of the war.

C. THE ALLEGED "GERMAN PLOT" OF MAY 1918

On April 12, 1918, the police rescued from an island near the coast of Galway a man who stated that he had survived the wreck of an American ship. This tale was soon proved to be fictitious and he was placed under arrest. When it was discovered that his name was Joseph Dowling, and that at one time he was a member of Casement's Irish Brigade, he was tried before a court-martial. It was learned that he had been put ashore from a German submarine and had mistaken the island for the Irish mainland. At his trial he made no statement and no evidence was adduced that proved the existence of any conspiracy between any Irishmen and the German Government. But British authorities loudly proclaimed that such a conspiracy had been disclosed in evidence which they kept secret. A portion of this evidence had been furnished from the files of the United States Secret Service.

On the night of May 17 a large number of leading Irish Nationalists were suddenly arrested. Seventy-three prisoners were quickly deported to England, where they were held for an indefinite time without charges or trial. Among them were Eamon de Valera, Arthur Griffith, Count Plunkett, W. T. Cosgrave, Darrell Figgis, Sean McGarry, Countess Marckievicz, Barney Mellowes, Pierce MacCan, George Nicholls, and Frank Lawless. The Government's explanation for this action was contained in the proclamation of Lord French, May 18. These Irish leaders had "conspired to enter into, and have entered into, treasonable communication with the German enemy." Drastic measures would be immediately taken to "crush the said conspiracy," and at the same time steps would be authorized to "encourage voluntary enlistment in Ireland." [9]

British newspapers, on May 20, went into great detail about the so-called "German plot." The account of the Dublin correspondent of the London *Times* was particularly graphic:

> Dublin opened its newspapers yesterday with a gasp of astonishment. It was not astonished, indeed, to learn that the Irish Government had discovered a German plot, but . . . at the boldness and firmness with which the Government acted on its discovery. . . . Not one in a hundred thousand of the Irish people knew anything about it until breakfast time. . . . Loyal and law-abiding men put down their newspapers with a sigh of profound relief.[10]

On the following day the *Times* reported that the main topic of conversation in Dublin was the "nature of the Government's proofs of the existence of a German plot." [11] The London *Daily Mail* had an editorial dealing with the same topic:

> It is clear that if the Government fail to convict a single one of the arrested persons of direct association with treasonable conspiracy, the accusation will be said to have failed miserably.[12]

There were no doubts in the minds of the editors of the London *Daily Telegraph*. The Irish leaders were guilty of treason, and inasmuch as the arrests had been made under the authority of the Defence of the Realm Act, they could be tried by court-martial and be given speedy punishment. Assurances were given to the readers of the *Telegraph* that "justification exists for the arrests . . . in the shape of astounding evidence." [13]

The London *Daily News* was not at all certain that the action of the Government had been wise and founded upon strict legality:

9. Beaslai, *op. cit.*, I, 188-191.
10. May 20, 1918.
11. May 21, 1918.
12. May 21, 1918.
13. May 24, 1918.

Action of so drastic a character taken on any less compelling ground would call for unsparing condemnation. For that reason it is of the first importance that the charge . . . should be formulated definitely and without delay, and a full and fair opportunity afforded them [the Irish prisoners] of making whatever defence they can make. In Ireland, no less than in England, accused prisoners are entitled to be considered innocent until their guilt is proved.[14]

Several days later the *News* expressed regret that no evidence against the Irish leaders had been produced:

It is now close on a week since the Government affected its coup in Ireland. . . . Meanwhile, the arrested persons have not been told what is the charge against them or what opportunity they will have of meeting it, or whether there is, in fact, any charge at all. . . . They [the Irish Government] may have abundant justification, but their delay in producing the necessary proof is unfortunate in the extreme.[15]

The *Westminster Gazette* agreed with the *News* that it was high time the Government gave to the public some of the evidence that led to the arrest of the Irish leaders:

It is impossible to find any man of any party who is not gravely disturbed by the Irish proceedings of the Government. . . . If a German plot has been discovered, and it has become necessary to arrest the Sinn Fein leaders, the arrests should have been accompanied by at least a *prima-facie* statement of the evidence against them. . . . We hope . . . the Government will stand firm against the suggestion of some Unionist papers that it is not necessary to produce any evidence.[16]

When the Government finally gave its alleged evidence of a German plot to the press, it was at once obvious that the public had been hoaxed. On May 25 the British newspapers printed this evidence in two parts.[17] The first part was a long and tiresome review of the relations between certain Irish revolutionaries and the

14. May 20, 1918.
15. May 24, 1918.
16. May 22, 1918.
17. The evidence against the Sinn Fein leaders was printed in full in the London *Daily Telegraph,* May 25, 1918, p. 7.

German Government leading up to the Easter Rebellion. It was not at all pertinent to an alleged German plot in 1918, and the fact that this stale, and in part forged, evidence was now exhumed as an exhibit against the imprisoned Irish leaders was really a confession of weakness. The second part of the Government's case against Irish patriots was so incredibly false that it carried conviction to no one who read it carefully. There was a lot of talk about plans to have munitions of war landed by German submarines at designated places along the Irish coast. This would make it possible for Irish revolutionaries to stage an insurrection when a German offensive reached its peak along the Western Front. The evidence then moved on to a direct lie about the activities of De Valera:

> According to documents found on his person, De Valera had worked out in great detail the constitution of his rebel army, and hoped to be able to muster half a million trained men. There is evidence that German munitions were actually shipped on submarines at Cuxhaven at the beginning of May. . . . It will be thus seen that negotiations between the executive of Sinn Fein organization and Germany have been virtually continuous for three and a half years. . . . In these circumstances no other course was open to the Government . . . but to intern the authors and abettors of this criminal intrigue.[18]

There was no attempt on the part of the Irish Government to publish any documents to sustain these grave charges of treason. None of the accused Irish leaders was ever tried in court or before a court-martial. The whole matter was such an obvious frameup that the Government did not dare to push charges that would have resulted in serious embarrassment. In England the press tried to support the Government as far as it could without being ridiculous. The London *Times* led in this fight against truth:

> Plain people here and in Ireland . . . will have no doubt that the statement issued by the Government today justifies beyond reasonable ground of cavil the arrest of the Sinn Fein leaders. Granted that it is not evidence of the guilty complicity in a German plot of any individual. Granted, too, that as the Government themselves point out, it is no more than an outline . . . [but] more than that cannot be made

18. London *Daily Telegraph*, May 25, 1918, p. 7.

public for . . . adequate reasons. We do not suppose that any patriotic person, here or in Ireland, will be disposed to question these grounds for reticence.[19]

The *Daily Telegraph* hysterically exclaimed that the scanty and dubious evidence given by the Irish Government to the press was sufficient "to justify the action of the British Government in appointing Lord French . . . and in striking off the heads of the traitorous Sinn Fein party at one blow." The *Daily News* regarded the matter in a far more serious vein. It was distinctly critical of the first portion of the Government's case against the Irish leaders. That was filled with old data that had long since lost its relevance:

> It is not merely irrelevant, but profoundly misleading, to recapitulate evidence of German intrigue in connection with the rebellion of April, 1916, as proof of Irish complicity in an alleged German plot in May 1918. The whole of this portion [part 1] of the Government statement is a singularly unfortunate confusion of the issue.

Part II of the evidence presented by the Government was as unconvincing as Part I. The data adduced against Bernstorff and Zimmermann with reference to plots in 1916 had little relation to events in the spring of 1918. The charges that the Government was trying to justify were not

> against Herr Zimmermann, or Count Bernstorff . . . but against Count Plunkett and De Valera and Countess Marckievicz and their fellow prisoners. Evidence much more specific than mere proof of German and German-American machinations are needed if the Government's recent action is to be vindicated. Is that evidence forthcoming? So far as the present document is concerned it is clearly not. . . . The single specific allegation . . . is the statement that, according to documents found on his person, De Valera had worked out in great detail the constitution of his rebel army. . . . There is a suggestion there of the existence of evidence of real importance. If such evidence cannot be made public, the least that can be demanded is that it should be examined by competent and impartial judges in whose findings the public would have implicit confidence. No plea of secrecy will avail against that suggestion.[20]

19. May 25, 1918.
20. London *Daily News,* May 25, 1918.

It is significant that most of the American press did not harbor the doubts so clearly expressed by the London *Daily News*. The Government's cheap stratagem of smearing the Irish leaders and thus destroying American sympathy for the cause of Irish independence had worked to perfection. Charges of treason are not easily forgotten, even though unproved, and Lloyd George hoped that any Irish pleas for independence that would be presented to the Peace Conference at the end of the war would receive scant support from President Wilson and the American public. As far as President Wilson was concerned, his hopes were completely justified.

As soon as the Government's charges of treason were presented against the Irish leaders, the American press voiced a sharp hostility against Sinn Fein and against any attempts adversely to affect the British war effort. Most American newspapers did not wait for the publication of the dubious evidence that the Irish Government made available on May 25. When the Irish leaders were arrested on May 17 it was generally assumed in America that they were guilty of some serious crime, and the action of the Government was strongly defended. In this regard the comments of the Chicago *Tribune* were typical:

> A Washington dispatch seems to confirm the British allegation that Germany, by making use of radical Irishmen in the United States, has been fomenting a plot to overthrow the British Empire. Our quarrel with Sinn Fein is that its votaries are doing everything in their power to bring about a collapse . . . [of Great Britain]. They cannot look to America for sympathy and assistance and needlessly sacrifice American lives.[21]

Frank H. Simonds, in the Atlanta *Constitution*, was certain that an Irish rebellion in 1918 would mean that

> there will be lost for Ireland now, and perhaps forever, all the sympathy and all the support which have been so real in the last half century. As far as America is concerned, future sympathy for Ireland must be predicated on Irish participation in the great war, and participation

21. May 22, 1918.

on the Allied side. Not in many years can Irishmen hope for American support.[22]

The Detroit *Free Press* was unsparing in its denunciation of Sinn Fein and the alleged German plot:

> Sinn Fein would have turned the world over to Berlin [by U-boat bases] if it could. It has succeeded in destroying its own influence with the great mass of the Irish people, who, as the words uttered by Mr. Dillon indicate, have welcomed the true significance of these Celtic Bolsheviki.[23]

The St. Louis *Globe-Democrat*, while it expressed "deep sympathy" for the plight of Ireland, had no use for "the Sinn Feiners. . . . We cannot look even with complacency upon an organization that seeks to take advantage of the world's peril to attain ends that are essentially selfish, however laudable they may be in principle." [24]

The very dubious evidence published by the Irish Government on May 25 seemed to strike an authentic note to many American ears. Even though De Valera had vehemently denied the existence of any German plot, most American newspapers regarded his conduct as distinctly suspicious. *The New York Times* was hysterical in its indictment of Sinn Fein leaders: "Few Americans of whatever descent . . . are not weary of and disgusted with Sinn Fein folly or madness." [25] The Philadelphia *Public Ledger* thought it was not unreasonable for the Irish Government to refuse to publish convincing evidence of the treason of Irish leaders: "It is obvious that at such a time as this the arrests would not have been made without ample evidence, and there are many good reasons for withholding it for the present." [26] The Rochester *Democrat and Chronicle* was tired of having people try to cast doubt upon the authenticity of the evidence presented by the Irish Government against Sinn Fein leaders: "Broad intimations of members of the

22. May 23, 1918.
23. May 23, 1918.
24. May 24, 1918.
25. May 28, 1918.
26. May 27, 1918.

Sinn Fein, or at least of their sympathizers, that the British Government fabricated the evidence of treason on which some of its leaders have been arrested, leave a bad taste in the mouth."[27] But *America*, the Jesuit weekly, entertained deep suspicions about this same evidence: "Up to this date (June 8), as far as can be learned from authentic sources, the British Government has not made public any evidence of a German plot in Ireland."[28]

While most of the American press accepted without serious question the fabrication of the Irish Government concerning the German plot, the American consul at Queenstown, C. M. Hathaway, caught the spirit of truth that was enshrined in Irish hearts. In a letter to Ambassador Page he discussed at length the reaction in Ireland with reference to the charges that had been leveled against the leaders of Sinn Fein:

> The Government's charge of a German plot and its arrests of Sinn Fein leaders in that connection is presumably a conspiracy to vilify Ireland and discredit the Irish cause abroad so as to relieve the British Government of the handicap of foreign sympathy (and particularly American sympathy) with Ireland's lack of freedom of self-determination. If anybody is guilty, as of course it is not impossible that a *few may be,* that man is in the wrong. This is however, so unlikely, and it is so probable that this is merely a piece of Government chicanery, that Irish sympathy remains too largely with the arrested men to warrant the Irish [Nationalist] Party's taking a decided stand against any who may be found guilty.[29]

The suspicions felt in Ireland relative to these charges of a German plot were also commented upon in a despatch from the American Embassy in London to the Secretary of State:

> The Government in its treatment of Sinn Fein leaders has not yet shown its hand clearly. Very little real evidence, if any, has been published and public opinion is becoming rather restive both here [London] and in Ireland. There is a general feeling that although the

27. May 26, 1918.
28. June 8, 1918.
29. C. M. Hathaway to Ambassador Walter H. Page, May 23, 1918, 800 I/138, *MS.*, National Archives.

Government's intentions are right, the evidence is not yet of such a character to justify its action if carefully investigated and subjected to the probable controversy following on full publicity. . . . The press . . . challenges the Government to prove the guilt of any of the suspects and they recall past examples of double dealing on the part of the British in an effort to show that the whole affair has been based upon the weakest sort of evidence in order to injure the cause of Ireland and interfere with the opposition to conscription.[30]

In *The New York Times*, May 26, a despatch from Washington made the following comment:

More evidence than that disclosed in the British Press Bureau's charges of the close connection between the Irish Sinn Fein and German influence is in the hands of the British and American Governments, according to an official statement made here [Washington] today.[31]

This "official statement" made in Washington to the effect that the American Government had important evidence against the Sinn Fein leaders led some Irish Nationalist leaders like T. P. O'Connor and Richard Hazleton to prepare a memorandum which they requested Senator Phelan to hand to Secretary Lansing.[32] If the American Government really had this evidence, the time had arrived when it should be made public:

The situation is in urgent need of being cleared up. If valuable time is allowed to pass, the effect of the damaging disclosures, if the materials for such are in the hands of the authorities, will be considerably lessened. If the American authorities have really important evidence in their possession, its immediate production would do more than anything else to influence public opinion in Ireland, for the charge of a "frame-up," which is believed in Ireland against the British authorities, would not be entertained against the American authorities. Either too little or too much has been said already on behalf of the American authorities—too little if important evidence of German-Irish plotting of a serious nature is in their possession, and too much if no important

---

30. American Embassy to the Secretary of State, May 28, 1918, 800 I/143a, MS., N.A.
31. *New York Times,* May 26, 1918.
32. Secretary Lansing to President Wilson, May 29, 1918, 841D.00/9a, MSS., N.A.

evidence exists. The arm of the Constitutional Party in Ireland is being paralyzed and that is not a situation which the American authorities can intend or desire.[33]

The President, of course, could not produce evidence which did not exist. He had stooped very low in his drive against the Sinn Fein leaders and against some important Irish-American leaders like Judge Cohalan. In 1916 the Department of State had forged evidence against Cohalan, and in 1918 Secret Service agents had fabricated confessions that had been vehemently repudiated by Liam Mellows and Patrick McCartan. Secretary Lansing could not tell T. P. O'Connor the real truth about the policy of the American Government, and it must have made both the President and Lansing very embarrassed to see how Irish Nationalist leaders regarded with deep suspicion the attitude of the Department of State.

In 1916 the American Government had taken the initiative in raiding the German Consulate in New York City and seizing documents that were quickly sent to London. In 1917 the Department of State had published some of these documents. In 1918 the British Government had taken the initiative and had secured some documents which they hoped the Department of State would publish and thus prevent charges of British bias being leveled against them. If the British Government had to publish these documents at once, would the Department of State assume responsibility for their production?

The attitude of the British Foreign Office is clearly revealed in the following notes that passed between Wilson, Lansing, and Ambassador Page. On May 10, 1918, Page wrote to Lansing that he had received from Admiral Hall copies of documents purporting to show a Sinn Fein conspiracy in Ireland:

> The Prime Minister who knows of the existence of the information but does not know its form, now wishes it to be made public in the interests of the Allied cause and consequently this will be done at an early date. In order to give the appearance of consistency in respect

33. Memorandum prepared by T. P. O'Connor and Richard Hazleton and handed to Secretary Lansing. *Wilson MSS.*, Library of Congress.

of previous disclosures of German telegrams, all of which have been made by our Government, Hall would, in communicating the documents to higher authority for publication, have to intimate that after interchanging information with the American Secret Service for a period of over a year, he is now in a position to decipher German messages himself. He greatly regrets that owing to superior orders he may be obliged to publish before copies of documents reach the President, which will not be for another week, but if he can hold back publication until after that date, he will do so in order that the President may, if he desires, make the contents public himself, or authorize their publication as coming from our authorities. Please acquaint me with the President's views . . . at the earliest possible moment.[34]

On May 18, Leland Harrison, Counselor of the Department of State, sent to Secretary Lansing the Sinn Fein documents:

Attached are the thirty-two documents which the British Government request you give out to the Press immediately. . . . If you are not prepared to do this, they then desire to publish them themselves. . . . It is presumed that the British Government desire to publish these documents in view of the natural inference to be drawn from the information contained in the last numbered documents that the Irish have continued their communications with Germany and have probably completed a plan for a second uprising, particularly in case the British should enforce conscription in Ireland. . . . In connection with the question of publication may I point out that in order to preserve as far as possible the fiction that the working out of German codes has been done by us, it would be desirable for the Department to give out this information.[35]

Secretary Lansing had many misgivings about the publication of these Sinn Fein documents by the Department of State. In a letter to President Wilson he remarked:

The enclosed papers are translations of decoded German messages relating to the Sinn Feiners' intercourse with the German Government through Sinn Fein agents in this country prior and subsequent to the rebellious outbreak at Dublin at Eastertime in 1916. These arrived

34. Ambassador Page to Secretary Lansing, May 10, 1918, 841.00/78, *MSS.*, N.A.
35. Leland Harrison to Secretary Lansing, May 18, 1918, Department of State, Office of the Counsellor, Record Group 59, N.A.

from London on Friday after you had departed for New York. Before these documents had reached us we had been importuned by the British Government, through Ambassador Page, to make them public. I assume that they are anxious to have this done so that they can employ them as evidence against the conspirators now operating in Ireland, some of whom have already been arrested. . . . By employing copies obtained from this Government the British Government would not be subject to embarrassing questions as to the authenticity of the documents and the nature of the German code. Our certification would be sufficient. . . .

My impression is . . . that it would be impolitic at the present time for us to assume the responsibility for the publication of these papers. The Irish situation is very delicate and anything which we might do to aid either side in the controversy would, I fear, involve us in all sorts of difficulties with the Irish in this country. . . . Publishing these papers at this time would be construed as a direct assistance to Great Britain in the matter of conscription in Ireland.[36]

President Wilson agreed with Secretary Lansing that American publication of the Sinn Fein documents would be impolitic:

I do not think that the British Government ought to use us to facilitate their fight for conscription in Ireland. I believe that the difficulties that would be created for them as well as for us by the publication in this country, by official release, would be greater than any of the alleged advantages; and I hope that you will reply to Page in that sense.[37]

The refusal of President Wilson to publish the Sinn Fein documents in the United States and thus assume responsibility for their authenticity created many difficulties for the British Government. In Ireland the suspicions concerning these data were widespread and deep. On June 12, Irwin B. Laughlin, in a letter to Secretary Lansing, said that the British Government had dropped "all discussion" of the alleged plot:

The general impression seems to be that the Irish policy followed by the Government has been a fiasco. The British Government's failure in handling the present situation is probably surpassed by the quandary the Irish Parliamentary Party find themselves in, as they have now

36. Secretary Lansing to President Wilson, May 19, 1918, *ibid.*
37. Wilson to Lansing, May 20, 1918, *ibid.*

completely placed themselves into the hands of the Sinn Fein by deserting their posts at Westminster.[38]

For centuries the only formula the British Government had ever used in treating manifestations of unrest in Ireland was stern compulsion. Under Lloyd George the same formula was rigorously applied. In the summer of 1918 civil liberties in Ireland ceased to exist. Not only were public meetings and assemblies forbidden, but even sports and athletic events were officially banned. When word of this repressive regime reached the ears of Senator Phelan, he requested President Wilson to make some brief statement of "Ireland's right to autonomous government (without necessarily defining the kind) and the prompt granting of it." [39] The President replied:

> I realize, of course, the critical importance of the whole Irish question, but I do not think that it would be wise for me in any public utterance to attempt to outline a policy for the British Government with regard to Ireland. It is a matter . . . of the utmost delicacy, and I must frankly say that I would not know how to handle it without risking very uncomfortable confusions of counsel.[40]

On July 4, at Mount Vernon, the President did stress the importance of self-determination for previously subject peoples, and many people in Ireland hoped that his words of bright promise might have some meaning for them:

> These are the ends for which the associated peoples of the world are fighting and which must be conceded them before there can be peace:
> I. The destruction of every arbitrary power anywhere that can separately, secretly, and of its single choice disturb the peace of the world. . . .
> II. The settlement of every question, whether of territory, of sovereignty, or economic arrangement, or of political relationship, upon the basis of free acceptance of that settlement by the people immediately

38. Irwin B. Laughlin to the Department of State, June 12, 1918, 800 I/162a, *MS.*, N.A.
39. Senator James D. Phelan to President Wilson, June 29, 1918, *Wilson MSS.*, Library of Congress.
40. President Wilson to Senator J. D. Phelan, July 1, 1918, *ibid.*

concerned and not upon the basis of the material interest or advantage of any other nation or people which may desire a different settlement for the sake of its own exterior influence or mastery.[41]

In September 1918 the British Government made a tragic joke of these high-sounding words by sentencing ninety-six Sinn Feiners to terms of imprisonment by courts-martial and civil courts. It was significant that none of these members of Sinn Fein were sentenced on the basis of any evidence produced by the British or American Governments relative to the alleged Irish-German plot of May 1918. That evidence was too questionable to bring before a court. But it was not difficult to find some ground upon which to build a case against Irish patriots, and they had small chance to escape British vengeance. Michael Collins continued to elude the watchful eyes of the British police, but he was a notable exception that proved the rigor of English rule. It was evident to most Irishmen that they were regarded by the British, and by some important American officials, as an inferior people that had few rights and no privileges. The American consul at Queenstown presented the matter to the American Embassy in his usual pithy manner:

> The naked skeleton of the Irish situation . . . seems to be that the native Irish race, comprising three-quarters of the population of this island, are held against their will in subjection by an alien race. While this condition continues, no settlement appears to be possible. . . . England must either grant full Home Rule or govern by force with no pretence to other right than that of the conqueror. . . . The situation with regard to the German plot charge by the Government has not changed except that the Irish attitude of scoffing incredulity has merely strengthened with the passage of three months without the production of anything they regard as proof, and indeed even an outsider is somewhat puzzled to understand just why such definite charges of German activities should have been produced and so little heard of them afterward.[42]

In America the false evidence of an Irish-German plot was used to bring in indictments against Jeremiah O'Leary and other Irish-

---

41. *The Messages and Papers of Woodrow Wilson* (New York, 1924), I, 500.
42. Charles M. Hathaway to Irwin B. Laughlin, American Embassy in London, September 12, 1918, 800 I/214, *MS.*, N.A.

Americans. Many persons believed that these indictments were merely the prelude to an open attack upon John Devoy and Judge Cohalan. Neither the Judge nor Devoy was intimidated by the tactics of the Wilson Administration. Their defiance of these worst aspects of Wilsonism was voiced in a typical editorial written by John Devoy:

> The *Evening Sun* of Saturday last reported that John Devoy would probably be indicted for this [Irish-German] "conspiracy." The statement was probably intended to frighten Devoy into running away, but he will not run away. He will stand his ground and fight this infamous Anglo-American conspiracy against Irish liberty, in court or out of it, wherever the fight may be brought, as long as there is breath left in him. And he has unshaken confidence that the fight for Irish freedom will be eventually won, no matter how many hard knocks he and others may be obliged to take, even to the forfeiture of life itself. And it will be won by the help of the American people, whose hearts are always true, no matter how grievously their judgment may for a time be warped by falsehood concocted for the purpose of deceiving them.[43]

While agents of the Wilson Administration were seeking some means to silence Devoy and Judge Cohalan, they had succeeded merely in stimulating Irish-American leaders to even greater exertions for the cause of Irish independence. On March 24, 1918, the Executive Committee of the Friends of Irish Freedom decided to hold another Irish Race Convention. It was scheduled to meet in the Central Opera House in New York City on May 18-19, with John Jerome Rooney acting as Temporary Chairman.

D. THE SECOND IRISH RACE CONVENTION, MAY 18-19, 1918

The Second Irish Race Convention that met in the Central Opera House in New York City, May 18-19, was an impressive gathering of brave spirits who were not intimidated by the dubious policy of the Wilson Administration towards Irish-Americans who dared to dream of Irish independence. Arrests in Ireland for participation in

43. *Cohalan MSS.*

an alleged German plot were in full swing, and in some American newspapers there were some very sarcastic references to the "Sinn Fein Convention" that was meeting in New York City.

After the convention had been organized, Justice Goff presented a resolution which called for "the application to Ireland now of President Wilson's noble declaration of the right of every people to self-rule and self-determination." President Wilson was requested to "exert every legitimate and friendly influence in favor of self-determination for the people of Ireland." The following day John A. Murphy presented another resolution which was immediately adopted:

> In this present crisis of our Race we solemnly affirm that in all things consistent with our loyalty as American citizens we will stand with and for our Race in Ireland in their struggle against the threatened extermination of the Race that now confronts them. We affirm that the present reign of terror attempted to be imposed on Ireland by the arrest . . . of more than five hundred of the Irish leaders, is an added outrage on the rights of a people, and will not find place or sympathy among the liberty-loving people of America.[44]

Inasmuch as the convention had been called by the Friends of Irish Freedom, it was necessary to proceed to the election of officers of that body. After some discussion the Very Reverend Peter E. Magennis, O.C.C., of New York City, was elected National President and Diarmuid Lynch, a recent refugee from Ireland, the National Secretary. It was during the sessions of this convention that Lynch made an address which clearly demonstrated that the leaders of Sinn Fein had no connection of any kind with a German plot. The New York press was careful to avoid any mention of this address. The *Sun* and the *Evening Post* had brief references to the convention and Liam Mellows was quoted as denouncing the charges of a German plot as "false as Hell!" John Devoy was also quoted as declaring that the "Sinn Fein arrests were based upon a frameup."[45]

44. *Gaelic American,* May 20, 1918.
45. New York *Evening Post,* May 20, 1918; New York *Sun,* May 19, 20, 1918.

Judge Cohalan closed the sessions of the convention with an address that emphasized the "Americanism of the Irish Race in America." He indicated the effective use the British Government made of propaganda, and pointed out the necessity of acquainting the American people with the facts concerning British misrule in Ireland:

> If you leave to the enemies of Ireland the supplying of the information by which American public opinion is to be convinced, you will have nobody but yourselves to blame, if, upon the misinformation which may be furnished, the case goes against you in that matter.[46]

There was a great deal of "misinformation" concerning the Irish in many circles in Washington, and this was especially true of the White House. At the close of the Irish Race Convention it had been decided that the plea for the application of the principle of self-determination to Ireland should be handed personally to President Wilson by a committee headed by Judge Goff. Later it arranged that the Very Reverend Peter E. Magennis, National President of the Friends of Irish Freedom, and Reverend Thomas J. Hurton, one of the National Vice Presidents, should take the plea to the President. Before they could take the trip to Washington, a letter reached the White House signed by Marguerite Maginnis. She was just

> a heart-broken young girl writing to the greatest man in the world today. . . . Ah, Mr. Wilson, your speeches have thrilled me as they have thrilled the world. Please won't you do something for my people, the Irish? The papers would make out that to be anti-British is to be un-American and therefore pro-German. . . . You are bigger than newspapers so I write to you.
> I don't believe there is any German plot. It would seem that the 1916 evidence is to be revived. 1916? That was before America entered the war. . . . My America demands an open and hasty trial for the Sinn Fein prisoners. . . . You can do something. . . . England would not dare to refuse you any request you may make.[47]

46. *Cohalan MSS.*
47. Marguerite Maginnis to President Wilson, May 21, 1918, *Wilson MSS.*, Library of Congress.

As soon as the President read this letter he wrote a hasty note to Tumulty: "Here is a letter which it seems to me dangerous for me to answer. You have a true instinct in such matters. How would you advise that I handle it?"

Tumulty, despite his Irish background and the advantage of his position as secretary to the President, did very little for the cause of Ireland. As soon as he received the President's brief note he penned a characteristic reply:

> At the Sinn Fein meeting held in New York this week at which speeches of the most seditious character were made, one of the orators of the evening was a man named Maginnis. I would not be surprised if this girl were in some way related to this individual. I suspect that the hand of some able Sinn Feiner is back of this letter and that an attempt is being made to draw you out. I do not think you ought to recognize it in any way or that you should personally acknowledge it and to say that it will be brought to your attention at the earliest possible moment.[48]

On May 24 the delegation from the Irish Race Convention called at the White House and requested an audience with the President. They were given a quick brushoff by Tumulty, who explained his action to the President:

> A committee headed by Rev. T. J. Hurton called at the Executive Office and asked for an appointment with you. They represent the Sinn Fein element that had a convention in New York recently and wish to present a memorial in that matter. It seems to me that it would not be wise for you to receive them or even to receive the memorial.[49]

It was later decided that Tumulty could receive the memorial pleading for self-determination for Ireland. He was also successful in blocking the attempt of Mrs. Mary F. McWhorter to present to the President an appeal from Irish-American mothers who had sons in the armed services. This memorial also was a plea to extend to Ireland the principle of self-determination:

48. Joseph P. Tumulty to President Wilson, May 23, 1918, *Wilson MSS.*
49. Tumulty to Wilson, May 24, 1918, *ibid.*

These mothers have cheerfully given their boys for the sacred cause of American freedom, as well as the cause of the oppressed races of the earth, and they are positive that even though you have never mentioned Ireland in your public declarations on behalf of these oppressed races, nevertheless they can depend on you to see that no injustice is done to Ireland at the Peace Conference because she happens to be held in bondage by one of our co-belligerents. . . . Many of these mothers feel that if they could get an interview with you, Mr. President, and in that interview present Ireland's case in the name of their boys for your consideration, that you would take up the cause of the Irish people in Ireland and see that they also are included among the peoples for whom you so nobly advocate the right of self-determination.[50]

Needless to say, this memorial from the Irish-American mothers with sons in the American armed services was not presented to President Wilson by Mrs. McWhorter. On July 18 she was received by Tumulty at the executive offices in the White House and the memorial was placed in a convenient pigeonhole. Scant regard was paid to memorials that emphasized the importance of self-determination for the people of Ireland.[51]

E. CARDINAL O'CONNELL MAKES AN IMPASSIONED PLEA FOR SELF-DETERMINATION FOR IRELAND

The British Government clearly realized the strength of the feeling in the United States in favor of self-determination for Ireland. With the help of the Wilson Administration, it had pretended to discover

50. *Cohalan MSS.*
51. It is interesting to note that in his memorandum addressed to the President, May 23, 1918, Tumulty characterized the speeches made at the Second Irish Race Convention as "most seditious." Apparently, any plea for Irish self-determination was seditious. He is, of course, quite incorrect in his remark that "one of the orators" at the convention was "a man named Maginnis." The Very Reverend Peter E. Magennis, O.C.C., was elected National President of the Friends of Irish Freedom, but he was unable to attend any of the sessions of the convention. The volume by Patrick McCartan, *With De Valera in America*, p. 46, makes the mistake of citing Father Magennis as one of the speakers. This is merely a minor error in a book that is noted for its venom and unreliability. (It might be noted that Father Magennis held the rank of Very Reverend by virtue of the fact that he was the General of the Carmelites.)

evidence of a German plot that involved a large number of the leaders of Sinn Fein. When this scheme backfired, it was thought expedient to enlist the assistance of the English Catholic clergy in an effort to convince American clerics that the British Government had friendly feelings for Ireland. The stubbornness and intractable nature of the Irish people made it difficult for Lloyd George to show his beneficent disposition.

In October 1918 the Right Reverend Frederick W. Keating, Bishop of Northampton, England, paid a sudden visit to America, and upon his arrival in New York City he immediately began his campaign of propaganda. As his secretary he enlisted the service of Shane Leslie, who was an unofficial agent of the British Government in the United States. Leslie had many American connections, and his pleasing personality and fluent pen made him a very valuable contact man for Bishop Keating. He was familiar with every aspect of British propaganda in the United States, and it was not surprising that as soon as the Bishop arrived in America he promptly began to lecture Americans on the real truth about Home Rule in Ireland:

> The Home Rule question is not the fault of England, but of Ireland. If Ireland can only agree upon an acceptable form of Government, England will not only willingly, but gladly grant it. The trouble is that what suits one faction will not suit the other, and each wishes to impose its ideas upon the others. The result is the turmoil which has been brought about and which has been the cause of much distress. . . . But my prime reason in making this tour is to try to establish a uniformity of policy among the English-speaking Catholics . . . that the reconstruction of the war-shattered world shall be conducted with the Christian thought uppermost, and without thought of giving sole consideration to reasons of a political or economic nature.[52]

A few days later, addressing a meeting at the Catholic University of America, Bishop Keating again remarked:

> For the moment, indeed, the horizon is overclouded by maddening political intrigues which have put Ireland in a false position before the world. . . . But this I can say, that the British public in general,

52. New York *World,* October 20, 1918.

and British Catholics in particular, are determined that the findings of the Irish Convention shall not remain a dead letter, and we shall give our support *en masse* to the Government when it incorporates those findings in a new and final Home Rule measure.

Monsignor Barnes, Chaplain at Oxford University, then requested permission to make the following remarks: "Irish extremists . . . have done much to throw back our hopes. The Sinn Fein party . . . have alienated English sympathies more than ever. . . . For an Ireland alone and unprotected, outside the British Empire, I can see no future." [53]

Shane Leslie, as Keating's secretary, endeavored to clarify the situation even further by the following comment: "Bishop Keating . . . would not have taken the opportunity to come to this country unless he believed that he was in agreement with the majority of the Bishops in America upon the Irish question." [54]

The impact of this British propaganda seemed apparent when Cardinal O'Connell entertained Bishop Keating in Boston. He referred to the statements made by Keating and Monsignor Barnes concerning Home Rule for Ireland and then made the interesting comment: "We accept both these statements made by . . . eminently representative Englishmen, occupying at least for the moment some official position, as being the real voice of the real people of England." As a final observation on this matter he said he looked forward to the fulfillment of the Irish settlement mentioned by them as "one superb act of splendid, generous and just recognition of the right" of the Irish people to some form of self-determination.[55] To the leaders of the Clan-na-Gael and the Friends of Irish Freedom, this statement of His Eminence meant that an important Prince of the Church had fallen victim to British propaganda. He would soon show that this was not true.

On November 2, 1918, a press despatch from Washington announced that Senator Phelan had presented to President Wilson

53. New York *Herald,* October 25, 1918.
54. *Cohalan MSS.*
55. Boston *Pilot,* November 9, 1918.

Plea for Irish Self-Determination

a petition from the priests of the Roman Catholic archdiocese of San Francisco requesting support of Ireland's plea for self-determination. The signatures heading the petition were those of the Most Reverend Edward J. Hanna, Archbishop of San Francisco; the Right Reverend Thomas Grace, Bishop of Sacramento, and the Right Reverend John J. Cantwell, Bishop of Monterey and Los Angeles.

When Joseph McGarrity, of Philadelphia, read this press statement he hurried to New York to talk the situation over with Judge Cohalan. The Judge knew of the intimate ties that existed between Senator Phelan and President Wilson and he knew that they would be completely satisfied with some form of Home Rule for Ireland. The Judge had long dreamed of Irish independence and he was resolutely opposed to any political settlement that would keep Ireland in English chains. The Catholic clergy in America had been distinctly cautious about taking any firm stand on the matter of self-determination for Ireland, and Judge Cohalan frankly informed McGarrity that he was not greatly impressed with the press statement concerning the stand of Archbishop Hanna. The fact that Archbishop Hanna had worked through Senator Phelan aroused suspicions that he might take political advice from the Senator.

The Judge, of course, was very anxious to secure the support of the Catholic hierarchy in this matter of self-determination for Ireland, but he wished to be very sure of his ground before taking any active step in that regard. An opportunity to take action arose very soon when the Friends of Irish Freedom decided to hold a meeting in New York City on December 10 for the purpose of pushing a program calling for Irish self-determination. Word came to the Judge, through Matthew Cummings and John Curley, that Cardinal O'Connell would be glad to speak at the projected meeting on December 10. He immediately went to see His Eminence in Boston and extended a cordial invitation which was accepted at once. But difficulties arose in New York City. When the Judge returned to New York City he asked George J. Gillespie, who was in close touch with important clerical dignitaries, to request the Vicar General, Monsignor Joseph F. Mooney, to approve the Cardinal's visit and address. When the Vicar General was loath to extend this approval, Judge Cohalan enlisted the assistance of Judge Goff and Judge Gavegan.[56] Under the pressure of the three judges the Vicar General finally gave way and sent the invitation to Cardinal O'Connell.[57]

The news that Cardinal O'Connell would speak at the meeting on December 10 was greatly disturbing to some Catholics in New York City. When Dr. William J. Maloney heard this announcement he rushed to the residence of Judge Cohalan and

> with great vehemence argued and pleaded against the coming of the Cardinal to speak. It would be a political blunder of far-reaching importance. It would make the Clan-na-Gael the tail of the kite of the Catholic Church. It would give undue prominence to the Catholic Church in the Irish movement: the effect on the American people would be disastrous.[58]

56. In an undated letter to Judge Cohalan, John Devoy makes the following comment concerning the difficulties of securing clerical consent for Cardinal O'Connell to speak at the Race Convention in New York City: "I have always known that personal feeling and jealousy count for even more among big Churchmen than among laymen. But the Boston man [Cardinal O'Connell] is head and shoulders above them all." Monsignor Mooney was Administrator of the New York Archdiocese, and the opposition to the invitation was based on the fear that the Cardinal wanted to be appointed to New York.

57. The situation with reference to securing Cardinal O'Connell's consent to speak in New York City on December 10 was quite complicated and required all of Judge Cohalan's tact and powers of persuasion to arrange matters so that a clerical explosion did not take place. In a recent letter to me, March 11, 1955, Monsignor Patrick A. O'Leary remarks: "It was the Cardinal's stand that brought the American bishops and clergy to espouse the cause [of self-determination for Ireland] and it was the Judge [Cohalan] who got the Cardinal to come. It was not easy to arrange this, for the Cardinal had to be invited by the head of the Archdiocese. Cardinal Hayes, then auxiliary bishop and very influential in the archdiocese, was very much opposed to O'Connell and would have nothing to do with him, but the Judge was able to prevail upon Monsignor Mooney . . . to invite the Cardinal."

58. Dr. William J. Maloney was an adroit schemer with a smooth tongue and a fluent pen. He aspired to a leading role in the part that America would play in the struggle for self-determination for Ireland. His ardent argument against having Cardinal O'Connell speak at the convention on December 10 was made to Judge Cohalan, John Devoy, and Diarmuid Lynch and was immediately recorded by Lynch. In 1917 and 1918 Maloney pretended to be a warm admirer of Judge Cohalan, and he was often a visitor at the Cohalan residence. Later he believed it was to his interest to break with

When Maloney's objections to the presence of Cardinal O'Connell at the meeting were brushed aside, he grew very angry and began an intrigue against Judge Cohalan. It happened that Joseph McGarrity had arranged for a mass meeting in Philadelphia on December 10, and Justice John W. Goff had consented to serve as chairman. But when Goff heard that Cardinal O'Connell would attend the convention in New York he canceled his engagement in Philadelphia and decided to remain in New York where, because of his seniority in the Irish movement, he would be drafted to serve as chairman. This change of plans greatly irritated McGarrity, who had counted upon the presence of Justice Goff in Philadelphia. Dr. Maloney carefully nursed these embers of discontent until McGarrity, in a mood of deep resentment, blamed Judge Cohalan for the change in Justice Goff's plans. Cohalan had nothing whatever to do with this change, but McGarrity refused to listen to reason and thereafter regarded the Judge with suspicion and hostility.[59]

---

the Judge, and his criticisms were petty and unfounded. We have already seen his attack upon the Judge in July 1921, when he claimed to have written the press statement which defended Judge Cohalan against the false accusations of Secretary Lansing. [See *ante*, pp. 236-237] This statement was signed by the Judge, and the Cohalan manuscripts give evidence to show that Maloney had nothing to do with its preparation.

Maloney was an intimate friend of Patrick McCartan and had a great deal to do with slanting the narrative, *With De Valera in America*, against Judge Cohalan. McCartan was an inept imitation of Maloney, with little of his talent for intrigue and none of his ability to talk and write with a semblance of sincerity. His editorials in the *Irish Press* were cheap models of irresponsibility, and on January 31, 1919, John Quinn wrote him a long letter protesting against a series of statements appearing in McCartan's periodical. One of these had dealt with a statement concerning Sir Roger Casement: "Casement, in the shadow of an English scaffold, sought aid from Mr. John Quinn and received a sneering, choicely-worded denial." This assertion, said Mr. Quinn, was "false in every respect. Casement never communicated to me after the libel episode. I never heard from him from England. . . . I did my best to save him by interesting Americans . . . in him and his pardon." After indicating a lengthy list of allegedly false statements made by McCartan, Mr. Quinn concludes his letter: "If you as the editor of the *Irish Press* think that such bitterness, malignity and falsehood as are contained in the editorial referred to helps the Irish cause in America, or anywhere else, you are of course entitled to that opinion." *Cohalan MSS.*

59. With characteristic inaccuracy Patrick McCartan, in his book, *With De Valera in America*, p. 58, states that Judge Cohalan was "the advertised Chairman of Cardinal O'Connell's meeting." Judge Cohalan's name had not

At the meeting which crowded Madison Square Garden to the bursting point, Cardinal O'Connell, who was introduced by Hon. Charles S. Whitman, Governor of New York, acting as temporary chairman, made an address which attracted wide and favorable attention. It was an eloquent tribute to the Irish people:

"The Irish people through all the painful vicissitudes of their history have been faithful, as no other people in all the world, to the Christian faith. The most Christian country in all the world today, according to the testimony even of her enemies, is Ireland. . . . Can any of us among the Church's leaders ever remain silent and inactive when there is at stake the welfare of the people to whom we owe our very daily bread and the roof that shelters us? There is no legitimate length, no limit within Christian law, to which I and every prelate and priest of America should not be glad and happy to go when the cry of the long-suffering children of the Gael comes to us, and when as now, before the tribunal of the whole world, the sacred justice to every nation and every people is to be given a public hearing.

It is because the people of Ireland have solemnly kept their sacred word, given to their great Apostle, to be faithful to Peter's successor as they would be faithful to Christ, that they have felt the heel of a foreign despot mercilessly grinding them down into the very dust of humiliation. . . . In God's name let us now speak out fearlessly for God's cause, for the cause of justice to all, weak and strong, small and great, or let us be forever silent. . . .

This war, we were told again and again by all those responsible for the conduct of the war, was for justice for all, for the inviolable rights of small nations, for the inalienable right, inherent in every nation, of self-determination. The purpose of this meeting tonight is very specific. The war can be justified only by the universal application of those principles. Let that application begin with Ireland. . . . If these principles are not applied in her case, no matter what else may be done there will be no complete justice, no genuine sincerity believable, and the war not bringing justice will not bring peace." [60]

---

been advertised as the chairman of the convention. In the *Gaelic American*, December 7, 1918, an announcement was made that Justice Edward J. Gavegan would be the chairman. It was later arranged to have Governor Whitman act as temporary chairman and Justice Goff as the permanent chairman. The name of Justice Cohalan had never been considered in that regard.

60. The address of Cardinal O'Connell was published in pamphlet form and widely distributed.

These impassioned words of Cardinal O'Connell rang round the Catholic world and focused attention upon the peace conference that was about to begin its sessions at Versailles. John Devoy gave further emphasis to the importance of self-determination for Ireland and alluded to the important role that should be played by President Wilson:

> We don't know that President Wilson intends to bring the Irish Question directly before the Conference; he has never said that he will. We don't know whether he only intends to bring it privately before the English representatives at that Conference; but we do know that his solemn declarations committed him irrevocably to bringing the case of ALL PEOPLES—all oppressed peoples, before that Congress. If he leaves Ireland out I am afraid he will never live long enough to live it down.

Towards the close of the proceedings, Justice Goff introduced Justice Cohalan as "an old friend of yours, a tried friend of Ireland, as true a heart as ever beat for Ireland." The Judge had been seriously ill with the "flu" that was then scourging America, but he refused to miss a meeting which he had been so instrumental in calling together in Madison Square Garden. He had long been an able and forceful champion of the rights of the Irish people and it was entirely fitting that he should repeat his many pleas for Irish self-determination. After referring to America's professed war aims and the position of England at the peace conference at Versailles with regard to the rights of the Irish people, he remarked upon the last election in Ireland in which the Sinn Fein Party had shown such impressive strength:

> Does that show what self-determination in Ireland will mean when it comes to be fairly decided, not with an army in occupation, not with a second army of constabulary, not with a thousand hidden sources of power that are used all the time against fair election—but openly and fairly when the time comes—and we hope it will come—when the Peace Conference will decree that a plebiscite of the adult population of Ireland should be taken fairly in Ireland, and that according to that the government of Ireland in the future should be fixed and determined. . . .

If England wants to give the measure of her sincerity let her say to the Peace Conference that she will withdraw her troops from Ireland; that she will permit a plebiscite to be taken in Ireland; and that she will agree to abide by the decision in Ireland; and no greater act of statesmanship could be performed by any English statesman than that very act.[61]

The meeting closed with the adoption of resolutions calling upon President Wilson, then on board the steamer *George Washington* en route to France, to "demand at the Peace Congress Self-Determination for the people of Ireland." Irish-Americans realized that at Versailles there would be many ardent pleas from many oppressed peoples for some form of self-determination. They did not seem to realize that President Wilson had no deep interest in the Irish Question and had no intention of embarrassing the British delegation at Versailles by pushing vigorously for some type of Irish independence. As a matter of fact the President was a phrase-maker and not a real peacemaker, and many of his slogans had explosive implications of which he was but dimly aware.

In the *Diary* of Secretary Lansing there are many allusions to Wilson's fondness for glittering generalities whose meaning was quite vague:

> There are certain phrases in the President's "Fourteen Points" which I am sure will cause trouble in the future because their meaning and application have not been thought out. . . . When the President talks of "self-determination" what unit has he in mind? Does he mean a race, a territorial area or a community? Without a definite unit which is practical, application of this principle is dangerous to peace and stability. . . .
>
> The President is a phrase-maker par excellence. He admires trite sayings and revels in formulating them. But when it comes to their practical application he is so vague that their worth may well be doubted. . . . In fact he does not seem to care just so that his words sound well.[62]

With regard to self-determination, it is obvious that President Wilson had not given careful consideration to the many meanings

---

61. *Cohalan MSS.*
62. December 20, 1918, *Lansing MSS.*, Library of Congress.

of that all-inclusive term, and he was greatly embarrassed when Irish-Americans insisted that he should find some generous application of it for the Irish people. Irish race conventions were anathema to him, and cablegrams telling him how to act at Versailles gave him a feeling that he was being pushed beyond endurance. In a letter to John J. Splain, Judge Cohalan remarked that the recent mass meeting in Madison Square Garden was the "greatest meeting ever held in America for the cause of Ireland." [63] This was undoubtedly true, but as far as the President was concerned it was merely another irritant that increased his dislike of the loud chorus of Irish-American sentiment for Irish independence. He would have favored some expression of Home Rule that would have left the British Government in secure control of the destiny of Ireland. Irish independence was to him unthinkable, and the dream for which Irish patriots were willing to die in the Easter rebellion of 1916 appeared to him as a nightmare. At Versailles he became an ardent champion of Poles, Jugoslavs, and Czechs who were seeking some form of self-determination. For the Irish, he assumed the role of stepfather who persistently closed his ears to all pleas for mere justice, and he clearly showed to a cynical world that racial discrimination and British bias were the real cornerstones of his Irish policy. The stunning Democratic defeat of 1920 indicated how American voters felt about this policy.

63. Judge Daniel F. Cohalan to John J. Splain, December 12, 1918, *Cohalan MSS.*

9 JUDGE COHALAN IS SHARPLY REBUFFED BY PRESIDENT WILSON

A. PRESIDENT WILSON REJECTS A SUGGESTION TO RECRUIT TROOPS IN IRELAND FOR THE AMERICAN ARMY

While Judge Cohalan and other outstanding Irish-Americans were endeavoring to exert pressure upon the Wilson Administration in favor of a program of self-determination for Ireland, there were some important senators who believed that such a program was not favored by a large number of Irishmen. It might be best to proceed with caution in dealing with Irish affairs, and it would be advisable to work with President Wilson and not against him. In a letter to Gerald F. M. O'Grady, Senator Thomas J. Walsh summed up the situation as follows:

> A letter was received from you some time ago indicating your intense interest in securing self-government for Ireland. I have long hoped for such a result, partly because of inherited sentiment . . . and largely because of my study of English misrule in that country. . . . I am sure that it would be for the best interests of America, and for all of us engaged in the war with Germany, that the Irish question should be settled on a basis of justice. It is not an easy matter, however, to solve owing to the dissensions among the Irish themselves. . . . The Sinn Feiners will be content with nothing but an independent Irish Republic. The last number of the *Literary Digest* quotes the Tuam *Herald* as saying that such a demand is the most pernicious nonsense. That, as I understand it, is the attitude of the Nationalists, headed by John Dillon and asserted in repeated conferences I have recently had

with him and T. P. O'Connor. They want Home Rule in the same sense that Canada and Australia enjoy Home Rule, remaining integral parts of the British Empire.

In the midst of all these contentions it is extremely difficult to say just what ought to be done, but President Wilson is deeply interested in the situation; he is extremely desirous of bringing about a settlement that will be acceptable to the great bulk of Irish people, and I have no doubt every influence that he can bring to bear to that end will be put forth.[1]

Senator Walsh seemed unaware of the fact that Home Rule had been tabled by the Lloyd George Government with very little chance that it would be put into effect unless Ireland responded in a favorable way to rigorous conscription. British policy made such a response highly unlikely. In September 1918, ninety-six Sinn Feiners "were sentenced to terms of imprisonment by courts-martial and civil courts, and in October seventy-one sentences were passed for offenses of a political nature." [2]

When coercion did not drive the Irish youth into rapid enlistment in the British Army, there was a strong inclination in certain military circles to exert more vigorous pressure. After studying the situation in Ireland with great care, James D. Whelpley, of the United States Military Intelligence, made the following pertinent comment:

> General Shaw is the head of the Irish Royal Command. He is a purely military type and represents the extreme militarist point of view in the handling of Irish affairs. It is understood that from him came the suggestion that if conscription was enforced in Ireland, that the people should be rounded up as they came out of the churches from Mass and forced into military service.[3]

Dr. Charles McCarthy, a distinguished American scholar who had made an extended visit to Ireland, thought that conscription

---

1. Thomas J. Walsh to Gerald F. M. O'Grady, July 30, 1918, *Thomas J. Walsh Papers, Library of Congress.*
2. Dorothy Macardle, *The Irish Republic,* pp. 258-259.
3. Edward Bell to Leland Harrison, Counselor of the Department of State, enclosing a report from James D. Whelpley, 800 I/222, *MSS.,* National Archives.

could be handled in a much more adroit manner. It might be possible to induce the British Government to "grant the American Army the right to recruit in Ireland. I am quite sure the Sinn Fein element would approve. I found no pro-German spirit in Ireland, and I am quite sure we could get 100,000 soldiers from Ireland in this manner. . . . There is a possibility that in the middle of October terrible conditions may occur if the British insist upon dragging out the Irish who refuse to fight under the British flag." [4]

Secretary Lansing was greatly impressed with this memorandum of Dr. McCarthy, which he thought contained "suggestions of a constructive nature in dealing with the problem of Ireland." He regarded McCarthy as a man of "extraordinary ability," and he believed his suggestions were "certainly valuable" with reference to the Irish Question.[5] The President promptly replied that he did not share Secretary Lansing's "judgment about Professor Charles McCarthy." He had read the memorandum on "Irish Conditions" and did not see how any of McCarthy's suggestions "could be acted on with advantage." [6]

President Wilson's strong opposition to the suggestion of Professor McCarthy stopped all further action in favor of recruiting in Ireland soldiers for the American army. Lansing had been impressed with the professor's evident scholarship, but the President knew a good deal about college professors, and McCarthy's memorandum seemed more like the term paper of a graduate student than a serious study of an important problem.

After November 11 conscription in Ireland ceased to be an important issue, and the President began to think in terms of an approaching peace with Germany. A peace conference would have to be called for the purpose of settling the problems of peace, and Irish Americans began to press for self-determination or independence for Ireland.

4. Report of Dr. Charles McCarthy on "Irish Conditions" enclosed in letter from General M. Churchill, Director of Military Intelligence, to Leland Harrison, October 7, 1918, 841D.00/8, *MSS.*, N.A.
5. Secretary Lansing to President Wilson, September 13, 1918, 841D.00/15A, *MSS.*, N.A.
6. President Wilson to Secretary Lansing, September 17, 1918, 841D.00/16½, *MSS.*, N.A.

B. THE PROBLEM OF IRELAND COMES BEFORE THE AMERICAN CONGRESS

It was apparent to many Irish Americans that strong pressure would have to be exerted upon President Wilson in order to induce him to present to the peace conference the plea of Ireland for self-government. On December 12, 1918, hearings were held by the Committee on Foreign Affairs of the House of Representatives on the resolution introduced by Thomas Gallagher, of Illinois, which requested the members of the American delegation to the peace conference to "present the right of Ireland to freedom, independence and self-determination."

Judge Cohalan did not appear during these hearings. His viewpoint was ably presented by Richard F. Dalton, who insisted that not only

> as a matter of right and justice, but as a matter of wisdom for mankind, for the benefit of Ireland, for the benefit of the United States, for the benefit of England herself, it is essential that the Irish question be settled, and it can only be settled by reference of it to a fair plebiscite of the adult population of Ireland. . . . I submit that the resolution as drawn . . . would simply be a respectful expression of the opinion of the American people to their delegates abroad that self-determination should be applied to Ireland.[7]

In the statement of Diarmuid Lynch to the Committee on Foreign Affairs, a sharp edge of bitterness could be clearly felt through the thin folds of language:

> Ireland has her back to the wall and looks the whole world square in the face. . . . She will be satisfied only with a settlement secured in accordance with the wishes of her own people, expressed through a plebiscite of her entire adult population, without any restriction whatsoever. . . . The case of Ireland was drawn up for presentation to the peace conference by Irish leaders most competent to write and present it, but each and every one of these leaders is today imprisoned

7. Statement of Richard F. Dalton before the House Committee on Foreign Affairs, December 12, 1918, *Hearings* on H.J. Res. 357, pp. 17-18, 55-56.

in England. . . . Ireland is shut off from the world and prohibited by the civil, naval and military power of England from sending her representatives direct to Versailles, there to present her case to the peace conference. . . . Ireland asks only that her wrongs cease and . . . that right be substituted for might, and that she be allowed to work out her own national destiny.[8]

C. THE IRISH PEOPLE CAST AN IMPRESSIVE VOTE IN FAVOR OF AN IRISH REPUBLIC

While Diarmuid Lynch was presenting to the Committee on Foreign Affairs the case of Ireland, Bishop Cohalan, of Cork, delivered on October 22, 1918, an important sermon which placed the issue of self-determination squarely before the people of his diocese. First of all, he asked the significant question: "What is the cause of British misgovernment of Ireland?" His answers to this question were detailed and penetrating:

> The causes are in part racial and in a large part religious. . . . Let me draw your attention to some of the characteristics of British rule in Ireland:
> 1. Any Irish industry which threatens to compete with English industries is crushed or is always on insecure ground.
> 2. The development of Ireland is restricted or prevented lest a rich and prosperous Ireland might look for independence.
> 3. England plays on the divisions in Ireland according to her purpose and to suit her own purpose.
> 4. Exceptional coercive law, one might say, has been the rule since the Union.

After discussing the effect of English rule, Bishop Cohalan looks to the future:

8. Statement of Diarmuid Lynch, December 12, 1918, *Hearings,* pp. 87-89. See also *House Document No. 1832,* 65 Cong., 3d sess., 87-89. According to a report published in *The New York Times,* Judge Cohalan told the members of the Committee on Foreign Affairs that the delegation of which he was a member spoke "for the majority of 20,000,000 Americans of Irish descent, and was pleading in behalf of a government which was well organized and firmly supported by its constituents." *New York Times,* December 13, 1918.

I hope we will win liberty for Ireland without sacrificing any more lives, but I refer to the situation as one fact that the Great Powers should keep in mind—a great fact because these are the things that will not be forgotten tomorrow or the next day. . . . Looking into the future I say that if the question of Ireland is not settled in a generous way, settled in a way that will meet the sentiments of the younger people, it will not be a lasting settlement. . . . There are three or four solutions of the Irish question before the world. One of these is that Ireland should be set up as a Sovereign independent nation, absolutely distinct, call it a Republic or a Kingdom as you will.[9]

There was some colorful comment in the British Parliament and in the British and American press to the effect that Bishop Cohalan, of Cork, was a brother to Daniel F. Cohalan. It was also intimated that Bishop Cohalan, in Ireland, owed his high ecclesiastical office to the pressure of the German Foreign Office upon the Vatican. In this way Germany could repay the Cohalans for their role in the background of the Easter Rising. Needless to say, these assertions were completely false.

On the day after Bishop Cohalan delivered his sermon, the Executive Committee of Sinn Fein sent an appeal to President Wilson for self-determination:

Taking our stand upon the separate and distinct Nationality of Ireland which is as well defined and incontrovertible as that of any other nation in Europe . . . we, the Executive of Sinn Fein, speaking on behalf of the Irish Nation, assert the right of Ireland to Independence and claim representation as a distinct and separate unit in the League of Nations.[10]

Not to be outdone by Sinn Fein, the Irish Nationalist Party introduced in the British House of Commons a motion in favor of self-determination for Ireland. In a speech at Manchester on October 27, T. P. O'Connor discussed the implications of this

9. The Cork *Examiner*, October 23, 1918.
10. The Appeal of the Executive Committee of Sinn Fein to President Wilson, 800 I/228, N.A.

motion: "Whatever takes place in the House of Commons on that motion is not the end of the chapter. We have another tribunal, when the great council of nearly all the Powers of the world meets to resettle the whole map of Europe—Ireland cannot be left out." [11]

The Nationalist Party next sent a letter to President Wilson acquainting him with the motion that had been introduced in the House of Commons calling for self-determination for Ireland:

> We felt, Sir, that we were justified in making this demand upon the British Government in your name and in the name of the principles in joining in this war for which you and your country stand. . . . Finally, Sir, in challenging the opinion of the British Government with regard to the rights of our people and as to the accord of their policy with your principles, were we not but repeating a challenge that you have already given to the statesmen of every one of the other Powers of the world? . . . We claim that this war must be looked at from your own standard of "broad-visioned" justice.[12]

It was evident that the cause of Ireland would be successful at the Peace Conference only if it were strongly supported by President Wilson. To prepare for this support, Bishop John Carroll, of Helena, Montana, wrote a letter to Senator Thomas J. Walsh in which he expressed the hope that the senator would insist "on President Wilson's principles of 'justice to all nations, small and great alike,' and 'self-determination' being applied, not only to Belgium, Poland, etc., but also to the down-trodden land of our forefathers." [13] Under the spur of this letter, Senator Walsh wrote a long communication to the President arguing in favor of Irish self-determination:

> I am sure you will not overlook the opportunity in the intimate conferences you are sure to have with the British statesmen to impress upon them the necessity of a speedy solution of the question of self-

11. The Cork *Examiner*, October 28, 1918.
12. T. P. O'Connor to the United States Ambassador at London, November 9, 1918, enclosing letter to President Wilson, 800 I/241, *MS.*, N.A.
13. Bishop John Carroll to Senator Thomas J. Walsh, November 19, 1918, *Walsh Papers*, Library of Congress.

government for Ireland. We shall not escape the harsh judgment of posterity if we do not insist on the same measure of justice for the people of Ireland in the matter of their government that we have declared our purpose to exact . . . for the peoples heretofore held unwilling subjects of the Central Powers. . . .

A vast multitude of the people in this country, not alone those of Irish descent, regard the continuance of English rule in Ireland as unjustifiable, and the exasperating course that has been pursued in relation to Home Rule as highly discreditable.[14]

The President immediately replied that he appreciated "the importance of a proper solution of the Irish question" but until he reached Paris and found "his footing in delicate matters of this sort" he could not "forecast with any degree of confidence" what influence he could exercise. He assured the senator that he would "keep this important interest in mind and shall use my influence at every opportunity to bring about a just and satisfactory solution."[15]

In a letter to Bishop Thomas J. Shahan, who had strongly advocated self-determination for Ireland, the President made much the same reply:

It will be my endeavor in regard to every question which arises before the Peace Conference to do my utmost to bring about the realization of the principles to which your letter refers. The difficulties and delicacy of the task are very great, and I cannot confidently forecast what I can do. I can only say that I shall be watchful of every opportunity to insist upon the principles I have enunciated.[16]

There was little doubt that the question of self-determination for oppressed peoples was a very "delicate one." Secretary Lansing, at Paris, was very aware of this fact. In his *Diary* he made the following entry:

The more I think about the President's declaration as to the right of 'self-determination' the more I am convinced of the danger of putting

14. Senator Thomas J. Walsh to President Wilson, December 2, 1918, *ibid*.
15. Wilson to Walsh, December 3, 1918, *ibid*.
16. President Wilson to Bishop Thomas J. Shahan, December 3, 1918, *Wilson MSS*.

such ideas into the minds of certain races. It is bound to be the basis of impossible demands on the Peace Congress, and create trouble in many lands. What effect will it have on the Irish, the Indians, the Egyptians, and the nationalists among the Boers. . . . The phrase is simply loaded with dynamite.[17]

Sinn Fein realized that the phrase self-determination was loaded with political dynamite and were prepared for a loud explosion that would be heard round the world. On November 25 the British Parliament was dissolved and polling day was fixed for December 14. Sinn Fein carefully drafted an election manifesto which strongly called for independence and an Irish Republic:

> Sinn Fein gives Ireland the opportunity of vindicating her honour and pursuing with renewed confidence the path of national salvation by rallying to the flag of the Irish Republic.
> Sinn Fein aims at securing the establishment of that Republic
> 1. By withdrawing the Irish Representation from the British Parliament, and by denying the right and opposing the will of the British Government or any other foreign Government to legislate for Ireland.
> 2. By making use of any and every means available to render impotent the power of England to hold Ireland in subjection to military force or otherwise.[18]

As Sinn Fein prepared to contest the elections, it was obvious that it faced tremendous handicaps. More than a hundred of its leaders, both men and women, were in jail. A large part of Ireland was under rigidly enforced military rule, and Sinn Fein itself and every other national organization had been banned. All Republican papers had been suppressed, and the election machinery and the Post Office were securely under British control. It was significant that of the seventy-three Republican candidates, forty-seven were in jail. Some of these candidates managed to have their election addresses smuggled out of prison, but these were promptly confiscated in the Post Office.

In spite of widespread British intimidation the election results were a surprising victory for Sinn Fein. Out of one hundred and

17. The Lansing *Diary*, December 30, 1918, *Lansing MS*.
18. Dorothy Macardle, *op. cit.*, pp. 919-920.

five candidates returned for Ireland, seventy-three were Republicans. Only six seats were won by the Parliamentary Party. T. P. O'Connor was returned for a Liverpool constituency. John Dillon, the leader of the Parliamentary Party, lost his seat in Mayo to De Valera by a crushing majority. Twenty-four of the thirty-two counties of Ireland had returned none but Republican members. Even the London *Times* admitted that the general election in Ireland had been regarded by all parties as a national plebiscite and "admittedly Sinn Fein swept the country." [19]

As soon as the news of this sweeping victory reached America, William J. Maloney, Patrick McCartan, Reverend T. J. Hurton, Monsignor Coghlan, and Joseph McGarrity formed a group that wished to exploit in every way the far-reaching implications of this impressive vote in Ireland. A meeting was held in the residence of Judge Cohalan which was attended by Judge Goff, Judge Gavegan, Judge Rooney, Robert Ford, John Devoy, Richard F. Dalton, Diarmuid Lynch, Rev. Peter E. Magennis, Rev. T. J. Hurton, William J. Maloney, Joseph McGarrity, and Patrick McCartan. Judge Cohalan believed that it was unwise for any group in America to anticipate the action of the Irish Constituent Assembly, which was scheduled to meet on January 21, 1919. Patrick McCartan heatedly exclaimed that the recent election in Ireland was really a national plebiscite in favor of the establishment of an Irish Republic and he thought that the Friends of Irish Freedom should be directed to hold, on the earliest date practicable, meetings in every city to congratulate the Irish people upon the erection of this republic. The majority of the group in attendance at the Cohalan residence disagreed with the viewpoint of McCartan, and it was decided to await the action of the elected representatives of the Irish people—in other words, the Constituent Assembly.[20]

In accordance with this viewpoint, on December 30, Judge Cohalan sent the following cablegram to De Valera:

Accept heartiest congratulations upon results of election. Ireland's overwhelming verdict in favour of President Wilson's policy of Self-

19. January 9, 17, 1919.
20. Patrick McCartan, *With De Valera in America*, pp. 63-65.

Determination for all peoples will greatly strengthen her position with lovers of liberty throughout America.[21]

McCartan, who had played a very minor role in the movement in America in favor of Irish independence, now saw an opportunity for self-advertisement and was determined to use it to the fullest extent. With the assistance of Maloney he prepared a proclamation "to the Citizens of the Republic of Ireland who are at present resident in the United States and Canada." In this proclamation it was stated that the recent election in Ireland was really a declaration of independence, and the "Irish people in America and Canada" were summoned to be ready and strong to aid the Irish Republic "lest it be overwhelmed by the imperial forces that are even now gathered to destroy it."

McCartan next sent a note to Secretary Lansing which announced Irish independence: "I have the honor to inform you that, exercising their inherent right of Self-Determination, the sovereign people of Ireland, on December 28, 1918, by more than a two-thirds majority, severed all political relations with Great Britain. . . . The United Kingdom of Great Britain and Ireland is at an end." [22]

Judge Cohalan was deeply interested in the establishment of an Irish Republic and had worked most zealously for more than two decades to further that objective. He was fearful that recent Irish visitors like McCartan and Maloney might endanger the success of his efforts. To indicate to Irish voters the support of a large majority of Irish Americans with reference to self-determination for Ireland, Judge Cohalan arranged for the Clan-na-Gael to hold a meeting on the evening of January 5 in the Central Opera House. In his address to the meeting the Judge remarked:

> We meet tonight for the purpose of congratulating the people of Ireland upon the fact that they have self-determined themselves and decided that they will live under no government except that chosen by themselves. . . . Ireland . . . is calling upon the opinion of the world

21. *New York Times,* December 31, 1918.
22. Patrick McCartan to Secretary Lansing, January 3, 1919, 841d.00/17, MS., N.A. McCartan signed this note as the Envoy of the Provisional Government of Ireland.

to strengthen and to enforce her point of view, to help her over the short road that remains between the position in which she is tonight and the position of absolute independence.[23]

At this same meeting Liam Mellows struck the same key note. Irish independence was still an aspiration that had to be achieved:

> They [the Irish people] have exercised so far as lay within their power, the right of Self-Determination, and they have determined that Ireland shall and must be free and independent. . . . Ireland has won a victory, but not the great victory that we want, that we hope for, and believe in. The road to that victory that has to be travelled is hard and thorny still.

McCartan and Maloney were determined to steal some of the limelight that Judge Cohalan and his friends were bathed in at this moment. Suddenly they decided to call an extra meeting to congratulate the people of Ireland upon their recent decision for self-determination. On January 6, under the auspices of the Irish Progressive League, the meeting was held in the Central Opera House. This League was a radical organization with some distinctly dubious members. One of the principal speakers was Norman Thomas, even then known for his advanced views. As was to be expected, the meeting on January 6 was unrestrained in its support of an Irish Republic, and a cablegram was sent to Eamon de Valera, addressing him as President.

The viewpoint of Judge Cohalan and John Devoy with reference to these hasty actions on the part of McCartan and Maloney was well expressed in an editorial in the *Gaelic American:* "It is not the business of the Irish in America to dictate plans, but it is their duty and their privilege to follow those made in Dublin by the elected representatives of the people of Ireland. Those plans will be formulated by a National Assembly in Dublin." [24]

23. *Gaelic American,* January 11, 1919.
24. *Ibid.*

D. THE THIRD IRISH RACE CONVENTION, PHILADELPHIA, FEBRUARY 22-23, 1919

The meeting of the Clan-na-Gael in New York on January 5 was merely a prelude to the Irish Race Convention, which was summoned to meet in Philadelphia on February 22-23, 1919. It was felt that such a convention would have a definite influence upon American policy at the Peace Conference at Versailles. It was also believed that this convention would give encouragement to the movement in Ireland for self-determination.

This movement was moving fast towards important decisions. On January 7, 1919, twenty-six elected Republican representatives met at the Dublin Mansion House and decided to convene Dail Eireann as an independent Constituent Assembly of the Irish nation. When the first Dail Eireann met on January 21,[25] a provisional constitution was read and unanimously adopted. Next, the Declaration of Irish Independence was read:

> Whereas the Irish people is by right a free people, and whereas for seven hundred years the Irish people never ceased to repudiate and has repeatedly protested in arms against foreign usurpation, and whereas . . . the Irish electorate has in the General Election of December, 1918, seized the first occasion to declare by an overwhelming majority its firm allegiance to the Irish Republic: now, therefore, we, the elected Representatives of the ancient Irish people in National Parliament assembled, do, in the name of the Irish nation, ratify the establishment of the Irish Republic and pledge ourselves and our people to make this declaration effective by every means at our command.[26]

The Dail then appointed three delegates to the Paris Peace Conference—Eamon de Valera, Arthur Griffith, and Count Plunkett. In an address to the Free Nations of the World, the Dail asked them to support "the Irish Republic by recognizing Ireland's national status and her right to its vindication at the Peace Congress." The

---

25. When the Dail met, thirty-six of the seventy-three Republicans elected in the general election in December 1918 were in jail.
26. Dorothy Macardle, *op. cit.*, pp. 272-273.

impossibility of securing permission from the British Government for the attendance of De Valera, Griffith, and Plunkett at the Peace Conference was recognized by accrediting Alderman Sean T. O'Kelly to Paris to serve as the envoy of the Government of the Irish Republic. On February 8 O'Kelly wrote to President Wilson in Paris to convey to him an invitation from the Corporation of Dublin to visit Ireland.[27] The President's reply was a polite negative. Some weeks later (February 22), O'Kelly wrote to Premier Clemenceau asking him to "fix a date" when the Irish delegates to the Peace Conference would have an opportunity to present the case of Ireland. Clemenceau never bothered to return an answer to this communication.

In the meantime the Clan-na-Gael and the Friends of Irish Freedom were preparing to summon another Irish Race Convention that might help to exert pressure upon President Wilson in Paris. In her account of the calling of this convention, Dorothy Macardle, relying upon the untrustworthy narrative of Patrick McCartan,[28] makes the mistake of attributing to McCartan, Joseph McGarrity, and Father Peter Magennis the main responsibility for calling the Philadelphia convention. After some words of criticism of Judge Cohalan, she remarks: "It was by the efforts of such men as these [McCartan, McGarrity, and Father Magennis] and of influential women like Mrs. McWhorter, of Chicago, that a great Irish Race Convention was summoned to meet in Philadelphia." [29]

As a matter of fact, McCartan, McGarrity, and Father Magennis had very little to do with summoning this convention. It was the

---

27. *Ibid.*, 277-280.
28. *With De Valera in America*, pp. 79-84.
29. Dorothy Macardle, *op. cit.*, p. 279. Mrs. Mary F. McWhorter was the National President of the Ladies' Auxiliary of the Ancient Order of Hibernians of America and was a close friend and an ardent admirer of Judge Cohalan. In a letter to the Judge, February 8, 1919, she remarks: "You are the guiding star and the inspiration of all that is best and truest in the ideals of our race. . . . You have never faltered in your allegiance to our dear dark Rosaleen; you have never forgot your dear Motherland. . . . You have always remained faithful to the old land and hence you are the ideal American Citizen. May our Heavenly Father reward you and may his Blessed Mother have an especial watch and guard over you and your dear ones." *Cohalan MSS.*

Clan and the Friends of Irish Freedom under the leadership of Judge Cohalan and John Devoy that organized and led the drive for a convention. Along with Diarmuid Lynch, they had bent every effort to make the Friends a strong organization that would command the respect of politicians of both parties. Judge Cohalan was constant in his attendance at the meetings of the Friends, and in introducing him as the speaker before a large gathering in the hall of the Innisfail branch, Monsignor James W. Power aptly observed:

> A good rule by which to size up a man's character is to know the friends he has and the enemies he makes. An Irishman who is loved by the English, like Carson, would not be much of an Irishman. On the other hand, the Irishman or sympathizer with Irish rights who would be hated by Englishmen and whose head they would like to get, would be the right stamp of the Irishman we need today. Such a man is the man I am about to introduce as the next speaker, and from what I know of him I can say that since the redoubtable Shane O'Neill, no man is hated and feared by England more than the Honorable Justice Cohalan, and for that reason, no man is more admired and better loved by his own.[30]

There is little doubt that Judge Cohalan and John Devoy had a major part in the calling of the Philadelphia convention, and it is significant to note that not only did the Friends of Irish Freedom really inaugurate the movement behind this convention but that forty per cent of the regular members of the Friends were residents of New York City.

When the Friends of Irish Freedom decided to hold the Philadelphia convention, they asked Judge Cohalan to lead a delegation to Baltimore to request the attendance of Cardinal Gibbons. Cohalan had been in close touch with the Rev. John F. Fenlon, S. S., who was Secretary of the Catholic University at Washington. Father Fenlon was an intimate friend of the Cardinal and was trying to draft a resolution which he hoped the Cardinal would propose to the convention. After working on it for some time he was dissatisfied with its phraseology and sent it to Judge Cohalan to put in final form. He would like to get it into the hands of Cardinal

30. *Cohalan MSS.*

Gibbons within a few days.[31] He also intimated that His Eminence, with reference to self-determination for Ireland, would "go as far as President Wilson and no farther." [32]

The difficulties in dealing with the Cardinal were well expressed by former Congressman Michael Donohoe of Philadelphia, a member of the committee that waited upon His Eminence:

> Judge Cohalan was the spokesman of the committee with an occasional low-toned, precise remark by Judge Goff. Judge Cohalan handled the case with rare skill for the great old prelate was throughout the interview cautious and conservative and at first apparently opposed to going beyond the Home Rule programme. His first response to Judge Cohalan's proposal was something like this: "I think the plan outlined by the late Mr. Redmond . . ."
> Cohalan: "But as your Eminence knows, President Wilson has emphatically declared for self-determination for all peoples."
> The Cardinal made several attempts to moralize on the danger of going too far, the virtue of moderation, etc., but he never got further than a few sentences before the Judge would shoot in a quotation from Wilson or Lloyd George that left the dear old saint without a leg to stand on. At last: "Of course, I'll have an opportunity of studying the resolution."
> Cohalan: "Oh, of course, your Eminence, there will be nothing in the resolution you cannot approve of."
> This is a brief account of what was a delightful fencing match that ended most happily.[33]

The role played by Dr. William J. Maloney at the convention is an intriguing one. He first endeavored to persuade Judge Cohalan not to attend the convention. He pretended to be fearful that the Judge's health would be impaired by such attendance. When this plan failed, he then begged Judge Cohalan to go at once to Paris, where his presence at the Peace Conference would be of inestimable value to the cause of Ireland. The Judge saw through these cheap stratagems and attended the convention, where he became the permanent chairman. When Maloney saw that he

---

31. Monsignor Patrick A. O'Leary to the author, March 11, 1955.
32. Rev. John F. Fenlon to Judge Cohalan, February 13, 18, 1919, *Cohalan MSS.*
33. *Cohalan MSS.*

could not prevent Cohalan's presence at the convention, he determined to dominate it by securing a place on the Committee on Resolutions. As a member of the committee he was so noncooperative that Michael J. Ryan became infuriated and remarked that "if the British had a man on the resolutions committee he would be doing exactly what Maloney was then doing." [34]

Shortly after the convention was formally opened, Judge Cohalan was instrumental in having a cablegram sent to Eamon de Valera, Arthur Griffith, and Count Plunkett advising them of the work of the convention. De Valera was not long in sending an important reply.

The high point of the convention was the brief address of Cardinal Gibbons and the resolution he presented for the approval of the delegates. In his address he emphasized the fact that Ireland wanted

> freedom to breathe the air of heaven. She wants freedom to develop the riches of her soul. She wants freedom to carve out her own destiny. . . . Liberty is a necessary part of justice; it is not a favor or a privilege. Nations as well as individuals have a right to liberty. Ireland's right to liberty is as clear as sunlight. . . . Just as in the war we took the side of Belgium and France and England because it was the side of liberty and justice, so for the very same reason should we now take the side of Ireland. All Americans should stand as one man for Ireland's inalienable right of self-determination.

The Cardinal then offered the resolution which had been largely drafted by John Devoy and Judge Cohalan. It called upon the Paris Peace Conference to "apply to Ireland the great doctrine of national self-determination" and to recognize the right of the people of Ireland to select for themselves, without interference, the form of government under which they wished to live.[35]

With characteristic inaccuracy Dr. McCartan states that

> on the evening of the Convention, in Maloney's room in the Bellevue-Stratford Hotel, in Philadelphia, McGarrity brought to Maloney and I

---

34. Monsignor Patrick A. O'Leary to the author, March 11, 1955.
35. *Cohalan MSS.*

[sic] a copy of the resolution to be proposed by the Cardinal. We were all three dismayed by it. I angrily contended that Cohalan had deceived us again. In effect the resolution, spread over many foolscap pages, denounced all entangling alliances with foreign nations, repudiated any League of Nations, and omitted to recognize the fact that an independent Government now existed in Ireland.[36]

As a matter of fact the resolution proposed by Cardinal Gibbons made no reference whatever to "entangling alliances with foreign nations" nor to any "League of Nations." It is obvious that the McCartan narrative is a tissue of misstatements and should not be accepted as reliable history. It is worth while to note that the resolution proposed by Cardinal Gibbons was seconded by Norman Thomas and supported by speeches given by Archbishop Messmer of Milwaukee, Rabbi Krauskopf, Rev. James Grattan Mythen, and Henry Goddard Leach. It was then unanimously adopted by the Convention.

At the close of the convention on Sunday evening, February 23, the chairman, Judge Cohalan, remarked: "There never was a gathering which will be more resultful for the cause of the Independence of Ireland and for the welfare and good of America, than this which I now declare closed." [37] On the following day, Eamon de Valera issued from his hiding place near Dublin the following statement:

We challenge England to allow Ireland the principle of free Self-Determination. Let that principle be applied to this island as a unit, and if a decisive majority of the whole people declare not for a separate, independent statehood, then we shall be silent. If England accepts the principle of Self-Determination for this island it will settle the Irish question forever.[38]

36. *With De Valera in America*, p. 82.
37. *Cohalan MSS.*
38. New York *World*, March 13, 1919. On March 30, 1919, in Manchester, the Irish Self-determination League of Great Britain was founded. A message from De Valera was read, and Harry Boland, who was present, "appealed for their moral and financial support in influencing public opinion on behalf of Ireland's claim to Self-determination." *Irish Independent,* March 31, 1919.

It was significant that De Valera was talking about the application of the principle of self-determination in an Irish national plebiscite to be held in the near future. He was following the trail blazed for him by Judge Cohalan, who was satisfied that the principle of self-determination, if implemented in the right way, would solve the Irish Question.

E.   PRESIDENT WILSON REFUSES TO PROMISE TO PRESENT TO THE PEACE CONFERENCE IRELAND'S PLEA FOR SELF-DETERMINATION

After the adjournment of the Irish Race Convention it was decided to send to Washington a delegation of distinguished Irish-Americans for the purpose of presenting to President Wilson the resolutions adopted by the convention. The leader of this delegation was Judge Cohalan. They arrived in Washington on February 25 and soon discovered that the President was "too busy" to see them. He had used this same formula in refusing to receive three previous important Irish-American delegations. They were finally informed that the President would accord a brief reception to the committee on the following Tuesday night in New York City after his scheduled address in the Metropolitan Opera House. The members of the committee, including Judge Cohalan, occupied seats reserved for them on the stage of the opera house and listened with deep interest to his address. After the address had been concluded, the committee waited in the clubroom of the opera house for a half hour, when they were told that the President "would not enter the room . . . if Justice Cohalan was present." When all the members of the committee, with impressive unanimity, declared "they would leave sooner than have Justice Cohalan leave alone . . . he said: 'The cause is bigger than any one man; the cause is bigger than I am. For its sake I will leave the room without question.'" [39]

When the President finally met the members of the committee, Judge Goff presented to him the resolutions adopted by the convention and then observed: "Mr. President, representing as we do

39. *Cohalan MSS.*

many millions of your fellow American citizens, I ask you to present to the Peace Conference at Paris the right of Ireland to determine the form of government under which she shall live." The President immediately replied that he did not believe "he should be called upon to answer such a question." Frank P. Walsh then expressed the opinion that the President should "use his powerful influence to see that the delegates selected by the people of Ireland were given every opportunity to present Ireland's cause to the Peace Conference." The President resented this pressure and replied to Mr. Walsh: "You do not expect me to give an answer to this request now?" Walsh murmured "No," and the audience with the American Chief Executive came to a fruitless end.[40]

F. DR. MCCARTAN PUSHES A CAMPAIGN OF SLANDER AND MISREPRESENTATION AGAINST JUDGE COHALAN

It would take a long book to correct the many slanders and misrepresentations launched by Dr. McCartan against Judge Cohalan. There is not space in this narrative for a detailed refutation of these misrepresentations, but some of them are such patent misstatements that they demand some correction. In dealing with the attitude of Judge Cohalan relative to self-determination, McCartan remarks:

> Cathal Brugha, the Minister of Defence in the Cabinet of the Dail, wrote to Diarmuid Lynch urging that Cohalan should demand nothing but recognition for the Irish Republic from the United States. Here was, at least, one member of the Cabinet who was not with de Valera in seeking self-determination from England.[41]

40. Statement given to the press by Judge John W. Goff and printed in the New York *Tribune*, March 5, 1919. It is interesting to note the pressure that was exerted upon the President to induce him to receive the committee from the Irish Race Convention. In response to a request from Senator Thomas J. Walsh on behalf of the committee, the President informed Tumulty: "Please express my great regret that I am obliged to decline to see all delegations. Time barely suffices to transact necessary public business [Feb. 24, 1919]." *Wilson MSS.* On February 28, 1919, Representative Jeannette Rankin also wrote in favor of an audience with the Irish Race Convention committee. *Wilson MSS.*
41. Patrick McCartan, *op. cit.*, p. 92.

It happens that this letter to Lynch was signed by both Brugha and Michael Collins. In the correct text of the letter there is no mention of Judge Cohalan and there was nothing in it that would "debar 'self-determination' as a means to that end [Irish independence]" It is also a matter of fact that at the time this letter was written (February 15, 1919), there was no Cabinet of Dail Eireann in existence.[42]

Another typical misstatement of McCartan deals with the organization of the Friends of Irish Freedom:

> At the first meeting of the Friends of Irish Freedom after the Convention it was discovered that without the knowledge of McGarrity, who was Chairman of the Organization Committee of the Convention, Cohalan had named a National Executive of 15. The supreme control of the organization was vested in this body. . . . The Friends of Irish Freedom had become his [Cohalan's] personal machine under his complete control; and it worked smoothly.[43]

It was at this meeting held on March 12, 1919, that the new National Executive Committee of 15 was elected. Both Dr. McCartan and Joseph McGarrity were present. Therefore the statement in McCartan's book is an obvious mistake. If McGarrity was present at the meeting on March 12 he knew all about the election of a new National Executive Committee and participated in this election. Inasmuch as the election was held under the jurisdiction of the National Council, it is incorrect to say that the situation was dominated by the National Executive Committee. It is also important to note that on no occasion between March 1919 and November 1920 was any objection raised at any meeting of the National Council with reference to the conduct of affairs by the National Executive Committee.

On March 23, 1919, a large meeting was held in the Metropolitan Opera House to further the cause of Irish independence. The Opera House was especially chosen to point up Wilson's cheap attempt to humiliate Judge Cohalan at this same forum on March 4. As usual,

---

42. Statement of Diarmuid Lynch, *Cohalan MSS*.
43. *op. cit.*, pp. 90-91.

Dr. McCartan incorrectly reports the address of Judge Cohalan and leaves the impression that the distinguished jurist made only a passing reference to the establishment of an Irish Republic. Quite the opposite was true. The gist of Cohalan's speech was reported in the New York daily press as follows:

> Today we are celebrating the fact that the Irish Republic has come into existence, but we pledge ourselves to carry on the fight until the existence of the Irish Republic is recognized by every country on earth, including the country against which the fight has gone on for 750 years. . . . There will be neither a just nor a durable nor a permanent peace unless the people of Ireland who have set up this Independent Republic receive from all the nations of the earth the recognition to which they are entitled, and unless, with the making of peace we have an opportunity of saluting this latest and newest of Republics as a sister republic of this great nation of America.[44]

To Irish-Americans all over the continent, it was evident that Judge Cohalan had accomplished a Titan's task in marshaling sentiment in favor of Irish independence, and they would have repudiated with vehemence the slurs of McCartan. This devotion to Cohalan was strongly manifested on March 9 at the Emmet celebration in Brooklyn. When Cohalan's name was mentioned

> by former Justice John W. Goff in the course of a statement of the work of the committee appointed by the great Irish Race Convention to see President Wilson on behalf of Ireland, the audience jumped to its feet and cheered and applauded until the building almost rocked. Again, when Justice Cohalan was introduced to address the great gathering the audience rose as if one impulse moved every man and woman in the big auditorium, and gave him a welcome such as a hero returning from a victorious campaign might feel elated at receiving.[45]

It was highly unfortunate that such an outstanding Irish-American, who had accomplished so much for the cause of Irish independence, should be brazenly sniped at by an Irish doctor who

---

44. Address of Judge Daniel F. Cohalan at the meeting held in the Metropolitan Opera House, March 23, 1919, *Cohalan MSS.*
45. *Cohalan MSS.*

seemed convinced that it was his duty to shoot Cohalan in the back and then poison the American mind against any real recognition of his tremendous services. His work as a poisoner had some permanent effects, because he forsook the scalpel for the pen, and his sharp and misleading words of abuse are still read in a book that is a perfect example of scurrility in print.[46]

G. CONGRESSIONAL PRESSURE WITH REFERENCE TO IRISH SELF-DETERMINATION AROUSES THE ANXIETY OF PRESIDENT WILSON

The cause of Ireland was very popular in Congress. In the third session of the 65th Congress there were eight resolutions introduced with reference to self-determination for Ireland or "requesting the Ministers Plenipotentiary of the United States of America to the International Peace Conference to present to the said Conference the right of Ireland to freedom and independence." The House Joint Resolution No. 357, introduced by Representative Gallagher, of Illinois, had been favorably received by most members of the House of Representatives, and after some amendments it was scheduled to be voted upon in the early days of March 1919. It expressed the "earnest hope of the Congress of the United States . . . that the Peace Conference, now sitting in Paris, in passing upon the rights of various peoples, will favorably consider the claims of Ireland to the right of self-determination." [47]

46. Among prominent Irish-Americans in New York City it was widely believed that Dr. McCartan and William J. Maloney were often in close contact with Joe Tumulty, President Wilson's private secretary. This suspicion is confirmed in the following correspondence. On March 8, 1919, McCartan sent a letter to Ben S. Allen, an official in the U.S. Food Administration, enclosing a copy of a cablegram he had sent to the Irish representative at Paris. On March 11 Allen sent this cablegram to Tumulty with some interesting comments: "The people who are using the Cohalan business for the purpose of playing politics are making the most of it. I am assured that the Irish Envoy is trying to checkmate this use of the Irish question as a football in American politics. I know that he and his friends have a plan to put the Cohalan-Walsh-Borah combination out of business. . . . If you are interested in getting some of the inside dope on this situation, I should like to ask Dr. Maloney down to Washington to talk it over." *Wilson MSS.*
47. *House Rept. No. 1054*, 65th Cong., 3d sess., p. 1.

In the Senate, Mr. Phelan had introduced a similar resolution (S.J. 203), and this action gave deep concern to the President and the Department of State. On February 3, 1919, Frank L. Polk, Acting Secretary of State, cabled to Secretary Lansing, in Paris, and outlined the course of action he had followed relative to these Congressional resolutions:

> There is pending in the Foreign Relations Committee a resolution of sympathy for Irish freedom. One proposal goes as far as requesting the President to instruct the Peace Delegates to present the matter for consideration in Paris. I have been able to delay the matter in committee for over a month, but I understand it may be forced out this week unless I can tell the Committee the President would prefer to have it held in Committee. Both sides are playing politics with the resolution in order to get the Irish vote and I hesitate to recommend that the President interfere. I however feel that I should ask you to lay the matter before him and request that you give me at earliest possible moment his views.
>
> The Irish party here are shortly to hold a convention and intend to select delegates to go to Paris to present the Irish cause. Ex-Senator O'Gorman, Bourke Cockran and others of that caliber mentioned as delegates. I think I have been able to discourage this movement, but any prophecy in regard to any Irish meeting is dangerous. If the question of passports for the delegates does not come up now, it is reasonably certain to come up later, and I suggest that this matter should also be given consideration.[48]

On February 5 Tumulty sent a cablegram to the President concerning a House resolution with reference to Irish self-determination:

> Flood says passage of some kind of Irish Resolution inevitable and could not be stopped without open and active opposition on your part and then he believes it would pass. Found as drawn Resolution was joint which would require your approval or veto. Had him promise Resolution would be made concurrent, which will require action by Senate.[49]

48. Frank L. Polk to Secretary Lansing, February 3, 1919, 841d.00/11a, *MS.*, N.A.
49. Tumulty to President Wilson, February 5, 1919, *Wilson MSS*.

The President was deeply worried about this Congressional pressure relative to self-determination for Ireland. On February 15 Secretary Lansing sent a hurried telegram to Polk: "The President does not think it would be wise for him to intervene in the matter discussed in your telegram but has instructed me to advise you to keep up the utmost pressure to see that the matter is not acted on at this Congress." [50]

Thanks to this pressure from the Department of State, it was possible to keep in the Senate Committee on Foreign Relations the Phelan resolution, but the sentiment in the House of Representatives was too strong to be checked. Representative Flood was able to substitute House Concurrent Resolution No. 68 for House Joint Resolution No. 357. This amended resolution read as follows: "It is the earnest hope of the Congress of the United States . . . that the Peace Conference, now sitting in Paris, in passing upon the rights of various peoples, will favorably consider the claims of Ireland to the right of self-determination." On March 4 this new resolution was adopted by the overwhelming vote of 216 ayes to 45 noes.[51]

After winning this victory in the House of Representatives, Irish-American pressure groups now devoted their attention to the Senate, where they had a doughty champion in the person of William E. Borah.[52] Borah was enthusiastic in his support of Irish self-determination, and he was equally fervid in his fight against the League of Nations. In this regard he had touched a responsive chord in the breasts of Judge Cohalan and a host of other Irish-Americans. On March 24 he wrote a typical letter to John W. Hart, of Menan, Idaho. It was a scathing indictment of the proposed League of Nations:

50. Secretary Lansing to Frank L. Polk, February 15, 1919, 841d.00/16, MS., N.A.
51. *Congressional Record*, LVII, 5057.
52. See the letters from Thomas Mannix to William E. Borah, March 24, 1919, Joseph J. McCaffery to William E. Borah, March 26, 1919, and the list of resolutions adopted by the Friends of Irish Freedom, March 16, 1919. *Borah Papers*, Library of Congress.

I thank you cordially for your letter but it was no surprise to me. There is too much red blood in your system to subscribe to this treacherous, un-American scheme. Taft is doing the same thing now that he tried to do when he was President—surrender the government to certain sinister influences. There has not been an American administration since that of Buchanan more under the influence of the interests which are not in harmony with the welfare of the people generally. It is quite natural that he should come under the dominating influence of any scheme which intends to transfer the sovereign power of this government to aliens. . . .

I hope, Hart, that you will write a letter to Hays. I am getting tired of this creeping, crawling, smelling attitude of the Republican Party upon an issue which involves the independence of this Republic. . . . The doctrine of treachery and disloyalty ate away the moral fiber of the Democratic Party for fifty years, and when the people awaken to the fact that this is a studied and deliberate attempt to transfer the sovereignty of this government to a tribunal controlled by aliens, they will damn forever the parties which connived at such a scheme. . . . The white-livered cowards who are standing around while the diplomats of Europe are undermining our whole system of independence and self-control will have no hearing when the American people come to know the facts.[53]

It was not just among Republican senators that a strong sentiment against the League of Nations was beginning to develop in Congress. A surge of opposition in the ranks of Democratic senators soon became manifest, and it was significant that many of these senators came from the Far West, where the Irish-American pressure groups were not as powerful as they were in the industrial East. On March 28 three Democratic senators sent to President Wilson a letter that must have given him deep concern for his program at Paris, which featured the League of Nations. Senator Peter G. Gerry was from Rhode Island, Senator Key Pittman from Nevada, and Senator John B. Kendrick from Wyoming. Their communication to the President stressed two issues—Irish self-determination and the League of Nations. It is so important as showing how political winds were blowing in the Senate that a lengthy quotation is justified:

53. Senator William E. Borah to John W. Hart, March 24, 1919, *Borah MSS.*

It has occurred to a number of your friends who send this letter that they ought, in justice to you and in the fulfillment of their public duties, to call your attention to the necessity of seeing that some progress is made before the Peace Conference adjourns towards a solution of the vexing question of self-government for Ireland.

It is difficult at your distance from our shores to appreciate, and your brief stay on this side on your return at the close of the late session, could not give you much opportunity to become fully cognizant of the intensity of the feeling that now prevails throughout our country on the subject referred to. We assure you that it has become a very serious matter. It may be that the subject is more prominently in the public mind because of the efforts of those who are endeavoring to arouse sentiment against the plan of a League of Nations to excite the prejudices of those of our citizens of Irish birth or descent, or it may be that Ireland is generally regarded as pre-eminently entitled to the right of self-determination in respect to her government. Doubtless both considerations have contributed to give to the question the serious aspect it has attained.

It is not alone that the future of our party imperatively demands that something be done before the work of the Peace Conference comes to an end to meet the reasonable expectations of the Irish people, but we all concur in the view that the prospect of early ratification of the treaty by the Senate will be jeopardized otherwise.

It is quite generally believed here that Great Britain is most desirous of launching the League. Indeed, it is persistently offered by its opponents here that we pay a heavy price for the privilege of aiding her in keeping the peace of the world, indeed, that we get practically nothing in return for very considerable sacrifices. Anyway, she is asking much more from the Conference than we are. If these views are even measurably true, she ought to be quite willing to give assurances in some form that Ireland should at least be accorded the same measure of self-government as is enjoyed by the favored colonies. . . . We are agreed that, in view of the considerations adverted to and your attitude so frequently and forcibly stated as to the rights of submerged nationalities, it would be a happy thing if you could, in some way, ask some action along the line suggested.[54]

Throughout the United States a spirit of opposition to the League of Nations was fast rising, and Judge Cohalan had quickly perceived this fact. In the New York *Sun* some of the editorials were

54. Senators Peter G. Gerry, Key Pittman, and John B. Kendrick to President Wilson, March 28, 1919, *Wilson MSS.*

growing increasingly critical of the idea of a League, and Judge Cohalan wrote to Frank A. Munsey, president of the *Sun*, and expressed his hearty agreement with these editorials. On February 24, 1919, Mr. Munsey wrote to the Judge to express his appreciation of this approval:

> I am glad the editorial appealed to you. It should have appealed to all men who have eyes that see. Only a blind man could fail to see that the Wilson League scheme is playing directly into the hands of England. And England would be a dull nation indeed if she did not accept a good thing when it is thrown at her. Apparently she knows her job. I wish we knew our job today as well as the earlier statesmen of this country knew theirs.[55]

55. Frank A. Munsey to Judge Cohalan, February 24, 1919, *Cohalan MSS*.

10 THE SENATE REJECTS A TREATY WHICH MAKES NO PROVISION FOR IRISH SELF-DETERMINATION

A. THE AMERICAN COMMISSION FOR IRISH INDEPENDENCE LABORS IN VAIN IN PARIS TO SECURE A HEARING FOR IRELAND

The Irish Race Convention which met in Philadelphia on February 22-23, 1919, chose an American Commission for Irish Independence which was instructed to visit Paris for the express purpose of presenting to the Peace Conference the case of Ireland. One of the chief items on the agenda of this commission was to secure permission from Lloyd George for Eamon de Valera, Arthur Griffith, and Count Plunkett to go to Paris and plead for Irish self-determination.[1] It was evident that this delegation from Dublin could not secure any favors from Lloyd George unless strong pressure was applied by the American Government. The American Commission for Irish Independence, consisting of Frank P. Walsh,[2] Ed-

1. *Ante,* pp. 296-297.
2. Frank P. Walsh (Chairman of the American Commission for Irish Independence) was a native of St. Louis, Missouri, a lawyer by profession and prominently identified with labor organizations as counsel. He had been a member of the Federal Industrial Commission, appointed by President Wilson, and had been a joint chairman, with ex-President Taft, of the War Labor Board.

ward F. Dunne,[3] and Michael J. Ryan,[4] had high hopes of inducing President Wilson to exert the necessary pressure.

On April 16 the American Commission for Irish Independence sent a letter to President Wilson asking for a hearing at the Peace Conference of the case of Ireland to be presented by De Valera, Griffith, and Count Plunkett:

> If these gentlemen were furnished safe conduct to Paris so that they might present their case, we feel that our mission would be, in the main, if not entirely, accomplished. May we, therefore, ask you to obtain from Mr. Lloyd George, or whomsoever may be entrusted with the specific details of such matter by the English Government, safe conduct for Messrs. De Valera, Griffith and Plunkett from Dublin to Paris.[5]

On the following day [April 17] President Wilson sent word to Mr. Walsh that he would see him that afternoon. During this brief audience there was little time to present the case of Ireland, but Walsh hoped there would be other sessions with the President.[6] In the meantime it would be important for the Irish-American delegation to visit Ireland to get a firsthand picture of the real situation there. Finding it impossible to secure an audience with Lloyd George, they went to the hotel where Colonel House was residing and complained that the British Prime Minister

3. Edward F. Dunne was an ex-Mayor of Chicago and an ex-Governor of Illinois. He had been educated at Trinity College, Dublin. He had long been an ardent champion of the cause of Ireland.
4. Michael J. Ryan was a prominent citizen of Philadelphia, where at one time he had served as City Solicitor. In State government he had held office as Public Service Commissioner. In 1915 he had been a candidate for the Democratic nomination for Governor of Pennsylvania. He was a member of the Clan-na-Gael and had been President of the United Irish League.
5. Frank P. Walsh, Edward F. Dunne, and Michael J. Ryan to President Wilson, Paris, April 16, 1919, *Colonel House Papers,* Yale University Library. On April 18, The American Commission for Irish Independence wrote to Judge Cohalan to report that "things were proceeding in quite a satisfactory manner. We have had interviews with the President and Colonel House, and hope to have something to report very shortly." *Cohalan MSS.*
6. *Congressional Record,* September 3, 1919, 66 Cong., 1 sess., 4668.

had not only failed to make an appointment to see them this week, as promised, but in their opinion he had no notion of seeing them at all. I am not surprised that George should try to wriggle out of this situation as he has so many others. [Sir William] Wiseman was so disgusted that he left nothing of denunciation for me to add.[7]

Finally Colonel House prevailed upon Lloyd George to let the Irish-American delegation have passports to Ireland,[8] and they arrived in Dublin on May 3. According to the American Ambassador in London, John W. Davis, one of the delegation, Michael J. Ryan, was

> on all occasions [during the visit of the delegation to Ireland] violent, and once or twice advocated action similar to that adopted in Easter Week in 1916. Messrs. Walsh and Dunne, I understand, although they did not advocate armed rebellion, missed no opportunity of stating that they represented over 20,000,000 of American people, all ready to help to their utmost in assisting Ireland to achieve its objective—i.e. an Irish Republic.[9]

In Galway, Mr. Ryan assured his audience that "the people had but to be patient and as certain as tomorrow follows today, they would secure their freedom and independence." Prior to their departure from Ireland, the Irish-American delegation issued this statement to the press:

> We are deeply appreciative of the universally generous welcome accorded to us as the accredited representatives of the Irish Race in America. The passion of the Irish people for freedom burns with its age-old intensity, but we find, in addition to this, under the most disinterested and able leadership in Europe today, they are putting their ideal into practical form in a manner which must challenge the admiration of the world and secure the favor and support of all right-thinking peoples.[10]

7. The *Diary* of Colonel House, April 29, 1919, *House MSS*.
8. *Ibid.*, April 30, 1919.
9. Ambassador John W. Davis to the Secretary of State, May 28, 1919, 841d.00/57, *MSS*., National Archives.
10. Edward L. Adams, American Consul at Dublin, to the Secretary of State, May 13, 1919, 841d.00/57, *MSS*., N.A.

On May 17 the Irish delegation to the Paris Peace Conference (Eamon de Valera, Arthur Griffith, and Count Plunkett) issued from the Mansion House in Dublin a communication addressed to Premier Clemenceau with reference to the Irish Question:

> We must ask you to call the immediate attention of the Peace Conference to the warning which it is our duty to communicate, that the people of Ireland, through all its organic means of declaration, has repudiated and does now repudiate, the claim of the British Government to speak or act on behalf of Ireland, and consequently that no treaty or agreement entered into by the representatives of the British Government in virtue of that claim is or can be binding on the people of Ireland. . . .
>
> We request you to notify the Peace Conference that we, the undersigned, have been appointed and authorized by the duly-elected national government of Ireland, to act on behalf of Ireland in the proceedings of the Conference and to enter into agreements and sign treaties on behalf of Ireland.[11]

On this same day (May 17) Frank P. Walsh, Chairman of the Irish-American delegation, wrote to Secretary Lansing asking that safe conduct be extended to the representatives of the Irish Republic so they could attend the meetings of the Paris Peace Conference.[12] Three days later the Irish-American delegation wrote to President Wilson requesting an audience that would enable them to present suggestions which Eamon de Valera, Arthur Griffith, and Count Plunkett had conveyed to them.[13] Walsh also wrote to Colonel House and called his attention to the letter which the delegation had sent to Clemenceau. He expressed the hope that the Colonel would "throw the weight" of his influence "in its favor." After receiving this letter Colonel House took up with the President

> the question of the Irish-American delegation. The President and Lansing were in favor of giving them a brusque refusal to their request, which was that the British Government be asked to give safe conduct to the delegates of the Irish Republic so they might come to Paris

11. *House MSS.*
12. Frank P. Walsh, *et al.*, to Colonel House, *ibid.*
13. Frank P. Walsh, *et al.*, to President Wilson, May 20, 1919, *Congressional Record*, September 3, 1919, 66 Cong., 1 sess., 4669.

and be heard by the Peace Conference. I suggested that they be politely told that the British Government had already intimated to us that they would not grant such a request, and largely because the Irish-American delegation had made incendiary speeches in Ireland while they were there.[14]

Colonel House was far more sympathetic with the cause of Ireland than were President Wilson or Secretary Lansing. He was annoyed therefore when Mr. Walsh sent a letter to the President before showing it to him:

> Colonel House informed Mr. Walsh that he very much regretted that he had made public his letter to the President before showing it to him as it contained a remark attributed to himself that was not in accordance with his recollection. He did not say that Mr. Lloyd George was ready to give safe-conducts to the three Irish Delegates, but that he thought that Mr. Lloyd George *might* give safe-conducts. He said that under the circumstances he had been obliged to publish a denial. Mr. Walsh made a very incoherent explanation in which he stated that he had called early in the day to see Colonel House, but not finding him at home, he had given the letter which had been sent to the President the night before. Mr. Walsh remarked that he felt his responsibility as a representative, and, as such, the necessity of acquainting his followers in the United States of what had actually taken place.[15]

Two days later the members of the Irish-American delegation called on Colonel House to express their regrets for the misunderstanding that had occurred:

> He [Mr. Walsh] added that they had no desire to start a controversy. Colonel House interposed that nothing would suit the British better than a row between himself and the Irish delegation, or between himself and Mr. Lloyd George. He said he was sorry that the journalists had not correctly reproduced his exact words. In any case he felt that Mr. Walsh had come closer to the truth than Mr. Lloyd George. The latter had recently submitted to him a letter for publication, but as it contained many inaccuracies he had been obliged to tell Mr. Lloyd George that, if the letter were published, he would be obliged to

---

14. *Diary* of Colonel House, May 20, 1919, *House MSS.*
15. Notes of a conversation between Colonel House and Frank P. Walsh, May 21, 1919, *ibid.*

give out a denial. Under these circumstances Mr. Lloyd George desisted from his intention. Mr. Lloyd George, Colonel House said, claimed that he had approved of the trip of the three Irish-American delegates to Great Britain and Ireland on the strength of Colonel House's recommendation. Colonel House said that he had not given such recommendation but had merely introduced them to Mr. Lloyd George as gentlemen and distinguished Americans.

Mr. Walsh replied that he had done nothing ungentlemanly unless it were ungentlemanly to tell the exact truth about what was going on in Ireland. Mr. Walsh then handed Colonel House a statement which he said represented the position of himself and his colleagues. Colonel House after reading it said that he could not subscribe to one paragraph: he had not said to the Irish members of the Delegation that he would ask Mr. Lloyd George to give them safe-conducts. What he had said was: Sir William Wiseman thought Mr. Lloyd George might give them safe-conducts. Colonel House asked Mr. Walsh whether he had received a reply from the President, to which Mr. Walsh stated that Mr. Close had written him a letter informing him that his communication to the President would be answered by Mr. Lansing, but up to the present he had received nothing from Mr. Lansing.

Colonel House remarked before the end of the interview that he would do all he possibly could for Ireland.[16]

The Lansing letter was sent to Mr. Walsh on May 24. He criticized the members of the Irish-American delegation for having made in Ireland remarks that gave "the deepest offence" to the British Government. "In view of the situation thus created, I regret to inform you that the American representatives [to the Paris Peace Conference] feel that any further efforts on their part connected with this matter would be futile and therefore unwise." [17]

This letter from Secretary Lansing did not unduly dismay the Irish-American delegation. On May 28 they sent a long letter to the President in which they included a large number of cablegrams they had received from all parts of the United States insisting upon the granting of an opportunity for the case of Ireland to be pre-

16. Notes of a conversation between Colonel House and the Irish-American delegation, May 23, 1919, *ibid.* Colonel House went out of his way to be courteous to the Irish-American delegation. See *Congressional Record,* 66 Cong., 1 sess., 4689-4691, for comments of Michael J. Ryan.
17. Secretary Lansing to Frank P. Walsh, May 24, 1919, *Cong. Record.*, 66 Cong., 1 sess., 4870.

sented to the Peace Conference. These cablegrams voiced vigorous protests against Article X of the Covenant of the League of Nations. This article would "prevent the giving of aid by outside advocates of liberty to oppressed nations, which practice has obtained among civilized peoples from time immemorial." [18]

When this letter from the Irish-American delegation was turned over to the official representatives of the American Government at the Peace Conference, they sent their answer to the President in the form of a joint negative response: "We are of the opinion that the request of Mr. Walsh[19] should not be granted for the reason that it is not within the province of the American delegation to request the Peace Conference to receive a delegation composed of citizens of a country other than our own." [20] On May 31 Mr. Grew, on behalf of the American delegation, sent a formal note to Walsh and Dunne which repeated the above formula.[21]

The Irish-American delegation countered with a request for permission to appear before the American Delegation to the Peace Conference for the purpose of presenting the resolution adopted by the Irish Race Convention on February 23, 1919, "with a brief argument in support thereof." [22] When this request was ignored, the Irish-American delegation filed with Secretary Lansing a report on "Conditions in Ireland with a Demand for the Investigation of this Situation by the Peace Conference." In this report there was a sharp condemnation of the Mountjoy Prison in Dublin. Political prisoners were locked in steel cages that had been built

> in the yards of the prison. These cages are exact duplicates of those used for wild animals in the larger zoological gardens such as Lincoln

18. Frank P. Walsh and Edward F. Dunne to President Wilson, May 28, 1919, *House MSS.*
19. On May 24, Michael J. Ryan, one of the members of the Irish-American delegation, became so disgusted with the evasive tactics of President Wilson that he decided to return to America.
20. Secretary Lansing, Henry White, E. M. House and Tasker H. Bliss to President Wilson, May 31, 1919, *House MSS.*
21. Joseph C. Grew to Frank P. Walsh and Edward F. Dunne, May 31, 1919, *Congressional Record,* 66 Cong., 1 sess., 4672.
22. Frank P. Walsh and Edward F. Dunne to Joseph C. Grew, June 2, 1919, *ibid.,* 4673.

Park and the Bronx. . . . The political prisoners in the jail, without exception, were men of the highest standing: journalists, lawyers, business men, skilled tradesmen and laborers. Many of them confined for months have not been informed of the charges against them. All of them are denied the right of trial by jury. . . . We took statements covering hundreds of cases of outrage and violence committed by the officers and representatives of the English government in Ireland.[23]

The persistence of the American Commission on Irish independence finally bore fruit in an interview between President Wilson and Frank P. Walsh and Edward F. Dunne. During the course of this interview the President made a revealing remark: "You should understand that no small nation of any kind has yet appeared before the Committee of Four, and there is an agreement among the Committee . . . that none can come unless unanimous consent is given by the whole Committee." This remark merely confirmed the strong suspicion expressed in a letter from Sean T. O'Kelly to John Devoy relative to an agreement between Wilson, Balfour and Clemenceau concerning the Irish Question.[24]

Near the close of this interview on June 11, under repeated questions of Frank P. Walsh, the President made the following statement that indicated his embarrassment over the question of Irish self-determination:

You have touched on the great metaphysical tragedy of today. When I gave utterance to those words I said them without the knowledge that nationalities existed which are coming to us day after day. Of course, Ireland's case, from the point of view of population, from the point of view of the struggle it has made, from the point of interest it has excited in the world, and especially among our own people, whom I am anxious to serve, is the outstanding case of a small nationality. You do not know and cannot appreciate the anxieties I have experienced as the result of these many millions of peoples having their hopes raised by what I have said." [25]

23. Frank P. Walsh and Edward F. Dunne to Secretary Lansing, June 6, 1919, *House MSS.*
24. *Gaelic American,* March 15, 1919.
25. Dorothy Macardle, *The Irish Republic,* p. 297.

After this interview with the President, Walsh was encouraged to send him a letter protesting against the brutalities that were an everyday occurrence in Ireland under English administration. It was also hoped that the President would place these facts before the Peace Conference and request an investigation by an "impartial tribunal." [26]

There was no "impartial tribunal" in Paris to hear complaints against the brutal English administration in Ireland. On June 28 the peace treaty with Germany was signed at Versailles, and President Wilson and the American delegation prepared to return to America. Meanwhile, Judge Cohalan, as requested by the Friends of Irish Freedom, had appointed John A. Murphy, of Buffalo, as a supplementary member of the American Commission for Irish Independence. Murphy[27] sailed from New York on June 20 and arrived in Paris after the signature of the Treaty of Versailles. On July 22 he sent a note to Clemenceau requesting an audience, but the French premier never bothered to send an answer.

The American Commission on Irish Independence had completed its task, and Sean T. O'Kelly, the Irish representative at Versailles, sent to Judge Cohalan[28] a warm testimonial relative to the work of the commission:

> I think it would not be amiss if I wrote you a few lines to let you and the members of the Committee of the Philadelphia Convention know how highly I appreciate their work, and of the indescribably valuable service they have rendered to the Irish Cause since they came here. The organization of the Philadelphia Convention was a big idea, and the success which attended it has marked it as the turning point in the tide of the new movement for Irish Independence so far as the United States is concerned. . . .

26. Frank P. Walsh and Edward F. Dunne to President Wilson, June 17, 1919, 841d.00/63, *MSS.*, N.A.
27. Mr. Murphy was a prominent business man of Buffalo, New York, who had long been an active member of the Friends of Irish Freedom. He had been instrumental in holding large meetings of the Friends in Buffalo, and had induced Bishop William Turner to take an active part in these meetings. On May 17 a large mass meeting had been held in Buffalo with Judge Cohalan as the principal speaker.
28. The task of selecting the members of the American Commission for Irish Independence had fallen to Judge Cohalan.

To my mind, however, the conception of the American Commission on Irish independence, and the sending of that Commission to Paris was even a greater achievement. . . . I personally ascribe the greater part of our success in the last few months to the work of the Commission that the Philadelphia Convention Committee formed and sent here. The success of this Commission has, to my mind, been so great that I believe when the history of these times is being written, a truthful historian must surely say that the American Commission on Irish Independence has by its achievements written one of the brightest pages of this bright era of Ireland's history.

The visit of the Commission to Ireland I judge as one of the happiest inspirations; and as far as one can judge from here the effect of that visit on the spirit of the people at home has been such that I believe there will never again be a doubt in the minds of the people of Ireland as to what the nature of their political demand should be.[29]

Mr. O'Kelly was a little too enthusiastic about the work of the American Commission for Irish Independence. It had really accomplished very little. Not even were hearings on the Irish Question permitted at Versailles. Of course there was no investigation of British brutality in Ireland. President Wilson had been deeply concerned about the alleged plight of African natives under German administration, and he had pressed for a transfer of the German colonies to British control. The misfortunes of oppressed minorities in Europe had greatly disturbed him, and he had rejoiced in the fall of the German and Austrian empires. Their destruction had meant the liberation of Czechs, Esthonians, Finns, Latvians, Lithuanians, Jugoslavs, and Poles and the erection of new states that gave substance to their dreams of independence. He had, however, resolutely closed his ears to the cries from hard-pressed and broken Ireland. It is true that he had consented to an audience with the members of the Irish Commission for Irish Independence who had paid a visit to Paris to plead the cause of Ireland, but he had privately confessed to a friend that "his first impulse was to tell them 'to go to Hell.'"[30] After seven centuries of barbarous mis-

---

29. Sean T. O'Kelly to Judge Daniel F. Cohalan, Paris, June 27, 1919, *Cohalan MSS.*
30. Thomas A. Bailey, *Woodrow Wilson and the Great Betrayal* (New York, 1945), p. 27.

treatment the Irish, apparently, should have been used to the lash, and the President was a little annoyed that they should complain of atrocities. Whatever he thought, it is a matter of record that he made no effort to accomplish anything for Ireland at a peace conference that was supposedly dedicated to the establishment of a new and just political order in the world. His indifference to the cause of Ireland was a clear indication that he was a phrasemaker and not a real peacemaker.

But there was one prominent Anglo-Irishman who still cherished a belief that President Wilson had done his best for Ireland. In a letter to Tumulty, Shane Leslie poured forth his soul:

> Since I saw you last I have been close enough to the Irish to realize the depth of their unfortunate resentment to the President. In spite of their many utterances of open hostility I think they do not relish being made the instrument of Republican vengeance. The President is still their only potential friend. I do not believe they have broken yet with all that the President stands for. . . . Certainly they realise what poor company they are joining in adding to the President's enemies. I feel more strongly than ever that the President did as much as the Irish had the right to ask of him but that his good will and generous hints were disregarded and he has been unjustly left open to criticism. Allied diplomacy like the Republican Party seems to favor a collision between the President and the Irish in view of the next election.
>
> In private protest to all this I am anxious to become an American citizen and be done with it all. For three years I have done my utmost to retain Irish confidence in the President but English policy gives me no choice between Sinn Fein and becoming an American. Could you enable me to enlist in the American forces now engaged in Russia or Siberia? [31]

B. THE IRISH QUESTION TAKES ON STRONG POLITICAL OVERTONES

Shane Leslie had completely misread the President's attitude towards the Irish Question. He did not realize that in the White House there had been no real sympathy for Irish aspirations. The President's impulse to tell the American Commission for Irish Independ-

31. Shane Leslie to Joe Tumulty, April 8, 1919, *Wilson MSS.*

ence "to go to Hell" was indicative of his feeling towards the Irish. He had stifled that impulse because it was a political imperative to curry favor with Irish-American voters. But he would never let politics injure his pet project of a League of Nations. He knew that Irish-American leaders were strongly opposed to Article X of the League Covenant and would demand a far-reaching amendment, but he had no intention of acceding to such a demand. When Senator Martin, of Virginia, intimated that it would be difficult to muster a two-thirds vote in the Senate in favor of the Treaty of Versailles, the President snapped back: "Martin! Anyone who opposes me in that, I'll crush." [32] He would soon learn that Judge Cohalan and many other Irish-Americans could not be crushed by Presidential pressure.

As far as the League of Nations was concerned, President Wilson, since November 1915, had been in favor of some league of nations to insure world peace, and in 1918 it had become the chief item in the program he intended to push at Paris. In the previous year some American publicists, realizing the strength of American isolationist sentiment, had feared that Republican leaders would use this sentiment to good political advantage. In this regard Herbert Croly sent him the following warning: "There seems to be a tendency among Republicans all over the country, but particularly in Congress, definitely to oppose the participation of the United States in a League of Nations under any conditions." Croly believed that Republican leaders would "try to make political capital" out of this issue, and he urged the President to "appeal to public opinion behind their backs and to make sure you have it." [33] The President replied that he was deeply interested in educating public opinion "by making some speeches through the country," and he indicated agreement with Croly's viewpoint that we "cannot afford to leave anything undone which would make us secure in the support of the great popular opinion of the country." [34]

After trying to enlist the assistance of the Carnegie Endowment for International Peace in a campaign to educate American public

32. Thomas A. Bailey, *op. cit.*, p. 13.
33. Herbert Croly to President Wilson, January 23, 1917, *Wilson MSS.*
34. President Wilson to Herbert Croly, January 25, 1917, *ibid.*

opinion in favor of a League of Nations,[35] the President decided to make a personal appeal to the American voters in the Congressional elections of 1918. In a letter to Edward W. Pou, Chairman of the Committee on Rules in the House of Representatives, he alluded to this appeal which he was about to issue to American voters: "I hope with all my heart it may be effective." [36] But his appeal fell very flat and the election returns indicated that in the new House of Representatives there would be 237 Republicans, 191 Democrats and 7 Independents. In the Senate there would be 49 Republicans and 47 Democrats. It was evident that the average American voter felt deep misgivings about the Wilson leadership. The Covenant of the League of Nations, which was deeply imbedded in the Treaty of Versailles, was bound to arouse the hostility of millions of Americans who were still wedded to the Washington tradition of political isolationism. If large numbers of Irish-Americans joined in this fight against the League because it might prevent, as they feared, the eventual independence of Ireland, it was obvious that the Wilson program was due for rough sledding in the Senate.

This rough sledding began early on the morning of March 4, 1919, when Senator Lodge presented to the Senate a pronunciamento drawn up by Senator Brandegee which boldly announced that the signatories were opposed to the Covenant of the League of Nations "in the form now proposed." This so-called round robin was signed by 37 (soon to be 39) Republican senators or senators-elect. Thirty-three votes would be sufficient to defeat the passage of the Treaty of Versailles.[37]

Republican senators hurled another challenge in the President's face. Ordinarily, when the short session of Congress ended on March 4, the new session would not begin until the following De-

---

35. See comments of Professor Rocco M. Paone in his doctoral dissertation, *The Presidential Election of 1920*, pp. 12-13, in the Georgetown University library.
36. President Wilson to Edward W. Pou, October 26, 1918, *Wilson MSS*.
37. *Congressional Record*, 65 Cong., 3 sess., LVII, 4974. See also Selig Adler, "The Congressional Election of 1918," *South Atlantic Quarterly*, XXXVI (1937), 447-465; Denna F. Fleming, *The United States and the League of Nations, 1918-1920* (New York, 1932), chap. ii.

cember. By resorting to a filibuster in the last days of the short session, the Republicans had been able to "kill" some important appropriation bills. This procedure would compel the President to call Congress into extraordinary session in the late spring so that these appropriation bills could be passed before the new fiscal year began on July 1.

Before Congress met in this extraordinary session which began on May 19, 1919, the current of opposition to the League of Nations was rising rapidly and this was very apparent in the Senate. On February 21 Senator Borah delivered an address on "Americanism" which his biographer calls "one of his great anti-League efforts."[38] It was an address that delighted Irish-Americans. Borah was a bitter foe of British imperialism, and he asked a series of leading questions that revealed a strong anti-British inclination: "What has England given up in this League of Nations? What has she surrendered? . . . Did she surrender the freedom of the seas? . . . Has she surrendered her claim for the largest navy? What has she surrendered?"[39]

Borah soon became the leader of the Republican "irreconcilables" in the Senate. There was a lot of fire, fury, and brains in this little group of "bitter-enders." Frank B. Brandegee, of Connecticut, had a sharp wit that infuriated his Democratic opponents, and they often winced as he lashed them on the League issue. Albert B. Fall, of New Mexico, was not an intellectual giant, but he was a steadfast opponent of the League and his vote could always be counted upon by his colleagues. Medill McCormick, of Illinois, former publisher of the isolationist Chicago *Tribune,* disliked the League with a bitterness that bordered on hysteria. There was never any doubt about his vote. Hiram W. Johnson, of California, able politician who had long dominated the scene in his native state, and an astute forecaster of political weather, was one of the most vehement opponents of the League and his influence was strong and far-reaching. George H. Moses, of New Hampshire, small-town newspaper editor, was a political manipulator of undoubted

---

38. Claudius Johnson, *Borah of Idaho* (New York, 1936), p. 228.
39. *Ibid.,* p. 229.

genius which often helped Senate "irreconcilables" to wreck the best-laid plans of Democratic senators in favor of the League. The intellectual peer of all the irreconcilables was Philander C. Knox, of Pennsylvania, who before entering upon a Senate career had already won distinction as an Attorney General under Theodore Roosevelt and as Secretary of State under Taft. His speeches were models of clarity of expression and keenness of thought.

Along with these "bitter-enders" was a formidable group of "strong reservationists" and a respectable number of "mild reservationists." The leader of the "strong reservationists" was Henry Cabot Lodge, who was Chairman of the Senate Committee on Foreign Relations. In 1919 Lodge was an outspoken opponent of the Wilson League of Nations. But he was fearful of a "blank negative to any League." It was possible for him to conceive "of a League that could do great good if properly guarded and in exact accord with our feelings." [40] Ex-senator Beveridge did not approve this cautious policy recommended by Senator Lodge. To him it looked like "hedging" on an issue of momentous importance.[41] This was also the viewpoint of Senator Borah, who frankly expressed his feelings to Beveridge: "We seem to be afraid to take a stand upon a great vital problem, and therefore we apologize and compromise upon a question which involves the very existence of our government." [42]

The pressure of these "irreconcilables" was so strong and persistent that Lodge had to bend before it. To confirm this pressure, Judge Cohalan and other prominent members of the Friends of Irish Freedom held a series of large mass meetings which adopted resolutions in favor of Irish self-determination. In this regard an "Irish Republic" was demanded. Other resolutions denounced Article X of the League of Nations as a danger to the eventual independence of Ireland.

On March 23 there was a "monster meeting" of Irish-Americans in the Metropolitan Opera House in New York City. In his address

40. Henry Cabot Lodge to Albert J. Beveridge, February 27, March 8, 1919, *Beveridge Papers,* Library of Congress.
41. Albert J. Beveridge to Senator Lodge, March 25, 1919, *ibid.*
42. Senator Borah to Albert J. Beveridge, January 28, 1919, *ibid.*

to this large audience Judge Cohalan stressed the fact that "English diplomacy never sleeps. England has won much by force, more by commerce, but most of all by diplomacy. Her diplomacy takes a thousand forms, but all of them are used in the interest of England, whether it is for the purpose of breaking down a nation, a people or a man." [43] On March 30 he was the principal speaker at another large meeting in Boston in Faneuil Hall. He was insistent that the Paris Peace Conference deal in a friendly way with Irish aspirations: "If the Peace Conference adjourns without seeing that the Irish Republic is recognized, there will be no just peace. What we Americans should do is this—do what can be done and what should be done to see that the Peace Conference recognizes the Irish Republic." [44]

On April 27, in New Haven, there was an Irish-American rally in Poli's Palace Theater, and once again Judge Cohalan was the orator of the evening.[45] But the Judge was not content with influencing public opinion by a series of meetings which passed resolutions calling for the erection of an Irish Republic. He knew that the Senate would convene on May 19 and that the Irish Question would come up before the new Senate Committee on Foreign Relations. It was important for him to keep in close touch with the friends of Ireland on that committee. He knew very well that in Senator Borah, Ireland had a doughty champion. On May 8 he wrote to the Senator and invited him to visit New York City for the purpose of meeting the more important Irish-American leaders. Borah wrote immediately that he was "exceedingly anxious" to arrange for such an interview because there were "some matters which I feel I ought to talk over with you and other

---

43. *Cohalan MSS.*
44. *Ibid.* With reference to Judge Cohalan's address in Boston, Father Thomas J. McClusky, S.J., remarked, in a letter of March 31: "You made a great and most favorable impression. The reception and the applause showed this at the meeting and the press has spread it through this country and the world." *Cohalan MSS.*
45. John J. Splain wrote to Judge Cohalan, May 1, 1919, to congratulate him upon his "splendid address" which had an "excellent effect" upon the audience in New Haven. *Cohalan MSS.*

friends." But the pressure of business was so great in Washington that it was "impossible to leave the city in the near future." [46]

As a result of this pressure from Irish-Americans like Judge Cohalan, Borah hurriedly prepared a resolution which he introduced in the Senate on May 29, which urged the American Peace Commission in Paris to "secure a hearing for the representatives of the Irish Republic." In a letter to Judge Cohalan, Borah expressed the fear that if his resolution was defeated, such action "would hurt us over there and here too." [47]

In order to assure the passage of the Borah resolution, more Irish-American mass meetings were held. One was scheduled to take place in Portland, Oregon, on June 1, and Andrew C. Smith requested Borah to send some message to the meeting. Borah responded with a sharp attack upon the League of Nations:

> The right of self-determination which we were assured was involved in this war is wholly excluded from the League Covenant. In this instrument the people have no voice, no opportunity to be heard. . . . There is no method, no means by which a subject people struggling for their liberties can ever be heard. The denial of a hearing to the representatives of Ireland discloses in an unmistakable way that the principle of self-determination has been rejected by the framers of this league. The league created an autocracy based upon the combined military power of five great nations. Under Article X this military force is to be used to hold intact the territorial boundaries of the members of the autocracy. This not only means the subjection of all small nations to the dictation of the autocracy but it means the use of the man power of the United States to settle the territorial disputes and dynastic quarrels of Europe.[48]

The widespread public opinion in favor of the Borah viewpoint made a profound impression upon the Senate Committee on Foreign Relations, which soon turned in a favorable report relative to the right of the representatives of Ireland to receive a hearing at the Paris Peace Conference. Judge Cohalan congratulated Bo-

---

46. Senator Borah to Judge Cohalan, May 14, 1919, *Borah MSS*. See also Borah to Judge Cohalan, May 23, 28, 1919.
47. Senator Borah to Judge Cohalan, May 29, 1919, *ibid*.
48. Senator Borah to Andrew C. Smith, May 31, 1919, *Borah MSS*.

rah upon securing this favorable action, but he believed it was most advisable to have the Borah resolution voted upon at the earliest opportunity.[49]

On the following day (June 6) the Senate adopted this resolution by the surprising vote of 60 yeas to 1 nay.[50] It was now obvious how political winds were blowing in the Senate, and if the President had been wise he would have given careful consideration to this fact. But he still cherished the illusion that he could dominate the scene in the Senate: "Martin! Anyone who opposes me in that [the ratification of the Treaty of Versailles], I'll crush." He was finally able to crush only the League and himself.

C. JUDGE COHALAN COMPELS THE SENATE COMMITTEE ON FOREIGN RELATIONS TO HEAR A PRESENTATION OF THE CASE OF IRELAND

Judge Cohalan was delighted with the adoption of the Borah resolution in the Senate. It had aroused "great enthusiasm and it is now of importance that the matter should be brought to the attention of the Peace Conference without delay."[51] The members of the American Commission at the Peace Conference were furnished with copies of the Borah resolution, but they made no attempt to bring it before the Big Four. The resolution may have had some influence upon President Wilson, who consented to see two members of the American Commission for Irish Independence on June 11. This private conference accomplished nothing for the cause of Ireland, and the President granted it merely as a gesture for placating the Irish vote in America.

But Judge Cohalan still had faith in the pressure of large public

49. Judge Daniel F. Cohalan to Senator Borah, June 5, 1919, *ibid*.
50. *Congressional Record*, 66 Cong., 1 sess., LVIII, June 6, 1919, 733. The second paragraph of the Borah resolution declared that the Senate of the United States "expresses its sympathy for the aspirations of the Irish people for a Government of their own choice." On June 17 the Irish Dail Eireann sent a warm response to the Borah resolution and declared that the ties that bound Ireland and America were "indissoluble."
51. Judge Cohalan to Senator Borah, June 10, 1919, *Borah MSS*.

meetings upon the minds of Senators who soon would have to vote upon the ratification of the Treaty of Versailles. On the night of June 10 he spoke at a meeting in Mechanics Hall in Boston, and on the 14th he paid a visit to Washington for another address in opposition to the League of Nations.

Irish-Americans in the Senate, like Senator Phelan, were greatly worried about the impact of this rising tide of adverse public opinion concerning the League. On June 26, in the Senate, he made a speech which he hoped would partially stem this adverse tide. He assured Irish-Americans that the League would really blaze a trail for Irish self-determination. If the League were widely adopted by the nations of the world, England would not have to fear that Ireland, if independent, could be used as a base of hostile operations against English ports:

> Ireland fears the guarantee of territorial integrity will prevent her from securing outside help for which she has vainly looked for centuries and which England has without a league been able to repel. . . . On the other hand, if Ireland wins independence by the moral pressure of the world and her own steadfast purpose to be free, the League will ensure her in her freedom. Once established, the principles of the League . . . become an accusing arraignment against England until she accords self-determination to the best qualified of her dependencies.[52]

Irish-American leaders responded to Senator Phelan's arguments by holding an "extraordinary meeting" in Madison Square Garden on the night of July 10. The Covenant of the League of Nations was subjected to a tremendous barrage of fiery arguments, and the enthusiasm of the audience rose to a fervor that shook the rafters of the Garden. It was evident that Senator Phelan might speak for President Wilson but certainly not for Irish-Americans.

The next move of Judge Cohalan was to rally sentiment against the League by having the Senate Committee on Foreign Relations hold extensive hearings on the Irish Question.[53] At first the members of the Committee were dubious about the advisability of this pub-

---

52. *Congressional Record,* 66 Cong. 1 sess., LVIII, 1787-1788.
53. Judge Cohalan to Senator Borah, July 11, 1919, *Borah MSS.*

lic presentation of the case of Ireland. Senator Borah wrote to Judge Cohalan in this regard: "It has been thought that it would be impossible to have hearings for all who wish to be heard, and it would be impracticable to discriminate." [54]

But Judge Cohalan was determined that the case of Ireland should be presented before the Senate Committee on Foreign Relations, and he began to manipulate certain forces that would control the situation. On July 26 the Democratic State Committee of Massachusetts adopted a resolution which expressed the fact that it was

> unalterably opposed to the attempt of England and her Allies to force upon the American people a so-called Covenant of a League of Nations which attempts to commit this Republic to recognize and hold forever the title of England to own and rule Ireland against the expressed will of an overwhelming majority of the Irish people." [55]

But despite this pressure exerted upon the Senate through the untiring efforts of Judge Cohalan, there was still some doubt as to whether hearings would be held upon the Irish Question. Some members of the Senate Committee on Foreign Relations were distinctly dubious about such a procedure. According to Daniel T. O'Connell, head of the Irish Bureau in Washington, the Chairman of the Committee, Senator Lodge, along with Brandegee and McCumber, were undecided about what should be done. Senator Moses was strongly in favor of a hearing before the committee made its report, but Brandegee was "frankly set in opposition" to this delay in the formal vote of the Senate upon the Treaty: "He believes there are enough votes to defeat the League and is desirous of meeting the issue at an early date." [56]

Judge Cohalan did not agree with this opinion of Brandegee.

54. Borah to Cohalan, July 14, 1919, *ibid*. In commenting upon the campaign carried on by Judge Cohalan against the League of Nations and in favor of Irish self-determination, Senator James A. Reed, in a letter to the Judge, July 19, 1919, remarks: "I think the fight is going along in fine shape. Your work is splendid." *Cohalan MSS*.
55. Resolution adopted by the Democratic State Committee of Massachusetts, July 26, 1919, *Wilson MSS*.
56. Daniel T. O'Connell to Judge Cohalan, August 19, 1919, *Cohalan MSS*.

He wanted the Irish Question to be discussed at length before the Committee and in this way secure valuable publicity for the case of Irish self-determination. He now pushed his efforts with new vigor, and he could use certain funds to good advantage. The Victory Fund drive that had been inaugurated in February 1919 was terminated on August 31, 1919. The net proceeds of this fund, as received by the Treasurer of the Friends of Irish Freedom, amounted to the impressive total of $1,005,080.83. Part of these proceeds could be used in a sustained attack upon the League of Nations.

Through the efforts of the Friends, as inspired by Judge Cohalan, more than half a million pamphlets on the Irish Question had been distributed in the United States.[57] Judge Cohalan threw himself into this campaign with tremendous vigor. A brief account of his activities in this regard is given in the memoir prepared by Daniel T. O'Connell:

> After our New York headquarters closed for the day, I worked with a matchless strategist, Justice Daniel F. Cohalan of the New York Supreme Court. Every night, by long-distance 'phone, we discussed our plan for the next day. Every Friday Judge Cohalan left for Washington to confer with Senators. Rushing from office to office in taxis, telephoning and walking, this physical and mental marvel never tired. I was exhausted when the time came for him to board the train for New York, after outplaying the British Embassy at their own game of "secret diplomacy." Few men can say so much in a few words as Judge Cohalan. Few have such a magnetic personality; fewer still have this man's sagacity and resource. The veteran Senator Lodge once said to me: "I consider Judge Cohalan one of the ablest men who ever came to Washington to plead a cause. The citizens of Irish blood are fortunate in having him as a leader." [58]

57. In this fight against the League of Nations in 1919 the Friends of Irish Freedom issued:
       700,000 pamphlets entitled "The Irish Republic Can Pay Its Way";
       500,000 colored maps of Ireland showing the Republican victory in the 1918 election;
       100,000 pamphlets by Edward F. McSweeney entitled "America First."
58. *Cohalan MSS.* See also Daniel T. O'Connell to Judge Cohalan, August 5, 1919, *Cohalan MSS.* O'Connell took charge of the Irish Bureau in Washington in the early part of July 1919. He was a Boston lawyer who was "well known for his work in Massachusetts both for Irish freedom and at the bar." See Washington *Times,* August 10, 1919. On September 13,

Provision for Irish Self-Determination

As a result of these activities, Judge Cohalan had his way, and hearings on the Irish Question were held before the Senate Committee on Foreign Relations. The members of the American Commission on Irish Independence (Frank P. Walsh, Edward F. Dunne, and Michael J. Ryan) testified at length upon the right of Ireland to self-determination and upon their recent experiences in Paris and in Ireland. On September 3 Judge Cohalan testified before the Committee. As a representative of the Irish-American element in America, he wished to emphasize the fact that the "Belgian atrocities have been duplicated a hundredfold in Ireland." As far as American foreign policy was concerned, the Irish-Americans wished to point out that

> under the Monroe Doctrine as it has been established, we have grown in wealth, prosperity and power as no nation in the history of the world has grown. . . . We Irish think that there should be no abandonment of the policy laid down by Washington in his Farewell Address of keeping away from permanent, entangling alliances with any of the countries of the Old World.[59]

D. IN HIS FAMOUS APPEAL TO THE AMERICAN PEOPLE PRESIDENT WILSON TRIES IN VAIN TO SQUARE THE CIRCLE OF THE LEAGUE OF NATIONS

The day after Judge Cohalan testified before the Senate Committee on Foreign Relations, President Wilson began a western tour which he hoped would counteract the pressure that Irish-Americans had exerted upon Congress. It was significant that in none of his speeches, during this trip, was any reference made to Irish self-determination. He talked a lot about "rehabilitated Poland"; "rescued Bohemia"; and "redeemed Jugo-Slavia." He went into great detail about the number of delegations that came to see him from oppressed peoples:

1919, Victor Herbert wrote to Judge Cohalan and remarked: "You have really done wonders for the cause and justly have gained the love and admiration of every true Irishman." *Cohalan MSS.*

59. *Congressional Record*, 66 Cong., 1 sess., LVIII, 4662-4664.

> Almost every day of the week that I was not imperatively engaged otherwise I was receiving delegations. Delegations from where? . . . Groups of men from all over the world. . . . Did you ever hear of Adjur-Badjan, for example. A very dignified group of fine-looking men came in from Adjur-Badjan. . . . They knew . . . what America stood for, and they had come to me . . . with outstretched hands and said: "We want the guidance and the help and the advice of America." And they all said that, until my heart grew fearful, and I said to one group of them: "I beg that you will not expect the impossible. . . . We will do the best we can. We will stand as your friends." [60]

It had been the President's impulse to tell the American Commission for Irish Independence "to go to Hell." To the delegations from Adjur-Badjan and other little-known and unpronounceable places he was extraordinarily polite and understanding. For the people of Ireland he had little sympathy and no desire to be their champion in a fight for self-determination. He and Sir Edward Carson had many thoughts in common.

He was quite loquacious about Article X in all the addresses he made on his western tour. The Covenant of the League was dear to his heart, and Article X was the keystone of this new arch of world peace:

> You have heard a great deal about Article X of the covenant of the League of Nations. Article X speaks the conscience of the world. . . . You have heard it said . . . that we are robbed of some degree of our sovereign independent choice by articles of that sort. Every man who makes a choice to respect the rights of his neighbor deprives himself of absolute sovereignty, but he does it by promising never to do wrong.[61]

At St. Louis the President grew warmly enthusiastic about Article X:

> The solemn thing about Article X is the first sentence . . . that says we will respect and preserve against external aggression the territorial integrity and existing political independence of other nations. . . . When you read Article X, therefore, you will see that it is nothing but

---

60. President Wilson's Address at Bismarck, North Dakota, September 10, 1919, *The Messages and Papers of Woodrow Wilson* (New York, 1924), II, 860.
61. *Ibid.*, pp. 746-747.

the inevitable, logical center of the whole system of the covenant of the League of Nations, and I stand for it absolutely.[62]

President Wilson might stand for the covenant of the League "absolutely," but there were millions of Irish-Americans who could not be persuaded to take a similar stand. From their viewpoint it seemed clear that Article X helped to freeze the status quo all over the world, and this status quo meant Irish subjection to England. Irish independence could be accomplished only through help outside Ireland, perhaps armed help. Under Article X, America would be bound to prevent this outside help from making Irish independence a reality. No real Irish-American could favor a covenant containing such an article, and the Friends of Irish Freedom sought new means of acquainting the American people with the dangers of the League. During the week of August 11-16, 1919, full-page and half-page advertisements were inserted in many newspapers throughout the country indicating the menace of the League to American liberties. When the President was on his western tour, each day in the city in which he spoke the newspapers carried advertisements asking what the founding fathers would have said to the surrender of American sovereignty through the agency of the League. On the days following his addresses there would be other large advertisements entitled "Then and Now," which contrasted Wilson's Fourteen Points with what was written into the Treaty of Versailles. His failure to secure self-determination for Ireland was stressed again and again. There is no doubt that the President saw these large advertisements, and it is quite likely not only that they underscored the hollow nature of his promises but that the pungent quality of the sharp phrases ate through the thin walls of his sensitive nature and helped to bring on the physical collapse that he suffered upon his return to Washington.

In this concerted drive against the League of Nations, Judge Cohalan was the principal leader. It was evident to him that unremitting pressure would have to be exerted upon the Senate, and he constantly thought of new devices that would help to bring wavering senators into line. One evening Daniel T. O'Connell

62. *Ibid.*, pp. 766-767.

phoned Judge Cohalan from Washington and expressed the opinion that Senator Frelinghuysen, of New Jersey, was weakening on the League issue. The Judge immediately got in touch with the other members of the Advertising Committee of the Friends of Irish Freedom, and it was decided to launch a postal-card campaign. Seventy-thousand cards were prepared for mailing to the Senator. Within two days, more than half of this number of cards were in the mail. On the back of each card was a demand that the Senator work for the defeat of the Treaty of Versailles, and each card bore the signature and address of a voter in New Jersey.[63] There is no doubt that this pressure was highly effective not only upon Senator Frelinghuysen but upon other senators who were uncertain of the stand they should take.

Large meetings of protest were held throughout September and October 1919, and earnest efforts were made to secure speakers whose words of denunciation carried weight with the average American voter. James McGurrin, one of the young leaders in the fight for Irish freedom, invited Senator Borah to be the speaker at a large rally in New York City. Pressure of business in Washington prevented the Senator from accepting this invitation, but he wrote a letter which could be read at the meeting. It was unsparing in its criticism of the League of Nations:

> The League of Nations in its present form is a complete autocracy. At no place and at no time are the people given a voice in this scheme of world peace, and in no way and by no process are the subject peoples permitted to have a hearing. In addition to being an autocracy it is an autocracy so arranged in its machinery that it may be controlled by European powers and against the only real Republic in existence today.
>
> When this League is organized five dominant powers (an alliance) will dominate and control as subject peoples nearly one half of the inhabitants of the globe. There is not to be found in the covenant a single line or phrase giving these subject peoples a right to be heard as to their independence or their freedom. There is no machinery provided

---

63. In the *Cohalan Papers* there is a considerable amount of interesting data on this advertising campaign directed by Judge Cohalan. It was very effective in molding the minds of large numbers of Irish-Americans with reference to the dangers of the League.

in the covenant by which these subject peoples can set up their own form of government or be permitted to live their own lives. So far as the terms of the League are concerned these peoples must live in subjection for all time to come. And we agree to do our part in keeping them in subjection. Ireland, Egypt, Korea, India and all subject peoples alike can find no door or escape from this autocratic machine save that of war with all the great powers combined against them. . . .

Let's fight it [the Covenant] now and fight it for all time as our fathers fought tyranny and autocracy before. . . . We should raise the banner once and for all. No compromise now or hereafter until the last vestige of this new scheme of autocracy has been wiped out.[64]

On the very day that Borah wrote this letter to Mr. McGurrin, the Senate rejected by a close vote the amendment offered by Senator Johnson which would deprive the British Empire of six votes in the League Assembly. But this defeat was merely a prelude to final success for the enemies of the treaty. On November 6 Senator Lodge reported to the Senate a series of fourteen reservations. Each one of these reservations was voted upon separately, sometimes after a protracted debate. One of these reservations specifically dealt with Article X of the Covenant. Finally, on November 19, 1919, the Senate was called upon to vote upon approving the Treaty of Versailles with the Lodge reservations attached. When the result was announced, 39 ayes, 55 nays, the galleries began to grow hysterical. The treaty with the reservations had lost, but the negative votes were not enough to ensure the approval of the treaty with no reservations. The "irreconcilables" now moved into a dominant position. The critical moment came when Senator Lodge permitted Senator Underwood (a Democrat) to move approval of the treaty without any reservations. This motion was quickly defeated by a vote of 38 ayes to 53 nays. Seven Democrats had now moved into the opposition along with Republican "reservationists" and "irreconcilables." The President's hold upon his party was beginning to break.

After the treaty was defeated, Senator Lodge wrote the following brief note to Judge Cohalan:

64. Senator Borah to James McGurrin, October 27, 1919, *Borah MSS.*

Thank you so much for your kind telegram which I greatly appreciate. They were obliged to choose between the treaty with my reservations or kill it themselves. They decided to kill it themselves—or, rather Mr. Wilson did, and if there was any killing to be done I am glad that they did it. I tried to ratify it with American reservations. Because American reservations were on, they destroyed it.[65]

Judge Cohalan was glad to have the treaty killed, with or without reservations, and in this spirit he sent the following telegram to Senator Borah: "Heartiest congratulations. Greatest victory for country and liberty since Revolution largely due to you." [66] Borah's reply was a well-earned tribute to the significant activities of Judge Cohalan: "You have rendered in this fight a service which no other man has rendered or could have rendered. Your country will always be under a debt of gratitude to you." [67]

While Judge Cohalan had been busy earning this glowing tribute, there were certain Irishmen visiting America who were endeavoring to "drown his honor in a shallow cup and sell his reputation for a song." In the days of Omar Khayyam it had been an old Persian practice to employ smear procedures to ruin an enemy's reputation. Irishmen like Patrick McCartan and Dr. William J. Maloney improved upon this practice by smearing their friends and the Friends of Irish Freedom with abuse that could only hurt the cause of Ireland. When this abuse was parroted by Eamon de Valera, it was obvious that a rift would soon be created in the ranks of Irish-Americans devoted to the ideal of Irish independence. It was highly unfortunate that De Valera listened to the advice of McCartan and Maloney, who wished to discredit Cohalan and then pose as the real leaders of Irish-American opinion. If De Valera had possessed more knowledge of the mathematics of practical politics, he would have known that the odds were against any petty scheme

---

65. Senator Lodge to Judge Cohalan, November 20, 1919, *Cohalan MSS.*
66. Judge Cohalan to Senator Borah, November 19, 1919, *Borah MSS.*
67. Borah to Cohalan, November 22, 1919, *ibid.* On November 28, 1919, Michael E. Hennessy, of the Boston *Globe*, wrote a brief letter to Judge Cohalan concerning Senator Lodge: "It may interest you to know that you have made a very favorable impression on Senator Lodge. The last three times I have seen him he has referred to you in terms of high admiration." *Cohalan MSS.*

to impair the reputation of a distinguished jurist who for decades had devoted all his efforts to advance the cause of Ireland. The fact that he worked hand in glove with McCartan and Maloney is an indication of his lack of stature as a statesman. Even a novice in politics knows better than to bite the hand that feeds him. But De Valera was not only ready to inflict a savage bite upon the hand of Cohalan; he was also ready to inspire a drive against the Judge that he hoped would eliminate him as the outstanding leader of the Irish-American element in America. The story of this dubious intrigue is told in the next two chapters.

11 PRESIDENT DE VALERA COURTS A QUARREL WITH JUDGE COHALAN

A. EAMON DE VALERA AND THE LEAGUE OF NATIONS

After De Valera's sensational escape from Lincoln Prison on February 3, 1919, it was hoped by Michael Collins, Arthur Griffith, and other Irish leaders that he would stay in Ireland and help prepare a program that would command success. But he was determined upon a secret visit to America, where he could carry on a propaganda campaign and raise money badly needed in Ireland. On June 11 he landed in New York and was soon in touch with Judge Cohalan and John Devoy.[1]

The issue of the League of Nations was immediately discussed by De Valera and prominent Irish-Americans at the home of Judge Cohalan. In 1918 and in the early part of 1919 De Valera had not been opposed to the idea of a League, and the first official declaration on behalf of the Irish Republic, March 31, 1919, in the form of a letter to Clemenceau, announced the fact that Ireland was ready for membership in the League. Needless to say, such entry would be based upon an acknowledgment of Irish independence. On May 26 De Valera, Griffith, and Count Plunkett had addressed another letter to Clemenceau protesting against "the form in which the covenant [of the League of Nations] is now drawn up" because it

1. De Valera's entry into the United States was a complete surprise to the Department of State. On June 23 John W. Davis, American Ambassador in London, sent a cablegram to the Department asking about De Valera: "Press reports indicate Valera now in the United States. How did he get there? Is Department likely to give him a passport to return here?" 841d.00/58, MS., National Archives.

"threatens to confirm Ireland in the slavery against which she has persistently struggled since the English first invaded her shores."

But the mind of De Valera refused to exclude the possibility of the creation of a League of Nations which might prove palatable to Ireland. If he had been a realist he would have recognized the fact that the Covenant of the League, as perfected in Paris, was in final form, with no chance of any early amendment that could possibly favor Ireland. When it was suggested to him that it would be advisable to discuss this League issue with Judge Cohalan he refused to do so. Diarmuid Lynch knew all about this meeting between De Valera and the outstanding Irish-Americans in New York City, and he was shocked at De Valera's negative attitude:

> The situation thus created was passed over in silence out of deference to the office held by de Valera. This silence was a great mistake. Men present on that occasion had a right to demand a full explanation of this unwarrantable attitude; had they grappled with the situation then and there, the machinations of the few disturbing elements would in all probability have been exposed and the whole position clarified at the outset of President de Valera's campaign in America.[2]

The "few disturbing elements" referred to in this statement of Diarmuid Lynch had particular meaning in connection with the activities of Dr. William J. Maloney and Patrick McCartan. They were determined to become the intimate advisers of De Valera and plan his program in America. Judge Cohalan and John Devoy would be very small items in this program. It was not long before McCartan paid a visit to the Irish Bureau in Washington and spoke a word of warning to the Director, Daniel T. O'Connell, about any criticism of the League:

> Senator Thomas J. Walsh, of Montana . . . was at that time an ardent supporter of Wilson and the League. At a critical moment he made a speech likely to win support from those of Irish blood who did not understand the real workings of the scheme, and I came out instantly with a counterstatement. I was then visited at the Bureau in Washington by

2. Statement by Diarmuid Lynch, National Secretary of the Friends of Irish Freedom and one of the heroes of the Easter Rebellion of 1916, *Cohalan MSS.*

Dr. McCartan, who, with some agitation, gave me a message from de Valera ordering me not to speak further against the League. I resented this. Later in the day, he (Dr. McCartan) left a written message: "The President asked me to tell you to be careful with your statements on such things as Senator Walsh's resolution, as he might be forced to repudiate you, and that would do harm to the whole movement. I told him politely to mind his own business.[3]

As for De Valera himself, the question of a League of Nations soon became anything but academic. At Fenway Park, in Boston, soon after his arrival in America, he gave his views on a League:

> We want a just League of Nations, founded on the only basis on which it can be just—the equality of right among nations. . . . A covenant for a League of Nations can be framed at Washington as well as at Paris. Now is the time to frame it. It is not enough for you to destroy, you must build.[4]

De Valera had completely misread the American attitude towards the Covenant of the League of Nations. It was impossible for any persons in Washington to frame a new covenant. President Wilson was entirely satisfied with the Covenant as he had helped to fashion it in Paris. He alone had the responsibility for conducting American foreign relations, and he was not going to scrap what he had taken so much trouble to build merely because De Valera was not satisfied with it. And the "irreconcilables" in the Senate would have nothing to do with a League of Nations. They were bitterly opposed to any surrender of American sovereignty, and they were able upon two occasions to secure the defeat of the League in the Senate.

After De Valera had been in the United States for some time, he began to realize that Irish-Americans were almost a unit in their opposition to the League. On May 24 Dr. Maloney had inspired an editorial in the *Irish Press* with the revealing caption: "Defeat of the League of Nations Will Not Free Ireland." By the end of June, Maloney and McCartan could clearly read the senti-

3. *Cohalan MSS.*
4. *Ibid.*

ment of Irish-Americans against the League, and McCartan published an editorial in the *Irish Press* which struck a very different note:

> If the United States accepts the League of Nations she will declare herself an open and avowed enemy of Irish independence under any shape or form. The League of Nations is nothing more or less than a perpetual declaration of war on Irish liberty, and the sooner the friends of Ireland realize this the better.[5]

This was the note that Judge Cohalan had long sounded, and De Valera would have heard it clearly soon after he had landed in America if he had wisely consented to discuss this matter with the Judge. But De Valera had no desire to listen to counsel. He wished to lay down the law for Irish-Americans to follow and, like President Wilson, he was ready to "crush" any opposition. He soon discovered that he could not "crush" Judge Cohalan, who for decades had led, in the United States, the fight for Irish freedom. But if he could not crush Cohalan he could at least make it very uncomfortable for him, and this he did upon all occasions. In a letter to Arthur Griffith, De Valera related his difficulties with the Judge:

> I labour under no misapprehension as to the relations between us. They are unfortunately only too well defined by the Judge's attitude from the beginning. So clear were they from the first, that I was actually considering the question of whether it would not be better for our cause that I should return, or go elsewhere. Separate as one would imagine our personal interests were—separate, too, as the parts we would naturally have to play, even in the closest co-operation here, I realised early that nevertheless, and big as the country is, it was not big enough to hold the Judge and myself.[6]

It is interesting to contrast this letter to Arthur Griffith with the statement made by De Valera to the Council of the Friends of Irish Freedom on December 10, 1919: that "Judge Cohalan and John Devoy had given him every assistance in their power"; that "he

---

5. June 28, 1919.
6. Piaras Beaslai, *Michael Collins and the Making of a New Ireland* (London, 1926), II, 4.

had had several conferences with them and always found them ready with advice and help"; that "nobody had tried to 'trip him up,' and he hoped there would be an end to all such mischievous statements." [7]

It is certain that in the early summer of 1919 Judge Cohalan showed no desire to "trip him up." On the contrary, the Judge made every effort to be of assistance. Knowing that Parnell had spoken before the Congress of the United States, Cohalan tried to secure the same privilege for De Valera. He discussed this matter with Senator Borah, who was willing to go ahead with the project. But De Valera insisted that before going any further an effort should be made to secure the support of Democrats in the Senate. Judge Cohalan, knowing the loyalty of most Democrats in the Senate to President Wilson and realizing that the President himself would be strongly opposed to the appearance of De Valera before either branch of Congress, expressed the opinion that Borah alone should handle the matter. De Valera was adamant in his refusal to work through Borah, so Cohalan, De Valera, and Harry Boland, one of De Valera's aides who had recently arrived in America, had a conference with both Borah and Senator Phelan. Phelan said he would have to discuss everything with his Democratic colleagues in the Senate, with the result that a prompt negative was soon announced. It was difficult for De Valera to realize that Democrats in the Senate like Phelan and Thomas J. Walsh were not disposed to advance the cause of Ireland in the face of strong Presidential opposition.[8]

B. DIFFICULTIES CONCERNING THE DISBURSEMENT OF THE IRISH VICTORY FUND

On January 14, 1919, as we have already seen, the Friends of Irish Freedom initiated a drive to collect an Irish Victory Fund. This fund would enable the Friends more effectively to carry on its

7. *Cohalan MSS.*
8. *Cohalan MSS.*

campaign to further the cause of self-determination for Ireland. The Irish Race Convention (February 22-23, 1919) endorsed the raising of this fund and fixed the total at the impressive figure of one million dollars. The purposes for which this fund would be raised and disbursed were clearly set forth in the circulars distributed by the Friends of Irish Freedom.

> To educate public opinion—
> a. To urge that the objects for which America entered the war may be fully attained.
> b. To urge and insist upon the recognition of the Republican form of government established in Ireland.
> c. To urge that America shall not enter into any League of Nations which does not safeguard all American rights.
> d. To maintain and preserve the American ideals of government and to oppose and offset the British propaganda which is falsifying and misrepresenting the facts of American history.
> e. To maintain for the foregoing purposes a widespread and professional publicity campaign.
> f. To defray the expenses of the Irish-American delegation to the Peace Conference.[9]

The drive to raise this Victory Fund was eminently successful. When the campaign ended on August 31, 1919, with large total of $1,005,080.83, the question soon arose as to the disbursement of this fund. It seemed of fundamental importance to carry out the purposes outlined in the circulars issued by the Friends of Irish Freedom. On May 7, 1919, there was a meeting of the National Executive of the Friends of Irish Freedom. Although he was not a member of the National Executive, Mr. McGarrity was permitted to attend the meeting, and he promptly made a motion to send $50,000 to Ireland to defray the expenses of the representatives of the Irish Republic then in Paris. Judge Cohalan objected to this motion because of the insufficiency of the funds at that time in the treasury of the Friends of Irish Freedom, but a motion of P. A. Moynahan was unanimously adopted which provided that $10,000 be sent at once to the American Commission for Irish Independ-

9. *Ibid.*

ence. The members of the commission would apply this sum to meet the expenses of any Irish representatives in Paris.[10]

McGarrity did not take his defeat gracefully, and the word was soon spread in Philadelphia that Judge Cohalan had been opposed to sending *any* of the Irish Victory Fund to Ireland. This statement was a plain untruth, and it reveals the length to which men like Maloney, McCartan, and McGarrity were willing to go in order to discredit Cohalan. It was not long before a vigorous campaign of misrepresentation was waged against Cohalan, Devoy, and other prominent members of the Friends of Irish Freedom.

To clarify the situation with respect to the disbursements of the Irish Victory Fund, John Devoy, at the meeting of the National Council of the Friends on June 11, 1919, moved the following resolution, which was seconded by Judge Cohalan:

> Resolved that 25 per cent of the fund at the disposal of the National Council be sent to our friends in Ireland to carry out the necessary work of sustaining the Irish Cause and defending it against English attacks; that as soon as, in the judgment of the National Council the condition of the fund will justify an increase, a larger proportion to be determined by the National Council may be sent; that a first instalment of $50,000, in addition to the $10,000 already transmitted, be forwarded as soon as possible; and that this action of the National Council be not published in the daily or weekly press, or made known to anyone not an officer of the organization.[11]

Father Hurton and Joseph O'Neill, of Philadelphia, proposed an amendment to this resolution allocating seventy-five per cent of the money raised to be sent to Ireland. This amendment received no support and was withdrawn. In accordance with the Devoy

---

10. Because of a misinterpretation of the cablegram transmitting this sum to the American Commission for Irish Independence, the members of the commission thought the $10,000 had been sent to defray expenses of the American delegation. They advanced, however, to the Irish representatives for current needs about $3,800. Later on (June 25, 1919), the Friends of Irish Freedom cabled to Mr. O'Kelly, in Paris, the sum of $10,000, and on November 8, 1919, $10,000 was given to James O'Mara for transmission to the Irish envoys in Paris. *Cohalan MSS.*
11. *Cohalan MSS.*

resolution, the following sums were paid to representatives of the Irish Republic:

> September 2, 1919—to Sean Nunan—$40,000
> January 2, 1920—to Harry Boland— 10,000
> February 26, 1920—to Harry Boland— 15,000

The extensive and successful advertising campaign carried on against the League of Nations in the summer and autumn of 1919 made heavy inroads upon the Irish Victory Fund, and there were many other incidental expenses. For the period January 1, 1919, to December 31, 1920, a partial list of disbursements gives an interesting picture of the activities of the Friends of Irish Freedom:

Books, pamphlets, news bulletins, office equipment and supplies	$113,303.00
Postage and expressage	22,605.56
Salaries—headquarters staff	27,431.16
Organizers' salaries	35,644.42
Advertising, publicity, and public meetings	96,641.45
Bureau of Information, F.O.I.F.	124,466.05
Protestant Friends of Ireland	77,486.27
Traveling expenses, President de Valera	26,748.26
To Ireland, per Representatives of Dail Eireann	115,046.61
Subscription to Irish Bond-Certificates	25,000.00

The total disbursements from the Irish Victory Fund from January 1, 1919, to December 31, 1920, were $887,284.74.[12]

C. DE VALERA AND THE IRISH BOND DRIVE

Shortly after the arrival of De Valera in America, a conference was held with Irish-American leaders with reference to a bond drive in the United States. De Valera announced that one of the main purposes of his visit to America was to raise funds for the cause of Ireland. He hoped to be able to float a loan of $5,000,000. This could best be effected by an issue of "Irish Bonds." Judge Cohalan, Mi-

12. These figures are taken from the official report of the Friends of Irish Freedom. *Cohalan MSS.*

chael J. Ryan, Richard F. Dalton, and Judge Goff, all able lawyers, immediately pointed out that any attempt to sell in the United States bonds of a republic which had no international recognition would be regarded as a violation of American "Blue Sky" laws. These laws were in force in many states as a protection to investors, and they were comprehensive in scope.[13]

In the face of these objections, De Valera continued to insist that an important part of his mission in the United States was to float "bonds," and he was determined to carry out his instructions to this effect. It is significant, however, to note that in a letter to Diarmuid Lynch, Patrick McCartan, and Liam Mellows, April 29, 1919, De Valera spoke of floating a loan in the United States through the sale of registered *certificates*.[14] The De Valera suggestion to raise money in America through the sale of bonds was strongly supported by Joseph McGarrity of Philadelphia, but in the end the counsel of Cohalan was followed and a committee consisting of Cohalan, Thomas Hughes Kelly, Bourke Cockran, Richard F. Dalton, and John D. Moore was appointed to look into the matter. The committee suggested raising funds through the sale of "Bond-certificates," and De Valera reluctantly accepted this suggestion.[15]

13. In dealing with the beginning of this bond drive, McCartan, on page 141 of his book, *With De Valera in America*, makes one of his usual misstatements: "As Michael J. Ryan had favoured in Ireland the floating of such a loan in the United States, President de Valera asked Ryan to give the others his opinion on the loan. Ryan, in a long statement, maintained the loan was impossible. Cohalan followed in the same strain: a loan was impolitic: it was illegal: it contravened the Blue-Sky laws." As a matter of fact, Ryan and Cohalan were not opposed to the floating of an Irish loan. They opposed raising this loan by selling bonds of the Irish Republic, which had no legal status.
14. *Cohalan MSS.*
15. Although President de Valera finally decided to follow the advice of the committee of outstanding Irish-Americans to raise funds from the sale of bond-*certificates,* Patrick McCartan, in his book, *With De Valera in America,* constantly refers to the sale of "bonds." On page 143 he speaks of the sale of "bonds"; on page 147 he states that De Valera issued and sold *"bonds* of the Republic of Ireland"; and on page 218 he discusses the drive to raise money in America and makes a statement to the effect that "the popular appeal sold *Bonds* of the Irish Republic."

In a letter to Judge Cohalan, July 14, 1919, Bourke Cockran deals with the difficulties of trying to sell in America the bonds of the Irish Republic. He had talked with some important Irish-Americans, and "the idea that a loan could be floated on normal financial grounds they scouted as pre-

Before any further action could be taken in connection with organizing a bond-certificate drive, the British Government, on September 12, issued a proclamation suppressing the Dail Eireann. As soon as McCartan heard of this action by the British Government, he got in touch with Joseph McGarrity and Dr. Maloney and secretly made preparations for a mass meeting of protest in New York City. Judge Cohalan and other prominent Irish-Americans were not consulted. The meeting was to be held on the evening of September 14, in the Lexington Theater.

The theater was packed, and the action of the British Government was roundly denounced, but Irish-American leaders in New York resented the fact that McGarrity had rushed up to New York from Philadelphia and together with Maloney and McCartan had secretly made preparations for the meeting. McGarrity then had the impudence to present to the National Council of the Friends of Irish Freedom on October 3 the bill for the expenses of the meeting ($1,515).

John Devoy regarded the actions of McGarrity, Maloney, and McCartan as indefensible and paid his respects to them in an editorial in the *Gaelic American:*

> The most dangerous English propaganda that ever menaced the Irish Cause is now being carried on here in America under the pretence of zeal for the Irish Republic. Its object is to sow dissension in the Irish movement at a time when unity is absolutely necessary, and to destroy confidence in the leadership when that leadership is achieving results most beneficial to Ireland and most injurious to England. If it should succeed, the Irish movement in America would be destroyed or rendered powerless and Ireland, when she most needs American help, would be deprived of it. . . . It can only be beaten by making our people fully acquainted with its insidious and treacherous character. . . . It does not matter to the slanderers that the men they falsely accuse have given the most ample proof of sincerity by standing up for Ireland when the whole power of the Washington Administration was exercised remorselessly for their destruction.[16]

---

posterous, insisting that money might be raised for such a purpose [Irish self-determination] as a matter of sentiment but never as a cold financial investment." *Cohalan MSS.*

16. November 5, 1919.

This bitter editorial in the *Gaelic American* had little effect upon McGarrity, who strongly pressed for the payment by the Friends of Irish Freedom of the expenses of the meeting on September 14 in the Lexington Theater. On November 7 the National Council voted this disbursement, but McGarrity's actions helped to widen the rift in the ranks of Irish-Americans. John Devoy was particularly incensed when McGarrity moved, at a meeting of the National Council on November 7, that "the total expenses of the bond-certificate campaign be defrayed from the funds of the Friends of Irish Freedom." Inasmuch as it had been estimated that the bond-certificate drive would cost about $1,000,000, McGarrity's motion, if approved by the National Council, would take every cent out of the treasury of the Friends. The chairman ruled that the McGarrity motion was out of order and it was not voted upon,[17] but everyone present realized that McGarrity had really issued a declaration of war against Cohalan and his friends.

But De Valera was more cautious than McGarrity. The Friends of Irish Freedom had ample funds he could use to advantage. For the time being, they should be conciliated and flattered. On September 20, 1919, he addressed a letter to the National Trustees of the Friends. He informed them that the preliminary arrangements "for the placing of the Bond-Certificates for subscription with the American public are now made." The next task was to complete the necessary organization "so as to be able to make an intensive drive not later than the first week of December." It had been estimated that "the total expenses of collecting the $10,000,000 will run into $1,000,000." He thought these expenses should not exceed $600,000. But some immediate cash was desperately needed. It would be a happy idea for the Friends of Irish Freedom to "give in advance their subscription for the amount in Certificates which the organization proposes to take."[18] The trustees recommended, September 29, a "loan to the American Commission for Irish Independence, through President de Valera, of a sum not to exceed

---

17. *Cohalan MSS.*
18. De Valera to the National Trustees of the Friends of Irish Freedom, September 20, 1919, *ibid.*

$100,000," and on October 3 the National Council of the Friends unanimously adopted this recommendation.[19] De Valera now had the funds that were imperatively necessary for beginning the bond-certificate drive.

Frank P. Walsh was appointed by De Valera to head this drive for a loan, but the man upon whom he really counted to make the drive a success was James O'Mara, who was hurriedly brought over from Ireland. O'Mara proved unusually adept in handling the complicated details of fund raising, and the campaign got off to an excellent start. But there were soon some alarming whispers of a new organization that would really take care of the bond drive, and Diarmuid Lynch was importuned to resign his position as National Secretary of the Friends of Irish Freedom and join the staff at the bond-certificate headquarters. He refused to take this step, but he co-operated loyally in pushing the bond drive. He turned over to the headquarters all the data that would be of service in preparing their campaign, and he furnished the addresses of the 70,000 members of the Friends.

But there was continued talk of a widening rift between Irish-American groups, with the hint that De Valera would help to organize an association that would be a rival of the Friends. At the meeting of the National Council of the Friends on December 10, 1919, John Devoy demanded that President de Valera "state to the National Council the exact truth of the situation in New York." If De Valera was dissatisfied with the roles played by Judge Cohalan and Devoy he now had an opportunity to air his grievances. His reply to Devoy's direct question is a revelation of his tendency to engage in double-talk:

> As far as himself and his colleagues were concerned any accusations as regards lack of support were false; Judge Cohalan and John Devoy had given him every assistance in their power; that he had had several conferences with them and always found them ready with advice and help; nobody had tried to "trip him up," and he hoped there would be an end to all such mischievous statements.[20]

19. *Ibid.*
20. Minutes of the meeting of the National Council of the Friends of Irish Freedom, *Cohalan MSS.*

It is interesting to contrast this specific statement with the declaration of hostility contained in the letter De Valera wrote to Arthur Griffith from which I have already quoted (page 343).[21] Another letter to Arthur Griffith was equally hostile:

> It is time for plain speaking now. A deadly attempt to ruin our chances for the bonds, and for everything we came here to accomplish, is being made. If I am asked for the ulterior motives I can only guess that they are—
> (1) To drive me home—jealousy, envy, resentment of a rival— some devilish cause I do not know what prompts.
> (2) To compel me to be a rubber stamp for somebody.
> The position I have held (I was rapidly *driven* to assert it or surrender) is the following:
> (1) No American has the right to dictate policy to the Irish people.
> (2) We are here with a definite objective. Americans, banded under the trade name (the word will not be misunderstood), Friends of Irish Freedom, ought to help us to obtain the objective, if they are truly what the name implies.
> It is not, however, from fundamentals like this the trouble arises. The trouble is purely one of personalities. I cannot feel confidence enough in a certain man to let him have implicit control of tactics here, without consultation and agreement with me.[22]

The Friends of Irish Freedom, under the leadership of Judge Cohalan and John Devoy, had paid the entire cost of De Valera's trips throughout the United States and had advanced $100,000 to help the bond-certificate drive. The tremendous services of Cohalan and Devoy had been so helpful that on December 10, 1919, De Valera himself had acknowledged the big debt he owed them. To some historians his letters to Arthur Griffith might be evidence either that at times he was a master of mendacity or merely that in America he had been easily confused or badly advised.

Cohalan clearly realized the fact that De Valera was not familiar with the American scene, and he made many allowances for the strange actions of the President of the Irish Republic. In January

21. *Ante,* p. 343.
22. Beaslai, *op. cit.,* II, 6-7.

1920, when the bond-certificate drive opened in New York, Cohalan addressed meetings in the Lexington Theater and in the Central Opera House. He was eager to be of every possible service to the cause of Ireland, and he did not permit personal slights from the De Valera clique to dampen his enthusiasm. It was not long before he realized that his friendly gestures towards De Valera had merely awakened contempt.

D. HEARINGS BEFORE THE HOUSE COMMITTEE ON FOREIGN AFFAIRS ON A BILL TO PROVIDE SALARIES FOR A MINISTER AND CONSULS TO IRELAND

The deep devotion of Judge Cohalan to the cause of Ireland was indicated in a most positive manner by the time that he spent in countless endeavors to place the question of Irish self-determination before the American people. He was the outstanding member of the Friends of Irish Freedom, inspiring the policy that the organization adopted, and he was the driving force that caused a large number of meetings to be held in favor of Irish freedom. He was never too busy to attend these meetings, and the pressure he exerted upon members of Congress was constant and highly successful. He was always emphasizing the fact that he was the spokesman for 20,000,000 Americans, and there is no doubt that he was an outstanding figure upon the American scene. In his contacts with Congress he was persuasive and influential.

On December 12-13, 1919, there were important hearings upon the bill introduced by Representative William E. Mason, of Illinois, to provide salaries "for a minister and consuls to the Republic of Ireland." The appropriation for this purpose was very modest—$14,000.

The debates upon this bill and the comments during the hearings revealed a clash between the opponents of the bill, who declared that no action should be taken with regard to Ireland until the President had taken steps in favor of Irish recognition, and the supporters of the bill, who believed that Congress had an important role in the procedure of recognition. Representative Mason himself opened the discussion by strongly arguing in favor of the view that "Congress has equal power with the President in taking the 'first step' in recognition of a new State." [23]

Judge Cohalan did not go as far as Mr. Mason in his support of the bill before the House of Representatives, but he cogently contended that recognition of new governments "is not in any sense a power that belongs peculiarly and solely to the President of the United States." He believed that the President, "acting up to the full measure of his power, can not really bring about the full recognition of any other country." In the first place, if the President is "to recognize a government in any one of those countries [France, Britain, or Brazil], before a minister or ambassador can take his position in that country, that action of the President will have to be had and it must be passed upon by the Senate of the United States." If the President would receive Dr. McCartan as the

> Minister from the Irish Republic, I would hold that we would not have gone the full length that we would have to go in recognizing the Irish Republic until also a Minister had been appointed by the Senate of the United States and his salary also provided for by the Congress of the United States.

The comments of Judge Cohalan drew a question from Representative Connally, of Texas: "Suppose that we should pass this resolution and send a representative over there to Ireland . . . and suppose that these Britishers should be contrary about the matter and still continue to hold Ireland?"

Judge Cohalan replied immediately:

> I think, Mr. Connally, that I know England so well and I know Ireland so well . . . that if the United States were to do just that . . . it would not alone be doing the just thing and the right thing, and the thing which eventually public opinion will compel them to do, but the most friendly act which has been done in hundreds of years to the people of England.

23. *Hearings Before the Committee on Foreign Affairs of the House of Representatives,* December 12-13, 1919, p. 8.

The statement of Judge Cohalan that the government of Ireland was both *de facto* and *de jure* evoked from Mr. Connally another question:

> Mr. Connally. Let me ask you this further question, as an American citizen. Supposing we should pass this resolution and Great Britain should take offense at it, and our action should eventuate in war; as an American citizen would you be willing for America to go to war to maintain the freedom of Ireland?
>
> Judge Cohalan. In any contingency, whether we were weak or strong, when a situation has been presented to the American people that appeared to them to be just, I have never found any red-blooded American citizen who was not in favor of doing that which would maintain justice, even though it would bring war.
>
> Mr. Connally. Then I understand you to answer my question in the affirmative?
>
> Judge Cohalan. Undoubtedly, under the circumstances.
>
> Mr. Connally. That you are willing for the United States, if her action in this regard should eventuate in war with Great Britain, that you are in favor of the United States going to war with Great Britain to liberate Ireland?
>
> Judge Cohalan. I will put it this way—
>
> Mr. Connally. My question was very direct.
>
> Judge Cohalan. I am going to answer your question, and there will not be any doubt as to my reply. I say yes. . . . I insist and reiterate that, as an American citizen, I would be in favor absolutely of doing that which was just.[24]

Representative Henry D. Flood, of Virginia, an ardent supporter of Irish self-determination, expressed the opinion that the recognition of new states was a "purely executive function and not a legis-

24. *Ibid.*, 18-40. Francis P. Jones, in his account of these hearings before the House Committee on Foreign Affairs, makes the following comments upon the remarks of Judge Cohalan: "It has been my privilege to listen to many men on many occasions expound the case of Ireland, but at no other time have I ever listened to so masterly an exposition as that of Judge Cohalan. It was noteworthy that he was able to meet with immediate effect every question asked by any member of the committee, and that on each occasion he not only amply demonstrated his complete possession of all of the facts of the case, but demonstrated a knowledge of constitutional procedure and law superior to that of any member of the committee." *Gaelic American*, December 20, 1919.

lative function." As far as the initiative in the matter of recognition was concerned, Mr. Flood was undoubtedly right.[25] But Judge Cohalan was arguing that the mere matter of extending recognition was meaningless if Congress, through its power of appropriating funds, did not grant the money necessary to implement the recognition power. Recognition, therefore, was not solely an executive function.

Mr. Flood, believing that the President had the sole power with reference to initiating the procedure of recognition, offered an alternative resolution which read:

> *Resolved*, By the House of Representatives, the Senate concurring, that they participate with the people of the United States in the deep interest they feel for the success of the Irish Republic which is struggling to establish its liberty and independence, and that it will give its constitutional support to the President of the United States, if he may deem it expedient to recognize the sovereign independence of that republic.

The introduction of the Flood resolution precipitated a series of conferences between leading Irish-Americans and President de Valera. He favored the Flood resolution, but Judge Cohalan continued his efforts in support of the Mason bill. On December 13, Bourke Cockran, during his testimony before the Committee on Foreign Affairs, was asked about his attitude towards the Flood resolution. He promptly replied:

> There is no substantial difference between Mr. Flood and myself about the action that should be taken by the committee. His resolution is just as effective, I think, as the bill that has been presented by Mr. Mason. . . . The difference between the two measures is not substantial. For while one specifically expresses the desire of the House for Irish independence, the other does the same thing by implication. Personally, and because of its explicit declaration that Congress believes Ireland should be free, I think I prefer Mr. Flood's measure.[26]

25. *Ibid.*, 18. For the development of the recognition policy of the United States see Julius Goebel, *The Recognition Policy of the United States* (New York, 1915), and Charles C. Tansill, "War Powers of the President of the United States with Special Reference to the Beginning of Hostilities," *Political Science Quarterly*, March 1930, 1-56.
26. *Ibid.*, 186.

But Mr. Flood's measure had no chance of securing any wide support in the House and never came up for a vote. The Mason bill was treated likewise. On April 8 Daniel T. O'Connell wrote to Judge Cohalan and complained that Stephen G. Porter, Chairman of the House Committee on Foreign Affairs, did not wish any immediate action on the Mason bill.[27] In anticipation of this situation, De Valera had drafted a resolution which Mason introduced as House Concurrent Resolution No. 56. It read as follows:

> *Resolved,* by the House of Representatives, the Senate concurring, that as the people of Ireland by ballot, in orderly election, have established an independent republic of Ireland, we respectfully urge upon the President the propriety of acting upon the principle of national self-determination and of according official recognition to that Republic and to its duly elected Government.[28]

In the third week in May, Mr. Mason informed Daniel T. O'Connell that this resolution had little chance of being given favorable action by the Committee on Foreign Affairs. On May 22 a conference was held at the Irish National Bureau attended by Mason, De Valera, Judge Cohalan, and Congressmen Kennedy, of Rhode Island, and Smith, of New York. According to O'Connell, at this meeting "the developments of the day were explained in detail to President de Valera. He agreed that a flat defeat of the Mason substitute would be inadvisable, and it was better to get a resolution of substantial merit [approved by Congress]." President de Valera personally dictated a new substitute. As revised, it read as follows:

> *Whereas,* the American people have always sympathized with the aspirations of every people seeking political freedom; and
> *Whereas,* the people of Ireland have shown unmistakably their desire to govern themselves; and
> *Whereas,* the conditions in Ireland consequent upon the denial of that right today endanger world peace; and
> *Whereas,* in particular, the unrest caused by these conditions is inevitably reflected in these United States of America, tending to weaken the bonds of amity and the ancient ties of kinship which bind so

27. Daniel T. O'Connell to Judge Cohalan, April 8, 1920, *Cohalan MSS.*
28. *Congressional Record,* 66 Cong., 2 sess., LIX, 7127.

many of our people to the people of Great Britain and Ireland; therefore, in the interest of world peace and international good-will, be it *Resolved,* by the House of Representatives, the Senate concurring, that the Congress of the United States views with concern and solicitude these conditions and expresses its sympathy with the aspirations of the Irish people for a government of their own choice.

On May 27 this substitute resolution drafted by De Valera came before the Committee on Foreign Affairs and was defeated by a vote of 12 to 7. After some new amendments this resolution (No. 57) was approved by the committee. It is significant that this resolution did not provide for the recognition of the Irish Republic. It merely expressed *sympathy* for the "aspirations of the Irish people for a government of their own choice." [29]

But even this modified resolution was not permitted by Mr. Porter, Chairman of the Committee on Foreign Affairs, to come to a vote, so all the efforts of De Valera and his Irish-American supporters came to naught. The hostile action of the House of Representatives, as expressed by Mr. Porter, made a deep impression upon Judge Cohalan, and that is the reason why, at the subsequent Chicago convention, he pressed upon the Committee of Resolutions a plank merely expressing "sympathy" for Irish aspirations.[30]

29. *Cohalan MSS.*
30. In commenting upon the political realism of Judge Cohalan at the Chicago Convention, Daniel T. O'Connell remarks: "Those attacking Justice Cohalan for having offered a 'sympathy' resolution at Chicago, which is regarded as the cause of the present controversy, did not know that the Mason 'sympathy' resolution before Congress was drafted by President de Valera. The shafts of attack were intended to fall mainly upon Justice Cohalan. Following the practice, which we did not deviate from until, in self-defence, the present controversy required a truthful, straightforward presentation of facts, neither Justice Cohalan nor the writer sought to avoid attacks on themselves, by making these extreme critics publicly realize that they were actually attacking President de Valera. The President remained silent and allowed the attacks to continue." *Cohalan MSS.*

E. PRESIDENT DE VALERA PROVOKES A TEMPEST IN IRISH-AMERICAN CIRCLES

While members of Congress made bold speeches in favor of the recognition of an Irish Republic, De Valera was making cautious addresses on the League of Nations. McCartan, in commenting upon these exercises in double-talk, makes the following observation: "President de Valera . . . dealt with the League in such a way that neither its supporters nor its opponents could dispute the justice of his position. . . . To speak without giving offence . . . seemed almost impossible. Yet President de Valera gave offence to none." [31]

But on February 6, 1920, in an interview with the New York correspondent of the *Westminster Gazette*, he gave offense to thousands of Irish-Americans. After stating that he was "ready for concessions to Britain provided domestic independence is granted," De Valera made some revealing remarks upon the Monroe Doctrine and the Platt Amendment and their application to Cuba:

> Now, if it were really her independence and her simple right to life as a national State that Britain wanted to safeguard, she could easily make provision for that without infringing upon the equally sacred rights of the neighbouring nation to its independence and its life. The United States by the Monroe Doctrine made provision for its security without depriving the Southern Latin republics of their independence and their life.
>
> The United States safeguarded itself from the possible use of the Cuba Island as a base for attack by a foreign Power by stipulating that the Cuban government shall never enter into any treaty or other compact with any foreign Power or Powers which shall impair or tend to impair Cuban independence, nor in any manner authorize or permit

---

31. Patrick McCartan, *With De Valera in America*, pp. 145-146. De Valera was being carefully watched by the office of the United States Attorney General. On November 3, 1919, the Allies Committee of Los Angeles sent a telegram to the Department of State protesting against the "revolutionary speeches of De Valera." In reply, the Attorney General, A. Mitchell Palmer, informed the Secretary of State, December 1, 1919, that up to date De Valera had not "made any speeches which bring him within the purview of any Federal statute." 841d.00/103, MSS., N.A.

any foreign Power or Powers to obtain by colonisation or for military or naval purposes or otherwise, lodgment in or control over any portion of the said island.

Why doesn't Britain do with Ireland as the United States did with Cuba? Why doesn't Britain declare a Monroe Doctrine for her neighbouring islands? The people of Ireland, so far from objecting, would co-operate with their whole soul.[32]

The Platt Amendment to which President de Valera referred in his interview reads as follows:

> I. That the government of Cuba shall never enter into any treaty or other compact with any foreign power or powers which will impair or tend to impair the independence of Cuba, nor in any manner authorize or permit any foreign power or powers to obtain by colonization or for military or naval purposes or otherwise, lodgment in or control over any portion of said Island.
>
> III. That the government of Cuba consents that the United States may exercise the right to intervene for the preservation of Cuban independence, the maintenance of a government adequate for the protection of life, property, and individual liberty, and for discharging the obligations with respect to Cuba imposed by the treaty of Paris on the United States, now to be assumed and undertaken by the government of Cuba.
>
> VII. That to enable the United States to maintain the independence of Cuba, and to protect the people thereof, as well as for its own defence, the government of Cuba will sell or lease to the United States lands necessary for coaling or naval stations at certain specified points.[33]

In his book, published in 1932, McCartan correctly says that this *Westminster Gazette* interview "was clearly an intimation that the President of the Republic of Ireland was prepared to accept much less than complete sovereignty for Ireland. . . . The choice of the *Westminster Gazette* seemed appropriate to inform Lloyd George that Ireland's President was willing to degrade her claim to the level of a domestic issue of England." [34]

32. *Westminster Gazette,* February 7, 1920, p. 5. McCartan, p. 150, publishes a long excerpt from this interview which appeared on February 7. The wording of this excerpt is characteristically inaccurate.
33. *The Statutes at Large of the United States,* XXXI, pt. II, 895-898.
34. *With De Valera in America,* p. 151.

De Valera realized that he had made a bad mistake in the *Westminster Gazette* interview, so he hurriedly sent McCartan to Dublin to explain the situation as best he could.[35] McCartan discovered that Countess Marckievicz, Cathal Brugha, and Count Plunkett showed "marked hostility" to the De Valera interview. It was clear that

> De Valera, without consultation with any of his colleagues, and without compulsion from anyone, had given up our claim to the sovereign status proclaimed by the men of Easter Week and reaffirmed by the Dail of January 21st. . . . De Valera had acted without authority, and he had reduced our claim to that of a vassal State before the comprehending eye of the Governments of the free nations of the world. . . . Certainly de Valera could not have selected a better "instrument" for "the task set me"; for in my mind our fight for recognition was centred on compelling Cohalan to come out for the sovereign Republic. . . . And I had *forgotten* to mention to them not only Cohalan's stand for recognition at the Mason Bill Hearing but also the remark at that Hearing of the former Chairman of the Committee of Foreign Affairs, that recognition of our Republic was only a matter of time.[36]

It was very evident to the friends of De Valera that he had made a bad mistake in his statements in the *Westminster Gazette,* but they quickly banded together to defend him. John Devoy, who had been slandered by these same followers of De Valera, felt the time had come to show that the President of the Irish Republic was a man whose tongue often outran his judgment. In the *Gaelic American,* February 14, 1920, he reprinted the *Westminster Gazette* interview with critical comments. A week later he returned to the

---

35. *Ibid.,* 153. The explanations of De Valera's interview which McCartan delivered to the Irish Cabinet were as follows: "First, he [De Valera] had wanted to start England talking so that some basis of settlement might be considered; secondly, in the interview he quoted only one paragraph of the Platt Amendment relating to Cuba, to show that Ireland was willing to discuss safeguards for English security compatible with Ireland's independence; and lastly, that only his enemies, and Devoy and Cohalan, had put a hostile construction on the interview in pursuance of the campaign they had started against him when he arrived in the United States, and which overtly and covertly they had since continued."
36. McCartan, *op. cit.,* pp. 153-155.

attack. Under the authority of articles III and IV of the Platt Amendment, an American army had been sent to Cuba in 1906 to insure order, and it had been retained there for three years. Discussing this fact, Devoy commented:

> Study of these facts will hardly recommend the Platt Amendment as a model on which to readjust the relations between England and Ireland. The spirit of justice and fair dealing which animates the American people has never characterized the English and the leopard does not change its spots. Such powers in the hands of the British Government would certainly be abused. . . . I am told that I attacked President De Valera. I did not do any such thing. What I said was mild, fair and friendly criticism of a public proposition involving the vital interests of the Irish National Cause, on which every Irishman has a right to express an opinion.[37]

De Valera realized that he was in a tight spot. Without consulting anyone, he had stated in a public interview that Ireland would be willing to have the British Government settle the Irish Question by an arrangement closely modeled upon the Platt Amendment that governed relations between the United States and Cuba. Then, to draw a red herring across this hot trail, he immediately made a bitter attack upon Judge Cohalan. In the *Gaelic American*, John Devoy had written some sharp strictures upon the policies advocated by De Valera. De Valera was certain that these strictures had been inspired by Judge Cohalan, to whom he wrote as follows:

> After mature consideration I have decided that to continue to ignore the articles in the *Gaelic American* would result in injury to the cause I have been sent here to promote. The articles themselves are, of course, the least matter. It is the evident purpose behind them, and the general attitude of mind they reveal is the menace. I am answerable to the Irish people for the proper execution of the trust with which I have been charged. I am definitely responsible to them, and *I alone* am responsible. It is my obvious duty to select such instruments as may be available for the task set me. It is my duty to superintend every important step in the execution of that task. . . .

37. *Gaelic American*, February 21, 1920.

I am led to understand that these articles in the *Gaelic American* have your consent and approval. Is this so? . . . You are the officer of the Friends of Irish Freedom, who, de facto, wields unchallenged the executive power of that organization. . . . You are the officer who has accepted its most important commissions, and spoken not merely in its name, but in the name of the whole Irish Race in America. It is vital that I know exactly how you stand in this matter.[38]

To this hysterical letter, Judge Cohalan made a dignified reply:

Your communication dated February 20th was handed to me by Mr. Boland on Saturday afternoon. I was amazed at its contents. In spite of its tone and because of the position which you occupy, I am responding to it. The *Gaelic American* is edited, as you know, by Mr. John Devoy, for whose opinions and convictions I entertain the highest respect. I control neither him nor them. . . . Into any controversy you may have with Mr. Devoy or others I refuse to be drawn.

May I venture to suggest that you evidently labor under a serious misapprehension as to the relations which exist between you and me. I know no reason why you take the trouble to tell me that you can share your responsibility to the Irish people with no one. I would not let you share it with me if you sought to do so. . . . What I have done for the cause of the Independence of the Irish people recently and for many years past, I have done as an American, whose only allegiance is to America, and as one to whom the interest and security of my country are ever to be preferred to those of any and all other lands. . . . I have no appointment from you or any other spokesman for another country, nor would I under any circumstances accept one. . . .

The people of Ireland have placed themselves unequivocally upon record as favoring complete Independence for their country. . . . A British Monroe Doctrine that would make Ireland the ally of England, and thus buttress the falling British Empire so as to further oppress India and Egypt and other subject lands, would be so immoral and so utterly at variance with the ideals and traditions of the Irish people as to be as indefensible to them as it would be intolerable to the liberty-loving peoples of the world. . . .

Are you not in danger of making a grave mistake when you talk in your communication of selecting "instruments" in this country, and of "levers" and "power end" and "other end of the lever" through which

---

38. Eamon de Valera to Daniel F. Cohalan, February 20, 1920, *Cohalan MSS.*

you hope to accomplish your purpose here? Do you really think for a moment that American public opinion will permit any citizen of another country to interfere as you suggest in American affairs? Do you think that any self-respecting American will permit himself to be used in such a manner by you? If so, I may assure you that you are woefully out of touch with the spirit of the country in which you are sojourning. . . .

I respectfully suggest in closing that you would be well advised if you hesitate before you jeopardize or imperil that solidarity of opinion and unity of action among millions of American citizens which you found here amongst us when you came, which have been the despair of England's friends and have already accomplished so much for America and for Ireland.[39]

This letter was so cogently phrased that De Valera never attempted to answer it. It was easier to have some of his lackeys smear Judge Cohalan and John Devoy with abuse that had no foundation in fact. But John Devoy was a hard man to smear successfully, and he fought back with a vigor that surprised his opponents. In a letter to a colleague he discusses in full the tactics of De Valera and his followers:

I want no fight if we can avoid it but I would not sacrifice the fundamental principle of the movement even to avoid a fight with him [De Valera] because we'd be worse off in the end than if we fought it out now. . . . I am also convinced that he meant to fight us all along and was only waiting for a good opportunity. He selected the wrong time and the wrong issue because his judgment is very poor, but he is filled with the idea (although he says differently) that the great ovations he got here were for him personally and practically gave him a mandate to do what he pleases. His head is turned to a greater extent than that of any man I have met in more than half a century. Every move he has made or that has been made in his name, in my judgment, shows a deliberate intention to attempt to sidetrack both the Clan and the Friends and to substitute for both an organization subject to his orders. . . .

His persistent attempts to get us to stop the Victory Fund Drive to make way for the Bonds and Joe's [Joseph McGarrity] fight to get most of the money sent over was to my mind then, as much as it is to-

39. Judge Cohalan to Eamon de Valera, February 22, 1920, *ibid.*

day, for the purpose of depleting our resources for work here, where the real battle is being fought now, and to cripple us. . . .

D. V's letter shows how much he has been filled up with misinformation about us here. He has been "informed" that C[ohalan] directed the policy of the G. A. [*Gaelic American*] so instead of dealing with me he writes to the man he has been told is my MASTER. . . . We cannot deal ON HIS TERMS with a man who undertakes to command us.[40]

Neither Judge Cohalan nor John Devoy wished to have an open quarrel with De Valera, and they were still ready for active co-operation with him in any movement to further the cause of Irish independence. On St. Patrick's Day, in New York City [March 17, 1920], there was an impressive parade. Judge Cohalan was the Grand Marshal, and he yielded the place of honor on the reviewing stand to De Valera. That evening, at a banquet given by the Friendly Sons of Saint Patrick, the Judge introduced De Valera in a very friendly manner: "I have the honor of introducing now as the speaker to the toast of 'Ireland,' a man who is a soldier, who is a scholar, who is a patriot, and who is the elected head of the Republic of Ireland—Eamon de Valera." [41]

At this banquet given by the Friendly Sons of Saint Patrick, Judge Cohalan had asked the audience to give to De Valera a "most cordial welcome." He was constantly making friendly gestures in order to preserve the unity of the Irish-American movement in favor of Irish independence. Perhaps a meeting of outstanding Irish-Americans would help to prevent a serious split in the ranks of the friends of Ireland! The Judge, therefore, suggested a conference of about one hundred important men identified with the Irish movement. The conference would meet in New York City on March 19.

40. John Devoy to a Colleague, February 26, 1920, *ibid.*
41. *Ibid.* On February 24 Devoy wrote to Judge Cohalan a brief note dealing with the situation: "The *News* this morning has another screed, evidently given out by Harry [Boland]. He tries to cover his tracks by saying he has nothing to say—after saying it. . . . Cunningham will give you Philadelphia *Record* with McCartan's inspired editorial commending D.V. for getting rid of you and me. I wonder what political job do I hold? I would like to get the salary." *Ibid.*

President de Valera attended this conference flanked by Joseph McGarrity, Harry Boland, and James O'Mara. As the temperature of the meeting soon rose to explosive heights, De Valera asked if the audience wished him to produce a letter "showing that for six months his opponents had been scheming to oust him, and that this meeting had been called as a chance not to be missed to achieve that purpose." At this point someone in the audience shouted: "Who wrote that letter?" Harry Boland replied: "John Devoy." Boland also vouchsafed the information that the letter had been written to John A. McGarry. De Valera then requested McGarry to produce the letter, which he refrained from doing. McCartan intimates that the letter was not produced because of the clamor in the hall against reading its contents.[42] The real reason why McGarry did not choose to read the letter was the fact that it did not sustain the De Valera contention.[43]

There were many persons in the hall who were ready to rush to the defense of De Valera. Rossa F. Downing, a Washington lawyer who followed in the train of the Irish President, presented a long argument trying to prove that "the best thing for Ireland was that she be put under an English protectorate." Her geographical position as well as her small population clearly proved that "the English alliance was a natural one." Downing was evidently endeavoring to present a variation on the Platt Amendment theme.

An intimate picture of the heated atmosphere of this conference on March 19 is given by a prominent member of the Friends of Irish Freedom:

> Joseph McGarrity, of Philadelphia, who had become obsessed with the idea that *he* was the real leader of the Irish Race in America, became so obstreperous in his talk and action that Chairman Ryan threatened him with expulsion from the Conference unless he showed better manners. President de Valera himself became so excited at one point that he blurted out he had not been in America a month when he concluded that there was not room in the country for Justice Cohalan and himself! Bishop Turner, of Buffalo, mildly rebuked him by saying that Justice Cohalan could not be expected to leave his native land be-

---

42. *Op. cit.*, p. 169.
43. *Cohalan MSS.*

cause President de Valera had come in. President de Valera stated that he had long been a student of the principles of democracy, and that in his opinion the Irish-American leaders whom he had met had yet to learn the ABC of democracy. John Devoy retorted that the "exhibition which Eamon de Valera had given was the whole alphabet of autocracy." At one point Harry Boland went into hysterics and had to retire from the room to compose himself.[44]

Another revealing account of the proceedings of this conference is given in a letter from John P. Grace to Andrew J. Ryan:

> I am half inclined not to answer your letter, as I have believed from the beginning of the unfortunate differences which have arisen between President de Valera and Justice Cohalan that the least said the better. It all came to me several months ago as a startling revelation. Things had been going along on the surface so magnificently. Under the leadership of Justice Cohalan, the Irish in this country had been united as never before. . . . It was Justice Cohalan who formed in the last few years the center of unity around which I and so many thousands in America gathered to the fight. . . . His leadership was quite different from everything that had ever been attempted; he brought to the cause in his splendid personality a knowledge and profoundly sane conception of American life in its relations to Ireland. . . .
>
> I attended a conference at New York on March 19, and I confess before Heaven that President de Valera was that day revealed to me as either laboring under some psychopathic condition or that the evil spirit himself had taken hold of the Irish movement. I am sure it was the consensus of opinion . . . that whatever President de Valera's qualities might be, his leadership was an accident. He had clearly fallen into the hands of men moved by selfish, and some by sinister motives, and they had convinced him that he was the man to lead the movement in America and not Justice Cohalan.
>
> For ten hours that day [March 19] about one hundred of us . . . were tortured by such an exhibition of intolerance and ingratitude as I have never witnessed before. Justice Cohalan, humbling himself under insults repeated constantly during those ten hours . . . did everything humanly possible or imaginable to bridge the chasm. De Valera had not only been the aggressor, but repeatedly the aggressor, and perhaps encouraged to go a little further as each new aggression was overlooked. . . .

44. This memorandum describing the atmosphere of the March 19 conference was written by John J. Splain, of New Haven. *Cohalan MSS.*

De Valera's attitude was one of infallibility; he was right, everybody else was wrong, and he couldn't be wrong. . . . Bishops and priests, Protestants and Catholics, aged men born in Ireland and young men born here . . . worked for those ten hours to bring President de Valera to the point of amenability. Justice Goff, Hon. Bourke Cockran, Judge Collins, Bishop Turner, Lindsay Crawford, and numbers of others literally begged President de Valera on our knees, in effect, not to persist in his apparent determination to have a public test of strength with Justice Cohalan. . . . I beg to repeat that, not having seen him before, as for those ten hours he unfolded himself, I thought the man was crazy.[45]

In McCartan's book, *With De Valera in America,* there is a badly garbled account of this conference on March 19; the statement is made that Judge Cohalan, "amidst shouts for peace, went forward to De Valera, made a retraction of his charges, and offered his hand. De Valera shook it." [46]

McCartan's statement that Judge Cohalan made a "retraction of his charges" against De Valera and "then offered his hand," is merely one of his almost countless inaccuracies. Judge Cohalan had nothing to retract. Mr. Grace put the situation very clearly in his letter to Andrew J. Ryan: "De Valera had not only been the aggressor, but repeatedly the aggressor." He should have been the one to retract a series of baseless charges. Judge Cohalan did shake hands with De Valera, because he was anxious to restore the unity in Irish-American ranks that had existed before the arrival of the President of the Irish Republic. He was more than ready to meet his detractors halfway in an effort to promote the cause of Ireland. He soon discovered that his efforts were purposely misunderstood, and the drive to break him and John Devoy proceeded at full speed, with De Valera giving it his most zealous support.[47]

45. John P. Grace to Andrew J. Ryan, June 28, 1920, *ibid.*
46. Pp. 168-169.
47. Mary C. Bromage, in her recently published volume entitled *De Valera and the March of a Nation* (London, 1956), rehearses many of the old, disproved charges made in the book published by Dr. McCartan, *With De Valera in America.* It is to be regretted deeply that she was not familiar with data that would have radically changed her narrative.

12 IRISH-AMERICAN UNITY IS SPLIT THROUGH THE EFFORTS OF DE VALERA AND HIS LIEUTENANTS

A. THE LEAGUE OF NATIONS ONCE MORE

The quarrel forced by De Valera upon Judge Cohalan was the beginning of a serious rift in the ranks of Irish-Americans, whose unity had been the product of unceasing efforts on the part of the Judge and John Devoy. They would now have to be prepared for new attacks upon them and the smears that would be abundantly used by some of De Valera's lieutenants. But Judge Cohalan did not permit these attacks to prevent him from continuing his fight against the League of Nations. The Treaty of Versailles would come once more before the Senate in the early months of 1920 and the Judge renewed his pressure upon senators like Borah and Johnson.

Senator Borah was fearful of the many peace organizations and internationalist groups that were favorable to the League, and at times he sharply criticized their tactics. On December 19 Judge Cohalan wrote to Borah in praise of one of his statements. He believed it might be expedient to warn these ardent League advocates that "searching investigations will be made of their activities." [1] A few days later he wrote again to Borah to protest against any financial arrangements that would postpone the payment of debts owed to the American Government by Allied countries. There was a

1. Judge Cohalan to Senator Borah, December 18, 1919, *Borah MSS.*

movement on foot to remit these Allied debts and thus saddle the American taxpayer with additional obligations. He thought that "regard for our own country should require us to be just before we are generous and make us think of America before we think of foreign countries." [2]

Both Borah and Cohalan clearly realized that a strong fight would be made finally to push the Treaty of Versailles through the Senate. The list of organizations behind the League was very long, with an estimated membership of some 20,000,000 persons.[3] Because of the pressure exerted by these organizations, Senator Lodge agreed to hold a series of bipartisan conferences upon the question of the League. To these conferences the Democrats sent Senators Hitchcock, McKellar, Owen, Simmons, and Walsh. The Republicans were represented by Kellogg, Lenroot, Lodge, and New.

The Democrats were anxious to present modified reservations regarding the League, and Lodge thought that it was essential to permit Democratic senators to feel that "we should be glad to hear their proposals." [4] But Lodge had to be careful not to offend the sensibilities of Borah, who might lead a bolt from Republican ranks. This caution on the part of the Republican leader annoyed Hitchcock, who complained to Mrs. Wilson that Lodge spent much of his time "with the moderate Republicans hoping to keep them quiet." [5] Borah watched every move of Lodge with suspicion and warned him that if any compromise were agreed upon with the Democrats, he would "no longer respect or co-operate with the party organization in the Senate." [6] Lodge responded to this pressure by abandoning bipartisan conferences, and he announced to the press that there could be "no compromise on principle." [7]

On February 10 the Treaty of Versailles came once more before

2. Cohalan to Borah, December 22, 1919, *ibid.*
3. *New York Times,* January 11, 14, 15, 1919; Henry C. Lodge, *The Senate and the League of Nations* (New York, 1925), p. 193.
4. Senator Lodge to L. A. Coolidge, January 1, 1920, *Lodge Papers,* Massachusetts Historical Society.
5. Senator Hitchcock to Mrs. Woodrow Wilson, January 5, 1920, *Hitchcock Papers,* Library of Congress.
6. Senator Borah to Senator Lodge, January 24, 1920, *Borah MSS.*
7. New York *Tribune,* January 27, 1920.

the Senate, and the battle of November was renewed. Many Democratic senators had felt the pressure exerted by Irish-American societies, and they endeavored to convince prominent leaders of these societies that President Wilson and the Covenant of the League of Nations were in no way opposed to the principle of self-determination as applied to Ireland. Senator James Hamilton Lewis wrote to Tumulty to assure him that in Chicago the Irish-Americans were not being led astray. He had recently spoken before a large Irish-American group, and it was generally conceded that

> the matter brought forth by me was a complete refutation of the charges [brought against the President and the League]. . . . I also demonstrated how the "reservations of Lodge" were in the language of the old neutrality laws under which Irishmen were jailed in the conflict between France and England. . . . I showed how under these very words used in the reservations, as taken from the old neutrality laws, Secretary Hay had forbidden contributions of Irish to the Boer cause and removed a consul who was an American-Irishman who happened to be of Irish birth, at Pretoria, South Africa. . . . From every place one meets the great results of this first complete historical disclosure of the fraud . . . of the Republican leaders in their attempt to check the Irish of this Middle West.[8]

It is evident that Senator Lewis completely misread the political situation in many parts of the country. There was a strong tide among Irish-Americans against the League, and occasional talks by Lewis would not check its flow. According to Judge Cohalan,

> reports from all over the country are entirely satisfactory as to the rising state of popular opposition to the whole British scheme [the League of Nations]. . . . One thing that may save the situation is the stubborn vanity of the President, and his friends, knowing this, are trying by flattery to urge him to accept as a triumph what will be, of course, an absolute defeat for him.[9]

Absolute defeat of the Treaty of Versailles seemed very probable, as the debates in the Senate showed that there was little

---

8. Senator J. Hamilton Lewis to Joseph P. Tumulty, February 16, 1920, *Wilson MSS.*
9. Judge Cohalan to Senator Borah, February 2, 1920, *Borah MSS.*

chance for a compromise that would be acceptable to the President. This fact delighted Judge Cohalan, who wrote to Borah that he was "greatly pleased with the situation . . . in Washington. I believe a final triumph for America is in sight." [10] But Borah was still a little fearful: "The fluid forces with which we have to deal may develop anything at almost any time." [11] Judge Cohalan continued to nurse his hopes that the Treaty would be beaten in the Senate. The sooner it was "brought to a head and disposed of the better in order that public opinion throughout the country may come to understand what it means. I think it will be the overshadowing issue in the coming campaign." [12]

In the early days of March it was evident that the Treaty would soon "be disposed of" in the Senate. On the day before the final vote there, a diversion was attempted by Senator Gerry in the hope that Irish-American opinion would be favorably influenced. A reservation [the fifteenth] was suddenly presented to the Senate favoring "the aspirations of the Irish people for a government of their own choice." When "such a government is attained by Ireland, a consummation it is hoped is at hand, it should promptly be admitted as a member of the League of Nations." [13]

This reservation was adopted by the Senate in a close vote of 38 to 36, with the "bitter-enders" and over half the Democrats present voting for it.[14] On the following day the final vote was taken in the Senate on the Treaty. It passed by a vote of 49 to 35, but it lacked the necessary two-thirds majority and therefore was rejected.

Judge Cohalan, of course, was delighted with this result. In a letter to Senator Hiram W. Johnson, he expressed his warm approval of the course followed by the Senator and indicated that Johnson was his choice for the Republican Presidential nomination:

> Let me again formally congratulate you on the splendid work you have done for our country in helping to defeat the proposed League of

10. Cohalan to Borah, March 2, 1920, *ibid.*
11. Borah to Cohalan, March 3, 1920, *ibid.*
12. Cohalan to Borah, March 8, 1920, *ibid.*
13. *Congressional Record*, 66 Cong., 2 sess., LIX, pt. 5, 4501.
14. Thomas A. Bailey, *Woodrow Wilson and the Great Betrayal*, pp. 263-264.

Nations. More and more the people are beginning to appreciate how destructive the League would have been to the best interests and highest ideals of our country, and the men who have fought so successfully against it have endeared themselves to millions of our countrymen.

I hope for you in the near future the greatest honors which can come to an American.[15]

B. BACKGROUND OF THE REPUBLICAN CONVENTION AT CHICAGO

Hiram Johnson's Presidential bee buzzed loudly in the bonnets of thousands of the Friends of Irish Freedom. The *Irish World* was ardently in his support, and when he won the Presidential primary in Michigan, it carried a large caption: "Glorious News from Michigan."[16] The *Gaelic American* was equally enthusiastic in his favor:

> The English crowd who are behind Hoover are putting in tremendous work and spending enormous sums of money to defeat Johnson. . . . Our people are working hard for Johnson in New Jersey, Maryland, Nebraska and Indiana, with bright prospects of victory, but they ought to redouble their efforts to ensure it. The triumph of Johnson in these States will give him such strength in the Convention that his nomination will be assured. Go to the primaries and vote for Johnson.[17]

At a meeting of the National Council of the Friends of Irish Freedom, a committee was appointed to "wait on the Republican and Democratic Conventions to request a plank in the party platforms favoring recognition of the Republic of Ireland." Judge Cohalan hoped that this pressure might lead to some good result, but he received no co-operation from De Valera. This fact was made very clear in a statement by Daniel T. O'Connell, head of the Irish National Bureau in Washington:

> The President [De Valera] has several times been quoted as saying that he went to Chicago when he found those charged with the

15. Judge Cohalan to Senator Hiram W. Johnson, March 23, 1920, *Cohalan MSS*.
16. April 10, 1920.
17. April 24, 1920.

responsibility of seeking adoption of a plank here making no preparations. . . . President de Valera knew better than anyone else. Practically all details of legislation and national political matters went through the hands of the writer. Not once did President de Valera ask for information as to the plans for Chicago. He had been fully informed regarding the Mason legislation. He had only to intimate that he wished for information regarding Chicago, to receive all available information. . . . A great deal of preliminary work in behalf of Ireland was done at Washington before the party leaders left for Chicago.[18]

On May 22 Judge Cohalan had a conference in Washington with President de Valera relative to the Chicago convention. At this conference, John E. Milholland strongly urged that the Friends of Irish Freedom advance $50,000 for the purpose of making "a tremendous display at Chicago to drive through the Republican Convention the resolution in favor of recognition." Judge Cohalan opposed this expenditure and these tactics, but De Valera sent Milholland to Chicago to exert what pressure he could command. Frank P. Walsh and other Irish-Americans close to De Valera advised him not to attend the Republican convention, but he disregarded this advice, much to the consternation of his friends. The situation is graphically described by McCartan:

> Frank P. Walsh, Bourke Cockran and others had advised President de Valera that it would be improper for him and dangerous to intrude upon the Convention. The risks he ran I made abundantly clear to him in a talk in which I supposed he meant his presence in Chicago to remain secret. So when I saw, in the New York *World,* that his departure with Sean Nunan for the Republican Convention had leaked out, I at once wrote through a third party advising him to leave Chicago immediately. . . . Before my letter could reach him, he ordered me by telegraph to join him in Chicago. So there we were—President de Valera, Mellows, Nunan, and I—all four of us, members of a foreign mission, trespassing on American hospitality. And our trespassing did not end with our presence.
> We opened offices, with huge circus posters outside on Michigan Boulevard; headquarters at the Blackstone Hotel—at the Convention

18. *Cohalan MSS.*

centre. . . . There was no chance of offending America that we did not take.[19]

In defense of his presence in Chicago, De Valera, in a press interview, remarked: "At all times, we have known that the American people were sympathetic with the Irish struggle for freedom. My mission in this country is to get action in accordance with that sympathy. If I do not get action I will consider that I have not attained the object of my Mission." [20]

On June 5 Judge Cohalan arrived in Chicago and immediately set to work, with some members of the Friends of Irish Freedom, to draft a plank which he hoped the Republican convention would adopt. The failure of the Mason Bill in Congress indicated that it would be idle to draft a plank that would specifically call for the recognition of the Irish Republic. The plank, as finally drafted by Cohalan and his friends, was a simple declaration in favor of self-determination for Ireland:

> *Resolved:* that this Republican Convention desires to place on record its sympathy with all oppressed peoples, and its recognition of the principle that the people of Ireland have the right to determine freely, without dictation from outside, their own governmental institutions and their international relations with other States and peoples.[21]

The plank drafted by De Valera and his clique called for the recognition of the Irish Republic. It is amazing that, in the face of the defeat of the Mason Bill in Congress a few days before, De Valera could still believe that the Republican Convention would adopt a plank that the American people, as represented in Congress, had rejected.[22]

19. Patrick McCartan, *With De Valera in America*, pp. 190-191.
20. *New York Times,* June 8, 1920.
21. *Cohalan MSS.*
22. The last paragraph of the plank as drafted by De Valera and his associates read as follows: "We pledge our party to the policy of according to the elected government of the Republic of Ireland full, formal and official recognition by the government of the United States, thus vindicating the principle for which our soldiers offered up their lives."

The dubious tactics employed by De Valera in Chicago are told in some detail by Daniel T. O'Connell:

> The nature of the plank which President de Valera proposed to introduce was not disclosed to Judge Cohalan until Tuesday, June 8, when in a most roundabout manner a copy was obtained. President de Valera wished, and had been encouraged to believe, he, personally, could argue before the Committee on Resolutions for the adoption of his plank. Such a plea was foredoomed to failure. Senator Watson said to several who approached him that it was wholly preposterous to think it possible to have the executive, or official representative of any other nation, argue before an American political convention committee in support of or opposition to a subject affecting the country's foreign relations.
>
> Justice Cohalan, realizing that the De Valera-Walsh resolution would be overwhelmingly defeated, and conscious that such a result would injure Ireland's cause, cordially approved the suggestion made by those in conference with him that President de Valera be urged to make such changes in the form of the resolution drafted by the President as would permit it having some chance to secure adoption. . . .
>
> Mr. Robert Emmet O'Malley. . . who had previously acted on a committee named to press the De Valera-Walsh draft, suggested a conference. . . . When Mr. O'Malley suggested Justice Cohalan attend the proposed conference, the Judge said perhaps it would be better to refrain from attending as so much antagonism was directed against him. Mayor John P. Grace, of Charleston, Hon. Joseph P. Mahoney, of Chicago, Judge Robert Crowe, of Chicago, John Archdeacon Murphy, of Buffalo, and Joseph P. O'Mahony, of Indianapolis, were named to confer with President de Valera and Frank P. Walsh. Justice Cohalan said he would abide by the conclusions of the committee. . . . It has been said by those attacking Justice Cohalan that he agreed to be present. Such an assertion is wholly groundless.[23]

The uncompromising attitude of De Valera with reference to the wording of his plank is clearly indicated by John A. Murphy, who attended the conference on June 8:

> The President submitted to us the plank he insisted should be adopted without change of any sort. But the one presented by Frank P. Walsh

23. *Cohalan MSS.*

next day to the Committee on Resolutions was much shorter; it was much milder in tone than the one we were told could not be changed in the least. Had discussion or compromise in the wording of the plank been invited or allowed, or unity sought, I am satisfied that it could have been obtained. Our committee were not at all set in the manner of phrasing the plank and would have accepted any reasonable wording in keeping with what WE knew must be the general form and tenor of a political plank.[24]

After receiving a sharp snub from De Valera, the Cohalan committee conferred with the Judge and with several additional members of the Friends of Irish Freedom, including Bishop Michael J. Gallagher, of Detroit. Bishop Gallagher had taken the trouble to see De Valera and had asked him to withdraw his plank. His plea had met with a terse refusal. Bishop Gallagher then informed De Valera that one member of the Friends of Irish Freedom had suggested that the President of the Irish Republic "go home." In recounting this incident to the committee of the Friends of Irish Freedom, Bishop Gallagher was struck by the unanimity of "noes" that greeted his remark. The voice of Judge Cohalan was the loudest one in this negative chorus.[25]

It was a great pity as far as Irish-American unity was concerned that De Valera did not go home immediately after the Chicago convention. He had no conception of political realities in America, and his insistence upon his plank revealed a stubborn, unperceptive quality that boded ill for the future. On June 9, when his plank calling for recognition of the Irish Republic came before the subcommittee on resolutions, it was defeated by a crushing vote of 11 to 1. Senator Borah was the only one who voted in its favor.

At four o'clock on the same afternoon (June 9) the Cohalan plank came before the same subcommittee and was approved by a vote of 7 to 6. On the following day the Chicago *Tribune* printed a tentative draft of the platform as approved by the subcommittee on resolutions. It contained the Cohalan plank. But when De Valera announced his opposition to this plank it was withdrawn and the

24. *Ibid.*
25. *Ibid.*

final platform as adopted by the Convention did not contain any plank dealing with the Irish Question. With the President of the Irish Republic it was always a question of rule or ruin, and he did a magnificent job of ruining Irish-American unity.

How well he worked in this regard at the Chicago convention was told in detail by Bishop Michael J. Gallagher in 1921:

> The most terrible mistake President de Valera has made in America and the most disastrous for Ireland was his rushing to Chicago (although he knew Justice Cohalan had been appointed by the Executive of the Friends of Irish Freedom, as Chairman of a Committee to look after the Irish plank in the Republican platform) and insisting that a plank drawn by himself should be adopted pledging the recognition of the Irish Republic and that nothing else would be accepted. The leaders of the Friends of Irish Freedom knew, as men experienced in American Conventions, that this plank . . . could not be forced through at that time. . . . The Friends of Irish Freedom leaders had tried for a whole year to get an implicit recognition bill—the Mason bill—through Congress and failed. . . . The Irish-American leaders, therefore, felt that under these circumstances it would be sheer folly to demand a recognition plank in express terms. . . . Accordingly, they negotiated and secured the adoption of the so-called Cohalan plank, in the sub-committee, by a vote of seven to six. . . .
>
> If this plank had been allowed to stand the Democrats would have had to adopt as good a one, and the result would be that the Irish cause would have been raised to a level hitherto unthought of in the minds of the whole American people. . . . But De Valera's offering one plank and the "Friends" another, subsequently, gave politicians a chance to say that the Irish did not know what they wanted. . . . De Valera denounced this plank [the Cohalan plank] as unacceptable, and had Milholland 'phone Senator Watson, the Chairman of the Resolutions Committee, that the plank was not wanted. The result was that Watson, in disgust, changed his vote over night, leaving the vote of the sub-committee six to six, which meant the defeat of the Cohalan plank and the dropping of all reference to Ireland in the Republican platform.[26]

26. Bishop Michael J. Gallagher to the Friends of Ireland in America, April 9, 1921, *Cohalan MSS*. The Friends of Irish Freedom published a large number of circulars containing De Valera's letter to Judge Cohalan, February 20, 1920; Judge Cohalan's answer, February 22, 1920; John Devoy's Letter to a Colleague, February 26, 1920, and Bishop Gallagher's Letter to the Friends of Ireland in America, April 9, 1921.

In his description of what happened at Chicago, McCartan twists the facts of the De Valera-Cohalan dispute so as to support the De Valera side of the case. But even in his garbled version of the affair there is an admission that at Chicago he, McCartan, had descended to vituperation instead of argument. After an unwarranted attack upon Bishop Gallagher he cooled off a bit and became more rational. As he phrases it in his book: "My madness then passed from me, and I felt sorrowfully that Ireland had cause to despair in us." [27]

Many Friends of Irish Freedom felt that they had good cause to despair in De Valera when they heard the details of the Chicago convention. Judge Lawless, of Virginia, regarded the situation as

> very serious and one calling for some dignified but positive action on the part of the National Council [of the Friends of Irish Freedom]. It appears to me that the President [De Valera] has acted not only unwisely but with an obduracy characteristic of the wrecker of the Democratic party and that his usefulness in this country is greatly impaired and probably at an end.[28]

John Devoy was

> quite satisfied with the Chicago fracas. We have left him [De Valera] a clear field and he can't put his defeat on us. Attempt to put defeat on your action in Chicago will strike every sensible man as absurd. Walsh has come out plainly enough to show his teeth. I am commenting editorially and putting responsibility on him, leaving D. V. out.[29]

Because of his deep solicitude for Irish-American unity, John Devoy was trying to spare De Valera as much as he could, but the temperamental President of the Irish Republic would not stay in the dignified category in which Devoy wished to place him. He seemed determined to impose his unwanted leadership upon Irish-Americans at times when it led straight to disaster. At San Francisco he repeated his blunders at Chicago.

27. *Op. cit.*, pp. 198-199.
28. Judge Joseph T. Lawless to Judge Cohalan, June 21, 1920, *Cohalan MSS.*
29. John Devoy to Judge Cohalan, June 28, 1920, *ibid.*

C. DE VALERA BUNGLES AGAIN AT SAN FRANCISCO

De Valera's defeat at Chicago did not dampen his ardor for political manipulation. He was determined to present to the Democratic convention at San Francisco a plank calling for American recognition of the Irish Republic, and he nursed the hope that he could persuade the committee on resolutions to permit him to make a personal appearance. His oratory and persuasive powers could do the rest.

He knew that Democratic Irish bosses like Charles F. Murphy, George E. Brennan, and Thomas Taggart would be present at San Francisco, and he expected significant assistance from them.[30] He was disappointed in this regard. As far as running the convention was concerned, President Wilson won an important victory when Senator Joseph T. Robinson was elected permanent chairman of the convention, with Senator Carter Glass as chairman of the Resolutions Committee. These lieutenants of Wilson would have scant sympathy with any resolution proposing recognition of the Irish Republic.

It was very apparent to the Friends of Irish Freedom that there was little hope that the Democratic convention would approve any plank dealing with Irish recognition. On June 25 Daniel T. O'Connell issued a statement to the effect that the Friends would make no attempt to act in a major role at San Francisco. The experience at Chicago would not be repeated. De Valera would have a clear field to present any plank he wished without any competition from the Friends.[31]

It was inevitable that the efforts of De Valera at San Francisco would be attended by failure. As early as March 1, 1920, Glass, Burleson, Underwood, Pomerene, and Robinson had arrived at an

---

30. Homer Cummings, a Wilson stalwart, feared that the Irish "bosses" might control the San Francisco convention. Murphy claimed that he controlled 310 votes in the convention, and Taggart and Brennan were supposed to dominate large blocs of votes. New York *Tribune*, June 25, 1920.
31. *Cohalan MSS.*

agreement on the platform that would be presented to the Democratic convention.[32] By June the proposed platform had been outlined in detail, and it did not contain any reference to Irish self-determination.[33] The members of the Resolutions Committee knew that President Wilson did not want any plank providing for the recognition of the Irish Republic, and Homer Cummings assured the President that "the Committee is in the hands of your friends." [34]

But De Valera refused to believe that he could not push through the committee a plank on Irish independence. On June 29 he and Frank P. Walsh appeared before the committee and warmly argued for recognition. They received some support from Senator Phelan but were strongly opposed by Tom Connally. The proposed De Valera plank was defeated in the full committee by a vote of 31 to 17. It was significant that none of the seventeen members who voted for it was willing to sponsor a plan to submit this De Valera plank to the convention in the form of a minority report.

In an effort to rally some support for his plank, De Valera and Walsh now organized a meeting of some three hundred persons to discuss the Irish Question. The atmosphere of the discussion soon became so heated that the police had to be called to quell the confusion.[35] It was evident that the topic of Irish independence was a most explosive one.

After extended conferences between De Valera, Frank P. Walsh, and some other De Valera adherents, it was decided to leave out of the proposed plank any mention of the recognition of the Republic of Ireland. Seven members of the Resolutions Committee agreed to sign this revised plank and present it as a minority report. When Edward L. Doheny attempted to place this plank before the convention, the most vociferous opposition was at once manifested. After an hour of boisterous confusion the vote was taken

32. Burleson to Woodrow Wilson, March 1, 1920, *Burleson Papers,* Library of Congress.
33. Burleson to Senator Pomerene, June 4, 1920; Gregory to Burleson, June 10, 1920, *ibid.*
34. Homer Cummings to President Wilson, July 1, 1920, "Cummings file," *Ray S. Baker Papers,* Library of Congress.
35. *New York Times,* July 2, 1920.

on the Walsh amended plank, which was defeated by a vote of 665 to 402.[36]

The tactics pursued by De Valera at San Francisco were revealed by Daniel T. O'Connell:

> It is now intimated that Mr. Walsh and President de Valera did not approve of the withdrawal of the "recognition" section [of the De Valera plank presented to the convention]. Mr. Walsh was in continuous attendance and consultation with the party leaders and delegates who were fighting for him, and President de Valera was in a hotel almost across the street from the convention.
>
> They had plenty of time, for hours before the vote was taken, to express disapproval or repudiation. Neither course was followed, and the delegates voted under the direction of a "steering committee" of fifty organized by Mr. Walsh, acting in harmony with his wishes and with Mr. Walsh present.
>
> The facts as recited are beyond contradiction. The withdrawal of their recognition plank was equivalent to an acknowledgment that Justice Cohalan was right when, viewing the two conventions with experienced, far-seeing vision, he foresaw defeat for such an extreme course.[37]

After all this confusion and useless fighting, the best that De Valera and Walsh could achieve was the insertion in the platform of a plank expressing sympathy with Irish aspirations.[38] The De Valera leadership of one section of Irish-Americans had proved to be a tragic failure. After looking into the situation carefully, John Devoy expressed his viewpoint to Judge Cohalan:

> It is quite evident to me now that his [De Valera's] action at Chicago was a maneuver to recover the ground he lost by the Cuban proposition—to make it appear that we are not really for the Irish Republic and he is. A lot of fools believe that and that is the cry of all the little factionists here. Where he will get his leadership when he has us all kicked out I don't know. There is not a man among them who is fit to lead a corporal's guard. His utter defeat in San Francisco has hurt him very badly, but there is already a campaign started to

36. *Cohalan MSS.*
37. *Ibid.*
38. *Ibid.*

show that the fact that over 400 delegates voted for his resolution (or plank) is hopeful for the future.

McCartan is weak and flimsy in the [*Irish*] *Press* this week. He is evidently flabbergasted. He puts his *memory* of occurrences against documentary evidence and goes into silly details about who was in certain hotel rooms and how easy it would have been to confer if conference was wanted.[39]

A few days later Devoy wrote another letter to Judge Cohalan relative to De Valera's tactics at Chicago: "We now see his reason for preventing action at Chicago. That despatch says he wanted to prevent us from 'selling the Irish vote to any candidate,' meaning he wanted to kill [Hiram] Johnson." [40] As far as Irish-Americans were concerned, the nomination of Hiram Johnson to the Presidency would have been a godsend. De Valera was too inexperienced in American affairs to appreciate this fact.

D. DE VALERA PRESSES HIS FIGHT AGAINST JUDGE COHALAN

With a record of two serious failures at party conventions in America to his discredit, De Valera now turned to the congenial task of undermining the Friends of Irish Freedom. In this way he could strike a sharp blow at Judge Cohalan. It might be expedient to strike at the Judge by way of Ireland.

De Valera's unhappy interview given to the American correspondent of the *Westminster Gazette* with reference to using the Platt Amendment as a guide to future Anglo-Irish relations had been a serious faux pas. Disturbed by the unfriendly reaction of Irish-Americans to this suggestion, De Valera sent McCartan to Ireland to explain his viewpoint. Several members of the Cabinet were in distinct disagreement with this viewpoint and they were not backward about expressing themselves. But they felt that they could not publicly repudiate De Valera. The situation is outlined in McCartan's book:

39. John Devoy to Judge Cohalan, July 4, 1920, *Cohalan MSS.*
40. Devoy to Cohalan, July 10, 1920, *ibid.*

When the Cabinet had finished with de Valera's Cuban business, I referred to my activities in the United States before De Valera came to end them. . . . I pointed out the need for prompt, decisive action then; and that if I had gone too far the Dail, when it met, was free to ignore or repudiate me. *"Repudiate* you!", repeated Collins, with a quick toss of his head; and his tone and gesture implied the idea was unthinkable.[41]

John Devoy was deeply interested in the reception that McCartan would get from Irish leaders. In a letter to Judge Cohalan he discusses this situation:

Now that McCartan's presence in Ireland has been made public and that Father Cullinane says he has been sent there to explain the situation here, it seems plain to me that De Valera wants them to endorse his action towards us and to reappoint McC. as Ambassador. . . . It is hardly possible to think that, with all the knowledge they now have of McC.'s conduct and of our objections to him, they would send him out again, but if D.V. insists on it they may do so. That would mean Maloney in charge here, constant interference in Washington and irritation and squabbling that would be very annoying and embarrassing. If they do it I see no remedy only a resolution by the National Council [of the Friends of Irish Freedom] declaring McC. *persona non grata* and demanding his immediate recall.[42]

Devoy was greatly disturbed when a group of Irish-Americans headed by the Reverend Patrick J. Healy, of the Catholic University, went to great lengths to heal the breach between him and De Valera. He was particularly distressed because Father Healy had appealed to "De Valera to stop me from defending the organization [Friends of Irish Freedom] from attacks inspired and encouraged by De Valera." [43]

De Valera's next move against Cohalan and Devoy was to send Harry Boland to Dublin to line up the Irish Revolutionary Brotherhood against their leadership of the Friends of Irish Freedom and their influence in the Clan-na-Gael. In Ireland it was difficult to understand what was going on in the United States, and many leaders

41. *Op. cit.*, pp. 154-155.
42. John Devoy to Judge Cohalan, April 29, 1920, *Cohalan MSS.*
43. Devoy to Cohalan, May 18, 1920, *ibid.*

felt that it was imperative to support De Valera. Piaras Beaslai, in commenting upon this situation, remarks:

> Mr. de Valera now despatched Harry Boland to Dublin. From the time of his departure to America to his death, Harry's ruling passion was a devoted personal attachment to De Valera. He arrived secretly in Dublin, was warmly greeted by Collins and painted the case of De Valera in the brightest colours, and that of his critics and opponents in the blackest hues. His representations, of course, carried great weight with Collins and the other I.R.B. leaders, and he was made the bearer of a message to the Clan-na-Gael expressing the dissent of the I.R.B. from the attitude of the "Gaelic American."

Soon after his return to America, Harry Boland announced publicly, that he was authorized to declare the Clan-na-Gael dissevered from the I.R.B. in Ireland. This statement was certainly inaccurate, and a clear case of exceeding his instructions. Collins was startled and annoyed when he saw the action Boland had taken. Boland also started what was called a "reorganized Clan." [44]

John Devoy soon realized what Boland intended to do. In a letter to Judge Cohalan he indicates what he was certain De Valera's lieutenant would endeavor to accomplish:

> Harry [Boland] is back here and there is a rumor he is going to "reorganize" the Clan or start a rival organization. . . . They mean war to the knife. It is an awful revelation. . . .[45]

Boland next circulated the lie that he had been authorized to dissever all ties between the I.R.B. and the Clan-na-Gael:

> Harry [Boland] admitted he was *instructed to cut the connection that had lasted for sixty years.* That is how he put it, but it ought to be forty-six. This shows they will stop at nothing and are determined to smash everything that stands in their way. . . . They are great men to have the fate of a country in their hands." [46]

Part of the campaign against Judge Cohalan and John Devoy took the form of vicious smears that circulated rapidly through Irish-American ranks. Diarmuid Lynch, National Secretary of the Friends

44. *Michael Collins and the Making of a New Ireland*, II, 20-21.
45. John Devoy to Judge Cohalan, July 15, 1920, *Cohalan MSS.*
46. Devoy to Cohalan, July 17, 1920, *ibid.*

of Irish Freedom, was also attacked without restraint. Smarting under this unjust assault, Lynch, on July 20, 1920, resigned his seat in the Dail Eireann. In his letter of resignation he frankly stated that in the dispute then raging in Irish-American ranks he was "generally in agreement" with Cohalan and Devoy.[47]

This statement was greeted with derision and he was subject to many further attacks. Through Devoy's *Gaelic American* these aspersions were warmly answered, but they were so numerous it was impossible to reply to all of them. Some of them came from lieutenants of De Valera who grossly abused American hospitality. A canard was circulated to the effect that Liam Mellows, when he first arrived in New York, had grievously suffered from neglect. Devoy quickly challenged the truth of this statement:

> The falsehood that Liam Mellows was badly treated has been going the rounds for a long time and it is not creditable to Liam Mellows that he has never uttered a word in refutation of it, but has allowed it to go on to the detriment of the National Movement and to the discrediting of a man for whom he once expressed a high regard [John Devoy]. The lie—an infamous and wholly unfounded lie—has not alone been circulated extensively in the United States, but it has gone to Ireland and is spread there for the same purpose—to injure the character of John Devoy. We now challenge Liam Mellows to say specifically over his name what injury was inflicted on him since he came to America.[48]

E. THE FIGHT FOR THE CONTROL OF THE FRIENDS OF IRISH FREEDOM

The De Valera fight against Judge Cohalan and John Devoy assumed many forms. It was not alone through smears, half truths and complete lies that De Valera's lieutenants carried on the struggle. They realized the honored place that Judge Cohalan had earned in the Irish-American movement for Irish independence. It

47. *Cohalan MSS.*
48. *Gaelic American,* July 24, 1920. Devoy had gone out of his way to be kind and generous to Mellows when he arrived in the United States after the Easter Rising. He paid him a salary equal to his own for work on the *Gaelic American* and sponsored him for the position of national organizer for the Friends of Irish Freedom.

would be impossible to destroy the esteem in which he was held merely through mendacity and double-talk, but his influence could be measurably lessened by seizing control of the Friends of Irish Freedom. This could best be achieved by placing in the office of National President one of the De Valera lieutenants.

In June 1920 the Very Reverend Peter T. Magennis, O.C.C., resigned as National President of the Friends and the way was now open for the election of a De Valera supporter. On July 30 the National Council held a meeting at which the resignation of Magennis was accepted, and then it proceeded to the election of the Right Reverend Michael J. Gallagher, Bishop of Detroit, as the new President of the Friends. On August 6 De Valera wrote a letter to Bishop Gallagher outlining his views as to a reorganization of the Friends —it was "necessary to democratize the system of control." The State Councils should have "real power and regularly function as the supreme authority except in regard to such matters as might be explicitly reserved for the National Council by the constitution." De Valera also urged the holding of another "Race Convention at some central point such as Chicago before the end of the fall." He also suggested that a special meeting of the National Council be held in Chicago.

To clear up difficulties that existed between Judge Cohalan, John Devoy, and De Valera, Bishop Gallagher had a conference with the President of the Irish Republic. Wisely, he took along with him Judge Hally. The conference had hardly begun before De Valera suggested that Bishop Gallagher resign, because he was "merely another retrenchment thrown up to retard his [De Valera's] triumphant advance and cover the retreat of the Cohalanites while they took up new positions." When the four-hour conference was over, Judge Hally remarked: "I'm sorry I came; I'm disillusioned; I thought the President of Ireland was a bigger man. His idea of harmony reminds me of Li Hung Chang's, who said the harmony he best loved to hear was the ring of the headsman's axe on the neck of his opponents."

Bishop Gallagher was strongly opposed to the holding of another Race Convention in the fall of 1920, and he did not approve of holding a meeting of the National Council in Chicago. The Council usually met in New York City, which was the focal point for a large majority of the Friends of Irish Freedom. The Bishop was not in favor of adopting the long list of amendments that were being pressed by De Valera's lieutenants. It was apparent that there was a scheme to seize control of the Friends of Irish Freedom for the purpose of furthering the plans of De Valera. His formula of rule or ruin was about to be invoked again.

John Devoy and Judge Cohalan were well aware of the schemes of the supporters of De Valera, and Devoy had some sharp correspondence with Harry Boland. Boland had written a bitter letter to Devoy about the stand taken by the *Gaelic American,* and Devoy lost no time in answering it:

> The last sentence in your letter in which you say of the *Gaelic American* . . . that "more scandal is poured into people's ears in one day than there is in any other institution that I know in the world," is very mean and wholly untrue. It is part of the fake case you are trying to build up against us to justify the hostile action that you have been taking in an underhand way for more than a year and which you propose to supplement and complete by an attempt to destroy us. It is you and your colleagues who have been pouring scandal and falsehood into people's ears all over the United States and Ireland.[49]

It seemed clear to Devoy that the leaders of the Friends of Irish Freedom had upset the "grand scheme" of De Valera and his followers to "make Walsh President and have him call a convention in which they would try to swamp us with their salaried officials of the Commission. We are not yet out of the woods, but we have the best of it."[50]

Devoy was correct in thinking that he and Judge Cohalan were "not yet out of the woods" as far as the schemes of De Valera were concerned. The Dail Eireann had followed the dictates of the President of the Irish Republic. It had inserted in its official records the report of the Acting Minister for Foreign Affairs concerning the situation in America:

49. John Devoy to Harry Boland, August 7, 1920, *Cohalan MSS.*
50. John Devoy to Judge Cohalan, August 7, 1920, *ibid.*

This portion of my report would be incomplete if I did not refer to the attitude of Supreme Court Justice Daniel F. Cohalan and John Devoy toward President de Valera and his mission. The ministry learns that these two men have never given their whole-hearted support to the President in his campaign. At the very outset they used their utmost endeavor to prevent a launching of the Bond Drive, and they attempted to force the President into the position of accepting their dictation in all matters of policy connected with his mission. The President has definitely refused to allow his judgment or his action to be dictated by these men and the success of his tour and of the Bond Drive are proof of his wisdom in the matter.[51]

This report made Devoy furious and he denounced it as completely untrue. He knew now how far De Valera was determined to go in his drive to crush any opposition to his American policy. Judge Cohalan and Devoy decided to meet this attack by concerting with other Friends of Irish Freedom as to the best procedure to follow. On August 12 Devoy wrote to the Judge and announced a meeting of the National Executive of the Friends of Irish Freedom at the end of the week. He thought it would be

> the most important meeting we ever held. We will hold a conference beginning at 4 o'clock Saturday afternoon at same place [Park Avenue Hotel]. We must carefully consider our plan of action in view of the situation revealed by that attack on us in the report of Dail Eireann's minutes. . . . D.V. is out to smash us, and he is nibbling away at the ramparts all the time. . . . He is the most malignant man in all Irish history.[52]

A few days after this letter was written a temporary truce was patched up between Devoy and Harry Boland; but Boland never meant to keep it, and it was not long before De Valera's lieutenants were moving ahead with their plans for control of the Friends of Irish Freedom. The *Irish World* continued its attack upon Devoy and Judge Cohalan. In a letter to the Judge, Devoy gives a brief picture of the situation:

51. *Ibid.*
52. Devoy to Cohalan, August 12, 1920, *ibid.*

The *Irish World* has the worst article yet, based entirely on that lie they got inserted in the records of the Dail Eireann. Harry [Boland] called up to get copies of this and last week's paper, apparently to have D.V. study them to see whether he will carry out the promise or not. It would not surprise me if he demanded that I should retract my comment of last week on the lie they sent over, which, of course, I will refuse to do. . . . I may be too pessimistic on account of the irritation over the *Irish World* but my experience with these men makes me suspicious of everything they do.[53]

Towards the last part of August it was apparent that De Valera and Boland had no intention of keeping the truce they had made with Devoy and Judge Cohalan. Devoy had never expected them to keep it:

D.V. and Harry are making a bad mistake in doing nothing, because we are getting credit for making peace, which is the uppermost thing in our people's minds just now. . . . Several friends are urging me to get [Austin] Ford indicted for criminal libel [for abusive articles in the *Irish World*], but the great objection is that men would say, "He was getting the worst of a public controversy and now appeals for protection to the law." But, on the other hand, it would be the best means of proving the falsehood of the propaganda against us and of the lies sent to Ireland.[54]

Harry Boland broke the truce to shreds by sharply criticizing Judge Cohalan. He made the statement that it was

treason for you [Judge Cohalan] to go to Chicago to upset the President's plans. . . . D.V. is obsessed with the necessity of safeguarding *his prerogative* and they are all crazy on that point. Lindsay [Crawford] and Diarmuid [Lynch] have told me of the amendments to the Constitution. They are all D.V.'s, but are presented by the Massachusetts State Council. They would hamstring the National Council and deprive it of all financial resources. . . . Harry wanted to know *what you are going to do,* and I asked him what *they* were go-

---

53. Devoy to Cohalan, August 25, 1920, *ibid.*
54. Devoy to Cohalan, August 27, 1920, *ibid.*

ing to do. This, I think, was one of the things that James [K. McGuire] objected to. He calls it "fighting." [55]

On September 7 ex-Governor Edward F. Dunne wrote to Devoy to inquire about the real meaning of a telegram from De Valera asking him to attend the meeting of the National Council of the Friends of Irish Freedom on September 17.[56] Devoy replied that De Valera hoped to control this meeting and to push through amendments that would change the whole structure of the Friends. It was evident that De Valera wanted "for himself the credit for all we have done in America and his whole mind is now concentrated on the effort to show that nobody in America amounts to anything and that he is the kingpin of the movement." [57]

When this long-awaited meeting of the National Council of the Friends of Irish Freedom was finally held on September 17, at the Waldorf-Astoria Hotel, De Valera was in attendance with his chief lieutenants. He was as temperamental as usual. When Mayor John P. Grace opposed the constitutional amendments that had been designed to assist De Valera to seize control of the Friends, De Valera took strong exception to some of the phrases of dissent and "left the hall, while his supporters rushed after him, seeking to break up the meeting with shouts of 'follow the President.'" [58] Several delegations went to his suite in the hotel and begged him to return to the meeting, but he refused to be placated. Harry Boland finally returned to the meeting and after a tirade of abusive remarks directed at the followers of Devoy and Cohalan, stated that De Valera wished "all those who wanted to help the Irish Republic to meet him in that room the following day." Only a few members of the National Council of the Friends agreed to accept this invitation.

To John Devoy it was obvious that De Valera was working hard to effect at the meeting a split in the ranks of the Friends:

55. Devoy to Cohalan, August 31, 1920, *ibid.*
56. Edward F. Dunne to John Devoy, September 7, 1920, *ibid.*
57. John Devoy to Edward F. Dunne, September 9, 1920, *ibid.*
58. Bishop Michael J. Gallagher to the Friends of Ireland in America, April 9, 1921, *ibid.*

The whole play was staged last night for a Split. Father Power's attempt to stampede the meeting with his squad of priests marching around shouting, "Break it up, break it up," being evidently intended as the signal, but its utter failure knocked out their plans. At an earlier stage in the meeting one of them was heard to say: "We haven't a gambler's chance here," and others said: "See how perfectly the Machine works." [59]

The Devoy-Cohalan machine did work quite well and the De Valera scheme to seize control of the Friends failed dismally. According to Devoy, "the general feeling in the city today is very good. There is deep resentment at D. V. and Harry [Boland], and some of the men on whom Harry was 'using his oil can' (as he puts it himself), are among the most angry."

The meeting on September 18 was an anticlimax. De Valera embraced the opportunity to criticize all his opponents, but he accomplished little. There was, however, a hint that a new Irish-American society more friendly to De Valera would be organized, and this was a herald of things to come.

But before he would devote his efforts to this new organization, De Valera wished to strike another blow at Devoy and Judge Cohalan. He could best do this by attacking the Clan-na-Gael. On October 22, 1920, Harry Boland gave a statement to the press concerning the Clan:

> Speaking with full authority in the name of the Supreme Council of the Irish Republican Brotherhood, I hereby announce that the Clan-na-Gael organization is no longer affiliated with the Brotherhood.[60]

It was evident to John Devoy that this mendacious statement meant that De Valera had declared "war to the knife" upon all his opponents.[61] We have already seen that Piaras Beaslai denied that

59. John Devoy to Judge Cohalan, September 18, 1920, *ibid.*
60. This press statement marked a new low in the De Valera attack upon Devoy and Judge Cohalan. It was treated with appropriate severity in the *Gaelic American*.
61. John Devoy to Judge Cohalan, October 23, 1920, *Cohalan MSS.*

De Valera and His Lieutenants

Boland ever received authority from the Irish Republican Brotherhood to make the statement that he gave to the press on October 22, 1920.[62] And John Devoy, during his visit to Ireland in 1924, talked with several persons who had been members of the Supreme Council of the I.R.B. in 1920. They assured him that Boland had never been delegated the authority he claimed he had received.[63] He had merely responded to the pressure exerted upon him by lieutenants of De Valera, and it is a revealing commentary upon the make-up of the President of the Irish Republic that he issued no statement clarifying the situation.

After having widened the split in the Friends of Irish Freedom, De Valera and his clique now took up the task of dissolving the Protestant Friends of Ireland. When Dr. Mythen, the active head of this organization, received a letter suggesting this dissolution, he replied:

> Your personal animosity to Judge Cohalan is none of my affair. When I, too, was under the same influence as you were, I felt very much the same way. I, too, have withstood Judge Cohalan on issues that had arisen within the Irish movement. If conditions arose again where I would feel justified in so doing, not for an instant would I hesitate to do so again. . . . Your covert charge against me, that I am permitting the use of the P.F.I. to be simply a tool for the use of Judge Cohalan, is a lie. . . . Never once has Judge Cohalan ever in any manner, shape or form, even suggested the manner in which our organization should be run or what manner of work it should do.[64]

The stage was now set for the launching of a new Irish-American organization that would be amenable to De Valera's desires. On October 20, 1920, he announced the birth of the American Association for the Recognition of the Irish Republic. The growth in membership of this new association was rapid, but its decline was inevitable when Irish-Americans realized that it had no real reason for existence. The movement towards recognition had been "shat-

62. *Ante*, p. 385.
63. *Cohalan MSS.*
64. *Ibid.*

tered" by De Valera's "Cuban interview of February 6th, 1920. Had the Association been started earlier it might have done much to justify its title." It had been organized not to promote the cause of Irish recognition but to embarrass John Devoy and Judge Cohalan. This fact is frankly admitted by McCartan.[65]

But if De Valera had failed to start an organization that had an important influence in the promotion of Irish recognition, he had been able to shatter Irish-American unity beyond repair. The Friends of Irish Freedom had been dealt a blow from which the organization never recovered. The rivalry between the Friends and the Association for the Recognition of the Irish Republic was not a friendly one, and even after his return to Ireland, De Valera continued to inspire hostility between the two organizations. In his letter of April 9, 1921, Bishop Gallagher clearly sets forth the situation:

> Let me add that the major part of this statement was written last December immediately after President de Valera launched his new organization. But when he disappeared I surmised that he had gone back to Ireland and therefore decided to continue my [Bishop Gallagher's] former policy of silence. I was foolish enough to cherish the hope that all men of Irish blood, interested in the liberation of Ireland, would remember how the Parnell split served her enemies. . . .
>
> If ever Ireland needed help from the power of American public opinion, it was during the last six months . . . . But America, the champion of freedom, . . . has done practically nothing. The reason is because President de Valera deliberately split the Irish movement in America, and all the energy of his followers has been wasted in the struggle to destroy instead of being expended for Ireland's cause against the common enemy. I nourished the hope that the friends of Ireland would soon see the folly of thus playing England's game, but it has been all in vain. The new organization is still spending thousands upon thousands of dollars trying to wipe out the Friends of Irish Freedom. Anyone who suggests that De Valera is not master of the people of Irish blood everywhere; or that, like ordinary mortals, he ever made a mistake in his whole life, is overwhelmed with billingsgate and foul abuse in the De Valera press. I have therefore

65. *Op. cit.*, pp. 216-217.

come to the conclusion that keeping silence about certain facts for the sake of more easily restoring harmony has not helped the situation but rather has given opportunity for misrepresentation. To form an intelligent judgment the truth should be made known. I am therefore writing this letter to those who may be interested that they may know the real facts of the case and then judge accordingly.[66]

In December 1920 De Valera returned to Ireland, and many members of the Friends of Irish Freedom carefully examined the record of his long visit to America and endeavored to estimate what he had actually accomplished during his eventful "Mission." The Irish bond-certificate drive had raised over five million dollars, but only half of this sum had reached Ireland and the other half had been returned to the subscribers. The needs of Ireland could have been taken care of through the activities of the Friends of Irish Freedom. During the six months ending August 31, 1919, the Friends had generously contributed more than one million dollars to a Victory Fund. There is little doubt that this fund could have been more than doubled.

There was really no need for all the excitement that De Valera and his lieutenants generated over the bond-certificate drive. But if the Friends for Irish Freedom had controlled the matter of fund raising, the role of De Valera would have been a very minor one. Such a role would have been very distasteful to him. He was obsessed with the idea that as the so-called President of the Irish Republic he could demand the instant and unquestioning allegiance of all men of Irish blood everywhere. He was amazed and infuriated when Judge Cohalan clearly intimated that his primary allegiance was to America. Aid to Ireland was based upon the view that Irish freedom would be an American asset. Ardent Americanism was the first article in the political creed of Judge Cohalan, and he

---

66. Bishop Michael J. Gallagher to the Friends of Irish Freedom, April 9, 1921, *Cohalan MSS*. The membership of the Friends of Irish Freedom in 1919 was impressive. There were 100,749 "regular" members, and about 175,000 "associate" members. After the split that was engineered by De Valera and his lieutenants, the "regular" membership declined to 20,000.

never permitted any reservations in this regard. It was a tragedy for the Irish-American movement when De Valera challenged this article.[67]

67. The unfortunate character of De Valera's activities in America is well expressed by Piaras Beaslai in his book, *Michael Collins and the Making of a New Ireland*, II, 21-22: "The case made by Devoy and Cohalan, put briefly, was that the Irish in America could only exert influence in American politics in their capacity of American citizens, to whom American interests were paramount, who sought recognition for Irish independence as something in consonance with American ideals of liberty. De Valera, on the other hand, maintained . . . that the Irish in America should be welded into an organised force, entirely under his own control as 'President of the Irish Republic.' . . . What he claimed was a right to 'dictate a policy' to Irish-Americans, by virtue of his office as 'President of the Irish Republic.'

"The fundamental fallacy of Mr. de Valera's position was his failure to recognize that, as President of an Irish Government fighting for its life, his place was in Ireland, and not in America. His claim to dominate Irish-Americans with an authority derived from the people of Ireland was obviously illogical."

13 THE BLACK AND TANS BEGIN A LONG CHAPTER OF ARSON AND MURDER

A. TERRORISM AND MURDER STALK THE IRISH COUNTRYSIDE

After the Paris Peace Conference had closed its sessions with no favorable action relative to Irish self-determination, tension throughout Ireland began to mount. It seemed apparent that Irish leaders would have to take the situation into their own hands and find some path to a satisfactory settlement. The Irish people would no longer submit to the old English rule of coercion, deportation, or death. The framing of an effective challenge to English misrule was primarily the task of Michael Collins, and he rose to the occasion with a resolute spirit and a bold plan that thrilled Irish patriots. English dominance of Ireland was made possible by large military forces stationed throughout the island. Something would have to be done to diminish the effectiveness of these forces.

Some of these English military units belonged to the so-called Royal Irish Constabulary. The members of this organization were not policemen in the ordinary sense of that term. The R.I.C. was a military force living in barracks in every part of Ireland. Their primary purpose was to "hold the country in subjection to England." [1] They were generally recruited from the ranks of the people,

1. Piaras Beaslai, *Michael Collins and the Making of a New Ireland*, I, 319-332.

and their intimate knowledge of many aspects of Irish life made them extremely effective as spies. This system of espionage was developed to such an extent that in every town and village the movements of prominent citizens were watched with care and duly reported upon. Irish self-determination would never be more than a mere phrase if the R.I.C. continued to function with their customary effectiveness. Plans to hamper their activities and wreck their system of espionage had been carefully considered by Irish leaders. It was Michael Collins who made these plans a reality.

As Director of Intelligence, Collins began to build an Intelligence Staff composed of men upon whom he could implicitly rely. This "Squad" consisted of Volunteers he could depend upon to carry out dangerous and difficult tasks. It was not long before these tasks were assigned and carried out with success.

Collins was particularly anxious to learn the procedures of the espionage system of the R.I.C. The members of his "Squad" infiltrated R.I.C. organizations and secured the keys to police and official cipher codes. Soon English official messages were tapped at various centers and decoded, and many confidential reports and secret documents found their way into his hands.

By concerted attacks upon outlying barracks of the R.I.C., the members of that organization were slowly pushed into the larger towns, and thus their espionage activities were becoming more and more limited. At times there was serious and open conflict between the Volunteers and English military forces. At Fermoy, County Cork, on September 7, 1919, a party of seventeen soldiers was attacked by Volunteers and disarmed. During the struggle one soldier was killed and three others were wounded. That night the military ran riot in the town of Fermoy, wrecking shops and assaulting civilians. The R.I.C. made no attempt to curb this lawlessness.

Through these well-planned activities, Collins "after one year's work, had effectually paralysed the British Government's political spy system in Dublin, a system which had worked so effectively for so many years, and defeated all the efforts of Irish Separatists in the past."² The English response was the suppression of the Dail Eireann as a "dangerous association" (September 10, 1919) and the establishment of a system of widespread and drastic coercion. Meetings of all kinds were forbidden, concerts were carefully controlled, papers were suppressed, and all activities were subject to the most rigorous scrutiny. Martial law prevailed in most of Ireland, and the situation gave the deepest concern to many Englishmen who feared the outbreak of a long and destructive civil war in Ireland. On December 14, 1919, the London *Observer* gravely remarked:

> Day by day the news from Ireland adds to the apprehensions of all who realize that Irish affairs are rising to a danger point. . . . The gravest duty that lies on the Government is to make possible the liquidation of this unreal and threatening phase. . . . All that can be offered of British goodwill is essential for success in this next and, we may soberly hope, final attempt.

This attempt on the part of the English Government was the "Better Government of Ireland Bill" introduced in the House of Commons on December 22, 1919. It proposed the establishment of separate parliaments for a divided Ireland, and the powers of these parliaments were distinctly restricted. On the following day Arthur Griffith sharply criticized this proposed new Home Rule bill:

> There is nothing for Irishmen in the English Premier's proposals. They are not intended to be operative. They are made to affect and mislead opinion in America. On February 13th, 1918, according to Sir Horace Plunkett's confidential report, the English Premier said to the representatives from his Irish Convention: "It is idle to propose partition now. You must accept the Unity of Ireland as a whole. Anything else would lead to failure." In the light of this America can understand how insincere are the present proposals. . . .
> The English Premier is again today in need of American aid. Since the end of the war his government in Ireland has acted as Russia never acted in Poland. . . . In the whole year 1917 there was

2. *Ibid.*, I, 379. Collins not only was Director of Intelligence but also was Minister of Finance in the Dail and Director of Organization in the Irish Republican Army.

a total of 719 acts of aggression against the Irish people; in the past six weeks of the present year there was a total of 3,187 such acts. These included 2,829 militaristic raids on private houses; 162 arrests; 126 sentences of imprisonment by paid magistrates and courts martial; 27 armed militaristic attacks on peaceful gatherings; 39 proclamations and suppressions, and 4 deportations without charge or trial. This shows the intensified provocative manner in which Mr. Lloyd George's Government is treating the country and which it seeks to make America believe it is anxious to conciliate.[3]

To influence American public opinion, Lloyd George likened the Irish movement for independence to the secession movement in the United States in 1861. Erskine Childers soon destroyed that false analogy:

We do not attempt secession. Nations cannot secede from a rule they have never accepted. . . . Lincoln's reputation is safe from your comparison. He fought to abolish slavery, you fight to maintain it. . . . We are a small people with a population dwindling without cessation under your rule. We have no armaments nor any prospect of obtaining them. Nevertheless, we accept your challenge and will fight you "with the same determination, with the same resolve" as the American States, North and South, put into their fight for their freedom against your Empire.[4]

The fight against English rule found important expression in the municipal and urban elections held on January 15, 1920. Of the twelve cities and boroughs of Ireland, eleven declared for the Republic. In Belfast alone, a Unionist majority was returned. Two of the counties in Ulster—Fermanagh and Tyrone—had a Sinn Fein majority. Of the 206 Councils elected in Ireland, 172 had a dominant Republican tinge. These Councils promptly pledged their allegiance to the Republic and to Dail Eireann, and all relations with the British Local Government Boards were severed. The Corporations of Dublin, Waterford, Limerick, Derry City, and Cork adopted at their first meetings a challenging resolution: "That the Council

---

3. This statement of Arthur Griffith is contained in the despatch from U.S. Consul at Dublin, Ireland, F. T. F. Dumont, to the Secretary of State, December 23, 1919, 841d.00/115, *MSS.*, National Archives.
4. *Irish Bulletin,* March 4, 1920.

declines to recognize the right of the English Lord Lieutenant to appoint a High Sheriff for the city." [5]

The English answer was immediate and drastic. On the night of January 20, 1920, the police and military terrorized the little town of Thurles in County Tipperary.[6] Several days later a considerable number of the inhabitants of the town were arrested and deported to England for imprisonment. As General Macready remarks:

> The arrest of persons suspected of complicity in outrage was authorised; those against whom evidence might later be forthcoming to be handed over to the civil power for trial, and those against whom no evidence could be produced to be deported and interned. Over sixty persons were thus arrested and deported to England as a result of the first sweep upon the last day of January, 1920.[7]

During the month of February 1920 some four thousand raids were made by the police and military against Irish homes. The reign of terrorism that existed in Ireland was in many cases worse than the regime of murder and oppression now associated with Russian rule behind the Iron Curtain. To stamp out every spark of Irish independence, the British Government hurriedly sent over to Ireland additional military forces. In addition to forty-three thousand British regular troops, the Royal Irish Constabulary was reinforced by large numbers of "rank and filers . . . with a special uniform . . . consisting of khaki coat, black trousers and cap . . . [who were] speedily christened the Black and Tans." These military forces were further augmented by another terrorist organization which consisted of ex-officers of the British Army and were "supposed to be a *corps d'élite*. They were named Auxiliary Cadets and were speedily known as the Auxiliaries." [8]

5. Dorothy Macardle, *The Irish Republic*, p. 327.
6. *The American Commission on Conditions in Ireland: Official Report*, pp. 6-34.
7. Sir Nevil Macready, *Annals of an Active Life* (London, 1924, 2 vols.), II, 439. In March 1920 Sir Nevil Macready was appointed Commander-in-Chief of the Forces in Ireland.
8. Patrick S. O'Hegarty, *A History of Ireland Under the Union, 1801-1922*, p. 740.

With this large military force under arms, the English Government made a determined attempt to crush all Irish resistance. A "typical night" in Dublin was given graphic description by Erskine Childers:

> As the citizens go to bed, the barracks spring to life. Lorries, tanks, and armoured searchlight cars muster in fleets, lists of "objectives" are distributed, and, when the midnight curfew order has emptied the streets . . . the weird cavalcades issue forth to the attack. Think of raiding a private house at dead of night in a tank (my own experience), in a tank whose weird rumble and roar can be heard miles away!
>
> The procedure of the raid is in keeping, though the objectives are held for the most part by women and terrified children. A thunder of knocks: no time to dress (even for a woman alone) or the door will crash in. On opening, in charge the soldiers—literally charge—with fixed bayonets and in full war-kit. No warrant shown on entering, no apology on leaving, if, as in nine cases out of ten, suspicions prove to be groundless and the raid a mistake. . . . Imagine the moral effect of such a procedure on the young officers and men told off for this duty! Is it any wonder that gross abuses occur: looting, wanton destruction, brutal severity to women? [9]

As an offset to the rough and brutal types of soldiers that filled the ranks of the Black and Tan organization, we have a description of the average soldier who had enlisted in the Irish Volunteers or the so-called Irish Republican Army. Inasmuch as this description is from the pen of an English Lieutenant General, it undoubtedly has some approximation of the truth:

> The captains of the Volunteers appear to have been almost all quite young men, farmers' sons for the most part, some of them schoolmasters, most with what, for their class, must be considered a good deal of education. . . . As a class transparently sincere and single-minded idealists, highly religious for the most part, and often with an almost mystical sense of duty to their country. . . .
>
> The Irish Republican Army seems to be particularly free from ruffians of the professional type, and the killings of police and others . . . were almost certainly done by members of the I.R.A. acting under military orders. . . . Behind their organization there is the spirit of a

---

9. Erskine Childers, London *Daily News,* March 29, 1920.

nation—of a nation which is certainly not in favour of murder, but which, on the whole, sympathises with them and believes that the members of the I.R.A. are fighting for the cause of the Irish people.[10]

B. THE BRITISH REGIME OF ARSON AND MURDER BECOMES MORE FIRMLY FIXED IN THE SUMMER OF 1920

The tide of terrorism that rolled over Ireland was allowed to abate for a short time in the early summer of 1920 so that the British Government might ascertain the American reaction to the British experiment in raw barbarism. If the Republican and Democratic conventions would approve of planks in their platforms that warmly supported self-determination for Ireland, it might be wise for British statesmen to change their policy towards Ireland. Britain had borrowed billions from the American Government to stave off national bankruptcy, and American desires had to be given some consideration. The Wilson Administration was too pro-British to express any deep concern about the plight of Ireland, but Irish-Americans formed a pressure group that demanded some action by Congress. Extended hearings had been held before Congressional committees, and resolutions expressing sympathy for Ireland had been introduced in Congress. These proceedings had been watched with deep interest by the British Government, and particular attention had been focused upon the party conventions to be held in June 1920.

This was the reason why Judge Cohalan had carefully phrased a plank which he expected the Republican convention in Chicago to approve. If De Valera had not played the fool at that convention, the Cohalan plank would have been accepted and the story of Ireland would have been very different. The Democratic Party would have adopted a similar plank, and this action would have been a warning to the British Cabinet to stop the terrorism they had let loose in Ireland.

10. Macardle, *op. cit.*, pp. 342-343.

The tragic consequences of De Valera's antics at the Chicago convention were pointed out by Bishop Gallagher in 1921:

> The most terrible mistake President de Valera has made in America . . . was his rushing to Chicago . . . and insisting that a plank drawn by himself should be adopted pledging the recognition of the Irish Republic. . . . The Irish-American leaders had . . . negotiated and secured the adoption of the so-called Cohalan plank . . . containing an acknowledgment of Ireland's right to absolute independence. . . . But De Valera was adamant and sent Frank Walsh down to the resolutions sub-committee to present his recognition plank where it mustered only one vote. . . .
> The Cohalan Independence plank was adopted by the sub-committee, thereupon De Valera denounced it as unacceptable. . . . This meant the defeat of the Cohalan plank and the dropping of all reference to Ireland in the Republican platform.
> This was immediately interpreted in England as the absolute repudiation of the Irish question by American statesmen . . . and was the signal for the opening of the saturnalia of arson, murder, lust and loot . . . that has raged in Ireland for the last eight months.[11]

On June 15 Mr. F. T. F. Dumont, the American consul in Dublin, sent a despatch to the Secretary of State concerning the effect of the fiasco at the Chicago convention upon Irish leaders: "The news that the Republican platform contained no plank favoring Irish freedom came as a shock to Sinn Feiners in Ireland. They had confidently counted upon Mr. de Valera's influence to have such a plank inserted." [12] A few days later Mr. Dumont was informed by Major Wilson, Chief Intelligencer Officer on the staff of the General commanding the Dublin Military District, that a

> new policy in regard to the Irish situation has just been decided upon by the British Government. . . . He states that the conciliatory policy of the Irish Administration is considered by the Government to be looked upon by Sinn Fein leaders as a sign of fright and weakness on

---

11. Bishop Michael J. Gallagher to the Friends of Irish Freedom, April 9, 1921, *Cohalan MSS*.
12. F. T. F. Dumont to the Secretary of State, June 15, 1920, 841d.00/209, *MSS*., N.A.

the part of the Government. . . . The Government at London proposes to have the Irish Administration take up actively the search for and prosecution of persons suspected of creating disorders in defiance of the Government in Ireland.[13]

By the middle of July the situation had grown worse

> day by day. . . . At the present time there is very little government in the constructive sense. Things are drifting to a dangerous point. . . . The "Intelligentsia" at the head of Sinn Fein would command any man's respect, especially if he is born a citizen of a republic. The pureness of the ideals and motives of these leaders cannot be gainsaid. . . . Sinn Fein found it difficult to believe that the Democratic Convention at San Francisco had refused the plank prepared by her leader, and was disgusted with the plank incorporated in the platform as to Ireland.[14]

In the middle of July Sir Horace Plunkett wrote to Colonel House that "the situation in Ireland is galloping to disaster."[15] It was certainly true that British terrorism was increasing in intensity. A party of the Black and Tans captured

> six unarmed Volunteers at Kerry Pike near Cork, cut out the tongue of one, the nose of another, the heart of another, and battered in the skull of a fourth. . . . Behind the whole programme of so-called unauthorised reprisals there was one military purpose and one only, that of rendering Ireland, in the words of the *Police Journal*, "an appropriate hell for rebels."[16]

13. Dumont to the Secretary of State, June 21, 1920, 841d.00/211, MSS., N.A.
14. Dumont to the Secretary of State, July 16, 1920, 841d.00/214, MSS., *ibid*.
 The terrible situation in Ireland led Shane Leslie to write to Secretary Colby on June 23, 1920: "I spent six months in an Ulster County with a Sinn Fein majority, which enjoyed perfect peace until the Government initiated raids which provoked reprisals. I have been in London vainly trying to get Dominion Home Rule put into action to which I am satisfied the majority of all Irishmen would not be opposed. However the Government have initiated a policy which leaves Sinn Fein the only refuge for moderates. This policy . . . is now deliberately fostering mutual massacre with a view to an ultimate appeal to the English voter." 841d.00/320, MSS., *ibid*.
15. Sir Horace Plunkett to Colonel House, July 19, 1920, *House MSS.*, Library of Yale University.
16. Frank Pakenham, *Peace by Ordeal* (London, 1935), p. 51.

A peak of barbarity was reached in August 1920 in connection with the treatment of Terence MacSwiney, Lord Mayor of Cork. On the evening of August 12 he was placed under arrest, along with several others, and was found guilty by a court-martial of having in his possession certain alleged incriminating documents. Arthur Griffith, Acting President of the Republic of Ireland, sent a cable to President Wilson asking for American intervention:

> I inform Your Excellency that the Lord Mayor of Cork, duly elected Deputy for Cork County, Ireland, was recently seized by the armed forces of England, arraigned before English military officers and forcibly deported from this country in an English war vessel and he is now in imminent danger of death in Brixton prison, London. I recall to Your Excellency the declarations made by the heads of Allied and neutral States when the Burgomaster of Brussels was treated with a lesser indignity and harshness.[17]

Bishop William Turner, of Buffalo, as the representative of "two hundred and fifty thousand Catholics who sympathize with Mayor MacSwiney," requested "immediate action" on the part of Secretary Colby.[18] On August 26 Cardinal O'Connell sent a similar wire to the Secretary of State: "I implore you in the name of humanity that our government do everything it can to prevent the death of the Mayor of Cork now dying in a British prison." [19] Norman Davis, Acting Secretary of State, sent a very dubious reply to Cardinal O'Connell: "I beg to inform you that from precedents established in cases of this character, the Department finds it is not in a position to make protestations to the British Government against the arrest and imprisonment of one who is not a citizen of the United States." [20] Mr. Davis had conveniently forgotten all about the frenzied American exertions to prevent the execution of the British nurse, Edith Cavell.

17. Arthur Griffith to President Wilson, August 24, 1920, 841d.00/227, *MSS.*, N.A.
18. Bishop William Turner to Secretary Colby, September 2, 1920, 841d.00/225, *ibid.*
19. Cardinal O'Connell to Secretary Colby, August 26, 1920, 841d.00/223, *ibid.*
20. Norman Davis to Cardinal O'Connell, August 30, 1920, *ibid.*

The situation in Ireland was clearly presented to the Secretary of State in the despatches of Mr. Dumont, U.S. Consul at Dublin:

> The bitterness of feeling [in Ireland] leads to horrors that can hardly be surpassed in a civilized country. . . . There is no doubt that the ill feeling between the two sides grows day by day and that much trouble will follow in the next few weeks. This is the normal result of enlisting British ex-service men for the Royal Irish Constabulary. These men, habituated to scenes of bloodshed in the Great War, are not policemen. They are entirely without sympathy for Irish aspirations and enlisted in the Constabulary for the adventure and excitement of the life. . . . The Black and Tans of today dominate and terrorize. . . . When all is said and done, and without regard to old quarrels between the Irish and Great Britain, the British Government is responsible for the present condition of affairs in Ireland.[21]

This responsibility for the reign of terror in Ireland was frankly admitted by Lloyd George at the Guildhall Banquet on November 9, 1920. In a revolting defense of the bloody reprisals of the Black and Tans and the Auxiliaries, he smugly remarked:

> There is no doubt that at last their [the Black and Tans'] patience has given way and there has been some severe hitting back. . . . Let us be fair to these gallant men who are doing their duty in Ireland. . . . It is no use talking about this being war and these being reprisals when these things are being done [by Sinn Fein] with impunity in Ireland. We have murder by the throat. . . . We had to reorganise the police and when the Government was ready we struck the terrorists and now the terrorists are complaining of terror.[22]

The callous manner in which Lloyd George boasted of his "reprisals" in Ireland inevitably reminds one of Shelley's sonnet in which he speaks of Castlereagh wearing the mask of murder and tossing human hearts to sleek, well-fed bloodhounds that walked with him. It should be remembered, of course, that Castlereagh was not responsible for the "Peterloo Massacre," but there is no doubt

---

21. F. T. F. Dumont to the Secretary of State, September 28, 1920, 841d.00/243, *ibid*.
22. Pakenham, *op. cit.*, p. 60.

that Lloyd George was directly responsible for atrocities that match anything contained in the famous Bryce Report.

On December 14 the new Lord Mayor of Cork sent an appeal to the American Ambassador in London to put an immediate stop to the march of murder across the bloody and wasted fields of Ireland:

> During the past week the people of Cork, men, women and children, have been held up in the streets of this city and robbed of all they possessed; hundreds of shops have been looted, unoffending citizens publicly whipped, shot, and it is to be feared in some cases, burned alive in their homes. The principal business quarter of the city has been bombed, burned and destroyed by the armed forces of the Crown, rendering thousands of people homeless and workless. In the name of humanity and of our tortured people seeking protection from such savage tyranny, we respectfully urge the immediate intervention of your government.[23]

The Wilson Administration had no intention of calling a halt to this British campaign of widespread murder and arson. At the end of January 1921 the American consul in Dublin sent a long despatch to the Secretary of State giving a detailed account of British terrorism:

> While these encounters [between the Irish Volunteers and the British Black and Tans and Auxiliaries] are termed "guerilla warfare" by the Sinn Fein and foreign press, it is a type of guerilla warfare to which civilized peoples have been unaccustomed since three centuries ago. . . . They [the Black and Tans] have turned thousands of Nationalists into Sinn Feiners and added hundreds to the "active list" of the Irish Republican Army. To maintain order thousands of new troops have been brought into Ireland and the country is an armed camp. . . .

23. Lord Mayor of Cork to John W. Davis, American Ambassador in London, December 14, 1920, 841d.00/274, *MSS.*, N.A. In a despatch to the Secretary of State, Mr. Dumont, U.S. Consul in Dublin, made some revealing comments upon this sack of Cork: "Damages from incendiarism in Cork up to December 12th have been variously estimated at from $2,500,000 to $5,000,000. . . . The Black and Tans are accused of cruelties, murders, arson and reprisals. It seems to me more than probable that in many cases these accusations have a foundation of fact. . . . The truth appears to be that the Government used wrong measures to meet a desperate situation." 841d.00/279, *MSS.*, N.A.

The jails are full and overflowing with the more prominent Sinn Feiners. . . . To my mind all this is useless effort. The South and West of Ireland is solidly Sinn Fein. . . . The present attitude of Mr. Lloyd George, Sir Hamar Greenwood and Sir Nevil Macready, which is that the "murder gang" of Sinn Fein must be hunted down and destroyed, leaves no hope of a near solution of the Irish question.[24]

C. THE AMERICAN COMMISSION ON CONDITIONS IN IRELAND

While the Wilson Administration watched with apparent indifference the long catalogue of British murders in Ireland unfold, the American public was not so callous with reference to planned terrorism. The American press told the story in great detail, and Irish-Americans denounced upon innumerable platforms these shocking atrocities. One of the periodicals that took the lead in a crusade against British policy in Ireland was the New York *Nation*. Dr. William J. M. Maloney was particularly active in influencing the *Nation* to support the cause of Ireland.[25]

A Committee of One Hundred and Fifty was soon created to look into this English atrocity program in Ireland. Thanks to the influence of Dr. Maloney, prominent members of the Friends of Irish Freedom like Judge Cohalan, John Devoy, Diarmuid Lynch, Richard Dalton, and John P. Grace were not asked to serve on this committee. Committee members included five State governors, eleven United States senators, thirteen members of the House of Representatives, four Roman Catholic bishops, four Methodist bishops, and many men well known in public life. Cardinal Gibbons served on the committee but not Cardinal O'Connell. So-called "liberals" like Jane Addams, Rev. John Haynes Holmes, Norman Thomas, Amos Pinchot, and Robert M. LaFollette accepted invitations to become members of this representative group which covered geographically 36 States of the Union.

24. F. T. F. Dumont to the Secretary of State, January 28, 1921, 841d.00/314, MSS., N.A.
25. See the special edition of the *Nation*, "Ireland and America," January 31, 1942, CLIV, No. 5, pt. 2, 125-148.

The Committee of One Hundred and Fifty selected a commission of eight who would hear testimony of witnesses who were acquainted with the Irish scene. A final report would then be made by this commission on the actual situation in Ireland. This small commission consisted of Jane Addams, well-known sociologist and social worker; Dr. Frederic C. Howe, outstanding authority in the field of economics; James H. Maurer, labor leader; Major Oliver P. Newman, sociologist; Senator George W. Norris, liberal statesman; Rev. Norman Thomas, lecturer and editor; Senator David I. Walsh, able statesman and former Governor of Massachusetts; and L. Hollingsworth Wood, lawyer and publicist. Dr. Howe served as chairman of the commission.[26]

The hearings before the commission were held in Washington from November 18, 1920, to January 21, 1921. The testimony of witnesses was shocking in the extreme. It was a long story of robbery, torture, and murder by the Black and Tans and the Auxiliaries. One high point in the proceedings was the testimony of Mary MacSwiney, a sister of the late Lord Mayor of Cork,[27] and the testimony of Muriel MacSwiney, his widow.[28] The testimony of Donal O'Callaghan, the Lord Mayor of Cork, was particularly revealing in its damning picture of the destruction of Cork by British troops and the Black and Tans.[29]

British officials realized that O'Callaghan could present a damning indictment of British policy, so they refused to grant him a passport to travel to America to testify before the American Commission on Conditions in Ireland. But where there's a will there's a way. He became a stowaway on board a ship bound for Newport News, Virginia. He was discovered by American immigration officials, and W. B. Wilson, Secretary of the Department of Labor, placed the matter of his entry before the Department of State. The decision of Norman H. Davis, Acting Secretary of State, was in his usual pro-British vein:

26. The American Commission on Conditions in Ireland: *Evidence on Conditions in Ireland* (Washington, 1921).
27. Pp. 183-264; 303-365.
28. Pp. 265-302.
29. Pp. 718-851.

I beg to advise you that the Department does not feel that it is in a position to make in favor of Mr. O'Callaghan an exception to the rule against allowing aliens to enter the United States without properly visaed passports. I, accordingly, respectfully request you to take the necessary steps in order to effect Mr. O'Callaghan's deportation from the United States.

Your Department is doubtless familiar with the President's Proclamation of August 8, 1918, issued pursuant to the Act of Congress approved the 22nd of May, 1918 (40 Stat. p. 559) and in connection with the case of Mr. O'Callaghan I beg to invite your attention to the following excerpt from that Proclamation: "I hereby designate the Secretary of State as the official who shall grant, or in whose name shall be granted, permission to aliens to depart from or enter the United States."

I feel that in the discharge of the functions entrusted to this Department by the above mentioned Executive regulations, which have the effect of law, it is my duty to take appropriate action looking to the enforcement of the law which was violated by Mr. O'Callaghan's improper entry into the United States.[30]

Secretary Wilson did not agree with this specious reasoning of Mr. Davis, and he permitted Mr. O'Callaghan to visit the city of Washington and testify before the American Commission on Conditions in Ireland. In a letter to the Acting Secretary of State he ably defended his course of action:

There has never been any doubt in my mind about the authority of the Secretary of State to control the passport regulations wherever and whenever passports are required, but the Executive Order which accompanies the Proclamation specifically provides that seamen shall not be required to have passports and places their admission under the jurisdiction of the immigrant inspectors of the Department of Labor. Mr. O'Callaghan is a seaman within the express meaning of the term as defined in the immigration laws . . . and the Executive Order accompanying the President's Proclamation.

In a communication from the Department of State to the Assistant Commissioner-General of Immigration under date of June 9, 1920, Mr. J. Stanley Moore, Chief of Visa Office, says:

"You are advised that it would seem proper that alien seamen ap-

30. Norman H. Davis to Secretary W. B. Wilson, January 11, 1921, *Wilson MSS.*, Library of Congress.

plying for permanent admission, and not provided with passports or other official documents showing their identity and nationality, should be admitted providing that it is established to the satisfaction of the Immigration officials that the identity and nationality of these aliens is proven."

The identity and nationality of Mr. O'Callaghan has been established to the satisfaction of the immigration officials. . . . From these it would appear that the Secretary of Labor would have the authority to admit Mr. O'Callaghan permanently. I have, however, decided that such a course would not be wise in the present circumstances, and have, therefore, permitted him to land for the purpose of reshipping, foreign, in accordance with the usual practice of the Department in such cases. Taking all of the law and the facts into consideration, I can not concur in the judgment of the State Department that Mr. O'Callaghan has improperly entered into the United States, or that the law has been violated in his case.[31]

The Department of State, having been easily bested in its bout with the Secretary of Labor, continued the controversy with Senator Thomas J. Walsh. In answer to his letter of inquiry of February 1,[32] Secretary Colby wrote to Senator Walsh in the same unhappy vein affected by Norman H. Davis. The action of the Department of State in the case of Mayor O'Callaghan had been based upon the statements of the Lord Mayor and "upon existing laws and regulations" applicable to all such cases. After repeating many of the opinions expressed in the letter of Norman H. Davis to Secretary Wilson, Secretary Colby concluded his letter to Senator Walsh as follows:

31. Secretary W. B. Wilson to Norman H. Davis, Acting Secretary of State, January 17, 1921, *ibid.*
32. Senator Thomas J. Walsh to Secretary Bainbridge Colby, February 1, 1921, *ibid.* On January 31, 1921, a group of priests in Butte, Montana, sent to Senator Walsh a telegram against British barbarity: "We the undersigned priests of Butte, Montana, during the late world war preached from pulpit and platform to our people urging that every sacrifice should be freely made in life and property to crush militarism threatening the democracy of the world. That preaching is now made a farce and a mockery in the eyes of our people and is destroying our moral influence with our people while British militarism in Ireland, the worst the world has ever seen, runs riot without protest from our government and is rapidly exterminating the race to which many of us belong." *T. J. Walsh Papers,* Library of Congress.

From the above it must be obvious that the position taken by the Department of State regarding Mr. O'Callaghan in no sense involved the question of permitting a political refugee to enter and remain in the United States. Such action was taken solely in compliance with a duty to execute the law, and was not dictated by any views on the Irish question.[33]

On February 5, Senator Walsh received a letter from Secretary Wilson which was in sharp disagreement with the viewpoint of Secretary Colby. He indicated that Section 3 of the Immigration Act of February 5, 1917, excluded from the United States "stowaways, except that any such stowaway, if otherwise admissible, may be admitted in the discretion of the Secretary of Labor." The Lord Mayor was a stowaway on the American steamship *West Cannon,* which arrived at Newport News, Virginia, on January 4, 1921. There was no doubt that the Secretary of Labor had the authority to admit him. When the Secretary of State (Mr. Colby) declined to waive passport requirements,

> the only discretion remaining with the Secretary of Labor was to send Mr. O'Callaghan back immediately or permit him to land for purposes of reshipment. . . . The latter discretion was exercised and the usual time allowed to Mr. O'Callaghan to find a vessel of his own selection upon which to reship foreign.[34]

It was very apparent to Senator Walsh that Secretary Colby in his letter of February 8 had been distinctly disingenuous. In a letter of February 10 he condemned Colby's communication as "entirely uncandid, if not misleading." Fortified with the information he had received from Secretary Wilson, he repeated the fact that the Secretary of State had the authority to admit aliens without pass-

---

33. Secretary Colby to Senator Thomas J. Walsh, February 8, 1921, *Walsh MSS.*
34. Secretary Wilson to Senator Thomas J. Walsh, February 5, 1921, *ibid.* Miss Anna Murphy, of New York City, wrote to Senator Walsh, February 14, 1921, and expressed the opinion that the reason for the anti-Irish attitude of Norman H. Davis was the fact that the previous summer he had received from an Irish waitress at a hotel at Stockbridge, Massachusetts, a sharp "blow in the face" after he had made "a scurrilous remark about the Irish." *Ibid.*

ports. With particular reference to stowaways, the Secretary of Labor could admit them upon his own responsibility:

> The situation plainly is that under the law you may admit or exclude Lord Mayor O'Callaghan as you see fit, at least with the concurrent action of the Secretary of Labor if, in view of later legislation, the provision in relation to stowaways in the Act of 1917 remains in force. If you have been misled into the belief that you were without discretion in the matter, I trust you will make a further study of the statutes to which your letter relates, and being convinced as I am satisfied you must be, that you are vested with full authority in the premises, you will exercise it in accordance with the time-honored principles of our country.[35]

This letter of Senator Walsh was so clear and cogent that Secretary Colby abandoned any further attempts at double-talk. He was merely the mouthpiece of President Wilson, who was intensely anti-Irish with no disposition to grant any favor to a spokesman for long-suffering Ireland. Fortunately, the Secretary of Labor granted Mayor O'Callaghan permission to land in the United States and then "find a vessel of his own selection upon which to reship foreign." This temporary entry permit allowed travel to certain areas, and thus O'Callaghan was enabled to hurry to Washington and appear before the American Commission on Conditions in Ireland. His testimony was of great value with reference to the reign of terror in Cork.

D. THE AMERICAN COMMITTEE FOR RELIEF IN IRELAND MAKES A MAGNIFICENT CONTRIBUTION

British brutality in Ireland had rendered homeless thousands of innocent persons, had deprived them of jobs, and had blasted their future. Many were on the verge of starvation. It was evident that the task of feeding these unfortunates and providing them shelter would rest upon the shoulders of charitable Americans. In 1921 the American Committee for Relief in Ireland was organized, with Morgan J. O'Brien as chairman. Cardinal Gibbons and Bishop Michael J. Gal-

35. Senator Thomas J. Walsh to Secretary Colby, February 10, 1921, *ibid.*

lagher were members of this committee, along with Senators David I. Walsh and Thomas J. Walsh.

The Friends of Irish Freedom, led by Judge Cohalan, enlisted with enthusiasm in this task of feeding, clothing, and housing thousands of Irish victims of organized cruelty. The sum of $25,000 was immediately advanced for this important work, and the branches of the Friends spared no effort to make the collection of relief funds a distinct success.

The work of the American Committee for Relief in Ireland can best be appreciated in terms of the following statistics:

> As of January 1, 1922, the relief fund raised in the United States amounted to $5,000,000. In Ireland, by January 1, 1922, $3,000,000 had been distributed through the agency of the Irish White Cross.

How the Relief Funds Were Spent

I

Belfast—Expelled Workers and Victims of British Raids

The Need—In July 1920 almost 10,000 Catholic wage earners were driven from Belfast industries. Again, in July 1921 and subsequent thereto, several hundred houses occupied by Catholic workers were destroyed.

The Result—Some 30,000 people were deprived for a year and six months of any means of livelihood. Nearly 2,000 persons were made homeless by the burning of their homes.

Relief—Weekly relief of $20,000 distributed in Belfast since March 1921 makes a total of $725,000.00
To build new houses for the destitute 50,000.00

Total for Belfast in 1921 .... $775,000.00

II

Victims of British Raids in Ireland Outside Belfast

Outside Belfast—At least 30,000 persons not engaged in the hostilities in Ireland have suffered directly or indirectly as a result of the conflict:

(1) About 1,000 buildings—farmhouses, shops—have been utterly destroyed; about 1,500 partially destroyed, many of them being rendered uninhabitable.

(2) Forty co-operative creameries utterly destroyed; 13 partially destroyed, leaving employees without any means of livelihood.
(3) Property to the value of more than $32,000,000 has been destroyed, as shown by the proceedings in the courts where claims for compensation have been filed.
(4) At least 6,000 men were imprisoned or interned; most of these were the sole breadwinners for hard-pressed families.
(5) Thousands of others were compelled to leave their ordinary pursuits and "go on the run."

III

For the children whose breadwinners were killed during the conflict in Ireland there has been set aside for their care and education the sum of $600,000.00

SUMMARY

(1) For relief in Belfast	$775,000.00
(2) For relief of personal distress outside Belfast	925,000.00
(3) Cost of providing shelter and for repair of houses and shops for over 600 families	700,000.00
(4) For relief of children whose breadwinners were killed	600,000.00
TOTAL	$3,000,000.00

The appreciation of the De Valera Government for this relief of persons in dire distress was conveyed in a letter from the Irish delegates sent to London to negotiate a treaty with the British Government. The delegates addressed their letter to Judge Richard Campbell (Secretary) and John J. Pulleyn (Treasurer) of the American Committee for Relief in Ireland:

> The Irish Delegates now engaged in negotiations for peace wish to express to you and ask you to convey to the other members of the American Committee for Relief in Ireland the profound gratitude which they, in common with their fellow-countrymen, feel towards the Committee and all those in the United States who have contributed towards its funds, for the generous assistance sent to Ireland for the relief of the suffering, loss and misery incurred by the Irish people in their struggle for national independence. . . .
> It is not only that the material aid that you have organized has been of incalculable benefit. You and your friends have helped to sustain

the spirit of our people and to make them realise that your great nation stood beside them with encouragement, sympathy and hope in the terrible ordeal undergone in the efforts to save their national institutions and the very fabric of their national life from destruction.[36]

36. Arthur Griffith, R. C. Barton, Michael Collins, George Gavan Duffy, and Eamon Duggan to Richard Campbell and John J. Pulleyn, October 29, 1921, *Walsh MSS*.

14 IRELAND ACCEPTS DOMINION STATUS AS A STEPPING STONE TO EVENTUAL INDEPENDENCE

A. THE MOVEMENT TOWARDS PEACE

The relief funds that poured into Ireland from America helped to sustain a population that had been pressed to the wall by a long regime of terror and murder.[1] The question of mere survival was uppermost in many minds in the autumn of 1920 when a letter appeared in the London *Times* from Brigadier-General George Cockerill, C.B., M.P., urging a truce and amnesty for Ireland and the holding of "a conference between plenipotentiaries of the two nations." Arthur Griffith promptly approved this suggestion, and the matter was further pushed by an American journalist, John S. Steele. It was stated that Lloyd George was interested in arriving at a truce with the Irish leaders, and Archbishop Clune, of Perth, Australia, had a conference with him on December 1. Archbishop Clune visited Ireland, and on December 4, after discussions with Michael Collins, agreement was reached upon a "tentative formula for a truce."

But this opportunity for a truce was scotched by the unfortunate activities of certain Irishmen who wished to have the glory of finding some road to a peaceful accommodation. Father Michael O'Flan-

1. The extensive and bloody character of the operations of the Black and Tans and the Auxiliaries is told in graphic detail in Piaras Beaslai, *Michael Collins and the Making of a New Ireland*, chaps. ii-x, and in Brigadier-General Frank P. Crozier, *Ireland Forever* (London, 1932), chaps. vi-ix.

agan, Vice-President of the Sinn Fein political organization, sent a telegram to Prime Minister Lloyd George which expressed an ardent desire for immediate peace, and this was buttressed by a resolution of the Galway County Council which deplored the reprisals of the Volunteers and called for peace. Lloyd George regarded these communications as an indication of impending collapse of the opposition in Ireland, and he decided that it would be expedient to postpone peace negotiations for a short while.[2] He had long been insistent upon the surrender of all arms by the I.R.A. before any peace negotiations could be commenced, and this factor alone destroyed any real chance for agreement.

In April 1921 Lord Derby paid a visit to Dublin with the naïve belief that a pair of horn-rimmed spectacles would safely cover his alias of "Mr. Edwards." He had a conference with De Valera, and so did Sir James Craig in May, but these talks were mere verbal skirmishes which accomplished little. In June, General Smuts found it convenient to take a trip to Ireland to see De Valera. Smuts had long been a "trouble-shooter" for Lloyd George, and his visit to Dublin had important political implications. The way had been paved for a formal invitation from Lloyd George to De Valera to attend "a conference here in London, in company with Sir James Craig, to explore to the utmost the possibility of a settlement."[3] On July 8 De Valera sent to Lloyd George a favorable reply, and on the following day a truce was announced that put an end to conflict in Ireland. It was to take effect on July 11, and thus ended the long reign of terror that had failed to break the Irish spirit.

On July 12 De Valera left Dublin for the London conference. He took along with him Arthur Griffith, Vice-President of Dail Eireann; Robert Barton, Minister for Economic Affairs; Austin Stack, Minister for Home Affairs; and Erskine Childers, Minister for Publicity. There were four meetings with Lloyd George, during which the important question of Dominion status for Ireland was exhaustively discussed. Lloyd George found De Valera a difficult person

2. Beaslai, *op. cit.*, II, 109-112.
3. *Ibid.*, II, 236-247.

to deal with, and he complained that it was "like trying to pick up mercury with a fork." De Valera remarked that the British Prime Minister could try the use of a spoon, but Lloyd George knew that it would have to be the spoon of Irish independence, and he was not willing to go that far.

On August 10 De Valera sent to Lloyd George a formal rejection of the British terms, and a series of letters and telegrams then passed between the two statesmen. Finally, De Valera accepted an invitation to another conference to be held in London on October 11. This meeting would determine the destiny of Ireland.

B. ON THE EVE OF THE DISARMAMENT CONFERENCE IN WASHINGTON, BRITAIN DECIDES TO ADOPT A CONCILIATORY ATTITUDE TOWARDS IRELAND

In America, the news of De Valera's rejection of the British terms aroused deep interest in Irish-American circles. Bishop Gallagher, President of the Friends of Irish Freedom, promptly sent a telegram indicating support of De Valera's stand:

> The Friends of Irish Freedom heartily congratulate you and through you the citizens of the Irish Republic, on your splendid declaration of today. In the recent past as an American organization working along American lines . . . we gave you the support essential at critical points in Ireland's struggle. . . . In the new crisis . . . the Republic will again require effective support and it will be yours in unstinted measure upon the same solid American basis.[4]

John Devoy sent a similar telegram of support:

> Permit the oldest active Fenian living to congratulate you and Dail Eireann on prompt and effective answer to Lloyd George's challenge and his threat to resume massacres implied in military measures announced by cable. Your action is a trumpet call to race in America which will bury differences and bring united action to enable Republic to defend Irish people in bitter struggle before them. Properly organized, the race abroad, on inspiration of and in conjunction with

4. *Cohalan MSS.*

people at home, each country devising own measures and acting under own leaders for a common purpose, can break British power, influence and trade and eventually destroy robber Empire unless Ireland is set completely free.[5]

Judge Cohalan also sent a message of congratulation to De Valera and to Dail Eireann. In commenting upon this conciliatory telegram the New York *American* remarked:

> It is declared here this [Judge Cohalan's telegram] means all circles of Irish people everywhere are encouraging the Dail Eireann and the Cabinet of the Irish Republic. The split in Irish ranks hitherto has hurt the cause of Erin. The healing of the breach indicated by Judge Cohalan's generous congratulations, say Sinn Fein leaders, will "strengthen the home people immensely." [6]

It was significant that these three telegrams of congratulation distinctly emphasized the viewpoint that Irish-Americans, on their own terms, would be glad to co-operate with the De Valera Government. Needless to say, the telegrams evoked no friendly response from the President of the Irish Republic.

It should be clearly understood at this point that John Devoy had no fixed determination to support the idea of an Irish Republic at any cost. His viewpoint in this regard is clearly expressed in a letter to Judge Cohalan:

> I think you ought not to push Bishop Gallagher into a position he may not be able to maintain. I don't think it is necessary for him to make a declaration for the Republic. It is quite enough for him . . . to remain President [of the Friends of Irish Freedom]. I also fear if we appear to be urging the people of Ireland to continue the fight without being able to give them the military supplies they need, we'll put ourselves in a very vulnerable position before the public and play into De Valera's hands. It is quite enough . . . to state our own firm adherence to the Republic and our determination to support those in Ireland who favor it.
>
> De Valera has put them in a cruel position by deliberately bringing about a situation favorable to compromise—almost making it necessary. They may not have supplies enough to continue the fight and

5. *Ibid.*
6. August 20, 1921.

that is his fault. He spent the money trying to destroy us here that ought to have supplied them with arms and ammunition.[7]

John Devoy and Judge Cohalan had not been content to send telegrams to De Valera and Dail Eireann congratulating them upon maintaining a firm stand against British pressure relative to Dominion status for Ireland. In those telegrams an argument had been made for Irish-American independence with reference to directives from the De Valera Government. To make their position crystal clear, John Devoy and Judge Cohalan sent over a representative in the person of James McHugh, a trusted member of the Clan-na-Gael, who later became a prominent member of the New York Bar. He would present their case to Arthur Griffith and Michael Collins. Collins was particularly interested in the American scene. De Valera had endeavored to persuade him to pay an extended visit to America for the purpose of raising additional funds and composing the differences between Irish-Americans. Collins had refused to undertake this American mission, but he was anxious to know all the details concerning the dispute between De Valera, on the one hand, and Judge Cohalan and John Devoy on the other. When Mr. McHugh returned to America, he told an interesting story about the attitude of Collins in this matter. Devoy wrote:

> He [McHugh] did his work splendidly, met every point they made and put our case in a way that left no room for evading the real issue. The result is that they made an offer that is impracticable—an effort to "get together," but the ice is broken and I am satisfied we can have our way.
> Mick [Michael Collins] assured him that D.V. is "playing the game" just as he wants; that there will be no compromise and that they are preparing intensively for a new campaign and will see it through. They claim that our men are in absolute control. They did not say it openly, but it evidently means that they have compelled him to toe the mark and are thus saving him by keeping up the appearance of unity. They made weak attempts to justify the attacks on us by saying they did not give Boland instructions to cut us off but gave him rather extensive powers which he stretched. . . . Boland is no longer Chairman. . . .

7. John Devoy to Judge Cohalan, July 11, 1921, *Cohalan MSS.*

Mick is a queer mixture of fighting man and Corkonian diplomatist, but is determined to see the job through. He has a great respect for your [Judge Cohalan's] ability, but finds fault with a lot of things that I did and said. He lays a lot of stress on keeping up an appearance of unity.[8]

Devoy had little faith in De Valera's zeal for a Republic:

I am quite satisfied that D. V.'s sudden zeal for the Republic is a case like Redmond's with the Councils Bill. . . . If he did not intend to compromise why make all the trouble here trying to smash every organization and man that stood for the Republic. Even yet he leaves the door open and is evidently trying to bluff Lloyd George to get an offer of Home Rule for all Ireland. But all the same, his action leaves us only one course. He can't turn back because the people won't let him and we must act as if he was acting consistently all along. We must even act with the fellows here who have been trying to break us up, to make an appearance of union.[9]

It was soon apparent to Devoy that compromise was really in the air of Dublin. As the correspondence between De Valera and Lloyd George increased in volume, it seemed evident that there would be no further conference in London except upon the basic terms of the British Prime Minister. This fact was early realized by Judge Cohalan, who expressed himself with clarity and force. John Devoy was in complete agreement with this viewpoint:

Your diagnosis of the situation in Ireland is correct. They are *all* in the Compromise plan and the people will accept anything they get. I am quite satisfied that De Valera arranged the whole thing—the series of mock heroic notes and the pretence of holding out for absolute freedom—with Lloyd George in those secret interviews, *if he hadn't done it before.* . . .[10]

It is not in Dublin alone that compromise was in the air. In London it was felt to be imperative that better relations be established with Washington. Lloyd George realized only too clearly that

8. Devoy to Cohalan, August 3, 1921, *ibid.*
9. Devoy to Cohalan, August 17, 1921, *ibid.*
10. Devoy to Cohalan, September 13, 1921, *ibid.*

England was at the greatest crossroads in history. America had emerged from the World War as a great naval power that would soon successfully challenge British supremacy on the high seas. This war had seriously imperiled the financial structure of the British Empire, and it was obviously impossible for the British Government to enter upon an arms race with the United States. The best that Britain could hope to achieve was naval parity, and this could be arranged only if cordial relations were maintained with America. American naval construction had been curtailed by President Wilson in 1919 after his "deal" with Lloyd George, under the terms of which America would reduce the rate of naval construction in return for British support of Wilson's project of a League of Nations.[11]

On March 4, 1921, the Harding Administration assumed office, and the British Government could no longer count upon the pro-British policy that President Wilson had consistently followed. It was imperatively necessary for Lloyd George to conciliate this new Administration in Washington. Large loans from the American treasury had enabled Britain to maintain financial solvency, and the Chancellor of the Exchequer ardently hoped that arrangements could be made with Washington that would ease the burden upon the British taxpayer. Heavy expenditures for new naval construction were out of the question, even though Winston Churchill in his most sonorous rhetoric announced that the British would not accept "any fettering restrictions which will prevent the British Navy maintaining its well-tried and well-deserved supremacy."[12]

Most British statesmen accepted the fact that British naval supremacy was a thing of the past, and soon even naval experts swung around to this viewpoint. On March 16, 1921, Lord Lee, newly inducted First Lord of the Admiralty, made a speech before the Institute of Naval Architects in which he proposed a naval agreement with the United States based upon the principle of

11. Harold and Margaret Sprout, *Towards a New Order of Sea Power* (Princeton, 1940), pp. 59-68.
12. *New York Times*, November 27, December 6, 10, 1918; R. A. Chaput, *Disarmament in British Foreign Policy* (London, 1935), pp. 70-72.

parity.[13] A month later, Lloyd George courted favorable American press opinion by inviting Adolph Ochs, publisher of *The New York Times*, to breakfast at 10 Downing Street.[14] The Prime Minister was beginning an active campaign to establish a close Anglo-American understanding. He soon discovered that the price of such an understanding would be the scrapping of the Anglo-Japanese Alliance that had existed since January 30, 1902. At first he was very reluctant to pay this price.

On June 20, 1921, an imperial conference convened in London. It was an unusually important imperial conference, because for the first time the Dominions were permitted to play a role in the formulation of British foreign policy. The role of Canada was particularly significant. Thanks to the support of Arthur Meighen, Prime Minister of Canada, the American Government had its wish gratified—the Anglo-Japanese Alliance was formally abandoned by Britain.[15]

The stage was thus set for an Anglo-American naval accord. On July 8 Secretary Hughes sent a cablegram to Ambassador Harvey inquiring "whether it would be agreeable to the British Government to be invited by this Government to participate in a conference on limitation of armaments, the conference to be held in Washington." [16] Cablegrams were also sent to Tokyo, Paris, and Rome with similar invitations. Acceptance meant that a disarmament conference would begin its sessions in Washington on November 12, and Lloyd George believed that the fate of England was closely tied to the results of the conference. Conciliation of America became the keynote of his policy, and success in this regard was gravely menaced by the situation in Ireland. He could not afford to have this reign of terror excite American public opinion to the point where Anglo-American amity was reduced almost

13. E. J. Young, *Powerful America* (New York, 1936), pp. 47, 53-54.
14. *Ibid.*, pp. 49-50.
15. John B. Brebner, "Canada, the Anglo-Japanese Alliance and the Washington Conference," *Political Science Quarterly*, March 1935, 45-59.
16. Secretary Hughes to Ambassador Harvey, July 8, 1921, *Foreign Relations*, 1921, I, 18.

to the vanishing point. This is the reason why he swallowed his resentment against De Valera and arranged for the conference in London that was to convene on October 11. He made this decision because he thought it was expedient to do so. Humanitarian motives are seldom basic considerations in the formulation of British foreign policy.

C. DE VALERA REJECTS THE ANGLO-IRISH TREATY OF DECEMBER 6, 1921, AND INCITES CIVIL WAR IN IRELAND

The story of the long and involved discussions in London that led up to the Anglo-Irish Treaty of December 6, 1921, is a twice-told tale that does not need to be repeated in this chapter.[17] It is obvious that the British representatives at this conference were far more experienced diplomats than the delegation from Ireland. De Valera had attended the London Conference in July, and his four meetings with Lloyd George gave him a clear idea of the difficulties that would arise during another conference. He suddenly decided not to attend this second conference and appointed a delegation that could not cope with the astute members of the group that represented Britain. The excuse that De Valera offered for nonattendance at the London Conference was that his presence in Ireland was essential "to preserve the symbol of the Republic." It was a great pity that he had not thought that way in 1919-1920, when he spent a year and a half in America. If he had remained in Ireland at that time he might have not only preserved the symbol of the Republic but also have confirmed Irish-American unity.

The Irish delegation to the London Conference was not impressive. Arthur Griffith had been an inspiring figure as a promoter of Irish nationalism, but he did not have the benefit of long experi-

17. For an extended treatment of the discussions during the London Conference see Frank Pakenham, *Peace by Ordeal*, chaps. vi-xix. See also Piaras Beaslai, *op. cit.*, chaps. xii-xiii; Lloyd George, London *Daily Telegraph*, December 23, 1922; Austen Chamberlain, London *Daily Telegraph*, March 29, 1932; Winston S. Churchill, *The Aftermath* (New York, 1929), chaps. xiv-xv.

ence as a diplomat at the conference table. He impressed both Lloyd George and Chamberlain with his studiousness and fidelity, and they perceived at once that he cared far more for realities than for empty symbols. They concentrated their attention upon him, and their efforts met with important success. Michael Collins had been strongly opposed to attending the conference but finally yielded to De Valera's unwavering insistence. He was a striking contrast to the taciturn Griffith. Vivacious, highstrung, and impulsive, he struck Austen Chamberlain as a person "full of fascination and charm." He essayed for a while the role of honest broker, but in the end he supported his old friend Arthur Griffith. Eamon Duggan was a Dublin solicitor who had played a part in the Rising in 1916 and had twice been imprisoned for his support of the Republic. He was earnest and able but he was no match for his British opponents. George Gavan Duffy had the advantage of a famous father who had been one of the organizers of the Young Ireland movement in the 1840s. The father had returned to Ireland as the recipient of many imperial honors, and his son carried on the family tradition. As an assistant to Sean T. O'Kelly, at Versailles, he had been able to gain a little experience in the dangerous crosscurrents of diplomacy. Robert Barton had served with the Royal Dublin Fusiliers during the World War but had left the Army at the time of the Irish Convention. He was a first cousin of Erskine Childers, who had attracted the favorable notice of De Valera. Barton had entered the Cabinet as Director of Agriculture and later received the appointment as Minister for Economic Affairs. He was sincere and industrious but was sadly lacking in experience as a negotiator.

The British delegation was composed of some of the outstanding men in public life. Lloyd George, at the Versailles Conference, had given the world a vivid picture of a protean personality that could quickly change to suit any turn of circumstance. There was little doubt that during the sessions of the Paris Peace Conference he had advanced in a significant manner the interests of the British Empire. Austen Chamberlain, famous son of a famous father, was far more than a mere politician. He was familiar with the currents in world politics and knew that it would be expedient for Britain to settle the Irish Question at the earliest possible moment. Lord Birkenhead had been anathema to most Irishmen because of his association with Sir Edward Carson in the fight against Home Rule in the stirring days of 1914. An able constitutional lawyer with ready information whenever it was needed, he could draft legal formulas quickly and expertly. He won Irish gratitude by his strong support of a fair Irish settlement.[18] Winston Churchill had not emerged from the World War with a reputation for sagacity and vision. His failures as the director of ill-fated naval operations were still familiar to most men in British public life. But his colorful personality commanded attention, and his verbal pyrotechnics lighted fires of admiration in thousands of hearts. In 1922, when he piloted through an uncertain House of Commons the Irish Free State Agreement, he accomplished a feat that revealed his unusual qualities. The other three members of the British delegation were not so favorably known. Sir Hamar Greenwood, Chief Secretary for Ireland, had earned the detestation of most Irishmen by his brutal policy of terror and murder. Sir Laming Worthington-Evans, Secretary for War, was a politician who never rose to the rank of statesman, and Sir Gordon Hewart, the Attorney General, was chiefly known for his graceful oratory and attractive literary style.

As one reads through the accounts of the sessions of the London Conference, it is apparent that the core of the controversy was one of symbolism, and certain phrases became part of a ritual that was constantly repeated—"Dominion Status," "Allegiance to the Crown," "Common or Reciprocal Citizenship," and "External Associate." The Irish delegation insisted that the British Government should recognize Ireland as a sovereign independent state, and the Irish Government, in turn, would agree to become an "External Associate" of the Commonwealth. In this capacity the status of Ireland would not be inferior to that enjoyed by "the sovereign partner states" of the Commonwealth. She would also be separately represented at imperial conferences. Ireland would not be a Dominion

18. Churchill, *The Aftermath*, p. 316.

Stepping Stone to Eventual Independence

nor "within the Empire." There would be no allegiance to the Crown, and there would be "reciprocal" and not "common" citizenship.

The sessions unexpectedly developed into long wrangles over many technical points, and even though the Irish delegation had ample instructions that authorized them to arrive at an agreement with the English negotiators, De Valera insisted that he be consulted at every stage of the proceedings. He had detailed in Dublin for constant counsel Austin Stack, Minister for Home Affairs, and Cathal Brugha, Minister for Defense. It was significant that both of these members of the Cabinet were hostile to Michael Collins.

But the Dail Cabinet at times was surprisingly unanimous in its decisions. On November 25 agreement was reached that "Ireland shall recognize the British Crown for the purpose of association as symbol and accepted head of the combination of Associated States." It was also agreed that Ireland should vote an annual voluntary contribution to the King's personal revenue, the British Civil List.[19]

One of the main difficulties that confronted the Irish delegation was the matter of the oath of allegiance. To solve this problem, De Valera himself dictated to Barton a draft of what he considered admissible as an oath: "I . . . do swear to bear true faith and allegiance to the Constitution of Ireland and the Treaty of Association of Ireland with the British Commonwealth of Nations, and to recognise the King of Great Britain as head of the Associated States." [20]

Barton carried this draft back with him to London. But the meetings of the conference were handicapped by the absence of Collins, who had resented some slurring remarks of Brugha and Stack in Dublin on December 3. Lloyd George realized the vital role that was being played by Collins, and he sent his secretary to the Irish delegation to insist upon a meeting with the full Irish delegation present. On December 5 Lloyd George announced his final terms, and the members of the Irish delegation discussed them in detail for many long and exhausting hours. Collins was a realist who refused to permit symbols to distort his picture of a future Ireland

19. Dorothy Macardle, *The Irish Republic*, pp. 372-573.
20. Denis Gwynn, *De Valera* (New York, 1933), p. 148.

that would slowly emerge from the position of an associate of the British Commonwealth of Nations to one of full independence. The proposed Anglo-Irish Agreement was not a final stage for Ireland; it was merely a stepping stone to the political status all Irishmen had fondly dreamed of: "The Treaty gives us freedom, not the ultimate freedom that all nations desire and develop to, but the freedom to achieve it." [21] Griffith shared this viewpoint. Although Sinn Fein had claimed that Ireland had already achieved its independence, it had never been clearly established that the political expression of this independence should take on a republican form. To become a monarchy by merely adopting the King of Great Britain as King of Ireland also, would make little difference to Griffith, who had expressed himself on this point very clearly.

When the final British terms were handed to Griffith on December 5, he remarked: "I will give the answer of the Irish delegation at nine tonight; but Mr. Prime Minister, I personally will sign this agreement and recommend it to my countrymen." When Lloyd George inquired if Griffith would sign the agreement even though every other member of the Irish delegation would refuse to do so, he replied: "Yes, that is so, Mr. Prime Minister." [22]

For some hours on December 5 it seemed as though two members of the Irish delegation would refuse to follow the lead of Griffith. Gavan Duffy and Barton held out to the last against signing the treaty, but pressure from Griffith and Michael Collins finally broke down their resistance, and shortly after 11:15 P.M. on December 5 word was brought to 10 Downing Street that the Irish delegation was approaching. After a brief discussion on some minor points on which agreement was quickly reached, the Irish delegation signed the treaty.

Griffith and Collins were not completely satisfied with the treaty, but they regarded it as a long step in the right direction. Not so with De Valera. He was at the Mansion House ready to preside at a meeting to celebrate the sixth centenary of Dante. His reaction

21. Frank Pakenham, *Peace by Ordeal*, p. 279.
22. Churchill, *op. cit.*, p. 321.

Stepping Stone to Eventual Independence

when he was presented with a copy of the treaty is graphically described by Piaras Beaslai, who was present on that occasion:

> Mr. Duggan . . . arrived at the Mansion House with the text of the Treaty as Mr. de Valera was preparing to go on the platform. They found him in a towering rage. [He had heard that a treaty had been signed without his express consent.] When they handed him the copy of the Treaty he laid it aside, declaring that he had no time to read it, and turned round to discuss whether he would wear his Chancellor's robe or not, muttering some remark about "soon being back at teaching." He presided at the Dante Commemoration without having read the Treaty. I was one of the speakers, and sat near him, and I was astonished at the state of suppressed emotion under which he seemed to labour. And all this time he had not taken the trouble to study the Treaty. Apparently the fact that a Treaty had been signed, without being first referred to him, was the source of his agitation. The nature of the Treaty, affecting the fate of the people of Ireland was of only secondary interest to him.[23]

To the Irish people the treaty was of vast importance. The Black and Tan terror was over and the British military forces would soon be withdrawn. Dublin Castle would no longer be a symbol of British repression. The hand of the British legislator, the British administrator, and the British judge would cease to exert terrific pressure upon Ireland. Ireland would have the "same Constitutional status in the community of Nations known as the British Empire as the Dominion of Canada, the Commonwealth of Australia, the Dominion of New Zealand and the Union of South Africa, with a Parliament having powers to make laws for the peace, order and good government of Ireland." There was an oath of allegiance to the King of England, "his heirs and successors by law, in virtue of the common citizenship of Ireland with Great Britain and her adherence to and membership in the group of nations forming the British Commonwealth of Nations." British imperial forces were to defend the Irish coast until the Irish Free State could assume this burden. In time of peace, certain harbor and other facilities were to be afforded to His Majesty's imperial forces, and in time of war

23. Beaslai, *op. cit.*, II, 308.

other facilities might be afforded. A large measure of fiscal autonomy was also granted to Ireland. In other words, a modified form of Irish self-determination was at last attained.

To De Valera, these concessions were not enough. The substance of freedom should be sacrificed for the shadow of independence. On December 9 a letter appeared in the Irish press from De Valera. He informed the Irish people that he believed the recent Anglo-Irish treaty was "in violent conflict with the wishes of the majority of the Nation as expressed freely in the successive elections during the last three years." Therefore, he could not "recommend the acceptance of this Treaty either to Dail Eireann or the country." When the Dail met to discuss the treaty, De Valera became highly excited and

> refused even to obey the Chairman. Jumping to his feet, he complained at once that the delegates had broken an understanding with himself that the "complete text of the draft Treaty to be signed would be submitted to him before signing." That statement provoked Griffith as Chairman of the delegates, to a vehement protest against any "suggestion that the Plenipotentiaries exceeded their powers." Collins also rose at once to make an indignant protest, while the Chairman of the Dail was powerless either to control the discussion or to insist that the agenda should be followed. Collins read out the credentials with which the delegates had gone to London. . . . It remained for the Dail . . . to ratify or reject the Treaty which they had signed. . . . For four consecutive days a fierce controversy then continued behind closed doors.[24]

During this heated discussion De Valera announced that if the Dail should reject the Treaty, he had prepared alternative proposals of his own. These proposals became famous as "Document No. 2." They were largely identical with the Treaty:

> Even the differences were so slight . . . that it seemed ridiculous to dispute about them. As De Valera's own considered alternative to the Treaty, "Document No. 2," disposed once and for all of any pretence that he opposed it on the ground that it had failed to secure recognition of the Irish Republic. It accepted formally almost all the

24. Denis Gwynn, *De Valera*, pp. 152-153.

provisions against which the subsequent campaign against the signatories of the Treaty was conducted. . . . The differences between the Treaty and De Valera's alternative were so slight that it seemed impossible that they could be upheld in face of public opinion when the Dail met in public.[25]

According to Piaras Beaslai, no more damaging blow could be struck at

> the Separatist position than the acceptance of "Document No. 2." The Treaty represented a compromise with a stronger party, reluctantly assented to as the best we could obtain. "Document No. 2," if agreed to, would have represented a voluntary offer from Dail Eireann, in which all our claim to be an independent Republic was abandoned. To ask men to face death in defence of Irish independence seemed a comparatively simple proposition; but to ask them to fight for what Mr. De Valera called the difference between "internal" and "external" association" with the British Empire, seemed a *reductio ad absurdum*.

De Valera recognized the weakness of his position and suddenly announced to the Dail that Document No. 2 was "withdrawn and must be regarded as confidential, until he brings his own proposal forward formally." Arthur Griffith at once challenged these dubious tactics:

> An effort has been made outside to represent that a certain number of men stood uncompromisingly on the rock of the Republic. . . . It has been stated also here that the man who made this position, the man who won the war—Michael Collins—compromised. . . . In the letters [instructions] that preceded the negotiations, not once was a demand made for recognition of the Irish Republic. . . . We went there

---

25. *Ibid.*, p. 154. In this same regard the following excerpt from Piaras Beaslai's *Michael Collins and the Making of a New Ireland*, II, p. 317, is pertinent: "The proposals [of De Valera] turned out to be the famous 'Document No. 2,' which varied from the signed Treaty about as much as Tweedledum from Tweedledee. I shall not waste time describing or discussing this strange document. The reader can study it for himself in the appendix, and compare its terms with those of the Treaty. He will find that the majority of the paragraphs are identical, word for word, with those of the Treaty, and that, where they differ, it is only a difference of phraseology." See also Hayden Talbot, *Michael Collins' Own Story* (London, 1922).

to see how to reconcile the two positions, and I hold we have done it. The President does not wish this document [Document No. 2] to be read. What am I to do? . . . Am I to keep my mouth shut, and let the Irish people think about this uncompromising rock of the Republic? . . .

During the last few years a war was waged on the Irish people . . . and for a portion of that time, when President de Valera was in America, I had at least the responsibility on my shoulders for standing for all that was done in that defence. . . . I would stand for it again under similar circumstances. . . . But in any contest that would follow the rejection of this offer, Ireland would be fighting with the sympathy of the world against her, and with all the Dominions—all the nations that comprise the British Commonwealth—against her. The position would be such that I believe no conscientious Irishman could take the responsibility for a single Irishman's life in that futile war.[26]

The unreasoning and hostile attitude assumed by De Valera during these debates in the Dail completed "the disillusionment" of many Sinn Fein leaders

who had cherished a pathetic faith in his straightforwardness. . . . It was with pain that some of us realised that Mr. de Valera was a very much smaller man, both in character and intellect, than we had taken him to be. . . . All the generous gestures, all the kindly words and ready concessions by Collins and Griffith, were only treated as weaknesses to be taken advantage of.[27]

The situation in Ireland during these tragic days has been well described by a distinguished Irish historian:

Into the great talk in the Dail, and the great talk in the country, and the formation of the Anti-Treaty Party, there went more hypocrisy, lying, and moral cowardice than one would have believed to have existed in this country. The opposition to the Treaty in the Dail was wholly dishonest. It had been made plain to the Deputies by Mr. de Valera, in public sessions and in private session, that they were negotiating for terms, and that he himself would not be bound rigidly by the oath to the Republic. They had before them, when they finally agreed to send plenipotentiaries to discuss terms, Mr. de Valera's own letters

---

26. Beaslai, *op. cit.*, II, pp. 317-318.
27. *Ibid.*, pp. 322-323.

to Lloyd George, in which he was obviously bluffing in order to save his face, in which every time he went a bit too far he immediately wriggled, and in which he mentions the word Republic only to assure Mr. Lloyd George that he was not asking England to recognise it. They knew, every one of them, what was going to be done, and not one of them dared to oppose it effectively or to expose it; because there was not one of them who did not know then, that the Truce came only just in the nick of time—that the war, if it had gone on any longer, might have ended in a complete collapse. . . .

The whole Dail was responsible for the treaty, and should have accepted its responsibility. It should not have put the responsibility on the country. But the members were not thinking of the country, but of their own little reputations. They wanted the Treaty to pass, but they wanted somebody else to vote for it. Men and women of the Dail who had thrown up their hats in the air for the Treaty on that first morning decided, after Mr. de Valera's pronouncement, that they could not afford to be less extreme than he; and so the split was made, made out of treachery and spite and moral cowardice.[28]

On December 7, 1922, the final vote in the Dail was taken and it resulted in a victory for the Treaty, 64 to 57. The following day De Valera attended the meeting of the Sinn Fein Executive and told them that they must "still fight on." His next step was to tender his formal resignation as President. Now he was ready to lead the party of opposition into a civil war that was to bring death and devastation to an Ireland that was just emerging from the blood bath administered by the Black and Tans.

To any impartial student of De Valera's career, it is obvious that his action in Ireland with reference to the Treaty was in line with the rule he had consistently followed in America—rule or ruin. He would suffer no opposition to his desires and would brook no interference with his plans even though they were designs for disaster. His cowardice in refusing to lead the Irish delegation to London to discuss treaty terms and his evident lack of character in the Dail debates with special reference to his "Document No. 2" bring back to memory the acidulous comment of John Devoy: "De Valera is the most malignant man in all Irish history." [29]

28. Patrick S. O'Hegarty, *The Victory of Sinn Fein* (Dublin, 1924), pp. 83-84.
29. John Devoy to Judge Cohalan, August 12, 1920, *Cohalan MSS.*

D. JUDGE COHALAN AND JOHN DEVOY DECIDE TO SUPPORT MICHAEL COLLINS IN HIS FIGHT AGAINST DE VALERA

The disingenuous character of De Valera's opposition to the Treaty was revealed in the attitude of Harry Boland. Before the signature of the Treaty, he was sent to America "to prepare the American people for the acceptance of something short of a Republic." [30] Naturally, therefore, when the press comments reached the United States with an outline of the terms of the Treaty, Boland promptly announced his approval of them. Joseph McGarrity, an ardent supporter of De Valera, was likewise in favor of the Treaty: "Ireland's sovereign independence is acknowledged by the British Cabinet and their action is approved by Britain's King. This much is certain." [31] James E. Murray, National Vice President of the American Association for the Recognition of the Irish Republic, expressed his delight at the terms of the Treaty: "I am delighted with the result of the Irish Peace negotiations. De Valera, who led the Irish people in this grim and heroic fight for liberty, will now take his position in history alongside of Washington." [32] Edward L. Doheny, President of the A.A.R.I.R., was one of the loudest voices in this chorus of praise for the Treaty:

> It is a great event throughout the British Dominions, but nowhere more portentous than here in America. It removes the greatest obstruction to a frank and friendly intercourse between this country and Great Britain. . . . It should have a beneficial . . . effect upon the deliberations of the conferees now meeting in Washington [Disarmament Conference].[33]

The Friends of Irish Freedom were much more cautious in their comments, and in some cases the observations were distinctly hostile. Bishop Gallagher, at the convention of the Friends on Decem-

30. Beaslai, *op. cit.*, p. 335.
31. *Irish Press* (Philadelphia), December 10, 1921.
32. Butte [Montana] *Independent*, December 10, 1921.
33. *New York Times*, December 7, 1921.

ber 10, 1921, remarked: "As American citizens, notwithstanding the compromise that has been reached, we cannot lower the flag of freedom." At the same convention John Devoy was called upon to express his opinion:

> The agreement will undoubtedly be altered to some extent; but whatever alterations are made in it, Ireland will remain under it an integral part of the British Empire. Parnell said that no man can set limits to the onward march of a nation; and this agreement won't set limits to the onward march of the Irish Nation to the only goal that is worth having—to the Irish Republic.[34]

Diarmuid Lynch, National Secretary of the Friends of Irish Freedom, and Laurence J. Rice, leader of the New York Clan-na-Gael, were outspoken in their criticism of certain sections of the agreement: "With Irish coastal fortifications under British control . . . with an Ireland swearing allegiance to a foreign King, the use of the term 'Irish Free State' is an insult to the dead who died fighting for an independent Irish Republic." [35] Judge Cohalan was distinctly caustic in his comments upon the Treaty:

> Lloyd George has won the greatest diplomatic triumph of his career. He has braced up the tottering British Empire for the moment by attaching to it an apparently satisfied Ireland. He hopes, largely as a consequence, as the London papers and their echoes here show, to proceed now to similarly attach America.[36]

The deep disappointment of Judge Cohalan and John Devoy at the terms of the Anglo-Irish Agreement did not cause them to rally to the support of De Valera. They had no confidence in his vision or integrity. His actions in the United States for a year and a half had indicated too clearly his overruling desire to dominate everyone around him. They nursed hopes that the Irish Free State would eventually gain its complete independence. With some of the views of Collins, both Judge Cohalan and Devoy were in strong

---

34. *Cohalan MSS.*
35. *New York Times,* December 8, 1921.
36. *Ibid.*

disagreement. Collins had written an interesting memorandum entitled "On the Wider International Aspects of an Anglo-Irish Settlement." In this memorandum he had remarked:

> A new era is dawning, not for Ireland only, but for the whole world. . . . The problem of associating autonomous communities can only be solved by recognising the complete independence of the several countries associated. . . . Into such a league might not America be ready to enter? [37]

When Collins broached these ideas to John Devoy, they evoked a spirited negative:

> In re suggestion that United States might enter Association of Nations of whose *bona fides* she was satisfied, American-Irish and many millions of other citizens are unalterably opposed to any Old World entanglements under any name whatsoever, knowing that highly-trained, unscrupulous British diplomats will overreach and hoodwink American amateurs. . . . America's only security lies in strict adherence to Washington's policy. . . .
>
> Although they remain [Irish] Republicans, our best men here, under existing conditions, favor giving the "Free State" a chance to do what it can for Ireland. Personally, I am utterly opposed to De Valera's attempt to upset the "Free State Agreement." . . . It is grotesque for De Valera to talk of his loyalty to the Republic. The first blow to the Republic was delivered by him in the Cuban interview; the second, and more deadly one, was his unpardonable action in rejecting the Republican plank at Chicago. . . . The third was his making the Split here on charges that were all impudent falsehoods, and using vast sums of money collected by us for the Irish Republic to keep the Split alive. You are fully aware of this and Stephen O'Mara's recent request to Splitters for return of money advanced to them is abundant confirmation. That money which should have gone to the support of fighting men in Ireland, was prostituted for an evil purpose and materially aided England's savage warfare on Ireland.
>
> These infamous actions of De Valera were approved or condoned by all of you. You all bolstered up an attempt to create an Autocracy and the present situation is the direct and inevitable result. You allowed De Valera to hold the funds here in his own name and he is

---

37. Frank Pakenham, *Peace by Ordeal*, p. 281.

now holding a vast balance and is fighting you, not for Ireland's sake, but to retain his grip as Leader, after proving his utter unfitness.

Adhering unalterably to my life-long Republican convictions, my earnest hope is that in such a struggle you may win, believing as I do that the defeat of De Valera's selfish campaign is absolutely necessary in Ireland's dearest interests.[38]

The attitude of Judge Cohalan, like that of John Devoy, was favorable to Collins. In a letter to Bishop William Turner, of Buffalo, Judge Cohalan clearly expressed his viewpoint:

> In common with all right-thinking persons, I am grieved beyond measure at the untimely death of Michael Collins. The shock was felt throughout the world. Such occurrences deal a serious wound to the moral character of the Irish people limitless in its effects.
>
> The ruthless and wanton destruction of other lives and real property by those misguided individuals who pretend to espouse a pseudo-Republic imposes a serious responsibility in the forum of conscience upon those whose malevolent inspiration and direction is the proximate cause of it all.
>
> May I recall to your mind the Park Avenue Hotel Conference in New York in 1920? What transpired in that meeting enabled you, with others, to scrutinize and observe closely the traits and tendencies of the central figures therein. How much like the conduct of Eamon de Valera on that occasion have been his actions since his return to Ireland. Crimination seldom serves to advance a cause. One's self-respect constrains its use except in rare instances.
>
> The present juncture of Irish affairs, however, warrants, yes—demands, that those of us who know the facts in the matter should point to those responsible for the disintegration of that solidarity of public sentiment in this country friendly to Ireland's cause. . . .
>
> It appears that the people of Ireland have reached a conclusion as to Mr. de Valera essentially like unto that which was arrived at concerning him very early in the progress of the cause in this country. . . . The much disturbed and distressed Irish people are, apparently, by no means discouraged as to their capacity to establish a real government in their own country. No one who has read the treaty provisions can fail to note its many serious limitations on Irish sovereignty and independence. The separation of the country into two parts as well as the veto power vested in the Governor General to be appointed thereun-

38. John Devoy to Michael Collins, February 16, 1922, *Cohalan MSS*.

der, evoke the disapproval of the advocates of Irish independence. Nevertheless, and notwithstanding, these provisions among others, the people of Ireland have decidedly expressed their approval of the plan as a whole. This fact seems to make it imperative for us who have been, and who intend to continue to be interested in Irish matters, to revitalize and reconsolidate our friends in America in order to aid the people in Ireland in their advance to the goal of a real Irish Republic.[39]

This condemnation of the actions of De Valera in inciting civil war in Ireland was strongly supported by Archbishop Michael J. Curley, of Baltimore. After a visit to Ireland, where he witnessed the destruction caused by De Valera and his followers, he expressed his opinions to an intimate friend:

I am delighted to know that the substantial people of Massachusetts are with the Irish people in their attempt to settle down to real living, and are not with the few in the country who are aiding the continuation of the most horrible system of destruction I ever witnessed.

I was in Ireland last Summer, and it makes the heart of an Irishman bleed to see the senseless stupidity of the De Valera people who seem to be bent on murder and destruction and on nothing else.[40]

Judge Cohalan was in cordial agreement with Archbishop Curley. He had seen De Valera at work in America and he was well aware of his genius for arousing bitter enmity between men of Irish blood wherever located. He was deeply disappointed when the Anglo-Irish Treaty merely secured Dominion status for Ireland. But he was certain that this treaty arrangement was a

step forward on the road to independence. It is only that and not in any sense an end by itself, or an achievement about which there will be any enthusiasm if the result is going to be only to tie Ireland more closely to England. I think you should make it clear on every occasion that while as between Collins and De Valera the real lovers of Irish liberty favor Collins, such favor is not an endorsement of any settlement with England but only an utter repudiation of De Valera as the author of the present situation in Ireland and the man whose actions

39. Judge Cohalan to Bishop William Turner, September 15, 1922, *ibid.*
40. Archbishop Michael J. Curley to Matthew Cummings, February 2, 1923, *ibid.*

Stepping Stone to Eventual Independence 441

have prevented a recognition by other nations of the Republic of Ireland.[41]

The civil war in Ireland was a shock rather than a surprise to Judge Cohalan. He had long realized that De Valera's opera-star temperament would make it most difficult for him to reconcile the many differences of opinion that existed in the minds of Sinn Fein leaders. The situation in Dublin required a President of unquestioned integrity. It was obvious that, during his tempestuous eighteen months in America, De Valera did not earn such a reputation. Indeed, at times he seemed merely a petty politician intent upon having his way even though his way seriously compromised the future of Ireland.

In his relations with De Valera, Judge Cohalan made strenuous efforts to find some common ground of mutual understanding. He had no axe to grind that would cut for him some path to preferment, and he had no thought of personal advantage. There was never any desire to court a quarrel with De Valera, and he anxiously sought to avoid one. But he resolutely refused to follow a policy that he felt would seriously injure the cause of Ireland. At the Chicago convention in 1920 the De Valera tactics were distinctly ill-advised and had tragic consequences for Ireland.

In a very real sense the quarrel between De Valera and Judge Cohalan was inevitable, and it stemmed from the fact that Judge Cohalan had a basic Americanism that was the very core of his being. His ardent support of the cause of Ireland was secondary to his devotion to American interests. He had always cherished a strong belief that an independent Ireland would be an important asset to America. His first loyalties were undoubtedly to America, and this fact deeply irked De Valera, who thought that all Irish-Americans should instantly respond when he sounded the horn of necessity.

Some biographers of De Valera and some Irish publicists whose pens have been dipped in ink generously supplied by the De Valera clique have twisted the story of Irish-American relations until the facts have been lost in pressurized history. I have attempted to pro-

41. Judge Cohalan to Matthew Cummings, March 13, 1922, *ibid.*

vide a new setting for the facts. I can only hope that students of Irish-American relations may gain a new perspective from my pages and will finally perceive and appreciate the unique contributions of Judge Cohalan and John Devoy to the cause of Ireland and the progress of the United States.

APPENDIX

The following letter was written to Judge O'Neill Ryan of St. Louis by the famous Irish patriot-priest Father Eugene Sheehy, who visited America in 1902.

September 6th, 1902

Park Avenue Hotel
New York
My Dear Judge:

I have been here these last two days—attended meeting D 14 Mr. P. Egan's former D.—will attend meeting District Officers tomorrow. Mr. Cohalan spoke at D meeting, dealing chiefly with Egan's defection in an exhaustive and masterly manner. His style is direct, logical & precise with the national characteristic of swiftness and happy readiness of speech. There is no mistake about the strength and flavor of his Nationalism. I shall be interested to see and hear more [of] him—he has captured me entirely—and I say this as my tribute. It does me the world of good to find the Irish American of this sort—therein is the *enduring* Hope that points to Destiny. My old friend Mr. D—— has been generous of his time to me since I came. *Past, present, Future* under Survey.

Kind wishes to Mrs. Ryan and Young Men.

Most sincerely,
Hon. Judge O'Neill Ryan   Eugene Sheehy

The three letters that follow are from Padraic H. Pearse to Judge Daniel F. Cohalan.

ST. ENDA'S COLLEGE,
RATHFARNHAM,
CO. DUBLIN,
IRELAND

P. H. PEARSE,
President
P.O. Box 1682
New York, N.Y.

New York,
6th May 1914

My dear Judge,

Before sailing for home I want to send you this line of farewell and of thanks for your great kindness to me during the past two months. I owe you thanks not only for your own generous subscription but for your unceasing and successful efforts to put me in touch with other good friends.

I would like you to accept the enclosed copy of a small book of Irish verse of mine which has been published since I left home and copies of which have just reached me. In return for great services ". . . I, being poor, have only my dreams" to give.

[Sincerely yours,
[P. H. Pearse]

28th Dec. 1914

Friend,

You told me to let you know if St. Enda's were in difficulty. Alas, the strain has reached, or almost reached, the breaking point. I greatly fear that I shall not be able to hold out until I feel free to resume my tour in America. It seems a terrible thing, after so much effort and sacrifice on the part of so many, to let the college go. My hope was that I could hold things together until I was able to go out to America again. But the continuance of the war and of the strained situation here and of your preoccupation with the Volunteer Collection seems to make an American visit impossible in the near future. What do you think I ought to do? I will hold on until I hear from you.

My best wishes for the New Year to you and yours.

Believe me,
Sincerely yours,
P. H. Pearse

ST. ENDA'S COLLEGE,
RATHFARNHAM
15th Oct. 1915

My dear friend:

Just at the critical moment for St. Enda's I was rung up by a city bank and told that £300 had been placed to my credit on instructions from New York. I knew that this was the reply of the three friends to whom I had written apprising them of the crisis that had arisen. I did not know, nor do I know yet, the individual or individuals to whose personal generosity I am indebted for this timely and effective help, but I know that your hand was in it, and I want to thank you. I have been enabled to surmount the crisis, and I do not now anticipate any difficulty in finishing yet another school year. We have a bigger school than last year, and on the whole a more promising lot of boys. So I am full of hope.

I don't quite know what to say to you. You have all been so prompt and so effective in your help that it leaves me without any adequate words. I do not trust myself to write what I feel about the *importance* of what you have done. To hold St. Enda's for another year means so much.

I am writing to John and to McG. too, for I know that it was they who co-operated with you. I wish I could shake hands with you all again.

I waited to send this letter by hand rather than by mail. It will, I hope, duly reach you.

Remember me to Mrs. Cohalan and to all the children. With kindest and most grateful regards to yourself,

Believe me,
Yours most sincerely,
P. H. Pearse

Patrick McCartan writes to Dan O'Connell concerning the League of Nations:

Nov. 7th, 1919

Dear Capt. O'Connell:

I did not expect to leave Washington so soon but have now to leave by the 4 o'clock train.

The President asked me to tell you to be careful about your statements on such things as Senator Walsh's (Mont.) resolution, as he might be forced to repudiate you and that would do harm to the whole movement.

If you were absolutely certain the Treaty would be rejected your statement was OK. On the other hand if the Treaty be adopted even with a few meaningless reservations your statement was detrimental to Ireland. If the League be adopted by the U.S. he considers it might be of some benefit to have the Senate on record that Ireland's case would be the first question considered by the League. However it is with regard to the future rather than the past he wishes to advise you and perhaps no such occasion is likely to again arise. I hope you will understand the point—namely that he merely wishes you to be careful. I always hate to write such things as they appear altogether different in writing from what they appear in a conversation.

Yours sincerely,
P. McCartan

On February 20, 1920, Mr. de Valera addressed to Judge Cohalan the following extraordinary letter, which was delivered by hand by Harry Boland.

Dear Justice Cohalan,

After mature consideration, I have decided that to continue to ignore the articles in the "Gaelic American" would result in injury to the cause I have been sent here to promote. The articles themselves are, of course, the least matter. It is the evident purpose behind them, and the general attitude of mind they reveal, that is the menace.

I am answerable to the Irish people for the proper execution of the trust with which I have been charged. I am definitely responsible to them, and I *alone* am responsible. It is my obvious duty to select such instruments as may be available for the task set me. It is my duty to superintend every important step in the execution of that task. I may not blindly delegate these duties to anyone whomsoever. I cannot divest myself of my responsibilities.

I see added force being applied, day by day, to the power end of the great lever of American public opinion, with which I hope to accomplish my purpose. I must satisfy myself as to the temper of the other end of the lever.

The articles of the "Gaelic American," and certain incidents that have resulted from them, give me grounds for the fear that, in a moment of stress, the point of the lever would fail me. I am led to understand that these articles in the "Gaelic American" have your consent and approval. Is this so?

The Friends of Irish Freedom organization is an association of

American citizens, founded to assist the Irish people in securing the freedom the Irish people desire. By its name, and by its constitution, it is pledged to aid in securing recognition for the established Republic. I am convinced it is ready to cooperate to the full with the responsible head of the Republic, who has been sent here especially to seek that recognition.

You are the officer of the Friends of Irish Freedom, who, de facto, wields unchallenged the executive power of that organization. You are the officer through whom its several resources are in the main applied. You are the officer who has accepted its most important commissions, and spoken, not merely in its name, but in the name of the whole Irish race in America. It is vital that I know exactly how you stand in this matter.

The whole question is urgent, and I expect you will find it possible to let me have a reply by Monday. To avoid all chance of miscarriage, I am having this delivered by Mr. Boland, personally.

I remain,
Very sincerely yours,
Eamon De Valera

On February 22, 1920, Judge Cohalan replied as follows:

Dear President De Valera,

Your communication, dated February 20th, was handed to me by Mr. Boland on Saturday afternoon.

I was amazed at its contents. In spite of its tone, and because of the position which you occupy, I am responding to it.

The "Gaelic American" is edited, as you know, by Mr. John Devoy, for whose opinions and convictions I entertain the highest respect. I control neither him nor them.

That he has the right to comment upon, or discuss your public utterances, or those of any man who speaks for a cause or a people, I assume you will grant. In any event, it is recognized by all Americans as one of our fundamental liberties. We have no law of lèse-majesté here, nor, as far as I can judge, is there talk of having one in the democratic and free Ireland in which we believe.

Into any controversy you may have with Mr. Devoy, or others, I refuse to be drawn.

May I venture to suggest that you evidently labor under a serious misapprehension as to the relations which exist between you and me.

I know no reason why you take the trouble to tell me that you can share your responsibility to the Irish people with no one.

I would not let you share it with me, if you sought to do so. That is a matter between them and you.

What I have done for the cause of the independence of the Irish people, recently and for many years past, I have done as an American, whose only allegiance is to America, and as one to whom the interest and security of my country are ever to be preferred to those of any and all other lands. What the extent and effect of that work may be will be decided by the members of the Race and by general public opinion.

I have no appointment from you or any other spokesman for another country nor would I under any circumstances accept one.

So long, and just so long as I can continue to work thus, I shall exercise such influence and talent as I may have in the same way and for the same ideals as in the past.

The people of Ireland have placed themselves unequivocally upon record as favoring complete independence for their country, and unless and until they by vote reverse that decision, I shall regard it as final, no matter what any man or set of men may say to the contrary.

With their demand for independence I am confident all Americans will finally agree, as it is not alone just, but in line with the ideals and best interests of our country, and essential to the permanent peace of the world, that all nations and peoples should be free.

If Ireland were to change her position, and to seek a measure of self-government that would align her in the future with England as an ally, in what I regard as the inevitable struggle for the freedom of the seas, that must shortly come between American and England, every loyal American will, without hesitation, take a position unreservedly upon the side of America.

A British Monroe Doctrine, that would make Ireland the ally of England, and thus buttress the falling British Empire, so as to further oppress India and Egypt and other subject lands, would be so immoral, and so utterly at variance with the ideals and traditions of the Irish people, as to be as indefensible to them as it would be intolerable to the liberty-loving people of the world.

I believe the people of Ireland were in deadly earnest in declaring for absolute independence, and no voice but that of the people themselves can convince me that they intend to take a position which will put them in hostility to America.

Should they, however, take such a step—as a free people undoubtedly have the right to do—I know that the millions of Americans of Irish blood, who have created this great movement in favor of Ireland's

Appendix

independence, which you found here upon your arrival, will once again show with practical unanimity that we are for America as against all the world.

Are you not in great danger of making a grave mistake when you talk in your communication of selecting "instruments" in this country, and of "levers" and "power end," and "other end of the lever," through which you hope to accomplish your purpose here?

Do you really think for a moment that American public opinion will permit any citizen of another country to interfere, as you suggest, in American affairs?

If so, I may assure you that you are woefully out of touch with the spirit of the country in which you are sojourning.

You point out that I have on occasion been called upon to speak, not merely in the name of the Friends of Irish Freedom, but in the name of the whole Irish Race in America. May I call your attention to the fact that it was always as an American, and for my countrymen, that I spoke?

You might have added that at those times, as at others, I have said nothing that took from the self-respect or dignity of those whom I represented, or that left any doubt upon my hearers that I believed many millions of Americans sympathized with that demand of Ireland for absolute independence, which you came here to voice.

I respectfully suggest, in closing, that you would be well advised if you hesitate before you jeopardize or imperil that solidarity of opinion, and unity of action, among millions of American citizens, which you found here amongst us when you came, which have been the despair of England's friends, and have already accomplished so much for America and Ireland.

Those millions do not desire to see a return of the conditions which, under the late Mr. Redmond, made political activities in Ireland a football in English party politics.

Yours very truly,
Daniel F. Cohalan.

BIBLIOGRAPHY

I. MANUSCRIPT SOURCES: OFFICIAL AND PRIVATE PAPERS
II. PRINTED SOURCES: OFFICIAL DOCUMENTS AND OTHER PUBLICATIONS
III. NEWSPAPERS AND PERIODICALS
IV. LETTERS, DIARIES, MISCELLANEOUS
V. BIOGRAPHIES, HISTORIES, SPECIAL STUDIES, ARTICLES

1. MANUSCRIPT SOURCES

Official Papers

A. DEPARTMENT OF STATE, WASHINGTON, D.C.

Great Britain:
   Instructions, Despatches, Notes, 1866-1922.
   London, *Embassy Archives,* 1914-1922.
   Miscellaneous Letters, 1866-1903.
Ireland: Consular Archives:
   Dublin: *Instructions, Despatches,* 1914-1922.
   Cork: *Instructions, Despatches,* 1914-1922.
   Queenstown: *Instructions, Despatches,* 1914-1922.
South African Republic and Orange Free State:
   Instructions, Despatches, 1899-1902.

Private Papers

B.
(*In the Division of Manuscripts, Library of Congress, unless otherwise noted.*)
Baker, Ray S.
Bayard, Thomas F.
Beveridge, Albert J.
Borah, William E.

Burleson, Albert S.
Cleveland, Grover
Cohalan, Daniel F., *Private*
Davis, J. C. Bancroft
Hay, John
Hitchcock, Gilbert M.
House, Edward M., *Yale University*
Lodge, Henry Cabot, *Massachusetts Historical Society*
McKinley, William
Olney, Richard
Schurz, Carl
Walsh, Thomas J.
White, Henry
Wilson, Woodrow

2. PRINTED SOURCES

Official Documents

A. UNITED STATES

Congress:
  Compilation of the Messages and Papers of the Presidents. Edited by James D. Richardson, 20 volumes, Washington, 1896-1927.
  Congressional Record, 1870-1922.
  Hearings Before the House Committee on Foreign Affairs on House Joint Resolution No. 357, 65 Cong., 3 sess.
  Hearings Before the Senate Committee on Foreign Relations, 74 Cong., 2 sess., January 10-February 5, 1936.
  House Report No. 1054, 65 Cong., 3 sess.
  House Document No. 1832, 65 Cong., 3 sess.
Department of State:
  Papers Relating to the Foreign Relations of the United States, 1870-1922.

B. GREAT BRITAIN

  Select Committee on the Corn Trade of the United Kingdom, *British Parliamentary Papers, 1812-13,* iii.
  Select Committee on the State of Ireland (Lords), *British Parliamentary Papers, 1825,* ix.
  "Report of the Select Committee on the State of Ireland," *British Parliamentary Papers, 1831-32,* XVI.

"Report on the Linen and Cotton Manufacture in Ireland," *British Parliamentary Papers, 1840*, xxiii.

"Report of Her Majesty's Commissioners of Enquiry into the Workings of the Landlord and Tenant Act of 1870 and the Acts Amending the Same," *British Parliamentary Papers, 1881*, xviii-xix.

"Report of the Special Commission to Inquire into Charges and Allegations Against Certain Members of Parliament and Others, 1888," *Cmd.-5891*

Documents Relative to the Sinn Fein Movement, London, 1921, Cmd.-1108.

Unofficial Documents

The American Commission on Conditions in Ireland. *Evidence on Conditions in Ireland* (Washington, 1921).

3. NEWSPAPERS AND PERIODICALS

A. AMERICAN

Atlanta, Ga.
  Constitution
Baltimore, Md.
  Sun
Birmingham, Ala.
  Age-Herald
Boston, Mass.
  Herald
  Pilot
  Post
  Transcript
Brooklyn, N.Y.
  Eagle
Buffalo, N.Y.
  News
Chicago, Ill.
  News
  Times-Herald
  Tribune
Cincinnati, Ohio
  Enquirer
Cleveland, Ohio
  News
  Plain Dealer
Dallas, Texas
  News
Des Moines, Ia.
  Register and Leader
Detroit, Mich.
  Free Press
  News
Emporia, Kansas
  Gazette
Indianapolis, Ind.
  News
  Star
Kansas City, Mo.
  Star
Los Angeles, Cal.
  Examiner
  Times
Louisville, Ky.
  Courier-Journal
Milwaukee, Wis.
  Journal
New Orleans, La.
  Times-Picayune
New York, N.Y.
  Evening Post
  Gaelic American
  Herald
  Journal
  Sun
  Times
  Tribune
Philadelphia, Pa.
  Public Ledger
Rochester, N.Y.
  Democrat and Chronicle
Washington, D. C.
  Herald
  Post
  Star

B. ENGLISH

Liverpool
  Daily Post
London
  Daily Herald
  Daily Mail
  Daily Telegraph
  News Chronicle
  Observer
  Standard
  Times
  Westminster Gazette

C. IRISH

  Cork *Examiner*
  Dublin *Evening Mail*
  Freeman's Journal
  Irish Independent
  Irish Times

Periodicals

A. AMERICAN

  America
  American Historical Review
  Catholic World
  Collier's
  Literary Digest
  Nation
  Political Science Quarterly
  Saturday Evening Post

B. ENGLISH

  Contemporary Review
  Nineteenth Century and After

4. LETTERS, DIARIES, MEMOIRS, MISCELLANEOUS

Asquith, Margot, *An Autobiography*. New York, 1922, 2 vols.
Blücher, Evelyn, Princess. *An English Wife in Berlin*. New York, 1920.
Castlereagh, Viscount, *Memoirs and Correspondence*. London, 1850-53, 12 vols.

Cavanagh, Michael, *Memoirs of Thomas Francis Meagher*. Worcester, 1902.
Creevy Papers, ed. by Sir Herbert Maxwell. New York, 1904.
Crozier, Brigadier-General Frank P., *Ireland Forever*. London, 1932.
Curry, Charles E., *Sir Roger Casement's Diaries*. Munich, 1922.
Denieffe, Joseph, *A Personal Narrative of the Irish Revolutionary Brotherhood*. New York, 1906.
Devoy, John, *Recollections of an Irish Rebel*. New York, 1929.
Devoy, John, *Post Bag*, vols. I-II, ed. by William O'Brien and Desmond Ryan. Dublin, 1948, 1953.
Duffy, Charles Gavan, *Young Ireland, 1840-1845*. London, 1896, 2 vols.
Duffy, Charles Gavan, *My Life in Two Hemispheres*. New York, 1898, 2 vols.
Gaffney, T. St. John, *Breaking the Silence*. New York, 1930.
Grey, Sir Edward, *Twenty-Five Years*. New York, 1925, 2 vols.
Healy, T. M., *Letters and Leaders of My Day*. London, 1928, 2 vols.
House, Colonel Edward M., *Intimate Papers*. Boston, 1926, 2 vols.
Lavery, Sir John, *The Life of a Painter*. Boston, 1940.
Lodge, Henry Cabot, *Selections from the Correspondence of Theodore Roosevelt, 1884-1918*. New York, 1925, 2 vols.
Macready, Sir Nevil, *Annals of an Active Life*. London, 1924, 2 vols.
Melbourne, *Memoirs of William, Second Viscount*, ed. by William T. Torrens, London, 1878.
Morley, John, *Recollections*. New York, 1917, 2 vols.
O'Connor, T. P., *Memoirs of an Old Parliamentarian*. London, 1929, 2 vols.
O'Hara, M. M., *Chief and Tribune*. London, 1919.
O'Leary, John, *Recollections of Fenians and Fenianism*. London, 1896, 2 vols.
Ryan, Desmond, *The Phoenix Flame*. London, 1937.
Senior, Nassau, *Journals, Conversations and Essays Relating to Ireland*. London, 1868, 2 vols.
Spring Rice, Sir Cecil, *Letters and Friendships*, ed. by Stephen Gwynn, Boston, 1929, 2 vols.
Swift, Jonathan, "Drapier's Letters," *Works*. London, 1907, VI.
Talbot, Hayden, *Michael Collins' Own Story*. London, 1920.
Thompson, Sir Basil, *Queer People*. London, 1922.
Wellington, Field Marshal Arthur, *Despatches, Correspondence and Memoranda*. London, 1878, VII.
Yeats, John Butler, *Letters to his son, W. B. Yeats, and Others*. London, 1944.

5. BIOGRAPHIES, HISTORIES, SPECIAL STUDIES, ARTICLES

Anonymous, "Daniel Florence Cohalan, 1865-1946," in *The Recorder,* American Irish Historical Society, X, December, 1947, 2-5.

Bailey, Thomas A., *A Diplomatic History of the American People.* New York, 1946.

Bailey, Thomas A., *Woodrow Wilson and the Great Betrayal.* New York, 1945.

Barton, Margaret, and Osbert Sitwell, *Victoriana: A Symposium of Victorian Wisdom.* London, 1931.

Beaslai, Piaras, *Michael Collins and the Making of a New Ireland.* London, 1926, 2 vols.

Birkenhead, Lord, *Famous Trials of History.* London, 1917.

Blum, John M., *Joe Tumulty and the Wilson Era.* Boston, 1951.

Boyd, Ernest A., *Ireland's Literary Renaissance.* New York, 1916.

Brebner, John B., "Canada, the Anglo-Japanese Alliance and the Washington Conference," *Political Science Quarterly,* L, March 1935, 45-59.

Bromage, Mary C., *De Valera and the March of a Nation.* London, 1956.

Butt, Isaac, *Irish Federalism.* London, 1874.

Callwell, Sir Charles E., *Field Marshal Sir Henry Wilson.* London, 1927, 2 vols.

Cecil, Lady Gwendoline, *Life of Robert, Marquis of Salisbury.* London, 1921-32, 4 vols.

Churchill, Winston S., *The Aftermath.* New York, 1929.

Churchill, Winston S., *Lord Randolph Churchill.* London, 1952.

Clancy, John J., *Irish Distress and Its Remedies.* London, 1881.

Colvin, Ian, *Life of Lord Carson.* London, 1934.

Corkery, Daniel, *The Hidden Ireland.* Dublin, 1925.

Costigan, Giovanni, "The Treason of Sir Roger Casement," *American Historical Review,* LX, January 1955, 283-302.

Crewe, Lord, *Lord Rosebery.* London, 1921, 2 vols.

D'Arcy, William, *The Fenian Movement in the United States, 1858-1886.* Washington, 1947.

Davitt, Michael, *The Fall of Feudalism in Ireland.* London, 1904.

Dennett, Tyler, *John Hay.* New York, 1933.

Duffy, Charles Gavan, *The League of North and South.* London, 1886.

Eversley, Lord George J. S., *Gladstone and Ireland.* London, 1912.

Fay, Sidney B., *Origins of the World War.* New York, 1929, 2 vols.

Fay, Rev. Sigourney, "The O'Connellite View of Ireland," *America,* XVII, June 9, 1917, 209-210.

Fleming, Denna F., *The United States and the League of Nations, 1918-1920.* New York, 1932.

Bibliography 457

Foster, John W., *The Practice of Diplomacy*. Boston, 1906.
Garvin, J. L., *Life of Joseph Chamberlain*. London, 1932, 5 vols.
Giffen, Sir Robert, *Economic Inquiries and Studies*. London, 1904.
Grenfell, Captain Russell, *Unconditional Hatred*. New York, 1953.
Griffith, Arthur, *The Resurrection of Hungary: A Parallel for Ireland*. Dublin, 1904.
Gwynn, Denis, *The Life and Death of Roger Casement*. London, 1930.
Gwynn, Denis, *The Life of John Redmond*. London, 1932.
Gwynn, Denis, *Young Ireland and 1848*. Dublin, 1949.
Gwynn, Denis, *De Valera*. New York, 1933.
Gwynn, Denis, *Traitor or Patriot*. New York, 1931.
Gwynn, Stephen, *John Redmond's Last Years*. London, 1919.
Harrison, Henry, *Parnell Vindicated*. New York, 1931.
Haslip, Joan, *Parnell*. New York, 1937.
Haynes, E. S. P., *A Lawyer's Notebook*. London, 1932.
Healy, T. M., *Why Ireland Is not Free*. Dublin, 1898.
Hendrick, Burton J., *Life and Letters of Walter H. Page*. New York, Garden City, 1923, 2 vols.
Hobson, Bulmer, *History of the Irish Volunteers*. Dublin, 1918.
Hone, Joseph M., *William Butler Yeats, 1865-1939*. London, 1942.
Horgan, John J., *Parnell to Pearse*. Dublin, 1949.
Hoy, Hugh C., *40 O. B. or How the War Was Won*. London, 1932.
Jenks, Leland H., *The Migration of British Capital to 1873*. New York, 1927.
Johnson, Claudius, *Borah of Idaho*. New York, 1936.
Keith, Arthur B., *The Belgian Congo and the Berlin Act*. Oxford, 1919.
King, David B., *The Irish Question*. New York, 1882.
Le Roux, Louis N., *Tom Clarke and the Irish Freedom Movement*. Dublin, 1910.
Lecky, William E. H., *The Leaders of Public Opinion in Ireland*. New York, 1903.
Leslie, Shane, *Henry Edward Manning*. London, 1921.
Leslie, Shane, *The Irish Issue in Its American Aspect*. New York, 1917.
Lloyd, Clifford, *Ireland Under the Land League*. London, 1892.
Lyons, Francis S. L., *The Irish Parliamentary Party, 1890-1910*. London, 1951.
Macardle, Dorothy, *The Irish Republic*. Dublin, 1951.
MacColl, René, *Roger Casement*. London, 1956.
MacDermot, Frank, *Theobald Wolfe Tone*. London, 1939.
Mackey, Herbert, *The Life and Times of Roger Casement*. Dublin, 1954.
Maloney, William J., *The Forged Casement Diaries*. Dublin, 1936.
McCartan, Patrick, *With De Valera in America*. New York, 1932.

McCarthy, Michael J., *The Irish Revolution*. Edinburgh, 1912.
McEnnis, J. T., *The Clan-na-Gael and the Murder of Dr. Cronin*. Chicago, 1889.
McGurrin, James, *Bourke Cockran: A Free Lance in American Politics*. New York, 1948.
Mitchel, John, *The Last Conquest of Ireland (Perhaps)*. New York, 1873.
Monteith, Robert, *Casement's Last Adventure*. Chicago, 1932.
Montgomery, W. E., *The History of Land Tenure in Ireland*. Cambridge, 1889.
Morley, John, *The Life of William E. Gladstone*. New York, 1903, 3 vols.
Nevins, Allan, *Henry White: Thirty Years of American Diplomacy*. New York, 1930.
Noyes, Alfred, *Two Worlds for Memory*. London, 1953.
O'Brien, George A. T., *Economic History of Ireland in the Eighteenth Century*. Dublin, 1919.
O'Brien, R. Barry, *Life of Charles Stewart Parnell*. New York, 1898, 2 vols.
O'Brien, R. Barry, *Thomas Drummond*. London, 1889.
O'Connor, Sir James, *History of Ireland, 1798-1924*. New York, 1925, 2 vols.
O'Connor, T. P., *The Parnell Movement*. New York, 1891.
O'Grady, Standish, *The Story of Ireland*. London, 1894.
O'Grady, Standish, *The Crisis in Ireland*. Dublin, 1882.
O'Hegarty, Patrick S., *A History of Ireland Under the Union, 1801-1922*. London, 1952.
O'Hegarty, Patrick S., *The Victory of Sinn Fein*. Dublin, 1924.
O'Hegarty, Patrick S., *A Bibliography of Roger Casement*. Dublin, 1949.
O'Neill, Brian, *The War for Land in Ireland*. New York, 1933.
O'Rourke, Canon John, *History of the Great Irish Famine of 1847*. Dublin, 1902.
O'Shea, Katharine, *Charles Stewart Parnell*. London, 1914, 2 vols.
Pakenham, Frank, *Peace by Ordeal*. London, 1935.
Palmer, Norman D., *The Irish Land League Crisis*. New Haven, 1940.
Parmiter, Geoffrey de C., *Roger Casement*. London, 1936.
Patch, Blanche, *Thirty Years with G. B. S.* London, 1951.
Paul, Herbert, *A History of Modern England*. New York, 1904-1906, 4 vols.
Petty, Sir William, "A Treatise of Ireland," *Economic Writings of Sir William Petty*. Cambridge, 1899.
Redmond-Howard, Louis G., *Sir Roger Casement*. Dublin, 1916.
Reynolds, James A., *The Catholic Emancipation Crisis in Ireland, 1823-1829*. New Haven, 1954.
Richey, A. G., *The Irish Land Laws*. London, 1881.

Sackville-West, V., *Pepita*. New York, 1937.
Severance, Frank H., "The Fenian Raid of 1866," *Buffalo Historical Society Publications*, XXV, 1921, 263-285.
Shaw, George Bernard, *Man and Superman*. New York, 1930.
Shippee, Lester B., *Canadian-American Relations, 1849-1874*. New Haven, 1939.
Sprout, Harold and Margaret, *Towards a New Order of Sea Power*. Princeton, 1940.
Stanwood, Edward, *A History of the Presidency from 1788 to 1916*. Boston, 1916.
Strauss, Eric, *Irish Nationalism and British Democracy*. London, 1951.
Sullivan, Alexander M., *The Last Serjeant*. London, 1952.
Sullivan, M. F., *Ireland of Today*. Philadelphia, 1881.
Tansill, Charles C., *Canadian-American Relations, 1875-1911*. New Haven, 1944.
Tansill, Charles C., *The Foreign Policy of Thomas F. Bayard*. New York, 1940.
Tansill, Charles C., *America Goes to War*. New York, 1938.
Taylor, Henry A., *The Strange Case of Andrew Bonar Law*. London, 1932.
Torrens, William T., Editor: *Memoirs of William, Second Viscount Melbourne*, London, 1878.
Trevelyan, George M., *Life of John Bright*. London, 1913.
Tyler, Alice F., *The Foreign Policy of James G. Blaine*. Minneapolis, 1927.
Walpole, Spencer, *Life of Lord John Russell*. London, 1891-1892, 2 vols.
Walsh, Patrick, *William J. Walsh*. London, 1928.
Ward, Herbert, *A Voice from the Congo*. New York, 1910.
Ward, Wilfrid, *Life of John Henry, Cardinal Newman*. New York, 1912, 2 vols.
Willert, Arthur, *The Road to Safety*. London, 1925.
Young, E. J., *Powerful America*. New York, 1936.

INDEX

Abercorn, Duke of, 142
Absentee ownership, in Ireland, 4, 19
Act of Union (1800), 9; O'Connell's fight for repeal of, 12-14, 20; repeal movement, 15-27
Acton, Lord, 93
Adams, Charles Francis, 35fn., 36fn., 37, 37fn., 39, 39fn.
Adams, Edward L., 314fn.
Adams, Henry, 116fn.
Addams, Jane, 409, 410
Adler, Selig, 324fn.
"Advanced Nationalists," 46, 48, 52
Afghans, 143
Aftermath, The (Churchill), 428fn., 430fn., 456
Agar-Robartes, Mr., 141
Agriculture, in Ireland, 4, 7, 18-19, 21, 25; co-operative movement and, 129
Albert, Heinrich, 195
Allen, Ben S., 306fn.
Allen, W. P., 38, 39
Allies Committee of Los Angeles, 359fn.
America (Jesuit weekly), 221, 222, 222fn., 223fn., 224fn., 263, 454, 456
America Goes to War (Tansill), 217fn., 459
American Association for the Recognition of the Irish Republic, 393-394, 436
American Civil War, *see* Civil War (U.S.)
American Commission for Irish Independence, 312-323, 329, 345-346, 346fn., 350; Wilson confers with members, 329; testimony of members before Senate Foreign Relations Committee, 333
American Commission on Conditions in Ireland, 409-414, 453; Official Report, 401fn.
American Committee for Relief in Ireland, 414-417
American Diplomacy and the Boer War (Ferguson), 114fn.
American Historical Review, 171fn., 454, 456
American Irish Historical Society, 456
American Land League, 57, 77
American National Red Cross, 115
American Revolution, 6, 7
Anderson, Indiana, 37
Anglo-American Joint High Commission, 106
Anglo-Irish Treaty (1921), 426-436
Anglo-Japanese Alliance, 425
Anti-Treaty Party, 434
Antrim County, Ireland, 141, 142fn., 150, 169, 173
Arana, J. C., 172
Arbitration Treaty, 112-113
Ardfert, Ireland, 187
Armagh County, Ireland, 141, 142fn., 150
Aristocracy, Irish, indifference to ideal of Irish nationalism, 29-30
Arthur, Chester, 81, 82
As It Was Said, 54fn.
Ashe, Thomas, 228, 253
Asquith, Cyril, 137fn.
Asquith, Herbert Henry, 137, 139, 144, 145-146, 150, 151, 152, 154, 155-156, 162, 163, 187, 208, 225; faithless pledges of, 161, 163

Asquith, Margot, 153, 153fn., 154, 454
Associated Press, 238
Association for the Exploration and Civilization of Central Africa, 169
Astor Hotel (New York City), 189
Atlanta *Constitution*, 261, 453
Aud (steamer), 198
Austria, 132, 152
Austria-Hungary, 149
Auxiliaries, 401, 407, 408, 410, 418fn.
Auxiliary Cadets, 401
Avondale, Parnell's estate at, 73, 92
Avory, Mr. Justice, 204

Bachelor's Walk, 149, 154, 155, 176
Bailey, Julian, *see* Beverley, Julian
Bailey, Thomas A., 107fn., 321fn., 323fn., 372fn., 456
Baker, Ray Stannard, 248, 249fn., 381fn., 451
Balfour, Arthur, 71, 87, 319; retires as Conservative Party leader, 138-139; Casement's scorn for, 171; visit to America, 226, 231
Ballymena, Ireland, 169
Balmoral, Ireland, 140
Baltimore, Maryland, 31
Baltimore *Sun*, 453
Barnes, Monsignor, 276
Barnes, Harry Elmer, xi
Barrington, Sir Eric, 172
Barry, John, 42, 96
Barton, Clara, 115fn.
Barton, Margaret, 63fn., 456
Barton, R. C., 417fn., 419, 427, 429, 430
Bayard, Thomas F., 75fn., 105, 105fn., 106, 106fn., 108fn., 109, 109fn., 110, 111fn., 112fn., 451, Arbitration Treaty, 112
Bayard-Chamberlain Treaty, 106-107
Beach, Thomas Willis, 67-68, 68fn.; comments about Parnell, 69
Beaslai, Piaras, 144fn., 199fn., 253fn., 257fn., 343fn., 352fn., 385, 392, 396fn., 397fn., 399fn., 418fn., 419fn., 431fn., 433, 434fn., 436fn., 456
Belfast, Ireland, 44, 142, 142fn., 400, 415, 416; linen exports, 5; shipbuilding, 9

Belgian Congo, 169-171
Belgian Congo and the Berlin Act, The (Keith), 170fn., 208, 209, 457
Belgrade, Yugoslavia, 149
Bell, Edward, 285fn.
Bellevue-Stratford Hotel (Philadelphia), 300
Bemis, Samuel F., xi
Beresford, Lord Charles, 142
Berle, A. A., 246
Berlin, Germany, 176, 177, 179, 181, 182, 185, 187, 189, 193
Bernardo, Carmelo, xi
Bernstorff, Count, 176, 192, 195, 238, 260
Bessborough Commission, 49, 49fn., 63
Bethmann-Hollweg, 181
"Better Government of Ireland Bill," 399
Beveridge, Albert J., 326, 326fn., 451
Beverley, Julian, 187, 188
Bibliography, 451
Biggar, F. J., 214fn.
Biggar, Joseph, 42, 44, 45, 63
Birkenhead, Lord, 175fn., 242, 428, 456
Birmingham *Age-Herald*, 203, 453
Birrell, 141, 151
Black and Tan's, 4, 213, 401, 402, 405, 407, 408, 410, 418fn., 431, 435
Black Creek, 35
Blackfeet, 11
Blackstone Hotel (Chicago), 374
Blaine, James G., 79, 79fn., 80, 83-84, 84fn., 459
Bliss, Tasker H., 318fn.
Blücher, Evelyn, Princess, 185fn., 454
Blum, John M., 209fn., 456
Blunt, Wilfrid Scawen, 25, 93
Bodkin, A. H., 204
Boer War (1899-1902), 113-120, 130, 371
Boland, Harry, 253, 301fn., 344, 363, 365fn., 366, 367, 389-393, 422, 436, 446; sent to Dublin by De Valera, 384-385; plans to reorganize the Clan-na-Gael, 385; Cohalan criticized by, 390
Booker, Colonel, 36
Borah, William E., 218, 306fn., 308, 309fn., 325fn., 326, 327-328, 331,

Index

344, 377, 451, 457; opposition to the League of Nations, 308-309, 325, 328, 336-337, 337*fn.*, 369-370, 372; pressure from Irish-Americans, 328; tribute to Cohalan, 338, 338*fn.*
Borchard, Edwin M., 234, 234*fn.*
Boston, Mass., 119, 120, 175, 327, 330, 342
Boston *Globe*, 338*fn.*
Boston *Herald*, 453
Boston *Pilot*, 40*fn.*, 108, 109, 113, 453
Boston *Post*, 242*fn.*, 453
Boston *Transcript*, 453
Boulogne, France, 53, 99
Bourne, Stephen, 48*fn.*
Boycott, Charles S., 62
Boyd, Ernest A., 122*fn.*, 456
Bragg, Commissioner, 109
Brand, Katherine, x
Brandegee, Frank B., 324, 325, 331
Branson, G. A. H., 204
Brazil, 172, 173, 174
Breaking the Silence (Gaffney), 189*fn.*, 455
Brebner, John B., 425*fn.*, 456
Brennan, George E., 380, 380*fn.*
Brennan, Thomas, 63
Brevoort Hall (New York City), 122
Bright, John, 86, 86*fn.*
British Guiana, boundary dispute with Venezuela, 111
British Parliamentary Papers, 9*fn.*, 10*fn.*, 11*fn.*, 49*fn.*
Bromage, Mary C., 368*fn.*, 456
Brooklyn, New York, 56; Emmet celebration in, 305
Brooklyn *Eagle*, 453
Brophy, Hugh, 33
Browning, 86
Bruce, Sir Frederick, 35*fn.*, 36, 36*fn.*, 37, 37*fn.*
Brugha, Cathal, 253, 303, 304, 429; shows hostility towards De Valera, 361
Bryan, William Jennings, 120
Buckle, George, 75*fn.*
Buckler, W. H., 247, 247*fn.*
Buffalo, New York, 35, 320*fn.*
Buffalo Historical Society Publications, 36*fn.*, 459
Buffalo *News*, 453

Bull (periodical), 239
Burke, Frank, 195
Burke, T. H., 70, 83
Burleson, Albert S., 380, 381*fn.*, 452
Burlingame, Anson, 116
Butt, Isaac, 41-42, 42*fn.*, 44, 45, 51, 456
Butte, Montana, 412
Butte *Independent*, 436*fn.*

Calais, France, 99
Callwell, Sir Charles E., 147*fn.*, 151*fn.*, 456
Campbell, J. H., 163
Campbell, Richard, 416, 417*fn.*
Campo Bello, 35
Canada, Fenians' invasion of, 33, 34, 35-36, 37-38, 40, 41, 114; Parnell's visit to, 57; Blaine's attitude toward, 79*fn.*; fisheries controversy between U.S. and, 105-107; plays role in shaping British foreign policy, 425
Canadian-American Relations, 1849-1874 (Shippee), 38*fn.*, 459
Canadian-American Relations, 1875-1911 (Tansill), 105*fn.*, 459
Cantwell, Right Reverend John J., 277
Caravats, 11
Carbery, Ethna, 124
Carbonari (Italian secret society), 31
Carders, 11
Carmichael, Otto, 226*fn.*
Carnarvon, Lord, 75
Carnegie Endowment for International Peace, 323
Carnegie Hall (New York City), 221
Carpenter, Mrs. Grace M., xi
Carrarol, Ireland, 59
Carroll, Bishop John, 290, 290*fn.*
Carroll, Professor, John, xi
Carroll, Mrs. Kieran, x
Carroll, Louis, xi
Carroll, William A., 52, 53*fn.*
Carson, Sir Edward, 87, 143, 143*fn.*, 144, 147, 150, 151, 154, 161, 162, 202, 225, 334, 428, 456; background, 140; Home Rule opposed by, 140-141, 161; Easter Rebellion, 201
Casement, Sir Roger, 158, 169-188, 198, 234, 236, 238, 256, 279*fn.*,

455, 456, 457, 458; Hobson defended by, 159; sympathy in U.S. for, 168; execution of, 168, 211, 242; background, 169-170; Congo report, 170-171; attacks on, in America, 171; scorn for Balfour, 171; opinion of Sir Edward Grey, 171; suspicion of British statesmen, 171-172; vacations in Ireland, 172; enlists in movement for Irish independence, 172; posts in British foreign service, 172; investigates conditions in rubber reserves of upper Amazon basin, 172-173; retires from British foreign service, 173; Cloghaneely Gaelic School subsidized by, 173; subsidies to Irish Nationalist publications, 173; praises the Gaelic League and Sinn Fein, 173; seeks German aid, 174, 176, 177, 190; opinion of Theodore Roosevelt, 174; dislike for Americans, 174; opinion of the Monroe Doctrine, 174; article by, in the *Irish Review*, 175; World War I and, 175; gun running at Howth and, 175-176; visits U.S., 176; mission to Germany, 178-186, 189, 190; confers with Devoy, 176; Findlay's plot to capture or kill him, 179, 181-182; returns decorations conferred on him by English government, 183; attempt to raise an Irish Brigade from prisoners in German prison camps, 184-186; health fails, 185; sum recieved by, from the Clan-na-Gael, 185*fn.*; imprisoned, 188; diary forged, 188; character defiled, 188, 207-209, 209*fn.*; Easter Rebellion and, 199, 202, 203-204; trial of, 204-206; found guilty of high treason, 206; final presentation of his case, 206; sentenced to death, 206; plea for clemency, 207-210; alleged homosexual behavior, 214*fn*.

Castlereagh, Viscount, 8, 9, 9*fn.*, 407, 454

Cathleen ni Houlihan (Yeats), 124-125

Catholic Association, 11-12

Catholic Church, 8; emancipation, 6-7, 11-12, 14; United Irishmen and the, 7; loyalty to England, 8, 11, 26; Mitchel's hostility towards, 26-27; Fenians opposed by, 30-32, 34, 39, 41; Papal decree condemning Fenianism, 39-40, 41; "No Rent Manifesto" opposed by, 65-66; Parnell denounced by, 99; Easter Rebellion denounced by, 201, 204*fn.*; conscription issue in Ireland, 247, 248*fn.*

Catholic Emancipation Crisis in Ireland, The, 1823-1829 (Reynolds), 458

Catholic University of America, 244, 275, 298, 384

Catholic World, 454

Catholics, denied right to serve in Parliament, 6, 11

Cattle industry, in Ireland, 4-5, 10

Caulfield, Congressman, 47

Cavanagh, Michael, 31*fn.*, 455

Cave, Sir George, 204

Cavell, Edith, 406

Cavendish, Lord Frederick, 70, 83

Ceannt, Eamon, 197, 199

Cecil, Lady Gwendoline, 87*fn.*, 456

Cecil, Lord Hugh, 142, 147

Cecil, Lord Robert, 226*fn.*

Central Opera House (New York City), 270, 294, 295, 353

Chamberlain, Austen, 427-428

Chamberlain, Joseph, 60, 69, 86, 86*fn.*, 457; Parnell's downfall aided by, 90-91

Chambers, Thomas, 52

Chaput, R. A., 424*fn.*

Chartists, 12

Chicago, Illinois, 371; bishop of, 32; Republican Convention (1920), 373-379, 403-404, 441

Chicago News, 453

Chicago Times-Herald, 115*fn.*, 453

Chicago Tribune, 203, 261, 325, 377, 453

Chief and Tribune (O'Hara), 70*fn.*, 455

Childers, Erskine, 148, 176, 400, 402, 402*fn.*, 419, 427

China, Opium War in, 22-23

Christensen, Adler, 178-179, 182, 183, 238

Index

Christiania, Norway, 179, 180, 182, 188, 238
Christie, Archbishop, 227*fn*.
Churchill, M., 286*fn*.
Churchill, Lord Randolph, 87, 87*fn*., 90*fn*., 140, 147, 456
Churchill, Winston S., 87*fn*., 424, 428*fn*., 430*fn*., 456; quoted on downfall of Parnell, 90; Black and Tan murder squads, 213; London Conference (1921), 428; Irish Free State Agreement piloted through House of Commons by, 428
Churchill Legend, The (Neilson), 150*fn*.
Cincinnati, Ohio, 54; Archbishop of, 32
Cincinnati *Enquirer*, 453
Citizen, The (paper), 26, 27*fn*.
Citizen's Army, 137
Civil War, U.S., 213; Fenians and the, 32
Clancy, Herbert J., xi
Clancy, J. J., 50, 51*fn*., 456
Clan-na-Gael, 41, 52, 77, 79, 105, 120-122, 130, 177, 276, 278, 294, 296, 297, 384, 385, 437; founded, 27, 38; supports Parnell, 53, 56, 57, 66-69, 77, 97; divided into two branches, 77-78; divisions united, 120; object, 121; program of action, 121; Cohalan and the, 121-122; Redmond repudiated by, 157; Irish Volunteers aided by, 157-159; remittances to the I.R.B., 159*fn*.; seeks aid of Germany, 176, 177; sum sent to Casement by, 185*fn*.; members of, dominate committees of the Friends of Irish Freedom, 189; Easter Rebellion and, 191; blamed for attack on Wilson Administration, 212; Third Irish Race Convention, 298; De Valera's attempt to sidetrack the Clan, 364, 392; Boland's reorganization, plans for, 385
Clan-na-Gael and the Murder of Dr. Cronin, The (McEnnis), 78*fn*., 458
Clapp, Verner W., x
Clare County, Ireland, 21, 61, 253
Clarendon, Lord, 21, 35, 35*fn*., 36*fn*.
Clark, Champ, 217, 221

Clark, Sir George, 248
Clarke, Tom, 144, 158, 176, 457; Easter Rebellion and, 197, 199, 200
Cleburne, Patrick, 32
Clemenceau, Georges, 297, 315, 319, 320, 340
Cleveland, Grover, 111*fn*., 112, 452; fisheries controversy with Canada, 105-107; British support for re-election of, 107-111
Cleveland *News*, 453
Cleveland *Plain Dealer*, 204, 453
Cloghaneely Gaelic School, 173
Clontarf, Ireland, 12, 14, 16
Close, Mr., 317
Clune, Archbishop, 418
Cockerill, George, 418
Cockran, Bourke, 115, 117, 117*fn*., 119, 119*fn*., 120, 177, 178, 189*fn*., 307, 368, 374, 458; conscription issue in Ireland, 246; De Valera's Irish Bond Drive, 348, 348*fn*.; testimony before House Committee on Foreign Affairs, 356
Coercion Act, 82
Coghlan, Monsignor, 293
Cohalan, Bishop, 288-289
Cohalan, Daniel F., ix-x, 119, 119*fn*., 120, 125, 126, 126*fn*., 127*fn*., 135, 157, 177, 180, 181, 182, 185, 186, 214, 221, 223, 224, 229, 231, 232, 252, 270, 277-279, 280*fn*., 283, 284, 287, 288*fn*., 289, 293, 294, 295, 297*fn*., 314, 320, 320*fn*., 321*fn*., 328, 337, 338*fn*., 340, 341, 361, 382, 383, 384, 409, 415, 421-423, 442, 443, 444, 446; quarrel with De Valera, xii, 340-396, 422, 441, 447; biographical sketch, 121; Clan-na-Gael and, 121-122; Irish Race Convention, 188, 189; Friends of Irish Freedom and, 189, 298, 353; Easter Rebellion and, 193, 193*fn*., 194, 196; Wilson's dislike for, 194, 213, 265, 302; crusade against, 196; *Gaelic American* largely owned by, 212; efforts of Wilson Administration to discredit and ruin him, 234-237; Second Irish Race Convention, 272; Maloney's intrigue against, 279; regarded with suspicion by McGarrity, 279; Third Irish Race

Convention, 298-301; principle of self-determination favored by, 302, 326; sharply rebuffed by Wilson, 302; McCartan's campaign against, 303-306; opposition to League of Nations, 310-311, 326, 330, 331*fn*., 335, 343, 369-373; selection of members of the American Commission for Irish Independence, 320, 320*fn*.; Irish-American rallies addressed by (1919), 326-327, 330; compels Senate Foreign Relations Committee to hear presentation of Ireland's case, 330-333; Daniel T. O'Connell's opinion of, 332; Lodge's opinion of, 332; testimony before Senate Foreign Relations Committee, 333; disavowed by McCartan, Maloney, and De Valera, 338-339; Borah's tribute to, 338, 338*fn*.; Lodge's opinion of, 338*fn*.; De Valera's Irish Bond Drive, 347-348, 348*fn*., 352, 389; friendly gestures toward De Valera, 352-353, 365; pressure exerted upon Congress, 353-358, 369; hearings before House Committee on Foreign Affairs, 353-358; political realism of, 358*fn*.; St. Patrick's Day parade (1920), 365; Friendly Sons of Saint Patrick banquet, 365; Republican Convention (Chicago, 1920), 373-379, 403, 404; criticized by Boland, 390; congratulates De Valera for rejecting British terms, 421; supports Collins in fight against De Valera, 436-442; attitude toward the Anglo-Irish Treaty, 437, 440
Colby, Bainbridge, 405*fn*., 406, 412-414
Collier's, 454
Collins, Michael, 254, 269, 304, 340, 368, 384, 385, 397-398, 417, 418, 422-423, 432, 433, 434, 437-438; London Conference (1921), 427, 429; Cohalan and Devoy support him in fight against De Valera, 436-442; death of, 439
Collins, Patrick A., 53, 109
Colum, Padraic, 206*fn*.
Colvin, Ian, 141*fn*., 143, 143*fn*., 147*fn*., 456

Committee of One Hundred and Fifty, 409-410
Compensation for Disturbance Bill, 60
Complete Grammar of Anarchy, The (Horgan), 142, 149*fn*.
Conciliation Hall, 18
Condon, O'Meagher, 39
Congested Districts Board, 87
Congo, *see* Belgian Congo
Congress, U.S., and the Fenians, 36, 37; Parnell and, 47, 57; fisheries controversy with Canada, 106-107; Arbitration Treaty, 112-113; World War I and, 216-217, 218; Congressional pressure relative to Irish self-determination arouses anxiety of Wilson, 306-308, 403; sentiment against League of Nations in, 309, 323-326, 331, 342, 369-372; Cohalan compels Senate Foreign Relations Committee to hear presentation of Ireland's case, 330-333; vote on the Versailles Treaty, 337; opposition to De Valera's appearance before, 344; pressure exerted upon, by Cohalan, 353-358
Congressional Record, 47*fn*., 48*fn*., 57*fn*., 106*fn*., 107*fn*., 116*fn*., 210*fn*., 216*fn*., 218*fn*., 308*fn*., 313*fn*., 317*fn*., 324*fn*., 329*fn*., 333*fn*., 357*fn*., 372*fn*., 452
Conley, Colonel, 189
Connally, Tom, 354-355, 381
Connemara, 74
Connolly, James, 197, 199
Conscription issue, in Ireland, 243-248, 255, 267, 285-286
Constantinople, Russia's desire to control, 152
Consular Despatches, 34*fn*.
Consumers' Co-operative Society, 129
Contemporary Ireland (Dubois), 74*fn*.
Contemporary Review, 454
Conyngham, D. P., 49*fn*.
Coolidge, L. A., 370*fn*.
Cooper Union (New York City), 54, 83
Co-operative movement, 129
Cork, Ireland, 5, 61, 102, 103, 136, 214*fn*., 400, 406, 408, 408*fn*., 410, 414

Index

Cork County, Ireland, 121, 248
Cork *Examiner,* 289*fn.,* 290*fn.,* 454
Corkery, Daniel, 4*fn.,* 456
Corn Law, Foster's (1784), 7
Corn Laws, repeal of (1846), 48
Cosgrave, William, 233, 253; arrested without charges or trial, 256
Costanzo, Joseph, xi
Costigan, Giovanni, 171*fn.,* 174*fn.,* 456
Cotton-goods industry, Irish, 7, 9
Council of Three Hundred, 133
County Clare Association of California, 218
Covenanters, 142
Cox, Samuel Sullivan, 57
Coyne, Martin, 237
Craig, Captain, 151
Craig, Sir James, 419
Craigavon, Ireland, 141
Crawford, Fred, 143
Crawford, Lindsay, 368, 390
Creevy Papers, The (Maxwell), 7*fn.,* 455
Creggs, Ireland, 99
Crewe, Lord, 104*fn.,* 150, 456
Crime and Outrage Acts, 26
Crimes Act (1882), 71
Crimmins, John D., 227, 228*fn.*
Crisis in Ireland (O'Grady), 64*fn.,* 458
Croke, Archbishop, 65, 73
Croly, Herbert, 323, 323*fn.*
Cronin, P. H., 78, 78*fn.*
Crooks, Will, 157
Crosbie, George, 136
Crowe, Robert, 376
Crozier, Frank P., 418*fn.,* 455
Cuba, 359-360, 361*fn.,* 362
"Cuba Five," The, 40
Cullen, Cardinal, 26, 31, 41; Fenians opposed by, 31
Cullinane, Father, 384
Cumann na nGaedheal, 131-133
Cummings, Homer, 380*fn.,* 381, 381*fn.*
Cummings, Matthew, 277, 440*fn.*
Cunard Steamship Company, 175
Curley, John, 277
Curley, Archbishop Michael J., 440
Curragh, The, 147
Curraghane, Ireland, 187

Curry, Charles E., 178*fn.,* 179*fn.,* 180*fn.,* 182*fn.,* 186*fn.,* 455
Cuxhaven, Germany, 259

Dail Eireann, 303, 304, 384, 390, 399*fn.,* 400, 419, 420, 421; first meeting, 296; delegates to Paris Peace Conference, 296-297; Borah resolution praised by, 329*fn.;* British proclamation suppressing the, 349, 399; Lynch resigns his seat in the, 386; follows dictates of De Valera, 388-389; Anglo-Irish Treaty, 432-435
Daley, John M., x
Dallas *News,* 203, 453
Dalton, Richard F., 188, 232, 287, 287*fn.,* 293, 409; De Valera's Irish Bond Drive, 348
Danton, Georges, 7
D'Arcy, William, 27*fn.,* 31*fn.,* 32*fn.,* 40*fn.,* 41*fn.,* 456
David J. Adams (fishing vessel), 105
Davis, Rev. H., 201*fn.*
Davis, J. C. Bancroft, 47, 47*fn.,* 82, 452
Davis, John W., 314, 314*fn.,* 340*fn.,* 408*fn.*
Davis, Norman H., 406, 410-411, 412, 413*fn.*
Davis, Thomas, 15, 17, 28, 30
Davitt, Michael, 55*fn.,* 56*fn.,* 62*fn.,* 63*fn.,* 64, 66, 69, 70*fn.,* 93, 103, 456; Land League conceived by, 51, 53, 54, 55, 66; arrested, 55; released, 56, 70; quoted on the Kilmainham Treaty, 70; Alexander Sullivan defended by, 78
Deak, Francis, 132, 133
Deasy, William, 38
Defence of the Realm Act, 257
"Deirdre of the Sorrows" (Synge), 126
Delagoa Bay, 114, 115, 170
Delamater and Company, 80
Denieffe, Joseph, 27*fn.,* 455
Dennett, Tyler, 113, 456
Derby, Lord, 419
Derry, Ireland, 142*fn.,* 150, 400; shirt-making in, 9
Derry County, Ireland, 141, 142*fn.,* 150

Des Moines *Register and Leader*, 453
Despatches, Correspondence and Memoranda of Field Marshal Arthur, Duke of Wellington, 19fn., 455
Detroit *Free Press*, 262, 453
Detroit *News*, 453
De Valera, Eamon, ix, 140, 228, 233, 293, 295, 301fn., 303, 449; quarrel with Cohalan, x, 340-396, 422, 441; Easter Rebellion and, 202; speech at Mansion House, Dublin, 241; criticism of the Lloyd George Convention, 241fn.; conscription issue in Ireland, 246; wins election in County Clare, 252-253; attitude toward secret operations of the I.R.B., 253; President of Sinn Fein, 254; elected President, Irish Volunteers, 254; arrested without charges or trial, 256, 260; lie about activities of, 259; appointment as delegate to Paris Peace Conference, 296-297, 312, 313, 315; challenges England to allow Ireland the principle of free self-determination, 301-302; attempt to discredit Cohalan, 338-339; visit to America, 340-396, 426, 441; League of Nations and, 340-342, 359; escape from Lincoln Prison, 340; Irish Bond Drive, 347-353, 364, 389, 395; gets funds from Friends of Irish Freedom, 350-351; tendency to engage in double talk, 351-352, 359; Cohalan's friendly gestures toward, 352-353, 365; hearings before House Committee on Foreign Affairs, 356-358, 358fn.; remarks concerning the Monroe Doctrine and the Platt Amendment, 359-360, 383; *Westminster Gazette* interview, 359-361, 383; carefully watched by office of U.S. Attorney General, 359fn.; Devoy's attack on, 361-362; attempt to sidetrack Irish-American organizations, 364, 383-396; smear campaign against Devoy, 364, 369, 385; quarrel with Devoy, 364-365, 365fn., 447, 384-396, 422; Devoy quoted on, 364, 382-383, 423, 435; St. Patrick's Day parade (1920), 365; Friendly Sons of Saint Patrick banquet, 365; Republican convention (Chicago, 1920), 373-379, 382-383, 403-404, 441; Democratic convention (San Francisco, 1920), 380-383; Friends of Irish Freedom discredited by, 383, 384, 446; McCartan sent to Ireland by, 383-384; Boland sent to Dublin by, 384-385; attack on Diarmuid Lynch, 385-386; fight for control of Friends of Irish Freedom, 386-396; Dail Eireann follows dictates of, 388-389; Association for the Recognition of the Irish Republic launched by, 393-394; truce with British leaders, 419; conference with Lloyd George, 419-420; rejects British terms, 420-421; London Conference (1921), 426-435; Anglo-Irish Treaty rejected by, 432-435; Cohalan and Devoy support Collins in fight against, 436-442

De Valera and the March of a Nation (Bromage), 368fn., 456
Devereux, Denis, 130
Devlin, Joseph, 137, 158, 165; conscription issue in Ireland, 246
Devoy, John, x, 30fn., 31fn., 33fn., 38fn., 40, 52fn., 53fn., 55fn., 66, 67, 68, 68fn., 69, 97, 120, 121, 122, 126fn., 130fn., 135, 137fn., 158, 158fn., 159, 159fn., 176fn., 177, 177fn., 178fn., 182, 184fn., 185, 185fn., 187, 188, 190fn., 191fn., 193fn., 196, 196fn., 199, 224, 229, 235, 237, 238, 252, 278fn., 293, 295, 319, 340, 349, 350, 351, 363, 368, 369, 378fn., 379, 384, 385, 386, 409, 421-422, 442, 455; hostility towards the Fenians, 40; Land League conceived by, 51, 53, 54, 55; opinion of Alexander Sullivan, 77-78; attitude toward the Gaelic League, 125-126; Synge criticized by, 126-127; *United Irishman* assisted by, 130; Irish Volunteer Fund, 159fn.; Casement's visit with, in New York City, 176; attends Philadelphia "demonstration" of protest against Bachelor's Walk incident, 176; Irish Race Convention, 188, 221; Easter Rebellion and,

Index

191, 192, 198; *Gaelic American* edited by, 212; Wilson criticized by, 212-213; Shane Leslie criticized by, 222-223; a convinced separatist, 224; expresses contempt for Wilson Administration, 239; Wilson Administration's drive against, 239-240, 270; methods and procedures of Secret Service agents criticized by, 251-252; Second Irish Race Convention, 271; importance of self-determination for Ireland emphasized by, 281, 300; Third Irish Race Convention, 298, 300; attack on De Valera, 361-362; quoted on De Valera, 364, 382-383, 423, 435; De Valera's smear campaign against, 364, 369, 385; quarrel with De Valera, 364-365, 365fn., 384-396, 422; attitude toward Mellows, 386fn.; supports De Valera in rejecting British terms, 420; supports Collins in fight against De Valera, 436-442; attitude toward the Anglo-Irish Treaty, 437

Devoy's Post Bag, 1871-1928, 53fn., 66fn., 67fn., 68fn., 69fn., 70fn., 78fn., 97fn., 98, 130fn., 157fn., 158fn., 159, 185fn., 188fn., 241fn., 455

Dictionary of Statistics (Mulhall), 19fn.

Dilke, Sir Charles W., 86fn., 88

Dillon, John Blake, 15, 28, 94, 95, 97, 98, 99, 103, 104, 151, 165, 248, 255, 262, 284, 293; loses faith in Liberal leadership, 162; conscription issue in Ireland, 246

Diplomatic History of the American People, A (Bailey), 107fn., 456

Disarmament Conference (Washington, 1921), 420-426, 436

Disarmament in British Foreign Policy (Chaput), 424fn.

Documents Relative to the Sinn Fein Movement, 180fn., 181fn., 192fn., 193fn., 199fn., 202

Doheny, Edward L., 381, 436

Doheny, Michael, 26; joins the Fenians, 28

Dolan, C. J., 134

Donegal, Ireland, 173

Donohoe, Michael, 299
Donoughmore, Lord, 6
Dowling, Joseph, 256
Dowling, Mrs. William A., x
Down County, Ireland, 141, 142fn., 150
Downing, Rossa F., 366
Doyle, Bishop, 11
Doyle, Michael Francis, 204-205, 207, 208-209, 209fn.
Driscoll, Pat, 187
Drummond, Victor, 80, 80fn., 81fn.
Dublin, Ireland, 9, 27, 31, 34, 45, 53, 53fn., 56, 65, 70, 72, 75, 87, 100, 103, 124, 125, 126, 127, 134, 140, 144, 161, 169, 173, 400; Archbishop of, 64; Easter Rebellion in, 198, 199, 202, 218; terrorism in, 402
Dublin County, Ireland, 199
Dublin Evening Mail, 14, 50fn., 60, 60fn., 454
Dubois, Paul, 74fn.
Duffy, Charles Gavan, 15, 15fn., 16fn., 17, 18fn., 20, 23, 25, 26, 26fn., 28, 123fn., 208, 427, 455, 456; breaks with O'Connell on question of federalism, 16; arrested, 16, 24; imprisonment, 16; released, 24
Duffy, Edward, arrested, 33
Duffy, George Gavan, 417fn.; London Conference (1921), 427, 430
Duggan, Eamon, 207, 417fn.; London Conference (1921), 427, 430
Dumont, F. T. F., 400fn., 404, 405fn., 407, 408fn., 409fn.
Dundalk, Ireland, 243
Dundas, 6-7
Dungannon Clubs, 133
Dunne, Edward F., 391; as member of American Commission for Irish Independence, 312-314, 318-319; background, 313fn.; testimony before Senate Foreign Relations Committee, 333
Dunsany, Ireland, 129
DuVal, Miles, xi

East Kilkenny, Ireland, 233
Easter Rebellion, 190-214, 218, 222, 223, 228, 252, 253, 256, 259, 266; background of the, 190-196, 289; Irish reaction to, 200-202; Amer-

ican reaction to, 202-204; leaders sentenced to be shot, 202, 204
Economic History of Ireland in the Eighteenth Century (O'Brien), 5fn., 458
Economic Inquiries and Studies (Giffen), 48fn., 457
Economic situation, in Ireland, 4-5; following the Act of Union (1800), 9-10, 25, 28
Edinburgh Review, 9fn., 10fn.
Education, in Ireland, 3
Egan, Maurice Francis, 244, 244fn.
Egan, Patrick, 63, 67, 443
Egypt, 170
Elder Dempster Shipping Company, 169
Emmet, Robert T., 121, 226
Emmet, Thomas Addis, 232
Emporia Gazette, 453
Encumbered Estates Act (1849), 25, 28
Endicott, William C., 109fn.
Engels, Friedrich, 25
England, *see* Great Britain
English Wife in Berlin, An (Blücher), 185fn., 454
Ennis, Ireland, 61
Enniscorthy, Ireland, 199
Erne, Lord, 62
Errington, George, 73, 74
Ervine, St. John, 42
Evening Mail, 60fn., 64fn., 66
Eversley, Lord, 72fn., 456
Evidence on Conditions in Ireland (American Commission on Conditions in Ireland), 410fn., 453
Exports, Irish, 10, 19, 20

Fall, Albert B., 325
Fall of Feudalism in Ireland, The (Davitt), 55fn., 56fn., 62fn., 63fn., 70fn., 456
Famine, in Ireland, 10, 14, 18-22, 25, 50; *See also* Starvation, in Ireland
Famous Trials of History (Birkenhead), 175fn., 456
Faneuil Hall (Boston), 119, 327
Fanny, The (boat), 143
Fay, Sidney B., 152, 152fn., 448
Fay, Rev. Sigourney W., 222-223, 226, 456

Fenian Movement in the United States, The (D'Arcy), 27fn., 31fn., 32fn., 40fn., 41fn., 456
Fenians, x, 25, 27, 29, 42, 52, 55, 66, 79, 114, 130, 176, 420; program, 29; ritualism of the, 29; hatred for A. M. Sullivan, 30; Catholic Church opposes, 30-32, 34, 39, 41; American Civil War and the, 32; in armed forces of England, 33; in prison in Ireland and England, 33, 34, 35, 36, 37, 40, 81-83; invasion of Canada, 33, 34, 35-36, 37-38, 40, 41, 114; activities of, threaten to cause a crisis in Anglo-American relations, 34-38; U.S. Congress and, 36, 37; in Canadian prisons, 36, 37; Manchester incident, 38-39; Papal decree condemning, 39-40, 41; Devoy's hostility towards, 40; divisions within their ranks, 41; disbanded, 41; Parnell and the, 43-46, 52, 76; alleged plots against England, 80, 81; Drummond's attitude toward, 81; Sackville-West and the, 81
Fenit, Ireland, 191, 192
Fenit Bay, 198
Fenlon, Rev. John F., 298, 299fn.
Fenway Park (Boston), 342
Feonin Erin, 27fn.
Ferguson, John H., 114fn.
Fermanagh County, Ireland, 141, 150, 400
Fermoy, Ireland, 398
Fifty Years of British Parliament (Lord Oxford), 138fn.
Figgis, Darrell, arrested without charges or trial, 256
Findlay, de C., 179-183, 186
Finerty, John F., 115fn.
Fish, Hamilton, 47
Fitzgerald, Dr., 97
Fitzgerald, Desmond, 228
Fitzgerald, John F., 226
Fitzgerald, John J., 246
Fitzmaurice, G. H., 247
Fitzpatrick, Mr., 166
Flannery, Father Edward, 212, 212fn.
Fleming, Denna F., 324fn., 456
Flood, Henry D., 216, 217, 307, 308, 355-357
Flynn, William J., 194, 195, 195fn.

Index

Ford, Austin, 390
Ford, Robert, 293
Foreign Policy of Thomas F. Bayard, The (Tansill), 75*fn.*, 108*fn.*, 459
Foreign Relations, 82*fn.*, 83*fn.*
Forged Casement Diaries, The (Maloney), 173*fn.*, 174*fn.*, 175*fn.*, 207*fn.*, 214*fn.*, 457
Forster, W. E., 66; attack on Parnell, 72-73
Fort Erie, Canada, 35
40 O. B. or How the War Was Won (Hoy), 457
Foster, John W., 118*fn.*, 457
Foster's Corn Law (1784), 7
France, World War I and, 150, 153, 216
Franklin, Vermont, 38
Franz Ferdinand, Archduke, 149
Freeman, The, 16
Freeman's Journal, 45, 60, 62, 65, 99, 99*fn.*, 102, 200, 241*fn.*, 255*fn.*, 454
Frelinghuysen, F. T., 82, 82*fn.*, 83, 83*fn.*, 84
Frelinghuysen, Senator, 336
French, Field-Marshal Lord, 255, 256, 260
French Revolution, 6, 7, 10
Friendly Sons of Saint Patrick, 365
Friends of Ireland in America, 378*fn.*, 391*fn.*, 404*fn.*
Friends of Irish Freedom, 189, 228, 233-234, 237, 270, 276, 277, 293, 297, 308*fn.*, 343, 346*fn.*, 349, 350, 351, 353, 366, 378*fn.*, 395*fn.*, 409, 421; opposes American intervention in World War I, 220; officers elected (1918), 271; Third Irish Race Convention, 298; misstatement of McCartan dealing with, 304; League of Nations opposed by, 326, 332, 332*fn.*, 335, 347; Victory Fund drive, 332, 344-347, 364, 395; Advertising Committee, 336; smeared by McCartan and Maloney, 338; funds used by De Valera, 350-351; De Valera's attempt to sidetrack, 364, 446; supports Hiram Johnson for President, 373; Republican Convention (Chicago, 1920), 374, 375, 377, 378, 379; Democratic convention (San Francisco, 1920), 380; discredited by De Valera, 383, 384; fight for control of, 386-396; membership statistics, 395*fn.*; relief funds, 415-416; supports De Valera in rejecting British terms, 420; attitude toward the Anglo-Irish Treaty, 436
Froude, James, 86

Gaelic American, 68, 78*fn.*, 126, 158, 212, 213, 221, 222*fn.*, 238, 238*fn.*, 239, 252*fn.*, 271*fn.*, 280*fn.*, 295, 295*fn.*, 319*fn.*, 349, 355*fn.*, 361, 362, 362*fn.*, 363, 385, 386, 386*fn.*, 388, 392*fn.*, 446; supports Hiram Johnson for President, 373
Gaelic League, 123-126, 127, 134, 144, 197; praised by Casement, 173
Gaffney, T. St. John, 185, 188, 189*fn.*, 455; appointed European representative of the Friends of Irish Freedom, 189
Gallagher, Edward J., 167
Gallagher, Bishop Michael J., 377, 378, 379, 391*fn.*, 394, 404, 404*fn.*; as President, Friends of Irish Freedom, 387, 421; member of American Committee for Relief in Ireland, 414-415; supports De Valera in rejecting British terms, 420; attitude toward the Anglo-Irish Treaty, 436-437
Gallagher, Thomas, 221, 287, 306
Galway County, Ireland, 21, 59, 199, 256, 314
Galway County Council, 419
Gardiner, A. G., 94*fn.*
Garfield, James, 79
Garvin, J. L., 86*fn.*, 457
Gathorne-Hardy, Mr., 45
Gavegan, Edward J., 278, 280*fn.*, 293
Geneva Red Cross Society, 115
George, Henry, 83
George Washington (steamer), 282
Georgetown University, x, xi; library, x, 324*fn.*
German Club (New York City), 176
Germany, World War I and, 152, 165, 166, 174, 175, 176, 178, 216; Casement seeks aid of, 174, 176, 177, 190; Clan-na-Gael seeks aid of, 176, 177; Casement's mission to, 178-

186, 189, 190; official attitude towards Ireland, 180-181; Casement's attempt to raise an Irish Brigade from prisoners in German prison camps, 184-186; Easter Rebellion and, 190-199; alleged "German Plot" (May, 1918), 256-270
Gerry, Peter G., 309, 310fn., 372
Gibbons, Cardinal, 227, 298-301, 409, 414
Gibbons, T. A., 50fn.
Giffen, Sir Robert, 48fn., 457
Gillespie, George J., 277
Gladstone, William E., 51, 63, 90, 92, 93, 94fn., 95, 96, 97, 458; Compensation for Disturbance Bill, 60; Irish Land Act (1881), 63-64; Land League denounced by, 64; defied by Parnell, 64-65; Parnell's offer to resign seat in House of Commons, 71; pursues policy of coercion and conciliation, 71-74; Arrears Bill, 72; Irish Home Rule and, 84-88, 93, 94, 97, 104; criticized by Salisbury, 89; Parnell's criticism of, 97
Gladstone and Ireland (Eversley), 72fn., 456
Gladstone and the Irish Nation (Hammond), 71fn., 75fn., 85fn., 86fn., 88fn., 89fn., 93fn., 94fn.
Glasgow, Scotland, 138
Glasnevin Cemetery, 31, 58
Glass, Carter, 380
Gleason, John H., 35
Gleason, Joseph, 35
God Save the King, 157
Goddard, Mr., 62
Godkin, Lawrence, 226
Goebel, Julius, 356fn.
Goff, John W., 189, 221, 232, 278, 279, 280fn., 281, 293, 299, 302, 303fn., 305, 368; Second Irish Race Convention, 271, 272; De Valera's Irish Bond Drive, 348
Gonne, Maude, 124
Gough, Brigadier General, 147
Grace, John P., 367-368, 368fn., 376, 391, 409
Grace, Right Reverend Thomas, 277
Grain trade, Irish, 10
Grant, Ulysses S., 48; Parnell rebuffed by, 46, 47

Granville, Lord, 73, 79, 79fn., 80fn., 81, 81fn., 82, 82fn., 83, 83fn., 84
Grattan, Henry, 65, 130; parliament and, 6, 8, 9; pro-British, 7; little sympathy for Tone's policies, 8
Gray, George, 112fn.
Gray, Sir John, 16
Great Britain, imperialism, 3-5, 18, 119; mercantilism, 5, 6, 7; economic recession in, 48-49; Arbitration Treaty, 112-113; Boer War, 113-120; Irish-Americans protest against British brutality in Ireland, 218-220; regards growing strength of Sinn Fein with apprehension, 252-256; Anglo-Japanese Alliance abandoned by, 425; Anglo-Irish Treaty (1921), 426-436
Green, Mrs. J. R., 172
Greenwood, Sir Hamar, 409, 428
Gregory, Lady, 124
Grenfell, Russell, 150fn., 457
Grew, Joseph C., 318, 318fn.
Grey, Sir Edward, 150, 150fn., 182, 183, 187, 194, 208, 210-211, 215, 217, 225, 455; Casement's opinion of, 171
Griffith, Arthur, 130-134, 173, 340, 343, 352, 399, 400fn., 417fn., 418, 419, 422, 433, 434, 457; challenges leadership of Redmond, 164-165; quoted on World War I, 165; denounced by Redmond, 165; arrested without charges or trial, 256; appointment as delegate to Paris Peace Conference, 296-297, 312, 313, 315; League of Nations issue, 340-341; as Acting President, Republic of Ireland, 406; London Conference (1921), 426-427, 430
Guedalla, Philip, 3
Gourteen, Ireland, 55
Gwynn, Denis, 12fn., 24fn., 140fn., 141fn., 146fn., 151fn., 152fn., 153fn., 154fn., 155fn., 161, 161fn., 163, 163fn., 166fn., 167fn., 171fn., 172fn., 173fn., 175fn., 176fn., 178fn., 184, 185fn., 187fn., 201fn., 207fn., 225fn., 231fn., 233fn., 248, 429fn., 432fn., 433fn., 457
Gwynn, Stephen, 86fn., 154, 160fn., 194fn., 455, 457

Index

Habeas corpus, writ of, suspended by English Government, 33, 34, 63
Hall, Admiral, 265, 266
Hally, Judge, 387
Hamburg, Germany, 143, 148, 175
Hamburg-Amerika Line, 175
Hamer, Philip, x
Hammond, John L., 71, 75*fn.*, 85*fn.*, 86*fn.*, 88*fn.*, 89*fn.*, 93*fn.*, 94*fn.*
Hand, Federal Judge, 239
Hanna, Archbishop Edward J., 277
Hansard's Debates, 156*fn.*, 157*fn.*
Harcourt, Lewis, 71, 72, 94, 94*fn.*, 95
Harding Administration, 424
Harold-Berry, Philip, 248, 248*fn.*
Harrington, Tim, 98
Harrison, Henry, 92*fn.*, 457
Harrison, Leland, 262, 266*fn.*, 285*fn.*, 286*fn.*
Hart, John W., 308, 309, 309*fn.*
Hart, Michael, 82
Hartington, Lord, 63, 72, 86
Harvey, Ambassador, 425
Haslip, Joan, 65*fn.*, 69*fn.*, 74*fn.*, 95*fn.*, 457
Hathaway, C. M., 263, 263*fn.*, 269*fn.*
Hawarden, 91
Hay, Adelbert, 115, 115*fn.*
Hay, John, 113, 113*fn.*, 115, 115*fn.*, 116, 116*fn.*, 117, 117*fn.*, 118, 118*fn.*, 119, 371, 452, 456
Hayden, John, 153
Hayes, Cardinal, 278*fn.*
Haynes, E. S. P., 207*fn.*, 457
Hazelton, Richard, 137, 264, 265*fn.*
Healy, Maurice, 136
Healy, Reverend Patrick J., 384
Healy, Timothy, 94, 98, 99, 99*fn.*, 103, 103*fn.*, 104, 136, 455, 457; conscription issue in Ireland, 246
Heffernan, John, xi
Hendrick, Burton J., 211*fn.*, 457
Hennessy, Michael E., 338*fn.*
Henry, Mitchell, 50
Herbert, Victor, 189, 232, 333*fn.*
Hewart, Sir Gordon, 428
Hibernians, Ancient Order of, 115, 237, 297*fn.*
Hicks-Beach, Sir Michael, 43
Hidden Ireland, The (Corkery), 4*fn.*, 456
History of Ireland (Keating), 27*fn.*

History of Ireland, 1798-1924 (O'Connor), 51*fn.*, 458
History of Ireland Under the Union, 1801-1922 (O'Hegarty), 6*fn.*, 9*fn.*, 12*fn.*, 13*fn.*, 14*fn.*, 17*fn.*, 20*fn.*, 21*fn.*, 23*fn.*, 24*fn.*, 26*fn.*, 30*fn.*, 32*fn.*, 43*fn.*, 124*fn.*, 129*fn.*, 130*fn.*, 131*fn.*, 133*fn.*, 134*fn.*, 145*fn.*, 160*fn.*, 163*fn.*, 165*fn.*, 197*fn.*, 198*fn.*, 401*fn.*, 458
History of Land Tenure in Ireland (Montgomery), 49*fn.*, 458
History of Modern England, A (Paul), 61*fn.*, 458
History of the Great Irish Famine of 1847 (O'Rourke), 22*fn.*, 458
History of the Irish Parliamentary Party, 51*fn.*
History of the Irish Volunteers (Hobson), 148*fn.*, 457
History of the Presidency from 1788 to 1916 (Stanwood), 120*fn.*, 459
Hitchcock, Gilbert M., 370, 452
Hoar, George F., 120
Hobson, Bulmer, 144, 148*fn.*, 157*fn.*, 158*fn.*, 159, 197, 457; as General Secretary and Quartermaster of the Irish Volunteers, 158; writes pamphlet to discourage Irishmen from enlisting in British Army, 172; correspondence with Casement, 173
Hoffman House, 119
"Hold the Harvest" (Parnell), 61-62
Holland, Amy, xi
Holman, Congressman, 47
Holmes, Rev. John Haynes, 409
Hone, Joseph M., 124*fn.*, 127*fn.*, 457
Hoover, Herbert, 373
Hopkins, Gerard Manley, 88
Home Rulers, 52, 53, 85, 131, 142*fn.*; *See also* Irish Home Rule League
Horgan, John J., 125, 125*fn.*, 137*fn.*, 142, 149*fn.*, 201, 457
Horigan, James B., x-xi
Horridge, Mr. Justice, 204
Houghton, W. H., 195
House, Colonel Edward M., 212*fn.*, 215, 216, 217, 227*fn.*, 235, 245, 246*fn.*, 247, 247*fn.*, 313-317, 318*fn.*, 405, 452, 455
House Committee on Foreign Affairs; hearings on bill to provide salaries

for a minister and consuls to Ireland, 353-358

House of Commons, O'Connell favors pressure in, 20; Parnell and the, 43-44; Easter Rebellion and, 201; conscription in Ireland enacted by, 255; motion in favor of self-determination for Ireland introduced in, 289-290; "Better Government of Ireland Bill," 399; Irish Free State Agreement, 428

House of Lords, destruction of veto power in, 137-138

House-Grey Agreement, 216, 217

Howe, Frederic C., 410

Howth, Ireland, 148, 155, 175-176

Hoy, Hugh C., 457

Hughes, Archbishop, 26, 27; Mass for McManus, 31

Hughes, Charles E., 425

Humphreys, Travers, 204

Hungary, 132

Hurton, Thomas J., 272, 273, 293, 346

Huxley, 86

Hyde, Douglas, 122-123, 123*fn.*, 124, 125, 127

Hyde Park, 208*fn.*

Immigration Act (U.S., 1917), 413

Imperialism, British, 3-5, 18, 119; American, 119

Indianapolis *News*, 453

Indianapolis *Star*, 453

Industrial Development Societies, 128

Industries, Irish, nationalism and, 127-128

Inishtooskert Island, 192

International Law, a Treatise (Oppenheim), 118*fn.*

Intimate Diary of the Peace Conference and After, 1911-1923 (Riddell), 255*fn.*

"Invincibles," 71

Ireland (periodical), 221

Ireland Forever (Crozier), 418*fn.*, 455

Ireland of Today (Sullivan), 49*fn.*, 55*fn.*, 459

Ireland, Past and Present (Conyngham), 49*fn*.

Ireland Under the Land League (Lloyd), 61, 66*fn.*, 457

Ireland's Literary Renaissance (Boyd), 122*fn.*, 456

Irish Affairs, 156*fn.*, 157*fn.*

Irish Agricultural Organization Society, 129

Irish Bulletin, 400*fn.*

Irish Citizen Army, 197, 199

Irish Citizens of America, 108

Irish Confederation, 23, 24

Irish Constituent Assembly, 293

Irish Distress and Its Remedies (Clancy), 50*fn.*

Irish Federalism (Butt), 42, 456

Irish Free State, 8, 437

Irish Free State Agreement, 428

Irish Freedom, 165

Irish Home Rule League, 41; See also Home Rulers

Irish Independent, 178, 186*fn.*, 201, 454

Irish Issue in its American Aspect, The (Leslie), 224*fn.*, 227*fn.*, 457

Irish Land Act (1881), 63-64

Irish Land and Irish Landlords, The (Gibbons), 50*fn.*

Irish Land Laws, The (Richey), 49*fn.*, 458

Irish Land League Crisis, The (Palmer), 51*fn.*, 62*fn.*, 458

Irish Literary Theatre, 124, 125

Irish National Land League, Parnell and the, 51-58, 61, 63, 67, 72, 89; founded, 55; objectives, 55; appeal for support of its program, 59; Irish elections and the, 59-60; rallying cry, 61; proceedings instituted against leaders, 63; denounced by Gladstone, 64; leaders arrested, 65; suppressed, 66

Irish National League, 72, 94

Irish Nationalism and British Democracy (Strauss), 5*fn.*, 8*fn.*, 25*fn.*, 29*fn.*, 459

Irish Parliament, 3, 72, 85; Catholics denied right to serve in, 6, 11

Irish Parliamentary Party, 1890-1910 (Lyons), 102*fn.*, 457

Irish People (periodical), 29-30, 32, 33

Irish Press, 279, 342, 343, 383, 436*fn.*

Irish Press Agency, 96

Irish Progressive League, 295

Index

Irish Question, The (King), 50fn., 66fn., 457
Irish Race Convention, 188-190, 221; Declaration of Principles and Policy, 189-190; Second, 252fn., 270-274, 274fn.; Third, 296-302, 312, 345
Irish rebellion (1798), 8
Irish Republic, The (Macardle), 158fn., 247fn., 253fn., 254fn., 255fn., 285fn., 296fn., 297fn., 319fn., 401fn., 403fn., 429fn., 457
Irish Republican Army, 402-403, 408, 419
Irish Republican Brotherhood, 11, 25, 53, 78, 130, 134, 392-393; founding of, 22, 25; Manchester incident, 38
Irish Review, 175
Irish Revolution (1916), 8, 134-135, 137, 167-168
Irish Revolution, The (McCarthy), 61fn., 458
Irish Revolutionary Brotherhood, 27, 384, 385
Irish Self-determination League of Great Britain, 301fn.
Irish Times, 103fn., 200, 243, 454
Irish Trade Mark Association, 128
Irish Volunteers, 144-145, 147-148, 155, 184, 402, 408; creation, 144; object, 145; slogan, 145; John Redmond and the, 145, 147-148, 158, 159-164; aided by the Clan-na-Gael, 157-159; sources of funds, 159fn.; attitude of Irish-Americans toward, 166; Easter Rebellion and, 197, 199; De Valera elected President, 254; officers, 254
Irish White Cross, 415
Irish World, The, 38fn., 45fn., 54fn., 78, 83, 159fn., 171, 188, 389-390; supports Hiram Johnson for President, 373
"Irishmen's Civil and Military Republican Union," 27

Jameson, Dr., 111
Jenks, Leland H., 48fn., 457
Jephson, Annie, 169
Johnson, Andrew, 36, 37
Johnson, Claudius, 325fn., 457
Johnson, Hiram W., 325, 337, 369, 372; support for Presidential nomination, 373, 383
Jones, Artemus, 204
Jones, Francis P., 355fn.
Journals, Conversations and Essays Relating to Ireland (Senior), 21fn., 455
Jowett, Benjamin, 86
Joyce, Robert Dwyer, 53

Kansas City, Missouri, Democratic National Convention (1900), 120
Kansas City Star, 453
Keating, Frederick W., 275-276
Keating, Geoffrey, 27fn.
Keating, John T., 238
Keith, Arthur B., 170fn., 457
Kellogg, Senator, 370
Kells, Ireland, 19
Kelly, Thomas Hughes, 348
Kelly, Thomas J., 38
Kendrick, John B., 309, 310fn.
Kenmare, Ireland, 31
Kenmare, Lord, 51
Kennedy, Congressman (R. I.), 357
Kenny, John, 176
Kenyon, Father, 31
Keogh, Judge and Mrs., 126
Kerekes, Tibor, xi
Kern, Senator, 216, 217
Kerry County, Ireland, 60, 187, 198, 199
Kerry Pike, 405
Kettle, Tom, 137
Kickham, Charles J., 30, 30fn., 53, 54; arrested, 33
Kilcawley, W. P., 237
Kilkenny city, Ireland, 253
Kilkenny County, Ireland, 29
Killarney, Ireland, 180fn.
Killeen, J. B., 55
Kilmainham Jail, 65, 66, 69, 70
Kilmainham Treaty, 69-70
Kinchassa, Congo, 170
King, Dr., 169
King, David B., 50fn., 66fn., 457
King Cotton Diplomacy (Owsley), 32fn.
King's Country, 21
Kitchener, Lord, 155, 161, 162, 164
Knights of St. Patrick (San Francisco), 219

Knox, Philander C., 326
Kossuth, Louis, 132
Krauskopf, Rabbi, 301
Krebs, Franz H., 209, 210, 210fn.
Kruger, Stephanus J. P., 111, 116, 118
Kubek, Anthony, xi

Lacy, Lawrence de, 199
Ladies' Land League, 70
LaFollette, Robert M., 409
Lage, William P., 234fn.
Lalor, James Fintan, 51-52
Lamont, Colonel, 108, 109
Land Acts, 49, 63, 72, 87, 128-129, 136
Land League, *see* Irish National Land League
Land League Manual (Clancy), 50, 51fn.
Land War in Ireland (Blunt), 93fn.
Lansdowne, Lord, 60, 151; instructs Casement to make survey of Congo basin, 170
Lansing, Robert, 196, 207, 207fn., 210fn., 211-212, 212fn., 227fn., 230fn., 231fn., 234, 239, 240, 242fn., 251, 264, 264fn., 265, 265fn., 266, 266fn., 267, 267fn., 291, 294, 294fn., 307, 307fn., 308, 308fn., 315, 317, 317fn., 318fn., 319fn.; attempt to discredit and ruin Cohalan, 234-237; misgivings about publication of seized Sinn Fein documents, 266; allusions to Wilson's fondness for glittering generalities, 282; McCarthy's suggestion that American Army recruit troops in Ireland, 286, 286fn.
Larkin, Michael, 39
Larne, Ireland, 143, 145, 148, 149, 155
Last Changes, Last Chances (Nevinson), 207fn.
Last Conquest of Ireland, The (Mitchel), 19fn., 21fn., 23fn., 458
Last Serjeant, The (Sullivan), 459
Laughlin, Irwin, 210-211, 267, 268fn., 269fn.
Lavery, Sir John, 455
Law, Bonar, 138-140, 142, 144, 147, 150, 151, 459; background, 139; Home Rule opposed by, 161, 162-163
Lawless, Frank, arrested without charges or trial, 256
Lawless, Joseph T., 379, 379fn.
Lawyer's Notebook, A (Haynes), 207fn., 457
Le Caron, Henri, *see* Beach, Thomas Willis
Leach, Henry Goddard, 301
Leader, The, 128
Leaders of Public Opinion in Ireland (Lecky), 457
League of Nations, 289, 301, 323-329, 334-335; opposition to the, 308-311, 318, 323-326, 328, 330-332, 335, 336-337, 342-343, 347, 369-372; De Valera's attitude toward, 340-342, 359
League of North and South, The (Duffy), 26fn., 456
Lecky, William, 86, 457
Lee, Lord, 424
Lee, Arthur, 114fn.
Leeds, England, 64
Leinster Hall (Dublin), 94, 96
Lenroot, Senator, 370
Leopold, King (Belgium), 169-170, 171fn., 209
LeRoux, Louis N., 158, 457
Leslie, Shane, 42fn., 94fn., 126, 221-222, 223, 226, 227fn., 236, 237, 238, 241, 241fn., 245, 245fn., 249, 249fn., 250, 405fn., 457; as Secretary to F. W. Keating, 275, 276; opinion of Wilson, 322
Letters and Leaders of My Day (Healy), 99fn., 455
Lewis, James Hamilton, 371
Lexington Theatre (New York City), 239, 349, 350, 353
Leyds, W. J., 114
Libau (steamer), 198
Liberal Party, 69, 70, 75, 85, 104, 134, 137, 138, 139, 141, 142, 145, 148, 150, 154, 156, 159; Dillon loses faith in leadership of, 162
Liberty, 195fn.
Library of Congress, ix, x, 35fn., 47fn., 106fn., 108fn., 109fn., 112fn., 114fn., 115fn., 116fn., 117fn., 205fn., 212fn., 219fn., 265fn.,

272fn., 285fn., 290fn., 308fn., 326fn., 370fn., 381fn., 411, 412fn., 451
Life of a Painter, The (Lavery), 455
Lifford, Lord, 51, 51fn., 52fn.
Limerick, 192, 199, 400; Bishop of, 64
Limerick County, Ireland, 21
Limerick Quay, 191
Lincoln Prison, 340
Linen industry, Irish, 5, 9
Literary Digest, 113fn., 284, 454
Literature, Irish, 123, 124-127, 128, 130
Liverpool, England, 169
Liverpool *Daily Post*, 454
Lloyd, Clifford, 61fn., 66fn., 457
Lloyd George, 139, 147, 151, 233, 241, 253, 254, 255, 275, 299, 312, 313, 314, 316, 360, 420, 423; Black and Tan squads, 4, 213; budget of 1909 rejected by House of Lords, 137; Home Rule issue and, 146, 225, 231, 232, 285; becomes Prime Minister, 225-226; conscription issue in Ireland, 243-244, 245, 285; policy of compulsion, 268; attempt to influence American public opinion, 400, 425; attitude toward reign of terror in Ireland, 407-408, 409; truce with Irish leaders, 418-419; conference with De Valera, 419-420; League of Nations and, 424; Washington disarmament conference, 425-426; London Conference (1921), 426, 429, 430, 437; at the Versailles Conference, 427
Local Government Act, 129
Lodge, Henry Cabot, 106, 114fn., 331, 337, 338fn., 452, 455; attitude toward the League of Nations, 324, 326, 370, 370fn., 371; quoted on Cohalan, 332; opinion of Cohalan, 338fn.
Lody (German spy), 180, 180fn.
Logue, Cardinal, 248fn.
Lokke, Carl, x
Lomasney, William Mackey, 68
London, England, terrorism in, 78
London Conference (1921), 426-435
London *Daily Express*, 207
London *Daily Herald*, 454
London *Daily Mail*, 257, 454

London *Daily News*, 258-259, 260, 260fn., 261, 402fn.
London *Daily Telegraph*, 257, 258fn., 259fn., 260, 454
London *Gazette*, 145
London *News Chronicle*, 454
London *Observer*, 399, 454
London School of Economics, 171fn.
London *Standard*, 110, 454
London *Times*, 51fn., 60fn., 62, 63fn., 64, 78, 86, 88, 89, 89fn., 90, 91-92, 110, 201fn., 257, 259, 293, 418, 454
Londonderry, Lord, 142
Los Angeles *Examiner*, 453
Los Angeles *Times*, 108, 453
Louisville *Courier-Journal*, 453
Lourenço Marques, Portuguese East Africa, 170
Lowell *Sun*, 167
Luby, Thomas Clarke, 30, 30fn., 32; arrested, 33
Lucy, Henry, 44
Lusitania, sinking of the, 194
Luthin, Reinhard H., xi
Lynch, Diarmuid, 228, 252, 252fn., 278fn., 288, 288fn., 293, 303, 304, 304fn., 341, 341fn., 348, 390, 409; Director of Communications, Irish Volunteers, 254; elected National Secretary, Friends of Irish Freedom, 271; Second Irish Race Convention, 271; statement to House Committee on Foreign Affairs, 287; Irish Bond Drive and, 351; De Valera's attack on, 385-386; attitude toward the Anglo-Irish Treaty, 437; resigns his seat in the Dail Eireann, 386
Lynch, W. F., 35
Lyons, Francis S. L., 102fn., 457

Maamtrasna incident, 74-75
Macardle, Dorothy, 158fn., 247fn., 253fn., 254fn., 255fn., 285fn., 296fn., 319fn., 401fn., 403fn., 429, 457
MacBride, John, 130fn.
MacCan, Pierce, arrested without charges or trial, 256
MacColl, René, 214fn., 457
MacDermot, Frank, 7fn., 457

MacDermott, Sean, 158; Easter Rebellion and, 197, 198, 199
MacDiarmuda, Sean, 144, 199
MacDonagh, Michael, 65fn.
MacDonagh, Thomas, 197, 199
MacDonald, Mr. (manager, London Times), 92
MacDonnell, Lord, 172
Mackey, Herbert, 457
MacNamara, John R., 115
MacNeill, Eoin, 144, 145, 181, 197, 199, 228
MacNeill, John, 123
Macready, Sir Nevil, 401, 401fn., 409, 455
MacSwiney, Mary, 410
MacSwiney, Muriel, 410
MacSwiney, Terence, 406, 410
Madison Square Garden (New York City), 246, 280, 281, 283
Magennis, Peter E., 271, 272, 274fn., 293; Third Irish Race Convention, 297; resigns as National President, Friends of Irish Freedom, 387
Maginnis, Marguerite, 272, 272fn., 273
Maguire, Edward, 39
Mahon, Sir Bryan, 255
Mahoney, Joseph P., 376
Mallow, Ireland, 13
Maloney, J. M. A., 231
Maloney, William J., 173fn., 174fn., 175fn., 207, 207fn., 214fn., 236, 237, 238, 278, 278fn., 279, 279fn., 293, 295, 306fn., 384, 409, 457; proclamation concerning Irish declaration of independence, 294; Third Irish Race Convention, 299-300; Friends of Irish Freedom smeared by, 338; Cohalan attacked by, 338-339, 346; determined to become intimate adviser of De Valera, 341; League of Nations, 342; mass meeting protesting British suppression of the Dail Eireann, 349
Malthus, 19
Man and Superman (Shaw), 18, 18fn., 459
Manchester *Guardian*, 248
Manchester incident, 38-39
"Manchester Martyrs," 38-39, 43-44
Manifesto to the Irish People, 145

Manning, Cardinal, 41, 42, 42fn., 93, 94fn.
Mannix, Thomas, 308fn.
Marckievicz, Countess, shows hostility towards De Valera, 361; arrested without charges or trial, 256
Marlowe, Nathaniel, 52fn.
Marshall, John, 235, 237
Martin, Senator (Va.), 323, 329
Martine, Senator, 218
Martineau, Harriet, 86
Martyn, Edward, 124
Mason, William E., 221, 353, 356, 357, 358fn.
Massachusetts Historical Society, 370fn., 452
Maurer, James H., 410
Maxwell, Sir Herbert, 7fn., 455
Maxwell, Sir John, 201
Maynooth, Ireland, 247
Mayo County, Ireland, 60
McAdoo, William G., 196
McCabe, Leo, 7fn.
McCafferty, John, 34
McCaffery, Joseph J., 308fn.
McCartan, Patrick, ix, 193fn., 228, 229, 229fn., 274fn., 279fn., 293, 293fn., 295, 297, 297fn., 300-301, 306fn., 348, 348fn., 359fn., 360, 360fn., 361, 361fn., 365fn., 366, 366fn., 368, 368fn., 374, 375fn., 379, 383, 394, 457; attack on, 240; inquisition by Secret Service agents, 251-252, 265; proclamation concerning Irish declaration of independence, 294; announces Irish independence, 294; Third Irish Race Convention, 297; campaign against Cohalan, 303-306; Friends of Irish Freedom smeared by, 338; Cohalan attacked by, 338-339, 346; determined to become intimate adviser of De Valera, 341; League of Nations issue, 341-342, 343, 445; mass meeting protesting British suppression of the Dail Eireann, 349; sent to Ireland by De Valera, 383-384
McCarthy, Charles (Fenian), 52, 53
McCarthy, Dr. Charles, 285-286, 286fn.
McCarthy, John, 187
McCarthy, Justin, 94-95, 97, 99, 103

Index

McCarthy, Michael J., 57, 61, 61*fn.*, 458
McClenahan, John, 27
McCloskey, Archbishop, 34
McClure, A. K., 109, 109*fn.*
McClure, John, 40
McClusky, Father Thomas J., 327*fn.*
McCormick, Medill, 221, 325
McCumber, Senator, 331
McEnnis, J. T., 78*fn.*, 458
McEvoy, Very Reverend Dr., 19, 20
McGarrity, Joseph, 182, 229, 238, 239, 240, 277, 279, 293, 364, 366, 436; regards Cohalan with suspicion, 279; Third Irish Race Convention, 297, 300; Friends of Irish Freedom and, 304; De Valera's Irish Bond Drive, 348; mass meeting protesting British suppression of the Dail Eireann, 349, 350; Irish bond-certificate drive, 350
McGarry, John, 228, 366
McGarry, Sean, 144; General Secretary, Irish Volunteers, 254; arrested without charges or trial, 256
McGee, Thomas D'Arcy, 26; refuses to join the Fenians, 27
McGinn, Richard, 188
McGuire, James K., 229, 232, 391
McGurrin, James, 119*fn.*, 189*fn.*, 336, 337, 337*fn.*, 458
McHugh, James, 422
McKellar, Kenneth, 370
McKenna's Fort, 187
McKinley, William, 113, 452; Arbitration Treaty, 112; Boer War and, 117, 117*fn.*, 118
McMahon, John, 37
McManus, Terence Bellew, 26; funeral, 31
McNeill, Ronald J., 142*fn.*
McPherson, Elizabeth, x
McSweeney, Edward F., 332*fn.*
McWhorter, Mrs. Mary F., 273, 274; Third Irish Race Convention, 297, 297*fn.*
Meade, General, 35
Meagher, Thomas Francis, 31*fn.*, 455; charged with sedition, 24; escapes to America, 26; refuses to join the Fenians, 27; American Civil War and, 32

Mearns, David C., x
Meath County, Ireland, 55, 199
Mechanics Institute, 31
Meehan, Father, 31
Meighen, Arthur, 425
Melbourne, Lord, 93, 93*fn.*, 455, 459
Mellowes, Barney, 199; arrested without charges or trial, 256
Mellows, Liam, 240, 295, 348, 374, 386; inquisition by Secret Service agents, 251-252, 265; Second Irish Race Convention, 271; Devoy's attitude toward, 386*fn.*
Memoirs of an Old Parliamentarian (O'Connor), 70*fn.*, 99*fn.*, 455
Memories and Reflections (Asquith), 152*fn.*, 156*fn.*
Mercantilism, British, 5, 6, 7
Messmer, Archbishop, 301
Metropolitan Opera House (New York City), 302, 304, 305*fn.*, 326
Meyer, Kuno, 182
M'Goey, John, 186
Michael Coffeys, 11
Michael Collins and the Making of a New Ireland (Beaslai), 144*fn.*, 199*fn.*, 253*fn.*, 257*fn.*, 343*fn.*, 352*fn.*, 385*fn.*, 393*fn.*, 396*fn.*, 397*fn.*, 399*fn.*, 418*fn.*, 419*fn.*, 431*fn.*, 433*fn.*, 434*fn.*, 436*fn.*, 456
Michael Collins' Own Story (Talbot), 433*fn.*, 455
Middletown, New York, 121
Migration of British Capital to 1873 (Jenks), 48*fn.*, 457
Milholland, John E., 374, 378
Military Intelligence, U.S., 285
Mill, John Stuart, 49
Milligan, Alice, 124
Milner, Lord, 151
Milwaukee *Journal*, 453
Mitchel, John, 17, 19*fn.*, 20, 21*fn.*, 23, 23*fn.*, 458; visits Galway, 21; *United Irishman* published by, 23; charged with sedition, 24; convicted and sentenced to Van Diemen's Land, 24; escapes, 26; publishes *The Citizen* in New York City, 26; expresses hostility towards Catholic Church, 26-27; refuses to join the Fenians, 27; moves to Tennessee,

27; organizes the "Irishmen's Civil and Military Republican Union" in New York City, 27
Modest Proposal for Preventing the Children of Poor People from Being a Burden to their Parents of the Country (Swift), 4
Molly Maguires, 11
Moloney, General, 166
Monroe Doctrine, 333; Casement's opinion of the, 174; De Valera's remarks concerning, 359-360
Monteith, Robert, 185-186, 187, 188, 199, 458
Montgomery, W. E., 49*fn.*, 458
Montreal, Canada, 57
Montreal *Gazette*, 37
Mooney, Monsignor Joseph F., 277, 278*fn.*
Moore, J. Stanley, 411
Moore, John D., 228, 228*fn.*, 229, 234
Moral and Pastoral Theology (Davis), 201*fn.*
Moran, David P., 127-128, 128*fn.*
Morel, E. D., 171, 171*fn.*
Morgan, J. H., 204
Morley, Arnold, 92
Morley, John, 44, 60*fn.*, 90*fn.*, 93, 93*fn.*, 94, 95, 96, 96*fn.*, 138*fn.*, 455, 458
Morocco, 174
Morrison's Hotel (Dublin), 53, 55, 65
Morton, Mrs. Grace Lee, xi
Mosley, E. A., 108, 109*fn.*
Moses, George H., 325, 331
Mount Vernon, 268
Mountjoy (boat), 143
Mountjoy Prison (Dublin), 318
Mulhall, Michael J., 19*fn.*
Mulleda, Henry S., 40
Munich, Germany, 185
Munsey, Frank A., 311, 311*fn.*
Murchison, Charles F., 108-109, 111
Murphy, Anna, 413*fn.*
Murphy, Charles F., 380, 380*fn.*
Murphy, John A., 271, 320, 320*fn.*, 376
Murray, Lord, 150, 151
Murray, James E., 436
Mutiny at the Curragh (Ryan), 147*fn.*
My Life in Two Hemispheres (Duffy), 16*fn.*, 18*fn.*, 455

My Political Trial and Experiences (O'Leary), 239*fn.*
Mystery of the Casement Ship, The (Spindler), 191*fn.*, 198*fn.*
Mythen, Rev. James Grattan, 301, 393

Nation (periodical), 15-17, 24, 28, 30, 106*fn.*, 409, 409*fn.*, 454
National Archives (N.A.), ix, x, 34*fn.*, 35*fn.*, 36*fn.*, 37*fn.*, 39*fn.*, 105*fn.*, 115*fn.*, 116*fn.*, 118*fn.*, 230*fn.*, 231*fn.*, 242*fn.*, 248*fn.*, 249*fn.*, 263*fn.*, 266*fn.*, 268*fn.*, 269*fn.*, 285*fn.*, 286*fn.*, 289*fn.*, 290*fn.*, 314*fn.*, 320*fn.*, 340*fn.*, 400*fn.*, 404*fn.*, 405*fn.*, 406*fn.*, 408*fn.*, 409*fn.*
National League of America, 77
National League of Ireland, 77
National Literary Society of Dublin, 122
National Press, 99
National Volunteers, 160, 162, 164, 197
Nationalism, Irish spirit of, 3-4, 8, 29, 122; O'Connell and, 15; the *Nation* and, 15-16; indifference of Irish aristocracy to, 29-30; Gaelic League and, 123-124; Irish literature and, 124-125; Irish industries and, 127-128; Arthur Griffith and, 131
Navan, Ireland, 55
Neilson, Francis, 150*fn.*
Nelson, Isaac, 60
Nelson, J. L., 112*fn.*
Nereide case, 235, 237
Neutrality for the United States (Borchard and Lage), 234*fn.*
Nevins, Allan, 118*fn.*, 458
Nevinson, Henry W., 207*fn.*
New, Senator, 370
New Haven, Connecticut, 327
New Ireland (Sullivan), 59*fn.*
New Ireland Review, 127
New Orleans *Times-Picayune*, 453
New Rochelle, New York, 126
New York *American*, 421
New York City, N. Y., 38, 54, 83, 120, 121, 195, 196; Irish element in, 84; Casement's visit to, 176; Irish Race Convention held in, 189-190

Index

New York *Evening Post*, 231, 232*fn.*, 271, 271*fn.*, 453
New York *Herald*, 34*fn.*, 202, 453
New York *Journal*, 453
New York *Sun*, 218, 271, 271*fn.*, 310-311, 453
New York Times, The, 39, 203, 207, 220*fn.*, 221*fn.*, 246*fn.*, 252, 262, 264, 264*fn.*, 288*fn.*, 294*fn.*, 370*fn.*, 375*fn.*, 381*fn.*, 424*fn.*, 425, 436*fn.*, 437*fn.*, 453
New York *Tribune*, 83*fn.*, 303*fn.*, 370*fn.*, 380*fn.*, 453
New York *World*, 109*fn.*, 117-118, 196, 227, 227*fn.*, 228, 236, 236*fn.*, 237, 275*fn.*, 301*fn.*, 374
Newman, Cardinal, 88, 88*fn.*, 459
Newman, Mrs. Agnes, 204-205
Newman, Oliver P., 410
Newport News, Virginia, 410, 413
Niagara River, 35
Nicholls, George, arrested without charges or trial, 256
"No Rent Manifesto," 65-66
Nolan, Colonel, 95
Norris, George W., 410
North Leitrim, Ireland, 134
Northcliffe, Lord, 208
Northumberland, 19*fn.*
Norton, George, 93
Noyes, Alfred, 458
Nunan, Sean, 374

O'Beirne, James R., 116-118
O'Brien, George A. T., 5*fn.*, 458
O'Brien, John P., 52
O'Brien, Michael, 39
O'Brien, Morgan J., 226, 414
O'Brien, Paddy, 233
O'Brien, R. Barry, 44*fn.*, 45*fn.*, 46, 46*fn.*, 52, 52*fn.*, 53*fn.*, 54*fn.*, 56*fn.*, 57*fn.*, 61*fn.*, 69*fn.*, 73*fn.*, 76*fn.*, 77*fn.*, 78*fn.*, 79*fn.*, 94*fn.*, 95*fn.*, 96, 96*fn.*, 97*fn.*, 98*fn.*, 99*fn.*, 458
O'Brien, Smith, 23; charged with sedition, 24
O'Brien, William, 53*fn.*, 65*fn.*, 93, 94, 97, 98, 99, 136, 447; "No Rent Manifesto," 65; Sinn Fein aided by, 137; conscription issue in Ireland, 246
O'Callaghan, Donal, 410-414

Ochs, Adolph, 425
O'Connell, Cardinal, 406, 409; plea for Irish self-determination, 276; Madison Square Garden speech, 277-281
O'Connell, Charles Underwood, 40
O'Connell, Daniel, 9, 9*fn.*, 12, 12*fn.*, 20, 222-223; fight for repeal of the Act of Union, 12-14, 20; conception of Irish nationalism, 15; arrested, 16; imprisonment, 16; breaks with Duffy on question of federalism, 16; break between Young Irelanders and, 16-18, 23; starvation in Ireland and, 18, 20-22, 23; compared with Parnell, 42, 58
O'Connell, Daniel T., 331, 331*fn.*, 332, 335, 341, 357, 358*fn.*, 373, 376, 380, 382; opinion of Cohalan, 332; background, 332*fn.*
O'Connell, John, 9*fn.*, 17
O'Connor, Dennis H., 81-82
O'Connor, Sir James, 51*fn.*, 458
O'Connor, T. P., 50*fn.*, 60, 64*fn.*, 70, 94, 95, 97, 98, 99*fn.*, 103, 153, 191, 233*fn.*, 244, 244*fn.*, 264, 265, 265*fn.*, 285, 290*fn.*, 293, 455, 458; sent to America to collect funds for the Nationalist cause, 232; conscription issue in Ireland, 244, 245, 245*fn.*
O'Donnell, Frank H., 51
O'Donnell, Patrick H., 189
O'Flanagan, Father Michael, 418-419
O'Gorman, Richard, 26
O'Gorman, Senator, 307
O'Grady, Gerald F. M., 284, 285*fn.*
O'Grady, Standish, 64, 129, 458
O'Growney, Father Eugene, 123
O'Hara, M. M., 70, 455
O'Hegarty, Patrick S., 6*fn.*, 9*fn.*, 12*fn.*, 13*fn.*, 14*fn.*, 17*fn.*, 20*fn.*, 21*fn.*, 23*fn.*, 24*fn.*, 26*fn.*, 30*fn.*, 32*fn.*, 42, 43*fn.*, 124*fn.*, 129*fn.*, 130*fn.*, 131*fn.*, 133*fn.*, 134, 134*fn.*, 145*fn.*, 160, 163*fn.*, 165*fn.*, 197*fn.*, 198*fn.*, 200, 401*fn.*, 435*fn.*, 458
O'Kelly, James, 52, 97
O'Kelly, Sean T., 297, 319, 320-321, 321*fn.*, 346*fn.*, 427
O'Leary, Jeremiah A., 188, 238, 239, 240, 252, 269

O'Leary, John, 26fn., 29, 29fn., 30fn., 52, 68, 455; contempt for A. M. Sullivan, 30; editorials written for the *Irish People*, 30; arrested, 33; President, Cumann na nGaedheal, 131
O'Leary, Patrick A., 237, 299fn., 300fn.
Olney, Richard, 452; Arbitration Treaty, 111-113
O'Mahony, John, 26, 27fn.
O'Mahony, Joseph P., 376
O'Malley, Robert Emmet, 376
O'Mara, James, 366; Irish Bond Drive and, 351
O'Mara, Stephen, 438
O'Neill, Lord Mayor, 246
O'Neill, Brian, 59fn., 458
O'Neill, John, 35, 36, 37-38
Oppenheim, L., 118fn.
Opium War (China), 22-23
O'Rahilly, The, 158, 158fn.
Orange Free State, 116
O'Reilly, John Boyle, 53, 108, 108fn., 109
Origins of the World War, The (Fay), 152fn., 456
O'Rourke, Canon John, 22, 22fn., 458
Osgoodby, George, 107, 108
O'Shea, Captain, 69, 90-92
O'Shea, Katharine, 43fn., 69, 72, 90-92, 458
Oskar II (Norwegian steamer), 178
Owen, Senator, 370
Owsley, Frank L., 32fn.
Oxford, Lord, 138fn.

Page, Walter H., 207, 211fn., 230, 231fn., 241-242, 242fn., 263, 263fn., 265, 266fn., 267, 457
Paine, Thomas, 7
Pakenham, Frank, 405fn., 407fn., 430fn., 438fn., 458
Pall Mall Gazette, 96
Palmer, A. Mitchell, 359fn.
Palmer, Norman D., 51fn., 62fn., 458
Paone, Rocco, xi, 324fn.
Papen, Captain Franz von, 176, 190
Paris, France, 53
Paris Peace Conference, 213-214, 261, 281-283, 286, 287, 290-291, 297, 303, 306-339, 397, 427

Park Avenue Hotel (New York City), 389
Parker, Raymond T., xi
Parliament, Grattan's, 6, 8, 9; Parnell as leader of Irish party in, 43-46, 48, 71, 72, 76, 79, 87, 94-101; *See also* House of Commons; House of Lords; Irish Parliament
Parmiter, Geoffrey de C., 206fn., 458
Parnell, Charles Stewart, 42-104, 120, 130, 136, 145, 149, 157, 344, 457, 458; compared with O'Connell, 42, 58; emergence as a statesman, 42-44; in Parliament, 43-46, 48, 71, 72, 76, 79, 87, 94-101; policy of legislative obstructionism, 44, 45; the Fenians and, 43-46, 52, 76; rebuked by Isaac Butt, 45; mother of, 46; visits U.S., 46-48, 56-57; rebuff from President Grant, 47; U.S. Congress and, 47, 57; and the Land League, 51-58, 61, 63, 67, 72, 89; address at Tralee, 53; Clanna-Gael and, 53, 56, 57, 66-69, 77, 78, 97; "last link" speech (Cincinnati), 54; hailed as "the New O'Connell," 55; Westport speech, 55; visits Canada, 57; defies Gladstone, 64-65; arrested, 65; "No Rent Manifesto" signed by, 65; Beach's interview with, 67, 68; Beach's comments about, 69; imprisonment, 69-70, 80; Kilmainham Treaty and, 69-70; released from jail, 69; Liberty Party and, 69, 70; offers to resign seat in House of Commons, 71; Crimes Act (1882) and, 71; Land Act and, 72; Irish National League founded by, 72; Forster's attack on, 72-73; National tribute to, 73-74; estate at Avondale, 73; Liberals and, 74; Maamtrasna incident and, 74; joins forces with Conservatives, 75, 84; extremists and, 76-77, 78, 88; Alexander Sullivan defended by, 78; inquiry by Parliamentary Commission, 67, 68, 88-90, 92; false charges leveled against, 88-89; Winston Churchill quoted on downfall of, 90; O'Shea's divorce suit and, 90-93, 97; criticizes Gladstone, 97; criticized by

Index 483

former supporters, 97; denounced by Catholic hierarchy, 99; death of, 99; devotion lavished upon, 100; Katharine Tynan's description of, 100; Redmond succeeds him as leader of Irish Parliamentary Party, 102-104
Parnell, Fanny, 61-62, 70
Parnell, John Howard, 46*fn.*, 47, 47*fn.*
Parnell Movement, The (O'Connor), 50*fn.*, 64*fn.*, 458
Parnell Parliamentary Commission, 66*fn.*, 67, 68, 88-90, 92
Parnell to Pearse (Horgan), 125*fn.*, 137*fn.*, 201*fn.*, 457
Parnell Vindicated (Harrison), 92*fn.*, 457
Parsons, Sir Lawrence, 161, 162
Patch, Blanche, 207*fn.*, 458
Paterson, New Jersey, 188
Paul, Herbert, 61*fn.*, 86, 458
Pauncefote, Sir Julian, 111
Peace by Ordeal (Pakenham), 405*fn.*, 407*fn.*, 430*fn.*, 438*fn.*, 458
Pearse, P. H., St. Enda's College founded by, 157; Easter Rebellion, 197, 199, 444, 445
Peel, Sir Robert, 13, 22
Penal code, in Ireland, 6
Pentonville prison, 211
Pepita (Sackville-West), 81*fn.*, 459
Percy, Lord Eustace, 236, 237, 238
Personal Narrative of the Irish Revolutionary Brotherhood (Denieffe), 27*fn.*, 455
Peruvian Amazon Company, 172-173, 207
Petty, Sir William, 4, 5*fn.*, 458
Phelan, James D., 211, 218-220, 241, 244, 244*fn.*, 264, 268, 268*fn.*, 276, 277, 307, 308, 344, 381; League of Nations favored by, 330
Phelps, E. J., 106*fn.*, 110, 110*fn.*, 111*fn.*
Philadelphia, Pennsylvania, Bishop of, 32
Philadelphia *Inquirer*, 203
Philadelphia *Public Ledger*, 262, 453
Philadelphia *Record*, 365*fn.*
Philosophy of Irish-Ireland, The (Moran), 128*fn.*

Phoenix Flame, The (Ryan), 51*fn.*, 55*fn.*
Phoenix Park, murders in, 72-73, 83, 88
Pigott, Richard, 88, 90, 92
Pinchot, Amos, 409
Pinkerton detective agency, 79
Pitman, Senator Key, 210, 309, 310*fn.*
Pitt, William, 6
Platt Amendment, 359-360, 361*fn.*, 362, 383; text of, 360
"Playboy of the Western World" (Synge), 125, 126
Plunkett, Sir Horace, 128-129, 227, 227*fn.*, 242, 243, 245, 246*fn.*, 248, 399, 405; arrested without charges or trial, 256; appointment as delegate to Paris Peace Conference, 296-297, 312, 313, 315; League of Nations issue, 340-341; shows hostility toward De Valera, 361
Plunkett, J. D., 108, 108*fn.*; Easter Rebellion, 197, 199
Poincaré, 152
Police Journal, 405
Poli's Palace Theater (New Haven), 327
Political Science Quarterly, 356*fn.*, 425*fn.*, 454, 456
Polk, Frank K., 212, 212*fn.*, 219, 219*fn.*, 230, 230*fn.*, 248, 249*fn.*, 307, 307*fn.*, 308, 308*fn.*
Pomerene, Senator, 380, 381*fn.*
Porry, John de, x
Porter, Stephen G., 357, 358
Portland, Oregon, 227*fn.*, 328
Portuguese East Africa, 170
Pou, Edward W., 324, 324*fn.*
Powell, Charles P., x
Power, Monsignor James W., 298, 392
Power, O'Connor, 46-48
Powerful America (Young), 425*fn.*, 459
Practice of Diplomacy, The (Foster), 118*fn.*, 457
Presbyterian Church, in Ireland, 8-9
Presidential Election of 1920, The (Paone), 324*fn.*
Pretoria, South Africa, 115, 371
Primrose League, 89
Principles of Political Economy, 49*fn.*
Protestant Friends of Ireland, 393

Pulleyn, John J., 416, 417fn.
Purcell, Mrs. C. Bernard, xi

Queenstown, 82, 175, 263
Queer People (Thompson), 208fn., 455
Quinn, John, 126-127, 127fn., 177-178, 182, 208, 226, 226fn., 279fn.; Lloyd George Convention (Dublin) favored by, 243

Randall, Congressman, 57
Rankin, Jeannette, 303fn.
Reading, Lord Chief Justic Viscount, 204, 245
Rebellion, Irish, *see* Irish rebellion (1798)
Recognition Policy of the United States, The (Goebel), 356fn.
Recollections (Morley), 138fn.
Recollections (O'Brien), 65fn.
Recollections of an Irish Rebel (Devoy), 30fn., 31fn., 33fn., 38fn., 52fn., 53fn., 55fn., 159fn., 176fn., 177fn., 178fn., 184fn., 185fn., 190fn., 191, 191fn., 193fn., 196, 196fn., 455
Recollections of Fenians and Fenianism (O'Leary), 26fn., 29fn., 455
Recorder, The, 456
Red Cross, *see* American National Red Cross; Geneva Red Cross Society
Redmond, John, 120, 126, 130, 134, 136-139, 140fn., 144, 145-146, 146fn., 208, 221, 224-233, 255, 299, 423, 457; succeeds Parnell as leader of Irish Parliamentary Party, 102-104; Irish Volunteers and, 145, 147-148, 158, 159-164; judicial and military inquiry demanded by, 149; betrayed by England, 150-157; repudiated by the Clan-na-Gael, 157; speech at Woodenbridge, 160; loyalty to England, 160, 166, 167, 224; National Volunteers organized by, 160; Giffith challenges leadership of, 164-165; Griffith denounced by, 165; Sinn Feiners denounced by, 165; popularity in America fades, 166-168, 224; attitude toward the Easter Rebellion, 201; death, 243
Redmond, William, 78, 233

Redmond-Howard, Louis G., 458
Redpath, James, 54
Reed, James A., 331fn.
Reid, Whitelaw, 115, 115fn.
Religion, in Ireland, 3; *See also* Catholic Church; Presbyterian Church
Renunciation Act (1783), 133
Repeal Association, 17, 18; collapse of the, 18
Republic, The (paper), 173
Resurrection of Hungary: A Parallel for Ireland (Griffith), 133fn., 457
Reynolds, James A., 458
Rhaetia, 175
Ribbonmen, 11
Rice, Laurence J., 188, 437
Richardson, Sir George, 143
Richardson, James D., 107fn., 112fn., 452
Richey, A. G., 49fn., 458
Richmond Prison, 16
Riddell, Lord G. A. R., 255, 255fn.
Riddleberger, Senator, 106
"Riders to the Sea" (Synge), 126
Ridgeway, Canada, 35
Rio de Janeiro, Brazil, 172
Road Round Ireland, The (Colum), 206fn.
Road to Safety, The (Willert), 178fn., 222fn., 459
Roberts, Lord, 142
Robinson, Joseph T., 380
Rochester *Democrat and Chronicle*, 262, 453
Rockites, 11
Rogers, Patrick, 12fn.
Ronayne, Joseph, 44
Rooney, John Jerome, 270, 293
Roosevelt, Theodore, 114fn., 326, 455; attitude toward the Boer War, 113-114; Casement's opinion of, 174; attitude toward the Home Rule issue, 227
Roscommon, Ireland, 13, 14
Roscommon County, Ireland, 99
Rosebery, Lord, 104, 104fn., 456
Rossa, Jeremiah O'Donovan, 33, 40
Rotunda Rink (Dublin), 144, 145
Royal Irish Constabulary, 397-398, 401, 407
Russell, George W., 124, 243
Russell, Lord John, 20, 21fn., 22, 459

Index 485

Russia, World War I and, 152
Ryan, A. P., 147*fn.*
Ryan, Andrew J., 367, 368, 368*fn.*
Ryan, Desmond, 51, 53*fn.*, 55*fn.*, 455
Ryan, John A., 204*fn.*
Ryan, John J., 237
Ryan, Michael J., 166, 224, 366; Third Irish Race Convention, 300; as member of American Commission for Irish Independence, 313-314, 317*fn.*, 318*fn.;* background, 313*fn.;* testifies before Senate Foreign Relations Committee, 333; De Valera's Irish Bond Drive, 348
Ryan, O'Neill, 189, 443

Sackville-West, Lionel, 81, 82*fn.*, 83*fn.*, 84, 84*fn.*, 105*fn.;* dismissal as British Minister to the U.S., 107-111
Sackville-West, V., 81*fn.*, 459
St. Albans, Vermont, 35
St. Enda's College, 157, 444
St. James's Hall, 86, 87
St. Louis *Globe-Democrat*, 203, 262
St. Patrick's Cathedral (New York City), 31
St. Patrick's Day (1920), 365
St. Teresa's Hall (Dublin), 124
Salisbury, Lord, 71, 75, 84, 86-87, 87*fn.*, 89, 90, 110*fn.*, 130, 142, 456; Gladstone criticized by, 89; attitude toward dismissal of Sackville-West as British Minister to the U.S., 110; Arbitration Treaty and, 111-113; Boer War, 118; policy of coercion and concessions, 128
Saltonstall, Leverett, 109
San Francisco, California, 31, 219, 244; Democratic Convention (1920), 380-383, 405
Sanford, Henry, 169
Santos, Brazil, 173
Saturday Evening Post, 195*fn.*, 454
Schenck, Robert C., 36
Schoonmaker, Commissioner, 109
Schurz, Carl, 112, 452
Scotland Yard, 207*fn.*, Casement's character defiled by, 188, 207
Scottish Borderers, 155
Sears, Louis M., xi
Secret Service, U.S., 193, 195, 196, 198, 234, 235, 250, 251, 256, 265, 266
Seeley, 86
Select Committee on the Corn Trade of the United Kingdom, 10*fn.*, 452
Select Committee on the State of Ireland (Lords), 9*fn.*, 10*fn.*, 11*fn.*, 452
Select Speeches (O'Connell), 9*fn.*
Senate and the League of Nations, The (Lodge), 370*fn.*
Senior, Nassau, 21*fn.*, 455
Serbia, 149-150, 152
Serbian Black Hand Society, 149
Severance, Frank H., 36*fn.*, 459
Sewall, 114*fn.*
Seward, William H., 34*fn.*, 35, 35*fn.*, 36, 36*fn.*, 37, 37*fn.*, 39, 39*fn.*, 116; conduct of foreign relations, 37
Sexton, Thomas, 95, 96
Seymour, Charles, xi, 212*fn.*
Shahan, Bishop Thomas J., 291, 291*fn.*
Shakespeare, William, 43
Sharkey, Mary Ann, xi
Sharkey, Mrs. Mary Ann, xi
Sharkey, Susan, xi
Shaw, Sir Frederick, 255, 285
Shaw, George Bernard, 18, 18*fn.*, 124, 207*fn.*, 459
Sheehy, Eugene, 443
Sheehy-Skeffington, Mrs. Hanna, 223, 224, 234, 240-241
Sheep industry, in Ireland, 4-5, 10
Shelley, Percy B., 407
Shipbuilding, in Ireland, 9
Shippee, Lester B., 38*fn.*, 459
Shirmer, 185
Shirtmaking, in Ireland, 9
Shortt, Edward, 255
Sievers, Harry, xi
Sigerson, Dr., 123*fn.*
Simmons, Senator, 370
Simonds, Frank H., 261
Sinn Fein, 133-134, 137, 144, 145, 164, 175, 197, 229, 233, 242, 248, 252, 256, 258, 259, 271, 285, 292-293, 404, 405, 405*fn.*, 408-409, 421, 430; object of, 134, 253; members denounced by Redmond, 165; praised by Casement, 173; England regards growing strength of, with apprehension, 252-256; new

constitution, 253; De Valera selected as President of, 254; leaders arrested without charges or trial, 256-265; hostility of American press toward, 261-263; appeal to Wilson for self-determination, 289; banned, 292
Sinn Fein League, 133
Sinn Fein revolution (April, 1916), 8
Sitwell, Osbert, 63*fn.*, 456
Skal, George von, 190
Sligo County, Ireland, 55
Sloane, T. O'Conor III, xi
Smith, Congressman (N.Y.), 357
Smith, Andrew C., 328, 328*fn.*
Smith, Sir Frederick, 204, 205, 242
Smith, Goldwin, 86
Smuggling operations, 5
Smuts, General, 419
South Atlantic Quarterly, 324*fn.*
Spalding, Archbishop Martin, 31-32
Spanish-American War, 113, 114
Spear, Samuel S., 35
Spencer, Lord, 71, 74-75
Spencer, Herbert, 86
Spender, J. A., 137*fn.*
Spindler, Karl, 191*fn.*, 198, 198*fn.*
Splain, John J., 283, 283*fn.*, 327*fn.*, 367*fn.*
Spring Rice, Sir Cecil, 114*fn.*, 194*fn.*, 225*fn.*, 226*fn.*, 455
Sprout, Harold, 424*fn.*, 459
Sprout, Margaret, 424*fn.*, 459
Stack, Austin, 253, 419, 429
Stalin, Joseph, 22
Stanley, Lord, 37*fn.*
Stanwood, Edward, 120*fn.*, 459
Starvation, in Ireland (1845-47), 10, 14, 18-22, 25, 28, 50; results of, 22-25
State Department, U.S., 36, 40, 47, 80, 193, 195, 210, 218, 219, 230, 234, 237, 248, 265, 266, 268*fn.*, 307, 308, 340*fn.*, 359*fn.*, 406, 410-413, 451, 452; Boer War and, 118, 119
Statutes at Large of the United States, The, 360*fn.*
Steele, John S., 413
Stephens, James, 26, 27, 29, 32-33, 124; arrested, 33; revolt against English armed forces, 33

Stewart, Charles, 46
Stockbridge, Massachusetts, 413*fn.*
Stockholm, Sweden, 189
Stone, Senator, 216, 217
Story of Ireland, The (O'Grady), 458
Strauss, Eric, 5*fn.*, 8*fn.*, 25*fn.*, 29*fn.*, 459
Suffrage, in Ireland, 6
Sullivan, Alexander M., 30, 59*fn.*, 204, 214, 459; Devoy's opinion of, 77-78
Sullivan, M. F., 49*fn.*, 55*fn.*, 459
Sullivan, T. D., 63
Summers, Mrs. Natalia, xi
Supreme Court, U.S., 235
Suvla Bay, 163
Swift, Jonathan, 4, 4*fn.*, 130, 455
Synge, J. M., 124, 125, 126, 127

Taft, William H., 326; attitude toward the Home Rule issue, 227; League of Nations favored by, 309
Taggart, Thomas, 380, 380*fn.*
Talbot, Hayden, 433*fn.*, 455
Tansill, Charles B., xi
Tansill, Charles Callan, xi, 75*fn.* 105*fn.*, 108*fn.*, 217*fn.*, 356*fn.*, 459
Tansill, Mrs. Charles Callan, xi
Tansill, Fred G., xi
Tansill, William R., xi
Tara Hill, Ireland, 13
Tasmania, *see* Van Diemen's Land
Taylor, Henry A., 139*fn.*, 459
Teller, Senator, 106
Temple, Philipps, xi
Templederry, Ireland, 31
Tennyson, Alfred, 86
Terrorism, in Ireland, 397-417
Thirty Years of American Diplomacy (Nevins, White), 118*fn.*
Thirty Years with G. B. S. (Patch), 207*fn.*, 458
Thomas, Norman, 295, 301, 409, 410
Thompson, Sir Basil, 207*fn.*, 455
Thornton, Sir Edward, 47, 79, 79*fn.*, 80, 80*fn.*
Thrashers, 11
"Three F's," 63, 64
Thurles, Ireland, 401
Tipperary County, Ireland, 21, 401
Tobias, Joseph F., 109
Tombs (New York City), 239

Index

Tone, Wolfe, 7-8, 16, 121, 130, 457
Tories, 19, 154; policy of "depopulation," 22
Toronto, Canada, trials of Fenians in, 37
Torrens, William T., 93fn., 455, 459
Towards a New Order of Sea Power (Sprout), 424fn., 459
Trade, Population and Food (Bourne), 48fn.
Traitor or Patriot (Gwynn), 207fn., 457
Tralee, Ireland, 53, 191
Tralee Bay, 191, 192, 194
Transvaal, and the Boer War, 113-120
Treason-Felony Act, 24
Trevelyan, George M., 86fn., 459
Triangle, The, 77-78
Trinity College, 140
Troy, Robert P., 219, 219fn., 220fn.
Tuam, Archbishop of, 55, 74
Tuam *Herald*, 284
Tuke, James H., 50
Tumulty, Joseph P., 205-212, 212fn., 218-219, 219fn., 227, 228, 228fn., 229-230, 230fn., 241, 241fn., 245, 245fn., 249fn., 273, 273fn., 306fn., 307, 307fn., 322, 322fn., 371, 456
Turner, Bishop William, 320fn., 366, 368, 406, 439
Twenty-Five Years (Grey), 153fn., 455
Twenty-five Years: Reminiscences (Tynan), 100fn.
Twisting of the Rope, The (Hyde), 124
Two Worlds for Memory (Noyes), 458
Tyler, Alice F., 79fn., 459
Tynan, Katharine, 100, 124
Tyndall, John, 86
Tyrone County, Ireland, 141, 400

Ulster, Ireland, 5, 62, 138-152, 156, 161, 163, 164, 225, 227, 400; economic situation in, 9
Ulster Day, 142
Ulster Volunteers, 142-143, 148, 149, 162
Ulster Women's Unionist Council, 140
Ulster's Stand for Union (McNeill), 142fn.

Unconditional Hatred (Grenfell), 150fn., 457
Underwood, Senator, 337, 380
United Brotherhood, 77
United Irish League of America, 166-167, 224, 313fn.
United Irishman (periodical), 23, 130
United Irishmen, 7
United States and the League of Nations, 1918-1920 (Fleming), 324fn., 456
United States of America, fisheries controversy between Canada and, 105-107; Arbitration Treaty, 112-113; Chinese immigration, 116; imperialism, 119; World War I, 215-217
Unlawful Oaths Acts, 26

Valera, *see* De Valera
Van Diemen's Land, 24
Vatican, 289
Venezuela, boundary dispute with British Guiana, 111
Versailles, Treaty of, 213-214, 281, 320, 324, 330, 336, 337, 369-372
Viceregal Lodge, 71
Victoria, Queen, 63, 75, 75fn., 84
Victoriana: A Symposium of Victorian Wisdom (Barton and Sitwell), 63fn., 456
Victory of Sinn Fein, The (O'Hegarty), 134fn., 200fn., 435fn., 458
Vienna, Austria, 149, 150, 152
Viereck, George Sylvester, xi, 195
Voice from the Congo, A (Ward), 459

Walpole, Spencer, 21fn., 459
Walsh, David I., 410; member of American Committee for Relief in Ireland, 415
Walsh, Frank P., 303, 374, 376, 379, 381-382, 388, 404; as member of American Commission for Irish Independence, 312-320; testimony before Senate Foreign Relations Committee, 333; Irish Bond Drive and, 351
Walsh, Gerald G., xi

Walsh, James J., 228
Walsh, Patrick J., 64*fn.*, 459
Walsh, Thomas J., 284-285, 285*fn.*, 290-291, 291*fn.*, 303*fn.*, 306*fn.*, 344, 370, 412, 412*fn.*, 413, 413*fn.*, 414, 452; supports League of Nations, 341, 342; member of American Committee for Relief in Ireland, 415
Walsh, William J., 64*fn.*
War for Land in Ireland, The (O'Neill), 59*fn.*, 458
War of 1812, 46
Ward, Herbert, 459
Ward, Wilfrid P., 88*fn.*, 459
Washington, George, Farewell Address, 333
Washington, Treaty of, 105
Washington *Herald*, 453
Washington *Post*, 203, 453
Washington *Star*, 57*fn.*, 117*fn.*, 202, 453
Washington *Times*, 332*fn.*
Waterford, Ireland, 5, 103, 400
Watson, Senator, 376, 378
"Well of the Saints" (Synge), 127
Wellington, Duke of, 13, 19, 19*fn.*, 93, 455
West, William, 34, 34*fn.*
West Cannon (steamship), 413
Westminster Gazette, 258, 359, 360, 360*fn.*, 361, 383, 454
Westport, Ireland, 55
Westport, New York, 229
Wexford County, Ireland, 5, 65, 199
Whelpley, James D., 285, 285*fn.*
Whigs, 19, 20, 86, 146; policy of "depopulation," 22
White, Henry, 112*fn.*, 116, 116*fn.*, 118, 118*fn.*, 318*fn.*, 452, 458
Whitefeet, 11
Whitman, Charles S., 280, 280*fn.*
Why Ireland is Not Free (Healy), 103*fn.*, 457
Wilhelm II, Kaiser, 111
Willert, Arthur, 178, 222*fn.*, 459
Wilson, Major, 404
Wilson, Sir Henry, 147, 147*fn.*, 151, 456
Wilson, W. B., 410-413
Wilson, Woodrow, 264*fn.*, 284, 285, 293, 299, 304, 343, 353, 354, 356, 381*fn.*, 406, 414, 452; dislike for Cohalan, 194, 213, 265, 302; Anglophilism of, 194, 213, 215; investigation of activities of Count Bernstorff, 195; attitude toward the Easter Rebellion, 204*fn.*, 213, 215; Casement affair and, 205, 205*fn.*, 208-214, 215; criticized by Devoy, 212-213; Versailles Peace Conference, 213-214, 261, 281-283, 286, 287, 290-291, 297, 303, 309-311, 313, 315, 317-338; World War I and, 215-217, 218, 226; attitude toward treatment of Irishmen by England, 219-220; Home Rule issue and, 227*fn.*, 228, 230, 230*fn.*, 231, 251; message to Russia, 228; Friends of Irish Freedom and, 233-234; attempt to ruin Jeremiah O'Leary, 239; pressure from Irish-Americans, 240-250, 287, 303, 303*fn.*; conscription issue in Ireland, 244, 244*fn.*, 267, 286; importance of self-determination stressed by, 250, 268; drive against the Sinn Fein leaders, 265, 272; attitude toward publication of seized Sinn Fein documents, 267, 267*fn.*; attitude toward Ireland's right to autonomous government, 268-269; pleas to, for application of principle of self-determination to Ireland, 272-274, 277, 289; appeal from Irish-American mothers to, 273-274; "Fourteen Points," 282, 335; rejects suggestion that American Army recruit troops in Ireland, 286, 286*fn.*; invitation to visit Ireland, 297; Cohalan rebuffed by, 302; resolutions adopted at Third Irish Race Convention presented to, 302-303; League of Nations, 308-311, 323-329, 334-335, 337-338, 342, 371, 424; extraordinary session of Congress called by, 325; conference with members of American Commission for Irish Independence, 329; western tour, 333-335; physical collapse, 335; opposed to appearance of De Valera before Congress, 344; Democratic convention (San Francisco, 1920), 380-381; Amer-

ican naval construction curtailed by, 424
Wilson, Mrs. Woodrow, 370, 370fn.
Wiseman, Sir William, 314, 317
With De Valera in America (McCartan), ix, 193fn., 229fn., 240fn., 274fn., 279fn., 293fn., 301fn., 303fn., 304fn., 348fn., 359fn., 360fn., 361fn., 366fn., 368fn., 375fn., 379fn., 384fn., 457
Wolfe, Henry F., xi
Wood, Mrs. Benjamin, 92
Wood, L. Hollingsworth, 410
Woodenbridge, Ireland, 160
Woodrow Wilson and the Great Betrayal (Bailey), 321fn., 323fn., 372fn., 456
Woolen industry, Irish, 5
Wordsworth, William, 194
Works (Swift), 4fn.
World War I, 149-157, 163-164, 165, 175, 176, 215-217, 226; Irish-Americans oppose American intervention in, 220-224
Worthington-Evans, Sir Laming, 428
Wynne, Father, 226
Wynn's Hotel (Dublin), 144

Yale University Library, 216fn., 246fn., 313fn., 405fn., 452
Yeats, John Butler, 174, 174fn., 455
Yeats, William Butler, 124-125, 126, 127, 174fn., 209fn., 455, 457
Young, E. J., 425fn., 459
Young, Thomas Lowry, 57
Young Ireland, 1840-45 (Duffy), 15fn., 455
Young Ireland and 1848 (Gwynn), 24fn., 457
Young Irelanders, 16-18, 20, 23, 24, 28

Zimmerman, Herr, 179, 180, 260